A History of the

African People

CHARLES SCRIBNER'S SONS : NEW YORK

Robert W. July

HUNTER COLLEGE

A History of the
African People

Facing title page and page 1: Near Tamanrasset in the Sahara, an Arab girl with a herd of sheep. Photograph from Three Lions, Inc.

Title page and page 173: Kariba Dam, Southern Rhodesia. © Photograph by Roy Greeth. Courtesy Rhodesia National Tourist Board.

Maps by Samuel H. Bryant

For E.A.J. and R.H.J.

Preface

The African continent is vast and its people various; to write its history is to confront at once the problem of achieving thematic clarity without distortion, of preserving narrative completeness while avoiding total congestion. The solution lies in perspective—particular viewpoints which give shape and focus to events otherwise dimly seen, but which necessarily deal more attentively with certain phenomena than with others. It is appropriate in this prefatory statement, therefore, to explain the priorities and perspectives of this book.

In the first place, I have been preoccupied to a considerable extent with modern Africa—almost two score newly independent nations quite precipitately created within scarcely a dozen years, and hard at work during the early phase of independence with the task of becoming vital modern societies. How they got where they are is surely a major question to which the historian of Africa must address himself, and this book has been written with that question continually in view.

In this connection there has arisen the difficult matter of emphasis. What is an appropriate division of the African time span? Which events demand extended treatment, and which may be relatively neglected for the moment? For me, the priority clearly belongs to the recent era of Africa's long-lived past. Beginning early in the nineteenth century a series of massive developments, both internal and external, shook the African continent, setting in motion forces the understanding of which is essential to any comprehension of the present-day African scene. Consequently, I have concentrated much attention on the last century and a half, partly because our present knowledge of the more remote past is still imperfect and incomplete, but also, it must be admitted, because it is this modern period which, to a very considerable extent, gives meaning to what we see unfolding in Africa today.

Next, although Africa is and has always been part of a wider world, this is a history of Africa's own people, not the story of the external image of a mysterious and remote continent. I have therefore given secondary emphasis to the activities of those many visitors —merchants and soldiers, missionaries and explorers, kings and proconsuls—whose contributions to Africa's history are not to be gainsaid but who were essentially outsiders and temporary residents. Rather, I have been interested to explain and describe the doings of Africa's own peoples, most of whom built their civilizations over thousands of years without reference to Europe and Asia. In analyzing Africa's periodic confrontations with intruders from other worlds, I have concentrated my attention, not on the stranger's view, but on the response and perspective of the African himself.

Further, a history of Africa's people must attempt to give some account of social phenomena as well as political events. Political activity gives shape and direction to society, but it is essentially an engine for the achievement of other objectives. How does man live? What are his aspirations for a better life? Why does he worship which god and how? These questions go to the heart of life, in Africa as in all the world's continents, and any review of her history must necessarily give them appropriate attention.

Finally, this is a history primarily of black Africa. I have not excluded the northern reaches beyond the Sahara but neither have I dealt with them systematically. North Africa has been treated primarily in terms of its relations with the sub-Saharan continent, the great desert looked upon more as a connecting link than a barrier between north and south. Thus, for example, I have discussed Egypt with reference to Kush and again in its later relations with the eastern Sudan, but I have not provided an ordered account of Egypt's internal history any more than an analysis of its important relations with Europe and the Near East.

Although, in dealing with a work of this scope, I have required, sought, and received aid from a wide range of sources, my first and most profound debt has been to Africa itself. There, for a decade beginning in 1958, I was able, first, to travel widely throughout the continent, and later, to live and work continuously over several years in both East and West Africa. This experience has been of utmost value to me in gaining insights and overviews, and, I hope, the ability to write with verisimilitude, for it meant not only a first-hand acquaintance with the land and the people, but also the opportunity to gather the judgments and experience of many African friends concerning Africa's history and civilization.

A number of individuals have been directly concerned in various ways with the preparation of the text. I am most grateful to Professor James R. Hooker for his perceptive comments which have helped improve the whole work, to Professors Donald Rothchild and Richard L. Sklar for their admirable suggestions toward bringing the last chapter into final form, and to Mr. Christopher Ehret for his guidance in preparing the map which covers distribution of African peoples and language groupings.

I must make mention as well of my debt to the directors of the Rockefeller Foundation who placed at my disposal the Foundation's splendid facilities at the Villa Serbelloni in Bellagio, Italy where this book was both started and finished.

By far the greatest help of all, however, has come from my wife who has been my active and productive collaborator at all stages. From the initial outline of ideas, through the vast travail of reading and writing, to the final polishing of editorial detail, she has greatly lightened my labors and brightened my pages through her astute historical judgment and thorough knowledge of Africa's history.

Contents

Illustrations

Maps

Part One: Ancient Africa

1: The Beginnings of African History

THE GEOGRAPHIC BASE

History begins with geography. The history of mankind has always shown the deep mark of environment; put another way, man's development can be seen as a struggle for freedom from the limitations of man's surroundings, that man might control and direct his environment rather than suffer its restraints. To understand the great movements of African history, therefore, it is necessary to grasp the essentials of Africa's geography.

Though Africa is the second largest of the continents, comprising 11,700,000 square miles, its size is not its most significant characteristic. More important is its location which places it uniquely among the world continental masses squarely across the equator with its northern and southern extremes almost equidistant from the equator at 37° 21′ North and 34° 51′ South respectively. Over 9,000,-000 square miles of Africa, or four-fifths of its area, lie between the two Tropics of Cancer and Capricorn.

The geographic location of Africa has contributed to its tropical climate which is warm but extreme only in certain locations and which lacks the violent fluctuations in temperature found, for example, in North America. More significantly, Africa's geographic position affects the pattern of rainfall which in turn has had a profound influence on African ecology and history. The latitudes adjacent to the equator north and south are covered by a blanket of low-pressure air which rises from the hot land in response to the near-vertical rays of the sun. Thus is created a region of heavy rainfall, and here —principally in the Congo River basin and the Guinea coast of West Africa—is to be found the verdant rain forest capable at once of sustaining high population density and resisting the inroads of unwelcome intruders. This rich growth does not extend across the continent to East Africa, however, where wind, sea, and topographical conditions limit precipitation and, hence, vegetation in that area.

Moving northward and southward away from the equator, the rainfall gradually diminishes through the zone of the trade winds until the subtropical high pressure belt is reached with a precipitation of less than ten inches a year falling on its vast desert regions. Once again, elevation on the eastern side of the continent causes variations. In the north, the Ethiopian highlands receive ample rain whereas in South Africa the Drakensberg Mountains on the east coast cause updrafts and abundant rainfall along a narrow coastal corridor, a condition which serves to accentuate the dryness to the west in the Kalahari Desert and South-West Africa. In the extreme northwest and southwest sections of the continent a Mediterranean climate prevails, more extensively in the north where it is shielded from the Sahara Desert by the Atlas Mountain barrier.

As a result of the gradual decrease in precipitation as one draws away from the equator, the rain forest quickly gives way to the savanna grassland which in its various forms is the characteristic vegetation of Africa. More than two-fifths of the continent is covered by varieties of grass in occasional combination with forest stands—a fact which accounts both for the abundance of wild game and the importance of Africa's pastoral societies. Even the so-called desert consists primarily of arid shrub and grass areas suitable for limited grazing; indeed, although Africa's deserts cover an additional 40 per cent of the continental surface, only 8 per cent is occupied by desiccated sand and rock wastes incapable of supporting vegetation. Similarly, scarcely another 8 per cent of the total continent is given over to the equatorial rain forest.

The progressive gradations in precipitation must be understood in terms of long-range averages, for a major characteristic of Africa's weather pattern is in fact the erratic fluctuation in the amount and timing of the rains from year to year. This fluctuation is caused by the unpredictable behavior of the intertropical front—the line of contact between the hemispheric air masses meeting along the equatorial zone. As the front follows the sun in moving north and south with the seasons, there are no physical features such as mountain ranges to define and regulate its cyclical drift. Hence the rains vary markedly from year to year, both in quantity and in the moment of arrival and departure. In one West African station, for example, the annual rainfall ranged from a high of 66 inches to a low of 24 inches over an eighteen-year period. Such dramatic shifts coupled with the typical pattern of violent soil-leaching downpours have forced low agricultural productivity and chronic food shortages, limiting population to what can be sustained in the worst years only.

African topography, helping to influence the continental weather, has been shaped by geological factors which render Africa unique among the world's land masses. The Mediterranean coast aside, Africa consists of a great block of ancient rock which has been little disturbed over 200,000,000 years except for periodic uplift and erosion. Africa thus becomes a vast complex of plateaus tilting slightly upward to the east and the south so that altitudes near sea level in Senegal or the Niger Delta rise gradually to the high veld of east and south Africa with its rolling plains several thousand feet in height. In the main these plateaus present an undulating landscape whose monotonous aspect is only occasionally broken by highlands like the Jos Plateau in Nigeria, the Futa Jalon in Guinea, or Mount Tahat in the Ahaggar region of southern Algeria.

Only one geologic feature has interrupted this pattern. During one of its periodic uplifts, the African block fractured on its eastern side forming the great Rift Valley fault system which begins its four thousand-mile course with the Gulf of Aqaba at the head of the Red Sea, continues through the Ethiopian highlands, then moves southward in two prongs that flank Lake Victoria east and west, finally joining again to form the Lake Nyasa depression and terminates on the eastern coast near the Mozambique city of Beira. Accompanying this gigantic series of faults has been widespread volcanic action forming such lofty peaks as Mount Kenya and Mount Kilimanjaro, as well as the Cameroons range in West Africa.

Africa's plateau system has resulted in another topographical feature of great historical importance. The ancient eroded tableland has produced a series of major rivers pursuing leisurely, meandering courses through much of their long passage, occasionally spreading out into broad shallow basins which once held inland seas, and

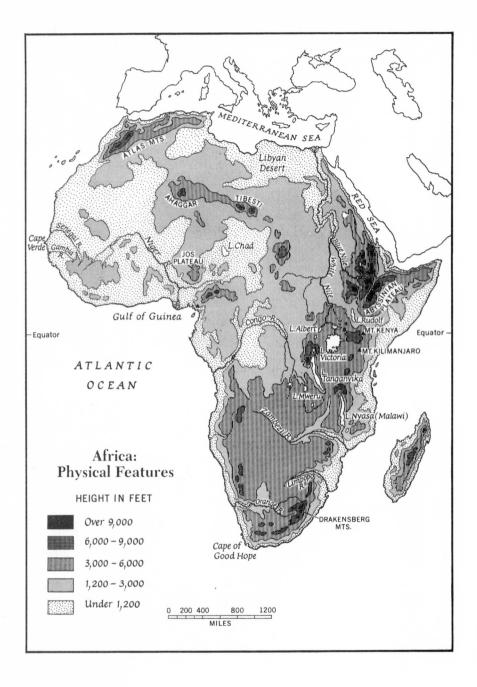

MEDITERRANEAN SEA

ATLAS MTS.

Libyan
Desert

AHAGGAR   TIBESTI

RED SEA

Cape
Verde   Senegal R.
        Gambia

Niger

JOS
PLATEAU

L.Chad

White Nile

Blue Nile

ABYSSINIAN PLATEAU

Gulf of Guinea

Congo R.

L.Rudolf

MT. KENYA

—Equator   Equator—

L.Albert

L.
Victoria

MT. KILIMANJARO

ATLANTIC
OCEAN

L.
Tanganyika

L.Mweru

L. Nyasa (Malawi)

Zambezi R.

Africa:
Physical Features

HEIGHT IN FEET

Limpopo R.

Orange R.

DRAKENSBERG
MTS.

Over 9,000

6,000 – 9,000

3,000 – 6,000

1,200 – 3,000

Under 1,200

Cape of
Good Hope

0 200 400   800   1200

MILES

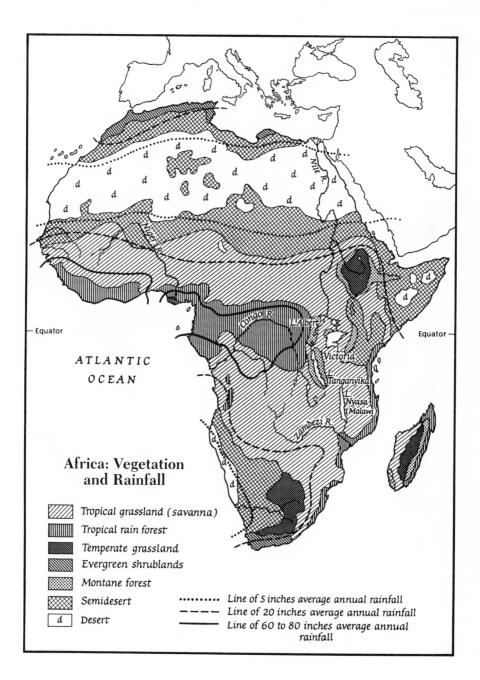

Africa: Vegetation and Rainfall

Tropical grassland (savanna)
Tropical rain forest
Temperate grassland
Evergreen shrublands
Montane forest
Semidesert
d — Desert

•••••••••• Line of 5 inches average annual rainfall
– – – – Line of 20 inches average annual rainfall
———— Line of 60 to 80 inches average annual rainfall

Equator

Equator

ATLANTIC OCEAN

Nile R.

Niger R.

Congo R.

L. Albert

L. Victoria

L. Tanganyika

L. Nyasa (Malawi)

Zambezi R.

finally spilling over the continental edge of the plateau in waterfalls and courses of rapids before emptying into the sea. The most celebrated of these cataracts is Victoria Falls on the Zambezi, but most other rivers have their falls—for example, the cataracts of the Nile, the rapids of the Congo below Stanley Pool, or the interior rapids and falls on the Niger and Senegal rivers. These rivers are navigable for long stretches in the continental interior, but their falls have greatly impeded penetration of the continent from the outside. It was not until the nineteenth century that Europe came to know anything substantial about the African interior, while only the occasional traveler from the Middle East was able to make his way into Negro Africa beyond the Sahara. For their part, the Africans were never tempted to travel beyond their own continent to explore other parts of the world and to spread knowledge of Africa's people.

Thus the geography of Africa has produced a continent with ample means for internal transport and communication via the great river systems and across the vast grassy plains. The desert areas have been difficult, but not impossible, to traverse, and in earlier times when there was greater rainfall, they supported a far greater human population than they do today. The rain forest, also difficult to penetrate, has been able to sustain high concentrations of population once man mastered the woodcraft necessary for a forest life. The Nile Valley aside, the weather pattern has tended to encourage a pastoral economy rather than agriculture of high productivity. Shifting cultivation and erratic harvests have not only restricted the population but have also led to political decentralization. Until the period of European colonization, large states usually emerged only with the appearance of chieftains of energy and resourcefulness; social cohesion has been limited by the particularities of tribal differences and the difficulties of maintaining lines of communication over long distances.

THE GENESIS OF MAN IN AFRICA

If history begins with geography, man begins, not with history, but with paleontology. Moreover, the present extent of archeological research places his beginnings squarely in Africa, and at a time of very great antiquity. The earliest known examples of primates—the order containing men, apes, monkeys, and lemurs—date back sixty million years, and fossil remains of more advanced primates of the super-family (hominoids) which produced both man and the great apes were concentrated in Egypt as long ago as forty million years. By Miocene times, a creature named *Kenyapithecus* had appeared in East Africa—an early specimen, *Kenyapithecus africanus* which was extant at least twenty million years ago, and a more evolved version called *Kenyapithecus wickeri* who thrived twelve to fourteen million years ago. The interesting fact about *Kenyapithecus* is that he co-existed with true apes while exhibiting structural characteristics which make him antecedent to modern man. Hence in Africa the family which was to produce man (hominids) had already branched off from the apes (pongids) as long ago as twenty million years, and a common ancestor for man and ape must therefore have lived in Africa at an even more remote past.

Over time the evolutionary descent from man's prehuman ancestor *Wickeri*, slowly unfolded. The record is obscure for want of information but clearly there were parallel lines of development involving true man and related types, some of which died out while the ancestor of modern man continued to survive. About two million years ago East Africa was the home of a creature who has been named *Homo habilis* by his discoverer, the distinguished archeologist, Dr. L. S. B. Leakey, and whose body structure, ability to make cutting tools, brain capacity, and erect carriage justified, in Leakey's judgment, his classification as the direct ancestor of true man. *Homo habilis* lived concurrently with another man-like being called *Zinjanthropus*, but skeletal similarities with modern man appear to place only *Homo habilis* in the direct line of descent, a premise supported both by his development as a meat-eating scavenger turned hunter and as a toolmaker of surprising ingenuity.

From this point forward, man's evolution was marked by a slow refinement of the simple tools of *Homo habilis* into a set of more efficient and specialized implements. Nevertheless about half a million years ago the most common type of implement had become the hand axe, a pear-shaped, chipped stone tool with a heavy base and a pointed or edged blade suitable for skinning animals or cutting meat into manageable chunks. Man seems to have avoided the cold, wet mountain slopes as well as the dangerous and difficult forest, preferring instead the shores of lakes and streams in open country where he could obtain water and lie in wait for the animals on which he preyed. During the long Paleolithic period, or Old Stone Age, man in his various early forms spread to Europe and Asia, bringing with him his characteristic hand axe which has been found in many western European sites and as far east as India. Africa, however, continued to be the center of greatest human activity as man gradually extended his range throughout the continent.

This relatively static, slowly evolving condition prevailed until perhaps 50,000 years ago when there began fundamental alterations in human development, associated with a basic shift in climate. The onset of the last ice age in Europe brought lower temperatures and moister weather to Africa, resulting in an extension of Mediterranean flora across the Sahara area. This environmental change in turn allowed man to spread rapidly into hitherto inaccessible areas, to increase in population, and to improve and further specialize his tools and food-gathering techniques.

During this later Paleolithic period, man in Africa began to use fire, long after its introduction in inclement Europe and Asia. Fire made practicable the utilization of caves and rock shelters for greater comfort and safety and these semi-permanent camp sites introduced the possibility of division of labor, perhaps between the sexes. In any event, once the idea of specialization had taken hold, it suggested its own development. The ubiquitous hand axe gave way to an extended battery of implements—chisels, gouges, awls, knives, scrapers, spearheads, and eventually, arrows. These tools often required handles which were made of wood or bone and fastened to the head with natural gum, sinews, or raw hide. Together they introduced vast changes in man's material circumstances and social patterns. Improved tools enabled man to extend his range into the forests for the first time, and, on the open plains where he continued to predominate, his hunting efficiency steadily mounted. Pitfalls, traps, spears with stone tips, throwing sticks, knives, and the bow meant a bigger and better supply of food. A wider use of material such as hides, bone, horn, ivory, bark, and resin led to greater efficiency and comfort.

It was during this period, about 35,000 years ago, that *Homo sapiens*, or modern man, made his appearance, rapidly becoming the sole survivor of the early types of man by approximately 10,000 years ago. Genetic evolution meant cultural evolution as well. A greater social complexity led to the need for improved communication and thus to the introduction of language. One profound effect of this technological revolution was that it enabled man for the first time to deal with the sheer necessity of survival on a part-time basis, thus providing a leisure which he could and did begin to devote to other pursuits—chiefly artistic activity, including personal adornment, as well as reflections of a religious nature. Here was the beginning of man's self-conscious preoccupation with his place in the world.

The end of the long millennia of the Paleolithic period came about ten thousand years ago at another important juncture in human development as man began to shift from an economy based on hunting and gathering to one based on cultivation. By this late date in man's history the races of Africa had begun to achieve their modern form. In the high veld of southern Africa, the predominant type at the opening of the Neolithic period, or New Stone Age, appears to have been the Bushman or his ancestor. This small, slightly built, tan-colored hunter and gatherer roamed the great grassland plateau in bands that varied in size depending upon the prevalence of water and game. During the more recent past, however, he has fallen on evil days. Unable to adapt his ancient hunting and foraging techniques to the exigencies of a more sophisticated world, he has been driven from his old range and, dwindling in numbers, now ekes out a marginal existence in the inhospitable wastes of the Kalahari Desert in southern Africa. Including his Hottentot cousins, he numbers today no more than 100,000 souls.

The closing millennia of the Paleolithic period were marked by a wet phase in the Sahara, and another followed between approximately 5500 and 2500 B.C. The well-watered Sahara now offered attractions to flora and fauna alike, and man followed plants and other animals to establish himself as a skilled hunter and fisherman along the many Saharan watercourses. From the north came the Caucasoids, ancestors to such modern peoples as the Berbers and Tuareg of North Africa and the desert, the Galla, Somali, and Beja of the East African "Horn", and most Egyptians of pharaonic times.

From the south, Negroid peoples moved into the Sahara, having apparently already occupied the West African forests, the Congo basin, and parts of eastern and central Africa, taking possession of the high plains alongside Bushmen with whom they share a common ancestry. In the Sahara the Negroids apparently specialized as fisherfolk. Their earliest traces have been found in the Egyptian Sudan at the site of modern Khartoum at a date as far back as 6000 years ago. At about the same time, other Negroes lived well to the west at Asselar, at the time an area of abundant fish and game but today a desert post some 250 miles northeast of Timbuktu. Between Khartoum and Asselar, additional Negro sites have been discovered, notably several in the Darfur area of western Sudan. The Negroids at Khartoum produced clay pots decorated with a characteristic wavy line, and these have been found at other sites along the Sudanese Nile as well as both east and west of the river. All in all, the evidence, though still scanty, suggests a widely spread Negro fishing and hunting culture in the Sahara during Neolithic times.

THE AGRICULTURAL REVOLUTION IN EGYPT

By definition the Neolithic period, beginning as long as ten thousand years ago, was characterized by the change from food gathering to food production, a change which had as profound implications for man as the previous revolution of specialization and division of labor. First, it brought a vast increase in population for it was now possible greatly to multiply and localize the supply of food. Even more significant was the shift from a nomadic to a settled form of social life. Hunting communities, obliged to move with the game and subject to seasonal water shortages, could never establish themselves long in one place and consequently could never produce and accumulate wealth above the bare necessities which they were obliged to carry with them. As cultivation was introduced, however, man could look beyond immediate toward ultimate objectives. He could accumulate and preserve food for future consumption, utilizing the time freed for some other purpose than subsistence. He could continue the process of specialization, exempting certain individuals from the task of food production to follow other pursuits—war-making and statecraft, artistic endeavors, the practice of religion, the development of writing, the improvement of technology, and in general, the acquisition of knowledge. Greater population density and a sedentary existence made possible for the first time an urban culture wherein exchange of goods and services and the communication of ideas became the natural order of things. This Neolithic food-producing revolution apparently did not have its beginning in Africa but rather in southwest Asia, for Africa by Neolithic times had ceased to be the world's prime center of human development. Nevertheless, when the Neolithic period made its appearance in Africa, it was in the spectacular form of the civilization of ancient Egypt. Elsewhere in the continent achievement was more modest, but wherever agriculture was introduced, it saw the steady decline of those older hunting cultures unable to adapt to the new order of things.

Agricultural production in Egypt appears to date from the sixth or early fifth millennium B.C. The predynastic people of Egypt were Caucasoid hunters who may at various times have spread from the Arabian peninsula but who in any case gradually developed a sedentary existence on the edge of the Nile Valley where they added fishing to their hunting activities and where they began to grow cereal crops. A number of independent groups occupied several river points stretching from the Delta south to Upper Egypt, but though there were differences in the details of their culture, the essentials were much the same. Hunting and fishing provided the basic support of the economy, but all communities cultivated both wheat and barley. Most possessed domesticated animals including cattle and sheep or goats. Flax was grown on which a textile industry subsisted. Silos were used for grain storage, pottery dishes were common, and serrated stone sickles were employed for harvesting. Housing was primitive, consisting of reed matting wind screens, and the communities were small and in some cases temporary. Being food producers, the people now had leisure time which they devoted to the refinement and elaboration of local arts and crafts. Economic self-sufficiency was still the standard and there were only the beginnings of an exchange economy between the settlements. There was as yet no thought of public works or the capital improvement of the land. Such an idea as controlled irrigation, for example, seems to have been unknown.

Gradually a changing environment forced more sophisticated responses. The Sahara wet phase was drawing to a close during the later Neolithic age and the desert tributaries were drying up. Settlements on the edge of the Nile Valley could no longer be maintained so that by the fourth millennium the communities were moving down the sides of the valley to the naturally irrigated flood plain of the Nile. The result was a dramatic increase in food production followed by a similar expansion in population. The older semipermanent village gave way to completely settled communities which grew in size and complexity. By the middle of the fourth millennium the culture of Egypt's Nile Valley had evolved in several important respects. First of all, the economy had shifted once and for all from a combination of farming and food gathering to a major reliance on agriculture, which was now aided by a certain amount of artificial irrigation. Secondly, the earlier near-isolation had been replaced by a lively long-distance trade with centers in the Aegean and the Middle East. Obsidian from Abyssinia, juniper berries and timber from Palestine, copper from Sinai, lapis lazuli from Afghanistan were exchanged for flint, stone vases, and other local products. Papyrus boats turned the Nile into a highway and the domestication of the ass made possible caravan transport to the Red Sea.

The establishment of agriculture and the expansion of commerce led in turn to further specialization within the economy, for increased production meant that merchants and craftsmen could be supported, and trade with distant places demanded the manufacture of local products in exchange. Flint was mined systematically, metal work was introduced, first with non-smelted ores and later through casting, stone tools were further refined, the production of elegantly worked stone vases increased, and new artificial substances were manufactured such as glazed pottery suitable for ornaments. Finally, a changing economy meant a rising level of personal prosperity. The old wind screens and round huts came to be replaced by substantial mud structures, rectangular in form and generous in size, with framed doors and windows. Graves, too, became larger and more lavishly furnished. Here was evidence of incipient inequalities in wealth which reflected the rise of a class structure.

The record was not one of unbroken progress and expansion, however, for with the development of settled, stable communities came competition for land, trade, and livestock. Towns were early fortified and local warfare became part of existence. Wars with outsiders also had to be endured. Hence there arose very early in the Nile Valley a condition which has characterized life in Egypt ever since—the search for political stability to insure economic prosperity. By the third millennium B.C. the Egyptian peasant from the fertile river flood plain could produce approximately three times as much food as he needed, but he required freedom from unrest to achieve this output. Consequently, he has always been willing to concede a substantial degree of authority to whatever political establishment could guarantee protection from internecine warfare and invasion, submitting to the confiscation, through taxation, of his surplus production in return for peace in the land.

1. Tropical rain forest

2. Saharan mountains

3. Desiccated desert wasteland

4. Savanna grassland during the dry season

When the pharaohs of the First Dynasty unified Upper and Lower Egypt and installed themselves as absolute temporal and religious rulers, they introduced for the first time this idea of a strong power at the center so necessary to the economic health of the river valley. With their rule, a divine kingship was imposed on the population with all its extravagances of royal prerogative. Princely palaces reflected great wealth but were nevertheless exceeded in their grandeur by the great tombs which contained not only the lavish accoutrements necessary for the needs of their royal inhabitants but large numbers of human victims who were obliged to accompany their royal master to the grave.

Nevertheless, the social and economic growth made possible by unification led to revolutionary changes which established ancient Egyptian civilization as one of the great cultural flowerings in the world's history. Not only did the population rise dramatically from the thousands to the millions, but further specialization introduced by the state was the basis of a growing class structure in a society of increasing complexity capable of producing and consuming a broadening variety of artistic and utilitarian goods. Making use of the surplus production of the peasantry, the kings supported a priestly and ministerial class, a professional army, large numbers of artists and craftsmen, laborers for the mines, quarries, and irrigation projects, as well as the hordes of engineers, artists, and workers who built the great palaces and monumental tombs of the pharaohs. The social structure became in essence a static hierarchy with a large serf population serving a ruling nobility and a king-god.

This social structure was the basis for Egypt's cultural revolution. The monumental architecture of royal palaces and royal tombs was supplemented by decorative arts of great beauty. Though pottery was widely used, it was largely utilitarian but the Egyptian stone vessels of the day have yet to be equaled by later civilizations in their technical and aesthetic perfection. The manufacture of linen had already so advanced by the First Dynasty that there has been little improvement ever since, and Egyptian jewelry is justly celebrated for its intricacy and variety of materials. Bone and ivory carving along with woodwork and leatherwork produced articles of everyday utility, but these crafts also yielded their share of artistic achievement in carved statuettes or engraved household articles.

Great steps were taken by scribes in the development of writing which began with simple pictograms for the keeping of records but which soon advanced to more complex, stylized hieroglyphs and a cursive script. Writing in turn led to systematic accumulation of knowledge and assisted in the development of precise scientific calculations necessary for the vital business of agriculture. A calendar was early invented as an aid in anticipating the annual inundation of the Nile, and this device was supplemented by other astronomical observations. The floodwaters were controlled by a network of banked fields and canals, and there was a system for raising water to higher ground above the flood plain. Farming implements were made of both stone and metal, for copper had become a common material in the manufacture of tools, weapons, and vessels. Indeed, copper woodworking tools effected a remarkable advance in cabinetry which involved not only a thorough knowledge of techniques such as joining but a refined use of carving and the inlay of mixed woods with ivory or ceramics.

An expanding economy and a society of increased sophistication required the constant import of raw materials for manufacture. Copper, malachite, and turquoise were brought in from Sinai, quantities of cedar and cypress from Lebanon, ebony, ivory, and resin from the south, and semiprecious stones from western Asia. Exports consisted of raw materials and manufactured goods, especially the celebrated Egyptian stone urns which have been located in Palestine, Crete, and as far off as the Greek mainland. Internal trade was also brisk judging from the extensive distribution of hallmarked pottery and the use of natural materials from widely scattered centers.

No doubt the daily life of the peasant remained simple, his possessions crude, but the more prosperous members of the community lived in comfort and, in the case of the nobility, in luxury. Rectangular houses with brick- or wood-vaulted roofs often contained well-appointed, separate living and sleeping quarters along with baths and toilets. Wooden beds and chairs were usually built low to the ground and upholstered in leather or cloth. Small stone tables served individual diners while alabaster chinaware alternated with rough pottery in presenting a wide variety of poultry, meat, fish, cereals, fruit, and drink, including wine and beer. Clothing was appropriately light, while cosmetics were much fancied as a complement to the jewelry of which the ancient Egyptians were unusually fond.

THE PATTERN OF RACES IN TROPICAL AFRICA

The spectacular cultural changes which the introduction of agriculture brought to Egypt resulted from the unique fertility of the Nile flood plain, making possible the application of political organization to economic productivity on a scale previously unknown. Elsewhere in Africa progress was much more modest. For one thing, there is considerable uncertainty as to when, where, and under what conditions the transformation from a food-gathering to a food-cultivating economy took place, but there clearly was no cultural revolution such as occurred in Egypt. The evidence, which is necessarily of a non-literary nature, comes severally from archeology, from the analysis of African languages, and from ethnobotany, with some assistance from the study of human blood types in relation to racial affinities. The available information has been interpreted and collated with impressive ingenuity, but it is scanty and sometimes contradictory, giving rise to hypotheses about Neolithic African society which tend on occasion to conflict with each other.

Since archeologists have been concerned longest with the reconstruction of Africa's beginnings, they have pieced together a persuasive picture of early civilizations in Africa which describes a relatively late and gradual metamorphosis from hunting societies to food producers under circumstances which contained none of the dramatic cultural changes of Egypt. During the early millennia of the Neolithic period, the greater rainfall in the Sahara area had made possible the development of communities in regions which are now wholly uninhabitable. The Negro population which had become established before the beginning of the fourth millennium before Christ at the confluence of the White and Blue Nile at Khartoum was duplicated by other Negroid and Caucasoid settlements located along Sahara watercourses arid since the onset of the dry phase midway in the third millennium B.C. What is today savanna grass and bush scrub was then forest and savanna respectively. Today's mid-Sahara was a habitable region of rivers and marshes and on these waterways Neolithic cultures were able to thrive.

The early Negro hunters and fishermen at Khartoum speared both fish and game with barbed bone harpoons, built wattle and daub shelters, but made no metal tools, kept no domestic animals, and practiced no cultivation. Sandstone grinders which they possessed were apparently used exclusively for the manufacture of red ochre powder although they would have been suitable for processing grain as well. By late fourth millennium these Negroes had been succeeded by another people, possibly of Negro stock, who were also hunters and fishers but who in their time began to domesticate animals, notably a dwarf goat. Khartoum, however, was no isolated phenomenon. The ready east-west communication along now dried-up rivers made possible the diffusion of this hunting and fishing culture throughout the Sahara. The center was probably not Khartoum, but rather the mid-Sahara of Tibesti and Ahaggar from whence social and cultural institutions were spread by migrations of people forced by the widening drought south to the savanna of West Africa, east to the Sudan, and northeast to Egypt.

As the desert slowly advanced, the peoples of the Sahara continued their move to more hospitable lands. During the third millennium, for example, Nubia was occupied by Caucasoid or Mediterranean pastoralists who probably came eastward from the Sahara. Others may have also scattered as far west as modern Mauritania as well as to Libya and the western Sudan. In any event there is slight but suggestive archeological evidence that the inhabitants of the desert fringes, prodded by the necessities of their changing ecology, were beginning to experiment with tropical agriculture. Certain Neolithic artifacts seem to imply cultivation. For instance, in the desert of eastern Mauritania the discovery of stone hoe-like implements, which might have been used for cultivation of yams and millet when there was greater rainfall, would mean that experimentation could have begun as early as the fifth millennium, resulting in full-fledged agricultural communities in the savanna by the first millennium B.C. There is no reason, moreover, to think that agriculture was slow to penetrate the forest belt of West Africa where the people were well equipped with woodworking tools and were residents of long duration. Indeed, recent discoveries deep in the forest area of western Nigeria have uncovered a human skeleton at a site which has been carbon-dated as being between nine thousand and eleven thousand years old.

While archeologists have tended to favor more recent dates for the introduction of agriculture in Africa, other observers have argued for a much more ancient beginning. Even the archeologists have been forced to push the inauguration of agriculture in the Middle East back at least to the ninth millennium, but agricultural geographers have insisted that plant crops evolved over a very long period, and that most were already in use by 3000 B.C., many in advanced forms indicating a long history of prior development. The present view of historical botanists is that Middle Eastern agriculture is of ancient origin, perhaps far back in Paleolithic times. Moreover, there is no reason to suppose that cultivation began exclusively in the Middle East with the domestication of cereals. It is possible that this stage was preceded by tropical gardening based on fruit and tubers, possibly in southeast Asia.

If the record of agricultural beginnings in Africa is unclear, it nevertheless seems very likely that early experimental cultivation began very long ago, longer than is usually accepted. Many crops are involved and their wide dispersion and development into different varieties argues for considerable antiquity. In the case of cotton, which is usually cited as having originated in Africa, the evidence indicates that cultivation in Africa occurred at least five thousand years ago and, being a non-food crop, was probably preceded by other, even more venerable, domesticated plants.

The possible ancient origins of agriculture in Africa, and the long-standing presence of Neolithic peoples of distinctive racial characteristics inhabiting the Sahara, savanna, and forest areas of the continent are sustained by analysis of Africa's languages. The present linguistic configuration in Africa finds the Afro-Asiatic speakers in the north and in the East African "Horn," the Negritic languages in West Africa but probing eastward almost to the Nile, the Central Saharan and the Nilotic groups in north central Africa roughly between Lake Chad and Lake Victoria, the Bantu throughout the subequatorial portions of the continent, and the click Khoisan languages in the extreme south. Of all these, the Bantu are by far the most homogeneous, having come from a common source and having developed their present variations over a period estimated at approximately fifteen hundred years, perhaps somewhat longer. By contrast, both the Afro-Asiatic and Negritic families contain languages which are far more diverse each from the others than are the members of the Bantu group. Hence on linguistic grounds it follows that the languages in West Africa and throughout the savanna must have been in the process of differentiation for a long time, far longer than among the Bantu. In the same way, the Afro-Asiatic group has been diverging from an ancient source over a very long period of time. Its Semitic branch has differentiations which had begun more than four thousand years ago, and the other branches—Berber,

Cushitic, Egyptian, and Chad—must have begun their move away from the parent tongue earlier still. Such a pattern can only mean that those portions of Africa north of the Congo rain forest must have been populated for a period of several thousand years. Moreover, the linguistic evidence suggests that the Afro-Asiatic speakers could have originated, not in Asia, but in the Nile Valley or the Sahara, since Africa contains four subfamilies to a single one for Asia.

Despite the comparative homogeneity of Bantu-rooted languages throughout the high plains of eastern, central, and southern Africa, the Bantu speakers of these regions exhibit a considerable variety of physical characteristics, culture, and social organization. This situation has emerged quite naturally from the commingling of an invading Bantu strain with various local stocks—Bushmen and Hottentots in southern Africa, Pygmies in the rain forest of the Congo basin, the Nilotes in East Africa, along with scattered pockets of Bushmen and Hottentots. The linguistic evidence suggests that the Bantu speakers originated in the central Benue River Valley from whence they migrated rapidly southward and southeastward about the beginning of the Christian era, occupying most of subequatorial Africa over the ensuing fifteen or more centuries. By the end of the eighteenth century, the Bantu spearhead was already probing deeply along the east coast of southern Africa where it came into fateful contact with the settlers of the Cape Town colony in the Zuurveld about four hundred miles east of Cape Town.

With the Bantu dispersion, the distribution pattern of populations in Africa achieved its modern form—that is, the form which obtained at the opening of the nineteenth century when the first serious European penetration of Africa took place. In West Africa, the Negro was the predominant type throughout the forest and savanna on the southern edge of the Sahara. North of the desert was the main body of Afro-Asiatic speakers—various Berber groups, Egyptians, and others—tempered by strong infusions of Arabs who had arrived during the spread of Islam beginning with the mid-seventh century A.D. In the eastern Sudan people of mixed Negro-Mediterranean strain gradually emerged, while East Africa developed similar hybrids when Mediterranean Caucasoids and varieties of Negroids were merged. In southern Africa, the Hottentot and Bushmen held sway over wide areas, undisturbed until the coming of the Bantu.

To these racial patterns the Bantu speakers brought their own

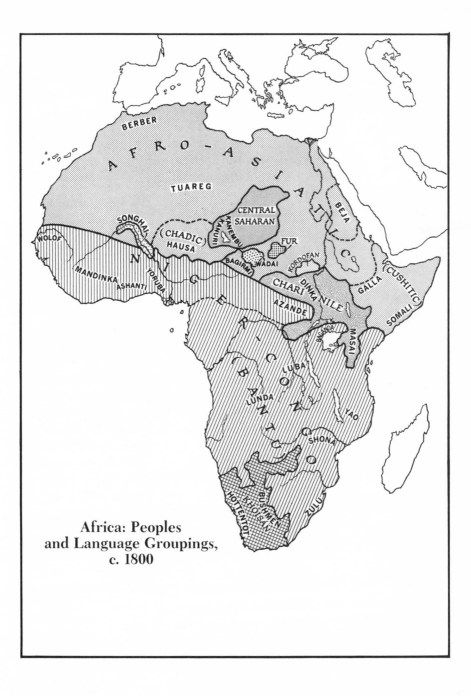

Africa: Peoples
and Language Groupings,
c. 1800

linguistic, genetic, and cultural characteristics which came to dominate the southern third of the African continent. All these developments took place over long periods of time so that assimilation and natural selection, no less than intrusion and annihilation, were factors in establishing the present racial pattern. For example, if the origin of the Negro is still a mystery to some, he might be explained very simply as the result of response to environment by a less specialized man during the long millennia of the Paleolithic period. Again, in the more recent past, the process of change from a hunting to a farming economy came slowly in subequatorial Africa, not necessarily by conquest and absorption, but also through gradual adaptation by Stone Age peoples of the techniques of their iron-using, Bantu-speaking, agricultural neighbors.

Suggestions for Further Reading

For a discussion of African geography see L. D. Stamp, *Africa, A Study in Tropical Development*, 2nd. ed. (New York: Wiley, 1964). Other volumes deal with geography in part; for example, Lord Hailey, *An African Survey, Revised 1956* (London: Oxford University Press, 1957); G. P. Murdock, *Africa: Its Peoples and Their Culture History* (New York: McGraw-Hill, 1959); or the relevant material in R. Oliver and G. Mathew, eds., *History of East Africa*, I (Oxford: Clarendon Press, 1963).

There is a growing literature on African prehistory. Standard works include Sonia Cole, *The Prehistory of East Africa* (New York: Mentor, 1965); J. D. Clark, *The Prehistory of Southern Africa* (Harmondsworth, Middlesex: Penguin, 1959); C. B. M. McBurney, *The Stone Age of Northern Africa* (Harmondsworth, Middlesex: Penguin, 1960); and H. Alimen, *The Prehistory of Africa* (London: Hutchinson, 1957; New York: Humanities Press, 1957). In addition see articles contained in *The Journal of African History*, 1962, vol. III, no. 2, particularly those by C. C. Wrigley, J. D. Clark, and W. B. Morgan. Wrigley also has an important article in *The Journal of African History*, 1960, vol. I, no. 2, entitled "Speculations on the Economic Prehistory of Africa." Indispensible is J. D. Clark, "The Prehistoric Origins of African Culture," *The Journal of African History*, 1964, vol. V, no. 2, and L. S. B. Leakey, "The Evolution of Man in the African Continent," *Tarikh*, vol. I, no. 3, 1966. Also useful is J. D. Clark and B. M. Fagan, "Charcoals, Sands, and Channel Decorated Pottery from Northern Rhodesia," *The American Anthropologist*, April, 1965. Much of this material is covered by G. P. Murdock, *Africa:*

Its Peoples and Their Culture History (New York: McGraw-Hill, 1959) with conclusions that are questioned by some other scholars.

The evidence offered by African linguistics is to be found in J. H. Greenberg, *Studies in African Linguistic Classification* (New Haven: Compass Publishing Co., 1955) [subsequently revised and reissued as *The Languages of Africa* (Bloomington: Indiana University, 1966)], which should be used in conjunction with M. Guthrie, "Bantu Origins: A Tentative New Hypothesis," *The Journal of African Languages*, I, 1962. See also, R. Oliver, "The Problem of the Bantu Expansion," *The Journal of African History*, vol. VII, no. 3, 1966; and Greenberg's "Historical Inferences from Linguistic Research in Sub-Saharan Africa," in J. Butler, ed., *Boston University Papers in African History*, I (Boston: Boston University Press, 1964).

For early Egypt the best works are V. G. Childe, *New Light on the Most Ancient East* (London: Routledge and Kegan Paul, 1954; New York: Norton, 1969); and W. B. Emery, *Archaic Egypt* (Harmondsworth, Middlesex and Baltimore: Penguin, 1961). A. J. Arkell, *History of the Sudan from the Earliest Times to 1821*, 2nd rev. ed. (London: Athlone Press, 1961; New York: Oxford University Press, 1961) is the best work on that subject.

2: Africa in the Ancient World

EGYPT AND KUSH

During the third millennium B.C. Egypt established her position as one of the major powers of the ancient world. A strong and absolute monarchy made possible the full exploitation of the rich soil of the Nile flood plain, and a rising national wealth led to some of mankind's greatest cultural and artistic achievements. For over two thousand years Egypt held her place as a major seat of ancient civilization in the West. Facing outward from Africa, she placed her imprint on the Mediterranean world, but she also faced inward to exert the authority of her ideas and institutions on the people of Africa.

The main line of Egyptian penetration to the south was along the great highway of the Nile, and the impetus was trade which only gradually led to conquest and occupation. Egypt's natural boundary on the south was the First Cataract of the Nile near the modern site of Aswan; below lay Nubia peopled by a brown-skinned stock similar to the Egyptians themselves or to the modern Beja or Somali. These people were primarily pastoralists, but Egypt had little interest in Nubian herds; rather she sought other products—gold from the Red Sea hills, hardwood and ivory to supplement her own dwindling supplies, granite for the massive tombs which Egyptian architects of the Old Kingdom were producing for her divine monarchs.

Egyptian influence in Nubia appeared early in dynastic times. The records of the First and Second Dynasties at the beginning of the third millennium refer to successful military expeditions to the south based on superior organization and weaponry, and graves of the Nubian people dating from this time contain copper tools which were of Egyptian design and origin. By the time of the great pyramid builders of the Fourth Dynasty (c. 2700–c. 2550 B.C.) Egypt was quarrying quantities of Nubian diorite for her mortuary sculpture without encountering local resistance, while during the Sixth Dynasty (c. 2420–c. 2260 B.C.) the pharaohs received homage from tribes south of the First Cataract despite the fact that no attempt had been made to occupy the country on a permanent basis.

Nevertheless, during the Sixth Dynasty which closed out Egypt's Old Kingdom, there was a record of increasing interest in the south. Canals were built around the First Cataract to enable boats made of Nubian timber to bring Nubian granite blocks north for the royal pyramids. Soldiers from the south were recruited into Egyptian armies engaged in campaigns against Bedouin tribes to the east. Finally, there were a number of expeditions made deep into what later came to be called the Sudan to explore and to trade. The name of one of these caravan leaders has survived, and thus we know of Harkhuf who undertook four journeys, each well over six months in duration, returning with quantities of ebony, ivory, frankincense, skins, and on one occasion a dwarf with which the pharaoh, Pepi II, was much impressed.

Harkhuf went south, not by boat, but across country with three hundred donkeys to the "Land of Yam." Perhaps the dwarf was in fact a pygmy thus implying a deep penetration to the south. More likely, however, Harkhuf journeyed only as far as Kerma just beyond the Third Cataract—an important market even in those ancient days where caravans from the south or from the El Fasher region of Darfur would have arrived with the goods which Harkhuf obtained. Hence whatever the extent of Harkhuf's own travels, there clearly were trade contacts with people far in the interior. These contacts did not necessarily imply peaceful relations for Harkhuf reported hostility toward his expedition on at least one occasion, and eventually punitive expeditions were required to subdue the southerners. With the death of Pepi II, however, the central authority in Egypt collapsed. Not only did this bring an end to the Old Kingdom but for a time it also terminated Egyptian interference with the peoples to the south who were now left free, sometimes to prey on their former overlords.

Egyptian interest in the Sudan, somewhat tentatively expressed under the Old Kingdom, became much more pronounced with the revival of strength during the dynasties of the Middle Kingdom. Coincident with the demise of the Old Kingdom and possibly caused by the withdrawal of Egyptian power north of the First Cataract, Nubia had been occupied by a race of pastoralists whose origins are obscure but who were a Caucasoid strain with possible Negroid characteristics. These so-called C Group people spread as far east as the Red Sea hills and were in possession of the Nile Valley south of the First Cataract when Egypt was united once again by the princes of Thebes who founded the Middle Kingdom about 2150 B.C. Egyptian unity led quickly to a revived interest in trade to the south which in turn brought conquest and occupation. Several military expeditions led to the establishment of a series of forts along the Nile as far as Semna, a strong point about twenty-five miles south of the Second Cataract where a permanent frontier was fixed.

The existence of fortifications certainly indicated that the local people did not take kindly to the Egyptian presence, but from the Egyptian point of view military strength was a necessary step in a carefully executed plan to develop a major trading center far down the river where ivory and gold could be obtained. The forts, which were fourteen in number, were of sturdy mud-brick construction reinforced with timber and were designed with multiple walls, towers, and revetments which made them virtually impregnable. Some were evidently sited to maintain peace-keeping garrisons while others were placed along the river at points where the traffic was vulnerable to attack. Clearly they were an important and successful device insuring a free flow of commerce through the Nubian province between the First and Second Cataracts in the face of a potentially hostile local population.

The object of this commerce was the land known as Kush with its center at Kerma about 150 miles due south of the frontier post of Semna. Here, beyond the Third Cataract, the river opens up for a long stretch of navigable water known as the Dongola reach. At Kerma the Egyptians of the Middle Kingdom built a trading post on what was at that time an island in the river. This trading station, which was probably the work of the pharaoh, Amenemet II (c. 1938–c. 1904 B.C.), was of typical reinforced mud-brick construction with the

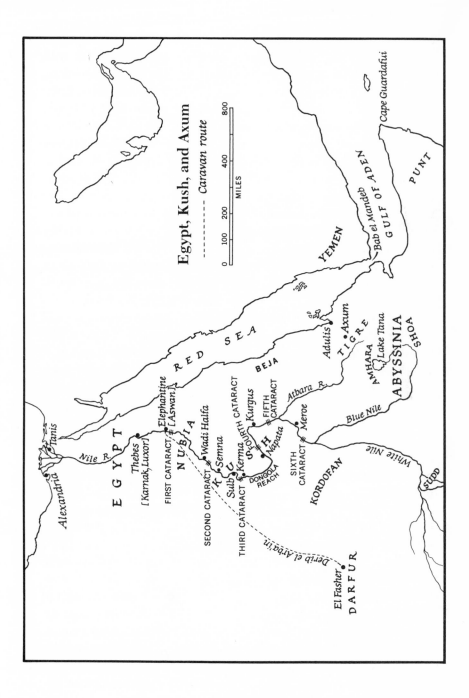

Egypt, Kush, and Axum

------ Caravan route

MILES

0   100 200   400   800

main building approximately 150 feet long and 75 feet in width. A second floor contained storage rooms as well as living quarters for guards and the community of Egyptian craftsmen who worked there. Nearby on the mainland a large cemetery with remains of both Egyptians and local residents suggests that the Egyptian post at Kerma, while fortified, was essentially a trading center and that the Egyptians lived peaceably over long periods among the local people on a basis of mutual commercial advantage.

Within the Egyptian compound were workshops where a variety of goods were produced, judging from the raw materials such as graphite, resin, mica, and rock crystal, which have survived along with supplies of partly manufactured glazed pottery and beads. What the remains at Kerma indicate is the beginning of a Nubian culture of local origin with an Egyptian overlay. Burial customs and practice appear to have remained Nubian, but the funerary chambers contained Egyptian statuary, and there is evidence that the local population favored a certain style of Egyptian jar long after it had gone out of fashion in the north. The artisans working at Kerma produced a wide variety of pottery, cabinetwork, jewelry, metalware, and ornamental objects which showed both Egyptian influences and local motifs. Surprisingly few goods were imported directly from Egypt, a fact which would indicate that the people of Kush by and large preferred the adaptations of the craftsmen based in Kerma. It is possible that the virility of the local culture reflected the fact that only a small number of Egyptians were ever permanently resident in Kush. It was therefore necessary to send occasional military expeditions to keep the peace which, however, finally broke down permanently when the Middle Kingdom fell before the invasion of the Asiatic Hyksos during the eighteenth century B.C.

The Hyksos occupation of Egypt had important repercussions for Kush. In the first place, it broke Egyptian colonial domination in the south, enabling Kush to gain her independence while maintaining her lucrative trade relations with the north. Paradoxically it also led to the first substantial infiltration of Egyptian culture into Kush. After a century of Hyksos domination, resistance rallied in Upper Egypt where the princes of Thebes were able to reassert their independence and eventually to unite Egypt once more under the New Kingdom. In their struggle against the Hyksos the Thebans relied upon Sudanese mercenaries who in time absorbed Egyptian ways and made Egyptian culture fashionable in Kush once they had returned home from the wars.

Egypt's fortunes continued to affect the Sudan, and her recrudescence during the brilliant Eighteenth Dynasty (c. 1580–c. 1340 B.C.) had profound political and social implications for the south. A series of military expeditions soon regained Nubia and Kush, then pressed far beyond the easily navigated Dongola reach—past the site of Napata which was later to become capital of the kingdom of Kush, and on to Kurgus where a frontier was established down river from the Fifth Cataract. It is possible that Egyptian power extended beyond the Fifth Cataract to Meroe, beginning as a military post and bringing the limit of Egypt's hegemony close to the Khartoum area where Negroes had been settled since Neolithic times. Indeed, trading expeditions were known to have penetrated far beyond that point. During the reign of Queen Hatshepsut who flourished early in the fifteenth century B.C., a merchant fleet sailed down the Red Sea to the Somali coast, then known as Punt, returning with a rich cargo of gold, rare woods, ivory, incense, skins, animals, and slaves, and it is likely that Punt was also reached at the same time by land caravans proceeding via the Nile Valley.

The New Kingdom occupation of the Sudan was as complete as it was extensive. After the initial military campaigns of the pharaohs, Ahmose and Thutmose I, peace descended upon the land and the emphasis of Egyptian public works shifted to serve religious instead of military purposes. During the long reign of Amenhotep III (c. 1405–c. 1370 B.C.), for example, a temple was completed at Sulb which rivaled in size and artistic merit its more famous contemporary at Luxor. Such military installations as were erected abandoned the design of the massive Middle Kingdom fortresses in favor of formalized structures often located most unstrategically at the center of sprawling urban areas inhabited by a now thoroughly Egyptianized population. The royal records show that tribute or taxes were regularly collected from local chieftains who no longer challenged Egyptian authority, that Egypt's military activities were directed exclusively toward Asia frequently with the aid of Nubian troops, and that the southern provinces were quietly administered by Egyptian viceroys. It is difficult to estimate how many Egyptians actually lived in the Sudan during the New Kingdom era, but the number was probably not great. At no time did the Egyptians develop a taste for emigration, and as the Sudanese became absorbed into Egyptian culture, the need for outside control was correspondingly reduced. Apparently the many temples helped maintain Egyptian ascendancy, and not only in religious affairs for surviving records suggest that a range of economic monopolies were granted to the priests by the pharaoh. One of these was the trade in gold which continued to be a major export to Egypt, being widely mined in Nubia and Kush as well as obtained from Negroes to the south. Other exports included the always popular ivory and ebony along with ostrich feathers, animal hides, perfumes and oils, and some grain and cattle. Slaves were also brought up from Nubia and Kush but the numbers do not seem to have been substantial at this time.

The rhythm of Egypt's history led once more to decline, this time to provide Kush with the opportunity to turn the tables on her former master. It was now more than five hundred years since the armies of Thutmose had moved irresistibly up the Nile, and a virile royal line had long since been replaced by a weak and corrupt administration divided by intrigue in which Nubian troops and officials played an increasingly important role. By the close of the Twenty-Second Dynasty, which came to power during the tenth century B.C., Egyptian authority had become so weakened as to enable Kush to exercise actual if not nominal independence. A royal line of Kush emerged which ruled from the capital established at Napata, which practiced many local customs such as Nubian burial rites, but which presumably considered itself the protector of an Egyptian civilization now in danger of corruption in the land of its genesis. The royal tombs at Napata grew steadily more imposing, and the rulers more wealthy and powerful. Substantial numbers of Egyptian scribes, priests, and craftsmen now lived and worked in the southern cities and the Egyptianized kings of Kush practiced traditional pharaonic religious and dynastic customs; for example, the marriage of royal brother and sister.

By the middle of the eighth century, the kings at Napata had extended their authority to include Upper Egypt; then under Piankhy (751–716 B.C.), the Kushite armies conquered the rest of Egypt, and the ancient country astride the Nile fell under the control of its Twenty-Fifth Dynasty made up of the kings of Kush. Piankhy's successors consolidated their control over Egypt but almost immediately came into conflict with another expanding power. From the rugged Assyrian hills of Nineveh emerged tough, disciplined armies equipped with iron-tipped weapons that soon proved irresistible. By the end of the eighth century, Assyria was master of the ancient Near East and was thwarted in an attempt to invade Egypt only when her troops were cut down by plague in Palestine in 701 B.C.

The Assyrian attack was merely postponed. In 671 B.C. Esarhaddon led his armies to Egypt and defeated the energetic and resourceful Kushite King Taharqa (688–663 B.C.) whose forces could not stand up to the Assyrian iron weaponry and fighting tactics. Taharqa was defeated but not conquered, however. Retreating to his capital at Thebes, he raised another army and reoccupied Lower Egypt as soon as the Assyrian forces had withdrawn. It proved to be only a temporary success. The Assyrians soon returned, defeated Taharqa a second time, reoccupied Memphis and other centers in Lower Egypt, then took Thebes in 666 B.C. forcing Taharqa to flee southward. A few years later an ill-conceived effort to retake Egypt by Taharqa's successor resulted in the devastation of Thebes by the troops of Asurbanipal, and the Kushite reign in Egypt came to a permanent conclusion after its brief hundred year ascendancy.

The military and political exploits of Egypt's Kushite kings were paralleled by a sensitive regard for cultural development. King Taharqa was particularly active in this respect. He erected monuments at Karnak, Thebes, and Tanis in Egypt proper, and raised or rebuilt a number of important temples in Kush. The description of one of these has survived—how it was constructed of sandstone with the help of Egyptian architects and craftsmen, how some of it was faced with gold leaf and how the landscaping included an artificial lake and gardens, how gold, silver, and bronze altars adorned its interior, and how the mighty king was able to dispatch the wives of defeated princes from Lower Egypt to serve in his temple far up the Nile.

This preoccupation with Egyptian civilization survived long after Kush had lost her political control over Egypt. The kings continued to use their Egyptian royal titles and represented themselves wearing the double crown of Upper and Lower Egypt. Court ceremony and religious practice remained Egyptian as did the official written language. The burial chambers of the royal pyramids were laid out in the classical manner with the traditional granite sarcophagi, the full complement of pots, tools, jewelry, and other articles needed in the spirit world, and the religious texts drawn from the Book of the Dead or the tombs of earlier Egyptian dynasties. Yet, at the same time, parochial influences were at work which were gradually to convert Kush from an outpost of Egyptian civilization to a self-contained Sudanic kingdom, slowly losing its virility as it was thrust more and more in upon itself and cut off increasingly from the refreshing influences of other cultures.

At first it was military and political considerations which contributed to isolation. In 591 B.C. an Egyptian army from the Delta defeated Kush and sacked Napata, sealing off the south with a garrison at the Second Cataract, and ending once and for all any lingering ambitions which the Kushite kings may have had to reoccupy Egypt. One direct result of this defeat was the transfer of the capital farther southward at Meroe, long a thriving river port located upstream from the Atbara confluence and only about 150 miles north of the site of present-day Khartoum. Though the immediate cause of the move was strategic, it was invited by other considerations. The Kingdom of Kush now reached well beyond the junction of the Blue and White Nile and may even have extended to the great papyrus marshes of the Nile known as the Sudd, as well as west into Kordofan. Hence Meroe with its central location and southern orientation was a more logical capital than Napata. Not only was Meroe a good port, but it lay within the best grazing land of a country whose basic economy rested with its herds of cattle, goats, and sheep. Finally it was at Meroe that Africa's first indigenous iron industry developed. A plentiful supply of ore and wood for fuel was available locally, and by the sixth century Meroe was becoming an iron-producing center from which knowledge of iron-working was to spread south and west throughout the African continent.

Not surprisingly in view of its economic assets, the Kingdom of Kush continued to thrive from its new capital. Meroe was well known to the ancients with its walled palace on the river's edge, its great temples with their massive masonry platforms, its rows of pyramids in which generations of kings and queens were buried, its furnaces and forges and the great slag heaps still visible today, and its sprawling urban clutter. For some time the culture remained uncompromisingly Egyptian; for example, during the reign of the great king, Aspelta (593–568 B.C.), despite the fact that he had probably been responsible for transferring the capital from Napata to Meroe. Gradually, however, isolation from the north began to leave its mark, and a century later the knowledge of Egyptian hieroglyphs was clearly declining. More serious, literacy was also failing as was the general quality of craftsmanship. Cultural decline reflected growing political weakness as well, for the royal records during the fifth and fourth centuries before Christ speak increasingly of the necessity for expeditions to suppress the Beja and other nomadic raiders pressing in upon the settled kingdom.

The slow deterioration of Meroitic culture was occasionally checked under vigorous rulers like King Ergamenes, or Arqamani, (c. 220 B.C.) and his immediate successors who enjoyed a period of considerable prosperity, possibly because they encouraged closer relations with Egypt and other parts of the outside world. At the same time, the relative isolation of Meroe had its advantages for it probably spared her the more abrupt demise of her northern neighbor, Egypt, who fell first before the might of Alexander and then succumbed to the Roman legions, while the land of Kush remained a cohesive independent political unit. In any event, sporadic contact with Egypt was maintained, sometimes with unfortunate results as when the Romans sacked Napata in 23 B.C. by way of retaliation for a raid on Aswan; sometimes more happily as when Netekamani (c. 12 B.C.–c. 12 A.D.) and his queen, Amanitare, borrowed Egyptian craftsmen to assist in their widespread building program. By Roman times Meroe had long since lost knowledge of Egyptian writing and had developed her own system of hieroglyphs. In other respects, there was little that remained of the Egyptian stylistic influences; witness the Lion Temple built at Naga by Netekamani—a low ungainly structure of hulking strength decorated with Meroitic designs and script, and even showing some evidence of inspiration from India, whose trade was now reaching East Africa via Axum in the Ethiopian highlands.

New and fresh contacts such as this might have revived the fading cultural strength of Kush. Artificial reservoirs built at the time indicate more than a casual Indian influence as does the appearance of cotton cloth at Meroe. Similarly, stylistic characteristics and artifacts from the Hellenistic world were being utilized and appreciated. It was not an age of growth, however, either in the Sudan or in the Mediterranean. Rome was disinterested in an impoverished kingdom far off in the sandy wastes of Africa, and as decay slowly spread throughout imperial Rome during the early centuries of the Christian era, poverty, depopulation, and stagnation became more and more general. Shut off from a dying world, Kush expired alone. While to the north Egypt slowly collapsed under the weight of famine, brigandage, nomadic attack, and urban unrest, Kush left no record of its final agony. It is necessary to turn to the Kingdom of Axum to learn that Kush was subdued by the Axumites during the early fourth century A.D., then revolted against her overlords, and was finally overrun some years later and totally destroyed by the armies of Ezana, Axum's great conquerer:

I made war on them . . . They fled without making a stand, and I pursued them . . . killing some and capturing others . . . I burnt their towns, both those built of bricks and those built of reeds, and my army carried off their food and copper and iron . . . and destroyed the statues in their temples, their granaries, and cotton trees and cast them into the [Nile]. . . . I planted a throne in that country at the place where the rivers [Nile] and [Atbara] join.

The story of Kush and Meroe does not end with the invasion and shattering defeat by Axum for there is yet to be explained the final fate of the Kushites and how their civilization, and possibly their descendants, may have survived in the hands of others. The evidence is circumstantial but suggestive. Axum had penetrated from the east and the people of Kush probably retreated westward into Kordofan and Darfur after the fall of Meroe. If northwestern Kordofan were part of the Kingdom of Kush during the Meroitic era, a retreat in that direction by a fugitive royal family would have been a natural move. A number of clues support this hypothesis. First, several Nubian-speaking groups in Kordofan and Darfur call themselves "people of Kush," and some maintain a tradition of having come from the east under royal leadership. Further, excavations in Kordofan have yielded evidence of Meroitic penetration after the defeat by Axum—pottery of characteristic design, Egyptian motifs in burial chambers, and a red brick pyramid similar to the last tombs of the kings of Meroe. Finally, Darfur contains a palace which might have been inspired by the late royal architecture at Meroe, while some of the tribes in the area use brands strongly reminiscent of the property marks of Meroe's rulers.

It is not unreasonable to suppose, therefore, that the remnants of the royal house of Kush and their followers retreated westward and regrouped in Kordofan and Darfur to form a new kingdom. What is more intriguing still, but much more speculative, is the pos-

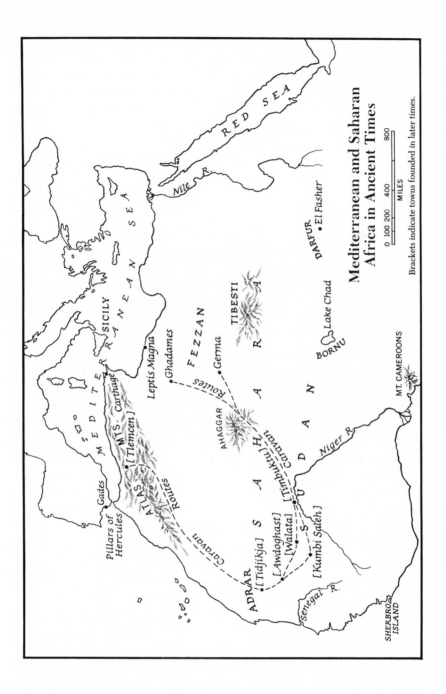

Mediterranean and Saharan
Africa in Ancient Times

RED SEA

Nile R.

MEDITERRANEAN SEA

SICILY

Leptis Magna

Ghadames

FEZZAN

Germa

TIBESTI

S A H A R A

DARFUR

•El Fasher

Lake Chad

BORNU

AHAGGAR

Routes

Caravan

Pillars of Hercules

Gades

ATLAS

Routes

Caravan

MTS. Carthage

[Tlemcen]

[Timbuktu]

[Walata]

[Awdoghast]

[Tidjikja]

ADRAR

S U D A N

[Kumbi Saleh]

Niger R.

Senegal R.

MT. CAMEROONS

SHERBRO ISLAND

0 100 200   400   800
MILES

Brackets indicate towns founded in later times.

AFRICA IN THE ANCIENT WORLD   39

sibility that Meroitic influences continued westward into the central Sudan and perhaps beyond. The great east-west highway along the southern edge of the Sahara could have easily accommodated the migration of both people and ideas. Thus might be explained the rise of several kingdoms west of Darfur in Tibesti and Bornu, and of others still farther removed—the Jukun in northern Nigeria for example—with ideas of divine kingship traceable perhaps to Egypt and Meroe. So many of the people of West Africa have traditions of an eastern or a northern origin—Yoruba tradition specifically cites Egypt and Arabia—that the idea of Egyptian and Meroitic influences becomes increasingly compelling. Finally, there is the matter of ironworking—transmitted to Egypt by the Assyrians, picked up and developed locally by Kush, and presumably disseminated south and westward from Meroe.

Unfortunately, the matter is not quite so simple. The linguistic pattern of West Africa is not hospitable to the idea of westward moving influences from the eastern Sudan during the post Meroitic era. The predominantly Negritic languages of the region are quite different from those of the central and eastern Sudan, and have been spoken in West Africa for a very long time. This does not preclude intrusion of people and ideas from the east but it does argue for a long-lived growth of indigenous ideas and institutions in the hands of West African Negroes living in the area for many thousands of years. Moreover, the matter of iron is troublesome since it was apparently mined and smelted in West Africa by at least the third century B.C., a fact which suggests either that it developed there independently or that it was introduced from some other source than Meroe which itself had only begun to use iron a scant 300 years earlier.

MEDITERRANEAN AFRICA

If knowledge of ironworking did not arrive in West Africa from the east, it may have come from the north, across the desert trade routes from Carthage which was founded by iron-using Phoenicians, probably late in the ninth century B.C. At first, the Phoenician interest in Africa was tangential for her merchants were concerned with the east-west trade in the Mediterranean, and African ports were but way stations where ships could put in for provisions and goods could be trans-shipped. Carthage was only one of many such entre-pôts, but it was extremely well situated at the narrow waist of the mid-Mediterranean, and with the decline of the Phoenician cities, the African colony emerged as the center of a trading empire of Punic settlements which stretched to the Pillars of Hercules at Gibraltar and beyond. The city of Gades on the Atlantic side of the Iberian peninsula was a Carthaginian outpost leading to trade farther north in Cornwall and Brittany. How far south the Carthaginian ships penetrated is uncertain. Carthage had inherited a number of Phoenician trading posts on the Moroccan coast beyond the Pillars of Hercules, and Herodotus reported active Carthaginian trading down the west coast of Africa. Moreover, there survives an account from the fifth century B.C. which tells of a Carthaginian admiral, Hanno, undertaking a long journey which may have led him to Sherbro Island on the Sierra Leone coast and possibly as far as Mount Cameroons.

The credibility of Hanno's account has been frequently called into question, but it does seem probable that Carthage attempted a certain amount of exploratory travel down the West African coast, and it is also reasonable to speculate that she might have had some commercial interest in overland routes south across the Sahara. On the whole, however, the small amount of evidence available is nega-tive. While the main items of trans-Saharan trade—gold, slaves, ivory, ostrich feathers, skins, and carbuncles—were to be found in the Punic markets, these items could also have been obtained in Mediter-ranean Africa. There survives a report of at least one Carthaginian said to have crossed the desert, but the report is second-hand and suspect. Though circumstantial, the fact might also be noted that no coins from the Mediterranean world have yet been found in the western Sudan, whereas many have been located in East Africa as far south as Natal. It would appear, therefore, that Carthage's African preoccupations were essentially agricultural, not commercial —that is, she was interested only in the Mediterranean coast and its Berber population as a source of food for her maritime establish-ments, and these ports were oriented northward, not southward.

Much the same judgment can be made of Rome after she had defeated Carthage and established herself as the chief power along the North African coast. Roman interest in Africa was even more ex-clusively limited to food production, and her administrative and mili-tary policies were keyed to this objective. African trade never bulked large for Rome. Her demand for gold, slaves, wild animals, and ivory was considerable, but these items were in good supply without the necessity of turning to trans-Saharan sources. Some Roman legions probably marched south to Tibesti and others may have crossed the desert to reach the Sudan, but these were isolated instances—discrete military operations rather than part of an effort to establish definite relations southward. Yet relations there were between the Sudan and North Africa; indeed, there had always been contact dating back to the prehistoric era when the Sahara enjoyed a moister climate and supported, first Negro fisherfolk along her watercourses, and later pastoralists on her slowly desiccating surface.

By historic times a regular connection between the sub-Sahara Sudan and Mediterranean Africa was being maintained and, Egypt and Kush aside, the contact followed two well-defined caravan routes. The first was in the east running from Germa and Ghadames in the Fezzan southwest to the Niger near the top of the great bend. The other was western, beginning in Morocco, descending southwestward along the Sahara side of the Atlas Mountains to the district of Adrar in modern Mauritania, then east to the trading centers in the region of the Niger bend. Writing in the fifth century B.C., Herodotus had spoken of the Garamantian people of the Fezzan proceeding south into the desert where they used four horse chariots to chase "Troglodyte Ethiopians." Presumably the troglodytes were the Tebu people of Tibesti, but the story of Herodotus had been discounted as improbable until the recent discovery of numbers of cave paintings in the Sahara representing horse-drawn chariots. At the time Herodotus composed his history, conditions in the desert may have been only slightly less severe than they are today. In any case they permitted the use of horses during historic times to maintain contact across the desert. It was the Hyksos who first introduced horses to Africa. By the beginning of the first millennium B.C. they were being used in the Fezzan and gradually they spread throughout all of North Africa and into the desert. Before this, it is probable that oxen were extensively employed for transport. Hence by the time the camel came into general use in the desert during the third and fourth century A.D., trans-Saharan communication had long been a reality.

When the Sahara had begun drying up during the later millennia of the Neolithic era, the Negroes gradually migrated south to the savanna, leaving the expanding desert in the hands of Berber pastoralists. It was these nomadic people who traversed the Sahara first by oxen, then later by horse-drawn chariot, and finally by camel. They discovered and cultivated the oases, dug the wells, and pursued a trans-Saharan trade along with their pastoral activities. The exchange of goods was accompanied by an exchange of ideas and an intermingling of blood. Thus, if the knowledge of ironworking and the use of certain plants came to West Africa from elsewhere, it may well have been the Berber who brought them south from the Mediterranean world. If certain religious and political ideas later came to be part of the way of life of the Hausa, the Fulani, or the Tokolor, these ideas could have been just as easily Berber as Meroitic.

THE ANCIENT LAND OF AXUM

To the south and east of the valley of the upper Nile, the land rises in a series of giant terraces to the heights of the Abyssinian plateau—a massive block of mountains which extends from the Nile to the Red Sea. Here, in this rolling upland, the Blue Nile traces its course in a great loop, racing from its source in Lake Tana in a five thousand foot descent through the cascades of its deep-cut gorge finally to join the more sedate White Nile at Khartoum. This mountainous country with its peaks so easily converted into fortresses and its river canyons impeding communication, has found internal cohesion difficult but freedom from invasion relatively easy to achieve. Its history has therefore tended to unfold in isolation from outside interference and influence, but often in a pattern of parochial dissension and division, a pattern which has frequently meant economic and political unrest as well as social stagnation.

Such isolation was not always the case, and to the ancient world the land of Ethiopia was regarded as an important outpost of the ancient civilization of the Middle East and Mediterranean basin. Much farther back in time, Ethiopia, like East Africa, had been host to a series of Stone Age peoples, including very likely Bushmen as well as Negroes, the latter possibly related to the hunters and fishermen of the Khartoum region. By the fourth millennium before Christ, agriculture had spread to the Abyssinian highlands where it was practiced by Cushitic speakers who had presumably migrated into the plateau area, driven perhaps by the drying out of the

Sahara. In the first millennium B.C. there occurred a major invasion from outside when Semites from the Yemen began to cross the Red Sea and occupy the northern plateau. Here they initiated major social and cultural changes which manifested themselves in such areas as language, art, and agricultural techniques. Over a period of time these Yemeni invaders conquered and settled among the local population giving the country their tribal names—Habeshat, from which was derived the word, Abyssinia, and Agaziyan, which yielded Ge'ez, the term for the classical language of Ethiopia. The indigenous people were Stone Age farmers whose relative lack of sophistication made it easy for the Semitic intruders to introduce an alien language and civilization. Thus was formed the early nucleus of the Ethiopian people with its blend of Cushitic and Semitic—an admixture both genetic and cultural.

The Yemeni Semites, once they became permanent residents of Ethiopia, established the kingdom of Axum on the northeastern Abyssinian plateau which descends in an abrupt scarp to the Red Sea. Trade with their ancient Arabian homeland continued and from their position on the shore of the Red Sea they became part of the commercial system which linked the Eastern Mediterranean, the Middle East, and the East African coast with the thriving markets of India. This was an ancient commerce based upon the demands of Pharaonic Egypt for the spices, the precious stones, and the incense of India needed to satisfy the king-gods on the Nile. East Africa too was an early supplier for the Egyptian market; even under the Old Kingdom there had been expeditions to the land of Punt in search of gold, ivory, ebony, and myrrh. That this trade continued to be important to Egypt was evidenced by the successful expedition of Queen Hatshepsut during the ascendancy of the New Kingdom one thousand years later.

The exact role of Axum in this early trade rests on supposition, for no direct evidence survives, but by the time that the Ptolemies succeeded to the Egyptian throne during the third century B.C., there were close relations between Egypt and Axum. The Ptolemies occupied the site of Adulis which later became the chief port for Axum, adding elephants to their other imports from the south for these beasts were in great demand at the time in support of Egypt's military campaigns against the Seleucids. Adulis became a possession of Egypt which colonized it and drafted the local people into the

Egyptian army, and Axum, though remaining independent, came under strong Egyptian influence.

By the time Egypt fell before the armies of Rome, Axum had become a major element in the trading complex of the Red Sea and the East African coast, and her commerce and authority steadily increased. The capital city of Axum was a wealthy, cosmopolitan center where the interior trade routes converged and caravans arrived regularly from the south and west with ivory and rhinoceros horn, animal hides and gold dust which were sent on for export to Adulis, now the port for Axum, along with locally produced spices and gum, as well as tortoise shell gathered along the coast. By the first centuries of the Christian era, Axum was said to control large areas of the African coast, ranging from the northern extremity of the Abyssinian plateau to the beginning of the East African "Horn." This expanding state resulted from energetic campaigning such as was evidenced by one Axumite king, the account of whose exploits has survived to the present. In a series of engagements he consolidated his control over the Tigre region of northeastern Abyssinia, extended the hegemony of Axum north and northwest as far as Egypt and south to the straits of Bab el Mandeb, and crossed to Arabia where he subdued tribes which had been plundering ships and caravans, thus securing trade routes by both sea and land.

It was in the middle of the fourth century A.D. that Axum achieved its greatest development both as the leading entrepôt and strongest military and political power in East Africa. King Ezana, who reigned long and successfully during this period, busied himself making safe the caravan tracks within his realm and extending his control to areas of chronic unrest where the ambush of traders was the chief occupation. In this way he subdued the Beja in the deserts north of Ethiopia and forced them to live within the Axumite kingdom, then proceeded with other campaigns aimed at chastising those who preyed on his commerce. His last expedition was also his greatest—the campaign against the people of Kush in response to their revolt against Axumite overlordship. Ezana's success was complete, driving his adversaries before him, sacking their cities, taking many prisoners, destroying their crops, and confiscating large quantities of livestock.

In commemorating his exploits Ezana had always spoken of his debt to the pagan gods of Axum, but in the case of Kush he ascribed his good fortune to the "Lord of Heaven, Who has helped me and given me sovereignty . . . and . . . has this day conquered for me my enemy." This was a significant change for it meant that the king had been converted to the Christian faith which had been making some headway in his realm since the early years of his reign. Ethiopian tradition states that the kings of Ethiopia are of Judaic stock in direct descent from Solomon and the Queen of Sheba, and goes on to offer a somewhat fanciful account of the country's Christian conversion, completely ignoring the role of Ezana. In fact, Christianity had been early introduced into Axum through mercantile relations with Byzantium, but it became the official religion of the state as a result of Ezana's conversion. This resulted from the devoted missionary work of a Syrian Christian named Frumentius who had been Ezana's tutor and who eventually became bishop at Axum on appointment by the bishop of Alexandria. However, Ezana's conversion seemingly had political as well as religious implications for it cemented good relations with the Roman emperor, Constantine, and ratified Axum's position as the commercial and cultural outpost of Hellenic civilization in East Africa.

Outside the court the conversion had little immediate influence for the majority of the people still worshipped their ancient gods. Nevertheless, by the sixth century after Christ, Christian influence had become well advanced and, because of the historical connection with Alexandria, the Ethiopian church followed the Egyptian Copts in their adherence to the Monophysite doctrine. This doctrinal divergence had no effect on relations with the Mediterranean world, for Byzantium, though it persecuted Monophysites in its own land, regarded Axum as a friendly Christian power. Ethiopian merchandise continued to play a major part in the international trade complex, and there is evidence that Axum's far-ranging commercial activities may have penetrated well inland, possibly tapping gold-bearing areas in Kenya.

Nevertheless, signs of decay were already apparent. The Mediterranean world, its strength spent, was slowly disintegrating. By the end of the fifth century A.D., the power of Rome lay destroyed in the West, the victim of successive waves of invasion combined with internal decay. In the East the old Graeco-Roman trade with India dwindled and died, and knowledge of East Africa's ports was lost. The agricultural population of Axum had always been dependent on outsiders to maintain its contacts with Mediterranean civilization;

hence, when the Muslim conquests of the mid-seventh century engulfed Egypt and North Africa, Axum was suddenly cut off and
thrown in upon itself. Arabs occupied Adulis and other Red Sea ports
fell to the rejuvenated Beja who scattered the Yemeni, Jewish, and
Greek merchants and severed the trade routes. Economic stagnation
led to cultural decline and political chaos. Greek was no longer
spoken, minted currency became rare, church construction ceased, and
pagan worship was revived. Gradually the Christian faith was naturalized and adapted to local conditions, producing the particular
brand of Christianity which developed in Ethiopia with its amalgam
of Coptic doctrine, indigenous pagan survivals, and Jewish practices
imported from Arabia before the rise of Islam. At the same time the
central power declined and the local nobility began to indulge in
civil strife. The pressure of the Beja forced the Axumites to turn
their attention inward, first to the hills of their native Tigre and then
by degrees to the less accessible parts of the Abyssinian plateau in
the Amhara and Shoa country to the south. Here the Axumites found
a population to whom they brought their Semitic language of Ge'ez
and their Monophysite Christianity, and gradually there emerged
an Ethiopian people born of the fusion of the Semitized Axumites
with the Cushitic highland peasant farmers.

Although the strength of Axum declined, its culture survived to
become part of another Ethiopian civilization which was to live in
isolation for a thousand years. Unfortunately the substance and
source of the ancient culture of Axum is little known. Certainly there
was influence from southern Arabia and from Greece—the earliest
known king of Axum had a Greek education and later kings issued
their public documents in Greek as well as Ge'ez. Essentially, however, these early Ethiopians developed their own civilization; witness,
for example, the pronounced artistic sophistication of local inspiration exemplified by the celebrated stone monuments of Axum. The
purpose of these monoliths has remained a mystery but clear to see
is their lightness and grace and the architectural motifs which indicate a secure knowledge of stone and wood construction of a post
and lintel design. Indeed, some of Axum's ruins suggest that at one
time she was the site of multi-storied castles with stepped walls and
battlements. Such seems likely for travellers reported that during
the sixth century the king of Axum lived in a formidable palace with
corner towers, bespeaking a power and elegance appropriate to the
importance of its royal inhabitant:

The king . . . was naked, wearing only a garment of linen embroidered with gold from which hung four fillets on either side; around his neck was a golden collar. He stood on a four-wheeled chariot drawn by four elephants; the body of the chariot was high and covered with gold plates. The king stood on top carrying a small gilded shield and holding in his hands two small gilded spears. His council stood around similarly armed and flutes played.

Suggestions for Further Reading

The rise and fall of Kush and its relations with ancient Egypt is dealt with systematically and thoroughly in A. J. Arkell, *A History of the Sudan from the Earliest Times to 1821*, rev. ed. (London: The Athlone Press, 1961; New York: Oxford University Press, 1961). This can be supplemented by periodical literature—for example, G. A. Wainwright, "Iron in the Napatan and Meroitic Ages," *Sudan Notes and Records*, XXVI, 1945; P. L. Shinnie, "The Fall of Meroe," *Kush*, III, 1955; and D. P. Kirwin, "The Decline and Fall of Meroe," *Kush*, VIII, 1960. See also P. L. Shinnie's *Meroe* (London: Thames and Hudson, 1967; New York: Praeger, 1966).

Some discussion of Meroe is contained in Basil Davidson, *The Lost Cities of Africa* (Boston: Little Brown and Co., 1959) which also deals with the question of influences brought to the Sudan across the Sahara from the north and the east. The standard work on the Saharan trade routes, however, is E. W. Bovill, *The Golden Trade of the Moors* (London: Oxford University Press, 1958). An antidote to the Europocentric view of cultural origins in West Africa is contained in J. Suret-Canale, *Afrique Noire, Occidentale et Centrale* (Paris: Editions Sociales, 1961). Also to be consulted are important articles by R. Mauny: for example, "Une Route Prehistorique à Travers le Sahara Occidentale," *Bulletin de l'Institut Français d'Afrique Noire*, IX, 1947; "Histoire des Métaux en Afrique Occidentale," *Ibid.*, XIV, 1952; "Une Age de Cuivre au Sahara Occidentale?" *Ibid.*, XIII, *1951;* and "Monnaies Anciennes d'Afrique Occidentale," *Notes Africaines*, Apr., 1949, no. 42. For the North Africa of Carthage and Rome, see C. A. Julien, *Histoire de l'Afrique du Nord*, 2nd. ed., I (Paris: Payot, 1964). In addition to the African references contained in Herodotus, see also W. H. Schoff, ed., *The Periplus of Hanno* (Philadelphia: The Commercial Museum, 1912), and G. Germain, "Qu'est-ce que le Périple d'Hannon?" *Hespéris*, XLIV, 1957.

While Arkell contains some references to ancient Axum, see instead Ernest Budge, *A History of Ethiopia*, I (Oosterhout, Netherlands: Anthropological Publications, 1966; New York, Humanities Press, 1966);

E. S. Pankhurst, *Ethiopia: A Cultural History* (Woodford Green, Essex: Lalibela House, 1955); A. H. M. Jones and E. Monroe, *A History of Ethiopia* (Oxford: The Clarendon Press, 1960); and R. Greenfield, *Ethiopia* (London: Pall Mall; New York: Praeger, 1965). Information on the role of Axum in the Indian Ocean trade is contained in W. H. Schoff, *The Periplus of the Erythraen Sea* (London: Longmans Green, 1912).

3: The States of the Western
and Central Sudan

THE WORLD OF THE DESERT AND THE SAVANNA

When the Sahara area began drying up about three thousand years before the time of Christ, it necessarily brought profound changes in the ecology of the region. Life did not end, however; it merely altered itself to meet the new conditions which confronted it. Like a receding tide, the water left the desert, taking with it much of the animal and vegetable world it had supported. During its wet phase, the Sahara had been a land of forests and lush meadows crossed by streams and dotted with lakes where the early Negro fisherfolk had fashioned their barbed-tipped harpoons and where later herds of cattle fattened on the rich pasture. Bit by bit the land grew more arid. In the Tassili Mountains deep in that region of the desert which is today the southeastern corner of Algeria, cave paintings have been discovered indicating not only an active human society many millennia ago but depicting as well an inexorable transition in the countryside—from herds of grazing cattle to a land of wild beasts, then later to a scrubland in which hunters stalked their prey while the pastoralists moved their livestock off to better feeding grounds.

During the Neolithic period, these settlements were spread

widely throughout the Sahara which also was the locale for a profusion of Africa's traditional wild life—lion, giraffe, elephant, antelope, and ostrich. By historic times, however, most of the flora and fauna had disappeared. Where once savanna grass had flourished, sub-desert bush prevailed, while deep in the interior even this type of scrub had given way to the desolate wastes of bare rock and drifting sand. Game still existed on a reduced scale for there were some animals capable of surviving for long periods solely on the moisture of their forage, while others limited their range to highland areas where water was available. Some districts like Ahaggar with its lofty peaks had permanent pools and occasional streams where crocodiles still thrived and air-breathing catfish managed to endure drought periods for months or even years at a time.

Most of the human population also migrated with the receding water supply, and so it was that the savanna came to be the *Bilad al-Sudan,* the land of the black people who abandoned their ancient Saharan sites and settled in the grasslands bordering the desert, eventually establishing themselves there as farmers and pastoralists. Not all the human dwellers of the desert departed, however. Scattered throughout the Sahara were nomadic people of Berber origin who like the wild animals were able to adapt themselves to the rigors of desert life. By the time of the first millennium after Christ, the dominant desert nomads had emerged as the Tuareg—fair-skinned Berbers whose men wore veils even while eating, and whose military state and individual toughness made them peculiarly capable of wresting a livelihood from the slender resources of their land. Constantly on the move in search of pasture and water, they migrated with the seasons, feeding their livestock in the more settled areas north and south of the desert during the hot months of the dry period. Their marginal existence, always vulnerable to the vagaries of the weather, made them both the natural foe and the dependent of the savanna people. During excessively dry weather they tended to raid and to occupy the moister regions, and in any event, they fostered a trans-Saharan trade, not so much for the goods it brought into their hands, but for the tribute which could be exacted from caravans traveling to and from the savanna which were obliged to pass along Tuareg trade routes and to rest at Tuareg oases.

Hence, the desert nomads were bound up in a vast rhythm of history with the peoples who lived to the north and to the south of them. In times of stress when conditions became severe and the savanna or Mediterranean states were weak, the desert encroached on the settled areas and the desert people predominated. Conversely, when the savanna was organized under a strong central regime, the settled area extended farther into the desert and the nomadic peoples frequently were forced to pay allegiance to a stronger power. It was a rhythm which aptly described the history of the Sahara and the Sudan until the era of colonial administration was ushered in at the opening of the twentieth century.

To the south of the Sahara, with its vast stony wastes, its areas of shifting sand, and its occasional mountainous masses peaked by gaunt outcrops, the land gradually becomes more congenial as first steppe scrub and then more abundant growth of grassland announce the presence of the true savanna. Beyond the savanna, approaching the equatorial low pressure zone, is the tropical rain forest stretching along the West African coast in a relatively narrow band of varying width. Into these territories the Saharan Negroes appear to have retreated before the force of the expanding drought, and settling there, they gradually evolved local variations on a common cultural and linguistic heritage over a period of several millennia. Rivers like the Niger and the Senegal combined with the open country to facilitate movement, and even the forest was no great impediment to migrating groups moving slowly in search of food or retreating to its shelter to avoid pursuit by some enemy.

In the savanna a slow evolution transformed a foraging into a food-producing economy. Agricultural methods were initially rudimentary and the range of crops limited, but local variations emerged which ultimately found some of the more resourceful people like the Hausa, Bambara, and Mandinka developing a deep-plowing technique for their millet and irrigation for cotton culture and other special crops. Animal husbandry became common, while beasts of burden from across the Sahara—the horse, the camel, and the donkey —provided locomotion for man and his goods. Stock raising became a way of life for some people, particularly the ubiquitous and peripatetic Fulani, but the utility of cattle was recognized by all—meat and dairy products to buttress a scanty diet, hides to be converted into leather, and muscle power for porterage.

The economy remained essentially agricultural, but it was by no means exclusively so. Knowledge of ironworking had come to West Africa in the closing centuries of the pre-Christian era, bringing with it implications for economic activity as well as for warfare and statecraft. By the time Arab explorers first began to visit the African interior in the tenth century A.D. they found there a highly developed craft production designed to feed the trans-Saharan trade to the north. In the bazaars and streets of the growing mercantile cities artisans wove their traditional cloth and produced artifacts and ornaments in cast bronze or worked gold and silver. These goods, added to quantities of raw gold, grain, gum, hides, ostrich feathers, ivory, kola nuts, and slaves, were shipped across the desert along the Tuareg-controlled trade routes in exchange for the silks, beads, mirrors, swords, horses, and foodstuffs of Mediterranean Africa. Most of all, however, the people of the savanna were interested in the salt that could not be obtained in their own land, and for this precious commodity they exchanged gold and slaves, particularly the former, which was the most sought-after product of the south, in the markets of North Africa.

Salt and gold—these were the driving forces behind the desert trade which grew during the centuries of the first millennium after Christ. The gold came in profusion—perhaps as much as nine tons a year—from a district called Wangara which was probably in fact two places—the Lobi area in Upper Volta and the region in modern Guinea and Mali located between the confluences of the Niger, Senegal, and Falémé rivers. Two methods of mining were employed. The first was to extract and refine gold-bearing ore dug from pits, while the second simply harvested the gold washed down along the stream beds by the annual flooding. In either case the gold was transported to a location where the salt caravans from the north had assembled, and here took place the celebrated silent trade, so widespread as to be frequently remarked by historians from Herodotus onward. Under this arrangement each side simply alternated in matching piles of gold and salt until a satisfactory exchange had been consummated, and during the whole transaction no word was spoken and none was necessary. It was a serious business for the southerners whose need of salt was so great that in some cases they offered gold for salt on an equal basis by weight, and it was not uncommon for salt to be broken into pieces and used for money among the Sudanic Negroes.

Such a lofty evaluation was ironic for most of the salt was mined in Taghaza, a dreary village far off in the northern desert, inhabited only by Negro slaves controlled by the Tuareg. Salt was so common in Taghaza as to be cut into building blocks for the walls of houses

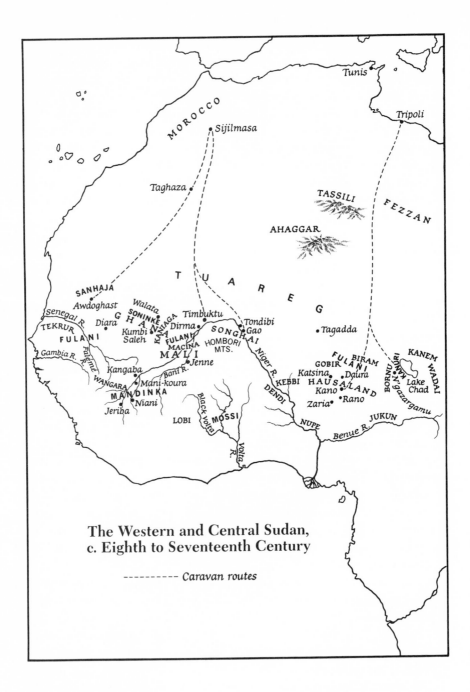

The Western and Central Sudan,
c. Eighth to Seventeenth Century

--------- Caravan routes

and mosques, and the miners of all this wealth were miserable wretches, often blinded as a result of the severe desert winds and subsisting on palm dates and camel meat brought by merchants who had come to collect their cargo of salt. That much of the profit fell to the traders was not surprising since they not only organized the enterprise but risked murder and extortion at the hands of the Saharan nomads or annihilation in the desert should their caravans be engulfed by columns of swirling sand or, losing direction in a trackless waste, wander aimlessly until the water gave out. By about 1000 A.D. there were four main routes, all dangerous even to the experienced traveler. Two in the west started from Sijilmasa in Morocco, one running through Taghaza to Awdoghast and the other proceeding straight south to Timbuktu and Gao. The other routes began in Tunis and Tripoli moving across the desert to Hausaland and Bornu respectively via the Fezzan.

Living in the savanna over countless centuries, the Negroes governed their communities through indigenous custom and law which was not only virile and workable in its own right but showed great resilience and flexibility in the face of invasion by both foreign people and ideas. The geography of the Sudan favored absorption and adaptation, for its easy lines of communication made it a natural meeting place where ideas, institutions, and blood strains could meet, fuse, and strengthen one another. Somehow, the fusion of local and exotic strains terminated in a hybrid more characteristically Sudanic than otherwise. For example, virtually every one of the medieval savanna kingdoms possessed traditions involving immigration of ruling dynasties from the north and east, but these rulers soon became absorbed and Negro kings held the reins of government during the apogee of such powerful states as Ghana, Mali, and Songhai. The bulk of the savanna population was the product of racial intermixture, and it was commonplace for villages of completely different tribal and cultural entities to coexist peaceably. Perhaps most illustrative of this process of blending and accommodation in the Sudan have been the Fulani with their hybrid background of Caucasian and Negro blood, their history of migration, and their intimate involvement in the affairs of Sudanic communities from the Senegal to the Benue.

The ability of the Sudanic civilization to adopt, absorb, and utilize outside influences was well exemplified by its early reaction to Islam. Islam arrived in the savanna via the trade routes, brought both by nomadic desert people and Arab merchants from the north. These latter established Muslim communities in the cities at the southern end of the caravan trails where mosques were raised, written Arabic introduced, and the wealth of Islamic learning laid open for all comers. Muslim interpreters were pressed into service in Ghana by its Negro kings and most of the state ministers were Muslim. In Mali the ruling dynasty numbered several practicing Muslims whose effective government was aided by Muslim officials and administrative practice. A similar pattern developed later in Songhai as well as in the Hausa states and the kingdom of Kanem to the east, aided perhaps by the Fulani who were already beginning to move through the savanna by the thirteenth century, A.D., spreading Muslim law and theology as a by-product of their wanderings.

Yet this Islamic impact was superficial. The vast majority of the people were untouched by the new faith and even the royal dynasties seemed to regard the teachings of the Prophet as an aid to more efficient administration rather than a divinely inspired way of life. The kings of Ghana remained pagan to the end, and the great Muslim rulers of Mali and her successors constantly shocked devout observers by their casual religious ritual or their continued accommodation of pagan institutions. In Mali the *mansa,* or king, gave scrupulous observance to Islamic practice but combined this with a tolerance for traditional customs at court and in the community at large; for example, certain accepted forms of public nudity or the practice of covering the head with dust when prostrating oneself before the ruler. In Songhai, the renowned conquerer King Ali of the *Sunni* dynasty, was a professed Muslim who nevertheless permitted himself to persecute the Muslims of Timbuktu. His successor, the *askia* Muhammad Toure, though encouraging Islamic institutions and relying heavily on Muslim advisers, failed to establish Islam as a state religion or to introduce it widely among his people.

The fact is there was no genuinely popular response to Islam among the people of the savanna until the religious upheavals of the nineteenth century. The Muslim way was able to make only slow progress over the centuries in the face of the virility of traditional customs. As for the rulers of the medieval kingdoms, they were glad enough to have the assistance of literate, educated advisers, but they were well aware that their political strength frequently rested, not on an alien system, but upon their mystical and spiritual powers as king, priest, and clan head under traditional African religious practice. Rejecting pagan ideas as godless and primitive, Islam was necessarily suspect in the eyes of the Sudanic rulers; hence, the double standard of the kings of Mali or the apparent paradox of *Sunni* Ali's hostility toward the religion he embraced as his own. Thus too may be explained Muhammad Toure's devoted encouragement of Islamic law and culture alongside his longstanding indifference to *jihads*, or holy wars, against pagan neighbors and his deference to traditional institutions as an important element in his celebrated imperial administration.

If Islam did take hold in any particular environment, it was in the great cities of the Sudan—Walata, Awdoghast, Kumbi Saleh, Gao, Kano, Timbuktu, and others—whose commercial preoccupations made them receptive toward outside influences and new ideas to an extent not to be found in the simpler bucolic world which surrounded them. If trade was the basis of their existence, a bourgeois culture and a cosmopolitan population was the hallmark of their character. Local farmers driving their produce-laden donkeys to market fought for space in the crowded streets with caravans from far to the north led by sharp-eyed Arab merchants. The king's horsemen, for all their military impressiveness, competed for the attention of passersby with squadrons of blue-clad Tuareg beating and cursing their furiously protesting camels. Naked servant girls hurrying along on some errand brushed past Muslim scholars quick to express a sense of puritan outrage at what they regarded as pagan indecorum. The cities were the places where the royal court sat with its galaxy of ministers, scribes, petty functionaries, and attendants, but they also abounded in craftsmen, students, slaves, scholars, and representatives of far-flung commerical enterprises. The African sections were marked by the characteristic round huts topped with thatched roofs, but large foreign quarters had also grown up to accommodate an expanding population of Muslims from the desert and beyond. Here were the mosques and the rectangular stone or mud houses with their interior courtyards, their heavy windowless walls on which were traced obscure symbols in geometric pattern, and their comfortable quarters where good food was prized along with good conversation, and a life of contemplation was aided by well-stocked libraries.

One feature of the Sudanic cities was the honored place which was given to women. In Kumbi Saleh they wore collars and bracelets, a form of adornment which was otherwise reserved for the king himself. In Walata they were renowned for their beauty and, though devout, were free to have lovers as they desired. The social position and personal liberty enjoyed by women never ceased to astonish Muslim travelers, nor yet did the widespread custom of uterine descent whereby the heir apparent to the throne was not the king's son but the son of his sister. The important position of women, in addition to the bourgeois-mercantile quality of urban society, was reminiscent of the cities of the European Renaissance, and like the European cities, those of the savanna maintained a quasi-independent status despite their location within a series of powerful empires.

Though similar in many basic respects, each metropolis had its particular character and period of greatness. Awdoghast, lying a two-week journey west of Kumbi, was a wealthy town where personal comfort and luxury held sway along with cultivation of the arts. Perched on the edge of the desert, it nevertheless had an abundant water supply which sustained fine herds of cattle and sheep and made possible a wide range of agricultural produce including wheat, millet, figs, dates, and grapes. Kumbi, the chief trading center during the ascendancy of the kingdom of Ghana, remained important even after its sack by the Almoravids in 1076, but the particular flavor of its Soninke Negro civilization and the richness of the royal house with its golden trappings ceased to exist after that time. Indeed, Kumbi finally collapsed when seized by the Soso in 1203 and was replaced during the thirteenth century by Walata, a hundred miles to the north, as the new terminus for the Saharan trade of the western desert.

Eventually Walata gave way to Timbuktu and Gao as the political center of gravity shifted eastward, first from Ghana to Mali, and then to Songhai. Gao, on the Niger bend, was reportedly a large and beautiful metropolis with an active trading life and abundant crops, including a special kind of cucumber which delighted that great voyager from North Africa, Ibn Battuta, when he visited the Sudan in the middle of the fourteenth century. Further up the Niger from Gao, Ibn Battuta identified Yufi [Nupe ?], a Negro city where white men were not welcome and which he did not visit, but his own travels took him eastward from Gao to Tagadda, another wealthy market town which imported fabrics and other goods from Egypt, and reportedly mined copper which, according to Ibn Battuta, was cast locally and shipped south and east to Hausaland and Bornu. The Hausa cities, Kano, Katsina, Zaria, and others, did not become important as caravan centers until the sixteenth-century decline of Songhai. They were located in combined woodland and farming country which produced abundant citrus fruit and cereal crops raised by the tall, black-skinned, broad-faced people of the region. Eventually Kano would become the leading market of the central Sudan with its houses of sun-baked mud, its vast market, its mosques, its great walls, and its complement of cultivated and prosperous merchants.

The most celebrated of these savanna cities, at least outside the Sudan, was Timbuktu, founded about 1100 A.D. by Tuareg nomads as a communications outpost just north of the Niger near the top of the river's great bend. Timbuktu had grown with the fortunes of Mali and had survived the persecutions of Songhai's empire builder, *Sunni* Ali, to become an important center of commerce and scholarship by the early sixteenth century. It was visited at that time by another renowned traveler, Leo Africanus, who set down a faithful description of its appearance and the life of its people just as it was being developed by the great *askia*, Muhammad Toure, as a regional capital where the Islamic civilization of the Sudan might thrive.

Leo noted the fine Sankore mosque and palace erected in the time of *Mansa* Musa (1312–1337), and spoke glowingly of the wealth and power of Muhammad Toure. He also commented on the many shops owned by merchants and craftsmen, growing rich on the lively trade in fabrics, spices, copper, gold, ivory, ostrich feathers, and slaves. An ample supply of water was available from wells and sluices which brought the overflow from the Niger, and this supply was sufficient to sustain a thriving agriculture. The population, which probably approached fifty thousand, was friendly and hospitable and given to celebrations which went far into the night with much singing and dancing in the streets. Most of all, Leo was impressed by the city's intellectual activities, for the king, Muhammad Toure, had attracted many learned and professional men to Timbuktu and supported their studies from his own treasury. Libraries were large and numerous and the Sankore mosque was doing double duty as a university as well as a place of worship. Located strategically at the end of trade routes which stretched as far as Venice, Genoa, and Cairo, Timbuktu flourished as long as the civilization it represented was able to provide peace and political stability for its trade. With the collapse of the Songhai empire, however, the fortunes of Timbuktu took a permanent turn which saw the once thriving city degenerate into an isolated dusty town, a handful of unimpressive mud buildings housing a listless population which time had finally passed by.

THE ANATOMY OF EMPIRE IN THE SUDAN

The great empires of the medieval Sudan have sometimes been regarded as ephemeral political entities without great intrinsic unity and lacking even frontiers to delineate the extent of their authority. In a purely time sense it seems unreasonable to impute weakness to states which lasted as long as Ghana's three centuries, Mali's effective existence from the advent of Sundiata in 1230 A.D. until the capture of Jenne by *Sunni* Ali over two hundred years later, the unbroken thousand-year reign of the ruling *mais* of Kanem-Bornu, or the long-lived stability of the Mossi states. Furthermore, the test of political vitality in these African kingdoms must be in terms of Africa's own traditional social institutions which made for an administrative and political structure vastly different from the concept of empire which developed, for example, in the West.

Political authority within the Negro civilization of the savanna had evolved over time at two differing levels, each of which was rooted in the idea of mutual relationships between individuals or groups. One level comprised the village community which was the essential economic unit of this rural civilization. Within the village, authority rested with such individuals as the heads of families, the members of the council of elders, and the chief. The formation of large imperial states was not only unusual but had little direct effect on political authority at this village level. Within their sphere the village leaders continued unchallenged, for the connection between the village and the enlarged state was made at quite a different level of political relation.

This second level was the lineage or the age grouping involving individuals who possessed common ancestry or identical age grade. The members of these groups, spread out over a number of villages, shared a fixed status such as rulers, nobility, serfs, and others, performed hereditary occupational roles long associated with their family group—farmers, merchants, craftsmen, hunters, and so forth —or in the case of the age set, inherited different civic functions as they passed through successive age grades. State-making occurred when the leader of one of these affiliations—the head of an age group, or the chief of a warrior clan, for example—succeeded by persuasion or more usually by force in imposing his authority on a growing number of independent villages. Such a configuration, based upon duties and responsibilities within a group membership constituted a vastly different form of polity than the idea of state defined by territorial dimension and the imposition of authority by one civilization, nation, or political association, upon another.

Under this system many political groupings based on lineage and age-set relationships could coexist within the same state, having little impact upon each other or upon the village community. A lineage could profoundly change its character, perhaps by adopting Islam, without having any marked effect on the rest of the society. The ruler was concerned, therefore, not with total domination of a particular territory but with maintaining clan relationships on which he could rely for such services as troop requisitions, tribute, labor on the royal lands, or servants for his court. In the Sudan, the state had no boundaries; only spheres of influence. It had no name; only the title of its ruler. It had no body of law; only the fixed obligations based upon kinship or other inherited status.

To be sure, the system had certain innate weaknesses, although such weaknesses have been apparent in other political configurations from the days of ancient Persia to more recent times. The savanna kingdoms infrequently possessed cultural and ethnic homogeneity; they were built on military conquest; imperial expansion often outran imperial administration; the problem of internal policing was never satisfactorily solved nor was the matter of orderly transfer of power through recognized succession. Hence when powerful outside pressures built up, these states, lacking internal cohesion, sometimes fragmented and disappeared, but in this respect they were only following where the empires of Alexander of Macedon and Charlemagne had already led.

THE KINGDOM OF GHANA

The earliest known kingdom of the Sudan was Ghana and its history well exemplified the ancient conflict between the Sahara and the savanna, involving both the religious asceticism of the desert and the desire for gold which has infected all men. Its origins have been lost but by the time it had come to the notice of Arab commentators late in the eighth century, Ghana was already a thriving state headed by Soninke Negro kings and renowned for its wealth in gold. Its traditions spoke of a founding dynasty from the north which was non-Negro, a not surprising statement considering Ghana's position near the southern edge of the desert bringing intimate involvment with the trans-Saharan trade and a growing rivalry with neighboring Berber groups. By the ninth century Ghana was approaching the fullest extent of its power and influence with territory extending to the south as far as the upper reaches of the Niger and Senegal, to the north as far as the desert and to the east as far as the Niger bend.

Control of the Wangara gold assured the prosperity of Ghana's kings, but Ghana suffered from the competition of Awdoghast lying to the west, which was controlled by Sanhaja Berbers and which was laying its own claim to become the major terminus for the commerce across the western Sahara. The vexation of the Awdoghast competition was temporarily laid to rest in 990 A. D., however, when the Soninke of Ghana captured the rival city during a period of internal dissension among the Sanhaja. This was the peak moment of glory. The market city of Kumbi Saleh became the chief mercantile and intellectual center in the Sudan and her king was renowned for his wealth and the splendor of his court. When he held audience, he appeared resplendent in garments of fine cloth and ornaments of gold, while his retainers and even the royal animals were similarly bedecked. His tariffs filled the royal treasury, while gold production in the realm was so great that the king was obliged to confiscate all but the gold dust in order to avoid currency depreciation, a process which greatly expanded the royal wealth.

Such prosperity was short-lived. During the eleventh century, the Sanhaja experienced a profound religious revival led by a particularly puritanical Muslim sect, the Almoravids, and the white heat of religious fervor was soon converted into a *jihad* with repercussions as far as Morocco and the states of Andalusia. In the Sudan, this holy war took the shape of a campaign which recaptured Awdoghast in 1055; then when some of Ghana's tributaries sought advantage from the situation and revolted, the weakened state of Ghana was unable to withstand another Almoravid attack and Kumbi fell in 1076. The Soninke garrison in Awdoghast had been put to death, and with the fall of Kumbi large numbers of people were massacred or forced to submit to Muslim conversion. For a time, it seemed as if Ghana might yet save itself when the Almoravid movement collapsed as quickly as it had arisen, but the basic damage had already been done. Mortally wounded by outside attack and internal unrest, its trade disrupted, its wealth pillaged, and its neglected land no longer productive, Ghana could not muster the strength for survival. The Soso chieftaincy of Kaniaga, a former vassal state which had already revolted successfully, moved to capture Ghana under the leadership of Sumaguru Kante, and in 1203 Kumbi was sacked and the independent kingdom of Ghana ceased to exist. The merchants of Kumbi, no longer able to pursue their affairs at the old site, moved about one hundred miles north toward the desert where a new commercial center, Walata, soon emerged as the major caravan terminus of the region.

THE RISE AND FALL OF MALI

The exploits of Sumaguru seemed to be the beginning of a new power centering on the Soso, but in fact the heir to Ghana's authority lay in another quarter. South of Kaniaga along the upper reaches of the Niger, were Mandinka Negroes occupying fertile farm land near the source of West Africa's gold supply, and these people were subdued by Sumaguru after his victory over Ghana. According to one tradition, Sumaguru put all the sons of the Mandinka ruler to death save one who was spared as an inconsequential cripple. This sole survivor, Sundiata, overcame his weakness, rallied local support, and fashioning a guerrilla army, eventually defeated and killed Sumaguru in 1235. The Soso were quickly absorbed, whereupon Sundiata advanced northward, sacked and annexed the remnants of Ghana in 1240, while at the same time taking control of the gold-bearing districts of Wangara. This was the genesis of the empire of Mali which, in a few short years, had established itself, extending its hegemony to include all of the former sphere of influence of Ghana.

Although the early Mandinka princes were said to be Muslims, it seems likely that Sundiata was a pagan, and it was on the traditional relationships within clans and lineage groups that he built his administration. To secure these relationships he maintained a shifting capital which successively moved among such river villages as Niani, Jeriba, Mani-Koura, or Kangaba, each of which presumably was called Mali while serving as Sundiata's headquarters. Significantly, these were agricultural communities, for Mali was rooted in a farming economy, but this by no means meant a neglect of the commercial possibilities of the trans-desert traffic. In addition to the gold supplies in the south, Mali reached out to control the salt of Taghaza as well as Saharan copper, and it was during the period of Mali's growth during the thirteenth century that Timbuktu began its development within the new kingdom as an entrepôt for desert caravans.

The precise extent of the empire under Sundiata is not known, but after his death in 1255 additional conquests were made by the *mansa*, Wali (1255–1270), and by Sabakura (1285–c. 1300) a freed slave of the royal household who seized power during a period of weakness within the ruling dynasty. Either Sundiata or Wali first brought Songhai under Mali suzerainty and Sabakura was apparently responsible for campaigns deep into Tekrur in the west as well as for the capture of Gao in the east. Nevertheless, until recently many of these conquests had been attributed to *Mansa* Musa (1312–1337), partly because Musa's devotion to Islam attracted the praise of Muslim historians and partly because of his glittering pilgrimage to Mecca in 1324–1325 which greatly spread the fame of Mali throughout Europe and the Middle East.

The progress of Musa's caravan has been recorded and savored by historians—the five hundred slaves bearing golden staffs, the hundred camels each loaded with three hundred pounds of gold, the spending spree in the bazaars of Cairo, and the scattering of bounty with such a lavish hand as to force a serious depreciation of gold on the Cairo exchange. So too has his sponsorship of as-Sahili, a poet and architect from Andalusia, who returned from Mecca with Musa's entourage to introduce an Arabian style to the religious and secular architecture of the Sudan. These events along with the number of Muslim scholars he brought back from the Middle East, emphasized Musa's Islamic persuasion and doubtless pleased Muslim historians who thereby may have tended to underestimate the accomplishments of Musa's royal predecessors. Moreover, they may have overlooked the degree to which the king, for all his devotion to Islamic religion and civilization, continued to rely upon traditional institutions for the administration of his realm. For example, when the propagation of the true faith threatened gold production in pagan Wangara, proselytizing was quickly abandoned. Moreover, despite the might and glory of Mali's great rulers, the integrity of local chieftaincies was scrupulously observed, and no attempt was made to eliminate traditional ritual at the royal court. Describing the audiences of the *mansa* a few years after Musa's death, Ibn Battuta approvingly commented on evidence of Islamic practice, but he was also obliged to observe the importance of customary usage—the *mansa* seated amidst the many traditional articles symbolic of royal authority, the elaborate ceremony with its liberal reliance on ritual magic, the rigid demands on time-honored protocol tendering homage to the ruler through prostration and dusting, and the royal Mandinka decorations for distinguished service which took the form of trousers of exceptional width.

The splendor of Mali reached during the reign of Musa continued for several decades but by the late years of the fourteenth century the problem of dynastic succession had intruded a fatal weakness into the government. Palace quarrels encouraged outside attack. As the fifteenth century opened, the Mossi were raiding the subject state of Macina, and later by 1450, Macina succeeded in regaining its independence from Mali. To the north the Tuareg occupied Timbuktu and Walata in 1433–1434, and in 1468 *Sunni Ali* of the rising power of Songhai captured Timbuktu, five years later reducing the supposedly impregnable town of Jenne. The rise of Songhai put an effective end to Mali's hegemony in the eastern Niger region, but her power lingered on fitfully in the west. Gradually deteriorating, however, it was finally snuffed out in the middle of the seventeenth century with the appearance of the Bambara states of Kaarta and Segu. Thus, after four hundred years, the great Mali empire had finally returned to the original status of a small chieftaincy on the upper Niger.

THE EMPIRE OF SONGHAI

By the time of Mali's final demise, Songhai, her imperial successor in the Sudan, had experienced her own brief moment of ascendancy —a century and a half which saw a rapid expansion across the western savanna, a short period of stability, and then an equally rapid decline into extinction. All this came as a climax to a long era of much more modest development. Like so many Sudanic peoples, those of Songhai had a tradition of northern intrusion on an indigenous people. According to this tradition, during the early Christian era Negro farmers and fisherfolk were settled along the Niger in what is today northwestern Nigeria. At some as yet undetermined moment they were invaded by northerners who may have been Berbers or even possibly refugees from Kush migrating westward after the fall of Meroe. At any event, these immigrants established the ruling Za dynasty but were soon absorbed into the local population, thus producing another example of a heterogeneous people living in the cosmopolitan Sudan.

After this early merger the Songhai people began to migrate up the river northward, eventually establishing themselves at Gao in a move which was of critical importance to the fortunes of the growing state. In the first place, it vastly improved the trading position of the Songhai, for the new location soon developed into a lively market town on which caravans converged from all directions. Next, it revolutionized Songhai's strategic position, placing her astride the east-west route of the Niger bend. Finally, it brought the Songhai into much closer contact with Islamic civilization, and the royal house, if not the general population, seems to have undergone conversion by the eleventh century. Rising wealth meant growing influence and expanding authority. Not long after the move up the river, the Songhai were already receiving the allegiance of a number of lesser principalities in their neighborhood.

At first this independent rise to power ran into difficulties. As early as the days of Sundiata, Mali may have exercised some degree of suzerainty over Songhai, and at the time of *Mansa* Musa, Mali clearly was in control of the younger state, placing great importance on the now thriving territory with its fine, large market city of Gao. The aggressive drive of the expanding Songhai could not be contained indefinitely by an alien power, however. Late in the thirteenth century the new *Sunni* dynasty established itself among the Songhai, and within a hundred years it began moving against a weakening Mali power. By the early fifteenth century Songhai had achieved its independence and was soon engaged, under the leadership of the *sunnis*, Muhammad Da'o and Sulaiman Dama, in subduing a number of Bambara groups and absorbing parts of Macina into the beginnings of a Songhai empire.

The main imperial thrust came with the long reign of *Sunni* Ali which began in 1464. With furious energy, he overran and ravaged the whole Niger country as far west as Jenne, blotting out the eastern half of the Mali state, and raiding deep into the homeland of the formidable Mossi whose independent kingdoms in the upper Volta basin had existed since the middle of the eleventh century. In many respects his activities paralleled the career of Mali's great conquerer, Sundiata. Both created an empire through quick military conquest, and both attempted to construct an administrative system based upon customary practice and thus to convert a passing military victory into a permanent political force. The pagan Sundiata largely ignored Islam in building the Mali empire and thus was ignored in turn by Muslim historians preoccupied with the contributions of Islamic civilization in the Sudan. *Sunni* Ali professed Islam, but persecuted the Muslim scholars of Timbuktu when he felt they were challenging his authority to rule as a magician-king at the head of the traditional hierarchy. Hence Muslim historians tended to be critical of his regime, and to ascribe the greatness of Songhai to his successor, the Muslim *askia*, Muhammad Toure.

This was to misplace the emphasis by half, for *Sunni* Ali not only established the bulk of the Songhai empire but developed a system for ruling his vast domains which was reasonably effective considering the difficulties he faced and which was never more than partially amended by his successors. He divided the empire into provinces under his appointed officials, coordinated the various traditional cults on behalf of the state, exercised constant pressure on divisive forces such as the Fulani of Macina and the tribes of the Hombori Mountains, and established a large and powerful fleet which ranged up and down the Niger maintaining lines of communication and keeping the peace. When he died in an accident in 1492, it was his governor of the Hombori area, Muhammad Toure, who usurped the throne and established the *Askia* dynasty, but the failure of an orderly succession aside, Muhammad Toure found himself at the head of a powerful and smoothly functioning state.

The *askia*, Muhammad, a Soninke Negro, introduced a number of innovations. He extended the work of conquest begun by *Sunni* Ali, pushing his influence westward as far as Diara in ancient Ghana, and raiding in the east to maintain his control of the caravan routes in the face of Tuareg or Hausa attack. He eliminated the threat of the old Za dynasty which had been displaced by the *Sunni* line, and added refinements to the imperial administration he had inherited. More than that, he reversed the official antipathy toward Islam, of which he became a devout follower after his pilgrimage to

Mecca in 1495. He encouraged Muslim scholars by granting them lands; he made them important advisers to his government, giving particular attention to the counsel of the celebrated North African theologian, al-Maghili; and he re-established Timbuktu as a seat of Islamic faith and learning after the persecutions of *Sunni* Ali.

There was a close association in the mind of *Askia* Muhammad between his attitude toward Islam and his vision of empire. The old system of administration established by *Sunni* Ali seemed out of date to the enthusiastic pilgrim returning from Mecca—inefficient in its decentralized reliance on local traditional authorities, ignorant and impious in its appeal to superstition and magic. Muhammad sought to convert a loose organization into a highly articulated empire. A vast array of ministers and regional administrators was appointed, taxation regularized, a professional army established, and the reins of government consequently centralized in the hands of the *askia*. Yet the very efficiency of these reforms contained the elements of weakness. The reliance on Islamic advisers divorced the king from his pagan people. The scrapping of the old system of obligation through clan and lineage destroyed traditional checks and balances without substituting new loyalties. The selection of provincial governors from the ranks of the royal household increased the possibility of revolt.

Consequently, the importance of *Askia* Muhammad's reforms can be overstressed. His administration, for all its innovation, still relied on the traditional authorities at the village level. Moreover, the Islamic institutions he encouraged took no deep root, and the countryside remained pagan. He himself felt no compulsion to undertake *jihads* against neighboring infidels and most of his military exertions were directed, not at extending the spiritual empire of the star and crescent, but at protecting the temporal power of Songhai. Finally, no more than his predecessors was he able to solve the problem of a lawful succession to the position of *askia*. With his fall from power in 1528, his empire embarked upon a period of uncertainty characterized by mediocre kings and palace revolutions, and this development in turn undermined the state and led to the final disintegration which came abruptly at the end of the sixteenth century.

Old and growing blind, Muhammad Toure was deposed by his son in 1528 in the first of a series of coups d'état which almost invariably brought disunity and weakness. During the sixty years that followed, eight *askias* reigned in Songhai. One of these, Daud (1549-

1582), was an able and successful ruler, but his success only under-scored the shortcomings of the others. Toward the end of Daud's reign, Songhai began to experience pressures it could not withstand. To the north, the sultanate of Morocco, among others, was suffering an economic decline occasioned by the development of new sea routes around Africa to the east which diverted commerce from western Europe away from the older Mediterranean passage. Morocco sought compensation elsewhere—a greater share of the trans-Saharan trade, and particularly control of the gold from the Sudan. During the sixteenth century the salt-producing center of Taghaza and other desert oases were periodically attacked and plans were made for an advance on Songhai in the hopes of gaining control of its gold supply.

Although these Moroccan threats were well known to the south, the people of Songhai felt secure in the protection of the desert; in-deed, for all its belligerency, Morocco had not been able to hold Taghaza, let alone march on the Niger. Nevertheless, in 1591 a col-umn of three thousand soldiers led by an Andalusian, Judar Pasha, succeeded in crossing the desert and appeared at Tondibi on the Niger above Gao. It was a much smaller force than the Songhai army but it contained a large proportion of European mercenaries equipped with muskets, which, in addition to superior discipline, were decisive against the bows and spears of the ill-organized enemy. Songhai was easily defeated, its army put into full retreat, and the Niger country rendered defenseless against the invaders.

Military defeat was quickly followed by political collapse. Morocco gained nothing from her adventure, for she found none of the wealth she sought and was unable to occupy and exploit Songhai. Nevertheless the invasion spelled the end of the Songhai empire. Gao and Timbuktu were occupied, the latter permanently for the Moroc-can soldiers eventually settled along the Niger bend ruling the region first as a protectorate, and then as they gradually became absorbed into the local population, establishing an independent albeit politically feeble state. Elsewhere Songhai split into its components. The Songhai themselves retreated down river to the Dendi home from whence they had originally come and where they succeeded in eluding the Moroccans. In Macina and Dirma, the Fulani raided the local farm-ing people, the Jenne region was attacked by the Bambara, while Tuareg visited their usual devastation all along the Niger bend. Political disintegration was followed by famine, and famine by plague. When some semblance of stability finally returned, political unity had been reduced to the level of village states which appeared by the hundreds. Raids and petty warfare became the hallmark of the times, trade suffered, and Islamic culture atrophied. It was not until the eighteenth century that larger states once more began to appear—the Fulani-controlled Macina and the Bambara kingdoms in Kaarta and Segu.

KANEM-BORNU AND THE HAUSA STATES

The pattern established by the kingdoms of the western Sudan was repeated with variations in Kanem-Bornu. An ancient residual population was subjected to a nomadic infusion which led to the development of a great state founded on military conquest and sustained by a complex system of administration. Eventually decline set in when an inflexible outdated government under flaccid leadership could no longer withstand the eternal hostility of predatory neighbors.

The original inhabitants of the Kanem region were the So people who probably comprised a number of individual tribal units loosely interrelated by language and culture, and whose customs such as divine kingship, an elevated position for women, and a sophisticated political hierarchy suggested a typical savanna culture in which ideas from afar gained easy access and were quickly absorbed. Not only ideas, but people, found their way to the land of the So in the neighborhood of Lake Chad. Between the seventh and ninth centuries A.D., the people in the Chad area were infiltrated by nomads from the Sahara of whom the Zaghawa were the chief group. These intruders, who may well have been forced southward by the Arab conquests in North Africa, established themselves as the ruling aristocracy over a wide area in the savanna around Lake Chad.

Under the impetus of the Zaghawa, the Kanuri-speaking state of Kanem took shape. Tradition places its beginning in the ninth century when Kanem's first king, Saif, founded the Saifawa dynasty which was to endure for a thousand years, but it was not until the eleventh and twelfth centuries that the historical record becomes intelligible. Islam appears to have been adopted by the royal house at the end of the eleventh century during the reign of the *mai*, or king, Umme Jilne, a beginning upon which succeeding *mais* built by developing closer relations with Muslim states to the north and east and encouraging pilgrimages to Mecca in a policy which presumably had commercial as well as religious objectives. By this time, this first Kanem-Bornu empire extended from the region of Kano as far as Wadai lying to the west of Darfur, while its influence reached out into the Fezzan along the trade routes to Tripoli. The royal succession was patrilineal but the queen mother had an important and powerful position within the hierarchy, and other pre-Islamic customs still surrounded the divine king; for example, his audiences were always conducted while he was hidden behind a curtain. The strength of Kanem rested in a large and active army, while government was conducted by a rigid bureaucratic hierarchy—an advisory council of nobility and members of the royal household, a network of provincial governors drawn from the king's relatives, and the important female element in the government which included the *mai's* first wife and his official "elder sister," as well as the queen mother—all with duties and privileges minutely regulated by protocol.

By the middle of the thirteenth century, the Kanuri state had extended southwest of Chad into Bornu, a development which assumed enlarged significance during the fourteenth century. For some time Kanem had been under pressure from the Bulala people, who had probably been vassals of Kanem but who finally pushed the Kanuri out of Kanem late in the fourteenth century. Under *Mai* Umar ibn Idris the ruling house abandoned its old capital at N'jimi and established itself in Bornu, but this was as much the result of a wasting power struggle within the royal household as it was a reflection of irresistible outside pressures. For about a hundred years the state remained weak albeit viable, and toward the end of the fifteenth century it began to revive and with this renaissance came the beginning of the second Kanuri empire.

Beginning with Ali Ghaji (1472–1504) and his son, Idris Katakarmabi (1504–1526), Kanem began to regain her former authority. It was Ali who put an end to the palace divisions which had torn the kingdom and who revived the army to the point where it was able to press outward on all fronts, dealing blows on the Bulala in the east, the kingdom of Jukun in the south, and the Hausa in the west. Idris Katakarmabi returned the Kanuri power to Kanem, but was less successful in an inconclusive attack on Kebbi.

Such military advances, however, were but a prelude to the reign of *Mai* Idris Alooma (1571–1603) under whom Kanem-Bornu reached the height of her power. During much of his long reign Idris Alooma was preoccupied with military campaigns through which he both consolidated the triumphs of his predecessors and added fresh conquests of his own. Thus he subdued dissidents in Bornu and secured his hold on Kanem, warred successfully against Kano and the Tuareg, and extended his power eastward, perhaps as far as Darfur. These numerous victories meant an army that was consistently superior to the forces it faced, a superiority which appeared to result primarily from the introduction of a corps of musketeers, but also from improvements in military transport.

Idris was by no means exclusively preoccupied with conquest, however. A devout Muslim, he made his pilgrimage to Mecca and established hostels in that holy city for the shelter of Bornu pilgrims, built brick mosques in the capital city of N'gazargamu in lieu of the older reed structures, and began to replace customary law and traditional tribunals with courts under Muslim magistrates following the dictates of Koranic law. His reforms extended to moral as well as juridical questions for he took a strong stand against adultery and obscenity. "So he wiped away the disgrace," observed a contemporary, "and the face of the age was blank with astonishment."

Military conquest and the encouragement of Muslim law seems to have been accompanied by no great change in the traditional political administration of the empire. The same complex hierarchy of officials aided the *mai* in governing; if anything, the system was more rigid than ever, based upon a pattern of fiefs granted to nobility and royal servants in return both for their loyalty and material assistance to the crown. The economy, moreover, had changed little from earlier days. The basic productivity of the land was agricultural, and the basic labor force was the peasantry supplemented by substantial numbers of slaves. Slaves were also an important commodity in the lively trans-Saharan trade, the Kanuri continuing their time-honored custom of raiding to the south for slaves to be shipped to North Africa—eunuchs and young girls were a specialty—in return for the horses of Barbary.

The Kanem-Bornu empire declined from greatness during the eighteenth century as it had done once before when ineffective kings, hampered by an over elaborate court life, found themselves unequal to the demand for vigorous leadership. When the crisis of an outside threat arrived early in the nineteenth century, it came from the Fulani who had already overrun Hausaland to the west, and it compelled ancient Kanem-Bornu to embark on a new period of reform and reconstruction in order to forestall disintegration and annexation by the new power that threatened her. As for the Hausa, the Fulani occupation brought revolutionary changes to a way of life which in many ways had been typical of the civilization of the savanna.

For long centuries the Hausa had occupied the area between Songhai and Kanem-Bornu. Their tradition postulated the familiar theme of a ruler who came from the north—in this case, Bayajidda, son of the king of Baghdad, who slew the serpent harassing the people and married the local queen, and whose grandsons became the kings of the major Hausa states of Gobir and Daura, Katsina and Zazzau (Zaria), Kano and Rano, and finally Biram. More than likely this tradition in fact refers to a series of invasions for, as with much of the Sudan, the Hausa country is open and easily penetrated, and the present-day Hausa give indication of repeated intrusion by outside groups which merged with a basic Negro stock.

Like their neighbors, the Hausa were agriculturalists. The broad flat plains of their countryside were well suited for the cultivation of corn, barley, rice, and cotton, while livestock fatted on the rich grass and citrus fruit grew wild in the low wooded hills. Most of the people lived in small farming villages but in time walled towns like Kano and Katsina had established themselves as centers of trade and of religious and secular thought. Like Kanem-Bornu, the Hausa states engaged in a brisk exchange with North Africa across the Sahara, the chief southern products being slaves and kola nuts, the latter always in great demand as one of the few stimulants permitted Muslims. Katsina and Kano rose to be the major Hausa entrepôts, but the other states also contributed to the trade in a well-conceived division of labor—Zaria to the south served as the slave raider, Rano was a center for industry, and Gobir on the edge of the desert protected Hausaland against the raids of the desert nomads.

Islamic culture and religion entered Hausaland gradually via the urban centers, probably having been first introduced through contacts with Bornu. Kano and Katsina were under Islamic influence by the late fourteenth century, but the degree of commitment was slight both among the general population and within the ruling class. Other states were even more lightly touched. Gobir was still pagan in the sixteenth century and Zaria was not converted until the nineteenth century *jihad* of Usuman dan Fodio. Indeed, dan Fodio's religious war was precipitated by his exasperation with what he felt was the casual attitude of the Hausa rulers toward Islam. Theology aside, the impact of Islamic civilization was considerable especially in the cities. When Timbuktu was enjoying a peak in the fifteenth and sixteenth centuries, a number of her scholars visited Hausaland, living and working in Kano and Katsina—for example, *al-Hajj* Ahmad who taught theology in Kano, Muhammad ibn Ahmad, a Sankore scholar who became a magistrate in Katsina, and al-Maghili who wrote an essay on the art of governing, advising Muhammad Rimfa (1463–1499), the king of Kano, that, "the eagle can only win his realm by firm resolve . . . Kingdoms are held by the sword, not by delays."

Until the Fulani achieved unity in Hausaland good advice and firm resolve had never been sufficient to bring together the Hausa states under a single ruler. This is surprising because the Hausa during much of their history were under pressure from powerful states —Mali and Songhai in the west and Kanem-Bornu to the east—and from time to time put forward resourceful local rulers like Queen Amina of Zaria or Sarkin Kanajeji who reportedly introduced iron helmets and chain mail to the armies of Kano. Outside pressure, however, usually meant periodic Hausa vassalage, now to Songhai at the time of *Askia* Muhammad, now to Kebbi during its sixteenth century ascendancy under Kotal Kanta, or from time to time to Kanem-Bornu, whereas regional leaders were generally unable to achieve more than the strengthening of their own state in relation to the others in the Hausa complex. Intramural rivalry dominated Hausa affairs over the years. Kano and Katsina were chronically at war with each other over which would dominate the southern end of the Sahara trade, and during the eighteenth century Gobir enjoyed a period of strength which she put to use largely in attacking her fellow Hausa states. It was in Gobir, on whose kings Islam had made little impression, that Usuman dan Fodio served as tutor to the royal princes, and eventually set in motion the forces of the Fulani *jihad* which was to bring ultimate political unity to Hausaland at the beginning of the nineteenth century.

Suggestions for Further Reading

The prime sources of information for the medieval Sudanic kingdoms are the accounts of contemporaries. Pre-eminent among these are H. A. R. Gibb, tr. and ed., *Ibn Battuta: Travels in Asia and Africa* (London: G. Routledge, 1929; New York: Cambridge University Press, vol. 1, 1958, vol. 2, 1962); Ibn Khaldun, *Histoire des Berbères*, 3 vols., tr. de Slane (Paris: P. Guenther, 1925); al-Bakri, *Description de l'Afrique Septentrionale*, tr. de Slane (Algiers: A. Jourdan, 1913); Leo Africanus, *The History and Description of Africa*, 3 vols. (London: Hakluyt Society, 1896; New York: Burt Franklin, 1963); as-Sa'di, *Tarikh es-Soudan*, tr. Houdas (Paris: E. Leroux, 1900); al-Kati, *Tarikh el-Fettach*, tr. Houdas and Delafosse (Paris: E. Leroux, 1913). See also T. Hodgkin, *Nigerian Perspectives* (London: Oxford University Press, 1960); D. T. Niane, *Sundiata: An Epic of Old Mali* (London: Longmans, 1965; New York: Humanities Press, 1965); H. R. Palmer, *Sudanese Memoirs*, 3 vols. (Lagos: Government Printer, 1928).

The major secondary works are E. W. Bovill, *The Golden Trade of the Moors* (London: Oxford University Press, 1958); J. S. Trimingham, *A History of Islam in West Africa* (London: Oxford University Press, 1962); M. Delafosse, *Haut-Senegal-Niger*, 3v. (Paris: Larose, 1912); S. J. Hogben and A. H. M. Kirk-Greene, *The Emirates of Northern Nigeria* (London: Oxford University Press, 1966); J. Rouch, *Contribution à l'Histoire des Songhay* (Dakar: Institut Français d'Afrique Noire, 1953); and Y. Urvoy, *Histoire de l'Empire du Bornu* (Paris: Larose, 1949). Also useful is J. F. A. Ajayi and I. Espie, eds., *A Thousand Years of West African History* (Ibadan: Ibadan University Press, 1965; New York: Humanities Press, 1965).

Additional works of more special focus include J. O. Hunwick, "Ahmad Baba and the Moroccan Invasion of the Sudan," *Journal of the Historical Society of Nigeria*, Dec., 1962; R. Mauny, "The Question of Ghana," *Africa*, v. XXIV, 1954; and *Tableau Géographique de l'Ouest Africain au Moyen Age d'après les Sources Écrites, la Tradition, et l'Archéologie* (Dakar: Institut Français d'Afrique Noire, 1961); E. P. Skinner, "The Mossi and Traditional Sudanese History," *The Journal of Negro History*, v. XLIII, 1958; J. D. Fage, "Reflections on the Early History of the Mossi-Dagomba Group of States," in J. Vansina, R. Mauny, and L. V. Thomas, eds., *The Historian in Tropical Africa* (London: Oxford University Press, 1964); and T. Hodgkin's series on the cities of the Sudan in *West Africa*, 1953, nos. 1883, 1884, 1890, 1891, 1896, 1897, 1903, 1904, 1905.

4: The Cosmopolitan World of East Africa

THE RISE OF THE CITY STATES

Sometime toward the close of the first century after Christ a Greek sailor from Alexandria was cruising along the East African coast taking note of the terrain, of the people in the various ports of call, and of the types of merchandise which his ship was engaged in exchanging. In itself this event was nothing extraordinary. The "Horn" of Somalia had been known to the Mediterranean world at least as far back as the expeditions which Egypt's Queen Hatshepsut had sent to Punt over fifteen centuries earlier, and since that time a lively trade had developed across the Indian Ocean involving the Mediterranean, Arabia and Persia, India, and the islands of the Indonesian archipelago as well as the Abyssinian kingdom of Axum and a series of East African entrepôts facing the Gulf of Aden and the Indian Ocean. What made the voyage of this particular mariner noteworthy was the fact that he had recorded and compiled his observations in the form of a guide to the ports and trade of the Indian Ocean, a guide known as the *Periplus of the Erythrean Sea* which has survived as the only testimony from ancient times giving a first-hand account of the East African coast.

The voyage began in the familiar waters of the Red Sea. Fitted out and stocked in an Egyptian port like Berenice, the ship first stopped at the busy emporium of Adulis, port city of Axum, where a wide range of goods—linen and cotton, unworked copper, brass, and iron, cooking utensils and tools, wine and olive oil—were exchanged for the local ivory, tortoise shell, and rhinoceros horn. Proceeding southward, the ship passed through the straits of Bab el Mandeb into the Gulf of Aden where a number of stops added to the stores of ivory and tortoise shell accumulating in the hold, but where incense, slaves, and Indian cinnamon could also be obtained. At last the rocks of Cape Guardafui were sighted and passed, and the travelers turned south into the Indian Ocean, cruising down the Somali coast.

The cheerless aspect of this forbidding land, its low cliffs and sandy wastes shimmering in the blazing heat, seemed to deny the possibility of human habitation, and indeed, after Opone, located a short distance beyond Cape Guardafui, there was no sign of life for hundreds of miles as the shoreline sloped southward and slightly to the west. Gradually the aspect began to change. South of the Juba River, the monotony of sand and stone was replaced increasingly by a flat coastal plain covered with tangled wild growth. Occasionally the terrain was punctuated by stretches of mangrove swamp; in some places, as at the site of Lamu and Mombasa, it was broken into island groupings by the action of rivers, inlets, and tidal creeks. The air was warm, but the fierce sun of Somalia was gone and the evenings were often freshly bathed with an onshore breeze.

This more genial coast with its milder climate and its many anchorages beckoned to the traveler who found not only water and shelter but human settlements as well—for example, the large offshore island which may have been Zanzibar where the crocodile was the only wildlife and the people fished with wicker baskets placed to trap the outgoing tide. A further sail of two days brought the ship to Rhapta, in those ancient days the farthest removed of the East African ports. Here the people were reported to be of great stature and given to piracy. They lived under what must have been regarded as primitive conditions in the eyes of Alexandrine sophisticates, for they exchanged their ivory and tortoise shell for manufactured iron tools and weapons unobtainable locally, and were pleased to receive in the bargain small gifts of wheat and wine. They seem to have been neither Bantu nor Bushman and they were ruled, at least nominally, by Arab kings living far off in the Yemen whose representatives had long come to Rhapta for its ivory and who had in many cases married and settled in the land. This was the extent of Mediterranean knowledge of East Africa. Beyond, reported the *Periplus,* "the ocean curves westwards . . . stretching out from the south and mingling with the western sea." Catching the summer monsoon, the visiting mariners turned from the mystery of the unknown and were soon headed toward the markets of India and Malaysia far to the east, where their ivory would bring a good price and a cargo of cotton, sugar, grain, and oil could be obtained for the return trip to Egypt.

These ancient contacts with East Africa, at once so extensive and so limited, implied no knowledge of the interior or communication with any people resident therein. It seems unlikely that the Bantu in their vast migration across central Africa had as yet reached the East African coast and, in any case, the forbidding terrain did little to invite exploration of the interior. The harborless shore of Somalia with its heat and its sand offered no temptation to linger, and even to the south along the tropical belt from Lamu to the Zambezi there were natural obstacles in the way of adventurers who might wish to push inland. Of the numerous East African rivers, only the Zambezi was of inviting dimension and it suffered from rapids, that chronic impediment of Africa's waterways. Overland travel was even less feasible. North of the Tana River lay the scrub and sand of Somalia, but to the south stretched the even more formidable Nyika—a belt of rising ground back of the coast more than one hundred miles deep and covered with a jungle of thorn bushes and trees—an impenetrable barrier across the path of those seeking the highland plateaus beyond.

The years passed, the traders kept coming, and the coastal entrepôts developed in size and number. By the end of the fourth century A.D. there were several settlements on the southern coast of Somalia, and Rhapta had grown in importance. It was apparently located on a river which might have been the Pangani or an arm of the Rufiji delta on the Tanzanian coast. From Rhapta some contact had now been made with the interior, for the snowy peak of Kilimanjaro was known to visiting seamen. South along the coast there had also been some exploration, since cannibals were reported living there as well as "Fish-Eating Ethiopians"—these groups possibly being early Bantu arrivals on the coast. But that was all. "South of these," reported Claudius Ptolemy in his *Geography,* "is the unknown land," where it was suspected but not known that other Ethiopians might dwell.

No physical record of these ancient settlements remains. Roman and other coins of the early Christian era have been found along the coast, but whether they came there at the time or later is uncertain. It is probable, however, that few Alexandrine Greeks visited East Africa after the collapse of Rome in the fifth century A.D., and that Persian and Arab seafarers monopolized the carrying trade thereafter, bringing quantities of the ever-popular African ivory to India and farther east where it was variously in demand—for palanquin litters and incense in China, as dagger handles, sword scabbards, jewelry, and ornaments in India. By the tenth century the East African entrepôts had added gold and iron to their exports, for as the knowledge of ironworking spread along the coast it was found that there were plentiful deposits of this metal which had always been much in demand in India. Leopard skins were another popular export, and faraway China was so fascinated by Africa's exotic animals to send an expedition during the fifteenth century in search of giraffes which were thought to be related in some fashion to the elusive unicorn.

If the *Periplus* was ambiguous as to the kinds of people living in Rhapta, later commentators were unanimous that the coastal inhabitants were Negroes. Negro slaves were being exported to Persia as early as the seventh century, and from the tenth century onward black men were consistently reported to be the inhabitants of the coastal towns. They were variously described as hunters, as fishermen, as cannibals, as traders, or as voluptuaries, as well as cultivators of a variety of tropical products including rice, millet, cucumber, coconuts, sugar, sorghum, camphor, and the ubiquitous banana. Although Arab Muslims lived in small colonies along the coast, the local people were as yet pagan worshippers of nature and practitioners of magic, ruled by kings whom they regarded as divine but who were nevertheless vulnerable to assassination if found tyrannical or unjust.

It is not clear what type of relationship was maintained between the Arab immigrants and the indigenous inhabitants of the East African coast—the Land of Zanj, as the Arabs called it. The traditional coastal chronicles, transcribed at a much later time, speak of early Arab settlements and Islamic conversion of the local population during the seventh century with consequent allegiance to the Caliphate, but such a development seems very unlikely. For example, the migration of the Shirazi from Persia, assigned in the traditional accounts to the tenth century, now seems to have taken place two hundred years later and to have come, not directly from

Persia, but south from Somalia. Similarly, the allegiance to Islam was probably a development of the thirteenth century paralleling the establishment of Muslim states in Indonesia, India, and Persia.

The pattern of outside influence, therefore, possibly followed a sequence beginning with Arab trading posts at or near local African towns and in time becoming a series of Arab-Muslim kingdoms established over a gradually Islamicized population. Alternatively, African trading centers may have developed in response to outside commercial demands with African royal houses slowly becoming Islamicized through the influence of Arab merchants living in these communities. In any event, Arab settlers, arriving in increasing numbers from the twelfth century onward, were continually being absorbed into a Bantu majority. According to a Portuguese account of the early sixteenth century, the people of Sofala were either black or mulatto; those of Mombasa, black, tawny, or white. The island of Kanbalu—possibly Zanzibar—was reportedly Muslim by the tenth century but in this case the process of assimilation worked both ways, for the population, though converted to Islam, spoke the local language. Mogadishu possessed a mosque in the thirteenth century, and by mid-fourteenth century the population of both Mombasa and Kilwa was staunchly Muslim. External contacts were by no means limited to Muslim Arabs, however. Waves of immigrants had crossed from Indonesia as early as the beginning of the Christian era, the clear evidence of their presence to be found in the Malagasy language and people of Madagascar and the presence in Africa of Malaysian plants such as the banana. There is, moreover, the visit to Ma-lin—the elusive Malindi of former times—by Chinese junks in 1417.

If there is some uncertainty as to whether these cities were governed by indigenous dynasties or Arab immigrants, there is little doubt that the prevailing culture, like the coastal people themselves, evolved essentially through a mixture of African and Middle Eastern characteristics. The basic language came to be Swahili with its Bantu base and its strong Arabic influences. The lack of coins and funerary inscriptions and the importance of African customs among the population and rulers of such towns as Kilwa and Mogadishu argue for African cultural development in combination with the Muslim. In one respect, however—in the domestic and state architecture which has survived—the inspiration is clearly of Arab, Persian, and perhaps Indian derivation with no discernible African character.

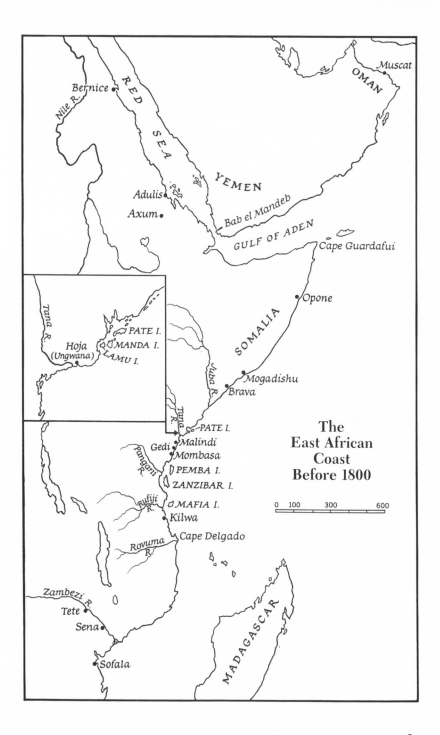

Bernice •

Nile R.

RED SEA

OMAN

Muscat •

YEMEN

Adulis•

Axum •

Bab el Mandeb

GULF OF ADEN

Cape Guardafui

SOMALIA

Opone •

Tana R.

Hoja
(Ungwana)

PATE I.

MANDA I.

LAMU I.

Juba R.

Mogadishu
Brava •

Tana R.

PATE I.

Gedi • Malindi

Mombasa

Pangani R.

PEMBA I.

ZANZIBAR I.

Rufiji R.

MAFIA I.

Kilwa •

Cape Delgado

Rovuma R.

The
East African
Coast
Before 1800

0   100   300   600

Zambezi R.

Tete •

Sena •

Sofala •

MADAGASCAR

The earliest of surviving structures is the Kizimkazi mosque on Zanzibar dating from the beginning of the twelfth century, but Kilwa on the Tanzanian coast has a thirteenth-century Arab palace and another ancient building which bears close stylistic similarities—though surely not equal antiquity—to the architecture of the Umayyad and early Abbasid caliphates of the seventh and eighth centuries A.D. The Kilwa palace occupies about two acres along a cliff overlooking the sea and is a complex of courtyards surrounded by rooms, sometimes with barrel vaulting, sometimes in double stories. The building material was coral rag set in lime mortar, but cut stone was used for roofing, decorative slabs, and architectural features such as doorways and stairs.

Many other coastal towns display architectural remains of Middle Eastern inspiration, particularly noteworthy in this respect being the Arab colony at Gedi on the Kenya coast which flourished between the fourteenth and sixteenth centuries. The town contained a mosque and a palace with a labyrinth of rooms designed for everything from state audiences, to private quarters for the women of the harem, and salesrooms for the commercial activities of the merchant-king. More modest domestic architecture consisted of houses of coral and mortar, singled-storied and flat-roofed, usually with four and five rooms comprising living and sleeping quarters, storage, bath, and kitchen facilities, in front of which was a courtyard employed for both recreation and commerce. It was a comfortable if not luxurious existence. There was none of the sophistication of the great cities of Arabia and India, but these coastal communities, though culturally provincial, were reasonably prosperous.

THE PORTUGUESE ON THE EAST AFRICAN COAST

The international trade on which the prosperity of the East African coastal markets rested reached its climax in the late fifteenth century. In addition to the traditional exchange with Arabia and the Persian Gulf, there were now substantial exports from East Africa to China, Indonesia, and India. During the twelfth and thirteenth centuries, moreover, a new element was added when Europe, reestablishing through the Crusades her ancient contacts with the Middle East, began to demand increasing quantities of Africa's gold and ivory.

With growing emphasis on gold and ivory exports, it was Kilwa which became at this time the major entrepôt of East Africa. By the end of the twelfth century Kilwa had gained control of Sofala far to the south beyond the Zambezi, and Sofala was the port through which flowed the gold from the inland mines associated with the Mwene Mutapa (Monomotapa) kingdom and the stone citadel of Zimbabwe. It is difficult to estimate the extent of Sofala's gold exports but they were substantial as was her yield of ivory. The value of her annual trade may have reached well over $1,000,000, based not only on gold and ivory but also on amber, pearls, coral, and copper. Portuguese explorers of the early sixteenth century remarked the quantities of beads, silk, and cotton cloth imported for the adornment of the local people, and excavations at Great Zimbabwe in the nineteenth century revealed substantial quantities of Indian beads and Chinese porcelain which had presumably made their way upcountry in exchange for the gold of the land.

Although Kilwa and Sofala led all the rest, prosperity was general along the East African coast. Kilwa's hegemony extended north only as far as Pemba Island, but her commercial success seems to have been shared by other centers well beyond the range of her political control. From Kilwa to Mogadishu there were almost two score towns sustained by a well-developed agriculture and a commerce based primarily in ivory. The coastal islands of Pemba, Mafia, and Zanzibar, lying within the Kilwa sphere of influence, produced a wealth of crops including sugar and citrus fruits, while the women, bravely decked in jewels and silks, reflected the local affluence. The island of Mombasa contained a busy port with a fine harbor behind which lay a bounteous land of roundtail sheep, fatted cattle, plump fowl, oranges, lemons, pomegranates, figs, and a plentiful supply of sweet water. Farther up the coast Malindi prospered, a fair city of fine stone houses set among rich orchards and fields of wheat, rice, and millet. Finally, there were the fortified island centers of Pate and Lamu and the large city of Mogadishu with its thriving trade, its multistoried houses, its central palace, and its long-standing freedom from invasion by sea. In addition to ivory these centers exported timber, pitch, and civet musk while imports included some foodstuffs and pottery along with the wide variety of cloth. Slaves were not a commodity at this time, and indeed, with the exception of the Sofala inland gold routes, there seems to have been little direct contact or organized caravan trade with the peoples of the interior.

Within a few short years all this prosperity went a-glimmering, as the coastal towns, unable to unite in adversity, quickly fell victim to the vigorous war making of Portuguese naval expeditions. Portugal, pursuing the expansionist dreams of Prince Henry, sought the double objective during the fifteenth century of throwing back Islam on behalf of Christ while achieving economic ascendancy through control both of African gold and a sea route to the markets of the East. Decades of exploration along the western coast of Africa culminated in 1487 when Bartolomeu Dias rounded the Cape of Good Hope and Pero da Covilha set out to explore the Indian Ocean ports by an overland route. Ten years later Vasco da Gama conducted his portentous reconnaissance of East Africa and western India, an exploration which suggested the possibility of a maritime empire in the Indian Ocean were Portugal able to gain control of a number of strategic points including the entrepôts along the East African coast.

It required only a few brief campaigns for Portugal to achieve her design of empire. In 1509, a combined fleet of Egyptians, Arabs, and Persians was destroyed and with it went the ability of Middle Eastern powers to offer effective resistance to Portuguese expansionism. Already commercial and military posts were being established on the Arabian, Persian, and Indian coasts, while East Africa was systematically brought under control—Kilwa made tributary in 1502, Zanzibar similarly reduced the following year, Sofala taken and both Kilwa and Mombasa sacked in 1505. Malindi, already in alliance with Portugal, was spared, but in 1506 a fleet occupied the islands of Lamu and Pate without opposition and devastated Hoja and Brava when these towns put up a stiff resistance. Mogadishu managed to hold off the attackers, who arrived late in the monsoon season, but in 1507 Mozambique was annexed, eventually to become the central point of Portuguese authority in East Africa. A short decade after da Gama's first appearance, Portugal had become master of the coast, a development which reflected not only the force of arms of the invaders but a fatal inability of the local rulers to put aside parochial divisions and face a common enemy in unity.

The Portuguese conquest, so easily achieved, was designed to divert the wealth of the coast to the royal coffers of Portugal; in fact it succeeded, not in transferring, but in destroying that wealth. The greatest blow was the loss of the coveted Sofala gold. The attack on Kilwa not only gutted and depopulated that city, thereby crippling her commerce, but also ended Kilwa's careful cultivation of the gold trade. The succeeding Portuguese occupation proved disastrous, for it brought on a passive resistance both on the coast and in the interior which quickly reduced the flow of gold to a trickle. Subsequent attempts by the Portuguese to effect an occupation of the interior failed in the main to achieve direct control over mining sites. Within ten years of her capture, Sofala had dwindled to the point that it was barely meeting expenses, and it has been estimated that the overall Portuguese trading losses during her two-hundred-year control of the East African coast ran as high as 40 per cent over revenue.

Portuguese administration north of Kilwa was consistently maladroit. Mombasa, suffering a second destruction in 1528, nurtured a deep resentment toward her overlords, a resentment which was shared by other towns chronically in a state of revolt againt the Portuguese garrisons which ruled them. When the Turkish power, extending southward from Egypt and Arabia during the latter part of the sixteenth century, attempted to infiltrate the East African coast, she was welcomed as a liberator by most of the coastal cities. The hard-pressed Portuguese were obliged repeatedly to defend their authority at Brava, Lamu, Pate, and other northern ports, and eventually to reorganize and centralize their administration at Fort Jesus which was erected at Mombasa at the end of the century.

It was to no avail. Held by the Spanish crown between 1580 and 1640, her far-flung possessions under increasing attack by Europe's rising mercantile powers, Portugal gradually lost control of her empire, East and West. By the middle of the seventeenth century, the Omani sultans had dislodged the Portuguese from Muscat and were raiding the East African entrepôts. A long period of strife ensued marked by local rebellion and growing attacks from the outside against a declining Portuguese power. In 1698 Fort Jesus fell to the Omani and thus for all practical purposes ended the period of Portugal's ascendancy in East Africa.

THE OMANI SUZERAINTY

Two hundred years of Portuguese occupation had contributed much to the decline of the coastal civilization. Portugal's rule had sought economic exploitation through military control, but this policy, poorly conceived and administered, had ended only in undermining commerce, denying its benefits with an even hand both to the exploited and to the exploiter.

Nevertheless, during this period the Portuguese were not the only calamity to visit the coast. In approximately the year 1580 there appeared before the Portuguese trading posts of Tete and Sena on the Zambezi, a Bantu group, the Zimba, who had abandoned their normal peaceful existence and embarked on an extended campaign of militant migration. In this respect they resembled the Jaga people who were invading the kingdom of Kongo during much the same years, or the Nguni and Sotho Bantu in their vast and desperate spasms of death and destruction during the migrations which were to follow the rise of Shaka early in the nineteenth century. The Zimba were no simple maurauders but practicing cannibals, according to a contemporary observer, whose sudden warlike impulse may have been related to political unrest in the Malawi kingdom located south and southwest of Lake Nyasa (Malawi).

In any event, the impact of the Zimba on the coastal towns was clearly devastating. First Sena and Tete were overwhelmed and their inhabitants consumed; then, a band of five thousand Zimba broke away from the main body and moved up the cost in the direction of Kilwa, "killing and eating every living thing, men, women, children, dogs, cats, rats, snakes, lizards," sparing only those who joined them in their insane orgy. Kilwa, already weakened by Portuguese attack and subsequent emigration, could not resist this additional onslaught. In 1587 some three thousand of her people were slain and eaten; the few survivors who had fled to the forest returned to find their city in ruins, a shattered remant of its former wealth and vitality.

Proceeding northward, the Zimba arrived at Mombasa in 1589 in time to witness its reduction by a Portuguese punitive expedition sent from Goa to subdue the inhabitants who were in the act of revolting with the help of Turkish allies. The Portuguese systematically reduced the defenses, then permitted the Zimba to hunt down the local population, many of whom dashed into the sea, preferring to take their chances with the Portuguese and the elements than with the ravenous hordes at their rear.

Their appetite yet unsatisfied, the Zimba pressed on to Malindi which they soon brought under siege. This time the defenders were more fortunate. On the point of breaching the defenses, the Zimba were suprised by the warlike Segeju people moving down the coast, who "came suddenly on their backes when they had gotten up the wall . . . and chased them with such a furie, that only the Captaine with above one hundred others escaped . . . And thus much of the Zimbas."

The demise of the Zimba did not end the woes of the East African cities. The Portuguese lingered on for another century eventually to be succeeded by the Omani Arabs, but this change merely substituted an Asian for a European overlord, a situation all the more ironic in that Omani intervention was at first actively encouraged by the East African communities. When, in 1650, Sultan-bin-Seif dislodged the Portuguese from Muscat and the Arabian coast, this event was applauded in East Africa's trading cities where the image of a Muslim-Arab kinship with the Omani led to dreams of a similar emancipation in Africa from western rule. An appeal to the Omani by Mombasa precipitated a series of raids in combination with local revolt, and although Portugal counterattacked by subduing the rebellious islands of Pate, Lamu, and Manda, she could do nothing to forestall the vast Omani fleet which lay siege to Fort Jesus for thirty-three months during 1696–1698. The Omani pressed their attack with no great vigor, yet eventually succeeded in reducing the fort despite a number of Portuguese relief expeditions. Only a faint spark still remained. Aided by internal divisions among the Arabs, Portugal once more took control of Mombasa in 1728, but this quickly proved to be a dying gesture for the following year the garrison was easily ousted by the Mombasans without even the necessity of Omani naval assistance. From that time forward, the Portuguese presence was effectively restricted to her coastal and inland posts in Mozambique south of Cape Delgado.

It was not long, however, before the East African coastal cities began to regret the encouragement they had lent the Arabs of Muscat, for the Omani soon proved no better masters than the Portuguese. Civil war in Oman during the early eighteenth century led a number of trading centers to renounce their allegiance to Muscat, and thereafter Omani suzerainty was maintained only with difficulty. During the Omani civil war, Pate, Malindi, Pemba, Mafia, and Kilwa were at various times in revolt. At mid-century both Mombasa and Kilwa were at war with Oman, and each regarded herself at the time as an independent state. Indeed Mombasa succeeded in sustaining her independence under the leadership of the Mazrui family from the time the first Mazrui became deputy governor in 1727 until the days of Sayyid Said one hundred years later. For a time Zanzibar displayed an unenthusiastic loyalty to Oman, but in 1784 when the Omani attempted a direct occupation of their African possessions, Zanzibar resisted and had to be subdued by force. Pate and Kilwa also submitted at this time, but Oman's control continued uncertain, leaving the coastal states substantially free to indulge their taste for local quarrels and to ignore the vexations of nominal rule from afar.

During the latter part of the eighteenth century there was one preoccupation in which all merchants—those of Oman and of the East African emporia alike—could agree. Slaving had never been an important part of the coastal trade during the Portuguese era and before, but in the middle of the eighteenth century the Dutch from the Cape Town area had begun to take slaves from Madagascar and Mozambique, and they were soon joined on the coast by French traders seeking labor for the plantations of the Indian Ocean colonies, Île de France (Mauritius) and Bourbon (later Reunion). Soon slaving had become a major economic factor on the coast, and the foundation had been laid for the slave trade of the nineteenth century.

The activities of the French were decisive in this respect. A French trader, Captain Morice, visited the coast and concluded a treaty with the sultan of Kilwa in 1776 whereby Morice was to be supplied with 1000 slaves a year. He also urged the extension of French power to the Kilwa area which he regarded as suitable for the establishment of a slave market as well as the development of plantations such as existed at Île de France. Morice looked on Zanzibar as another likely site for a slave depot and recommended its absorption into the French empire, arguing that 300 Omani defenders among a population of 40,000 would offer no serious deterrent. France, however, made no move against either Kilwa or Zanzibar for she was unwilling to risk alienating Oman in a move which would have complicated her struggle with the British in the Indian Ocean. Moreover, she already was receiving substantial supplies of slaves from East Africa. By 1790 the French were averaging approximately 1700 slaves a year from Kilwa and others were available in quantity at Zanzibar where a large and profitable slave trade had developed by the early nineteenth century. Slaving made an enormous difference in the ecology of the French islands—Île de France, which contained only 600 Negroes in 1735, possessed a slave population of 49,000 in 1807, and Bourbon had changed over the years in similar fashion, numbering almost 30,000 slaves by 1787.

Although the sale of slaves to the French was profitable, it was only a part of the total developing trade. The French captains who called at Zanzibar complained of discrimination in favor of Arab slavers bound for Muscat and other ports in the Red Sea and Persian Gulf, and a similar discrimination was practiced at Kilwa. By 1811, Zanzibar had become the chief center of the coastal trade and was exporting between 6000 and 10,000 slaves annually to Île de France, Muscat, and India, as well as quantities of ivory, rhinoceros horn, and other products from which the authorities realized a large revenue through customs. Though the Omani sultan received better than half of Zanzibar's annual tariff revenue, his fiat had little practical authority on the island and even less along the coast. Nevertheless, the booming trade was bound to attract the attention of the reigning sultan, Sayyid Said, who had fought his way to the Omani throne in 1806. At a later time, when circumstances were to permit such a move, this resourceful monarch would reassert an active control over his East African possessions and even move his seat of government to Zanzibar, thus establishing a new political configuration in East Africa.

ETHIOPIA—THE TRIALS OF ISOLATION

In the spring of 1520 a Portuguese mission arrived at Massawa on the Red Sea—an expression of Portugal's expanding interests in the Indian Ocean and its bordering complex of territories and waterways. The immediate objective was the establishment of relations with what was thought to be the land of Prester John, but perhaps the most enduring result was the narrative penned by one of the mission's members, Father Francisco Alvarez—the first foreign description of the remote highland kingdom of Ethiopia, and one of the few glimpses granted the outside world of a land which had grown in myth and mystery even as its true character had vanished into enigmatic legend. "The Ethiopians slept near a thousand years," Gibbon was to note with justice, and forgetful they were of the world about them, but by others they had not been forgotten so much as lost, particularly in the West whose civilization they had shared in ancient times.

If the mountainous inaccessibility of the Abyssinian highlands made for potential isolation, it was the rise of Islam which divorced the Ethiopians from their Mediterranean connections, turning their gaze southward and forcing them in upon themselves. Although no holy war was directed against Ethiopia, the seventh century expansion of Islam saw the fall of Egypt, the collapse of the Persian and Byzantine empires, and the beginning of Arab occupation of Red Sea bases. Beyond this, the Beja nomads of the Red Sea hills in one of their periodic eruptions, overran the Eritrean plateau late in the seventh century, cutting off the people of Axum from their northern and eastern contacts. Thus isolated, Axum lost complete touch with Hellenistic civilization, and apparently suffered political fragmentation and cultural decline as well. During the ensuing centuries, Ethiopia disappeared from the view of the West and, even in her own land, her history for a time gave way to legend.

Despite a ninth-century success in regaining its Red Sea outlets, Ethiopia maintained her prevailing southern orientation. The Axumites gradually migrated to the mountain districts of Amhara, Gojjam, and Shoa where they re-established their kingdom in the face of hostile pagans, particularly the Agau people. At first the Axumites were successful, partially subduing and converting the Agau. Late in the tenth century, however, there ensued a confused period of invasions and of revolt by the Agau who ravaged the country, slaughtering the clergy, and virtually obliterating the Christianity of the Axumites. At last the monarchy prevailed, but the nation which emerged from the ordeal was the result of fusion, not of conquest. Thenceforward the Christian Axumites formed the Abyssinian aristocracy while Ge'ez and Amharic came to be the dominant national languages. Slowly the Agau yielded to Christianity but only as their own religious practices were absorbed into church ritual, while they themselves emerged as the major ethnic element in the Abyssinian population. This cultural, political, and religious fusion was far enough advanced by the middle of the twelfth century for the Agau to gain control of the monarchy in the form of the Christianized Zagwe dynasty which ruled the Ethiopian state for approximately 150 years and presided over a religio-cultural flowering which was to be of great importance in shaping the character of Ethiopian civilization.

The physical expression of this flowering was projected most eloquently by the monolithic churches built in the highland fastness of Lasta during the reign of King Lalibela (c. 1181–c. 1221). These astonishing architectural monuments were cut directly from their mountain of volcanic stone, hollowed out and shaped into arcades, chapels, naves, and sanctuaries, pierced with windows, supported by columns and arches, and embellished with reliefs and architectural ornamentation—all carved from the living rock like a series of gigantic sculptures. Eleven churches in all, they were no mere eccentricity for they followed in the long tradition of religious architecture already widely practiced in Ethiopia and utilized ancient motifs such as the shaped arches inspired by the summit of the great stele at Axum.

The churches of Lalibela were more than an architectural triumph, however; they represented the emergence of the unique Christianity of Ethiopia and the close relationship of church and state which has come to characterize Ethiopian society. The Christianity of the Axumites had been drawn from the Coptic persuasion and their bishop consecrated by the patriarch at Alexandria, but ethnically and culturally they were Semites from Arabia. For their part, the Agau exhibited Judaic as well as pagan characteristics, perhaps because of influences derived from Yemeni Jews before the advent of Islam. The resultant clash of these two strains almost brought the end of Christianity in Ethiopia, but when at last the Axumites had prevailed, the Agau converts had succeeded in embedding many of their pagan practices and Judaic legends and customs in the body of ritual and dogma of the Ethiopian church. At the same time, a close relation developed between the religious and temporal power as each reached out for the aid of the other in the quest for survival. In the end, Ethiopian Christianity emerged as a way of life—metamorphosed in the heat of political strife and the passion of religious devotion, then for long centuries protected, unchanging, from the adulterating effect of outside influence.

The Zagwe dynasty of the Agau, of which Lalibela was the most illustrious representative, gave way to the restored Solomonid line about 1270 and Solomonid monarchs have ruled Ethiopia ever since. Under the early kings of this dynasty which claims descent from Solomon, Christian conversion was pursued as before, but increasingly it shared the royal attention with military campaigns against the numerous Muslim states—Ifat, Hadya, Bali, Doaro, Adal, and others —established by local Cushitic speakers like the Sidama along the southern and eastern edges of the Ethiopian plateau. These kingdoms, absorbing Islam from coastal Arabs, had emerged between the tenth and twelfth centuries while the Axumites and Agau were mutually

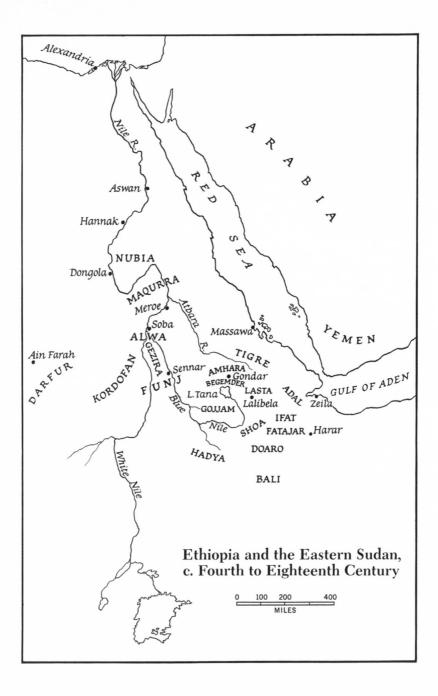

Ethiopia and the Eastern Sudan,
c. Fourth to Eighteenth Century

0   100   200   400
MILES

preoccupied, and they now pressed in upon the Ethiopians only to be repulsed and, for a time, reduced to vassalage.

Unlike the Zagwe period for which little historical information survives, the era of the restored Solomonid kings was marked by chronicles which provided at least an outline of events. Yekuno Amlak (c. 1270–c. 1285), the first of the "king of kings," shifted his base of operations from Lasta to Amhara and began to move against his Muslim neighbors, but major expansion at the expense of these states was not achieved until the reign of the militant Amda Seyon (1314–1344). The dynasty reached an early peak under Zara Yakob (1434–1468) who not only consolidated the gains of his predecessors, but greatly stimulated local religious activity and established relations with Rome in an effort to stand off both the external influence of Islam and the continuing effects of indigenous paganism. Zara Yakob's methods were often harsh. Aside from his commentaries on church doctrine and his program of church construction, he instituted a much-feared inquisition designed to stamp out heresy. Consequently, records his chronicle, "there was great terror . . . on account of the severity of his justice and of his authoritarian rule and above all because of the denunciations of those who, after having confessed that they had worshipped . . . the devil, caused to perish many innocent people by accusing them falsely."

The Ethiopian gesture toward the church of Rome coincided with Europe's own developing interest in Africa and Asia which brought the Portuguese to East Africa at the beginning of the sixteenth century seeking both to dominate the material wealth of the East and to destroy the spiritual world of Islam. An attempted liaison with the Christian kingdom of Ethiopia therefore was a natural outgrowth of Portugal's search for allies in a hostile land as well as the quest for that mythical Christian king, Prester John, whose existence had been rumored since the twelfth century, first in Asia and finally in Ethiopia. Thus it was that the Portuguese explorer Pero da Covilha had made his way to Ethiopia in 1494 at the conclusion of his travels to India, the Middle East, and East Africa, while a quarter century later the diplomatic mission which included Father Alvarez arrived to pursue closer relations between the two countries.

Although nothing came of the mission, the need for cooperation soon became apparent. The kingdom of Ethiopia was powerful and extensive as the sixteenth century dawned, stretching from Massawa in the north to the tributary states of Ifat, Fatajar, Doaro, and Bali in the south, but the Muslims were tireless in their opposition and needed only the unifying strength of effective leadership to shift the balance of power in their favor. Population pressure possibly originating in Somalia, a renewed sense of religious mission, and a developing Ottoman interest in East Africa finally came to a focus in the Muslim state of Adal during the early sixteenth century, and when Adal shortly produced a gifted general in the person of Ahmad ibn Ghazi (1506–1543), the Ethiopians soon found themselves facing a crisis of survival.

Ahmad, called Gran or left-handed, organized a powerful army, instilled it with the spirit of the *jihad* against the infidel, and in 1529 scored a decisive victory over the Ethiopian emperor, Lebna Dengel (1508–1540). This engagement was followed by a systematic devastation and occupation of Ethiopia which brought most of the country under Muslim control, laid waste to large areas, destroyed much of the intellectual and artistic heritage of the land, brought the forcible conversion of large numbers of people, and reduced the emperor to a hunted fugitive in the remote mountain districts of Tigre, Begemder, and Gojjam. In desperation, Lebna Dengel appealed to the Portuguese for help and in 1541, after the emperor had been succeeded by his son, Galawdewos (1540–1559), a contingent of four hundred musketeers arrived at Massawa and helped defeat the Muslims in an engagement near Lake Tana during which Gran himself was slain. Resting largely on the shoulders of one man, the Muslim menace was removed, suddenly, dramatically, and indeed, permanently.

The problems of the upland empire were by no means ended, however. The Muslim forces retiring to their capital at Harar were almost at once replaced by a new threat in the form of the pastoral Galla, Cushitic-speakers, who, in the middle of the sixteenth century, began to move northward from their nucleus in southern Ethiopia. They occupied the emirate of Harar, scaled the mountains on the east and south of the Abyssinian plateau and flooded Shoa, moving on to infiltrate Amhara and Lasta. Military action had no effect on this vast movement, nor were the Galla susceptible to assimilation into the more developed Ethiopian culture. Before their remorseless advance, the Ethiopians were forced to withdraw, and to share their country with the invaders with whom they lived side by side over the ensuing centuries, but always as strangers and potential enemies.

Coincident with the beginning of the Galla migrations there

was a Turkish occupation of Massawa and other coastal points which the emperor Sarsa Dengel (1563–1597) succeeded in neutralizing though not eliminating in 1589. Staggered and depressed by incessant invasion, the Ethiopian nation now faced yet another intrusion of a different sort. Portuguese aid against Ahmad Gran had caused renewed interest at Rome in converting the Ethiopians, and a Jesuit mission was soon dispatched with this end in view. At first success was slow in coming, but through the patient tact of Pedro Paez, the mission ultimately gained the conversion of the emperors Za Dengel (1603–1604) and Susenyos (1607–1632).

Unfortunately for the cause of Roman Catholicism, Paez died in 1626 and was replaced by a zealot, Alphonso Mendez, who sought at once to impose the Roman church on the whole country, forcing the emperor to do him public homage, rebaptizing the population, remodeling the liturgy, forbidding many ancient practices, and introducing others anathema to local custom. Such a move led straight to bloody rebellion, anarchy, and eventually to the deportation of the Jesuit mission. For a time Susenyos stoutly supported the Latin reforms as his country sank in self-destruction, but finally he could endure the spectacle no longer. In 1632, the emperor re-established the Ethiopian church. "Hear ye! Hear ye!" read his proclamation. "We first gave you this faith believing that it was good. But innumerable people have been slain . . . For which reason we restore to you the faith of your forefathers. Let the former clergy return to their churches . . . And do ye rejoice." Susenyos then abdicated in favor of his son, Fasiladas (1632–1667), and soon after died despondent still embracing the faith his people had rejected.

For the next two centuries Ethiopia withdrew into a sullen xenophobia in which regionalism, palace intrigue, and the unrelenting pressure of the Galla population led to internal decay, political fragmentation, and ultimate collapse of the central authority. Fasiladas established a fixed capital at Gondar, an inaccessible retreat in the mountains of Amhara, and this move effectively divorced the emperors from their people. The royal line in its growing weakness appealed for Galla support which further discounted imperial authority in the eyes of each local prince, or *ras*, only too ready to exercise independent rule. Galla mercenaries came to dominate the monarchy, and in 1755 a half-Galla king mounted the throne. The Galla were too divided among themselves, however, to impose national unity through their own rule, while the Ethiopians found themselves pressed into isolated islands by the expanding sea of Galla intruders.

By the middle of the eighteenth century, the throne had lost all authority, maintaining its existence only through the tradition of its sacred origin while de facto government rested in the hands of the Galla leaders and provincial chiefs. Civil war was continuous, and separatism steadily gained strength. Only the church remained national in identity, but its authority was at low ebb and its influence negligible in the face of militant war lords. By 1840, although the number of independent provinces had been reduced to four—Shoa, Gojjam, Amhara, and Tigre—the disintegration of Ethiopia appeared permanent.

Beyond the divisive thrust of the Galla intrusion acting on a land of mountainous inaccessibility, there was another factor which both aided and hindered national unity. The Ethiopian character had been shaped by a highland environment in which remoteness spawned parochialism and conservatism in a static society. The difficult years of isolation following the seventh century rise of Islam had forced the Ethiopians to come together in political unity and religious communion, but the process was long and difficult and had not been completed when Ahmad Gran's armies devastated the land and brought on the awesome apostasy to Islam. Eventually the old order was restored, but restoration came at a price. The church was no longer receptive to ideas from without—Roman or otherwise—and settled down to a defense of the status quo which could only lead to ignorance and inbreeding. The royal house abandoned the strength and flexibility of its peripatetic court for the brooding isolation of Gondar, and thus permitted each provincial *ras* gradually to establish his own local rule, protected by his mountain inaccessibility and the apathy of effete kings. Divorced from the outside world, Ethiopian society languished and the Ethiopian spirit atrophied.

Nevertheless, the fusion of Agau and Axumite had brought forth a national state consummated in the glory of the great kings of the Solomonid restoration while providing a spiritual brotherhood within the shelter of Ethiopian Christianity. During the most critical days of the Muslim invasion neither the monarchy nor the church ever lost faith in its traditions and responsibilities. The invaders were driven out and a new national strength emerged which reached full force in the uncompromising rejection of the Jesuit effort to westernize the Ethiopian church. Later, as the nation split into warring factions, both church and royal dynasty still retained enough prestige to survive in name if not in authority. When, during the nineteenth century, forces were set in motion in the direction of political unity, it was found that the Ethiopian spirit had not yet expired nor had the vision of an Ethiopian nation.

CHRISTIANS AND MUSLIMS IN THE EASTERN SUDAN

When Ezana and his Axumite armies sacked Meroe in the middle of the fourth century after Christ and sent its royal family reeling toward the west, there remained in the Nile Valley a Negroid people called the Nuba who not long before had arrived from Kordofan and settled among the people of Kush. Perhaps their arrival had hastened the decline of Meroe; at any rate, after the defeat by Axum the language and culture of the Nuba, or Nubian, immigrants gradually become dominant in the Nile Valley south of Egypt as these people spread downstream, merging with the indigenous population and establishing a new series of states to replace the fallen power of Meroe.

By the sixth century three kingdoms had come into being— Nubia, Maqurra, and Alwa—all of which were converted to Monophysite Christianity through the exertions of the Empress Theodora of Byzantium. For a time, however, it appeared as though the Arab invasion of North Africa might engulf these states. Following the conquest of Egypt, a campaign was launched which brought a Muslim army to the gates of Dongola, now the capital of the single kingdom of Maqurra which had embraced Nubia. Undaunted, the Nubian archers stood off the attackers and Maqurra secured a treaty in 652 which established a peace between Muslim Egypt and Christian Sudan, a peace which endured for six hundred years, and gave rise to a profitable northward-moving trade in slaves. To the south, Alwa stretched her hegemony from the site of ancient Meroe to take in most of the Gezira lying between the White and Blue Nile. Her capital of Soba, near the confluence, came to be a major slave market during this period.

For many centuries this Christian Nubian civilization prospered. Along the Nile, numerous villages with attractive churches and monasteries were set among gardens, vineyards, and pastures rich in produce. Even the crocodiles were said to be tamed by the smiling land. The kingdom of Maqurra may have spread its rule far to the west, for churches existed at Ain Farah in Darfur. Nevertheless it was Alwa which rose to be the more wealthy and powerful. Her land was broad and fertile and, as in the days of Meroe, stock breeding was a major occupation which yielded fine horses and camels as well as quantities of cattle. While there were always many pagans in the land, Christianity was well served. A thirteenth-century traveler reported four hundred churches and many monasteries to sustain the fact that the religion of Christ was the religion of ruler and state. The king was absolute and had the power arbitrarily to enslave his subjects who surprisingly accepted this ill treatment with never a word of protest.

Following several centuries of peace, prosperity, and cordial relations with Egypt, a change set in midway in the thirteenth century. The arrival of the Mamluk rulers in Egypt touched off a series of military campaigns into Maqurra which, though abortive, weakened the regime and destroyed much of the country's wealth. These expeditions led in turn to large-scale Arab immigration from Egypt, hitherto rigorously forbidden, which resulted finally in the political collapse of Maqurra early in the fourteenth century. More remote, Alwa lingered on, but by the fifteenth century her people had been overrun by infiltrating pastoral Egyptian Arabs. Resultant civil war and political chaos created a vacuum of authority which was filled early in the sixteenth century by a new power—the Funj sultanate.

The final disintegration of the Christian kingdoms of Maqurra and Alwa opened the way for the spread of Islamic religion and civilization throughout the eastern Sudan. Arabs from the north continued to filter into the land, driving their flocks before them, and gradually there arose a new strain made up of the local population combined with an Arab infusion. At the same time indigenous institutions tended to give way before Arab political organization and language, while Christianity and paganism were replaced by Islamic culture and religion. The fall of Maqurra and Alwa, therefore, represented a turning point in the history of the eastern Sudan, for thenceforward it was Islam and the Near East rather than Nubian Christianity which came to shape the lives of the people.

The Funj were a good case in point. Of obscure origin—possibly an offshoot of the White Nile Shilluk, possibly from a black nation of the upper Blue Nile—they appeared suddenly and dramatically in 1504–1505 to found their capital of Sennar on the Blue Nile and to establish their hegemony over the Sudan until the days of Muhammad Ali three hundred years later. They quickly subdued the Abdullabi Arabs who had taken over the collapsing state of Alwa, but were themselves just as quickly converted by Islam and brought into a close economic and cultural association with Egypt.

By mid-seventeenth century, the Funj were at the height of their power, exercising suzerainty over a series of vassals as far north as Hannak near the Third Cataract, and controlling directly the Gezira plain between the White and Blue Nile. A century later, however, Funj power began to decline as civil strife robbed the regime of its strength. By the time the armies of Muhammad Ali advanced on Sennar in 1821, not only the power but the will to resist had departed, and the Sudan fell to the invaders uncontested.

Suggestions for Further Reading

For a discussion of the East African coast it is best to begin with the chapters by Gervase Mathew and G. S. P. Freeman-Grenville dealing with the period up to 1840 in R. Oliver and G. Mathew, eds., *History of East Africa,* I (Oxford: Clarendon Press, 1963). James S. Kirkman, *Men and Monuments on the East African Coast* (London: Lutterworth Press, 1964; New York: Praeger, 1966) is a lively account based largely on archeological findings, and G. P. S. Freeman-Grenville, *The Medieval History of the Coast of Tanganyika* (London: Oxford University Press, 1962) deals exhaustively with that subject. The same author provides an invaluable selection of documents in *The East African Coast* (Oxford: Clarendon Press, 1962). The older R. Coupland, *East Africa and Its Invaders* (Oxford: Clarendon Press, 1938) is useful for the geopolitics of the Indian Ocean, while John Gray, *History of Zanzibar* (London: Oxford University Press, 1962) is standard for its subject. See also J. Strandes, *The Portuguese Period in East Africa* (Nairobi: East African Literature Bureau, 1961). These sources may be supplemented by substantial periodical literature including G. S. P. Freeman-Grenville, "East African Coin Finds and their Historical Significance," *Journal of African History,* v. I, no. 1, 1960; N. Chittick, "Kilwa and the Arab Settlement of the East African Coast," *Ibid.,* v. IV, no. 2, 1963; and N. Chittick, "The 'Shirazi' Colonization of East Africa," *Ibid.,* v. VI, no. 3, 1965. A recent examination of the slave trade is found in E. A. Alpers, *The East African Slave Trade* (Nairobi: East African Publishing House, 1967).

For Ethiopia, see A. H. M. Jones and E. Monroe, *A History of Ethiopia* (Oxford: Clarendon Press, 1960); Richard Greenfield, *Ethiopia, A*

New Political History (London: Pall Mall Press, 1965; New York: Praeger, 1965); E. Ullendorf, *The Ethiopians* (London: Oxford University Press, 1965); and Ernest Budge, *History of Ethiopia*, 2v. (Oosterhout, Netherlands: Anthropological Publications, 1966; New York: Humanities Press, 1966). These may be supplemented by E. S. Pankhurst, *Ethiopia, A Cultural History* (Woodford Green, Essex: Lalibela House, 1955) with its many fine illustrations, and by J. S. Trimingham's excellent *Islam in Ethiopia* (London: Frank Cass, 1965; New York: Barnes & Noble, 1965). Useful first-hand accounts include Richard Pankhurst, ed., *Travellers in Ethiopia* (London: Oxford University Press, 1965); and James Bruce, *Travels to Discover the Source of the Nile* (Edinburgh: Edinburgh University Press, 1964; New York, Horizon Press, 1964).

Sudanese history is dealt with in part by a number of works including A. J. Arkell, *A History of the Sudan from the Earliest Times to 1821*, rev. ed. (London: Athlone Press, 1961; New York: Oxford University Press, 1961); P. M. Holt, *A Modern History of the Sudan* (London: Weidenfeld and Nicolson, 1963; New York: Praeger, 1963); J. S. Trimingham, *Islam in the Sudan* (London: Frank Cass, 1965; New York: Barnes & Noble, 1965). For the Funj, see P. M. Holt, "Funj Origins: A Critique and New Evidence," *Journal of African History*, v. IV, no. 1, 1963; and O. G. S. Crawford, *The Fung Kingdom of Sennar* (Gloucester: J. Bellows, 1951). Also useful is J. Bruce, *Travels*, previously cited.

5: The West African Forest Civilization

THE LAND AND THE PEOPLE

The West African coastal area, stretching along two thousand miles from Senegambia to present-day Cameroun, contains people whose languages and customs suggest a common ancestry far in the remote past. Much less uniform is the land in which they live; even the rain forest which characterizes so much of the region along the coast varies greatly in nature and extent, between the Gambia tidewater and the hills of present-day Sierra Leone or from the dry slope of the Accra plains to the humid jungle swampland of the Niger Delta.

When European mariners first began to explore the West African coast during the fifteenth century, they divided it into the western or windward district extending from Cape Verde to Cape Palmas and the eastern, or leeward, coast which comprised the sheltered shoreline of the Gulf of Guinea. Such divisions had little meaning for the West African inhabitants. More significant were the varying stretches of forest, the pattern of river drainage, or the hilliness of the terrain. To the west in what is today Senegal, the Gambia, and Portuguese Guinea, the land is open and well watered by navigable streams which quickly abandon the mangrove swamps near the sea to range through fertile flatlands whose sandy soil is now employed in the cultivation of rice, millet, and groundnuts, and whose rivers give easy access to the interior.

The Senegambia is in fact not a true part of the West African forest for its latitude betrays a closer kinship to the savanna, but farther to the southeast the windward coast undergoes a marked change in character. In this region of modern Guinea, Sierra Leone, and Liberia a thick expanse of forest covers the coastal areas and at one time penetrated far inland before the advent of widespread bush farming. Here the rivers rush down from interior iron-bearing hills like the Futa Jalon only to lapse into sluggishness as they approach the coast, finally creeping to the sea through delta marshes. Unlike the Gambia, this country defies easy communication. Not only are the rivers difficult to navigate but in places the hills come right to a shoreline which offers no harbor save the excellent bay at modern Freetown, while overland travel must contend with a forest encouraged by an annual rainfall not infrequently well in excess of one hundred inches.

East of Cape Palmas the wooded area is less extensive and the terrain less severe. Gently rolling hills are covered by a relatively narrow band of forest which disappears entirely along the coast in parts of modern Ghana, Togo, and Dahomey, reflecting the lower precipitation in those areas. In the region of the Niger Delta, however, both rainfall and vegetation are abundant in a country which is both connected and divided by a network of waterways—a means of communication for the native of the land but a labyrinth to befuddle the unwary stranger. Elsewhere the coast is somewhat more hospitable with lagoons and inland waterways and occasional rivers like the Ogun and the Volta which permit some access to the interior.

Since it seems probable on anthropological and linguistic grounds that the people of the West African forest belt were long ago very closely related to one another, they may have moved into the region as part of the vast migration of Negroes who fled the Sahara as it grew progressively drier beginning about the sixth millennium B.C. Human habitation in the forest has been found dating back ten thousand years; the assertion of northern and eastern origin appears many times over in the traditions of West African people, while major languages like Yoruba, Edo, or Ibo have an antiquity of their own of at least four thousand years. Infiltrating the forest probably in response to population pressures from the north, the migrants would have found, first of all, shelter from attack, and then a fertile, well-watered territory capable of sustaining substantial numbers of people. The earliest intruders were probably hunters and fishermen, but as agriculture was mastered, the forest provided a genial environment for crop production.

The forest offered protection, but the price was often isolation. Over wide stretches the people lived in small self-sustained village states where economic self-sufficiency was keyed to survival and where social stability was secured at the expense of innovation. A rigid social order based upon mutual privileges and obligations insured a place for everyone. No one, not even the ruler, could become appreciably richer or more powerful than his neighbor. No one, not even the sick or the aged, would be forgotten by a well-developed sense of community responsibility. It was a society, however, which cherished the status quo, which utilized its religion to combat change, and which made war on new and unfamiliar ideas.

Yet generalization invites distortion, for not all the forest dwellers were isolated nor all the states small or backward. Benin was already a strong and extensive kingdom when the Portuguese discovered it in 1485, and subsequently the Yoruba of Oyo, the Ashanti, and Dahomey established stable centralized states with extensive political authority, widespread economic interests, and a highly sophisticated culture. It was the Yoruba of Ife who cast bronze portraits of their sovereigns, possibly as early as the twelfth and thirteenth centuries A.D., which are among the world's finest examples of naturalistic sculpture, which may have derived from the celebrated Nok terracottas of an earlier era, and which were forerunners of the splendid bronzes which Benin began to produce in the fifteenth century. Artistic output of a high order was never the monopoly of a few, however; witness the imagination and humor of the gold weights of Ashanti, the subtle music of the talking drums in what is today Ghana and Nigeria, the delicate Bulom ivory carvings so prized by the early Portuguese visitors to Sierra Leone, and the splendid wood sculpture produced by a wide range of West African people— Ibo and Yoruba, Dan and Guro, Senufo, Baule, or Mende—to name but a few.

Communication within the West African forest had none of the ease which characterized the movement of people in the savanna, but isolation was relative, not absolute, and trade was an important part of life in the forest belt. Village markets existed for the exchange of commodities produced locally, but there was also a long distance trade which dealt in specialty goods which were distributed widely along well-established trade routes. Salt manufactured on the sea coast was exchanged for iron or gold mined in the interior. Leather products of pastoralists living on the edge of the savanna were shipped south where they might find a market in cotton-growing, cloth-producing communities. Slaves and gold found ready purchasers in the kingdoms of the Sudan and later, when the Europeans began to visit the West African coast from the fifteenth century onward, gold and then slaves became major exports of the forest region south to the Atlantic trade.

Commerce of this sort led to a certain amount of economic specialization. Most people were farmers but some clans came in time to be associated with such occupations as mining, weaving, or smithing, while trading was the part-time occupation of many, especially women. Indeed, commerce became the specialty of certain tribal subdivisions like the Dyula who had their representatives located strategically along trade routes and who devoted their full time to merchandising, leaving cultivation of their lands in the hands of domestic slaves. On these routes towns developed whose main function was the exchange of goods, and here were to be found the large markets with a wide variety of products—gold dust, fabrics, kola nuts, shea butter, and salt along with food and other consumer goods to sustain the people whose main work was the conduct of business in the market. These centers engaged in more than economic exchange, however. They were also places for relaxation and the enjoyment of friendship, for the exchange of gossip, for romance or for intrigue. It was there that news of the outside world could be obtained, where fresh ideas first made their entry into the circumscribed universe of the forest villager.

A varying environment and a multiplicity of slowly diverging cultures makes difficult the portrayal of the typical forest society before the coming of the Europeans. The Ibo who dwelt east of the Niger and north of its delta were a vigorous farming people who lived in village neighborhoods of scattered homesteads governed by a headman and a council of elders. Such individualism among the Ibo betrayed a mistrust in political allegiances which transcended the local community, although it did not prevent a vigorous system of public policing by age-grade societies charged with carrying out the decisions of the elders. Family descent was patrilineal and family solidarity was strong, centering on the homestead with its heavy walls of red earth surrounding the barns and dwellings. If the householder was wealthy, his compound contained his own house behind which were ranged the huts of his several wives as well as numerous farm buildings for storage and livestock. Near the barn was sure to be a small shrine where rested the symbols of personal gods and ancestors, and these received regular offerings of food, palm wine, kola nuts, and prayer.

The Akan people living in the forest west of Yorubaland presented a somewhat different way of life. Though agricultural like the Ibo, they lived in compact villages divided into wards and family compounds, their family structure was rigorously matrilineal, and they typically organized themselves into complex states with a king and a full complement of attendant ministers. Royalty in the West African forest was a precarious profession, hemmed in by many limitations, however. The *alafin*, or king of Oyo, always stood the risk of a no-confidence vote by his council of state which according to the dictates of custom compelled him to commit suicide. Among a number of peoples it was the rare king who died of natural causes, but this may have reflected, not customary regicide so much as the natural uneasiness of crowned heads. Even in his prime, a king was limited by his advisers. An early Portuguese account records how a Sierra Leone king was obliged to consult his elders before initiating warfare, "and if it appears to them that the war is unjust, or that the enemy is very strong, they tell the king that they cannot help him, and give orders for peace despite the king."

Among the Wolof and Serer of Senegambia, royalty, if vigorously sustained, fared better. The Wolof king was elected by the nobility but once chosen he quickly concentrated formidable power in his hands and was surrounded by taboos and certain attributes of divinity. A warrior chief, he protected his authority by a retinue of soldier-slaves, dependents, and praise singers, appointed local chiefs who repaid him with a share of their tax revenues, and drew wealth from levies on merchants, cattle-tending Fulani, and conquered peoples. The Serer kings presided over a similarly centralized organization, and both Wolof and Serer political systems conceded important powers to the women of the royal clans. The king's mother controlled certain villages which paid her tribute, and presided in judgment over cases involving adultery. In the Wolof state of Walo it was possible for a woman to become the *bur*, or chief of state.

Both Wolof and Serer society was rigidly hierarchical. Among the Serer there were clearly defined classes of royalty, nobility, warriors, peasants, and crown servants, as well as special low castes in-

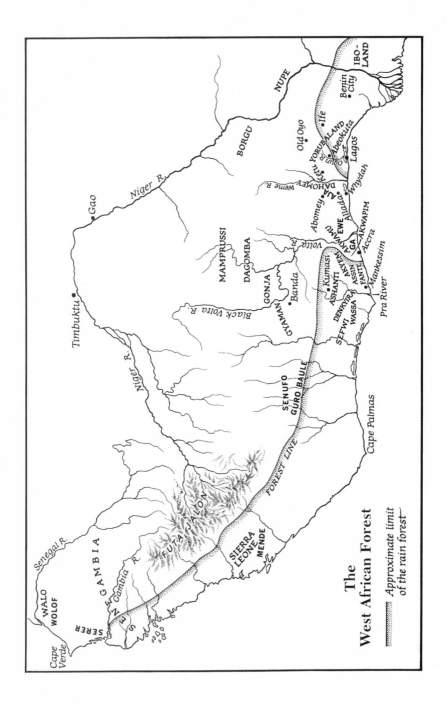

The
West African Forest

Approximate limit
of the rain forest

cluding smiths, butchers, leatherworkers, and praise singers. Slavery was widespread but it too was carefully divided into such groupings as slaves pawned for debt, hereditary house servants who could not be sold, and true slaves acquired through war or purchase. Slaves represented a large portion of the population and in certain instances they enjoyed great power and privileges—for example, those who dwelt in the royal household and served as advisers to the king.

Political life in the West African forest was by no means exclusively related to class structure or royal lineage. There were also the many secret societies, particularly in the region lying between Portuguese Guinea and the Ivory Coast, which exercised a profound influence on the life of the people. These cults, based on mystery, ritual, and magic, did not intrude directly upon chiefly prerogative, but their authority was so great in the shaping of local custom and the imposition of taboos affecting daily life as to constitute for practical purposes a very real check on the powers of the constituted government. Many societies existed, but the most widespread among a number of tribal groups were the *Poro* for the men and the *Sande* for the women, each concerned principally with sexual education and the metamorphosis from adolescence to adulthood, but associated in the popular mind with supernatural powers which enabled the societies to wield great authority in temporal affairs.

The *Poro* practiced rites which claimed death and resurrection for its candidates who emerged from initiation with a deeper spiritual strength as well as the authority to indict individuals in their villages for alleged breaches of the law or even to forbid others the performance of certain normal actions such as planting a crop or making a journey. Non-compliance generally found the offender being carried off into the bush by spirits, never to be seen again, a dreadful supernatural process which rarely failed to impress a people already convinced of the awful power of the society.

Among the Mende of Sierra Leone the secret societies were the de facto guardians of the ethical and moral standards of the people. They were concerned specifically with sexual values and practices, but the ultimate goal was the propagation of socially accepted behavior—womanly character and virtue, codes of male honor, or rules of public conduct on which there was common agreement as the ethical foundations for a healthy society. Hence these societies claimed a wide-ranging prerogative to dictate in such matters as public health, agricultural production, education, or political succession relying on their close liaison with the spirit world as a basis for their authority. In this respect they were not unlike the medieval church in Europe which also prescribed rules of conduct and codes of behavior based on spiritual authority, and which frequently compelled the temporal power to compliance.

IFE, OYO, AND THE RISE OF THE YORUBA

One of the most prominent examples of a West African people claiming an origin in the East comes from the Yoruba whose tradition has intrigued those who have seen influences from ancient Egypt in Yoruba art, customs, and religious practice. According to Yoruba myth, the national origin is traceable to Ife where Oduduwa, a prince of Mecca, came seeking refuge from Muslim persecution and remained to live among the local people. Oduduwa's children became the progenitors of the several Yoruba nations, including the Oyo who later became the founders of a large and powerful empire.

What can be inferred from this tradition is that there were invasions of the forest country from the north, one of these being associated with the name of Oduduwa and occurring about 1000 A.D. at a site called Ife. It is very probable that there were people already living in the forest and that the intruders came in a series of discrete waves, deferring to Ife as the spiritual source of the Yoruba people but granting it no political primacy. That Ife was an important center may be inferred from the splendid art she produced at this early period, but there could have been no genuine unity among the Yoruba who never even provided themselves with a national name—the term, Yoruba, originating during the nineteenth century, applied not by the Yoruba themselves but by outsiders to describe a series of city-states where variations of the same language were spoken.

Tradition began to give way to historical fact with the formation and development of the state of Old Oyo. Founded according to tradition by Oranmiyan, a son or grandson of Oduduwa, it probably dates from the late fourteenth or early fifteenth century A.D., after which it quickly became politically predominant throughout Yorubaland, its authority extending at its height during the eighteenth century north to the Niger, south to the sea, east as far as Benin, and west to include the kingdom of Dahomey. The Oyo empire was not a centralized monolith but consisted rather of layers of states with varying loyalties to the center. Most closely connected was metropolitan Oyo which was directly administered. Next came provinces closely allied with Oyo, then provinces with considerable local independence where Oyo exercised only suzerainty, and finally autonomous states which had been conquered by Oyo and were forced to pay tribute.

Clearly, this empire functioned as effectively as its system of communication, the vigor of its rulers, and the efficiency of its army. At the head of the state was the *alafin* of Oyo, a powerful monarch but by no means a thoroughgoing autocrat. Surrounded by a complex of palace and state officials, the *alafin* was considered sacred, but was in important respects the creature of the people, or at any rate, of those who wielded political power. These were the *Oyo Mesi*, the aristocratic leaders of the seven wards of the capital city who formed a council of state and were responsible for selection of each new *alafin*. This enormous authority also worked in reverse for the *Oyo Mesi* could condemn a deficient king to death by suicide, thus placing a powerful check on any tendency toward royal tyranny. Furthermore there was the *Ogboni*, a secret society of religious and political leaders who had the power to review decisions of the *Oyo Mesi*, including the repudiation of the *alafin*. In the provinces were *obas*, or princes, drawn from the local ruling lineages and exercising considerable autonomy provided it was accompanied by regular payment of tribute.

That the Oyo empire remained virile until late in the eighteenth century is tribute to the ability of numerous kings who, like the legendary Sango or Ojigi, the eighteenth century conquerer of Dahomey, were able to govern effectively despite the customary limitations placed upon their rule. There were other factors contributing to imperial strength, however; for example, the tradition that decreed death to defeated generals, a strong system of administration at least within metropolitan Oyo, a steady stream of revenue in tribute and taxes to feed the treasury, and a certain degree of cultural and linguistic cohesion among the people living near the capital.

Despite their imperial status, the people of Oyo lived simply. Their mud houses were roofed with foliage and modestly furnished. Dress was rudimentary, although personal cleanliness was scrupulously observed, and whenever a dirty or unkempt person was encountered it was sure to be a sign of mourning. The people were of an unassuming and virtuous disposition; crime was consequently rare and submissiveness to one's superiors was a standard rarely violated. Being compliant by nature, the Oyos were more diplomatic than forceful, even appearing in extreme circumstances to lack straightforwardness. This characteristic was accompanied by an ambiguity in speech as well as a shrewdness in commercial dealings for which they were widely renowned.

It was during the seventeenth century that the Oyo empire began to develop on a large scale, and under the warlike *alafin*, Ajagbo, reached out toward the coast. With the eighteenth century came the conquest of the kingdom of Dahomey when Dahomey attempted to dispute Oyo's coastal outlets. Under Ojigi (c. 1698– c. 1732) and his successors, first the slaving center of Allada and then Dahomey proper were invaded and devastated, but Oyo was unable to occupy the enemy territory and had to be content with tribute which consisted of men and women as well as military supplies and cash payments in cowries. Apparently at the height of her powers, Oyo was in fact already overextended and began to lose strength when the royal line came under the domination of Gaha, the *bashorun,* or head, of the *Oyo Mesi,* who seized power in 1754 and held it until he was overthrown about 1774. Although with *Alafin* Abiodun (1754–1789), the royal line had managed to re-establish itself and to maintain domination over an increasingly restive Dahomey, the Egba subgroup of the Yoruba successfully asserted their independence toward the end of the eighteenth century as did others including the Bariba people of Borgu, and the Nupe. By the opening of the nineteenth century, Oyo was facing a protracted civil war which was to sap the energies of the Yoruba throughout the century, and which was brought to an end only with the British intervention in Yorubaland in 1893.

Though there were complex factors at work, the decline of Old Oyo was the result of basic weaknesses within the Yoruba community. In the first place, the empire had become too unwieldy and its lines of communication and supply overextended, thus inviting revolt in the provinces. Such defections might have been offset by strong leadership within Oyo itself but in fact it was at this very time that internal dissension robbed the administration of its essential vigor. The rule of Gaha seriously weakened the web of authority around the *alafin,* and this in turn meant indecision within the government and a decline in the effectiveness of the army. Other pressures took their toll. For example, there was the rise of coastal trade, particularly in slaves, which swung the center of economic gravity southward away from Oyo; another factor was the growing influence of Islam in the north, but essentially the fault was internal. In the final analysis, as they were to demonstrate during their nineteenth-century civil wars, the Yoruba had little internal cohesion and were incapable of living and working together in peace.

THE PEOPLE OF BENIN

Benin lies in the West African forest east of Yorubaland. Not only was its territory adjacent, but it shared many close cultural contacts with the Yoruba including elements of a common heritage. The tradition of both the Bini and Yoruba people described how an early Benin state, lacking effective royal leadership, invited Oduduwa, the king of Ife, to send a prince to rule, and how the choice finally fell on Oranmiyan, who was later to found the state of Oyo. Oranmiyan reportedly decided that only a prince of Benin blood would suffice, and so he fathered a son through the daughter of a Bini chief, and this son, Eweka, became the founder of the future Benin empire. This myth suggests that the invasions of Yorubaland at the time of the establishment of Ife also affected the Bini, or Edo, who were either conquered by a wave of Yoruba immigrants, or possibly admired the efficiency of their neighbors sufficiently to invite a member of the royal line of Ife to rule as *oba* in Benin.

Whatever the cause, the royal infusion seems to have had a salutary effect. The reign of Eweka may be dated from about the fourteenth century during which time Benin slowly gathered strength. The capital was established at the site of Benin, while the kings asserted their authority over the nobility and secured primogeniture as the basis for royal succession. By the middle of the fifteenth century Benin had become a formidable state under Ewuare the Great (c. 1440–c. 1473) who extended its influence westward to its colony at Lagos and eastward as far as the Niger. The stability of the kingdom at this time is attested to by the superb artistic output of cast bronzes and carved ivory which were used not only for ornamental effect but to set forth the accomplishments of the Benin kings and state.

With its location near the seacoast, Benin was one of the earliest West African states to come into contact with the European explorers who were making their way down the West African coast during the fifteenth century. It was in 1485 that the Portuguese appeared at Benin in search of trade which was quickly instituted with pepper and slaves as the chief exports. At this time, however, Benin was a stable and established state, and the appearance of the Portuguese had little effect on her Edo-speaking population. In the first place, the slave trade never achieved important proportions in Benin whose indifference to such a commerce forced the traders to look elsewhere on the coast where better markets existed. Moreover, the Portuguese were careful to keep firearms from falling into Edo hands so that guns never played a major part in Benin's armament and expansionist policy. Finally, Portuguese efforts at Christian conversion were a pronounced failure in the face of a vigorous and complex state religion, and a people who remained resolutely pagan.

Though the importance of Europe may have been minimal, the early presence in Benin of Western traders and voyagers offered an unparalleled insight into the life of a West African community before there had been any infiltration of alien influence. The image of a virile society emerges. During its sixteenth century apogee, Benin City was a stronghold twenty-five miles in circumference, protected by walls and natural defenses, containing an elaborate royal palace and neatly laid out houses with verandahs and balustrades, and divided by broad avenues and smaller intersecting streets. The power of the *oba* was apparent in his wealth, his divinity, his domination over commercial transactions, and his large and lavish court. In this prosperous society, the wealthier classes dressed and dined very well. Beef, mutton, chicken, and yams were staples, while the less well off made do with yams, dried fish, beans, and bananas. No beggars existed in Benin, where those unable to keep themselves were normally supported by the king and lesser officials.

Trade with Europe remained peripheral, but the large and powerful state of Benin must have rested on more than an agricultural base, and it is therefore possible that there was a substantial trade to the northern markets of Hausaland. The nation was highly organized with a strong kingship rooted in indigenous religious and political practices, a complex and effective administration, and an army noted for its size and efficiency.

As with the source of Benin's growth, her gradual decline during the seventeenth, eighteenth, and nineteenth centuries is equally difficult to diagnose. Perhaps it was the custom of secluding the *oba* which developed during the reign of Ehangbuda late in the sixteenth century and which thus tended to place military and political power in the hands of the chiefs while the *oba* was limited to the exercise of religious authority. Perhaps it was the struggle over royal succession which often preoccupied rival groups of chiefs, for chiefly positions were not hereditary and had to be protected, frequently by dominating weak *obas* unable to exercise the power concentrated in the kingly office. Perhaps it was an administrative complexity grown unwieldy which encouraged civil war as a means to new balances of power within the state. Perhaps, during the nineteenth century, it was Fulani pressure in the north and European commerce in the south. In any event, internal disputes proliferated and were accompanied by breakaway movements of subject people until the last decades of the nineteenth century found Benin in full decline ready to be toppled by the British occupation of 1897.

THE KINGDOM OF DAHOMEY

The Yoruba had also maintained intimate connections with another powerful state which appeared at a later time on their western flank. During the early decades of the eighteenth century there arose the kingdom of Dahomey which, first as a vassal of Oyo and later as an independent nation, came to be one of the chief sources of supply for the West African slave trade.

Both linguistic and cultural influences from Yorubaland had long manifested themselves among the Aja and Ewe states lying to the west, but by the end of the seventeenth century, Old Oyo was reaching out to Dahomey to impose her political control as well. By 1698 Allada, the capital of the Aja states had been subdued; then between 1726 and 1730 Dahomey was conquered and remained tributary to the Oyo power for the next hundred years. Interestingly, it was at precisely the same time that Dahomey was establishing her own local hegemony within the Aja country and developing relations with European slavers which were to draw her into a deep economic commitment to the slave trade.

The rise of Dahomey and her simultaneous conquest by Oyo were not unconnected. During the seventeenth century, Allada and neighboring communities like Whydah were engaging in a rising round of civil wars, raids, and rebellions probably brought on by the unsettling impact of the transatlantic slave trade. The constant raiding inland by the coastal states soon made Dahomey strong in self-defense; first she repelled these attacks and then during the 1720's under King Agaja she conquered Allada and Whydah in an apparent attempt to introduce political stability and to end the unsettling effects of slaving. Thus she became the paramount power among the Aja states, a development which necessarily led to the invasion by Oyo, unwilling to see her tributary, Allada, so rudely handled by the upstart.

The terms of peace in 1730 permitted Agaja to retain both his army and internal self-government, but the Oyo suzerainty was deeply resented by the Dahomeans who felt themselves oppressed and who looked forward to the day when they would engineer a successful revolt. Meanwhile, the state was undergoing profound economic changes, for Agaja had reluctantly agreed to cooperate with the European slavers, and within a few years Dahomey had been converted into a major slaving power. Thousands of slaves were exported annually from her ports while Dahomean raids systematically emptied the interior of population. By the end of the eighteenth century, the national economy was largely dependent upon the slave trade; consequently when conditions began to change within the trade at that time, they soon brought forth a series of notable political repercussions within the kingdom.

The royal house of Dahomey ruled from its capital at Abomey on principles unusual in traditional West African societies, for power was highly centralized in the hands of the king. He appointed his chiefs with no relationship to lineage, rewarded officials with personal gifts rather than paying salaries, sustained the army from his own private treasury, and forbade the formation of secret ·societies as a challenge to the royal power. With warfare as a chief occupation, the army with its Amazon contingent occupied an important position within the state and Dahomey's administration was to a considerable extent monopolized by the military. Two of the most important posts, however, were the *mehu* and the *yovogan* who directed national trade and finance, which included slaving since slaving was a state monopoly. The king's festival held yearly came to be reported widely by European traders for its wholesale human sacrifices. The purposes were partly religious but the scale of bloodletting was also meant to impress African and European alike with the quality of Dahomean ferocity in a move calculated to improve the Dahomean position in the slave trade.

By the close of the eighteenth century a number of factors had brought a steadily declining prosperity. Slaves from Oyo were being diverted from Dahomey's ports, and her own expeditions were no longer able to bring back sizeable catches from the now empty country north of Abomey. At the same time European demands were dwindling, first as a result of the commercial uncertainties caused by the long-lived eighteenth century wars, and then in response to the abolition of the slave trade instituted by Britain in 1808. Depressed trade led to political unrest which found outlet in abortive attempts to throw off the Oyo yoke and to replace the ruling dynasty at home. King Kpengla (1774–1789) tried in vain to break the Oyo hold and to replenish his barracoons by raiding the Yoruba kingdom of Ketu. His successor, King Agonglo, was the victim of a palace assassination in 1797, but the revolt failed to unseat the royal line. Finally, in 1818, Gezo seized power from Agonglo's son, Adandozan, and during a long reign lasting until 1858, he attempted to regain a measure of Dahomey's diminishing prestige and wealth. First, freedom was secured from the failing Oyo kingdom in 1822, whereupon Gezo next turned to the problem of rehabilitating the Dahomean economy. His search for new sources of slaves as well as opportunities for legitimate trade soon resulted in a series of raids on the Egba stronghold of Abeokuta, and thus brought Dahomey squarely into the nineteenth-century Yoruba civil wars.

THE AKAN STATES OF ASHANTI AND FANTE

West of Dahomey in the forest area contained between the coast and the lower reaches of the Volta River and its Black Volta tributary, lies the country of the Akan states. Here in a series of migrations between the eleventh and thirteenth centuries A.D., small groups of Twi or Akan speakers moved south from the savanna, mixing with the people already living in the forest, and fanning out east and west of the Pra River to establish a series of village communities— Wassa, Sefwi, Denkyira, Ashanti, Assin, and Fante, among others. By the early seventeenth century the Akan had secured their preponderance in the region which was spread over with a series of small states trading among themselves and with their Ga-Adangbe neighbors as well as with coastal communities west as far as the Ivory Coast and east to Benin.

Beyond this local and regional commerce, an important international exchange was developing which would in considerable part command the attention and shape the history of the large body of Akan people. Already by the early fifteenth century a trade had developed to the north, for the salt, gold, kola nuts, and slaves of the forest were greatly in demand in the Saharan entrepôts. Toward the end of the fifteenth century, Portuguese explorers made contact with Akan coastal states and began an Atlantic-oriented trade which gradually grew in importance over the ensuing century and a half, offering manufactured goods, chiefly firearms, in exchange for gold. By the close of the seventeenth century, therefore, there were two major commercial preoccupations within the gold regions—a series of older interior routes heading north to Jenne, Timbuktu, or the cities of Hausaland, and the newer southern traffic to the coast. There, along the Gold Coast, a whole range of stations represented, among others, Dutch, British, and Danish interests, while Portuguese and French ships sailed Gold Coast waters though neither nation maintained permanent bases in the area.

This growing trade, directed both north and south, played an important role in the political configuration of the Akan people, the most dramatic and formative expression of which was the rise of Ashanti. After early migrations had taken them to the Pra River, the Ashanti gradually moved north to the site of present-day Kumasi where they founded a number of small village states. Drawn to this district because it was a junction of north-south trade routes and a region rich in gold and kola nuts, the Ashanti for a time were unable to exploit their advantage when they fell under the control of neighboring Denkyira about the middle of the seventeenth century. Quickly closing ranks, however, under the leadership of the Oyoko clan and its first three kings, Obiri Yeboa, Osei Tutu, and Opoku Ware, they fashioned the Ashanti kingdom which threw off the Denkyira controls and soon established itself as the foremost military state in the Gold Coast region and a major commercial power with commitments north to the savanna and south to the Atlantic.

The achievements of the Oyoko kings were of the greatest importance to the growth of Ashanti. Under Obiri Yeboa, who was killed in battle during the 1670's, the supremacy of the Oyoko clan was acknowledged by all dwelling in the Kumasi area and the other ruling lineages were taken into the Oyoko line which had founded the nuclear Amanto states of Ashanti—Kumasi, Bekwai, Juaben, Kokofu, and Nsuta. Osei Tutu solidified this beginning by establishing the spiritual unity of Ashanti in the sacred symbol of the golden stool; then he chose Kumasi as the nation's capital, and instituted a constitution which acknowledged the supremacy of the *kumasihene,* or king of Kumasi, who would henceforth be known as the *asantehene,* or head of the Ashanti state. The kings of the member states were integrated into the new political union in various ways—they became commanders of the national army and formed a council of advisers to the *asantehene,* they were obliged to supply the army with requisitions of troops and were expected to preside at the annual national festival. Nevertheless, in local affairs their authority continued unchallenged. Thus a fine balance was struck between loyalty to the center and freedom for the parts.

Once his reforms were complete, Osei Tutu began an expansion which claimed Denkyira as a major victim and which extended suzerainty to the coast. Most of the new territories were incorporated into the Ashanti union which had reached substantial proportions by the time Osei Tutu fell during a campaign against the Akyem in 1717. His great-nephew and successor, Opoku Ware, followed these accomplishments with further conquests deep into the northern gold producing regions of Banda and Gyaman, then south to subdue Akyem, Akwapim, and Akwamu, entering Accra in 1744. Further campaigns followed, and with Opoku Ware's death in 1750 Ashanti was unchallenged among the Gold Coast states.

National purpose and military organization aside, two factors contributed greatly to the Ashanti expansion. The first was the desire of these inland people to break through to the coast and take direct part in the Atlantic trade. The second was the desire for firearms to give authority to Ashanti economic and political aspirations. This interest in the Atlantic trade the Ashanti shared with other Akan—their Denkyira oppressors, for example—but few others appeared capable of grasping the relationship of economic enterprise and political unity and were consequently unable to meet the Ashanti in their new strength. The Denkyira were so devoid of a sense of survival as to allow firearms to pass through their territory to Ashanti, knowing that these weapons would soon be used against them. Some others less suicidal were able to echo, albeit faintly, Ashanti unity and economic purpose. Of these the Fante became the outstanding group along the coast and as such a potential rival to Ashanti expansionism in the eighteenth and nineteenth centuries.

Like other Akan, the Fante claim their origin in the savanna from whence they migrated in small groups, penetrating the forest and arriving near the coast where they established their capital at Mankessim. By the late fifteenth century the Portuguese knew of their existence as a small city state a short distance inland from the coast. Toward the end of the seventeenth century, however, there was a rapid expansion along the coast which was soon filled with a series of independent Fante states stretching from the Pra River to the Ga state in the west.

The Fante expansion was probably related both to population increase and to a desire to act as middlemen between the European trade and the interior markets. Nevertheless, such commercial ambitions would surely have been stillborn had not the Fante managed to combine their dispersion with a political union, apparently in response to the rising power of Ashanti fresh from its conquest of Denkyira between 1699 and 1701. Emulating Ashanti, the Fante states formed a league with a parliament composed of national representatives headed by the *braffo,* or ruler, of Mankessim who became the head of state. Like the Ashanti federation, the Fante union brought into being another large state among the Akan, but there was an important difference between the two. The Fante union was essentially pragmatic—a specific counter to the Ashanti threat—and lacked the sense of brotherhood and the symbols of national unity which brought the Ashanti into such long-lived cohesion. Fante unity therefore tended to rise and fall with the immediacy of an Ashanti move to the south, and at its best never approached the effectiveness displayed by the northerners. Nevertheless it did represent a concrete response to Ashanti expansionism within the balance of power of the Akan states.

Indeed, for a long time there was no Ashanti challenge to the Fante. Up to 1750 the Ashanti were preoccupied in the north and then until the beginning of the nineteenth century constitutional upheavals and civil strife at Kumasi kept them engaged at home. Early in the nineteenth century, however, there was a series of Ashanti invasions of the south, but by this time wars among the Akan were no longer largely intramural affairs, for they had come to involve increasingly the European commercial and military establishments liberally sprinkled along the coast. Thus the later history of Ashanti and Fante became part of the history of nineteenth-century European penetration in West Africa.

During the early nineteenth century the Ashanti administered a series of thorough defeats to the Fante which eventually brought British intervention in the dispute. Partly these defeats were the result of Fante disunity and weakness, but they also represented Ashanti success in creating a strong state under an effective central administration. Under Opoku Ware, Ashanti power had extended rapidly into regions which were not acceptable within the definition of the original Ashanti union; hence those who followed him as *asantehene* were faced with a critical problem of consolidation and imperial administration, a problem which was brilliantly solved by Osei Kwadwo (1764–1777) and augmented by his successors, Osei Kwame (1777–c. 1801) and Osei Bonsu (c. 1801–1824).

The Ashanti empire of the late eighteenth century sprawled over some 150,000 square miles of forest and savanna, from Cape Mount in modern Liberia to Dahomey, and from the coast north to Dagomba and Mamprussi. Administering this vast region with a population of three to five million called for radical measures which were soon introduced by Osei Kwadwo. In the first place, the hereditary chiefs of Kumasi were systematically eliminated and replaced by a bureaucracy which, although it in time became hereditary itself, was subject to royal appointment and control. Thus the imperial financial and political affairs were directed by ministers solely responsible to the throne, while the provinces were ruled by proconsuls similarly under royal surveillance. A national treasury was established in charge of tolls and other taxes, a state trading company and state-controlled mines drew financial power closer to the *asantehene*, while special political officers represented the king's will at home and abroad.

Beyond this, the *asantehene* moved to circumscribe the powers of the original Amanto states which were exempt from imperial reforms and still possessed a large degree of local autonomy as well as power within the Ashanti army. In part he attempted to limit the Amanto chiefs by developing new military formations of foreign mercenaries directly controlled by the crown. In part, pressure on the Amanto developed from the steady accretion of power at the center—the replacement of a king-in-council with ad hoc advisers, the cultural assimilation of subject people, and the imposition of an ideological uniformity throughout the state. Although the Amanto chiefs managed to salvage some of their declining powers, the authority of the *asantehene* grew steadily during the nineteenth century, giving rise to a complex, centralized, bureaucratic state unusual among West African societies.

Suggestions for Further Reading

For the people of the West African forest see G. P. Murdock, *Africa: Its Peoples and Their Culture History* (New York: McGraw-Hill, 1959); H. Baumann and D. Westermann, *Les Peuples et les Civilisations de l'Afrique* (Paris: Payot, 1962); C. Fyfe, *Sierra Leone Inheritance* (London: Oxford University Press, 1964); T. Hodgkin, *Nigerian Perspectives* (London: Oxford University Press, 1960); and J. F. A. Ajayi and I. Espie, eds., *A Thousand Years of West African History* (Ibadan, Nigeria: Ibadan University Press, 1965; New York: Humanities Press, 1965). For secret societies see Kenneth Little "The Mende in Sierra Leone," Daryll Forde, ed., *African Worlds* (London: Oxford University Press, 1954).

Brief attention to the larger West African kingdoms is given in J. D. Fage, *An Introduction to the History of West Africa*, 3rd. ed. (Cambridge University Press, 1962) which should be supplemented with *A Thousand Years of West African History* previously cited.

For more specialized coverage, see D. Forde and P. M. Kaberry, eds., *West African Kingdoms in the Nineteenth Century* (London: Oxford University Press, 1967); J. Egharevba, *Short History of Benin*, 3rd. ed. (Ibadan, Nigeria: Ibadan University Press, 1960; New York: International Publications Service, 1960); R. E. Bradbury, *The Benin Kingdom and the Edo-Speaking Peoples of Southwestern Nigeria* (London: Oxford University Press, 1957); S. Johnson, *History of the Yorubas* (Lagos: CMS Bookshops, 1921); M. Crowder, *The Story of Nigeria*, rev. ed. (London: Faber and Faber, 1966), *A Short History of Nigeria* (New York: Praeger, 1966); J. D. Fage, *Ghana: An Historical Interpretation* (Madison, Wisconsin: University of Wisconsin Press, 1959); W. E. F. Ward, *A History of Ghana*, 2nd. ed. (London: Allen and Unwin, 1958; New York: Humanities Press, 1966); W. W. Claridge, *A History of the Gold Coast and Ashanti*, 2v., 2nd. ed. (London: Frank Cass, 1964; New York: Barnes & Noble, 1964); R. S. Rattray, *Ashanti Law and Constitution* (London: Oxford University Press, 1929); E. L. R. Meyerowitz, *Akan Traditions of Origin* (London: Faber and Faber, 1952); I. Wilks, *The Northern Factor in Ashanti History* (Legon, Ghana: Institute of African Studies, University of Ghana, 1961); A. Dalzel, *The History of Dahomey* (London: Spillsburys, 1793); M. J. Herskovits, *Dahomey: An Ancient West African Kingdom*, 2v. (New York: Augustin, 1938; Evanston, Ill.: Northwestern

University Press, 1967); I. A. Akinjogbin, *Dahomey and its Neighbours, 1708–1818* (Cambridge: Cambridge University Press, 1967); C. Newbury, *The Western Slave Coast and Its Rulers* (Oxford: Clarendon Press, 1961); D. P. Gamble, *The Wolof of Senegambia* (London: Oxford University Press, 1957); and Abbé P. D. Boilat, *Esquisses Sénégalaises* (Paris: P. Bertrand, 1853). A recently expressed skepticism concerning the traditional relationship between Benin and Ife is found in A. F. C. Ryder, "A Reconsideration of the Ife-Benin Relationship," *The Journal of African History*, v. VI, no. 1, 1965.

Other useful articles include R. E. Bradbury, "The Historical Use of Comparative Ethnography with Special Reference to Benin and the Yoruba," J. Vasina, R. Mauny, and L. V. Thomas, eds., *The Historian in Tropical Africa* (London: Oxford University Press, 1964); W. Tordoff, "The Ashanti Confederacy," *The Journal of African History*, v. III, no. 3, 1962; and A. F. C. Ryder, "The Benin Missions," *Journal of the Historical Society of Nigeria*, v. II, no. 2, Dec., 1961.

6: The Great Migrations

THE CIVILIZATION OF ZIMBABWE

Not far beyond the town of Fort Victoria in southern Rhodesia, the road from Salisbury passes near the site of Great Zimbabwe—one of the notable monuments of Africa and once considered perhaps its greatest enigma. There are two buildings. Perched on a hilltop in this gentle rolling country is the "acropolis"—so called because its network of stone walls set among massive granite boulders strongly suggests a citadel. Below in the quiet wooded valley is the "temple," at least part of which appears to have had ceremonial, possibly religious, functions.

Europeans who came upon Great Zimbabwe in the nineteenth century were mystified by its strange aspect. Although there were other analogous ruins in Rhodesia, none was nearly so complex and, as it later developed, so ancient; moreover, stone monuments were not common in areas of Africa untouched by outside influence. Consequently, although nothing about Zimbabwe suggested European or Asian antecedents, these first observers were reluctant to hypothesize an African origin and put forth romantic alternatives variously involving Solomon and Sheba, Phoenician explorers, and other representatives of the ancient world.

What in fact they saw did nothing to encourage such speculation. The "acropolis," its walls seeming at once to grow out of and to support the rounded granite outcrops, resembled no known architectural style of Asia or Europe. Similarly unique, the "temple," which covered an area the length of a football field and two-thirds as wide, was enclosed by a stone wall thirty feet high and up to fifteen feet thick, and contained a series of interior walls all roughly circular or oval in pattern as well as a solid conical tower unexampled elsewhere in the world. Equally unusual were the major entrances which punctuated the segmented walls, eschewing arches or post-and-lintel doorways; the approximate, non-geometric aspect of the ground plan; and the exclusive use in all construction of stone bricks unbound by mortar. Despite this, the stonework was smoothly joined and in general good repair, a condition all the more astonishing in view of the evident antiquity of the complex.

In time a more thoroughgoing archeological study of the site of Great Zimbabwe yielded a less exotic, more credible explanation of its function and history. It was only the oldest and most sophisticated of a series of stone monuments situated in the Central African plains. Each had once been referred to as *dzimbahwe* or "great stone house," a term locally employed to denote the royal court, or kraal, and similar to a modern phrase used to identify a courthouse or a chief's tomb. Great Zimbabwe had served as the capital site of several major kingdoms, its stone construction reflecting the importance of its royal occupants while lesser folk dwelt in kraals of traditional mud and wattle, more comfortable but less imposing. The royal enclosure contained the palace of the king as well as dwellings for his wives and probably for his ministers. The conical tower marked the king's house while the labyrinth of walled passages protected the royal occupant from the profane gaze of the common people. Although in no way approaching the antiquity of Solomon, Great Zimbabwe probably dated from the ninth century A.D. It had been held at various times by successive peoples who enlarged and refashioned its buildings while erecting other *dzimbahwe* sites, and it achieved its final form during the eighteenth century while occupied by the kings of Changamire. About 1833, the civilization of the area, already in full decline, came to an abrupt end when the Ngoni destroyed the Changamire kingdom during their northward flight from the Bantu upheavals in South Africa.

Long before the time of Great Zimbabwe, the region between the Zambezi and Limpopo rivers had been occupied by bands of Bushman hunters and food gatherers into whose range a people—

possibly Bantu speakers and certainly using iron—moved early in the Christian era. Within four centuries they were joined by another group of iron-users who possessed primitive mining techniques which were applied to the region's widespread gold-bearing veins and which yielded very substantial quantities of ore. The genesis of these early intruders is unknown although there is some consensus in favor of Negro antecedents; similarly, there is uncertainty about the origin and identity of later migrants who arrived in Rhodesia south of the Zambezi early in the second millennium A.D. Some observers feel that they were the Karanga who sifted across the Zambezi from the Congo basin as possible predecessors of the modern Shona speakers of Mashonaland. In any event they occupied the site of Great Zimbabwe and contributed the dressed stone additions to the rough walls that had gone up beginning in the ninth century, founding at the same time one of the earliest states to be established in the country contained between the Zambezi and Limpopo.

A large-scale, centralized political authority made its appearance at the beginning of the fourteenth century with the arrival south of the Zambezi of the Mbire, a Bantu group migrating from the Lake Tanganyika region, which had developed advanced political institutions as well as skill in metal craft and masonry work. Apparently, the Mbire were instrumental in revitalizing the resident Shona kingdom which by the middle of the fifteenth century had come under the domination of the Rozwi, an influential ruling group responsible both for a pair of unusually able kings and a period of rapid territorial expansion. From Zimbabwe as a base, first Mutota, and then his son, Matope, fought a series of campaigns which yielded a vast empire by the time of Matope's death about 1480. Pressed by overpopulation and a shortage of salt and urged by upcountry Arab traders, both monarchs extended their rule from the Indian Ocean to the desert of Kalahari and from the Limpopo in the south to the Zambezi, each gaining in the process the appropriate praise name of *Mwena Mutapa*, or Master Pillager.

It was the brief burst of a golden age for the empire called Monomotapa by the Portuguese who had lately arrived at the coastal towns of Sofala and Kilwa. At Zimbabwe the architecture flowered both artistically and technically; there was a growing variety of decorated pottery, copper, bronze, or gold ornaments in use; while widespread distribution of imported Asian ceramics and glassware reflected a rising wealth. Disintegration soon set in, however. Over-

5. Timbuktu skyline

6. Bambara antelope
headdress

7. Carved stone church: Lalibela, Ethiopia

8. Royal palace at Gondar, Ethiopia

9. The Omani fortress at Zanzibar

10. Yoruba terra cotta sculpture from Ife

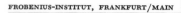

11. Iron sculpture shrine figure, Dahomey

12. Ashanti gold weight

13. Benin bronze: warrior and attendant

14. Great Zimbabwe: the royal kraal

extended communications, court intrigue, and a lack of cultural and ethnic homogeneity led to an early secession by the southern provinces led by its governor, Changa, who took the title of *changamire* and laid the foundations of what came to be called the Changamire kingdom. The core of the Mutapa domain remained in the north where it had already removed before the secession. It was primarily to this northern power that the Portuguese traders addressed themselves after their occupation of Sofala in 1505.

As usual, Portuguese presence raised difficulties for African states. Despite local resistance, the Portuguese gradually effected a penetration of the interior during the latter part of the sixteenth century—trading posts at Sena and Tete on the Zambezi, a network of interior stations and missions, and the acquisition of large tracts of land and mining concessions. In 1629 they succeeded in reducing the Mutapa king to the role of vassal to the Portuguese crown, a situation which endured until the end of the seventeenth century when the Changamire state conquered most of Mutapa, leaving only a small weak remnant in the Sena-Tete region. Thereafter, a much reduced Portuguese trade existed on sufferance by Changamire, but she, herself grew progressively weaker during the eighteenth century and fell victim to Zwagendaba's Ngoni invaders early in the 1830's.

The Karanga were a people devoted to small scale farming and animal husbandry but much of the wealth of the Mutapa and Changamire kingdoms derived from their substantial gold mining industry. An extensive network of open shaft mines had early produced quantities of gold which was exchanged through the coastal markets for Chinese porcelain, beads from India and Indonesia, and presumably Asian cloth as well. The presence of large numbers of Arab traders in the interior, the care with which the gold mines were guarded by royal edict, and the levying of export-import duties all testified to the importance of trade to the inland economy. When the Portuguese arrived, they made every effort to gain access to the gold sources which were, however, denied them both by the coastal traders guarding their monopoly and by the rulers of the interior states who rightly feared political domination. In their desperation the Portuguese ultimately contrived to force their presence on the people of Mutapa, but their clumsy statesmanship succeeded only in weakening the political structure of the kingdom without gaining them any substantial proportion of the gold supply.

Unquestionably Mutapa suffered from Portuguese interference, but there were also problems of political unity and administrative centralization which were intrinsic and which resembled the difficulties of other African nations—for example, the great empires of the Sudan or the kingdom of Ethiopia. The area of the original state created by Mutota and Matope was so vast that transportation and communication based on foot travel could not provide essential unity, while rivers were always serious barriers to the movement of armies. Moreover, there was no universally accepted system for the transfer of authority from one generation to the next, and the kings, for all their divine status, faced serious limitations on their authority. Thus the death of a strong ruler like Matope was followed at once by the split which created the two states of Changamire and Mutapa, and the latter soon suffered other losses of territory when provincial governors drawn from the ruling family successfully established independent kingdoms in their own right.

The king was revered as a god and lived on a most lavish scale with his court of wives, concubines, and officials. His audiences were held in public but he himself remained behind a screen which concealed him from suppliants who came creeping and clapping their hands to show proper homage. When the king died his queens and some of his ministers were dispatched to keep him company in the spirit world, while all the fires in the land were extinguished, for fire was associated with the royal authority and new fires could be kindled only with the flame of the new king. Yet this seemingly omnipotent personality was also the creature of powerful customary limitations. As a god, the king had to be of flawless aspect; hence if he became seriously ill or deformed he was expected to commit suicide. The royal compound, situated behind a high fence, tended to isolate the monarch and make him dependent upon his deputies—the legion of officials, courtiers, and queens, into whose hands much actual power devolved. The royal office was therefore powerful but its power lay as much in its symbolic strength as in the authority wielded by the royal incumbent.

Beyond the court, life was simple. Peasant farmers, living in mud huts behind stockades, cultivated their fields and tended their cattle in a timeless round. Local production of cloth and ornamentation must have been minimal in view of the constant demand for the textiles and ceramics of the East, but the wealth of Mutapa and her sister kingdoms was such that these things could be afforded at least by the wealthier classes. The Portuguese were impressed both by the trading and fighting ability of the people, and indeed their weapons were varied and well made. There being no written language, historical tradition was entrusted to a class of mediums whose accuracy was exceptional. To Portuguese ears the Karanga language had ·much appeal, particularly in comparison with what they regarded as the guttural harshness of Arabic. "[They] pronounce their words with the end of the tongue and the lips, that they speake many words in a whistling accent, wherein they place great elegance . . . Their stile of speaking is by Metaphors: and Similitudes very proper, and fitted to their purpose."

THE COMING OF THE BANTU

The civilization which produced Great Zimbabwe and the state of *Mwena Mutapa* was related to a major migration from West Africa which appears to have unfolded during the centuries of the Christian era with profound effects on the ecology and history of the southern third of the African continent. Knowledge of iron had made its way into West Africa by the third century B.C., long after the region had mastered agriculture. Hence any emigrants moving southward as a result of population increase caused by the food-producing revolution would have already become iron-using agriculturalists, thus providing them with a decisive advantage over Pygmy and Bushman hunters and enabling them to introduce dramatic improvements on the limitations of a Stone Age world.

About the time of Christ this migration began as Negro people from the central Benue River valley around the present border between Nigeria and Cameroun pushed south and southeast into the forest of the Congo River basin. These Bantu speakers seem to have been relatively few in number—perhaps only several hundred—but they were able to move quickly through the rain forest via the Congo drainage system until they emerged at the southern fringe of the forest in what is today the Luba country of northern Katanga. From this point, a lightly wooded area not unlike their original homeland along the Benue, the Bantu apparently developed rapidly in numbers and expanded in all directions—moving southward across the Zambezi to form the civilization which produced Zimbabwe, pushing eastward into the high plains where they fanned out in a complex movement which enveloped the plateau and the coast of East Africa, and doubling back through the forest to absorb the Pygmy people of the Congo. With iron spears they would have been formidable both as hunters and warriors, and their iron implements would have effected a revolution in cultivation, even in East Africa where cereals were probably already known. Thus they were in a position both to attract and to assimilate other people, imposing upon them their language until the population of Africa south of the equator had been converted substantially into iron-age speakers of Bantu.

The extent and the rate of advance of the Bantu migrants is difficult to date with any precision. They may have reached the East African coast near Cape Delgado by the fourth century A.D. in the person of Claudius Ptolemy's Ethiopians. Ironworkers were in the Zambezi Valley early in the Christian era, and the savanna north of the Zambezi contained agriculturalists perhaps as soon as the first century A.D. Below the Zambezi there were very early iron sites while a full-scale iron-age culture was established between the Zambezi and Limpopo by the end of the fourth century. There is no assurance that all this was the work of early Bantu settlers; however, the most plausible alternative is that these iron-age sites resulted from adaptation of an infiltrating Bantu economy and culture by resident Bushmen or Hottentots with the prospect of Bantu settlers soon to follow. Indeed, during the ensuing centuries the record of Bantu occupation of Rhodesia became evident with the development of the Zimbabwe culture, and the southward movement continued across the Limpopo with Sotho speakers pushing deeply into southern Africa by the beginning of the seventeenth century and perhaps much earlier.

Elsewhere the pattern has been somewhat more difficult to trace. In the Bantu heartland located in the Luba-Lunda region of the Congo, an elaborate culture began flourishing in the eighth and ninth centuries A.D., based on Katanga copper and trade with the East African coast. To the east in the area of the Great Lakes there is also evidence of Bantu migration, spreading north from a nucleus in the Zambezi Valley and establishing the iron age in Rwanda, Uganda, and western Kenya over a protracted thousand-year period beginning about the sixth century A.D. In this region, however, the Bantu movement was complicated by countermigrations southward by Nilotic peoples. In western Uganda and Rwanda, pastoral groups known as the Hima and Tutsi had established themselves over the

Bantu farmers by the end of the fifteenth century, but at this point the Hima kingdom was invaded by the Nilotic Luo who poured into Uganda and western Kenya establishing a series of states north and west of Lake Victoria. Of these, Bunyoro was at once the largest and most powerful, and Buganda the most compact and homogeneous, the latter thus early exhibiting a unity which was later to make it one of the most important powers in East Africa.

Farther to the east the Bantu migration encountered another Nilotic intrusion from the north in the form of pastoralists who presumably had come down the arid highland steppe along the Rift Valley even before the arrival of the Bantu, who thereby made the Bantu detour slightly southward in their movement to the east, and who eventually formed a north-south wedge between the Bantu of the Great Lakes and those of the eastern highlands and the coast. East of this Nilotic wedge, the Bantu centered on two nuclear points—the Taita hills near Mt. Kilimanjaro and the Shungwaya district lying between the Juba and Tana rivers in Somalia. These became dispersal areas for a number of important Bantu groups. From Shungwaya came the Kikuyu, the Segeju, and others, possibly as early as the thirteenth century A.D., while the Taita region was the place of origin for several tribes including the Chagga and Shambaa.

Although the process by which the Bantu expansion occurred is necessarily a matter of conjecture, there were at work a number of related factors shaping the pattern of migration. First of all, though farmers, the Bantu knew only an unsophisticated slash-and-burn cultivation which quickly exhausted the land and necessitated a virtually continuous movement by small groups of village units to new areas where better land was available. Furthermore, the Bantu farmers supplemented their agriculture with hunting—another factor which tended to keep them on the move. Rudimentary as it was, however, Bantu cultivation made possible a rapidly and steadily expanding population which in turn was a powerful propellant to further migration. Relocation took place in response to the laws of marriage, inheritance, and lineage, but movements also resulted when groups became dissatisfied over questions of political or economic rights, and broke away from the parent community to form a new clan or tribe in a new area. Hence soil exhaustion combined with population increase to produce a rapid, dynamic migration.

By and large the spread of the Bantu appears to have been

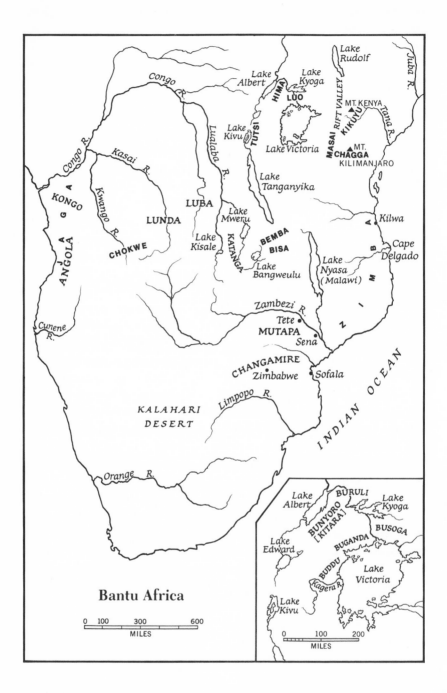

Bantu Africa

0 100 300 600
MILES

Lake Albert
BURULI
Lake Kyoga
BUNYORO [KITARA]
BUSOGA
Lake Edward
BUGANDA
BUDDU
Kagera R.
Lake Victoria
Lake Kivu

0 100 200
MILES

peaceful, and their absorption of indigenous peoples was through the persuasiveness of a more advanced culture rather than by force of arms. Occasionally, however, the process built up pressures; at any rate, the peaceful spread of peoples was punctuated from time to time with explosive marches by groups organized on a military footing. The basis for these eruptions is probably to be found in land hunger even though their immediate objective appears superficially to have been little more than destructive conquest. Three examples may be cited: the late sixteenth-century movements of the Jaga who burst into Kongo and Angola from a point somewhere in the African interior, the Zimba who devastated the East African coast during much the same years, and the early nineteenth-century population explosions in southern Africa following the military conquests of the Zulu chieftain, Shaka.

There is little evidence available to explain the destructive march of the Zimba. As for the Jaga, motivation is also uncertain although contemporary accounts of their tactics have survived. They lived in fortified camps permanently mobilized for war, their numbers were small but their military organization highly developed, and their conquest of more populous but less belligerent people involved the cultural and political absorption of captives into the Jaga complex. Thus a vast community and an enormous area was affected, all from the modest beginning of a handful of original Jaga warriors.

An analogous assimilation of conquered people was characteristic of Zulu expansionism and the series of military migrations it touched off; witness, for example, the Ngoni, Ndebele, Kololo, and others whose strength was so profoundly augmented by large-scale accretions of foreign elements as they ranged in a desperate search for security. In these instances the motive seems clearer. Land hunger and population pressures set the Zulu in motion and was at the heart of the military migrations that followed. It is not unreasonable to suppose that the Jaga might have been similarly motivated; that, in fact, all these militant movements were essentially an accelerated version of the more orderly and peaceful expansion of the Bantu peoples.

THE BANTU CULTURE

Although the Bantu speakers introduced an iron age and an agricultural civilization into a Neolithic hunting and gathering society, their way of life came to vary greatly from place to place, partly through the influence of the people with whom they came in contact, and partly because of the relentless pressure of environment. The Bantu of the Congo basin, therefore, developed different ideas of economy and statecraft from those of the cattle-rearing Bantu of the East African high plains; those of the Swahili coastal communities did not exhibit great similarity either sociologically or ethnically with the dwellers of the Great Lakes country.

There were many common traits as well, born of a common ancestry and the uniformity of man's instinctive response to the exigencies of everyday living. The basic economic occupation of the Bantu continued to be the agriculture they had brought with them, although with differing techniques geared to geographic location. In the Congo savanna the classic slash-and-burn cultivation continued, with fields used on a rotating basis for a few short years, then abandoned until a slow regeneration restored their fertility. Such wasteful methods insured shifting settlements and a low density of population, but in some areas there were important variations; for example, perennial cultivation by the Lozi in the Zambezi flood plain or the irrigation and terracing practiced among the highland Kikuyu and Chagga who may have learned these refinements through contact with other people in the area. Less restricted was the range of crops placed under cultivation—millet and sorghum among the Ethiopian cereals, bananas, yams, and taros representing the Malaysian imports, all overlaid with maize, manioc, sweet potatoes, and other New World food crops introduced after 1500.

One major variation was the stock raising economy practiced in the grazing country east of the Great Lakes which stretched from the upper Nile Valley to the plains of South Africa. In this vast area, environment dictated an economy based mainly on livestock, and in the struggle for existence, cattle ceased to be merely a food supply and became fundamental to the whole way of life of these people. Cattle represented wealth and social position, they were used to cement ties and redistribute wealth among kin, they solidified the authority of rulers, and they played a ritual role in all major moments of human existence—birth, puberty, marriage, and death. With important exceptions such as the Kikuyu or the centralized states around the Great Lakes, the people of the cattle complex lived close to the level of subsistence—their communities consisting of small clusters of insubstantial huts located in kraals where the livestock was sheltered at night; their possessions, aside from the all-important cow, consisting of a hoe, a spear, and a few skins for clothing or receptacles. Crafts were few and labor specialization rudimentary. Political organization was generally restricted to the village which itself was usually no more than an extended family. With such a paucity of material goods and only small scattered communities, there was no concept of trade; consequently barter was the only form of exchange and neither money nor markets existed.

Within the Bantu and Nilotic cattle complex there was little hunting or fishing, but elsewhere these were important adjuncts to a crop economy. Similarly, trade supplemented the agricultural pursuits of most societies dominated or influenced by the Bantu. The Rhodesian gold mines of the Karanga and their predecessors led very early to an important Indian Ocean trade conducted by Swahili and Arab merchants, and this exchange later dwindled only because of the tactless aggressiveness of the Portuguese. Trade was well developed among the Congo people where craft specialization gave rise both to a range of products and the need to exchange them. Basketry, weaving, pottery, ironwork, and wood carving were widespread, and many other specialists including hunters, sculptors, blacksmiths, musicians, or boatbuilders put an economic value on manual skills and created a market for labor. The use of a medium of exchange was widespread and its character various, taking the form frequently of consumer goods like salt or rafia cloth. Much of the Congo trade was intertribal, but in East Africa, societies like the Kikuyu maintained an important trade among themselves in agricultural and craft products available at well-stocked markets. There developed, however, a certain amount of exchange with neighboring people; for example, the Kikuyu supplied red ochre to the Nilotic Masai, whose customs forbade the taking of things from the earth.

In almost every part of the Bantu world the basic social and political unit was the village. A village chief usually held sway in varying degrees of authority with the assistance of a council of elders, and their function was to interpret and apply the clearly defined laws governing conduct, sometimes making use of the trial by ordeal when testimony was inconclusive. For some, like the Kikuyu, however, the organized village threatened an excess of authority and consequently their society was based on age groups with dispersed homesteads rather than compact communities. Scattered farms did not always mean a disinclination toward centralized authority, however, for the people of the Great Lakes kingdoms also favored dispersion; yet their states were highly developed, large-scale monarchies. Where centralized states existed, they arose out of groups of villages held together by recognition of a common royal or chiefly clan, but even here, the king often was limited to ceremonial or religious functions with political authority remaining at the village level. As always, environment played an important part in the shaping of political structure—witness the loosely drawn lines of authority among the Nguni speakers of South Africa in their well-watered ranges in contrast to the closer social and political ties among the Sotho groups, clustered around the infrequent water holes on their arid plateau. It seems clear that the process of state-making in the Bantu areas was much the same as it was elsewhere in Africa and outside, with circumstance or the determination of a small number of individuals often playing decisive roles.

Both state and society were closely related to religious thought and practice among the Bantu. The firm belief in a supernatural world, in the efficacy of sorcery and magic, in the need for ritual to propitiate the spirits, and in the existence of a metaphysical continuum between the living and the ancestors all contributed important sanctions to reinforce basic social values. Hence the institution of divine kingship drew authority from belief in the royal power over fertility, while the prominence given to the ancestor helped strengthen the essential unity of the group in a parlous world.

THREE BANTU SOCIETIES

The Luba and Lunda States

Lake Kisale is a small body of water in the northern Katanga about 300 miles west of the southern tip of Lake Tanganyika. Vast cemeteries have been discovered in this region dating from the eighth and ninth centuries A.D., and it appears likely that this was a center of population for a number of states which developed in the Congo savanna during the sixteenth and seventeenth centuries. At first these communities were little more than tiny chiefdoms, a whole series of which had established themselves by 1500 in a broad area surrounding Lake Kisale. At this time a conquerer, Kongolo, appeared and began a process of unification which was carried on by

his son, Kalala Ilunga, and which had culminated in the unified kingdom of Luba by the end of Kalala's reign.

Political unification, which was a new and important idea in the
region, was maintained within the Luba kingdom by a hierarchy
of chiefdoms intermediary between the king and the village. Several
villages formed a territorial chiefdom and these in turn were gathered
into provinces which, added together, made up the centralized state.
With the exception of some local headmen, all chiefs derived their
authority as *balopwe,* or members of the ruling lineage of Kongolo
and Kalala Ilunga, and in this way political cohesion was achieved.
Close relatives of the king usually held the major titles within the
central government, including the head of the army or police force,
for membership in the royal lineage was very important as a basis
for both the authority and the supernatural gifts to rule. The king
was deemed divine and his power was absolute, but in practice he
was limited by the prerogatives of the many members of his blood-
line holding important positions at court.

Luba kings after Kalala continued to extend their hegemony,
eventually penetrating to the east and south into non-Luba areas
which were ruled as tributary states rather than as integral provinces.
Eventually a period of internal unrest complicated Luba expansionism, but this was long after the Luba royal house had made the
important move of establishing itself in the neighboring territory of
the Lunda. Cibinda Ilunga, a son of Kalala, conquered the Lunda
state around 1600 and married its queen to become king of the Lunda.
Immediately he appears to have divorced himself from further contact with the Luba kingdom, so that he and his successors henceforward ruled a separate, independent state.

For some time the Lunda had been expanding in response to
natural population increase, establishing groups of breakaway villages
in a generally westward movement. With the imposition of Cibinda
Ilunga's rule, this imperial development was given a shape and
stability which improved on the administration created by the Luba
and eventually saw the Lunda kingdom expand to cover a vast area
in the central Congo west of Luba. The cohesiveness of the state
rested on the institution of perpetual kinship which linked all village
headmen to each other and to the king. To this was added the important concept of positional succession which allowed a new headman to inherit all of his predecessor's kinship relations as well as his
name. This arrangement worked, not only for people of Lunda origin,

but for non-Lunda groups as well, since their chiefs could be absorbed into the system through positional succession, thus becoming an integral part of the Lunda kinship pattern. With this arrangement went a good deal of local self-government, for the royal power refrained from interfering in provincial affairs as long as tax payments were regular. The king, who was known as *Mwata Yamvo*—the Lord of the viper—was represented by a district political official called the *cilool* who was nominated by the local headmen, who was endowed with the quality of perpetual kinship to the king, and who acted chiefly as a tax collector. As with the Luba, the Lunda king was divine and all powerful although his authority was in fact greatly reduced by the system of indirect rule practiced in the provinces. Withall, the flexibility of this system encouraged greater loyalty to the central authority than among the Luba and made possible large-scale expansion without the necessity of a large standing army.

Lunda influence spread far beyond the limits of actual rule. In Angola and in the Rhodesian plateau to the south and east, there was continuous infiltration of Lunda migrants, small groups discontent with conditions in their homeland who emulated adventurer-conquerers like Kalala Ilunga or Cibinda Ilunga and imposed their own rule elsewhere. Thus Lunda culture spread in many directions, introduced by ruling clans of Lunda to peoples of similar background; for example, Chokwe to the west, or Bisa and Bemba to the east below Lake Tanganyika. In this way Lunda culture and principles of government became widely diffused throughout central Africa and greatly conditioned the civilization of the peoples living in the Congo-Zambezi watershed until well into the nineteenth century.

Bunyoro and Buganda

In the area around the Great Lakes the development of large-scale political units came about by a process involving people other than the Bantu. Bantu farmers in the region were apparently organized in loosely connected clans whose relative affluence and rising population rested on the easily raised plantain. Into the area came cattle pastoralists, the Hima, who settled in Uganda to the north and west of Lake Victoria, and the Tutsi who came to rest farther south near Lake Kivu. Among the Hima there emerged the Chwezi clan or dynasty which developed ideas of a centralized state and put them into effect by organizing the kingdom of Kitara between Lake Victoria and Lake Albert. At the end of the fifteenth century, the Chwezi, already in a state of collapse, were overwhelmed by an invasion of Nilotic Luo from the region of the Bahr al-Ghazal tributary to the White Nile. The Luo may have been able to effect a peaceful infiltration; in any event they established their own ruling Bito dynasty and reorganized Kitara as the kingdom of Bunyoro. While some Hima remained in the Bunyoro area, others retreated southward where they may have given rise to another cattle clan, the Hinda, who were to be responsible for a number of kingdoms and principalities stretching from the region of Ankole south of Lake Victoria and perhaps as far as Burundi at the northern tip of Lake Tanganyika. For their part, the Luo established a ring of tributary states around Bunyoro—Buddu, Buganda, Buruli, Busoga, and others —which were ruled in most cases by sub-dynasties of the Bito clan. Hence, through the activities of the Hima and Luo, the Bantu area of the Great Lakes came to be organized by intruding Nilote minorities into a series of kingdoms in which loyalty to the crown rather than to kinship ties was the basis for new and more complex systems of political enterprise.

In Bunyoro this new loyalty was hard earned. The basic orientation of the people continued toward community and clan; furthermore, poor communications and a primitive military technology invited separatism under ambitious local leaders. Nevertheless, numerous devices were introduced which strengthened the idea and the fact of a central authority. First of all, the institution of the monarchy was related as closely as possible to the people as a whole—by divorcing the king from his connection with the Bito clan, by stressing the divinity of the ruler and identifying him with the prosperity of the nation, by making him the source of a vast political patronage surrounding the palace, and by concentrating a large share of the national economy in the form of an exchange of gifts between the king and his subjects. At the same time the chiefs were subordinated to the crown through non-hereditary appointment, through royal sanction of chiefly investiture, and through elaborate ceremony. Finally, the king's authority was strengthened by the system of royal tours whereby the court changed headquarters constantly, requiring that the local population maintain the royal entourage in royal fashion, and enabling the king to gain a first-hand view of affairs throughout his realm.

This growing sense of national unity evolved even more successfully in Bugunda despite her modest origins. While Bunyoro held the stage during the sixteenth and early seventeenth centuries, Buganda quietly gathered strength, its very smallness an asset. The Bantu, Hima, and Luo strains were merged into a homogeneous population securely fixed in a structure of Baganda clans which were in turn closely linked to the monarchy. Hereditary chieftaincies within these clans therefore added to national unity, but even more significant was the institution early in the eighteenth century of a royal bodyguard responsible to the *kabaka*, or king, and it was at this time that a major expansion developed which made Buganda master of the northwestern shoreline and hinterland of Victoria from the Nile to the Kagera River.

In the nineteenth century the Baganda people continued to expand northwestward at the expense of a declining Bunyoro, and as her domains increased her imperial administration took on additional refinements. For example, new territory, such as the southern province of Buddu, was governed by royal administrators, not by hereditary chiefs. Moreover, during the eighteenth century the kings of Buganda began to encourage large-scale external trade which remained a royal monopoly designed to augment the king's wealth and power. Royal wealth bought increasing loyalty to the crown and made possible the military strength to extend and to protect commercial enterprise. In Buganda the idea of centralization and economic growth had become firmly fixed by the middle of the nineteenth century.

The Kikuyu

If the trend toward centralization and territorial acquisition was the hallmark of some peoples, it was by no means the choice of the majority who remained members of small village societies regulated by lineage or age groupings. Nevertheless, decentralization did not necessarily mean a lack of political and social cohesion, a fact which the Kikuyu nation amply illustrated. The Kikuyu Bantu formed a large and active agricultural community situated to the south and east of Mt. Kenya, apparently having settled there after migrating from the Shungwaya area in southern Somalia. Despite their number, which today has swelled to 1,600,000, they endured no local chiefs, let alone a centralized state, and generally eschewed village life in favor of individual homesteads scattered about the countryside. Yet Kikuyu society was far from disorganized and a highly articulated coherence was in fact characteristic of the Kikuyu nation.

This essential unity was maintained through the family, the clan, the community, and the age group. Consanguinity and common ancestors were bonds which were strongly felt and which led to cooperation among individuals who might otherwise have been unresponsive to authority. Within the family the father was the head, and the law of the homestead lay in his hands. Beyond this an elaborate system of relationships was maintained among family and clan members which defined and governed their actions as individuals and established mutual obligations and rights. Indeed, among the Kikuyu the idea of individual initiative was sharply discouraged as self-seeking, whereas the concepts of corporate effort and group responsibility were regarded as the cardinal virtues.

Each family had its own council with the father as the head and it was he who represented the family in the government. If there was a village council, it consisted of the heads of the several families in the village. Similarly, there were district councils made up of the district elders, and from these groups were chosen the elders who comprised the national council. These groups consisted of the more mature members of the Kikuyu community, but the younger people were also represented through a special council which dealt as well with military affairs. These positions were elective according to an eligibility graded by age, and the group had the power to dismiss or suspend those office holders who had transcended the established rules of conduct. Hence a system of government developed which was egalitarian within the range of accepted practice, relying heavily on group discussion and the power of public opinion to bring about efficient but responsible government.

It was the institution of the age grade which furnished the capstone to national solidarity—a system which the Kikuyu shared with their Masai neighbors with whom they warred, traded, and occasionally intermarried. Each generation, men and women alike, was organized into an age group which gave two kinds of stability to the nation—a horizontal unity throughout the land provided by successive layers of age grades each performing its well-defined social and political roles, and a vertical stability by which the individual was guided through life's successive stages with security, a security which thus became the endowment of the Kikuyu community at large.

Suggestions for Further Reading

The literature on the migrations of the Bantu and other peoples is scattered. For a summary of the Bantu dispersion see R. Oliver, "The Problem of the Bantu Expansion," *The Journal of African History*, v. VII, no. 3, 1966. The linguistic evidence is discussed in J. Greenberg, *Studies in African Linguistic Classification* (New Haven: Compass Publishing Co., 1955); [later revised as *The Languages of Africa* (Bloomington: Indiana University, 1966)] M. Guthrie, "Bantu Origins: A Tentative New Hypothesis," *The Journal of African Languages*, v. I, 1962; and M. Guthrie, "Some Developments in the Prehistory of the Bantu Languages," *The Journal of African History*, v. III, no. 2.

The standard work on the archeology of Zimbabwe has been G. Caton-Thompson, *The Zimbabwe Culture: Ruins and Reactions* (London: Oxford University Press, 1931), but see also R. Summers, *Zimbabwe: a Rhodesian Mystery* (London: Nelson, 1963; New York: Tri-Ocean Books, 1963). Other accounts dealing with the central Africa of Zimbabwe are included in B. Davidson, *The Lost Cities of Africa* (Boston: Little Brown, 1959); D. P. Abraham, "The Early Political History of the Kingdom of Mwena Mutapa (850–1589)," *Historians in Tropical Africa* (Salisbury: University College of Rhodesia and Nyasaland, 1962); Abraham, "Maramuca: An Exercise in the Combined Use of Portuguese Records and Oral Tradition," *The Journal of African History*, v. II, no. 2, 1961; B. M. Fagan, "The Iron Age Sequence in the Southern Province of Northern Rhodesia," *The Journal of African History*, v. IV, no. 2, 1963; Fagan, *Southern Africa during the Iron Age* (London: Thames & Hudson, 1965; New York: Praeger, 1966); and R. Summers, "The Southern Rhodesian Iron Age," *The Journal of African History*, v. II, no. 1, 1961. See also B. Davidson, *The African Past* (London: Longmans, 1964); and Abraham, "Ethno-history of the Empire of Mutapa," in J. Vansina, R. Mauny, and L. V. Thomas, eds., *The Historian in Tropical Africa* (London: Oxford University Press, 1964).

For Bantu culture, see G. P. Murdock, *Africa: Its Peoples and Their Culture History* (New York: McGraw-Hill, 1959); J. Vansina, *Kingdoms* Herskovits, *The Human Factor in Changing Africa* (London: Routledge and Kegan Paul, 1962; New York: Knopf, 1962, Vintage, 1967); J. Kenyatta, *Facing Mount Kenya* (New York: Vintage, 1962); and P. Tempels, *Bantu Philosophy* (Paris: Présence Africaine, 1959).

The Luba and Lunda kingdoms are discussed in Vansina, cited above, but see also D. Birmingham, *Trade and Conflict in Angola* (Oxford: Clarendon Press, 1966). For Bunyoro and Buganda see R. Oliver and G. Mathew, *History of East Africa*, I (Oxford: Clarendon Press, 1963); J. H. M. Beattie, *Bunyoro, an African Kingdom* (New York: Holt, Reinhart, Winston, 1960), and "Bunyoro: An African Feudality," *The Journal of African History,* v. V, no. 1, 1964; and B. A. Ogot, "Kingship and Statelessness Among the Nilotes," Vansina, Mauny, and Thomas, cited above.

7: The Coming of Europe

As the fifteenth century dawned, few Europeans could foresee a future in which Western ideas and institutions would sweep across the seas and Europe would take possession of large areas on all the world's continents. Within Europe herself plague, famine, and warfare had dominated the preceding hundred years, filling men's minds with confusion and their hearts with despair. The great flowering of Italy's Renaissance was only just beginning; what was more immediately apparent was the enfeebled and divided leadership within the Church as two rival popes presided in Avignon and Rome. Beyond Europe, moreover, the prospect offered little encouragement for it had become increasingly clear that the Crusades were failing in their attempt to wrest the Holy Land from the grasp of Islam. By the end of the thirteenth century, Palestine had been retaken by Mamluk armies, thus permanently ending Christian control of Jerusalem. In the decades that followed, Ottoman Turks had overrun Asia Minor and driven into the Balkan peninsula, a move which would lead to the capture of Constantinople and the fall of Christian Byzantium in the middle of the fifteenth century and open the way to eventual Ottoman domination of eastern Europe.

Nevertheless the foundations were already taking shape for Europe's subsequent global ascendancy. For several hundred years there had been a steady recovery from the chaos following the collapse of the great empire which Charlemagne had left at his death in 814 A.D. The slow revival of trade and industry, the expansion of agriculture, the rise of towns, and the growth in population combined to produce economic strength and political stability reflected in the social order of the feudal system and the first steps toward national monarchies. Progress was particularly apparent in the vigorous assaults on Islam which by mid-twelfth century had recaptured control of the Mediterranean, which rolled back the Muslims in southern Italy and the Iberian peninsula, and which took control of important territories in North Africa and the Middle East through the lusty warmaking of the early Crusaders.

The Crusades helped create an appetite in Europe for the goods of the East and brought further wealth to Italian shipping centers already engaged in transporting the exotic products of Asia to Europe's expanding markets. By the early fourteenth century these international movements, which tended to break down parochial isolation, were being paralleled with far-reaching developments in Europe herself. Commerce and urbanism had begun to turn the countryside away from manorial self-sufficiency toward a growing involvement in an exchange, profit-oriented economy. Slowly, serfdom started its conversion to tenancy or freehold tenure, and, as the traditional interdependence between lord and peasant dissolved, it was the monarch who assumed the responsibilities and loyalties no longer exercised by the feudal nobility.

The setbacks of the fourteenth century thus proved to be but a temporary hesitation, for the essential thrust of Europe's growth remained undiminished, stimulated by her energetic acquisitiveness and crusading fervor. There was the continued demand for the luxuries and spices of the East and the lure of enormous profits to be gained from that traffic. There was the intensified search for precious metals, always scarce in Europe and now critically so as bullion drained away to pay for the products arriving from Asia. Finally there was the white heat of Christian faith, undimmed by adversity and eager to regain the initiative in the holy war against Islam.

In the Iberian peninsula were people with both the experience and the determination to combine a search for commercial profit with a renewed assault on Islam. For centuries they had slowly pushed back the Moorish invaders from Africa, restricting them finally to the southern enclave of Granada where their unhappy remnants would eventually be absorbed or expelled. In the liberated area, small Christian states gradually took shape and by the early fifteenth century had combined into three kingdoms, Castile, Aragon, and Portugal. It was these states—first Portugal and later Castile and Aragon joined to form the kingdom of Spain—which were to take the lead in initiating Europe's great imperial expansion into the world beyond.

THE IMPERIAL DESIGN OF PORTUGAL

Portugal possessed modest but important advantages for the imperial adventures on which she was about to embark. Her position in Iberia athwart the path of the Islamic thrust into Europe had given her a first-hand knowledge of the Muslim world, an essential tool for both Crusader and merchant adventurer. Moreover, Portugal was a nation of sailors; hence her people possessed the practical experience necessary for the marine reconnaissance of the East which would eventually turn the African continent and outflank the established trade routes through the Mediterranean and across Asia. Finally, Portugal produced at this moment a royal leadership which combined ingenuity with stability, thus enabling an essentially poor and weak state to achieve successes seemingly beyond her reach. Of most importance in this connection was Prince Henry the Navigator, the youngest son of the Portuguese king, John I.

Portugal's first move was direct—the conquest of Ceuta on the Moroccan coast in 1415. While this was a psychological blow and military defeat for Islam, it nevertheless did nothing to loosen the Moorish hold on the trans-Saharan gold trade. Clearly, if Muslim-controlled trade routes in Africa and Asia were to be captured, more resourceful and far-reaching means would be needed. Urged on by Prince Henry, Portugal experimented with ship design, map making, and systems of navigation, and gradually Portuguese exploration brought the West African coast into view. The first halting moves were made in familiar waters as Madeira was occupied in 1419; then, overriding the fear of the unknown, Henry's captains pressed on—Cape Bojador was passed in 1434, the Azores sighted in 1439, Cape Blanco reached in 1442, and the following year Arguin Island was discovered. By 1460, the year of Prince Henry's death, Portuguese caravels were moving along the Guinea coast beyond Cape Verde approximately as far as Sierra Leone.

Concurrently with exploration went the search for trade. In 1441, one ship returned to Portugal with some gold dust and Negro captives, and other captives soon followed, victims of slave raids but indicative of the possibilities for a more systematic commerce. In 1448 Arguin was fortified in the vain hope that the Saharan gold trade might be diverted to that coastal point. As the Portuguese moved down the coast, they probed inland up the Senegal and Gambia rivers where they made contact respectively with Tekrur and one of the Mandinka chiefdoms, but they were never able in this fashion to gain access to West Africa's gold. Much more successful were the ventures of Fernao Gomes, a Lisbon merchant who between 1469 and 1475 explored the coast under royal charter, reaching beyond Fernando Po and south of the equator. In 1471 the ships of Gomes located an area where abundant supplies of gold were to be had, a region they named Costa da Mina and which subsequently came to be known as the Gold Coast.

The gold of the Costa da Mina joined with other products, including pepper and modest numbers of slaves, to insure substantial Portuguese profits in West Africa, and they encouraged the crown to organize the trade in a series of state monopolies. Forts and factories were established intermittently along the coast as far as Benin, but the Portuguese kings were not the sort to rest content with their West African gains. The route to India still eluded detection, and when the energetic John II came to the throne in 1482 he determined to press forward with the business of exploration. In 1483, Diogo Cão discovered the Congo River and established relations with the kingdom of Kongo. Five years later Bartolomeu Dias rounded the Cape of Good Hope and the way to India was at last open to Portugal's mariners. Deterred by an exhausted and timorous crew, Dias got no further, but word concerning the wealth of India eventually trickled back to Portugal from Pero da Covilha who had left home at the same time as Dias and had finally reached Calicut by overland route. In 1497, therefore, a fleet under Vasco da Gama was dispatched which proceeded to Calicut via East Africa, collecting a variety of spices in India and establishing the tone of ill-tempered aggressiveness which came to characterize Portugal's long-lived presence on the East African coast. During the early sixteenth century successive naval expeditions annexed the major coastal towns of East Africa, established Portuguese power in India, defeated a number of Arab fleets in naval battles, and thus took direct control of the trade of the Indian Ocean. One hundred years after Ceuta, Portugal had achieved her grand design of a commercial and Christian empire in the East.

THE PORTUGUESE IN KONGO AND ANGOLA

On the way to asserting her imperial claims in the East, Portugal paused at the Congo River to indulge in a venture of cooperation between Europe and Africa. Persuaded perhaps that the Kongo kingdom was essential to the discovery of Prester John, Portugal sought an alliance with an equal and sovereign sister state which would benefit Portuguese commerce and permit Christian conversion and thus secure a friendly coastal base through which the realm of Prester John could be reached.

Initial Portuguese overtures were encouraged, and in 1491 a mission arrived at the court of Nzinga Kuwu, the *manikongo,* or paramount chief, of what was in fact a loosely drawn confederation of local states stretching south from the Congo about two hundred miles and inland as far as the Kwango River. The *manikongo* was greatly pleased with the tools and gifts which arrived in company with a complement of artisans and missionaries, and soon he and many of his court had embraced Christianity. Properly cultivated, such an auspicious beginning might have developed into a model of international cooperation, but instead a combination of neglect, self-interest, and circumstance brought the eventual political and social disintegration of the Kongo state.

First of all, there was the preoccupation of Portugal with her Indian Ocean ventures, a natural state of affairs which brought the temporary abandonment of the Kongo liaison at the close of the fifteenth century and a reversion of the *manikongo* to his traditional way of life. Next, the handful of Portuguese who remained in Kongo succeeded in the Christian conversion of Afonso, the heir apparent, but only at the expense of a political division within the nation. A further strain was added by the Portuguese living on nearby Sao Tomé island where a growing need for plantation labor soon brought them to the mainland in search of slaves and ready to support that search by interfering as needed in local matters. When Afonso succeeded to the throne in 1506, his own sincere desire to introduce the benefits of Western, Christian civilizations was consistently

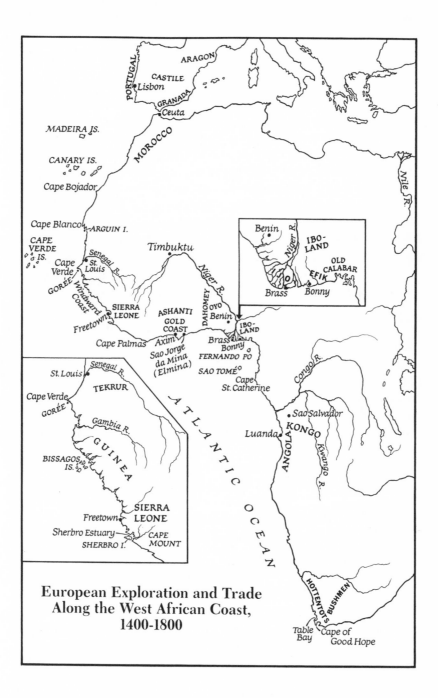

**European Exploration and Trade
Along the West African Coast,
1400-1800**

thwarted by the machinations of the Sao Tomé residents as well as by missionaries sent out from Portugal who regrettably came to be more interested in slaving than in educating and evangelizing the local people.

Within a few years the situation had deteriorated to the point where King Manuel of Portugal, responding to Afonso's complaints, dispatched a special agent to Kongo armed with a directive, the *regimento* of 1512, to guide him in advising Afonso on the administration of his government. A tight rein was at once to be placed on all Portuguese residents, but a major responsibility of the royal agent was the introduction of Portuguese custom and law and the propagation of Christianity in the realm—in short, the creation in Africa of Portuguese society in faithful replica. All this was to be managed with tact and discretion as was the policy on trade—witness the gentle hint contained in the royal instructions that it would indeed be unfortunate were the ships of Portugal's helping hand to return home empty when there were cargoes of slaves, ivory, and copper to be had.

This blueprint for assimilation might have succeeded in establishing an African kingdom strengthened by the best assistance—technical and spiritual—that Europe had to offer at the time. It was substantially accepted by the fully assimilated Afonso who had already abandoned such traditional practices as royal seclusion at meals and who stood ready to act on its recommendations concerning secular and religious education. Afonso, however, rejected Portuguese legal codes as too foreign for immediate application; his experience with the opposition to his dining with his court, European fashion, amply illustrated the need for gradual change and adaptation in the introduction of alien institutions.

There were more serious difficulties, however. The *regimento* was thoroughly opposed and undermined by those Portuguese whose interests it threatened, and Portugal, already deeply committed to her Asian enterprises, could lavish little attention, let alone resources, on a minor speculation on the West African coast. The essential weakness of the venture became apparent. Portugal's ulterior motives—her preoccupation with commercial profit and a way to Prester John—had to be served first. She preached equality of sovereign states but employed a double standard by insisting on commercial and religious monopoly and the right to attach Portuguese advisers to the Kongo government. She pledged assistance to a needy sister nation but demanded economic exploitation in return.

Afonso gradually lost control of the situation, engulfed by the intrigue and factionalism of the Portuguese, largely ignored by the authorities in Lisbon, and divorced from his people who were increasingly restive over the unceasing attrition of the slave trade. Afonso's death about 1545 inaugurated even more unsettled times. Divisions among the Portuguese and their steady pursuit of the traffic in slaves encouraged the cupidity of local chiefs which further undermined the authority of the *manikongo*. A state of rising chaos was climaxed in 1568 by the arrival of the Jaga, a militant group who burst into Kongo from the east, routing her army, sacking her villages, looting her supplies, slaughtering her people and devouring their flesh.

With Portuguese help, the invaders were finally ousted, but by this time the life had gone out of the ravaged kingdom. Beyond the Jaga depredations, constant slaving had decimated the population, destroyed the country's political unity, and corrupted the ruling group and its Portuguese advisers. Gradually the Portuguese slaving interests shifted their attention southward to the region of Angola. When the Kongo king acknowledged Portuguese suzerainty in recognition of the assistance lent him against the Jaga, this act had little practical meaning and was ignored in Lisbon. By the early seventeenth century most Portuguese had disappeared and with them went virtually all signs of the Christian life and culture they had initially introduced.

Increasing Portuguese attention in Angola was to prove as disastrous as had neglect in Kongo, and once again it was the slave trade which was at the root of an unhappy history. Interest in the region which the Portuguese called Angola rose during the sixteenth century as the unsettled conditions in Kongo set the slavers searching farther down the coast. In the early years of the century the small chiefdom of Ndongo had been founded by one who took the title of *ngola* and who acknowledged the paramountcy of the *manikongo* to the north. Gradually the chiefdom spread in size and power, and in 1556 it gained its independence from Kongo with the aid of Portuguese arms. In search of commercial exchange and personal prestige, successive *ngolas* had sought trading contacts and missionary assistance from Portugal, but were scarcely prepared for the act of the

Portuguese king who, in 1571, granted Angola as a proprietary colony to one of his followers. Although a system of royal governors was later instituted, there ensued years of chronic warfare to no ultimate advantage as a series of governments sought to impose their authority over the stubbornly resisting local people while concurrently searching for non-existent silver deposits. Slaving was a preoccupation that kept the country in a state of turmoil which was only heightened by such events as the late sixteenth-century arrival of the Jaga fresh from their Kongo adventures and the mid-seventeenth century capture of Luanda by a Dutch squadron. Indeed, the people of Angola were able to survive these crises, but not the unrelieved erosion of Portuguese neglect, local corruption, and an economy condemned to produce only slave labor for Sao Tomé and for the plantations of Brazil and other New World communities. During the 1850's, slavery was nominally abolished in Portuguese territories, but Angola's unhappy experience with the traffic in slaves was to continue virtually without stint until the eve of the First World War.

THE ARRIVAL OF THE DUTCH

As with the Portuguese, the Dutch appearance in Africa was but part of a grander geopolitical design. Portuguese expansionism did not go long unchallenged within Europe. Even as Portugal was laying the basis for her Indian Ocean empire through the voyages of Dias and da Gama, Spain was underwriting the explorations of Columbus which were to lead, among many other things, to her own New World empire based on gold, and, particularly, on silver. The success of these Portuguese and Spanish enterprises—combined in 1580 under the rule of Philip II of Spain—led, however, not to monopoly, but to greater competition. For the Portuguese, the long-range effect of Spanish control was disastrous for it encouraged Spain's enemies to mount a successful attack against the overextended network of possessions which Portugal's limited manpower had established with much effort in the East.

In the case of the Netherlands, also ruled by Philip as part of his initial inheritance, the situation was quite different. Within the Low Countries, antipathy toward Spanish rule on political, religious, and economic grounds erupted in a revolt by the northern Netherlands provinces which, after a long struggle, brought virtual independence in 1609. In the course of the conflict, the Dutch found themselves cut off from supplies of Asian goods arriving in Europe at Lisbon. Their natural response was to seek these goods directly, an effort which soon led to sharp mercantile-military competition with both Portugal and Spain.

In the East, Dutch industry and thoroughness combined with imaginative merchandising and superior seamanship to rout the Portuguese and hold off British mercantile pretensions while establishing a highly successful commercial empire centered on the Dutch East Indies and administered by the East India Company founded in 1602. Rising Dutch power struck with equal force in the Atlantic where the Dutch West India Company chartered in 1621 visited heavy damages on both the Spanish and Portuguese. Portuguese Brazil was occupied for a time during the first half of the seventeenth century while Spanish settlements in the Caribbean were repeatedly ravaged. Dutch merchantmen dominated the European carrying trade while her fighting ships were everywhere, convoying and protecting her efficient and numerous fleets of cargo vessels.

The reflection of these global operations was soon apparent in Africa. Dutch ships were prowling West African waters before the close of the sixteenth century, and initial reconnaissance was closely followed by stronger measures—at first raids on Sao Tomé and Sao Jorge da Mina, then the occupation of the island of Gorée in 1617 and the capture of Arguin in 1633. Four years later came the crowning indignity to Portugal's authority when Sao Jorge on the Costa da Mina was plucked from her defenders and converted into the Gold Coast stronghold of Elmina. These operations were designed to capture the Guinea trade from the Portuguese, and by the first quarter of the seventeenth century Dutch ships had blanketed the West African coast, dealing in gold and ivory and then increasingly in slaves for the plantations of America. It was the slave trade, for example, that accounted for the capture of Luanda in 1641, for Angolan slaves were much prized in Brazil where more than twenty-three thousand were brought into Recife during the decade up to 1645. Nevertheless, it was not these lucrative commercial activities which were to account for the most fateful of the Dutch enterprises in Africa.

In the spring of 1652 a small fleet of three Dutch ships dropped anchor in Table Bay at the bottom of the African continent and established the tiny community which was the beginning of European presence in South Africa. Initially there was no thought of African colonization, for these ships contained only a modest number of employees of the East India Company charged with developing a station midway between Europe and the East where merchantmen on the long journey to and from the Indies could put in for water and fresh food. The pragmatic Dutch were not concerned with local conquest or exploration. The empire to which they aspired lay far to the east, and the commander, Jan van Riebeeck, was given explicit instructions—lay out a truck farm and barter for cattle with the local people, build a small fort but avoid trouble with the Hottentot inhabitants of the region.

At first these instructions were followed with reasonable fidelity, but in time circumstances altered the nature and the activities of the community. In 1657, in a move to increase production, nine of the company employees were given the status of free burghers with farms on leasehold, and the same year slaves were imported from Java and Madagascar to augment the labor supply. Hindsight views these as momentous developments for at once they converted the settlement from a temporary expedient to a permanent colony, and established the institution of servile labor. Soon another fateful decision was taken when company herds were formed in order to supplement the unsteady Hottentot meat supply. This move led to disputes with the Hottentots over grazing rights and to eventual armed conflict which drove the Hottentots off their lands, and began the process of disintegration of their social and political institutions. At the same time the authorities made the first move in South Africa toward apartheid—an abortive attempt to avoid trouble between the settlers and the Hottentots by means of physical separation.

In time came other innovations. Strategic considerations argued for a strong and populous community at this South African station standing athwart the sea route between Europe and the riches of the East; consequently, an active immigration policy was instituted during the administrations of Simon van der Stel and his son Willem who directed the Colony between 1679 and 1707. Dutch and German settlers were recruited as was a body of French Huguenots, and in another portentous move, an effort was made to provide wives drawn from Dutch orphanages, thus foreclosing the possibility of mixed marriages and the rise of an Afro-European community. Simon van der Stel founded the village of Stellenbosch, and other communities soon followed based upon farm holdings granted in full ownership.

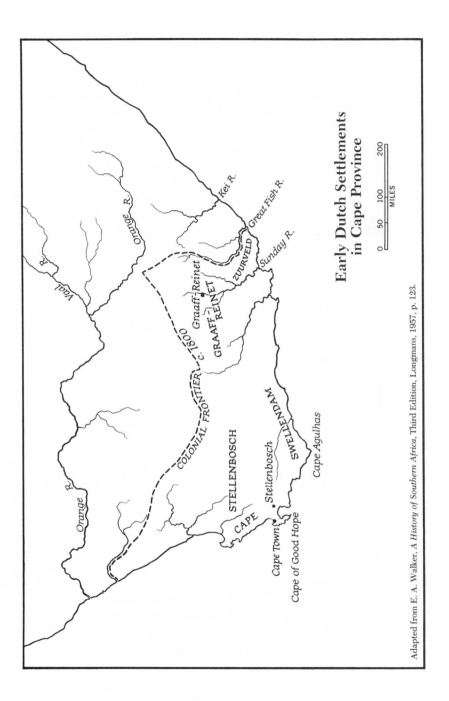

**Early Dutch Settlements
in Cape Province**

MILES
0 50 100 200

Adapted from E. A. Walker, *A History of Southern Africa*, Third Edition, Longmans, 1957, p. 123.

THE COMING OF EUROPE   159

Despite these measures the population rose but slowly, and by 1708 there were only 1700 free burghers and an equal number of slaves. Nevertheless the pattern for the Colony had been established—a permanent agricultural settlement in which labor was performed by a servile group under the direction of a privileged landowning class. This was a far remove from the original concept of a refreshment station sustained by hired employees of the Dutch East India Company.

Immigration was not encouraged after the era of the van der Stels but by that time the Company had already lost control of its venture. Henceforward the destinies of the Colony lay in the hands of its body of permanent settlers acted upon by the exigencies of their adopted land. In the area of initial settlement which was well suited to the truck- cereal- and viniculture required by the Company, a society emerged, based in agriculture and commerce, closely regulated by the rules of a paternalistic regime but accustomed to evading those rules through such devices as smuggling and bribery, living a leisurely life in which slaves performed physical labor and no one essayed intellectual activity, filling out each day with a changeless routine that, in Cape Town at any rate, tended to atrophy moral standards and coarsen social grace.

Beyond the hills encircling the Cape region, however, there slowly took shape another community which was to form the basis of the Boer people. Slave labor in the settled districts encouraged young people to move along to an area where land was available in quantity, and if the land were suitable only for grazing, this neatly fitted the increasing demand at Cape Town for supplies of fresh meat. Thus the *trekboer,* or frontier farmer, came into being. Moving eastward with his herds, he occupied territory over which the Company exercised only nominal control and he occupied it in great tracts of at least six thousand acres in order to sustain his cattle on the sparse prairie. In typical farming fashion, he had large families and each of his many sons in turn came to require his own six-thousand-acre homestead; hence, in only a few generations a vast region had been swallowed up as the *trekboers* probed far to the east, well beyond the practical limits of the Company's government.

On the frontier, life was more monotonous than difficult, and unspectacular durability was the essence of survival. In the *trekboer,* self-esteem joined with self-reliance, and physical toughness was matched by tenacity and endurance. With self-reliance, however, there emerged a deepening antipathy toward official authority and a tendency to confuse land occupation and land ownership. The isolation that shaped self-sufficiency also bred a smallness of spirit—suspicious of innovation, hostile toward the stranger, and comfortable only in the inhospitable wastes of a narrow but familiar world. It was a simple matter for these pioneers to draw from their Calvinist faith a sense of individualism that bordered on anarchy and to see in themselves the chosen people of the Old Testament wandering in the wilderness in search of the promised land. At the same time intermarriage and a sense of common destiny bound the frontier trekkers together in a cohesion which was ultimately to emerge in Afrikaner nationalism.

Both on the frontier and in the more established areas the settlers early developed the racial attitudes which have come to characterize the apartheid philosophy. At first, although efforts were made to keep Hottentot and settler apart, there was no discrimination against children of mixed unions who were granted full citizenship status as were freed Negro slaves. Nevertheless, despite the miscegenation involving European, Hottentot, and other strains which gave rise to the Cape Coloured population, the early settler regarded the Hottentot as stupid, lazy, and dishonest, an attitude which came to define unreliability on racial lines. The institution of slavery, moreover, introduced black men from both West and East Africa whose inferior social status was equated with skin color. The immigration of European women put an end to the mixed marriages which would otherwise have been inevitable, while the attitude of slaveowners toward their chattels tended to extend indiscriminately to all persons of color, regardless of status.

Among the stern self-centered trekkers of the interior even more rigid racial attitudes emerged. Within the isolated frontier farmstead with its European ownership and its labor force of slaves or landless Hottentots, absolute authority was necessary for survival in a social-economic structure made still more inflexible by the need to maintain white identity in a sea of color. Moreover, the appropriation of Hottentot grazing land which accompanied the process of expansion was more easily justified in terms of racial superiority, while the cattle-raiding practiced by indigenous Bushmen added its measure to the racial antipathy expressed in a campaign of extermination and enslavement against these Stone Age hunters. Under these circumstances it was no problem to interpret predestination on racial lines, and in time Calvinism gave doctrinal sanction to attitudes which had developed from extra-theological origins.

When, toward the end of the eighteenth century the Boer farmers trekking eastward came into contact with Bantu peoples slowly descending the East African coast, the pattern of racial attitudes had already been set among a land-hungry, independent-minded people. Land hunger was no less pronounced among the Xhosa vanguard on the Bantu frontier, and hostilities were not long in developing. The point of contact was the Zuurveld between the Sunday and Fish rivers, and although the authorities were able to arrange a truce and establish a boundary along the Fish River in 1778, the frontiersmen, already chronically at war with the Bushmen, were soon skirmishing with the Xhosa as well. Severe drought in 1791 and 1792 brought a fresh outbreak of hostilities and when the settlers became convinced that the government in faraway Cape Town was lending them insufficient aid while hindering their attempts at self-defense, they proclaimed the districts of Graaff-Reinet and Swellendam to be independent republics in 1795. Such a show of independence in this late eighteenth-century era of revolutions was short-lived for in the same year an English squadron occupied the Cape by arrangement with the Dutch government as protection against seizure by the French. The revolt was quashed in 1796, and although the British withdrew under treaty arrangement in 1802, they were back again four years later, this time to remain. A new complication had been added to the complexities of South Africa's intramural affairs.

THE BRITISH AND FRENCH IN WEST AFRICA

Both England and France were relative latecomers to the imperial adventures begun by Portugal, but having arrived last they also were to exercise the most pervasive influence as colonial powers. Nowhere was this more true than in Africa.

It was the slave trade which first brought British and French merchants in force to the West African coast. The Portuguese had traded for slaves as early as the fifteenth century and Spain's New World possession had provided a ready market in the sixteenth century. The interest of England and France, however, was linked to the growth of their own plantation colonies in America, and these did not become important producers much before the middle of the seventeenth century. As these colonies developed at a time when mercantilist theory proclaimed the necessity of a closed economic system embracing colony and mother country, official policy in both England and France required that the rising demand for slaves be satisfied exclusively through national resources. Hence this was the era of the British navigation acts and similar mercantilist restrictions by France, the period when the Dutch were ousted from New Amsterdam and their naval power steadily eroded by the rising competition from France, and particularly from England.

In West Africa British and French mercantile activity took the form of national trading monopolies like the Royal Africa Company chartered by Charles II in 1660 or the French West Indies Company created by Colbert in 1664. These interlopers, who were quickly joined by commercial interests representing Sweden, Denmark, and Brandenburg, successfully challenged the Dutch in West Africa and by the opening of the eighteenth century had taken over most of the slaving on the West African coast, exclusive of the Portuguese in Angola.· The French early established themselves in the region of the Senegal River, occupying St. Louis island at the mouth of the Sengal in 1659 and capturing the slave depot of Gorée from the Dutch in 1677. British establishments were concentrated on the Gold Coast where a series of fortified posts brought a direct confrontation with the Dutch bases such as Elmina and Axim. Elsewhere along the coast either the natural deterrents of poor anchorages and difficult navigation or the determination of the local people kept the traders at arm's length, forced to remain in their ships or to maintain unfortified trading posts under the watchful eye of African monarchs. This did not mean a lack of sympathy among Africans for the slave traffic but rather a desire to share in its control, and the volume of trade rose steadily through the eighteenth century, by which time the British commercial effort had far outstripped all competitors.

Paradoxically, it was in England during the late eighteenth century that the first steps were taken leading to the eventual abolition of the slave trade.

THE NATURE OF THE EUROPEAN IMPACT

The coming of Europe to Africa, an event so intimately connected with Europe's worldwide economic expansion, affected African communities in different ways and varying degrees. In xenophobic Ethiopia, Portuguese Jesuits struggled in vain for a foothold, but Portuguese soldiers may well have saved Ethiopian Christianity from annihilation at the hands of Ahmad Gran and his Muslim armies. On the East African coast, the Portuguese quickly subdued the ancient trading states, but made little impression on the local society and culture which remained staunchly Muslim, Arab, and African. In South Africa the Dutch overwhelmed the fragile culture of the Bushmen and Hottentots, destroying and displacing the former in a war of extermination, and transforming the latter from a loosely knit nation of pastoralists to landless rural laborers and urban drifters, and ultimately causing them to become lost in the Cape Coloured community. The inland kingdoms of Mutapa and Changamire were able in the long run to stand off Portuguese intrusion, but across the continent in the west, the people of Kongo and Angola were devastated by these same Portuguese, the Kongo kingdom disintegrating before the ravages of the slave trade which likewise decimated the population and depressed the economy of her Angolan neighbors. Indeed, disintegration in the Kongo region in time became the basis of a new socio-political system in which perpetual unrest, warfare, and slaving reduced the area to a series of independent villages, and prestige and power were based, as they came to be in the city states of the Niger Delta, on the number of slaves an individual possessed.

In West Africa, where Europe came early and remained late, the Western impact was also various, but nowhere did it lead to the total social disintegration that befell the indigenous people of South Africa or the political annihilation that was the fate of the Kongo kingdom. The Portuguese presence, for example, so fatal to Kongo, had but a minor influence in Benin where the intruders traded and proselytized with their usual vigor for almost three decades after their arrival in 1485, but where the slave trade was disappointingly limited as was the interest of Benin's *oba* in Christianity—an interest, moreover, prodded not by a yearning for spiritual elevation as much as by a desire for firearms. There was another reason. The *oba* was religious as well as temporal leader of his people, and had no enthusiasm for any limitation on his authority as head of a virile state.

Along the Guinea coast between the Gambia River and Cape Mount, Portuguese influence was somewhat more pervasive, but primarily in social and economic matters for the local rulers were jealous of their sovereignty and guarded it tenaciously. Here and there forts were built in small-scale replica of the Gold Coast castles, but it was impossible to practice mercantilist restrictions in the face of chiefly independence, and this unrestricted coast came to be the favorite base of operations for numbers of private traders, drawn from various European nationalities.

In their economic pursuits, however, the Europeans brought about some fundamental changes to this upper windward coast. In the first place, there seems to have been little or no slavery in this part of West Africa before the rise of the transatlantic trade, but by the late eighteenth century there had developed an indigenous slave class, primarily the property of mulatto chiefs like the Caulkers and the Clevelands who maintained slave labor in the form of sailors, porters, farm workers, and craftsmen, and who sold off these chattels in the international market if the occasion demanded. The rise of slavery, moreover, caused basic changes in law and criminal punishment. Under traditional law, fines, not imprisonment, had been the usual penalty for transgressors, but with the rise of slaving a wide range of misdemeanors came to be punishable by sale to Europeans. Finally—and most significantly—these early European contacts were the means through which a wide range of plants were introduced to West Africa. The Portuguese bought sugar from Madeira, corn, cassava, sweet potatoes, pineapple, and pawpaw from the Americas— all with profound implications for population growth and density.

European traders on the upper windward coast encouraged a local taste for European goods and also led to the rise of a small but important mulatto population, largely of English antecedents in the area of the Sherbro estuary, and Portuguese farther up the coast. Taking local wives, many of these traders tended to settle down within the compass of local custom, some even wearing tribal tattoos. The process was reciprocal, however, for there were Africans educated in Europe who clung tenaciously to the symbols, such as clothes or furnishings, of their European experience. Those who could afford a European education usually availed themselves of it, although the motive was often no more than the mastery of mercantile techniques. The cultural amalgam was often complex. Some individuals gave every outward sign of a European way of life but could not always change habits of mind or morals with their dress. Others broke under the impact of a foreign education and were unable to maintain themselves in either their old or new world. Still others were able to be thoroughly African or European, faithfully changing in response to circumstance. Many exhibited latent attraction to charms, witchcraft, and other superstitions, but this was only what was observed among many Europeans as well.

Farther up the coast in the French settlements of St. Louis and Gorée, a mulatto or creole community had arisen which was on the way to a much more thoroughgoing Westernization. Formed through the union of African—chiefly Wolof—women, and officials, artisans, and others, the mulattoes of Gorée and St. Louis quickly assumed important social and economic functions. The women, called *signares,* contracted common-law marriages with visiting Europeans which were defined with precise formality and which guaranteed the social status and economic independence of each *signare* upon the eventual return of her husband to Europe. Many *signares* therefore became respected and wealthy matrons while mulatto men, called *habitants,* had ample opportunities for careers in commerce or government service. These people were practicing Christians, and by the opening of the nineteenth century were on the way to adopting French speech and dress to match their French names and Gallic orientation. There were creole mayors of St. Louis and Gorée by the late eighteenth century, and when French citizenship was extended to the colonies during the French Revolution, the Senegalese sent their list of grievances to the Estates General just as did Frenchmen from the home country.

There were a few pure-blood Africans in St. Louis and Gorée who, like the mulattoes, identified themselves with Europe, but the overwhelming proportion of the population of the French communities of Senegal, to say nothing of the hinterland, contained Africans almost totally unaffected by European language, religion, or custom. Moreover, French political authority was limited to her two urban centers in addition to a few trading posts along the coast and up the Senegal River. This was typical of the European presence throughout West Africa. Rarely did it penetrate beyond the coast, for the seaboard states took pains to keep it out in order to maintain their middleman status between the European visitors and the markets of the interior. Nowhere was this development better illustrated than among the trading city-states of the Niger Delta.

These states had existed long before the coming of the Europeans, arising from a mutual need for exchange between the Delta fisherfolk and the people of the interior—the latter in quest of protein and salt, the former eager to offset their lack of bulk foodstuffs, clothing, tools, and household goods. In addition, the overpopulated Ibo of the hinterland exported manpower for agriculture, while various skilled craftsmen from upcountry were also much in demand among the Delta people. The whole system worked through a complicated web of markets operated by part-time petty traders and full-time merchants. When the Portuguese first arrived, the trade structure had therefore already been well established and the changes occasioned by the newcomers were in terms of products, rather than patterns of trade. The Europeans demanded and received ivory and slaves, and it was easy to alter the status of contract laborer to that of slave and to obtain slaves by other means in the overpopulated centers of the interior.

One of the chief vehicles of the slave trade in Iboland came to be the *Aro Chukwu* oracle. Known as the Long Juju, the oracle was widely recognized as the voice of Chukwu, the supreme deity, and the representatives of the oracle, therefore, exercised great power throughout Iboland. Scattered colonies of Aro, an Ibo subgroup, not only provided access to the oracle but, as the only centralized organization in decentralized Iboland, acted as a commercial network along which goods and travelers could pass with safety. Thus the Aro became the middlemen of Iboland, and as the demand for slaves arose, they utilized their special position to monopolize the slave trade as well. Universal belief in the power of the oracle established it as a final court of appeal in the settlement of disputes. The Aro who controlled the oracle passed sentence in terms of fines to be paid in slaves and soon they were the dominant force in the slave trade from which they gained great wealth and power.

Although the essential nature and function of the Delta trading states had predated the arrival of Europeans, their eventual size, political structure, and social makeup were certainly a direct result of the European presence. Traditional African societies usually revolved around the extended family bound together by blood ties. In the Delta states, by contrast, economic needs and European contacts led to another type of social structure—the House System. In order to meet the international demand for slaves, the original Ijo, Efik, or other people of Bonny, Brass, Old Calabar, and their sister states imported large numbers of slaves from the populous Ibo interior, retaining some of these as household chattels. In this way powerful trading houses arose consisting of a family of freeborn and its complement of bondsmen. Since all members of a house, slave or free, and their progeny, remained members of that house, it was possible for families to grow in size and influence while the original small fishing and trading village developed a cosmopolitan quality and scale Each house was ruled arbitrarily by its head, and the government, whether royal or republican, was in fact an oligarchy controlled by the most prominent traders. A rough-and-ready democracy existed, however, for heads of houses were elected by all house members, and it was possible for slaves to rise in the hierarchy through merit and succeed, as some did, to the headship of the house.

These burgeoning Delta states were an effective screen against European penetration to the interior, but they were also in part a response to European demands for strong and stable trading outlets. On the Gold Coast stability was sought through the construction of fortified posts but these castles gained no more than a minimal foothold, for their garrisons remained by sufferance, unable either to exert political authority outside their walls or to enforce their desired trade monopoly. Indeed, local rulers characteristically exacted the payment of tariffs, fines, and rents, while refusing the traders access to the interior, always maintaining their own jealous control over the inland trade. Typical was the situation reported by one seventeenth-century European agent in taking note of the authority of the Fante, "The blacks . . . drive a great trade with all interlopers without regarding the English and Dutch factors . . . Neither of those European nations dare oppose the natives' . . . for fear of being ruin'd themselves." Perhaps the degree of tenacity in opposition to European penetration was best exemplified by the stubborn defense of John Conny, a Gold Coast chief of the early eighteenth century, who stood off the Dutch when they tried to land an armed party and take his fort, succumbing only after seven years of combined diplomatic and military pressure.

THE EUROPEAN TRADE

In West Africa, the impact of Europe was most apparent in matters connected with trade. Except among the Delta states, political systems were scarcely affected. Outside the mulatto community of Senegal, there was little success in religious proselytization. Even on the coast where Europeans were most apparent the basic social organization remained largely unaltered after 350 years. In economic matters, however, the Western presence was more pervasive—sometimes superficially in the silver buckles or satin waistcoats of local kings, sometimes more significantly in the firearms which stepped up the destructiveness and attendant misery of local warfare. The introduction of "dash"—a gift designed to lubricate the channels of trade—came in time to be a characteristic aspect of West African life, but more portentous was the steadily growing demand at all levels of society for the manufactured products of Europe.

Even within the realm of economic affairs there were considerable variations of African response to Europe. A major element in the eighteenth-century rise of Ashanti militarism was the desire to break through to the coast and participate directly in the Atlantic trade. The kingdom of Dahomey arose in the wake of political instability among the Aja states caused by the slave traffic, while commerce in its various forms laid the basis for politics and prosperity among the city states of the Niger Delta. On the other hand the Yoruba interest in the overseas commerce remained peripheral, and Benin early revealed an indifference to Portuguese slaving ventures. Even the pattern of trade showed the effect of the interpenetration of two cultures. If European merchants encouraged the use of money as a medium and measure of exchange, traditional African barter continued to dominate commerce along the coast until the abolition of the slave trade. The African concept of trade called for the unit exchange of one item for another whereas Europeans were prompted by the profit motive. This basic difference led to the introduction of the sorting—a combination of goods such as textiles, alcohol, firearms, tobacco, and hardware given as a unit in equal exchange for an individual slave or a quantity of gold. The Europeans calculated the value of their sortings by a commercial standard called the trade ounce and gave themselves a healthy markup in the process, but the essential system of exchange continued on the basis of barter, while the markup soon resulted in a corresponding rise in the price of slaves offered by African dealers.

Many attempts have been made to assess the effects of the Atlantic slave trade on West African societies, but such judgments have been largely insubstantial and conjectural for want of concrete evidence. Occasionally there has been substantive detail as in the case of the *Aro Chukwu* oracle which played such an important role in the procuring of slaves and the maintenance of trade connections among the decentralized Ibo. More often, however, conclusions have been little more than personal opinions and sophisticated guesses based upon deduction from fragmentary statistics.

If one generalization may be risked, it could be said that, despite unexampled individual misery, despite devastation and depopulation in certain areas, the slave trade had relatively little impact on West African society taken as a whole. Certainly, although those affected by the trade were numbered in the millions, their loss to West African communities does not appear to have been significant. The attrition was spread over four hundred years from the mid-fifteenth century and ranged spatially from Senegal to Angola; much more concentrated by comparison was Europe's massive emigration to the Americas during a few short decades preceding the First World War. Moreover, though losses in West Africa were unevenly distributed in time and place and bore most heavily on the healthiest sections of society, major states such as Ashanti and Oyo remained virile, while centers like Iboland from whence many slaves were drawn seemingly suffered no important loss in population. No doubt an economy based on slaving was based insecurely, while nations devoted to slave mongering became brutalized and unproductive. Yet the conviction cannot be escaped that, by and large, Europe's initial impact on Africa was minimal—in no way comparable with the influence she was to exert when she returned again during the nineteenth century, this time with humanitarian and not predatory motives.

Suggestions for Further Reading

Portuguese activities along the coast of West Africa are recounted in James Duffy, *Portuguese Africa* (Cambridge, Massachusetts: Harvard University Press, 1959); and Jan Vansina, *Kingdoms of the Savanna* (Madison: University of Wisconsin Press, 1966). See also J. F. A. Ajayi and I. Espie, eds., *A Thousand Years of West African History* (Ibadan: Ibadan University Press, 1965; New York: Humanities Press, 1965). For the era of European expansion, the best brief account is J. H. Parry, *Europe and a Wider World, 1415–1715* (London: Hutchinson and Co., 1949; New York: Hillary House, 1949).
Southern Africa 3rd. ed. (London: Longmans, 1957; New York: Barnes & Noble, 1964). See also C. W. De Kiewiet, *A History of South Africa, Social and Economic* (London: Oxford University Press, 1941); and Leo

Marquard, *The Story of South Africa*, 3rd. ed. (London: Faber and Faber, 1968; *A Short History of South Africa*, New York: Praeger, 1968).

The great wealth of traveler accounts and contemporary commentary on the slave trade is brought together conveniently in several collections. See T. Hodgkin, *Nigerian Perspectives* (London: Oxford University Press, 1960); Freda Wolfson, *Pageant of Ghana* (London: Oxford University Press, 1958); C. Fyfe, *Sierra Leone Inheritance* (London: Oxford University Press, 1964); and B. Davidson, *The African Past* (London: Longmans, 1964; Boston: Atlantic Monthly Press, 1964). Useful secondary works include G. I. Jones, *The Trading States of the Oil Rivers* (London: Oxford University Press, 1963); and K. O. Dike, *Trade and Politics in the Niger Delta* (Oxford: Clarendon Press, 1956). The slave trade is examined in B. Davidson, *Black Mother* (London: Victor Gollancz, 1961; Boston: Atlantic Monthly Press, 1961).

Part Two: Modern Africa

8: The Genesis of Modern Africa

THE AGE OF REVOLUTION

Mid-twentieth-century Africa has been marked by great political, economic, and social change. A revolution of political freedom has transformed colonial status into national sovereignty for some two score African states. Economic development, long demanded by subject peoples of their colonial masters, has become a prime objective of independent African governments. At the same time, a major social revolution has gained momentum, challenging an older way of life, questioning traditional values and customary relationships, and presenting Africa with many of the same advantages and the same problems which the process of modernization has already brought to other parts of the world.

Modern Africa—the Africa of national patriotism and national independence, of economic planning and rising hopes for material prosperity—had its genesis during another revolutionary epoch in Africa's history. In the early decades of the nineteenth century, the people of Africa were also subjected to great and rapid change. Across much of the continent, the rhythm of more leisurely development was interrupted and altered, events were piled upon events in accelerated tempo, new directions were opened to African societies, and long-standing isolation from outside forces was irrevocably shattered. The thrust of new forces introduced Africa to its modern era, an era of which the present-day revolution of political independence and economic development is but the latest manifestation.

The new forces were various—in place, in substance, and in impact—but they tended to be related to events outside Africa, particularly events connected with the explosive expansion of European influence into all corners of the earth's continents. In most instances the early nineteenth-century European involvement in Africa was indirect, albeit important, but in West Africa it was immediate and portentous, introducing a new way of looking at the world which was greatly to influence the shaping of modern African societies.

At the beginning of the nineteenth century, in recently established coastal centers like Freetown or expanding older establishments such as St. Louis, there dwelt Africans dedicated in greater or lesser degree to reform of traditional communities and replacement of indigenous institutions with concepts and practices learned from the West. Their ideas had been shaped by Europeans—in part by English missionaries seeking to end the traffic in slaves, in part by Frenchmen extolling the democratic principles of the great Revolution of 1789—and they were convinced of the necessity for converting the world of West Africa into a replica of the European society they had come to admire. They absorbed and accepted Christianity along with the profit motive, and Western education hand in hand with Western dress. Far more than marginal repositories of European cultures, they saw their duty as West African leaders—churchmen, merchants, and public officials—to encourage the spread of Christian-European standards and institutions among neighbors and relatives and thereby to introduce revolutionary social and economic concepts which would bring about the modernization of West Africa. Although their drive for national independence was thwarted by the late nineteenth-century European colonial occupation of Africa, their advocacy of modernization slowly spread its influence and led to a major assimilation of Western ideas and standards. These in turn provided the basis for the eventual surge toward independence and the determination to secure a better life which reached a climax in the two decades following the end of the Second World War.

Concurrent with these developments in West Africa, and far to the south, another revolutionary change was taking shape, partly caused by immigrants from Europe but also deeply affected by basic mutations in indigenous African society. During the late eighteenth century, Boer farmers spreading out from the Dutch enclave at Cape

Town had come into contact with the Xhosa vanguard of the Nguni-speaking people, and the hostility which was generated from this early confrontation of Boer and Bantu was to lead to the racial separation, exploitation, and antipathy which characterizes South Africa in the twentieth century. The early Boer trekker was a dour, suspicious individual whose views on race had already become fixed by material uncertainty and an ungenerous nature, and whose mastery of European technology would ultimately insure his dominance over the black man in South Africa. By the opening of the twentieth century he had secured that dominance, in the process converting the African from independent pastoralist to landless laborer, both in the town and in the countryside.

Prior to this eventuality, however, Bantu society had already reformed itself almost beyond recognition, setting in motion political and ecological forces which profoundly affected African populations over vast areas in the southern, central, and eastern portions of the continent. The driving force was land hunger caused by population pressure among migrating cattle keepers, and the vehicle was the military outburst known as the Zulu *Mfecane*. The loosely knit Bantu societies slowly spreading toward the southern tip of the African continent were suddenly overturned and scattered by the concentrated onslaught of the disciplined, martial Zulu. Many groups were destroyed and many others absorbed by those nations which survived by adopting the centralized state and military tactics of the Zulu conquerers. The shock waves of the *Mfecane* spread outward from its nucleus on the eastern coast of South Africa, propelling group after group in a frenzied flight from extermination. Long-lived migrations drove people thousands of miles from their homelands, reorganized state systems along revolutionary lines, and established new nations of many diverse tribal remnants as far to the north as the swamps of the upper Zambezi or the plains bordering Lake Tanganyika.

Indeed, the great migrations from the south were not the only elements of change which touched the high Tanganyikan plains during the first half of the nineteenth century. Before the arrival of these militant Ngoni invaders, the East African plateau had been slowly shedding an introspective preoccupation with village stock- and crop-raising through a growing trade with the Swahili entrepôts along the coast. By the opening of the nineteenth century, slaving had joined the traffic in ivory, and the rising international demand for this merchandise had tempted groups of coastal Swahili and Arabs to adventure inland where they competed or cooperated with inland African traders. Over the years, increasing emphasis on slaving brought raiding and warfare which was further intensified by the introduction of firearms by the coastal traders. When the Ngoni appeared with their highly organized military state, they added their considerable measure to the spreading chaos of the interior plains. As in the south, the strong survived and the weak were annihilated, while new political and social configurations made their appearance. Some nations endured by adopting Ngoni military centralization, others by arming themselves with muskets. At the same time entirely novel groupings emerged, made up of adventurers and refugees torn loose by the troubled times from their more stable existence, and devoted to warfare and brigandage. Slaving visited death, destruction, and moral breakdown as did the great ivory hunts conducted by armed gangs led by Arab, Swahili, or African freebooters. Only in the northern plains and the region of the Great Lakes, politically stable and beyond the Ngoni reach, was the breakdown of order avoided.

If the nineteenth century put an end to East Africa's isolation from the outside world, it did little to prepare her people for the colonial occupation which was to follow. European influences were initially minor and indirect—the faintest indication of what was later to develop. Similarly, across the broad savanna of the sub-Saharan Sudan, Europe was a remote phenomenon to the farmers and herders caught in the great upheavals which altered their lives during this same era of change. Early in the nineteenth century accumulated social, political, economic, and ideological frustrations burst forth in Hausaland in the form of a *jihad* which created unity from diversity and placed the indelible mark of Islam on a vast area roughly coincident with the northern region of Nigeria. It seems likely that this *jihad* was part of a spreading expression of malaise throughout a Muslim world dismayed by the pretensions of a renascent West; in any event, it was followed by other similar risings to the west and the east which brought religious ferment and political revolution to the vast savanna from the Senegal to the Nile. New states came into existence at the urging of new leaders, a millennial figure of great influence arose in the Egyptian Sudan, and the Islamic faith, civilization, and way of life at last gained the allegiance of the vast savanna it had been seeking for centuries.

One other area of early ninteenth-century ferment remains—
the Nile Vally of Egypt. Here too the Muslim world was under pressure from Christian Europe, and here Africa made dramatic and
effective response.

MUHAMMAD ALI AND THE MODERNIZATION OF EGYPT

In Egypt, since the mid-thirteenth century, the Nile Valley
fellahin, or peasant, had forfeited his liberty in exchange for the
doubtful security and the certain tyranny provided by his Mamluk
overlords. The Mamluks, a special caste of Turkish and other Asian
slaves, had long formed an important element within the armies of
the Muslim Caliphate, their growing strength culminating in the
middle of the thirteenth century when the Mamluks in Cairo seized
power, and thus established themselves as Egypt's de facto rulers for
the next five centuries. For the Egyptian farmer the long-lived
Mamluk regime was an agony compounded of plague, famine, civil
war, and the tax collector's whip. In 1517 Egypt became part of the
Ottoman Empire, but this event had little long-range effect on
Mamluk' rule which eventually reasserted its oppressive ways much
as before. The Mamluks held the land under a feudal system designed
for maximum exploitation, and as their hold on the country became
progressively more corrupt and inefficient, the lot of the peasant grew
correspondingly critical. By the latter part of the eighteenth century great tracts of land were going out of cultivation for lack of
proper irrigation as two and one-half million people incongruously
scratched for the barest subsistence in this potentially rich earth.

In July, 1798, Napoleon landed an army in Egypt in a move designed to sever Britain's link to India. As imperial strategy it was well
conceived but the execution was faulty, and the French were gone
in less than three years, forced out by British arms and the complexities of governing a prostrate and backward people. For France
and Britain it was but an incident in their protracted struggle for
domination of the seas. For Egypt it was the cannon shot that ended
her weary centuries of stagnation and torpor. To be sure, it did not
put an end to Egypt's ordeal of tyranny and oppression at the hands
of foreign masters, for practical independence was not to come for
another century and a half. It did, however, introduce an age of

political stability during which peasant productivity was re-established; more than that, it forced the Egyptians out of the medieval into the modern world.

The instrument of this revolution was Muhammad Ali. A professional soldier who arrived in Egypt with a troop of Albanian cavalry in support of the resistance mounted by the Ottomans against the Napoleonic invasion, Muhammad Ali remained after the French had departed, eventually to become the founder of yet another dynasty of foreign princes. By 1805 he had survived a complex power struggle involving several Turkish factions and the Mamluks to emerge as the most powerful leader in the land. The following year the reluctant sultan in Istanbul was obliged to name Muhammad Ali Pasha as his viceroy or governor in Egypt. In 1811 he eliminated the Mamluks forever, slaughtering them in an ambush which left him without challenge to his plans to revive Egypt's economy and rebuild her political fortunes.

Personal power was the goal of this political realist, who once dismissed Machievelli as a tyro, and each move was carefully calculated to enhance his strength. The elimination of the Mamluks brought him control over Egypt, and a strong renascent Egypt was a stepping stone to pre-eminence in the Middle East and perhaps even to the sultanate at Istanbul. The French occupation, though brief and uncertain, had amply demonstrated Western technological superiority, particularly in its military manifestations; hence, Muhammad Ali set about with the aid of French technicians and military experts to reorganize his army and to create an officer corps on Western lines. Military instruction, however, suggested reforms of a broader educational perspective and led severally to the dispatching of young Egyptians for study abroad, the establishment of technical institutes in Egypt, and a massive program of translation into Arabic of the many essential European texts.

These were expensive innovations which could be paid for only through an enhanced public revenue, and increased revenue in turn rested upon a thorough rehabilitation of Egypt's obsolete, inefficient economy, replacing subsistence cultivation with a modernized system based upon cash crop production and local industry. Muhammad Ali attacked the problem with characteristic foresight and energy. Egypt's traditional agriculture relied upon the periodic overflow of the Nile into her floodplain where the precious water was captured through an arrangement of dykes, and the fields revitalized with annual deposits of rich alluvial soil. Nevertheless, frequent floods and drought could not be controlled by such archaic techniques which suffered the additional disqualification in Muhammad Ali's eyes of supporting only one annual crop during the high water period.

By the early nineteenth century the expanding industry of Europe was already consuming vast quantities of cotton—between 1800 and 1830 Britain's yearly imports rose from 50 million to 300 million pounds—and Muhammad Ali knew that Egyptian soil with proper irrigation was ideally suited to cotton culture. With the assistance of European hydraulic engineers, he installed a network of deep-cut canals, adding steam-driven pumps to bring the river water to the fields during the dry summer months. The result was two annual crops and a vast increase of cultivable acreage. High quality long-staple cotton came in time to dominate Egyptian exports while other cash crops, notably sugar, tobacco, and indigo, were produced, as well as summer rice and corn to supplement the traditional yields of winter wheat and barley.

A rising food and cash crop production was not to be wasted on the Egyptian peasant, however, for all increases in revenue were earmarked exclusively for economic and military development. A surprisingly modern system of state capitalism was instituted by the imaginative viceroy. First of all, the land was nationalized with the understanding that peasants, though nominally tenants, would be virtual owners of their tracts as long as they kept up their tax payments. This was no mean task for taxes were heavy and were supplemented by other burdens—forced labor requisitions for public works such as canals and dams, and a system of government monopolies for basic crops like cotton, tobacco, or sugar, whereby the state bought each year's output at a minimum rate and sold it on the world market for a substantial profit.

Such techniques brought a dramatic increase in national resources. Between 1800 and 1850 the population almost doubled while acreage increased from 3,200,000 to 4,150,000. Over the same period government revenue rose almost four times with exports and imports increasing tenfold. Muhammad Ali used these funds to pay for his increasingly efficient army and his extensive educational and industrial reforms—the schools, the textile mills, shipyards, iron foundry, and other manufacturing establishments, and the large numbers of foreign technicians imported to operate the complex machinery of the new Egyptian economy. It was an expensive but important principle, for the absence of foreign loans and concessions also meant the absence of foreign economic and political interference; failure to grasp this essential fact was later to plague the reign of Ismail, Muhammad Ali's grandson, and lead to eventual European occupation and loss of independence for Egypt.

The long-suffering, hard-working *fellahin* contributed to Muhammad Ali's success in another important respect when he became the highly efficient line soldier in the renascent Egyptian armies. An early experiment with Sudanese slaves proving impracticable, the governor turned to his peasants, and soon his French instructors had trained a modern army along Western lines which was the most powerful in the Middle East. For a time this force was deployed in support of Muhammad Ali's Ottoman masters, but eventually Turk and Egyptian came into conflict, and it soon became evident that the decaying power at Istanbul was no match for the Egyptian pasha who appeared ready and able to take the Caliphate and establish himself as sultan of the Ottoman Empire.

Muhammad Ali's very success had now become an embarrassment. His rising predominance in the Middle East troubled the British who preferred a weak and responsive Turkish power in control of the routes to India and the Far East. At home his growing industrial establishment protected by tariffs and sustained by a stable currency and up-to-date marketing methods vexed European merchants who sought free access to the Egyptian market for their own manufactured products. In the end it was the West, the source of Muhammad Ali's strength, which destroyed him. In 1838 Britain obtained the right of virtual free trade within the Ottoman dominions, and three years later the Treaty of London forced Muhammad Ali to conform—to abolish his protective tariffs and sharply reduce the size of his army. His nascent industrialization thus scuttled and his military force emasculated, the aging viceroy could no longer maintain his interest in economic reform, and most of his programs, particularly in education and industry, were permitted to lapse during the years preceding his death in 1848. Indeed, it is probable that some relaxation would have been necessary in any case for, after centuries of stagnation, the burdens of a rapid, forced modernization —a costly army, an initially inefficient industry, and an agricultural revolution which yet denied its benefits to the farmer—were probably more than the peasantry and the ancient land could have endured indefinitely.

Whatever its deficiencies, Muhammad Ali's program effected vast and permanent changes in Egypt. There was a fundamental shift away from subsistence farming to the much more productive cash crop agriculture which so greatly shaped the country's economic future. Although early industrialization failed and the educational innovations for the most part did not survive their founder, the ideas they engendered remained and grew. Egyptian students returning from Europe as well as Western teachers and technicians in Egypt stressed the virtues of Western civilization, while Muhammad Ali's extensive translation program not only introduced Western scientific and technical knowledge to the Muslim world but also enriched Arabic literature with new approaches to law, politics, history, and literary expression. Equally important was the emergence of the Egyptian civil servant—a European-educated bureaucrat whose stake in the survival of an Egyptian nation contained the seed of nationalism, yet who maintained the conviction that Egypt's progress was closely linked with Westernization. Perhaps, Muhammad Ali's greatest shortcoming was his failure to see need for a modernized, revitalized Islam to accompany and guide technical and economic modernization along lines acceptable in the Muslim world. Traditional Islamic thought and practice was left to continue, unchanged, resentful, and suspicious, and its reconciliation with Western technical superiority still remains a major problem of Muslim leadership in the Middle East today.

Muhammad Ali's revolution of modernization cast a long shadow forward. No less important to the shaping of modern Africa were those other early nineteenth-century phenomena—the *jihads* of the sub-Saharan Sudan, the population explosions in South Africa, the intrusion and dissemination of the tenets of Western civilization in West Africa, and the opening of East Africa to international commerce. It is now necessary that each of these developments be examined in detail through the chapters that follow.

Suggestions for Further Reading

Discussions of Muhammad Ali's role as a modernizer are not numerous. Brief accounts of various aspects of his career are available in a number of works—John Marlowe, *Anglo-Egyptian Relations, 1800–1953*

(London: The Cresset Press, 1954); Tom Little, *Egypt* (London: Ernest Benn, 1958; issued as *Modern Egypt*, New York: Praeger, 1967); Ibrahim Abu-Lughod, *Arab Rediscovery of Europe* (Princeton: Princeton University Press, 1963); Moustafa Fahmy, *La Révolution de l'Industrie en Egypte et ses Consequences Sociales au 19e Siècle* (Leiden: E. J. Brill, 1953); and R. O. Collins and R. L. Tignor, *Egypt and the Sudan* (Englewood Cliffs, New Jersey: Prentice-Hall, 1967). See also Helen A. B. Rivlin, *The Agricultural Policy of Muhammad Ali in Egypt,* (Cambridge, Massachusetts: Harvard University Press, 1961); Desmond Stewart, "Mohammed Ali: Pasha of Egypt," *History Today*, vol. VIII, no. 5, May, 1958; and R. L. Tignor, "Muhammad Ali, Modernizer of Egypt," *Tarikh*, vol. 1, no. 4.

9: Religion and Empire in the Western and Central Sudan

PRELUDE TO THE GREAT *JIHADS*
OF THE NINETEENTH CENTURY

The collapse of Songhai at the close of the sixteenth century marked the end of an era in the western Sudan. For the next two hundred years the movement toward political centralization was to give ground to particularism while the universality of Islam stood checked, no longer encouraged in the courts of kings. The invading Moroccans had strength only to destroy Songhai, and the state they substituted soon found itself engaged in a desperate defense of shrinking sovereignty along the Niger. In 1727 the kingdom of Segu made Timbuktu a tributary and by the end of the eighteenth century the Tuareg had taken control of the whole Niger bend, occupying Timbuktu and thoroughly destroying the power of the *arma*, as were called the descendants of the original Moroccan invaders. To the east the Hausa states continued divided and discordant, while Bornu was in decline, the victim of external pressure and the dry rot of ineffective leadership. Only along the upper Niger did a degree of stability emerge during the eighteenth century in the military oligarchies of the Bambara states, Segu and Kaarta, while to the southeast in the Volta watershed, the Mossi kingdoms—Wagadugu, Yatenga, and others—still flourished in their traditional strength.

In the many smaller states which arose after the breakup of Songhai, the rulers were either pagan or but nominally Muslim. The Mossi had always resisted Islam and so too did the ruling families of Kaarta and Segu. During the seventeenth century an independent Fulani state had flourished in Macina but it remained pagan until 1776 and in any event was dominated in turn during the eighteenth century by both the Tuareg and the Bambara of Segu. The Hausa kings carried their Muslim allegiance lightly, making small use of scholars and jurists and seeking maximum accommodation with the indigenous tradition and custom. Only Bornu could claim status as a major Muslim state, and even there many heathen practices were countenanced. Furthermore, it was not just the ruling dynasties who were indifferent to Islam, for the bulk of the peasant farmers stretching from the Senegal basin to Lake Chad still worshipped according to ancient animist custom.

Nevertheless, the eclipse of Islam was relative and there were important Muslim islands in the pagan sea. In the first place, there were the industrious Dyula merchants—Mandinka Muslims and professional traders—who maintained a network of market villages throughout the West African savanna and forest. These merchants, who carried on the long-distance trade in gold, salt, slaves, and other products, lived quietly among their animist neighbors, never attempting overt conversion but exercising the subtle influence of their way of life. Secondly, there were the Kunta Arab nomads from the southern Algerian desert who grazed their stock along the northern banks of the Niger and became in time the proselytizers of the people of the Saharan fringe. Finally, there were the Fulani. These people, part Berber and part Negro, had originated in the Futa Toro along the Senegal River, but their pastoral habits brought them eastward beginning about the thirteenth century, and gradually they became an integral part of Sudanic life as far as Adamawa in the Benue basin two thousand miles removed from their homeland. Although the cattle-raising Fulani remained on the whole animist, those who settled in the towns were primarily Muslim, and few were more thoroughgoing than the Torodbe, a clan of scholars and clerics who came to exercise a powerful influence as royal advisers and administrators. In consequence of the activities of these groups, Islam had become established in numerous urban areas, largely among merchant immigrants, but by the end of the eighteenth century it was the religion of the ruling classes only in Bornu and the adjacent states of Wadai and Bagirmi.

The loss of political influence suffered by Muslims following the fall of Songhai was less serious in the eyes of true believers than the spirit of accommodation which had long characterized the relations of Islam with West Africa's Sudanic peoples. Perhaps this was the force of necessity, for African culture had never been receptive to the demands of Islamic doctrine which was consequently obliged for survival to give ground to indigenous customs and thought. The Dyula traders were a good case in point. They lived peaceably side by side with pagans to whom they sold great quantities of Muslim amulets and by whom they were thoroughly accepted as part of the pagan African scene. Although they were a factor in spreading Islamic culture throughout West Africa, they were but a minor influence for mass conversion.

Such a permissive, conciliatory attitude was anathema to the evangelical, revivalist strain in Islam, a reforming impulse which came across the great desert from North Africa and struck deep roots among certain of the Fulani clans. The vehicle was the Qadiriyya brotherhood brought to the Sudan by the Kunta Arabs and embodying in the cult of *sufism,* or saint worship, a belief in the spiritual superiority of Islam, the correctness of Islamic law, and the need to restore the theocratic state of Islam in all its original purity. The Torodbe Fulani, religious teachers and Muslim scholars, became leading exponents of the Qadiriyya way, and scattered throughout the savanna, they represented points of potential political disaffection based on their disapproval of the prevailing religious laxity. To them there could be no compromise with unbelievers, no true Muslim could rest content living in the land of the infidel as servant and subject. Aside from religious conviction, they saw themselves educated in a superior culture yet lacking commensurate political authority, made to do the bidding of pagan overlords as scribes or counselors, forced to submit to taxation unsanctioned by Islamic law, and subjected to military conscription, possibly in support of a pagan war against true believers. Such a situation was intolerable and called for decisive action as prescribed in the Quran—first the *hijra,* or flight from the land of the infidel, and then the *jihad,* the holy war to extend the abode of Islam.

The frustration of hard-shell reformers like the Torodbe was poised against the resentment harbored by the pagan or nominally Muslim chief against the religious dogmatists in his realm. Their ill-concealed air of superiority was all the more vexing because their assistance was so often necessary in the affairs of state. Moreover, their religious exclusiveness was frequently accompanied by linguistic and cultural differences which made them unassimilated islands of foreigners in their adopted land. Finally, there was always the danger that advisers might develop excessive influence and arrogate authority, using it to subvert the state on behalf of an alien religion and way of life.

The uneasy balance in Sudanic society between pagan ruler and Muslim zealot was first upset during the eighteenth century in revolutions which saw the establishment of small-scale Islamic theocracies in Futa Toro and Futa Jalon. The high plateau of Futa Jalon had long been the home of pagan Susu and Mandinka people, but this grazing country proved attractive to pastoral Fulani from Macina who began to infiltrate the Futa toward the end of the seventeenth century. The Fulani, though lukewarm Muslims, found pagan rule vexing and finally were persuaded by their religious leaders, notably Ibrahim Musa, to embark on a *jihad* about 1725. A long complex struggle ensued which only ended in victory for the intruders in 1776 when their war leader, Ibrahim Sori, succeeded in establishing a Muslim government in Futa Jalon.

Meanwhile, an analagous development was unfolding in Futa Toro where another Muslim theocracy was founded in 1775. In this Senegalese Futa, a struggle for power arose between Torodbe Muslims and their pagan Fulani rulers, creating unrest which was compounded by the raiding of aggressive Moors from the north side of the Senegal River. Under Sulaiman Bal, the Torodbe began a *jihad* which unseated the Fulani Denyanke dynasty and installed the Torodbe as the new aristocracy with Abd al-Qadir as leader. In both the Futa Jalon and Futa Toro the revolutionary Islamic states proved unstable, for their elective governments patterned on early Islamic models were ill suited to the character of their quarrelsome people. The significance of these early *jihads* lay elsewhere, however—in the creation of theocratic governments controlled by Muslim scholars, and in the considerable conversion to orthodox Islam effected among the rank and file. Although the immediate influence of these states appears to have been limited to their own territory, their shape and purpose cast a long shadow forward across the Sudan.

USUMAN DAN FODIO AND THE SOKOTO *JIHAD*[*]

Far to the east of the original Fulani homeland in present-day Senegal, a situation was unfolding in Hausaland with all the classic ingredients of explosive religious revolution. For several centuries Fulani had been settled in the Hausa states—both the *Fulanin Gida,* the sedentary Fulani usually associated with the towns, and the *Bororoje* pastoralists of the Hausa countryside. The relation of these groups to Islam was complex. While the town dwellers were normally Muslim, their religious allegiance was likely to be nominal for many had become wealthy assimilated members of Hausa society, intermarried with the local people, speaking their language, and embracing their way of life. Nevertheless, also included among the urban Fulani were the clerical Torodbe whose orthodox view of Islam was intrinsically antagonistic to any political authority other than a Muslim theocratic state. For their part, the pastoralists included many pagans along with some practicing Muslims, the latter cleaving closely to their religion, in the midst of rural isolation, as a major standard for ethical and social behavior. Moreover, Torodbe scholars moved from place to place as itinerant teachers, thus spreading their religious views among the cattle-keeping Fulani.

There were other complicating factors defining the status of the Fulani. The dislike of Muslim scholars for the casual religious practices of the Habe dynasties of the Hausa states was both heightened and diluted by the fact that many Fulani clerics earned their livelihood as teachers and counselors in the very courts they despised. Furthermore, the full assimilation of the sedentary Fulani into Hausa society was checked by an abiding sense of group solidarity binding together a Fulani minority dwelling in a predominantly Hausa popu-

[*] SUDANESE STATES AND THE NINETEENTH CENTURY *Jihads*

Sokoto	Kanem-Bornu	Macina
Shehu Usuman dan Fodio	*Shehu* al-Kanemi	*Seku* Ahmadu Bari
b. 1754–d. 1817	d. 1835	b. *c.* 1775–d. 1844
Muhammad Bello	*Shehu* Umar (1835–1880)	*Seku* Ahmadu II d. 1852
Sultan of Sokoto		*Seku* Ahmadu III d. 1862
(1817–1837)		

Mandinka Empire	*Tokolor Empire*
Samori b. *c.* 1835–d. 1900	*al-Hajj* Umar b. *c.* 1797–
	d. 1864
	Ahmadu b. *c.* 1835–
	d. 1898

lation. Beyond this, the disinterest of pagan Fulani herdsmen toward questions of Islamic orthodoxy was offset by their outrage over what they regarded as excessive and discriminatory taxation by a Hausa government. Finally, it was always a source of irritation to a Fulani Muslim, proud of his culture and his literacy, to see political authority in the hands of those he regarded as his inferiors.

This complex set of tensions within Fulani society was further complicated by stresses among the Hausa. Excessive taxation was resented by the Hausa farmer no less than by the Fulani herdsman, corruption and arbitrary rule bore equally on all ethnic groups, while those Hausa who shared the religious convictions of the Fulani reformers shared as well their inclination toward the efficacy of revolution. Thus a highly unstable situation had developed in Hausaland by the late eighteenth century, a situation which was likely to explode as soon as an agent was introduced which upset the precarious equilibrium. Such an agent did in fact appear, and with him began the momentous events of the Sokoto *jihad* led by the great religious reformer, Usuman dan Fodio.

Usuman dan Fodio, called *Shehu,* or chief, by his followers, was through birth, education, and temperament the embodiment of the Muslim teacher and philosopher. Born in the kingdom of Gobir in 1754, a member of the Torodbe clan and Qadiriyya brotherhood, he seemed destined from the first to follow his father in a career as scholar and teacher. Throughout a long apprenticeship he was thoroughly trained by a series of learned men, gaining an intimate acquaintance with Quranic knowledge as well as a mastery of Muslim law, rhetoric, and classical Islamic history. In some cases his teachers gave him a good deal more than a careful but conventional education —from his uncle, Uthman Binduri, he came to understand the importance of the Quranic injunction, "enjoining the right and forbidding the wrong," at first by prayer and preachment, but if necessary, by deed; through his celebrated teacher, Jibril, he observed the actual, albeit unsuccessful, call to *jihad* against heresy and pagan practice.

By the time he was twenty Usuman dan Fodio had begun to teach at Degel, his home in Gobir, and soon he was traveling and preaching extensively, the burden of his message being the need to end misgovernment and unsanctioned religious practice and to be guided by the *Shari'a,* the law of Islam. In addition to licentiousness and lust, Usuman declared, the rulers of Hausaland were corrupt and sacrilegious, persecuting the true believers and debasing Muslim rites with pagan ceremonies. Over the years Usuman's persuasiveness brought a growing number of followers to Degel and finally gained him access to Bawa, the sultan of Gobir, whom he attempted to instruct in the true path of God. "None was his equal," his son, Muhammad Bello was later to attest. "People trusted him and flocked to him. . . . He instructed the *ulama* [learned men], and raised the banner of religion. . . . He spread knowledge and dispelled perplexity. . . . Revered by both great and small, he was a reformer at the head of his generation."

Fame brought power which in turn engendered fear. His demand for reform added to his adherents in Gobir as well as in adjacent Zamfara and Kebbi, and his copious writings enhanced his reputation still further. Religious reform, however, meant social reform and a direct threat to the established authorities, for their rule was based in no small part on their support of traditional Hausa social custom and religious practice. Sultan Bawa of Gobir allegedly planned to assassinate the *Shehu* in 1789, but instead of carrying out the threat, granted important religious and economic concessions at Usuman's insistence. Slowly circumstances moved on to extremity. At some point during the 1790's, the idea of *jihad* took shape in the *Shehu's* mind, and in 1795 he urged his following to arm themselves. The reigning sultan, Nafata, countered by denying all but Usuman the right to preach, prohibiting further conversions to Islam, and forbidding the wearing of the turban and the veil, those distinctive symbols of Usuman's people. When Yunfa succeeded his father, Nafata, in 1802, the final break came quickly, for the new sultan, though a former pupil of the *Shehu*, was determined to break the latter's power. In 1804, Yunfa attacked Abd al-Salam, a non-Fulani supporter of Usuman, killing and capturing many of his followers. To this aggression, the *Shehu* responded by ordering his people to emigrate from Gobir, and with this *hijra* in the purest Muslim tradition, the ultimate break had come. Only *jihad* could follow—war against the infidel.

After some initial setbacks, the forces of Usuman proceeded to conquer the Hausa states within a few short years. The *Shehu* provided the prestige of his spiritual leadership but left military affairs in the hands of his brother, Abdullahi, and his son, Muhammad Bello, while numerous Fulani leaders from points in Hausaland received flags from Usuman as army commanders charged with military activities in their several areas. Much of Kebbi was occupied in 1805 and the Fulani war camp was established at Gwandu. A year later Zaria was taken without a struggle and in 1807 both Kano and Katsina fell. In 1808 several armies converged on Alkalawa, capital of Gobir, and in the ensuing battle Yunfa was defeated and killed. This ended effective resistance in Hausaland which eventually was divided into two regions—Gwandu under the administration of Abdullahi and Sokoto under Bello.

By this time, although the *jihad* was far from finished, its character had already been substantially altered. Usuman and his pious followers were motivated from the first by a desire to achieve purity of religious devotion, a thoroughgoing social reform, and the renascence of Islamic culture in the Sudan. In this respect their purpose lay close to the substance of other roughly contemporary reformist movements in the Muslim world—for example, the Mahdiyya in the eastern Sudan and the Sanusiyya of Cyrenaica. The Sokoto *jihad,* however, required soldiers as well as scholars and in any event tended to attract individuals with something less than the *Shehu's* religious zeal. Fulani solidarity rallied many Fulani pagans to the cause, and others came, attracted by the prospect of personal gain. Gradually the *jihad* assumed a more secular character in which a Fulani aristocracy replaced Hausa kings and courts and the idea of a Fulani empire eclipsed the universalist concept of a better world under Islam. Needless slaughter and plunder attending most Fulani victories, persecution of Hausa by Fulani forces, and the appointment of Fulani to virtually all important posts alienated the Hausa population and sharpened the point of Fulani imperialism.

With the collapse of Hausa resistance the force of the *jihad* swung eastward to Bornu where some small territorial gains were made but where the Fulani were effectively checked by 1812 through the energy and ability of al-Kanemi, the leader of the Kanembu nomads from the Lake Chad area. In 1812 the *Shehu* retired from all active participation in government and when he died five years later, the leadership of the empire devolved on Muhammad Bello, Abdullahi somewhat reluctantly stepping aside. Conquest continued, now moving southward and eastward, and eventually extended as far as Adamawa in the east, and Nupe and Yorubaland to the south where, in the last instance, diplomacy rather than force of arms effected an occupation of the Yoruba town of Ilorin. When Muhammad Bello died in 1837 he was ruler of a territory roughly equivalent to what later became the northern region of Nigeria—a

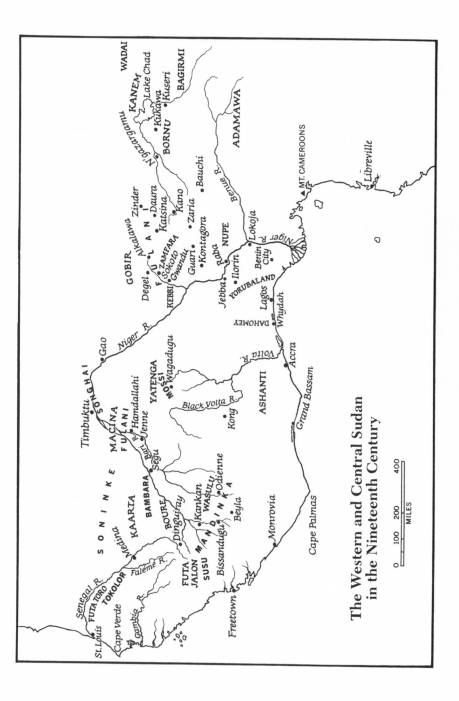

The Western and Central Sudan
in the Nineteenth Century

Fulani empire of Muslim emirates, or provinces, in Hausaland and beyond.

To a considerable extent the empire was the work of Bello. During the early years of the *jihad* he had supported his father's spiritual leadership with essential military persuasion, and when he succeeded to power as Sultan of Sokoto, he continued active campaigning, dispatching almost fifty expeditions during his reign to subdue dissidents or to extend the realm of Islam further into pagan territory. Yet Muhammad Bello ruled by persuasion as well as by force. A Muslim scholar scarcely less brilliant than Usuman, he found time to produce numerous tracts on science, law, morals, history, or Islamic doctrine in which he sought to explain the objectives and tactics of the revolution. As an administrator he attempted to introduce government according to the precepts of the *Shari'a*, frequently taking a personal hand in provincial affairs, checking the excesses of his troops in conquered territory, restraining corruption, and intervening in the decisions of his magistrates in the interests of justice. Sokoto became a center where Islamic scholars flourished, and the precepts of the *jihad* were from thence broadcast throughout the Sudan.

Muhammad Bello's many campaigns reflected a degree of restiveness with Fulani rule which continued after his death; nonetheless, the empire did not collapse and was intact when occupied by the British at the beginning of the twentieth century. This cohesiveness is remarkable not only in view of the traditional divisiveness of Hausaland but also in the fact that the emirates which succeeded the old Habe kingdoms, although essentially political states, were bound to Sokoto primarily by religious allegiance. Allegiance was relative, however. Whereas in Zaria, Kano, or Bauchi there was peace in the land, and in Adamawa and Ilorin the Fulani were on the offensive, in other regions outbreaks were chronic. In Nupe and Guari and again in Gobir and Kebbi the idea of independence from Fulani rule was never abandoned and unrest continued; more generally the Fulani success evoked a revival of Hausa language and culture while Habe governmental administration survived largely undisturbed by an overlay of Fulani, Muslim procedure.

The main feature of the Sokoto *jihad*, therefore, came to be the political, cultural, and religious unity of Hausaland, although a secondary consequence was the renascence of the traditional commerce of the Sudan. From the capital city of Sokoto, built by Muhammad Bello, to peripheral communities like Raba in Nupe, there was evidence of the increasing commercial exchange which effective policing could provide. The English explorer, Hugh Clapperton, remarked in 1823 that Sokoto trade, though modest, included exports of local brass, pewter, and cloth, while among imports were spices, perfume, and beads from Tripoli and Ghadames, goora nuts from Ashanti, and Tuareg salt exchanged for local corn. Ten years later, Macgregor Laird, visiting Raba, spoke enthusiastically of the horses, donkeys, and raw silk brought from North Africa by Arab traders, while at mid-century Heinrich Barth made frequent note of this rising trade throughout Hausaland.

For Barth, the major emporium was Kano, by reason of her combination of household industry and commerce. Various cloths were woven in the baked mud compounds and dyed in the municipal vats to be shipped off to consumers near and far—to the desert Tuareg for their veiling, to Timbuktu where Kano cloth was esteemed for its fineness, to Adamawa where its only competitor was nakedness, and to far-off Arguin Island on the Atlantic. Further, there were leather products, chiefly sandals and tanned hides much fancied in North Africa, as well as unprocessed goods including kola nuts, and of course, slaves.

Slaves were a major element of the economy within the Fulani empire both as an item of exchange and a source of agricultural labor. The demand in the great markets such as Kano and Katsina led to the depopulation of territories on the periphery of the empire where raiding armies such as those of Raba were long in the habit of swooping down on helpless villages, and the infamous Ibrahim Nagwamatse, Emir of Kontagora, ended his late nineteenth-century career of conquest and pillage with the taunting, "I shall die with a slave in my mouth." In Adamawa Barth reported many private individuals with over one thousand slaves, while provincial governors controlled many times more, most engaged in cultivation. At Kano toward the end of the century, domestic slavery was common and slaves of various tribal origins were an important element in the economic life of the community as craftsmen, merchants, and cultivators as well as integral members of their masters' families. Others who came to Kano were less fortunate, for many were marched off along the killing desert tracks to the markets of Ghat and the Fezzan.

SEKU AHMADU IN MACINA

Usuman dan Fodio and his followers sought reform through a return to the principles which obtained in the days of the Prophet and the early Caliphates. In this sense the movement was conservative, attempting to reach back to earlier orthodoxy as a model for the present and future. The widespread conversions which took place among the Hausa and neighboring people therefore were to an established Islamic practice; for example, strict reference to the precepts of classic law, adherence to the Qadiriyya way long familiar in the Sudan, or a penchant for regarding the *jihad* as a latter-day parallel to the reforms of Songhai's *Askia* Muhammad Toure and his great scholarly adviser, al-Maghili. Circumstance, however, made the Sokoto empire a much less thoroughgoing Islamic theocracy than that to which its founders aspired, or which subsequently developed west of Hausaland, in Macina lying upstream from Timbuktu and the lake region of the Niger.

Conditions in Macina in the early nineteenth century resembled those of Hausaland. There was the same mixture of true believers and infidels—of Muslim Fulani and pagan pastoral Fulani, of Soninke and Songhai people, long converted, poised against animist Bambara. The state of Macina was controlled by the long-lived Fulani Dyalo clan, and the government was essentially pagan in practice although the ruling *ardo* of Macina was in fact a Muslim. Further complications existed in that Macina, a Muslim state, was the vassal of pagan Segu, while the Dyalo clan had long been rivaled by the powerful Fulani Sangare family.

As in the case of Hausaland, such an uneasy equilibrium of antipathetical forces invited disruption and discord which came in 1818 in the form of a *jihad* led by *Seku* Ahmadu Bari, a member of the Sangare clan. The *seku*, or chief, who was born about 1775, was educated in the traditional Muslim manner and according to the precepts of the Qadiriyya brotherhood. In the course of subsequent travels he visited Hausaland about 1805 in time to observe the early stages of the Sokoto *jihad* from which he drew considerable inspiration for his subsequent activities in Macina. Returning home, he established himself as a teacher and gathered a following, then ran afoul of the *ardo* of Macina when one of his students killed the *ardo's* son. In seeking to chastise Ahmadu, the *ardo* asked for the aid of the pagan Bambara king of Segu, and this event triggered the classic response of *hijra* to a new headquarters established at Hamdallahi, followed by *jihad* which defeated the Bambara and led to the creation of an Islamic state with Hamdallahi as its capital. A number of Tuareg and Songhai principalities were overrun and the trading cities of Jenne and Timbuktu taken, although these latter, as long-standing centers of Muslim learning and activity, would seemingly have been immune to the molestations of a holy war.

The Macina empire of *Seku* Ahmadu ran along the Niger roughly from Jenne to Timbuktu and was bounded by Kaarta and Segu to the southwest and the Mossi to the southeast. Much smaller than the Sokoto empire, it was also more centralized and easily administered, and although its leadership was far less productive of theological scholarship than Usuman and his disciples, Macina soon developed into a rigorously governed theocratic state and scored notable successes in its permanent conversions among the pastoral Fulani, and to a somewhat lesser extent among the Bambara and other pagans. *Seku* Ahmadu headed a grand council charged with all legislative, executive, and judicial authority, organized an efficient provincial administration, and instituted taxation and distribution of war booty in conformity with the *Shari'a*. A strong puritanical element was apparent in the prohibitions which Ahmadu placed on spirits, tobacco, and dancing, an austerity which ultimately proved so vexing to the more relaxed urban Muslims that, with the death of Ahmadu in 1844, Timbuktu revolted and succeeded partially in easing the control of her internal affairs.

The disenchantment of the Timbuktu Muslims reflected the broad range of social and political complexities in the Macina area which had given rise to the movement of *Seku* Ahmadu in the first place. There were, for example, the differences between pagan and true believer, both within the Fulani community and between the Fulani and other people. There were the varying views of Islam separating the puritan reformer and the cosmopolites of the worldly trading centers. There were the rivalries between Fulani clans, and those between Muslims of different nationality—Soninke, Fulani, Arab, and others. The *jihad,* therefore, became a composite of many movements—for religious reform, for independence from pagan Segu, for dynastic control of Macina. Not the least of its characteristics was civil war, for clan fought clan while Muslim hand was turned against Muslim.

THE *JIHAD* OF *AL-HAJJ* UMAR

Seku Ahmadu designated his son, Ahmadu II, as successor, and Ahmadu in turn was succeeded by his son, Ahmadu III, in 1852. Despite the purity of religious purpose and practice which survived the reign of *Seku* Ahmadu, Macina soon ran afoul of the third great *jihad* of the western Sudan, that of *al-Hajj* Umar (b. c. 1797, d. 1864), the Tokolor warrior from Futa Toro who overran and absorbed the Niger kingdom in 1862, capturing and executing Ahmadu III in the process.

The conquest of Macina was the culmination of developments long unfolding. Born the son of a Muslim scholar toward the end of the eighteenth century, *al-Hajj* Umar, like Usuman and *Seku* Ahmadu, was given a sound Muslim education, then in his early manhood made an extended pilgrimage to Mecca, a journey of great consequence personally and to the subsequent history of Islam in the western Sudan. Pausing in Egypt, Umar met the scholars of the Azhar mosque in Cairo and doubtless observed the efforts of Muhammad Ali to strengthen the international position of his African Muslim state. In Arabia, the opportunity to visit the holy places would have played its part, while Umar must also have made note of the Wahabiyya activists in their reformist movement. Of great significance while at Mecca, moreover, was his initiation into the Tijaniyya brotherhood by Sidi Muhammad Ghali, a *khalifa*, or deputy, of al-Tijani, the founder of the order. Umar became an enthusiastic supporter of Tijani doctrine which was egalitarian and puritanical in spirit, strongly missionary in impulse, and thoroughly persuaded of the moral superiority of all Tijani adherents over the members of other brotherhoods. The way to God, argued the new message, need not be limited to an intellectual aristocracy as with the Qadiriyya. Spiritual salvation could be attained by anyone capable of the highest moral discipline, a state of mind which was revealed by indifference to material pleasures such as tobacco, alcohol, or an excess of wives beyond the Quranic sanction. Such direct, unambiguous teaching penerated deeply into the mind of Umar who became *khalifa* of the Tijaniyya for the western Sudan, and it was to play a central role in the subsequent organization and spread of his movement.

Returning home, *al-Hajj* Umar paused at Bornu long enough to marry a daughter of al-Kanemi, then stopped at the court of

Muhammad Bello where he remained several years, taking one of Bello's daughters as wife, and assimilating a full measure of the philosophy and tactics of the Sokoto *jihad*. The illusion of Islamic unity in the Sudan was furthered by his welcome to Macina in 1838, where he stayed briefly before passing on to Futa Jalon. There he paused for nine years, absorbed in the task of attracting and arming a following grounded in Tijani doctrine, a provocative activity which gradually aroused the uneasiness of the local rulers. If Umar's doctrine was novel, so too was his armament, for, unlike other Muslim religious leaders, he equipped his *talaba,* or disciples, with firearms obtained on the West African coast. In 1848 he performed the *hijra* to Dinguiray, a military base from which he launched his *jihad* in 1852.

Early successes led to control of several Bambara and Mandinka states in the upper Niger and Senegal basins and brought Umar to Futa Toro where he already had much support among his Tokolor countrymen, but where he also encountered French commercial interests on the Senegal River. This was the first time one of the Sudanic *jihads* had confronted a European power, yet it seems probable that Umar's holy war was at this stage concerned only with extending his Tijani empire at the expense of Muslim and pagan African states rather than with an attack on the infidel Europeans. The French, however, were nervous and rebuffed Umar's suggested cooperation which would have given him a free hand to pacify and control the Futa while gaining him access to arms through the Senegalese entrepôt at St. Louis. Umar's reaction to French mistrust was first an attack on river traders, possibly in quest of the arms withheld, and then a siege of the river fort at Medina where he was repulsed in 1857 in a brilliant defense by the St. Louis mulatto commander, Paul Holle.

Umar had already begun operations against the Bambara of Kaarta and occupied their capital in 1854. He now turned his full attention eastward and defeated Segu in 1861, thus placing himself in direct confrontation to his former hosts and co-religionists, the Fulani rulers in Macina. Ahmadu III of Macina had already been greatly disturbed by the move against Segu and had persuaded her king to embrace Islam and then, unsuccessfully, had come to her support. Such an expedient conversion was no protection against the full flood of Umar's *jihad* which engulfed Macina in 1862. Umar justified his move, which paralleled the Sokoto thrust at Bornu a half century earlier, on the grounds that Ahmadu, like al-Kanemi, had allied with an infidel against a true believer and thereby had committed apostasy.

Thus Macina was absorbed by the Tokolor empire of *al-Hajj* Umar, but this height of success was also the point of undoing for the great conquerer. His Tijani doctrines did not sit well with the Qadiriyya Muslims of Macina and an uprising developed in which Umar lost his life in 1864. His rule was carried on with great difficulty by his son, Ahmadu, who lacked his father's prestige and could control neither the partisan separatism of local people nor the independence of his own Tokolor governors. Nevertheless his political skill held the empire together at least in name until it was finally subdued by French arms, the final blow coming in 1893.

The influence of Umar's conquests transcended the life of his political empire. Certainly he effected no permanent cohesion in the Sudan as the post-mortem stresses within his realm amply demonstrated. Nonetheless, he did bring about widespread conversions to Islam, while the pre-eminence which the Tijaniyya brotherhood came to have throughout West Africa was largely traceable to his influence. Even in Hausaland the new movement has gradually come to supersede the Qadiriyya in a development which had its beginning in the visit which *al-Hajj* Umar paid to Sokoto in the 1830's.

AL-KANEMI AND HIS SUCCESSORS IN BORNU

The great *jihads* of the nineteenth century appeared to impose a vast Islamic unity throughout the western Sudan, but in fact relations between the major Muslim states were often seriously strained. The politics of empire did not always coincide with theological objectives, nor did worldly leadership necessarily agree with the aspirations of the more spiritually minded. Over the years Muslim Macina and Muslim Sokoto harbored small mutual esteem, while Macina found much political, if not spiritual, comfort in close relations with the pagan Bambara of Segu. For his part the religious reformer, *al-Hajj* Umar, showed no enthusiasm for fighting the infidel French but fell on his co-religionists of Macina with a gusto more appropriately reserved for the unbeliever. Similarly, the Fulani of Sokoto directed one of the major onslaughts of their *jihad* at the Muslims of

Bornu, a gross perversion of the holy war, the defenders were quick to point out.

By the opening of the nineteenth century, Bornu had lost most of the strength inherited from the days of her great *mai*, Idris Alooma. Her most recent kings had proved effete, her administration over-elaborate, and her armies ineffective. Former vassals such as Kano, Zaria, Daura, and Katsina no longer gave more than nominal allegiance, while Fulani dwelling within the borders of Bornu were becoming restive, stimulated by the revivalism of their cousins to the west. When the *jihad* of Usuman dan Fodio was set in motion in 1804, the Hausa rulers of Kano and Daura appealed for assistance to their suzerain, the *mai* Ahmad (1793–1810), but the meager aid forthcoming was soon smashed along with the troops of Kano, and Kano fell to the Fulani. This success encouraged the Fulani of the western provinces of Bornu to rise in revolt, a movement which was so successful that it led to the establishment of a series of small emirates in western Bornu as well as the capture and sack of the capital city, N'gazargamu, in 1808.

In this moment of extremity *Mai* Ahmad, already in flight, called on the assistance of another of the many remarkable leaders which the Sudan produced during this age of religious revolution. Al-Kanemi, Muslim scholar and leader of the pastoral Kanembu people, had already been engaged in an informal war against the Fulani. Now, with official sanction, he moved his forces against the intruders, relieved N'gazargamu twice, in 1809 and 1811, and, although the frontier emirates were permanently lost, put an end thenceforward to serious Fulani designs on his country.

Al-Kanemi had therefore saved Bornu from what appeared to be certain extinction. Concurrent with his military action, however, this versatile leader had challenged the legitimacy of the Sokoto *jihad,* condemning it as an illegal exercise in imperialism. In the eyes of Usuman and Muhammed Bello, the government of Bornu had permitted pagan practice among its people, and worse, had given aid to pagan Hausa kings. Such an apparent approval of paganism was paganism itself, they argued, and consequently the fit object for a holy war. Al-Kanemi, with long residence and travel in North Africa and the Near East and with a sound reputation for scholarly theological commentary, contended that pagan practices performed in ignorance or weakness did not indicate paganism, that weakness was the unfortunate lot of all people, including the Fulani themselves. If all were to be condemned as unbelievers because of their sins, he insisted, there would be no true believers left to judge the infidels. "Tell us therefore why you are fighting us and enslaving our free people. . . . We have indeed heard of things in the character of the Shaikh [Usuman dan Fodio], and seen things in his writings which are contrary to what you have done. If this business does originate from him, then I say that there is no power nor might save through God. . . . Indeed we thought well of him. But now . . . we love the Shaikh and the truth when they agree. But if they disagree it is the truth which comes first."

Al-Kanemi's military argument was more persuasive than his theology, particularly with the peripatetic Fulani who were numerous only in western Bornu and who drifted home after each successful campaign, making difficult the permanent occupation of N'gazargamu. Al-Kanemi retook most of the lost provinces, settling his Kanembu followers on the land thus acquired and supplying them with slaves captured in battle. His frontiers stabilized, he then turned to the refurbishing of a government much in need of repair, for as military leader, he was now the effective ruler of the state. Assuming only the modest title of *shehu,* he was content to rule from behind the throne, permitting the *mai* and his court to carry on their sterile round of activities undisturbed. By-passing the nobility, he ruled through the *kokenawa,* provincial administrators of common birth, and via the courts for which he served as chief justice. Reforms were much the same as those attempted by his critics in Sokoto—the re-establishment of a Muslim theocracy in conformity with the precepts of the *Shari'a*— and indeed his reforms may have been more thoroughgoing than those of Sokoto whose people had been less touched by Islam.

During the later years of his rule, al-Kanemi returned to the wars but with little profit. Between 1816 and 1824 he pressed a bloody but inconclusive struggle with Bagirmi, a former vassal state lying to the southeast, and then took the offensive against Sokoto, hoping to regain the Hausa territories but earning only a bad mauling for his trouble. Internally there was an unhappy incident when in 1814 the titular *mai,* Ahmad Dunama, tried unsuccessfully to slip away from the *Shehu's* watchful eye and had to be deposed, an event less important in itself than as a forecast of things to come.

Al-Kanemi died in 1835 bequeathing a rejuvenated Muslim Bornu to his people and to his son and successor *Shehu* Umar (1835–

1880). It was, however, during Umar's long reign that the final disintegration of Bornu played itself out, for the vitality of al-Kanemi was evidently personal and could not be instilled into the ancient, failing kingdom. In 1846 *Mai* Ibrahim, chafing under the limitations of his subordinate position, precipitated civil war by plotting with the sultan of Wadai who invaded the kingdom and burned Kukawa, the capital built by al-Kanemi. Umar, who had been absent campaigning in the province of Zinder, was able to expel the Wadai army, but in the process of the war, Ibrahim was executed and his son, Ali, installed as a puppet by the Wadai army, was killed in battle. Thus in futility ended the thousand-year reign of the mighty Saifawa dynasty.

From that point forward Umar ruled directly although he eschewed the title of *mai,* resting content with the simple designation of *shehu.* Interestingly, however, once he became titular head of state, Umar assumed the characteristic aloofness which had so weakened the effectiveness of the last *mais,* retiring into the inaccessibility of religious and royal ritual, and in the process losing control of his government to a set of viziers who became de facto rulers—*al-Hajj* Bashir until 1853, and Abd al-Karim thereafter. Such a withdrawal from the responsibility of rule, frequently characteristic of African monarchies, more than offset the long march toward centralization in Bornu's government. A king with only ceremonial functions and an aristocracy with privileges but no power led to administrative disorganization and regional particularism. During Umar's last years the realm was in thorough disarray—the western provinces virtually independent, and Kanem to the east under the control of militant Wadai. After 1880 the decline continued under three of Umar's sons, ending once and for all in 1893 when independent Bornu fell before the armies of Rabih, a conqueror from the eastern Sudan.

SAMORI AND RABIH

Viewed in their entirety, the great *jihads* may be regarded as an attempt by Muslim scholars—chiefly Fulani—to re-establish the primacy of Islam in the western Sudan as they felt it had once held sway in the days of the *askia,* Muhammad of Songhai. Thus they tried to restore the classic purity of the Islamic state, to purge the religious system of corrupt syncretistic and polytheistic forms, and to extend the domain of *dar al-Islam,* the abode of the true faith.

Examined in still larger context, other factors may have played their part—the decline of Muslim prestige and authority throughout the world relative to the West, and the falling off of the trans-Saharan trade in the face of newer routes headed southward to the sea. Whatever their differences, therefore, the theological orientation of the *jihad* leaders binds them each to the others while separating them from other late nineteenth century Sudanic leaders whose motivation and activities seemingly derived from different sources. Of these latter, two stand out for particular attention—Samori Toure and Rabih Fadlullah.

Samori was born between 1832 and 1835 in the Beyla region of what is today the southeastern corner of Guinea. His father was a peddler and cattleman who traced his descent to the Muslim trading community of the Dyulas, but his mother came from local farming stock; hence, Samori's early upbringing was probably essentially pagan. His paternal ancestors had long before migrated from the Macina area to Kankan in the Niger watershed, a Mandinka center of growing commercial importance during the eighteenth and nineteenth centuries. Here, in the mercantile aspirations and activities of the Dyula traders, lies the key to Samori's career.

For several hundred years the Dyula Mandinka had developed their own commercial empire linking the forest and the savanna, living quietly in the market towns but gradually growing wealthy, powerful, and restive. In the nineteenth century, prodded by the success of Islamic revolutions to the north, they established a number of small states in the southern Sudan, notably Kong and Odienne, which were concerned with trade to the south in salt, kola nuts, and slaves, and which were only secondarily interested in the propagation of Islam. Young Samori early followed his father's career as a petty trader, and in time was converted to Islam, less out of religious conviction, it seems, than as a defense against the pagan people among whom the traders were constantly moving. By 1865, Samori had begun to adopt more aggressive tactics, organizing a personal following with the object of establishing Dyula law among the many warring principalities in the Mandinka country. Bit by bit his unusual military prowess led to the development of a unified state between the forest and the Tokolor empire which *al-Hajj* Umar had built to the north.

During the early expansionist phase, Samori avoided any conflict with Europeans, for his interests lay elsewhere, but his rising strength necessarily placed a barrier before European expansion into the savanna, and since Samori's appearance coincided with a growing European—particularly French—interest in the West African interior, a confrontation was sooner or later inevitable. Samori's mercantile orientation southward led to cordial relations with the English at Freetown from whence came firearms for his armies after 1879. The British government, moreover, was cool toward extending its authority inland whereas French visions of glory, in compensation of the humiliating loss to Prussia and Bismarck in 1871, called for an active advance from Senegal into the Sudan which might lay the basis for a vast empire stretching eventually from the Atlantic to the Red Sea.

By 1873 Samori had taken Kankan and established his capital at Bissandugu, his territory gradually blanketing the upper Niger basin in the regions of Boure and Wasulu. During the 1880's the French advance was intermittent and uncertain, and in any event, was directed largely to the north against the Tokolor state of Ahmadu, the son of *al-Hajj* Umar. Samori was able to maintain his position through skirmishing and diplomacy—courting the British in order to offset the French, concluding friendship treaties with France herself, and urging cooperation on Ahmadu as the best means of dealing with the intruder. It was in vain. Ahmadu could not bring himself to work with a rival African power, the British ultimately were not willing to oppose French pretensions in the interior, and France by 1891 had decided once and for all to push on with her imperial plans. Ahmadu was defeated by 1893, and Samori, though conducting a brilliant guerrilla action which enabled him to remove his state intact far to the east in the region of Kong, was finally run down and captured in 1898, dying two years later an exile in Gabon.

If Samori's initial motivation was commercial and his ultimate fate bound up in the European imperial thrust into Africa, his career differed from that of the great *jihad* leaders in other important respects. Chief among these was his relation to Islam. The son of a pagan, Samori was converted more through expedience than conviction; yet once converted he seems to have taken his religious obligations seriously. He carried on theological studies dutifully over the years and exhibited in his personal conduct the indices of his faith. Moreover, he encouraged Islam throughout his realm—destroying animist shrines and fetishes, building mosques and Quranic schools, assuming the title of *almami,* or leader of the faithful, and compelling the observation of a number of Quranic usages.

How deep was this Muslim commitment is a question. As an illiterate and an imperfect Muslim scholar, Samori was ill-equipped to build a Muslim theocracy and indeed made no such attempt. Beyond this, in his extensive military activities he treated Muslim and pagan alike with fine impartiality, thereby earning the implacable enmity of Muslims in parts of the Sudan where his memory remains unpleasantly alive today. When he took the town of Kong in 1895, the Muslim scholars were slaughtered at the doors of the mosque and those who survived were later executed. If this was done in the name of military necessity, it also indicated an aloofness from religious scruples and commitments, along with a ruthless nature apparently indifferent to human life. Only a few years ago, a leading Muslim from Bamako remarked that Samori's sole endearing trait was his love for his mother.

Samori must be regarded, therefore, as a political, not as a religious figure—the architect of a resurrected Mali empire rather than a soldier of the Lord, Allah. Alternatively and in another light, he appears as an early nationalist leader trying to build and hold together a Mandinka state in the face of the growing pressure of French expansionism. His gifts were military and administrative. His governmental organization was highly sophisticated and practical— the hierarchy from village to district to region to central government with the *almami* at the apex, the shrewd balancing of military against civil authority and local autonomy against centralized control, the astute decision to organize each district to include a heterogeneous population slow to unite in revolt. Even more impressive were his military talents—in logistics no less than in tactics, in thoroughness of plan as well as determination in the field. His *sofa,* or professional soldiers, were supplemented by a conscripted army of citizens all drilled in the scorched earth, hit-and-run tactics which were always the only possible means of success against the French artillery. His diplomacy kept the guns coming from Freetown, but he wisely supplemented this supply with workshops capable of turning out spare parts and effecting repairs. When the French set out to dispose of him in 1891 they anticipated a campaign of a few weeks in duration. Instead they were drawn into a seven-year struggle in which Samori held off the attackers with his best troops while his auxiliaries conquered and organized a completely new state into which he was able to retreat with his government and armies intact, leaving only a thoroughly ruined countryside to be occupied by his

French pursuers. Even his military intelligence was exceptional. Asked how he repeatedly discovered the French movements without giving away his own, he growled, "It is because I eat alone."

Nonetheless, a career of military conquest brought forth less admirable traits. Samori's political survival depended on guns and these, along with North African horses, were best obtained in exchange for slaves. A substantial portion of Samori's operations, therefore, consisted of fearful slave raids which devastated the countryside, bringing death and bondage to its population. Moreover, between 1891 and 1893, his grand retreat before the French from Bissandugu to the area of Kong was characterized by a systematic destruction of the land and its villages, culminating with the sack of Kong and the slaughter of its population in 1895. Understandably, such tactics have tarnished Samori's memory in parts of West Africa, although the age of African national independence has tended to excuse his actions as the necessary, if unfortunate, by-product of a desperate stand against foreign invasion.

The apotheosis of Samori as an early leader of African resistance to European penetration does not seem to have been granted to that other statemaker in the nineteenth-century Sudan who eventually fell before French arms. Possibly this is due to the paucity of information which survived the career of Rabih, information, moreover, supplied primarily by his conquerers and critics. Rabih first appeared in the Bahr al-Ghazal region of the southern Egyptian Sudan as a lieutenant of the powerful slave trader, Zubair Pasha. When Zubair's son was defeated and killed in 1878 by the forces of General Gordon, seeking to stamp out the slave trade in the eastern Sudan, Rabih was suddenly a soldier without a patron. Rallying a few hundred survivors, he retreated westward, carrying on a precarious existence as a brigand but gradually building up an army that enabled him to advance from successful raids to permanent conquest, first of Bagirmi in 1891 and then of the failing Bornu kingdom in 1893. Destroying the capital of Kukuwa, Rabih built a new seat of government but otherwise added little to the administration he had inherited. Master of the Chad basin, he tried unsuccessfully to extend his domain westward at the expense of Sokoto, and was obliged to content himself with consolidating the territory already conquered. His efforts were ultimately in vain. As in the case of Samori, Rabih ran afoul of European powers making determined probes deep into the Sudan. In 1900 Rabih was killed and his forces defeated by a French army at Kuseri, and although resistance continued briefly after his death, Rabih's kingdom was soon absorbed into the colonial holdings of France, Britain, and Germany.

A hard-bitten, self-made man, Rabih, like Samori, survived through his military prowess. How far his interests extended to the propagation of Islam is uncertain, however. His attitude toward the Mahdi of the eastern Sudan was ambivalent for he ignored the Mahdi's overtures while at the same time pursuing his conquests as a Mahdist army leader. There was, moreover, a Mahdist group in the western Sudan, and during the years of Rabih's ascendancy he maintained correct though hardly cordial relations with its leaders. It seems fair to conclude, therefore, that Rabih's motivation was more military than religious.

Suggestions for Further Reading

The standard general works which deal with the period of the *jihads* are by J. S. Trimingham, both his *Islam in West Africa* (Oxford: The Clarendon Press, 1959), and *A History of Islam in West Africa* (London: Oxford University Press, 1962). Other general works which contain relevant material include E. W. Bovill, *The Golden Trade of the Moors* (London: Oxford University Press, 1958); Vincent Monteil, *L'Islam Noir* (Paris: Éditions du Seuil, 1964); and J. D. Hargreaves, *Prelude to the Partition of West Africa* (London: Macmillan and Co., 1963; New York: St. Martins, 1963). A. A. Boahen's *Britain, the Sahara, and the Western Sudan* (Oxford: The Clarendon Press, 1964) offers a good summation of current theses concerning the origins of the Sokoto *jihad* and another interesting analysis is available in the preface of T. Hodgkin, *Nigerian Perspectives* (London: Oxford University Press, 1960). For the Sokoto *jihad*, M. Last, *The Sokoto Caliphate* (New York: Humanities Press and London: Longmans, 1967) is basic, while I. M. Lewis, ed., *Islam in Tropical Africa* (London: Oxford University Press, 1966) contains numerous references to the *jihads*. Another recent account is *The Fulani Empire of Sokoto* (London: Oxford University Press, 1967) by H. A. S. Johnston. See also the chapters by J. O. Hunwick in J. F. A. Ajayi and I. Espie, eds. *A Thousand Years of West African History* (Ibadan: Ibadan University Press, 1965; New York: Humanities Press, 1965); S. J. Hogben and A. H. M. Kirk-Greene, *The Emirates of Northern Nigeria* (London: Oxford University Press, 1966); and Lady Lugard, *A Tropical Dependency* (London: Frank Cass, 1964). *Afrique Noire, Occidentale et Centrale* by

J. Suret-Canale (Paris: Editions Sociales, 1961), gives brief accounts of the *jihads* in what later became the French controlled areas of the savanna.

The accounts of travelers like Heinrich Barth, Hugh Clapperton, and others are basic sources for the period of the *jihads* and later, but more convenient is the excellent selection contained in Hodgkin, cited above, which also includes excerpts from the writings of the leaders of the Sokoto *jihad*, including the Muhammed Bello-al-Kanemi correspondence.

The main work on Bornu is in French: Y. Urvoy, *Histoire de l'Empire du Bornou* (Paris: Larose, 1949), but information is available in many of the volumes cited above. Similarly, the main writings dealing with Macina and the Tokolor *jihad* are in French, for example, A. Hampaté Ba and J. Daget, *L'Empire Peul du Macina, 1818–1853* (Bamako: Institut Français d'Afrique Noire, 1955); F. Carrère and P. Holle, *De la Séné-gambie Française* (Paris: Firmin Didot, 1855); M. Delafosse, *Haut-Sénégal-Niger*, 3v. (Paris: Larose, 1912); and E. Mage, *Voyage dans le Soudan Occidental* (Paris: Hachette, 1868).

The career of Samori Toure is touched upon in the relevant volumes noted above, but see also E. Peroz, *Au Soudan Français* (Paris: Calmann-Lévy, 1889), A. Kouroubari, "Histoire de l'Imam Samori," *Bulletin de l'IFAN*, v. XXI, July–Oct., 1959, and an article by R. Griffeth in *Tarikh*, vol. 1, no. 4.

Information on Rabih is even more limited. In addition to those appropriate works cited above, there is E. Gentil, *La Fin de l'Empire de Rabeh* (Paris: Hachette, 1902); O. Meynier, *La Mission Joalland-Meynier* (Paris: Editions de l'Empire Français, 1947); and A. D. H. Bivar, "Rabih ibn Fadlullah—The Autograph of a Despot," *Nigeria Magazine*, no. 68, March, 1961.

Several useful articles dealing with the *jihad* period should be noted: H. F. C. Smith, "A Neglected Theme of West African History: the Islamic Revolutions of the Nineteenth Century," *Journal of the Historical Society of Nigeria*, v.2, no. 2; F. H. El-Masri, "The Life of Shehu Usuman dan Fodio before the Jihad," *ibid.*, v.2, no. 4; M. Waldman, "The Fulani *Jihad*: a Reassessment," *The Journal of African History*, v. VI, no. 3, 1965; and T. Hodgkin, "Uthman dan Fodio," *Nigeria Magazine*, Oct., 1960.

10: The Eastern Sudan: Egyptian Expansion-ism and the Mahdist Revolution

INVASION FROM THE NORTH

Muhammad Ali Pasha's motivation was always simple, his tactics complex. The building of a mighty Egyptian state as the vehicle of personal power was the lifetime objective of the great modernizer (1805–1848), but the means to this end were various. "You are aware," he wrote in 1823 to his forces invading the Sudan, "that the end of all our effort and this expense is to procure negroes." African slaves drilled into an efficient and loyal army would offset the losses suffered in his taxing campaigns against the Wahabiyya in Arabia and offer an inviting replacement for his insubordinate Albanian troops. There were other attractions, however. He hoped to gain access to the famed, if illusory, gold of the Sudan, deal a final blow to the Mamluk remnants who had survived the massacre he had engineered in 1811, and extend his hegemony south along the Nile as had the pharaohs of old, thereby placing his hand firmly on the profitable commerce of the Red Sea. For these reasons the Sudan was tempting to an ambitious ruler, and all the more so since its gradual decline into a number of petty moribund states promised success at little cost to any determined invader.

Necessarily, there were logistical problems involved in transporting a fighting force through hundreds of miles of difficult, little-known country, and had a serious and sustained military opposition been mounted, the intruders might easily have met disaster. A heterogeneous army of four thousand Turks and Albanians, Maghrib Arabs and Egyptian Bedouins, Barbary Coasters and Negro Africans was colorfully decked out in a great variety of costumes in which the bright-hued pantaloons, slippers, and short jackets of the Turks predominated, but which also exhibited Kurdish cavalry in steel breastplate and conical hat, Bedouins clothed in chain mail and helmet, and Arabs in their traditional flowing robes. A mercenary army, it was commanded by Muhammad Ali's third son, the twenty-five-year-old Ismail, who was assisted by an officer corps which included an American marine recently converted to Islam and the cause of Muhammad Ali. Uniformity and well-drilled precision were conspicuously absent in this motley assortment, but, fortunately for Ismail, its variety extended to its armament which included all-important artillery and a contingent of riflemen to sharpen its striking power.

The guns soon proved their utility. In the autumn of 1820 the army moved out from Aswan and swept past Dongola, lately deserted by its Mamluk contingent. Soon Ismail was confronted by the Shakiyya people whose warlike habits and splendid horsemanship were cancelled out by a medieval weaponry, and who were consequently slaughtered by the Turkish firepower in two engagements, their ears sent back to Cairo by the basketful for promised bounties. As it happened, the gallant but futile effort of the Shakiyya was the only opposition offered Ismail's troops by the demoralized and divided principalities along the Sudanese Nile. The army continued its march upstream, usually proceeding at night to the sound of kettledrums but often breaking ranks to wander off into the desert or to pause and plunder the local inhabitants. The next major objective was Shendi, a trading center not far beyond the ancient site of Meroe—a ragged, dusty, sun-scorched town where a splendid assortment of goods was on display but where slaves were the central item of commerce. Quickly securing the submission of the local ruler, Ismail pressed on, crossing the Nile into the Gezira and entering Sennar unopposed in June, 1821. The unkempt appearance of town and inhabitants matched the ineffective bewilderment of Badi, the last of the Funj sultans whose pathetic final act of independence was the transfer of his faltering realm to the invaders.

In the summer of 1821 another column effected an easy conquest of Kordofan and the essential Sudan was now controlled by Egyptian power which would later add the wide spaces of Darfur in the west and the unknown and inaccessible reaches south of the Sudd—that vast papyrus swamp choking the Nile below her Bahr al-Ghazal tributary. The occupation had been simple—perhaps too simple—but from this point forward complications began to accumulate for invader and invaded alike. Sennar had been a shock, the famed capital a shabby village of grass huts housing a ragged population, docile yet sinister. Soon the summer rains poured down on the northerners, sapping their energy and eroding their morale, forcing them to sleep in the black mud and robbing them of even the will to bury the growing number of comrades dead with fever. In Cairo, Muhammed Ali was calling for gold and slaves but the response was disappointing for the gold supplies were exhausted and only half those slaves shipped on to Egypt survived the trip.

The Egyptian administration was not content merely with opportunities for slaving, however, and shortly proceeded to institute a comprehensive system of taxation, the severity of which amounted to confiscation, threatening the supply of slaves in the Sudan where specie was scarce and payment came in kind. The declining morale of the invaders was now matched by the disillusionment of the Sudanese whose initial reaction to the northerners had not been unfavorable. Numbers of Egyptian soldiers were ambushed and others murdered in their beds as they slept. Great migrations of people moved off to the wilderness, chiefly along the Ethiopian marches, placing the protection of distance between themselves and the Egyptian tax collectors. At Shendi, Ismail was assassinated in October, 1822, when first he imposed an impossible assessment on the local ruler and then publicly insulted him. The incident set off a widespread revolt along the river from Shendi south, a revolt which might have succeeded even in the face of the northern firepower had the local people been able to suppress parochial differences and unite in adversity. With Ismail's death, the commander of the Kordofan army assumed responsiblity for the occupation and soon his forces were burning, ravaging, slaughtering, and enslaving in a vicious outburst of retribution until the Sudan lay ruined and prostrate, its villages gutted and its land depopulated, denied even the sense of despair which had initially triggered rebellion. With the end of bloodletting came renewed taxation and further migrations, but in 1825 at last a more reasonable regime was instituted and the exhausted Sudan settled back to peace and the hope for some measure of rehabilitation.

THE ECOLOGY OF POVERTY

The troops of Ismail, pushing their boats through the Second Cataract of the Nile at Wadi Halfa, entered a grudging land where civilization blossomed only under careful cultivation, where great kingdoms—Kush, Maqurra, Alwa, Funj—had flourished in their time, but where an implacable environment was ever ready to take advantage of weakness and return the land to its primeval state. The country was a vast rocky plain, broken by occasional hills and crossed by dry ravines, a virtual desert almost as far south as the confluence of the White and Blue Nile, and thereafter a savanna scrubland suitable for the support of nomadic peoples with their camels, sheep, or cattle. Gradually the terrain below the confluence became more verdant, permitting cultivation of millet, groundnuts, and garden crops on terraced hillsides and well-tended orchards, but the basic agriculture continued to be stock raising.

Through this difficult land flowed the great river, tracing a serpentine green-edged ribbon across the sandy wastes, but in no sense a highway by reason of the half dozen cataracts which obstructed travel over its thousand-mile course between Aswan and the confluence. The Egyptians were able to move their craft up the river only with difficulty, and once they occupied Sennar and subdued the Funj, a far deeper penetration into central Africa was prevented by the Sudd which was not to be breached for another eighteen years. The land they traversed was hot and dry, the rainfall like the vegetation gradually increasing southward but arriving in a seasonal fall which punctuated, but did little to relieve, the shimmering, blasting heat.

Muhammad Ali had invaded the Sudan in search of wealth, but little could be wrested from the parched land, its worn-out gold mines and sparse population. Along the Nile flood plain, in the Gezira, and on the Kordofan steppe country, simple villagers devoted themselves to a timeless round of planting and gathering, their narrow lives defined by the rains, the floods, and the droughts, their daily routine absorbed in the trudge to the fields and the primitive, unchanging techniques for working their crops, their thoughts fixed in a static pattern conditioned by an age-old bondage to the land. Needs were simple and life was close to nature—meals elementary and repetitive, crafts limited to supplying necessary tools for agriculture, clothing, or housekeeping, buildings designed to accommodate no frivolity beyond basic shelter and protection, and society organized in a rigid family hierarchy which smothered individuality and initiative.

These sedentary people were an admixture of many strains, the Arab being only the latest. Although their language and culture in most cases had become essentially Arab and their religion Islamic, their ethnic characteristics remained stoutly indigenous, the Arab blood absorbed in the dominant Sudanic type—Nubian in the north, with Negroid people, such as the Funj, predominating in the central Sudan. Among the sedentary groups along the Nile, the Danaqla were Nubian speaking, yet the closely related Ja'aliyyin occupying the river valley north of the confluence, were Arab speakers. Among the nomadic cattle keepers the evidence of Arab blood was somewhat more apparent. In the east, it is true, the Beja characteristically maintained their ethnic and cultural purity, adopting only the religion of the Arabs, but among the other pastoralists ranging both east and west of the Nile the Arab proportion was ethnically greater, a fact which, when added to the effects of a desert life, helped set off the nomads from the sedentary farmers.

Prominent among the pastoralists were the Baqqara, Arab camel herders turned cattlemen, who ranged west of the river in Kordofan and Darfur, intermarrying with the farming population to form a virile nation of stock raisers, hunters, and slavers. These hard-driving, hard-riding individualists, self-reliant but ignorant and narrow in their isolation, would in time indulge their love of booty and aversion to taxation by providing formidable support for the Mahdist revolution of the 1880's. Despite their verve, they were indolent by nature, content to idle away their time in gossip, leaving the work at camp to the women and slaves, but engaging in periodic bursts of activity, now hunting or making war with a furious recklessness, now indulging their fondness for dancing, with celebrations which sometimes lasted for two days or more.

Superimposed on the agricultural economy of the Sudan was a pattern of trade following routes which moved north from Sennar to Egypt, and west-east to connect Darfur with Suakin on the Red Sea. The routes to the north by no means followed the course of

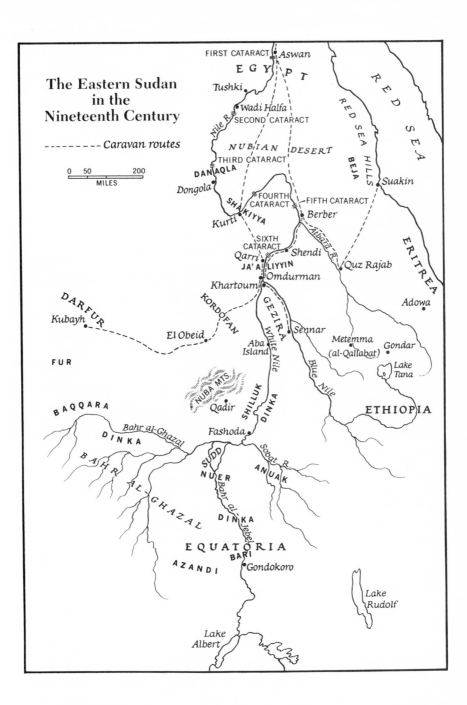

The Eastern Sudan
in the
Nineteenth Century

-------- Caravan routes

0   50   200
MILES

FIRST CATARACT • Aswan
E G Y P T
Tushki •
• Wadi Halfa
SECOND CATARACT
R E D   S E A
RED SEA HILLS
Nile R.
N U B I A N   DESERT
THIRD CATARACT
DANAQLA
BEJA
Dongola •
SHAIKIYYA
FOURTH CATARACT
FIFTH CATARACT
Kurti •
Berber •
Suakin •
SIXTH CATARACT
Atbara R.
ERITREA
Qarri •
Shendi •
JA'ALIYYIN
Quz Rajab •
Omdurman •
Khartoum •
DARFUR
KORDOFAN
GEZIRA
Kubayh •
Adowa •
FUR
El Obeid •
Sennar •
White Nile
Metemma
(al-Qallabat)
Gondar •
Aba
Island
Blue Nile
Lake
Tana
NUBA MTS.
SHILLUK
DINKA
ETHIOPIA
BAQQARA
Qadir •
DINKA
Bahr al-Ghazal
Fashoda •
B A H R
Sobat R.
A L   G H A Z A L
SUDD
NUER
ANUAK
Bahr al-Jebel
DINKA
E Q U A T O R I A
BARI
AZANDI
• Gondokoro
Lake
Rudolf
Lake
Albert

the Nile with its long stretches of rapids and its great S-shaped loop which added hundreds of miles to the journey. Instead caravans struck out overland from Qarri to Kurti or alternatively followed the river through Shendi and Berber and then took the long trek through the Nubian desert directly to Aswan. Such travel, though common, was hazardous and uncomfortable—water was dangerously scarce while the monotony of the daily round alternated inexorably between the scorching noonday heat and the intense cold of the desert night. The west-east track normally originated at Kubayh in Darfur and proceeded to El Obeid where the road turned north to Shendi, for the route directly to Sennar was threatened by the Shilluk people along the White Nile. From Shendi the caravans doubled back southeast to Quz Rajab from whence they moved northeast to Suakin on the coast.

These routes, converging on Shendi, established that river town as the prime market of the Sudan, and indeed, its stalls contained a surprising variety of goods from three continents—spices from India, steel blades from German manufactories, leather from Kordofan, Egyptian soap, Venetian glass, Ethiopian gold, and Dongola horses, among many other items—the appeal of these products being fully matched by a port town's recreational diversions designed for the taste and appetite of men who had been weeks in the desert. Other entrepôts along the river—Berber, for example—were smaller versions of Shendi with its noisy clutter, its incessant argumentation and bargaining, its polyglot population of Muslim and pagan, Negro and Arab, its prostitutes, and its "bouza" grog shops.

The chief preoccupation of these market centers was commerce in slaves, both for the internal and external trade. For the most part the recruits came from afar, from Christian Ethiopia which provided women much prized for their beauty and loyalty, and from the pagan areas southwest of Darfur. Many bondsmen remained in the Sudan as servants, field hands, or retainers, but most went on to Egypt and Arabia. It is estimated that Sennar exported some fifteen hundred slaves each year to Egypt, while Darfur produced as much as six thousand annually, mostly girls destined for domestic service or harem residence. A goodly number of these naturally found their way to the Shendi market where a young male already marked with smallpox brought fifteen dollars but where girls were worth twenty-five. Treatment of slaves seemed to vary greatly. Although normally regarded only as livestock, they were reasonably well cared for, and their ultimate fate in Egypt and Arabia not infrequently involved manumission.

The fall of the Christian kingdoms to infiltrating Arabs from Egypt during the fourteenth and fifteenth centuries was accompanied by the introduction of Islam to the Sudan, but the uniformity it supposedly imposed was illusory, for intruding Islam was obliged to adapt itself to local customs even as traditional ways bent before the impact of the new faith. Thus, as the invading Arabs intermarried with the local people and merged their racial characteristics, so universal, flexible Islam adjusted to local practices and absorbed their animist elements into its own religious system.

In one respect, however, it was local conditions which imposed their uniformity on Islam. In the Sudanese peasant a wretched poverty was matched by an absolute and superstitious ignorance. Religious practice, therefore, was characterized by emotional appeals to magic, while orthodox Islam with its system of abstract truths had little attraction. Consequently the Sudanese became highly receptive to the concept of *sufism*, in which mystical devotion to a Muslim saint, living or dead, enabled the follower of that saint to partake of his *baraka*, or God-given supernatural power, and placed that follower in closer relationship to an otherwise remote and unapproachable deity. Islam in the eastern Sudan came to be identified with saint worship and the rise of religious brotherhoods, the external index of religious devotion showing itself not as the mosque, but rather the whitewashed, domed tomb of the saint. In the western Sudan, the Fulani clerics employed *sufism* primarily as a vehicle for puritan reform. In the east it was the emotional appeal of *sufist* mysticism which captured the heart of the peasant.

EGYPT IN THE SUDAN

The Sudan was but one of many enterprises in which Muhammad Ali was interested, and it was a minor one at that. Nevertheless, since his interest was essentially in the extraction of wealth, it was imperative that the initial occupation be followed as quickly as possible by a peaceful administration designed to restore some prosperity to the wounded land. Beginning in 1825 a series of able administrators bent their energies to that end. The first of these, Mahu Bey Urfali, ruled only one year, yet in that short time he set the tone of government which was followed by his successor, Ali Khurshid and Ahmad Abu Widan, who between them governed the Sudanese provinces until 1843.

Mahu's policy was based on reason, and reason dictated that the prostrate, frightened land be wooed by conciliation. To induce the people back from their refuge in the Abyssinian foothills, he promised a three-year tax holiday, imposed a tight rein on his army, sent food into the stricken Gezira, and took the shrewd if unexpected step of consulting Sudanese notables concerning his plans. Khurshid elaborated and enlarged on this beginning. On Mahu's recommendation he employed a local *shaikh*, Abd al-Qadir, as adviser, and Qadir was helpful in urging his people back to their fields, and later prevented a serious policy error when he persuaded the Egyptians to drop their plans for the forced military conscription of Sudanese freemen.

Khurshid's ultimate objective was a stable body of cultivators and pastoralists engaged in an expanding productivity which would serve as the basis for Egyptian taxation. That his administration was smiled upon in Cairo is attested to in the responsibilities and honors bestowed on him by Muhammad Ali. Beginning with Sennar province, he gradually was given control of Berber, Kordofan, and Dongola —all ruled from his capital at Khartoum. Throughout his domains a concerted effort was made to follow Muhammad Ali's bidding that the Sudan pay for itself, but since money was scarce, the payment of taxes was often difficult and the process of collection a grim business. There were taxes on land and taxes on livestock, taxes on water wheels and custom duties on exports and imports. In Dongola, where Egyptian administration meant protection from Shakiyya raiders, collection was usually no great problem, but in the south Khurshid devoted much effort to attracting fugitives back to their lands and was obliged to exempt numerous chiefs from assessment in return for their cooperation in leading the exiles home. Tax gathering was usually accomplished through the use of Shakiyya irregulars supplemented occasionally by Egyptian cavalry, but in lean years even payments in kind were a great hardship; in 1835, the Sudanese pastoralists were obliged to part with their slaves in lieu of the usual levy in cattle.

The Egyptians were by no means content to tax the inefficient peasant as they had found him, but sought rather through a wide range of developmental schemes to improve the productivity of the land—to apply, in short, the Egyptian concept of modernization to this Egyptian colony. Agriculture, the basis of the economy, was fostered in a number of ways. Skilled workers were sent specifically to grow opium, indigo, and cotton, while more generally experienced Egyptian farmers and artisans were requisitioned from all Egyptian provinces on orders from Muhammad Ali himself. Irrigation was undertaken, Egyptian bullock-driven water wheels introduced, and improved pest control taught to the Sudanese. Many new crops were tried, and since their choice was often based on faulty information, most failed; for example, coffee, which was unsuited to the hot plains; silk because the mulberry seed would not grow in the Sudan; and wool when the Sudanese sheep could not be made to produce even a minimum quality for weaving. Some experiments were more successful, however. Indigo became a major crop; sugar cane, though unpopular with the Sudanese farmers, showed profit; while various types of fruit made good headway.

On the whole these were but minor additions to the two basic agricultural products of the Sudan—cattle and gum arabic—in which the northerners were interested. Draft animals for Egyptian farms and factories were cheap and abundant in the south, and demands were constantly coming from Cairo for new shipments which had to be kept within reasonable limits to forestall renewed emigration back to the wilderness. Since gum, which came from the widespread acacia and was used in the manufacture of paper and confectionery, presented no such problems, this Egyptian state monopoly proved most profitable over the years. The acacia was also widely used in boat building, but its utility was not unlimited. When Muhammad Ali asked for samples suitable for rifle butts, it was found that nine hours and forty minutes were necessary to saw through one piece, the arsenal report concluding solemnly, "This shows that . . . this wood is indeed very hard."

Despite Egyptian exertions, the struggle for economic development in the Sudan came to very little. While military governors generally made poor production managers, the Sudanese peasant clung tenaciously to his traditional techniques of cultivation, successfully withstanding the efforts of the Egyptian experts to convert him to the ways of scientific agriculture. Many schemes, moreover, were illusory; witness Muhammad Ali's lifelong search for gold supplies long ago exhausted, or the fruitless attempts to develop iron mining in Kordofan. Beyond this, as the pasha grew older, his energies flagged and his alertness was blunted with the result that a vacillating policy in Cairo soon enfeebled the administration in the Sudan. The death of Abu Widan in 1843 inaugurated a period during which no fewer than eleven administrators sat in Khartoum over twenty years. In 1848 Muhammad Ali died but this brought no relief for he was succeeded, first by Abbas I (1848–1854) under whose indifferent administration the Sudan atrophied, and then by Muhammad Said (1854–1863) whose capricious, lethargic nature perpetuated the drift which had set in during the last years of Muhammad Ali. Nevertheless, it was these unproductive years that witnessed an event of great importance in the history of the Sudan —the breaching of the Sudd and the penetration along the Bahr al-Ghazal and the upper Nile.

THE SOUTHERN SUDAN AND THE SLAVE TRADE

The prime motive for Muhammad Ali's initial penetration of the Sudan was his desire for slaves to fill the ranks of the Egyptian army. He was soon disillusioned as to the utility of black troops outside their native land, but since the Egyptians and Turks fared ill in the south, these slave regiments, called *jihadiyya*, or regular soldiers, came in time to be the major support for the Egyptian administration in the Sudan. The harvesting of slaves, therefore, continued to be a major activity of the governors at Khartoum who organized armed raids annually into the Nuba hills in Kordofan, the mountains of western Ethiopia, or among the Dinka and Shilluk people living along the White Nile. Success was far from automatic, for local resistance was stubborn and resourceful; yet when Muhammad Ali dispatched an expedition in 1839 to explore the upper reaches of the White Nile, it was not a further search for slaves but curiosity over the river's source and the lure of gold which provided the initial impulse. The immediate consequence was the adventitious rise of an ivory trade, at first largely conducted by Europeans, and it was only later that large scale slaving came to dominate the relations of upper and lower Sudan.

The Nile expedition, first of three led by a Turkish naval officer, Salim Qapudan, failed to discover the Bahr al-Ghazal channel to the west, but managed to find its way southward through the swampy maze of the Sudd, pushing up river as far as the future site of

Gondokoro. The initial reaction was disappointing, for Muhammad Ali's El Dorado still eluded him, but soon certain compensating factors became apparent. Great quantities of ivory were found to be available almost for the asking, while the local people, screened off until this moment from external influences, were an immediate attraction to European missionaries. Herein lay the seeds of future discord, hatred, and contempt. The intruders from the north, eager to exploit the area and possessing the technical superiority to do so, were at first totally ignorant of local custom and then learned to profit from its weaknesses. The indigenous people, fixed in their traditional ways and indifferent to the potentialities of change, fell victim to the invaders who used them and eventually enslaved them. The possibilities for progress were great, but human frailty led instead to human tragedy.

Through circumstance and habit, the local residents were peculiarly vulnerable, for their isolation had been complete and long-lived. To the east lay the Ethiopian highlands while the north and west were shut off by the Nuba hills and the swamps of the Bahr al-Ghazal watershed. On the south lay more mountainous country and the impenetrable equatorial forest. Hemmed in by these barriers a vast plain sprawled across the map, intersected by sluggish rivers, parched and bare during the dry season, flooded and covered with high grass during the rains, and capable of sustaining a scattered population only at a minimum level of subsistence.

Within this remote, barren, and cheerless land dwelt peoples with a splendid sense of isolation and a sublime self-confidence, but their isolation had shielded them from developments around them, particularly technological advances, and their self-confidence was that of individualism rather than of unity. Most were Nilotes—Luo speakers who had spread north from the Bahr al-Ghazal to form the farming and pastoral communities of the Shilluk and Anuak people along the White Nile and the Sobat rivers, Nuer and Dinka, tall slim-hipped pastoralists spread widely through the Sudd and White Nile regions, or the more sedentary Bari located in the neighborhood of Gondokoro. Whatever their origins or occupation, these people all shared an aversion for organized government and lived instead in small mutually antagonistic social units, the pastoralists indulging in a kind of organized feud in which cattle raiding played a basic role. In the western part of this area were Sudanic-speaking groups who had migrated from the Lake Chad-Chari River area, as well as

Negroes from the southwest, all of whom were sedentary farmers but none save the Azande people any more friendly to strong leadership or united effort than their Nilote neighbors.

These were the people encountered as Salim led his first expedition up the Nile, and in its initial stages the confrontation was encouraging. The Shilluk, who knew the northerners, were not especially cordial and there were some early misunderstandings with the Nuer and Dinka, but on the whole the travelers were received by the wonder-struck inhabitants as nothing less than messengers from the gods. In the Bari country, the people were not only friendly but culturally more developed, and quickly produced quantities of cattle and ivory which they agreed to exchange for beads.

Gradually the bloom of cordiality faded in the face of growing familiarity. European traders soon appeared, drawn by the reports of ivory along the Bahr al-Jebel, or upper White Nile, but in time they were challenged increasingly by Arab merchants from the Sudan and Darfur. As the competition increased, the available supplies of ivory were exhausted, necessitating the organization of elephant hunts and the establishment of permanent colonies which relied on the local people for subsistence. Suspicion and hostility soon prevailed. The southerners could not accommodate the newcomers within their traditional systems of land holding and communal assistance—what the one regarded as a necessary sharing of the meager fruits of the land the other saw as dishonesty and avarice. By the 1860's the trade had come under the control of the Arabs who looked on the local people as savages, called them *abid*, or slave, and resorted increasingly to superior force to resolve disputes. The local people responded with a rising truculence born of fear and uncertainty, and unaccustomed to solidarity in the face of adversity, they were easily divided and exploited, their helplessness merely intensifying the scorn and impatience of those who had come to make profit from the land.

For a time the traders were held off by the southerners, pinned down to river posts, and prevented from penetrating the interior in a widening quest for fresh supplies of ivory. By the 1850's, however, the wars between tribal sections which had initially complicated the search for ivory were being turned to the traders' advantage. Rivalries were encouraged and alliances formed with different groups eager to enlist the military assistance of the outsiders. Soon the trading post had become the sole point of stability in a sea of chaos, and its master the most powerful authority in his district.

The process was simple and effective. Raiding among the divided inhabitants, the armed bands employed by the traders captured supplies of cattle which were exchanged for ivory and the service of porters. In the process prisoners were taken and used in lieu of money to pay the wages of the armed retainers. Thus a commerce in slaves soon developed as a by-product of the ivory trade for a single slave was worth three months pay. For their part, the traders found it increasingly profitable to engage directly in slaving as they probed ever deeper into the virgin country away from the river.

In the Bahr al-Ghazal watershed, the trading camps developed into formidable strongholds, called *zeribas*, which were provisioned by the local people in return for a military support that soon reduced them to a state of vassalage. Here the slave trade was far more extensive than along the upper Nile, and the many slaves brought in by raiding parties were quickly bought up by numerous itinerant Danaqla and Ja'aliyyin traders, called *jallaba*, who swarmed down from Kordofan by the thousand, each to purchase a few slaves for eventual sale in North Africa. Superior armament usually spelled success for the raiders but occasionally they were badly defeated, particularly by the Dinka who had long experience in the thrust and parry of cattle raiding. In time one of the most powerful of the *zeriba* chiefs came to be al-Zubair Rahma Mansur who built a commercial empire based on the slave trade and ultimately became so powerful that the government in Cairo, despairing of controlling Zubair, appointed him instead as governor of a Bahr al-Ghazal province it in fact did not control.

BACKDROP TO THE MAHDI

In 1863 Ismail Pasha became viceroy of Egypt, an event which should have recalled the progressive days of Muhammad Ali, but instead led to the eventual loss both of Egypt's independence and her conquests in the Sudan. Ismail's troubles stemmed as much from personal shortcomings as from circumstance. He was intelligent, charming, energetic, and sympathetic to the process of modernization begun by his distinguished predecessor, but he was also impulsive and capricious in decision and totally bereft of judgment in financial matters. He introduced many public improvements but rarely saw them through to completion, while his efforts at national development eventually bankrupted the economy and opened the way to European intervention in support of his foreign creditors. Under Ismail, the Egyptian empire extended itself far into Africa, but ill-advised campaigns in Ethiopia in 1875–1876 destroyed the effectiveness of the army, rendering it incapable of providing the empire with adequate protection when the moment of crisis arrived.

It was during the years of Ismail's rule that the ground was prepared for the Mahdist revolution in the Sudan, and in this respect the Egyptian government's policy toward the slave trade was fundamental. Ismail's pro-Western orientation led him to favor abolition of the slave trade, but the inauguration of such a policy had profound ramifications in the Sudan. There, economic orthodoxy strongly supported by religious sanction had elevated slavery to the level of a natural law and established the slave trade as an honorable occupation. More specifically, two powerful groups were challenged—the Danaqla merchants who controlled the trade on the upper Nile, and the *zeriba* chiefs and their *jallaba* middlemen in the Bahr al-Ghazal.

Initial efforts at control were ineffectual, but in 1869 Ismail engaged the British explorer, Samuel Baker, to extend effective Egyptian rule along the Bahr al-Jebel, and four years later appointed Charles George Gordon to succeed Baker as the governor of the recently constituted upper Nile province of Equatoria, raising him to the position of governor-general of the Sudan in 1877. Baker was not a happy choice for his heavy-handed methods not only antagonized Muslim slavers resentful over restrictions imposed by a European Christian, but succeeded even in alienating the southerners he was charged with protecting when he seized their cattle for food.

Gordon's administration of Equatoria was somewhat more accommodating, but as governor-general his first duty was to put an end to the slave trade in all areas, and by 1879, when Ismail was deposed, he had made substantial progress in that direction. In Equatoria he declared the ivory trade a government monopoly and forbad the formation of private armies, thus compelling many of the merchants to retire from business. In the Bahr al-Ghazal, where Zubair had already been eliminated, his son and successor, Sulaiman, and the other slavers were crushed after a hard campaign and their *zeribas* destroyed.

Such progress came at a price. The Bahr al-Ghazal lay devastated, its inhabitants scattered, and the *jallaba* driven into Kordofan and Darfur where they bided their time in sullen resentment over the loss of their goods and means of livelihood. Along the White Nile the commercial hegemony of the Danaqla was under increasing pressure from an apparently malign Egyptian administration directed by European unbelievers. Beyond this, the Egyptian government was in full decline supported by an army which had lost its authority as a fighting force. By the time of Ismail's fall from power a potentially explosive situation had developed in the Sudan.

THE MAHDIST REVOLUTION

On June 29, 1881, the Mahdi declared himself and shortly thereafter performed the *hijra* from the land of the infidels to his refuge at Qadir in the Nuba hills of southern Kordofan.

Before that moment he had been Muhammad Ahmad, a Muslim ascetic, who was born a Danaqla in 1844 and who early showed preference for a life of religious study over the traditional boat building trade of his family. Like so many Sudanese, Muhammad Ahmad's religious interests led not to the formalized Islam taught at al-Azhar in Cairo, but to the mysticism of a *sufist* brotherhood, and in 1861 he joined such an order, the Sammaniyya, when he was only seventeen years old. In the years that followed he gained a reputation for extreme piety and humility to the extent that when he went to live at Aba Island on the White Nile in 1870, he soon gained a large following among the local people attracted by his asceticism. His puritanical leanings were so pronounced that they caused Muhammad Ahmad eventually to break with his *shaikh*, Muhammad Sharif, and ally himself with another leader of the Sammaniyya order, a man presumably of less worldly nature but in any event of such an advanced age as to be susceptible to an early succession. When the old man died in 1880, Muhammad Ahmad became the acknowledged leader of his group—the possessor of a powerful *baraka*, or supernatural power, and an individual of proven piety whose growing appeal was especially strong among the people of Kordofan.

In a general sense, the Mahdist revolution in the eastern Sudan was a manifestation of the broad wave of spiritual unrest which swept the Muslim world during the late eighteenth and nineteenth centuries and resulted in such movements as the puritan, revivalist Wahabiyya in Arabia and the *jihads* of the West African Sudan. More particularly, it was a response of the people of the eastern Sudan, mired in their poverty and born into discontent, to gain some counterpoise to their misery and sense of frustration. Already fervent advocates of mystical *sufism*, they also subscribed to the doctrine of a Second Coming. Though such a belief varied throughout the Muslim world, in the Sudan it took the form of Mahdism whereby in the last hours of the world, a Mahdi or God-guided one would come to confirm the faith and proclaim justice. He would then fall before the Dajjal or Anti-Christ who in turn would be destroyed by Christ the Prophet as the world ended in the triumph of the true faith.

At the moment that Muhammad Ahmad became a leader of the Sammaniyya, there was a rising Mahdist expectation in the land, reflecting specific dissatisfaction with the lax morality and worldliness of Egyptian administrators as well as a more generalized sense of despair over the lot of mankind. It was not unnatural, therefore, that the new leader, with his reputation for extreme piety and his constant call for the renunciation of worldly vanity, was soon being regarded by some as the expected Mahdi. His own followers began saying that the Mahdi would come from among them, while one in particular, a new adherent from the Baqqara nomads of Darfur named Abdallahi ibn Muhammad, claimed to recognize Muhammad Ahmad as the Mahdi.

Doubtless these intimations influenced Muhammad Ahmad, but his own nature, rooted in emotional puritanism, required an inner conviction of divine calling, even as the movement he was to lead needed the genuine impulse of messianic expectations which could never have been transmitted by a counterfeit. In time such conviction came in a series of visions which Muhammad Ahmad was at pains to point out were revealed to him while he was in a state of wakeful good health. The secret was first communicated to his disciples; then after a trip to Kordofan to test popular opinion and settle on a place of refuge, the historic announcement was made, and Muhammad al-Mahdi called on his adherents to rally to his person.

The remove to Qadir was consciously patterned in parallel to the flight of the Prophet from Mecca to Medina, and at Qadir the forces of the Mahdi steadily grew, partly in response to the appeal of his religious message, partly because of economic and political discontent, and partly because of the success of his arms against ineffectual Egyptian efforts to bring him to terms. Within a year he had won several important victories, gathered large quantities of war booty, and increased the number of his adherents from the few hundred who had assisted his departure from Aba to many thousand. Broadly these *ansar*, so called after the helpers of the Prophet Muhammad at Medina, fell into three categories. There was the growing body of disciples who came to the Mahdi out of religious conviction, persuaded of the need for reform leading to a new theocratic state. There were, moreover, the many Danaqla, Ja'aliyyin, and other disaffected traders and their mercenaries—particularly the *jallaba* sulking in Darfur and Kordofan—who saw in the Mahdi a means to regain their former economic and political ascendancy. Finally, there were the Baqqara pastoralists who had suffered at Egyptian hands, first in the person of Zubair who conquered their Darfur homeland in 1874 and then through the subsequent Egyptian administration which sought to impose onerous and unfamiliar taxation. In time another important element was added to his forces—black *jihadiyya*, professional soldiers captured in battle who served their new master as faithfully as they had the Egyptians. These troops greatly strengthed the Mahdi's forces through their use of firearms which were expressly denied the *ansar* as a violation of the prophet's injunction concerning weaponry.

By the summer of 1882 the Mahdi had shifted from the defensive phase of *hijra* to the militant offensive of *jihad*, and there was much to commend this change. The government forces were plagued by bad leadership, difficult communications, and the confusion in Egypt caused by the Urabist army uprising of 1881–1882. Their line troops, moreover, had no heart for a fight in opposition to a holy war which compelled the support of all Muslims. The Mahdi, on the other hand, was campaigning on home ground amidst friendly people caught up in the emotional surge of his cause. His guerrilla tactics were ideally suited to the capabilities of his own forces—ill-equipped but zealous levies from the local people who could move quickly, live off the land, harass marching columns, and bottle up the Egyptians in the towns to be cut off and starved out at leisure. In January, 1883, El Obeid, the provincial capital of Kordofan, surrendered after a difficult siege, thus bringing a vast increase in wealth, power, and territory to the Mahdist cause.

The fall of El Obeid greatly raised the Mahdi's prestige but more impressive still was the annihilation in November, 1883, of the expeditionary force sent south under the command of a British soldier, William Hicks, for the purpose of regaining Kordofan. This last vain effort by a failing Egyptian government to reassert its rule in the Sudan persuaded waverers that the northerners were finished. The following month the province of Darfur capitulated and in April, 1884 Bahr al-Ghazal came over. Meanwhile the Beja had been persuaded to join the Mahdist cause bringing with them the Red Sea hill area, save only the port city of Suakin. By early 1884 it was clear that the Mahdi must prevail throughout the Sudan unless decisive action were taken, action which was beyond both the resources of the Egyptian regime and the determination of the British who had occupied Egypt during the summer of 1882 at the time of the Urabist revolt.

The final scenes of the Mahdist triumph, which took place at Khartoum early in 1885, involved the British more than the Egyptians: British governmental confusion, the force of British public opinion, and the activities of the energetic but unpredictable Gordon who had returned to the Sudan in February, 1884 as governor-general. Gordon's instructions called for him only to explore means for evacuating the Egyptians in the Sudan, for the British were not willing to become involved in the interior and had committed troops solely for the protection of the Red Sea port of Suakin. Gordon, however, regarded his function as more executive than advisory and his erratic actions precipitated a crisis. First, he mistakenly announced a policy of evacuation, thus convincing waverers in the Sudan of Egyptian weakness. Then, after the Mahdi had rejected an offer of cooperation, Gordon proclaimed his intention to establish a strong government and defeat the Mahdi, presumably with the aid of troops Britain was not prepared to provide. Remaining stubbornly in Khartoum, the governor-general was cut off as the sedentary people along the river north of Khartoum at last rose to join the Mahdi. In May, Berber was taken and the Mahdi's forces closed in on the doomed city. Pressed by public opinion at home, the British government finally organized a relief expedition which made its way south as the Mahdist army massed for attack. The British reached the Khartoum area on January 28, 1885, but it was already too late. Two days earlier the defenses had been breached, the garrison overwhelmed, the city taken, and Gordon slain despite the Mahdi's orders that he be taken alive.

EPILOGUE: THE *KHALIFA* ABDALLAHI

With the fall of Khartoum the initial objective of the Mahdi had been achieved as most of the Muslim Sudan came under his control. At this point, however, facing the problems of consolidation and the further extension of his *jihad,* he died suddenly in June, 1885, and a completely new phase of the Mahdist movement now unfolded. There was, first of all, a short power struggle which culminated in the accession of the *Khalifa* Abdallahi as the Mahdi's successor. Abdallahi was the same Baqqara adherent who had first recognized the Mahdi, and who had subsequently risen to prominence in the movement. His position as commander of the powerful Baqqara forces in the Mahdist army was decisive in bringing about his election, but it also indicated potential divisions among the Mahdist leadership which occupied the attention of the *Khalifa* immediately upon his assumption of power.

The chief division lay between the Baqqara nomads and the Danaqla and Ja'aliyyin river people, including the Mahdi's own kinsmen known as the *Ashraf.* Abdallahi met this problem with characteristic resourcefulness. He gradually circumscribed the power of the *Ashraf* by political and military means, finally eliminating them in the course of suppressing an abortive conspiracy in 1891. At the same time he attempted with varying success to tame his unruly Baqqara kinsmen by forcing them to migrate to the region of his capital at Omdurman on the Nile where he could more successfully keep their refractory tendencies under control. By 1891 his authority over the land had become firmly established, but in the process the ideal of a Muslim theocracy governed according to the Muslim law of the *Shari'a* had been converted into a conventional secular autocracy.

In defending his frontiers, the *Khalifa* was much less successful, although at first his affairs went reasonably well. A drawn-out war with Ethiopia between 1887 and 1889 ended in the defeat of Ethiopia and the death of her King Yohannes, while in 1887 an attempt to re-establish an independent sultanate in Darfur was crushed. Less fruitful was the effort to carry the *jihad* into Egypt, a move which ended disastrously at Tushki above Wadi Halfa in 1889. Indeed, this was a portentous defeat for it demonstrated a Western military superiority which, when later combined with growing Western interest in the African interior, was to culminate in the downfall of the *Khalifa's* Sudan as an independent African nation.

The final days of the Mahdist state were a reflection more of forces in Europe than in Africa. In the early 1890's the Belgians in Leopold's Congo began to probe the Congo-Nile watershed, and in 1895 the French decided to send an expedition into the Bahr al-Ghazal. The following year the British suddenly moved south from Egypt, presumably to protect the Italians in Eritrea from a Mahdist attack after their defeat at Adowa by the Ethiopians in March, 1896. A series of engagements followed in which the defenders were successively driven back to Omdurman and there, just north of the city on September 1, 1898, they suffered the final blow which put an end to the Mahdist regime in the Sudan. The *Khalifa* survived for another year before he and his shattered forces were finally destroyed, but by that time his conqueror, General H. H. Kitchener, had moved on to confront the French at Fashoda and another era had opened in the varied fortunes of the eastern Sudan.

Suggestions for Further Reading

Standard histories covering the nineteenth-century Sudan are P. M. Holt, *A Modern History of the Sudan,* 2nd ed. (London: Weidenfeld and Nicolson, 1963; New York: Praeger, 1963); and K. D. Henderson, *Sudan Republic* (London: Ernest Benn, 1965; New York: Praeger, 1965). Vivid accounts are to be found in Alan Moorehead, *The White Nile* (London: Hamish Hamilton, 1960; New York: Harper, 1961) and *The Blue Nile* (London: Hamish Hamilton, 1962; New York: Harper, 1962).

The Egyptian occupation is examined in Richard Hill, *Egypt in the Sudan, 1820–1881* (London: Oxford University Press, 1959); while the southern Sudan is dealt with in Richard Gray, *A History of the Southern Sudan, 1839–1889* (London: Oxford University Press, 1961). See also Robert Collins, *The Southern Sudan, 1883–1898* (New Haven: Yale University Press, 1962). Information on customs and traditions among some of the people of the southern Sudan is available in the writings of E. E. Evans-Pritchard and others but most briefly in M. Fortes and E. E. Evans-Pritchard, eds., *African Political Systems* (London: Oxford University Press, 1940); Daryll Forde, ed., *African Worlds* (London: Oxford University Press, 1954); and Lucy Mair, *Primitive Government* (Baltimore: Penguin, 1962).

The standard work on the Mahdist state is P. M. Holt, *The Mahdist State in the Sudan* (Oxford: Clarendon Press, 1958), and this should be supplemented with J. S. Trimingham's valuable *Islam in the Sudan* (London: Frank Cass, 1965; New York: Barnes & Noble, 1965).

11: Population Explosions
in Southern Africa

MFECANE—THE ROAD FROM ZULULAND

Shaka Zulu is properly regarded as one of the great revolutionary figures in Africa's history. Like Philip of Macedon, he introduced changes in war making that spawned empires and altered the face of his world; yet he was as much the creature as the master of the events he precipitated.

The vast migration of the Bantu people, spilling over sub-equatorial Africa in the centuries after Christ, had crossed the Limpopo River before the opening of the fourteenth century and by 1800 its Xhosa vanguard was established far down the eastern coast near the bottom of the African continent. The shape of the land determined the nature and extent of this population movement. To the east between the coast and the Drakensberg Mountains lay a fertile valley attractive to a pastoral people who could grow corn and millet to supplement their essential stock-raising economy. By the end of the eighteenth century, these Nguni-speaking sections of the Bantu had reached the Fish River and were in contact with those other pastoralists—the *trekboers* moving eastward from the Cape Colony. Farther to the west, the Sotho speakers had fanned out broadly across the plateau below the Limpopo, those to the east penetrating almost to the Orange River while further west the Tswana, pressed against the inhospitable Kalahari Desert, were more limited in their southward movement. Finally, on the western side of southern Africa lay the Kalahari itself and adjacent arid steppes, a last refuge of the Bushman and Hottentot and a formidable barrier which held the Bantu advance well to the north.

If geography affected the rate of penetration of these colonists, it also helped to shape their daily lives—placing its mark on political institutions, social customs, and economic practice. The South African plateau was ideally suited to their pastoral existence, but it was in its political manifestation that the adaptation to the land was best exemplified. A slow migration by cattle keepers was most efficiently carried out by small independent groups each organized around a royal clan, an arrangement which allowed a working balance between social cohesion and individual expression. Warfare was a small-scale affair involving either grazing rights and cattle, or defense against Hottentot and Bushman raids. There was no need for excessive political centralization. Along the eastern corridor families and settlements were scattered across the well-watered land. Inland on the dry veld, a greater concentration was called for around the few available waterholes, but even here the authority of chiefs was limited by a popular assembly and a system of advisory councils, and everywhere chiefly power was forced to bow to the superior authority of public opinion.

Such an arrangement, centralized in conception but loosely administered in practice, readily led to political division as a solution for disputes arising from problems of royal succession and arbitrary rule or conflicts over land rights. Indeed, this had been the essential process of the Bantu dispersion—population growth bringing on social and political stresses which in turn were the basis for emigration and a new buildup of population. The system worked as long as there was free land for expansion, but there was bound to be trouble when the pressure of a rising birth rate could no longer be safely drawn off through migration and a fresh wave of colonization.

It was precisely this form of pressure which seems to have been developing, particularly among the Nguni speakers toward the end of the eighteenth century. A fertile, disease-free country permitted an uninhibited natural increase which within the confines of the narrow coastal shelf brought population densities that could not long be endured by a pastoral society in need of ample grazing grounds. As land became scarce, the nature of warfare changed from a quasi-recreational pastime to a serious struggle for survival, necessitating the institution of a much more rigorously controlled politico-military system. Large-scale, strongly armed political configurations were called for and emerged. In the northern Drakensberg corridor of Zululand appeared three federations under strong leaders—the Ngwane under Sobhuza, the Ndwandwe of Zwide, and the Mthethwa led by Dingiswayo.

Political change necessarily led to social change, but most significant of all was a thoroughgoing revolution in military tactics which profoundly altered the shape of traditional society even as it sought to subserve changing political needs. First to go was the age-old custom of puberty rites involving circumcision, and consequent seclusion and vulnerability of fighting youth over protracted periods. Henceforth, proclaimed Dingiswayo—for it was the Mthethwa who perhaps first instituted the change—young men would be organized into military regiments based on age grades, and the achievement of their manhood would be accomplished on the field of battle, where it could be as effectively demonstrated as it was urgently needed. The new regimental organization soon became widely utilized, for it provided not only greater military efficiency but created a unitary, nationalized army which transcended parochial loyalties and converted the somewhat hypothetical powers of the chief into something more real.

Dingiswayo, however, lacked the ruthlessness and imaginative turn of mind necessary to carry these innovations to their logical conclusion, and it remained for his successor, Shaka, to respond to the demands of the changing times. Here was an outstanding military talent driven by consuming ambition and controlled by a pitiless, unbending, and cruel nature. Born out of wedlock, the unwanted son of the chief of the Zulus, Shaka in maturity became physically powerful but psychically crippled by the need to compensate through recognized achievement as a man for the years of ridicule and humiliation endured as a result of his clouded origins. His military prowess soon brought the favor of Dingiswayo who assisted Shaka, despite his disqualifications, to succeed his father as chief of the Zulus, then an insignificant people within the Mthethwa hegemony.

Once in control, Shaka moved swiftly and surely, putting into effect plans which had been long maturing. The traditional warfare of his day had been a casual business conducted by spear-throwing warriors who advanced in loose formation, hurling first invective and then their weapons, retiring when disarmed to fight another day. Little permanent damage was done by these war games which were designed, not for slaughter but for cattle raiding. Shaka's innovations were shattering. In place of a handful of light spears, he provided his troops with a short heavy stabbing *assegai*, or spear, which was used as a sword at close quarters and discarded in battle only on pain of death. The Zulu regiments were thoroughly trained and disciplined to fight en masse by direction, never as individuals. They adopted and refined the "cow horn" formation, somewhat reminiscent of the Macedonian phalanx, which employed a massive center with swift enveloping wings capable of attacking a flank and engulfing the enemy rear in a pincer movement. The close-formation advance behind a wall of giant cowhide shields was adequate protection against thrown weapons; then at close quarters, the heavy stabbing *assegai* came into murderous play, combining with the iron discipline and coordinated tactics to spread dismay and disaster among the enemy. Precision and discipline were provided by constant drilling, for Shaka placed his army on a permanent war footing, segregating his troops in training camps where they practiced and perfected their skills all the year round. Total warfare was the essence of Shaka's military reforms, and none less well prepared could stand before his attack.

What followed changed the face of southern and central Africa. By the time Shaka became chief of the Zulu, the Ndwandwe had routed Sobhuza's forces which retired northward and eventually established themselves as the Swazi nation. Then, about 1818, the victorious Ndwandwe under Zwide met Dingiswayo's Mthethwa in a climactic battle during which the Mthethwa were routed and Dingiswayo killed. Whether by design or accident, Shaka and his Zulus took no part in the fighting, but whatever the circumstances, Shaka thenceforward stood unrestrained by obligation to any overlord, free to work for his own cause and to put his new ideas and military strength to the test. Thus began the *Mfecane*—the crushing.

Shaka added the remnants of the Mthethwa to his Zulu forces, then stood off the Ndwandwe hordes in the pivotal battle of Gqokoli Hill, his tactics and the discipline of his troops succeeding brilliantly against heavily superior numbers. Another engagement followed in which the Ndwandwe were routed and split, their power shattered, leaving Shaka master of Zululand. Zwide and a small contingent survived to renew the dispute with Shaka another day, but two other groups under Soshangane and Zwangendaba, abandoned their lands to the victors, moving northward eventually to place their mark on the territories lying beyond the Limpopo.

Shaka's significance lies less in his career subsequent to this point than it does in the type of state he was able to develop as well as in the widening ramifications which the *Mfecane* had throughout southern and central Africa. Initially, the Zulu nation had been tiny, but with the fall, first of the Mthethwa and then the Ndwandwe, it grew rapidly by accretion, and as a result of subsequent campaigns, many additional tribes and their territory were grafted on to the rapidly expanding Zulu state. The traditional pattern of Nguni society made this process easy, for each tribal unit was already organized along territorial lines with loyalties in terms of the chief, not the lineage, and tribes had long contained people from many different unrelated clans. What Shaka did was greatly to accelerate this process through military conquest, insuring allegiance to the center by controlling and limiting the authority of territorial sub-chiefs, and ruling through his military *indunas,* the common-born leaders of his regiments.

Shaka's major political innovation, however, was the establishment of military barracks on the king's domain, which did much more than create an irresistible fighting machine: it brought together youth from all parts of the land and bound them together irrevocably in a common age grouping and a mutually shared mortal danger. All were dependent upon the king for their livelihood, all viewed him as the focal point of personal loyalty, all were imbued with a sense of Zulu nationalism which would stay with them for the rest of their days. Under Shaka, therefore, the Nguni state system with its centralization in embryo became a highly integrated political unity containing a thoroughgoing cultural assimilation, and herein lay the basis for a latter-day Zulu national cohesiveness and pride.

Shaka's whole system was built on force, and this was both his strength and his weakness. The purpose of the state was the formation of a strong military establishment, and the purpose of this in turn was political aggrandizement. Year after year, the Zulu armies went forth to battle, and soon the territory between the Tugela River north toward Delagoa Bay was Zulu, while south of the river Natal lay devastated and Pondoland was under continuing pressure. In 1826 the remnants of the Ndwandwe were annihilated in a final battle, and several smaller groups were absorbed. By 1828, plans were maturing for a major push to the south against the people between Natal and the Cape Colony frontier. Not only would this put all of the Nguni under Zulu control but it would bring contact with the Europeans and access to their trade goods and military knowledge. A decade of warfare had taken its toll, however. Even the most sanguine were tired of unrelieved campaigning and bloodletting; even the most savage spirits were shaken by Shaka's remorseless brutality. While the armies were far from home on campaign, an assassination plot was conceived and Shaka was cut down by his brother, Dingane, much to the relief of friend and foe alike. Shaka's career had lasted a brief ten years but in that short span a whole new nation and way of life had come into being; more than that, the ramifications of his conquests would carry on long after his death and far beyond the limited frontiers of Zululand.

Dingane became the new Zulu king and, despite the wave of reaction which raised him to power, he soon resumed the militarist policies of the great conqueror. Dingane's problems, however, were to originate in another quarter. A colony of British merchants and missionaries had for some years been gathering at Port Natal, which became a natural rallying point for Zulu dissidents as well as a potential colony of the Cape government. More serious still, the Boer cattlemen of the Great Trek, singling out Natal as an ultimate destination, had defeated the Zulus in 1838 and forced Dingane to evacuate all territory below the Tugela River. From that point forward the European influence slowly overwhelmed the Zulu state. The withdrawal north across the Tugela so undermined Dingane's prestige that he was unseated in 1840 by his brother, Mpande, who thenceforward carried on a conciliatory policy toward the Boers. Finally, during the 1870's, the Zulus unwittingly became an issue between the British and the Boers, which ultimately led to the defeat of Cetewayo, Mpande's successor, in 1879. Thus ended, for practical purposes, the independent Zulu nation.

CENTRAL AFRICA AND THE GREAT NGONI TREK

Long before the final demise of the Zulu kingdom, the effects of the *Mfecane* were being experienced over a range of a thousand miles to the north, as far as the region of the great lakes of Nyasa and Tanganyika. The violent defeat of the Ndwandwe by Shaka caused the movement of a number of people, including two sections of Zwide's defeated force, destined to play an important role in the subsequent history of central Africa. One of these groups under Soshangane came to rest near Delagoa Bay during the 1820's, then moved inland where it came into conflict with the other fugitives led by Zwangendaba. Ousting his rival who was sent reeling westward, Soshangane created the Gaza empire which imposed its rule from the Zambezi to the Limpopo and reduced the Portuguese trading settlements in Mozambique to tributary status. In time, however, the Gaza state came under increasing pressure from European imperial interests, and in 1895 it was finally incorporated into Portugal's African holdings.

The fate of the defeated followers of Zwangendaba was of more epic proportions—first, a long series of great victories and bitter defeats experienced in the process of a monumental migration which lasted a full generation and covered a march of a thousand miles and more; then, the establishment of major kingdoms comprising many diverse peoples, all in a world far removed from their original home in northern Zululand.

Such great achievements had modest beginnings. Zwangendaba's Jere people were but a minor group torn loose from their lands by the force of the *Mfecane*. Fleeing into southern Mozambique, they were badly mauled by Soshangane about 1831, passing into the Shona country of the Changamire empire where once again they suffered defeat, this time by another body of migrating Nguni speakers. Defeat was not unrelieved, however, for the Jere, or Ngoni, as they began to be called, brought Zulu fighting tactics with them which enabled them to subdue most local people encountered, many of whom were not only defeated but absorbed, thus expanding the size and strength of the Ngoni as their migration proceeded. In Mashonaland they devastated Changamire and sacked Zimbabwe, turning from thence north to cross the Zambezi in November, 1835, at which point a new phase in Ngoni history began.

North of the Zambezi, the Ngoni entered a region free of other southern marauders, inhabited partly by strong states related to the Lunda but also by decentralized villagers who were an easy prey for the invaders. Zwangendaba's hordes swept through the countryside, halting to engulf defenseless communities and ravage their lands, then moving on to new pastures to repeat the process. Although marked by protracted pauses of several years each, the line of march moved steadily northward, passing to the west of Lake Nyasa until a point was reached east of the southern tip of Lake Tanganyika. Here Zwangendaba paused and built a center called Mapupo, for his people were weary, there were ominous divisions developing within the nation, and the old chief was ill and flagging in energy. About 1848 he died at Mapupo. It was twenty years since the great migration had begun far to the south in the defeat of the Ndwandwe.

Zwangendaba's own outstanding qualities of leadership aside, what had given the Ngoni cohesion and strength was the manner in which they dealt with those they conquered—that total political and cultural assimilation of one people by another which has frequently characterized African societies. Like the Lunda concept of positional succession or the extension of the original Ashanti royal clan to embrace former adversaries, the Ngoni system found a place for the vanquished which brought much-needed strength to the state and offered a new life to those who might otherwise have been faced with slavery and death. War captives were merely added to the homesteads of the original Jere families, becoming lowly but fully-recognized relatives of their adopted masters. The young men were initiated into age-grade fighting regiments without prejudice and could rise to highest prominence solely on military ability. As more captives were taken, they too were absorbed, and so the nation grew through accretion and natural increase. Political unity was maintained by means of the original Ngoni clan pattern which developed in complexity to take account of the naturalized adherents who far outnumbered the first migrants from Zululand. The military efficiency and fighting tactics of Zululand, and Jere social structure and cultural values survived, secure in the devotion accorded by all to the idea of Ngoni nationhood.

Nevertheless in time stresses developed. The death of Zwangendaba removed one major cohesive force while the growing size and complexity of the nation encouraged cleavages which were as natural as they were characteristic of the long-lived process of the Bantu dispersion. Eventually secessions took place which broke the Ngoni into five different groups, and in this form the final stage of the Ngoni migration was effected. Zwangendaba's death brought on a successional struggle which culminated in a complicated series of splits. First, a small group of dissidents fled northward along the

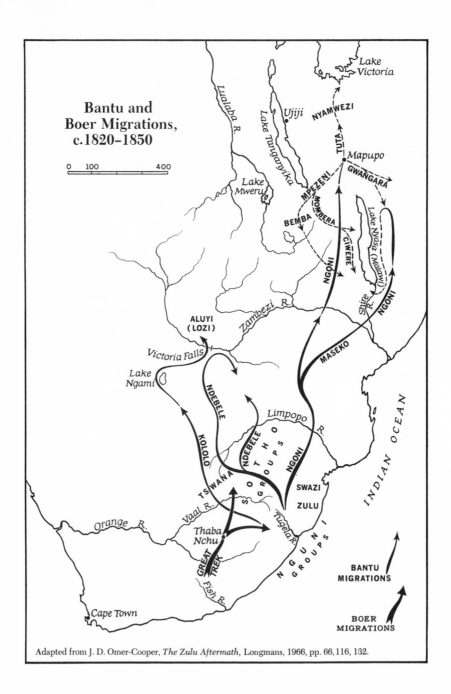

**Bantu and
Boer Migrations,
c.1820–1850**

0   100   400

Lake
Victoria

Lualaba R.

Lake Tanganyika

Ujiji

NYAMWEZI

TUTA

Mapupo

MPEZENI

GWANGARA

Lake
Mweru

BEMBA

MOMBERA

NGONI

CIWERE

Lake Nyasa (Malawi)

Shire R.

NGONI

ALUYI
(LOZI)

Zambezi R.

MASEKO

NGONI

Victoria Falls

Lake
Ngami

NDEBELE

Limpopo R.

KOLOLO

NDEBELE

S O T H O   G R O U P S

NGONI

TSWANA

SWAZI

Vaal R.

ZULU

Orange R.

Tugela R.

INDIAN OCEAN

Thaba
Nchu

N G U N I   G R O U P S

BANTU
MIGRATIONS

GREAT TREK

Fish R.

BOER
MIGRATIONS

Cape Town

Adapted from J. D. Omer-Cooper, *The Zulu Aftermath*, Longmans, 1966, pp. 66, 116, 132.

eastern side of Lake Tanganyika. Known as the Tuta, they captured and absorbed many Nyamwezi, a people with whom they later co-operated, while contributing their share to the chronic unrest which so greatly assisted Arab slave procurement in the region of the Tabora-Ujiji route. Another section, called the Gwangara, escaped to the eastern side of Lake Nyasa where they came to dominate what is now southeastern Tanzania, although ultimately dividing into two separate kingdoms. Meanwhile, the main body of Ngoni split in half, one group under Mpezeni moving westward into Bemba country and then eastward to the Fort Jameson area of modern Zambia; the other led by Mombera doubling back on Zwangendaba's route and settling in the highlands west of Lake Nyasa. The fifth Ngoni state broke off from Mombera and finally took possession of territory in the Dowa uplands in the southern part of present-day Malawi. A sixth group of migrants, generally classified as Ngoni and called Maseko after their leader, had journeyed northward independently of Zwangendaba and, after many difficulties, finally established themselves in the Shire country south of Lake Nyasa.

Thus the effects of the *Mfecane* came to central Africa in the form of wars and raids, but it was also responsible for the introduction of Ngoni culture and polity and the revolutionary idea in much of eastern and central Africa that people of different language and background could be welded into large-scale and lasting state systems. While the Ngoni kingdoms disappeared in the course of the European occupation of central Africa during the last part of the nineteenth century, the sense of common identity which they engendered has lingered on.

THE SEARCH FOR SECURITY—
SEBETWANE AND MZILIKAZI

The upheavals in Zululand greatly intensified the social and political instability of the southern Bantu, tearing peoples from their lands and sending them scrambling for safety to become both pursued and pursuer, both refugees from a rapacious power at their rear and aggressors devouring all in their path. Throughout the plateau west of the Drakensberg scarp ran the shock waves of the *Mfecane*, gathering intensity as they proceeded, dealing death and destruction, emptying habitable land, drawing together frightened fugitives of diverse background into centers of desperate defense, and dispatching others in a headlong flight from fear that became an orgy of violence and bloodshed.

It was quickly apparent that the effects of the *Mfecane* could not be contained within the narrow limits of the coastal shelf east of the Drakensberg Mountains. The early skirmishing between Ndwandwe and Mthethwa soon involved other people, for example, the Hlubi, costing them their cattle and their grazing grounds and forcing them over the scarp and up onto the plateau where the Sotho speakers predominated. At once the Hlubi fell on the Tlokwa, ousting them from their territory and sending them on a migration devoted to warfare and pillage. Among those attacked in turn by the Tlokwa were a Sotho group led by a young and resourceful chief, Sebetwane, who, seeing no future in a strife-ridden land, determined to move on to less demanding latitudes where his losses in cattle might be recouped and security obtained.

There followed a long odyssey toward the northwest in which Sebetwane's Kololo people, as they began to call themselves, fought their way through the Tswana country, sometimes victorious sometimes defeated, alternately losing their cattle and gaining new herds, enduring the rigors of the Kalahari, and finally after years of wandering arriving on the Zambezi above Victoria Falls. Here they encountered new hazards in the form of hostile people and an unfamiliar terrain, for this was the flood plain of the Zambezi, virtually submerged during part of the year and requiring mastery of radically different fighting techniques and methods of agriculture. Somehow the Kololo managed to adapt themselves to this new land and succeeded in subduing the local people in 1838, while beating off attacks of other marauding Nguni-speaking groups.

Once the Kololo had established themselves and eliminated outside threats, there remained the difficult problem of administering the more numerous indigenous Aluyi with their different culture and language. This was accomplished by fusion between the two groups through intermarriage and the elevation of local leaders to positions of prominence. The Aluyi soon accepted the name of Kololo and willingly adopted the language and traditions of the southerners. A strong peaceful state emerged which greatly impressed David Livingstone when he first visited the Kololo kingdom in 1851, but in fact its strength proved more apparent than real. When Sebetwane died suddenly that same year, a problem of succession arose which could not

15. Shaka's *indunas*
conducting parley

Illustrated London News, DECEMBER 6, 1902

16. The queen's kraal, Swaziland

Les Bassoutos, BY E. CASALIS

17. Moshesh in 1833

18. Cavalryman of the Central Sudan, early nineteenth century

Narrative OF DENHAM, CLAPPERTON AND OUDNEY

The Pictorial Edition of the Life and Discoveries of David Livingston, BY J. E. RITCHIE

19. A slave market in the eastern Sudan

20. An audience of
the *mai* of Bornu,
early nineteenth
century

Costume Antico e Moderno, BY FERRARIO, 1815

21. Kano in 1850

© GEORGE RODGER, MAGNUM PHOTOS

22. Dinka villagers

23. Yoruba wood mask

CHURCH MISSIONARY SOCIETY, LONDON

24. Bishop Crowther

25. Africanus Horton

AUTHOR

Graphic, 1876

26. Procession of Dahomey chiefs, their retainers and slaves

O mwata Kazembe, BY A. C. P. GAMITTO

27. *Mwata Kazembe, 1831*

Tippu Tib, BY H. BRODE, 1907

28. Tippu Tib, *c.* 1885

Graphic, 1873

29. Zanzibar waterfront about 1875

30. King Yohannes IV
of Ethiopia

31. The victor at Adowa: Menelik with his chiefs

Illustrated London News, MARCH 28, 1896

be satisfactorily resolved. Fissures appeared between the Kololo and their local subjects, and in 1864 the former, already reduced by malaria, were overthrown and scattered. Kololo influence survived, however, for the Lozi, as they now called themselves, in effect continued to use the language of the intruders as well as elements of their customs. "We hear everyone around us speaking Sesuto," an observer remarked years later, adding, "The same customs, the same manner, the same dress, the same sociability and official code of politeness . . . It really requires an effort of mind to believe oneself on the Zambezi."

Of the many threats which Sebetwane endured in his flight toward security, the most persistent was that of Mzilikazi and his Ndebele. This Nguni-speaking people spread terror and destruction in broad strokes across southern Africa during the years of their wandering, yet they too were fugitives, seeking refuge from attack, conquering in their rush to avoid being conquered. Their flight began, like many others, in Zululand where Mzilikazi committed the gross indiscretion as one of Shaka's military leaders of refusing to turn over to his overlord a number of cattle captured in a raid. This was bald rebellion, and Mzilikazi and his small group soon found themselves in headlong flight over the mountains to escape the avenging Zulu regiments.

This incident occurred about 1821, and for the next fifteen years the Ndebele became involved in a running struggle for survival which did not end until they had safely established themselves in Matabeleland. At first they paused in the northern Transvaal from whence their hunting parties ranged widely in search of cattle and captives among the less martial Sotho and Tswana. In 1825, however, Mzilikazi was on the move southwestward in search of better range and greater security from Shaka's regiments. For almost ten years the Ndebele maintained themselves near the site of present-day Pretoria. It was a heavily settled area when they arrived but the systematic destruction of towns and seizure of livestock quickly depopulated the countryside. The local people were decimated, their men put to the sword and their women and children absorbed to add their strength to the Ndebele military state. Those who escaped lived wretchedly in marginal areas which they disputed with wild beasts, leaving the accessible land in the hands of the conquerors.

Still, security was elusive in this land of shifting fortune. Mzilikazi's growing nation lacked the stability that comes with

longevity, and to his south were outlaw bands of Griquas and Hottentots whose mounted riflemen were more than a match for a massed
assegai charge and whose hunger for cattle drew them inexorably to
Mzilikazi's massive herds. Soon the Ndebele were under attack which
they stood off with difficulty while their peril was compounded by a
new Zulu punitive campaign ordered by Dingane. Once again the
order was given and the Ndebele began moving westward into
Tswana country.

In 1836 a new peril appeared in the form of the Boer trekkers.
Attacked by the Ndebele who mistook them for Griqua raiders, they
struck back, routing the charging regiments with their rifle fire and
eventually sacking Mzilikazi's towns and confiscating large numbers
of cattle. This devasting rout precipitated a long march to the north
across the Limpopo where, after more difficulties including a brush
with the Kololo of Sebetwane, the exhausted Ndebele settled permanently in the country that had once been the domain of Changamire.

That the Ndebele survived as a unit and eventually emerged
stronger than ever in Matabeleland reflected the toughness of the
military-political state which evolved during their migration. Leaving
Zululand with the classic Shakan battle techniques, Mzilikazi organized his people into military regiments which constituted individual settlements of soldiers with supporting civilian population,
each commanded by a military leader and considered as part of the
king's household. The older men served as reserves to a permanent
standing army which was augmented from time to time by newly-
formed age regiments to which captive people were added. In this
military hierarchy there was no room for traditional chiefs, and absolute power rested with Mzilikazi, the king, who owned most of the
cattle, distributed marriageable girls among his warriors, and ruled
through his regimental *indunas*. Upon the settlement in Matabeleland,
the military towns grew into permanent geographic divisions and
service in the age regiments became hereditary. The cohesiveness of
the state was now enhanced by two additional factors. In the first
place, the regional governors were the military leaders whose non-
royal origins precluded their organizing secession movements. Moreover, a class system slowly emerged which gave primary rank to the
descendants of the original Ndebele, thus preserving Ndebele culture and language in the face of the massive infusions of conquered
peoples. Nevertheless, when Mzilikazi died in 1868, these safeguards

did not prevent a dispute over the succession which went to his son, Lobengula, only as the outcome of civil war.

MOSHESH AND THE DIPLOMACY OF SELF-DEFENSE

Not all the victims of the *Mfecane* ran; not all sought to solve the problem of national security by adopting the violent tactics of Shaka. In Basutoland, security through the consolidation of diverse peoples was still the objective, but this was to be effected by diplomacy rather than by warfare. In the long run a policy of conciliation succeeded where violence failed—a new nation was conceived during the turbulent years following the rise of Shaka and that nation survives today, modest but independent.

The Basuto nation was the work of a most unusual and gifted statesman. During the early years of the nineteenth century, Moshesh, the young prince of an obscure Sotho sub-tribe, began to take account of the defensive possibilities of the flat-topped hills which were common to the mountainous region just west of the Drakensberg scarp opposite Natal. He saw that these heights could be defended against large numbers of attackers if properly provisioned and fortified. With a small group of young men he therefore established himself on an upland called Butha Buthe, and soon had the opportunity to test the validity of his strategy.

The repercussions of the *Mfecane* had thrown the Hlubi across the Drakensberg front and dislodged the powerful Tlokwa under their queen regent, Mma Ntatisi, and her son, Sikonyela. In their predatory migration, the Tlokwa attacked Butha Buthe on two occasions and were repulsed only with difficulty, carrying off Moshesh's cattle and driving his people to the brink of starvation. It was clear that, although the principle of defense was sound, a better site than Butha Buthe was needed, one where not only an army but a whole people could stand off attack indefinitely. When such a place was finally located about 1824, Moshesh led his people to the new site, called Thaba Bosiu, in a brilliantly executed march through bandit- and cannibal-infested territory. Now, at last, he had a firm base on which to build a viable state.

Although military defense was an essential element of Basuto policy, the success of the nation rested ultimately on the wisdom and diplomatic skill of Moshesh himself, and Moshesh's statesmanship in turn was based upon several major principles. In the first place, the psychology of military defense and the need for survival argued for the primacy of peaceful negotiation over warfare. Again and again, Moshesh resorted to diplomacy in place of force and, more often than not, his patience was rewarded. The starving tribal remnants infesting the environs of Thaba Bosiu were won over from cannibalism and brigandage by the offer of food and shelter. The tough, vengeful Zulus were neutralized through a judicious use of tribute. In 1831, after repelling a fierce Ndebele assault on his stronghold, Moshesh completely disarmed the attackers by offering them cattle in place of the usual insults.

This was no policy of weakness, but rather a shrewd strategy designed to exploit human vanity or to offer an adversary the opportunity for graceful withdrawal from an embarrassing position. If such means failed, Moshesh had recourse to his second principle, that of dividing his opponents; for example, his successful elimination of the Tlokwa by inducing other groups to attack this aggressive people, and at a later time, his persistent efforts to woo the British as a counterbalance to the menace he saw in the Boer settlers.

Finally, Moshesh possessed the imagination and flexibility to profit from the strength of his enemies, to use their techniques on behalf of his own cause. From the Griqua raiders he learned the use of firearms, guerrilla tactics, and the swiftness of horse-borne sallies, military skills which later stood him in good stead against the Boers in contradistinction to the suicidal *assegai* charges of the Ndebele. To meet European diplomacy Moshesh encouraged missionaries to settle in his territories where they were able to render invaluable assistance in the complex dealings with Boer and Briton, but without being permitted to dominate and divert Basuto policy.

To some extent these were elements of a negative posture of defense, the positive side of which was the creation of a healthy, strong Basuto nation. Here again Moshesh successfully brought into play his diplomatic talents. Persuasion, not force, held the loyalty of the many different people who came to live in the mountain refuge with its center at Thaba Bosiu. Small heterogeneous groups were permitted to retain their own leaders under the surveillance of members of Moshesh's ruling family. Larger groups were essentially self-governing, required only to acknowledge the ultimate authority of Moshesh. Cultural differences were gradually overcome by propinquity, and national bonds grew strong in a spirit of mutual need and respect. Above all was the example of Moshesh himself, always the man of peace, always the diplomatist, always placing reason before choler. In the difficult days of the Boer expansion, Moshesh was to be the salvation of the Basuto nation.

THE BOER TREKKERS

The land hunger which precipitated the Bantu *Mfecane* was also the ultimate force behind the Great Trek of the Boer cattlemen, but there were other important factors working as well. First of all was the attitude toward race, long in formation within the Cape Colony, which equated status with pigmentation. As the nineteenth century opened, the Colony numbered approximately 75,000 inhabitants, but only one in three was a free white man—the others being slaves or members of a dubious floating population of Hottentots, half-castes, freed bondsmen, and runaways—and under the circumstances it was easy to assign an inferior position to men of color. On the eastern frontier, such racial thinking was firmly fixed in the bleak philosophy of the Boer farmers whose narrow world was based on the essential inequality of man. Secondly, there was the chronic distaste for authority which obsessed the *trekboer's* mentality. Already he had moved far to the east, vexed even by those uncertain and flaccid controls imposed by the Dutch East India Company. The administration of the British could only strengthen resentment and suspicion, especially since the new regime appeared to represent viewpoints outrageous to Boer principles regarding individual freedom and racial inferiority.

British rule, therefore, was a deeply disturbing factor, for it introduced concepts genuinely foreign to the South African society that had evolved over 150 years in relative isolation from European intellectual developments. For one thing there was the idea of administrative efficiency, particularly with respect to land registration, which attempted a systematic linkage of individuals to the land for purposes of taxation, orderly settlement, and more efficient farm management. To the Boer this smacked of tyranny, as did another British innovation, rule by law. The introduction of a professional judiciary independent equally of interested parties and executive pressure was a novelty which might have been better endured had the new magistrates been of higher competence. Unhappily, British zeal for reform did not extend to the desire to pay for it, with the result that officials were no more efficient and far less representative than they had been formerly. Worst of all, the British brought with them humanitarian impulses which preached such heresy as emancipation for slaves, and equality before the law for all men. These notions shook a world long accustomed to a rigid caste system, and the paternalistic dispensing of ad hoc justice.

At first, the application of British rule seemed to favor the frontier farmer. To combat vagrancy, it was decreed in 1809 that Hottentots have a fixed address, thus virtually compelling them to take service and making extremely difficult the establishment of a free labor market. A few years later an ordinance permitted the apprenticing of Hottentot children to farms where they had grown up. The vagrancy code, however, also provided legal safeguards insuring equitable contracts, and in 1812 the so-called Black Circuit court heard evidence in support of charges by Hottentot servants and passed sentence on white masters where accusations of mistreatment were proved.

Such steps were but a prelude to the far-reaching Fiftieth Ordinance of 1828 which sought nothing less than the complete overhaul of the codes governing the legal and civil status of the colored population. Urged by Dr. John Philip, superintendent in South Africa for the London Missionary Society, the Ordinance banished vagrancy and pass laws, at once guaranteeing freedom of work and the end of color discrimination by law. In 1834, with the abolition of slavery in the British Empire, former bondsmen automatically were brought under the provisions of the Fiftieth Ordinance, and the same year an attempt by the legislative council in Cape Town to institute a new vagrancy law was disallowed in London.

Frequently reforms were tactlessly applied or gained little advantage to compensate for the ill-will they engendered. The thoroughgoing and necessary revision of the administration of justice undertaken in 1828 was offset by a needless abolition of the old *heemraden* courts which were popular and familiar and could have been easily adapted to the new system. At the same time, the inauguration of a policy making English the sole official language in the country gained nothing but resentment, and led to the eventual emergence of the Afrikaans language in South Africa. The abolition of slavery, moreover, was poorly implemented in the Cape Colony. Not only were farmers irritated by the prospect of former slaves possessing legal equality, but many were deprived of proper compensation through faulty administration and some forced into bankruptcy as a result.

British administration also interfered fatefully on the frontier, where Boer and Bantu contended with each other for possession of the same land. Rising population pressure meant chronic unrest which government policy was unable to soothe. First, the establishment of a fortified frontier in 1812 led to the outbreak of war and the substitution in 1819 of a neutral zone between the Great Fish and Keiskamma rivers. Unoccupied land such as this was no less than an invitation to violence which burst forth in 1834 after several years of drought had sorely tried black and white alike. In the fighting, the Xhosa were driven back and in 1835 Governor Benjamin D'Urban annexed the land between the Great Fish and Kei rivers as Queen Adelaide Province, to be available for further Boer colonization. The natural jubilation of the frontiersmen, however, was soon converted to a high pitch of exasperation for, responding to missionary pressure, the government in London reversed D'Urban's policy and returned the annexed territory to African hands. The year was 1836, and the Great Trek, which had already started informally, now began in earnest.

The Boer farmers had had enough of official policy. The philosophy of the Fiftieth Ordinance extended to the Bantu was anathema to these people; neither would their land-hunger, long deprived, be satisfied by a pattern of permanent settlement with its entanglement of quitrents, land sales, survey charges, title deeds, and crown lands. A much more attractive alternative, more in keeping with their past history and spirit of independence, was a move on to new lands beyond the reach of the unsympathetic authorities and their hateful edicts. If the government chose to allow the Africans to remain in the coastal lands, they would move inland where their scouts reported vast expanses of unoccupied tracts. Here where there was no Fiftieth Ordinance and a servant knew his place, they could build a new life.

Altogether one out of every five Dutch-speaking South Africans joined the Trek, drawn mostly from the less settled eastern regions. The parties went off in varying sized groups, sometimes only a handful of families, sometimes in larger companies. Their ox-drawn wagons contained all their belongings, moving along at the rate of about six miles a day which was the best that could be expected from grazing cattle, sheep, and goats. There was work for everyone. The men were busy with the livestock, repairs for the trek gear, hunting, and standing guard. The women cooked, mended, and cared for the children, while small boys were expected to help with the herds. It was desperately hard work in the face of a perilous present and an uncertain future. Variously searching for mountain passes, cutting tracks, dismantling wagons for the backbreaking passage across the mountains, enduring fevers, loss of livestock, dwindling supplies, and uncertain harvests, many were to perish and all would suffer.

Avoiding the heavily populated coastal strip, the trekkers moved inland, crossing the Orange River and skirting the mountain stronghold of Moshesh's Basutoland. Here in Transorangia they paused, uncertain whether to strike north across the Vaal River or alternatively to turn east over the Drakensbergs into the valley of Natal. The land was empty and the Boer parties at first largely unopposed, but the reason was ominous for the silence was that of fear and devastation, not of peaceful solitude. The effects of the *Mfecane* were in full force—the high plains had been cleared by the rampaging Ndebele, Sikonyela's Tlokwa were harassing Moshesh's fortress, Griqua parties were raiding across the Orange River, while the Zulu regiments of Dingane held the coastal belt in a grip of terror. As intruders, the Boers could have these new lands, but only if they were able to take them by force.

While the individual parties were congregating at Thaba Nchu in Transorangia, an engagement was fought to the north near the Vaal River which gave a taste of things to come. In October, 1836, a party of trekkers beat off a series of furious attacks by Ndebele regiments, taking a murderous toll with their firepower but losing all their livestock in the engagement. Retiring to Thaba Nchu with difficulty, they there joined a growing debate as to the future direction and leadership of the Trek. It was finally agreed to turn east to Natal under the experienced frontiersman, Piet Retief, but before the Drakensberg Mountains were reached, the group split, one wing led by Andries Potgieter turning north and crossing the Vaal. By this time there were already more than two thousand trekkers, all of an independent turn of mind, resistant to the idea of a coordinated, disciplined movement which their perilous circumstances demanded.

Thereafter success vied with disaster. Potgieter fell on the Ndebele in the autumn of 1837, defeating them so decisively that Mzilikazi decided to abandon his territories to the victors and take his people to the less fiercely contended regions beyond the Limpopo. Thus the Transvaal fell to the trekkers, but Retief's contingent suffered a far different fate beyond the mountains. Asking that his group be accommodated in Natal, Retief met a qualified acceptance from Dingane who required only that Retief regain some cattle taken by Sikonyela, the Tlokwa chief. When this was achieved with relative ease and the trekkers had already begun to descend the scarp into Natal, Dingane became alarmed and put Retief and his party to death when they returned with the cattle in February, 1838, then turned his troops on the Boer wagon trains, scattering them and almost succeeding in wiping them out. In the long run it was a vain effort, for *assegai* charges could not contend with rifle fire. With the assistance of reinforcements led by Andries Pretorius, the Boers counterattacked and in December, 1838 routed the Zulus at Blood River, bringing about Dingane's eventual downfall and the accession to power of the tractable Mpande. The Zulu hold on Natal was broken.

THE SHAPE OF THINGS TO COME—
SOUTH AFRICA AT MIDCENTURY

There was no precise end to the Great Trek. Settlers continued to cross the Orange River in their wagons, but already by 1840 the tone of the movement was beginning to change from a quest for new land to the consolidation of territory already acquired. The backbone of Bantu resistance had cracked with the defeats of Dingane and Mzilikazi, but military subjugation of the African nations would prove to be the least of the trekkers' problems. Both the *Mfecane* and the Great Trek were convulsive responses to population pressure and land hunger, and when the clamor and the dust of battle had subsided, it was found by Bantu and Boer alike that the people and the land were still there and the old problems persisted, albeit in vastly new dimension. The Great Trek, moreover, had been a flight from British authority—indeed, almost an anarchistic rejection of authority in any form—yet an ordered society and a stable government would be essential if the gains of the trekkers were to be consolidated. As always, dilemma was not to be resolved in flight.

In Natal, the Boers had no sooner won their haven from oppression than trouble began to pile upon trouble. The trekkers, handy with a rifle or a woodsman's axe, lacked either sympathy or experience for government. Insubordination and disloyalty undermined authority and rendered futile any rational solution to economic problems rooted in the matter of land distribution. Farmers could not be prevented from moving over the frontier into Bantu country, cattle raids and hunting parties were unrestrained, many forays returned with Zulu orphan children under an apprenticeship which was tantamount to slavery, and attempts were made to clear Natal of her tens of thousands of Africans by driving them south into Pondoland. The land distribution policy, reflecting cherished Boer principles of the rights of free men, dealt out six-thousand-acre farms with an open hand which took no account of valuation, occupancy, and tax assessment, let alone such refinements as land surveying.

Having fled from the jurisdiction of the Cape government, the settlers had embarked on a course which would shortly bring them back into conflict with the British. Whatever misgivings there may have been in London over the rise of an independent nation potentially attractive to rival European powers, it was Natal's relations with her neighboring peoples that precipitated British intervention. British troops occupied Port Natal in 1842 after a large-scale commando raid had penetrated Pondo country; then as a bankrupt and ineffective Boer government struggled to maintain its dwindling authority, the British decided to annex Natal which became a dependency of the Cape Colony in 1845. At this, many of the original trekkers moved inland to the high veld, for with British rule came the policy of racial equality which had already set the frontiersmen in motion once before.

In the interior the situation, no less desperate, was more confused, partly because the trekkers were spread over a wide area, partly because of the presence of other powers such as the Griqua states and Moshesh's Basutoland, and partly due to the ambivalence of the British government. The Boers had settled variously in the Transvaal, in the Winburg region between the Vet and Vaal rivers, in the Griqua territories across the Orange River, and along the Caledon River in land which Moshesh claimed as his own. Everywhere they resisted authority, including their own; nowhere could they bring themselves to establish effective government. In the Transvaal they set up a republic in 1844 with Andries Potgieter at its head, but it was years before this state in name became a state in fact, and the Boer trekkers themselves were never able to bring the Transvaal and her sister Orange Free State into single political union.

The region of Griqualand was a particularly sore spot. Here, north

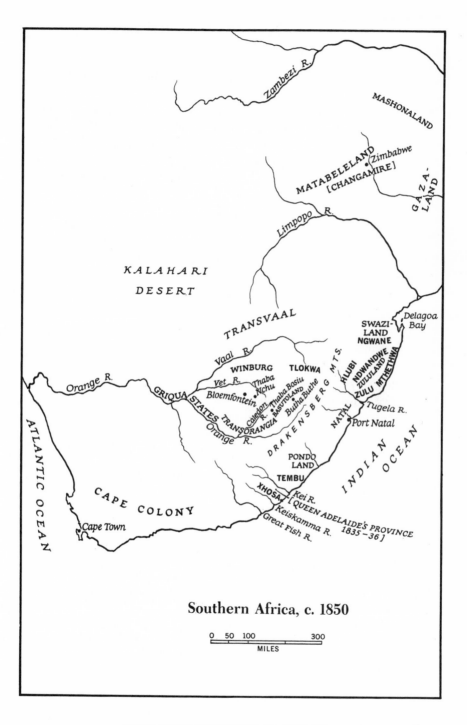

Southern Africa, c. 1850

0 50 100   300
MILES

of the Orange River, half-caste refugees from the Colony had mixed with Hottentots and Bushmen fragments to form communities strung along a thin strip of arid land, and by the early 1820's the Griqua population had risen to approximately 3000. Despite its low rainfall, Boer farmers had long found this territory attractive for seasonal pasture, and well before the Great Trek they had begun to settle there more permanently in numbers which would eventually overwhelm the Griquas. In 1845 trouble broke out between the settlers and the Griqua chiefs which required the intervention of British troops. By the time peace had been restored, it was apparent to Governor Sir Harry Smith at Cape Town that the Boers would never accept Griqua rule, and therefore in 1848 he declared the Orange River Sovereignty as a dependency of the Cape Colony.

This annexation of the region between the Orange and Vaal rivers included Griqua, Boer, and Moshesh's Basuto settlements and was part of an overall attempt to solve the frontier problem, but it ran afoul of changing fashions in Britain regarding imperial responsibilities. Free traders who thought colonies expensive encumbrances combined with liberals subscribing to the doctrine of self-determination and together they raised questions about a deepening involvement in a worldwide colonial establishment. In addition, missionary influence was at low ebb after an expedition up the Niger in 1841 resulted in almost 50 European deaths from malaria. Reacting to these factors, Parliament began to favor withdrawal and retrenchment, and this mood hardened as far as South Africa was concerned when fresh hostilities broke out on the frontier in 1850. In 1852 the British concluded the Sand River Convention which recognized the independence of the Boers beyond the Vaal. Two years later the Bloemfontein Convention did the same for those settled between the Vaal and Orange rivers. The trekkers had at last succeeded in establishing the independent states they had set out to found.

British diplomacy and imperial strategy also had profound implications for the Basuto nation of Moshesh where the pressure of settlers had been steadily building up around the edges of his mountain stronghold. As a result of a treaty with the British in 1846, Moshesh set aside land along the Caledon River where the major Boer settlements had developed, but this arrangement was considered inadequate by those farmers located deeper in Basuto territory and they refused to give up their homesteads. Boer farms and Basuto villages were soon interspersed to a degree that made a fixed boundary difficult. When the Orange River Sovereignty was established, the question of boundary had been left unsettled, then was later defined by the British resident at Bloemfontein, H. D. Warden, to the intense dissatisfaction of the Basuto, many of whom now found themselves isolated across the frontier from their own people.

Moshesh, who had long foreseen the danger of fixed boundaries, was unable to control his polyglot followers and fighting broke out. Worse still, Moshesh found himself facing a British power whose aid he had consistently courted as an antidote to Boer expansionism. In 1852, with characteristic deftness, he combined force and diplomacy to induce the withdrawal of a British expedition, but within two years the British had washed their hands of the problems of the interior, and Moshesh found himself alone facing the Boer republic of the Orange Free State. The wars which broke out in 1858 and 1866 ended disastrously for the Basuto with the loss of virtually all their fertile land. As his state tottered on the brink of total disintegration, however, Moshesh once more sought British aid, and this time in the face of annihilation, he secured an annexation in 1868 which saved the Basuto nation.

The salvation of Basutoland was gained at the price of independence, economic no less than political, for the territory which Moshesh was able to salvage was a rocky height of limited resources and heavy population, and henceforth the Basuto people would be dependent upon their white neighbors for their livelihood. Herein lay the pattern which emerged from the *Mfecane* and the Great Trek. Two people, Bantu and Boer, sought land to accommodate rising numbers, hampered by an outdated, inefficient system of husbandry. The Boer, being technically more advanced, was able to defeat the Bantu, pushing him by degrees off the land. The wars, those fought by the trekkers as well as the so-called Kaffir Wars along the Cape Colony frontier, were always over possession of land, and the outcome of each encounter saw the African faced with further losses, ever less able to maintain his herds, sow his crops, or fuel his fires. In 1857, the Xhosa and Tembu gave dramatic and macabre emphasis to the process when, driven by superstition and frustration as their herds withered away in starvation and disease, they slaughtered their stock and scattered their grain in response to the vain prophecy that this would rid the land of the hated white man. The sequel of 25,000 dead of starvation and many thousands more driven into the Colony in search of survival was symbolic of the breakup of the old way of life—a social and economic submission to match political subjugation.

The land had been the foundation on which traditional society rested. When one went, the other went. The African people, however, remained, obliged to embrace a new pattern of life, a pattern which was no longer theirs, but that of the white man. Deprived of his ownership, the African still remained on the land as squatter, tenant farmer, and laborer. He herded cattle and planted corn as before, but the cattle might be his master's, his corn pledged against future taxes, and his labor the property of others much as that of the serf in the medieval manors of Europe. Beyond this his growing taste for European consumer goods further mortgaged the African's resources to the new way of life.

The tragedy, however, was not so much in the disintegration of a traditional society which had its own shortcomings, as it was in two other factors. The first was the subservient position of the African, locked in a social status wherein his meager share in the fruits of his labor was perforce established by others. Related to this was the system itself, as hopelessly behind the times as it was ahead of the Bantu society it had replaced. Obsolete agricultural techniques were applied to an infertile land, while capital accumulation, immigration, and foreign investment lagged in a land of wars, droughts, and insect plagues. Religious fundamentalism was no substitute for education and the spirit of inquiry. Rugged individualism led, not to political freedom, but to political fragmentation which in turn complicated the already difficult process of economic planning.

Even as modern science applied to problems of economic productivity was changing the face of nineteenth-century Europe and America, technology and industry remained unknown in this far corner of the world. The Cape Colony continued poor and the Boer republics many times poorer, eking out an existence on the sale of wool and hides which could not pay for much-needed roads, railways, harbors, and local industry. The labor of the African—unskilled and inexpertly applied—consequently benefitted no one, neither master nor servant. Each was bound up with the other, and both were caught in the toils of an ineffective, superannuated system.

The *Mfecane* and Great Trek had changed the face of South Africa, obliterating traditional society and throwing black and white into a complex of mutual interdependence. In the next stage of her history, South Africa would finally turn to the problem of economic reform—an industrial revolution based on the discovery of mineral resources which was to replace poverty with wealth and show the way- to national unity. It would not solve the problem of racial harmony, however. It would succeed only in shifting the center of tension from the farm to the city.

Suggestions for Further Reading

The *Mfecane* and its consequences are set forth in detail in J. D. Omer-Cooper, *The Zulu Aftermath* (London: Longmans, 1966; Evanston, Ill.: Northwestern University Press, 1966). Some further details are available in two articles by the same author in *Tarikh*, v. I, nos. 1 and 2, but see also D. R. Morris, *The Washing of the Spears* (New York: Simon and Schuster, 1965). For further information there is a sizeable collection of contemporary missionary and explorer accounts as well as numerous anthropological and historical studies of the African peoples involved. See, for example, J. A. Barnes, *Politics in a Changing Society* (London: Oxford University Press, 1954); A. T. Bryant, *Olden Times in Zululand and Natal* (Cape Town: C. Struik, 1965; New York: Tri-Ocean Books, 1929); E. Colson and M. Gluckman, eds., *Seven Tribes of British Central Africa* (Manchester: Manchester University Press, 1959; New York: Humanities Press, 1959); D. F. Ellenberger and J. C. Macgregor, *History of the Basuto, Ancient and Modern* (London: Caxton, 1912); M. Gluckman, "The Kingdom of the Zulu," M. Fortes and E. E. Evans-Pritchard, eds., *African Political Systems* (London: Oxford University Press, 1940); David Livingstone, *Missionary Travels and Researches in South Africa* (London: John Murray, 1857; New York: Humanities Press); M. Read, *The Ngoni of Nyasaland* (London: Oxford University Press, 1956); E. Ritter, *Shaka Zulu* (London: Longmans, 1955); I. Schapera, ed., *The Bantu-Speaking Tribes of South Africa*, 4th. ed. (London: Routledge and Kegan Paul, 1953; New York: Humanities Press); and G. Tylden, *The Rise of the Basuto* (Cape Town: Juta, 1950).

The standard work on the Great Trek is E. A. Walker, *The Great Trek*, 4th. ed. (London: A. and C. Black, 1960; New York: Barnes & Noble, 1960); but several general histories contain material on this period. See E. A. Walker, *A History of Southern Africa*, 3rd. ed. (London: Longmans, 1957; New York: Barnes & Noble, 1964); L. Marquard, *The Story of South Africa*, 3rd. ed. (London: Faber and Faber, 1968; *A Short History of South Africa*, New York: Praeger, 1968); and C. W. De Kiewiet's splendid *History of South Africa, Social and Economic* (London: Oxford University Press, 1941). The background of racial problems in South Africa is treated in W. M. Macmillan, *Bantu, Boer, and Briton*, rev. ed. (Oxford: Clarendon Press, 1963).

12: The Humanitarian Revolution: Europe's Second Coming to West Africa

THE ENLIGHTENMENT AND WEST AFRICA

The initial impact of Europe on Africa was minimal; her second coming momentous. The first arrivals—explorers, then merchants, their thoughts on gold, Prester John, or the passage to India—brought little but an acquisitive disposition which led eventually to the Atlantic slave trade and untold misery for millions of West Africans. Those who came later did so expressly to put an end to the traffic in human beings. In achieving this purpose, they struck a fundamental blow for humanity. They also set in motion forces which would recast the face of West African society in a growing revolution, the most recent expression of which is found in the independence movements and the drive for modernization among the African peoples in the middle of the twentieth century.

That West Africa was to undergo a profound social and cultural upheaval flowed from the fact that Europe was already in the mid-passage of a similar revolution. By the middle of the eighteenth century, the first faint stirrings of medieval mercantile enterprise had long since joined with the humanism of Italy's Renaissance in a flood of vitality encompassing an ever-widening range of human activity. The slow and painful growth of commerce had now developed into colonial systems flung far across the oceans, as powerful, unified nations—first Portugal, then Spain, and finally the Netherlands, France, and England—vied with each other for control of the world's riches. At home royal as well as private patrons encouraged learning and the arts, while experimental science gradually replaced magic and metaphysics as the basis for knowledge of natural phenomena. Religious conviction may have been shaken by the new scientific thought and severely strained by the upheavals of the Reformation, but in the end it had emerged, if more diverse, all the more strengthened in its diversity. The vast learning of the ancient world lay open once more, and the human spirit was more open to receive it. In Europe, dogmatism was giving way to skepticism, and resignation to optimism, while social rigidity was replaced by social dynamism.

Optimism suggested, not human perfection, but human perfectibility. Wars, plagues, famine, brutality, and tyranny indicated the extent of current igorance, stupidity, and man's chronic inhumanity to man; yet Europe's eighteenth-century Enlightenment was confident that human reason offered the key to a more perfect world. Through rational thought the laws of nature had been revealed. It remained only for man to learn to live in harmony with them, and progress would inevitably follow. The idea of progress, moreover, had no limits, and even the less enlightened corners of the world were capable of grasping perfection. Implicit in Enlightenment thinking, therefore, was a humanitarian duty to bring the fruits of European civilization to the many unfortunate peoples still languishing in outer darkness.

As the eighteenth century drew to a close, Europe's Enlightenment touched West Africa in two ways, both of far-reaching consequence. First, there was the great Revolution of 1789 which transformed French society and eventually rearranged the map of Europe. From the crucible of revolution emerged the noble principles of liberty, equality, and fraternity—liberty to think, to speak, and to worship according to personal conscience, equality in the pursuit of happiness, and the mystical fraternity of all men seeking a better life. The Revolution also produced that outburst of patriotic feeling which argued national independence as the way to individual liberty, but which also insisted paradoxically that French culture was pre-eminent; therefore in practice French nationalism was the greatest nationalism, and colonial peoples should be encouraged to forget their own history and way of life that they might be assimilated into the higher civilization of France.

On the Senegal coast, the modest trading centers of St. Louis and Gorée, far from being abandoned to their own devices, were encouraged to share the fruits of the revolutionary democracy unfolding in France. The slave trade was abolished and the slaves freed, all became citizens of the new French nation, and an invitation was tendered to send representatives to Paris. The Senegalese responded with appropriate revolutionary fervor and in 1793 subscribed an unsolicited sum to help toward the defense of the "motherland." During the reaction of the Napoleonic period, most of these liberal gains were wiped away, but already firmly fixed, both in France and in her small West African colony, was the idea that Senegal was French in fact and in spirit, and that liberty meant not independence from France but freedom to enjoy the fruits of French civilization, as much in Africa as in France herself.

Among other things, the Napoleonic era witnessed the re-emergence of slavery and the slave trade within France's overseas possessions, but it was precisely in the final abolition of the slave trade in the nineteenth century that the European Enlightenment made its second major impression on West Africa, and in the process changed the future course of her history. From small beginnings, the slave trade had developed into a big business by the middle of the eighteenth century, profitable both to the indigenous entrepreneurs along the West African coast and the slavers from Europe, and essential to the plantation economies of the Americas. Slaves were assembled locally through purchase, barter, raiding, kidnapping, and warfare. Brought to the coast, they were sold directly to the captains of the slave ships awaiting them or, more commonly, to European or African brokers who gathered the slaves in barracoons to be held until a sale could be effected. Thereupon began the infamous Middle Passage to the New World, a six to ten week voyage during which the slaves were chained, row upon row, in narrow, airless holds, lying in their own filth, deprived of normal movement and fed the meanest of diets, made occasional sport of by their captors, and subject to every malady attracted by the conditions of their unfortunate confinement. One out of every three or four failed to survive the passage, succumbing to disease and maltreatment, while the rest faced the ultimate terror of the slave auction and the prospect of permanent exile in a strange land, far from friends and family.

The total volume of this lucrative traffic is unknown, but during the eighteenth-century heyday of the trade, at least seven million slaves reached American shores while the following century saw an additional four million crossing the Atlantic from West Africa. Profits were reckoned in terms of 100 per cent and more; hence, the importance of this commerce may explain in part why the eighteenth century, for all its self-styled enlightenment, appeared undisturbed by the conditions under which the slave trade and slavery in the colonies were conducted.

Not everyone was undisturbed, however. Though isolated, there were voices raised in protest—clergymen and literary figures mostly, and as a group, the American Quakers. John Locke opened his first *Treatise on Civil Government* with an attack on slavery, and in 1748, Montesquieu remarked acidulously, "It is impossible for us to suppose these creatures to be men, because, allowing them to be men, a suspicion would follow that we ourselves are not Christians." Others were even more eloquent in action. In 1772 slavery was ruled illegal in England and Ireland, largely through the exertions of Granville Sharp, whose dogged industry and faith in English law led to the celebrated opinion of Lord Mansfield freeing the slave, James Somerset. The consequences were profound. First, there was the loss of property valued at hundreds of thousands of pounds, mostly the slaves of West Indian planters resident in Britain. Beyond this was the prospect that the end of slavery in the British Isles was but the first step toward its abolition throughout the empire. Next, there were the complications arising out of thousands of freed slaves cast loose in society without any means of support. Finally, there was the impact that Granville Sharp's success was to have on the subsequent fortunes of West Africa.

COLONIZATION, CHRISTIANITY, AND COMMERCE

However tentatively, as the nineteenth century dawned, Europe's posture toward Africa was changing; the slaver was giving way to the humanitarian. Granville Sharp's personal crusade had achieved its desired result, but it had also set in motion its predicted consequences. In Britain a rising chorus of criticism against the slave system led finally to an organized movement launched during the 1780's to abolish the slave trade. For twenty years men like Sharp, Henry

Thornton, James Stephen, and Thomas Clarkson hammered away at the evils of the slave trade while in the crucial arena of Parliament the fight was carried by the eloquent and indefatigable William Wilberforce. More generally, support grew as the British economy shifted from a mercantilist preoccupation with the West Indian sugar plantation based upon slave labor toward a free trade emphasis on cheaper imports of food and raw materials to sustain a growing manufacturing establishment at home. In 1807, the slave trade was abolished, and the reformers were able to turn their attention to slavery in the empire which finally fell to their attack in 1834 with the passage of the Abolition Act during the previous year. Meanwhile, the Somerset case and the freeing of slaves by British forces during the American Revolution had led to the accumulation of a population of indigent Negroes in London, destitute, homeless mendicants whose plight stirred the humanitarian spirit of Granville Sharp to action a second time.

Sharp's immediate solution was private philanthropy, but it was soon evident that a broader, more systematic and permanent solution was needed. Never wanting in imagination, Sharp hit upon the idea of repatriation and, the objects of his concern being of African descent, it seemed reasonable that they be resettled in the land of their origin. It mattered not that few if any had ever seen Africa or that former slaves were unlikely to possess the skills and judgment necessary to make a success of a new settlement in a strange land. Private contributions were raised, the government agreed to underwrite part of the expense, and in the spring of 1787 a group of over four hundred set sail for Sierra Leone where they established a self-governing community, named by Sharp the Province of Freedom, on the site that later was to be known as Freetown.

Idealism and good will in London, however, were no compensation for settler inexperience, the hostility of the local inhabitants, and the ravages of fever. The colony foundered and was saved from extinction when it was reorganized in 1791 as the property of the Sierra Leone Company, a joint stock enterprise of British philanthropists headed by Henry Thornton. Substituting a benevolent despotism in the person of Governor Zachary Macaulay for the ineffectual democracy of the settlers, the Company kept the colony alive, being greatly assisted in this respect by two much-needed infusions of immigrants. In 1792 there arrived from Nova Scotia some 1200 former slaves freed by the British army during the American Revolution, who, suffering from the intolerance of Tory emigres, had not been successful in establishing themselves in Canada and who consequently seized the opportunity to gain homesteads in West Africa. Eight years later the Nova Scotians were followed by five hundred Maroons, runaway Jamaican slaves who had finally surrendered to the authorities in 1795, and after a brief, unhappy stay in Nova Scotia, had agreed to repatriation in Sierra Leone. With this nucleus, the Company hoped to develop a commercially profitable venture, but in fact it lost heavily and eventually was forced to turn over its undertaking to the British government. In 1808 the settlement of less than two thousand became a crown colony, a development of great significance for it coincided with the abolition of the slave trade and provided a convenient center for the repatriation of the tens of thousands of Africans who were soon being rescued by the British antislavery naval patrols operating in West African waters.

Herein lay the germ of a very different kind of European enterprise in West Africa. The abolitionists had hoped to establish missions among the indigenous inhabitants, and in 1799 the Church Missionary Society was founded by Wilberforce and others with this purpose in view. These missions were to introduce Christianity, but also to encourage local agricultural production to take the place of slaving and thus develop a healthy, mutually beneficial commerce between Europe and West Africa. Slavery would shrivel and die, the abolitionists reasoned, while Western, Christian culture would gradually take hold, leading the Africans from what was regarded as a primitive barbarism to the higher civilization of the West.

In fact, circumstances played a variation on this theme, although the ultimate effect on West Africa was much as had been foreseen. The missionaries found their calling, not in tribal society, but among the recaptives who were pouring into Freetown harbor as a result of the exertions of the British antislavery squadron. Originating from West African points scattered between Senegal and the Congo, these repatriates were settled in villages surrounding Freetown where, under missionary guidance, they became converts to Christianity, and began to emulate the Nova Scotian settlers in their assimilation of Western culture. Although very few of the inhabitants native to Sierra Leone were affected, the rise in the Freetown area of a Christian community of African repatriates, learning English, and gradually becoming Europeanized, was a development of greatest consequence and cast a long shadow forward.

Sierra Leone was not the only West African experiment in the rehabilitation of former slaves. Some two hundred miles southwest of Freetown on the Grain Coast, another settlement struggled for survival. In 1822 a small group of American Negroes arrived off Cape Mesurado, their voyage underwritten by the American Colonization Society which had come into existence some years earlier dedicated to the proposition that free blacks and manumitted slaves in the United States might gain a new start in life in Africa. There, it was argued, they would be safe from the discrimination and persecution which was their frequent lot in America, although the free American Negro looked on colonization more often than not as the enemy of abolition and racial equality, and was largely hostile toward the movement.

The early days of Liberia, so named for the freedom it signified, were a repetition of the difficulties encountered at Sierra Leone as disease, poor leadership, local hostility, limited numbers, and inexperience almost led to extinction. Once again, a single individual came forward to save the day. Yehudi Ashmun, a young white New Englander, assumed control when the authorized agent of the Colonization Society virtually deserted his charges. Like Zachary Macaulay at Freetown, Ashmun forced the reluctant colonists to work together, fought off attacks by the local tribal groups resentful of intrusion and slowly brought an organized, permanent community into being. By the time Ashmun departed in 1828, Liberia, though weak, was established.

After these early years, the similarity between the two philanthropic ventures ended. While Sierra Leone grew rapidly as a repatriation center, Liberia drifted aimlessly, weak, impecunious, and ignored. The problem of slavery in the United States was of a magnitude which could find little relief in the resettlement of a few thousand Negroes; moreover, the political heat raised by the slavery issue made impossible any substantial assistance to the Liberian venture by the United States government. During the thirty years between the founding of the colony and the Civil War, only $5,000,000 was subscribed publicly and privately in America, and most of this sum went to defray the transportation expenses of the emigrants. Few American Negroes were interested in colonization unless it was the price of manumission, and as late as 1850 the Liberian settlements numbered less than three thousand individuals. By that time, however, despite a faltering economy, political instability, and chronic troubles with the local people, Liberia had become an independent Negro nation. As the colony of a private philanthropic society, it lacked sovereignty, and when its status was challenged under international law, there appeared to be no viable alternative to a grant of independence. In 1847 Liberia received its independence and thus began the history of an insecure, unwanted nation, small, weak, unstable, and frequently on the verge of collapse, yet somehow surviving to serve, among other things, as a symbol of the freedom to which others in Africa would in time aspire.

SENEGAL—THE JACOBIN HERITAGE

Both the British and the French were unenthusiastic imperialists in the decades following the fall of Napoleon. Adam Smith's dry assertion that slave labor was more costly than free labor was matched by his conviction that colonies were a needless expense, and this view came to dominate the councils of economy-minded governments in England and France. Paris retained, but did little to develop, the few overseas possessions which survived Waterloo—Martinique and Guadaloupe in the Caribbean; Reunion Island in the Indian Ocean; and her trading posts in Senegal, these last returned at the conclusion of peace in 1815 after intermittent occupation by the British during a century of chronic warfare.

Senegal was the object for a time of a program designed to develop a wide range of agricultural products desired in France, but this mercantilist project fell victim to mismanagement, and its failure merely strengthened the views of those who regarded colonies as a drain without compensation on the national treasury. The local mulatto population was preoccupied with trade up the Senegal River, chiefly in gum used in France for sizing and dye-fast, but for this activity there was no great official enthusiasm since it implied costly military action against the tough, warlike Moors and Tokolor people who controlled the interior. Beyond this, there was a mild interest in coastal trade which brought French shipping to such places as Grand Bassam on the Ivory Coast, Whydah in Dahomey, and Gabon.

Reaction in Paris, however, did not necessarily suggest abandonment of the revolutionary impulse to extend Western civilization in its Gallic mutation to those parts of the world still deprived of its light. To the governor charged with resuming French administration after the British occupation went unequivocal instructions. "The prime mover of the new colony," announced the ministry in Paris, "must be European culture driven by French energy, becoming through example, through persuasion, and through the appreciation of new achievements, the soul of the African."

Within the settled communities of Gorée, St. Louis, and the entrepôts along the Senegal, the French efforts at cultural assimilation were received with cordiality by both the *métis*, or mulattoes, and the small number of Africans who, like the mulattoes, were engaged in the river traffic. Typical of this group was Gabriel Pellegrin, a leading *métis* who had in his youth helped organize an insurrection unseating an unpopular governor to the cry of "Long live Robespierre," but who in middle age was a respected merchant, mayor of St. Louis, and trusted negotiator in commercial relations with the people of the interior. Another was the Abbé Boilat whose seminary training in France led to the priesthood and an attempt, albeit abortive, to establish secondary education on the French model in St. Louis. Still another was Paul Holle, a St. Louis mulatto who exchanged an early career as civil servant to become a celebrated Senegalese soldier and defender of the French post at Medina against *al-Hajj* Umar in 1857. Holle was a forthright protagonist for French civilization in Africa which he encouraged not only with arms but with words, urging the administration to subdue the interior by military force, to educate the people away from what he regarded as the retrogressive effects of Islam, and to step up economic development that the great potentialities of the country might be realized.

Such views were widely held by the small but important population of assimilated mulattoes and Africans, but for the most part the people of Senegal were as yet untouched by French culture. Most of those living in the cities were Wolof-speaking Muslims; household servants, artisans, and laborers, as well as a shifting number of Africans from upcountry whose cultural habits and religious practices made them indifferent to Western ways. Despite the final abolition of slavery in 1848 and the extension of French citizenship, it was to be another half century before the African people of the settled communities—let alone the interior—began to respond to the full cultural, economic, and political implications of the French presence in Senegal. Meanwhile, they remained subservient to the mulatto oligarchy which dominated Senegalese life during the second half of the nineteenth century.

THE BIBLE AND THE PLOUGH

By midcentury, a small but highly significant change was underway on the West African scene. Dotting the coast, a number of cities had sprung into existence, African in population but with growing European orientation, centers from which a Western way of life slowly began to extend itself outward, carried in the baggage of the African residents of these towns as they moved across the countryside as traders, missionaries, or government officials. St. Louis, Monrovia, Cape Coast, Accra, Lagos—government seats and market towns— they were developing that admixture of peoples and ideas which marks the authentic cosmopolitan center.

Freetown in Sierra Leone was the prototype. Over the years thousands upon thousands of rescued slaves had been put down in her harbor to be repatriated in the satellite communities which surrounded the growing port. By 1850 Sierra Leone contained more than forty thousand of these liberated Africans, drawn from many points along the West African coast but dominated by large numbers of Yoruba, victims of the increased slaving occasioned by the civil wars which gripped Yorubaland intermittently after 1821. Uprooted and torn from their traditional way of life, the immigrants quickly accepted the standards they found at Freetown, sending their children off to study English and other subjects at mission-directed schools, while striving to emulate their Nova Scotian and Maroon predecessors in absorbing elements of a Westernized, Christianized culture. Beginning life anew as laborers, apprentices, and farmers, they nevertheless turned naturally to trade as a means to self-betterment, and gradually there emerged a social and economic hierarchy reflecting middle class standards of achievement.

At the bottom of the scale were the newest arrivals, unskilled laborers and cultivators struggling with an unfamiliar existence and suffering the stigma ever reserved for the newly arrived immigrant. Those who advanced beyond this stage became small traders and craftsmen, and higher still were the successful merchants with their European houses and furniture, their libraries, and their air of mid-Victorian domestic comfort. At the apex were the few large-scale merchants with extensive economic interests, community leaders notable for their public service as jurors, or in a few cases, as members of the colonial legislative council. Such were William Henry Pratt and John Ezzidio, Ibo and Nupe recaptives respectively, whose energy and imagination led to mercantile success and important trading contacts with England. Another was the self-made and industrious William Grant who rose to become a leader in Freetown circles as merchant, legislative councilor, newspaper owner, and spokesman for the community of creoles, as the Freetown Africans in time came to be known.

Although creole culture dominated the city, Freetown nevertheless maintained a cosmopolitan quality. The creoles, in their urge to become Westernized, adopted European dress, Christian worship, and Western education, at the same time developing their own patois, Krio, which varied from English, while retaining a number of their traditional customs. Others were less assimilated, however. On the streets, stately Wolof women glided by in their mantillas, while half-naked Kru laborers jostled Fulani in their long white robes. The European community was small but important because of its association with government. British administrators generally lived in open-veranda houses, and the prevailing architectural standard was the one- or two-story clapboard building with shingled, steeply pitched roof, the simple hut inhabited only by those who could afford no better. Freetown still relied largely on the outside world for its amenities. There was little machinery and a chronic shortage of skilled craftsmen. Church clocks were infrequently in working order, the government wharf possessed no crane for unloading, and even wagons and wheelbarrows were rarities. After 1852 the situation improved considerably as regular steamship service was instituted with England.

The creoles of Sierra Leone were more than casual, passive agents for the spread of European civilization in West Africa, however, for they soon found themselves pressed into service as active participants in the continuing struggle of the abolitionists against the slave trade. Despite the exertions of the naval squadrons, the trade had not died out, and African chiefs had failed to recognize the superiority of legitimate commerce over slaving. At first, European enterprise took the form of a series of expeditions to investigate the interior, and particularly to determine the course of the Niger, as a means of opening up the country to legitimate trade from Europe. Such was the motivation which lay behind the major explorers of the early nineteenth century—Mungo Park, René Caillié, Denham and Clapperton, the Lander brothers, and Heinrich Barth—but while their exertions yielded much new information concerning the West African interior, they had little impact on the problem of abolition.

By the 1830's leadership of the antislavery movement had passed on to new hands, and chief among these were Thomas Fowell Buxton, who had succeeded Wilberforce as the parliamentary spokesman for the abolitionists, and Henry Venn who became secretary of the C.M.S. in 1841. Buxton and Venn saw that the slave trade would die only when it was replaced by something more profitable to West Africans; hence, said Buxton in his influential volume, *The African Slave Trade and Its Remedy*, it was necessary to explore the interior with an eye to the establishment of permanent missions which might conclude trade treaties with local chiefs while providing training in crafts and modern agricultural methods for their people. Manned at first by European technicians and missionaries—for Christian conversion was an essential part of Buxton's plan—the stations would eventually be operated by Africans trained especially for the purpose.

The object, said Venn, was the establishment of an independent West African middle class society in faithful replica of Venn's own Victorian England. Ignorant chiefs governing primitive villagers subsisting on the edge of famine were always tempted to sell off surplus population, he continued, but West African communities of scientific farmers, merchants, and small-scale industrialists, reinvesting their surplus profits in an expanding economy, would combine an economic interest in the conservation and utilization of manpower with Christian strictures against slavery, and thus the iniquitous trade would wither away in the face of a beneficent Western Christian civilization. It was one of the first arguments for the idea of technical assistance—economic aid and specialized training to the end of creating independent, productive, modernized communities of West Africans.

European merchants already operating in West Africa had little sympathy for this brand of economic and religious philanthropy, and indeed Buxton's plans received a severe setback in 1841 when a government expedition to establish an agricultural station on the Niger ended in disaster, a third of the European members perishing of fever. The idea persisted, however, and Venn turned a weakness to advantage by insisting that it was not the European but the already Christianized, Westernized African, primarily the repatriate in Sierra Leone, who was best qualified by training, background, and physical resistance to disease, to play the major role in West African regeneration. Let British business interests invest in a profitable venture of expanding trade, let British philanthropy underwrite the expenses of establishment and training, but let the mission stations be directed and staffed by Africans.

Sierra Leone, therefore, became a major center for the development of the apostles of modernization: formally trained missionaries to staff the proposed inland stations and institute what Buxton called, "the Bible and the plough," along with less formal representatives of Westernized Africa, merchants and others among the liberated Africans who began to drift back to their homeland along the coast east of Badagry after 1839. In Freetown, Fourah Bay College was established by the C.M.S. in 1827 for the training of mission teachers, and its first pupil, Samuel Ajayi Crowther, was also to become the foremost African exponent for the assimilation by West Africans of Henry Venn's Victorian bourgeois culture.

Crowther was indeed the classic product of British philanthropy. A Yoruba rescued by the antislavery squadron when still a boy and repatriated at Freetown in 1822, he showed a quick intelligence and sober application that commended itself to the missionaries in Sierra Leone and earned him educational opportunities which led to an early career as mission teacher. After a number of years of work in the Freetown area, he accompanied the Niger expedition of 1841, then went to England for seminary study, and after being ordained, was posted to the C.M.S. mission at Abeokuta in 1845. When, with Crowther's active assistance, the C.M.S. succeeded in establishing a number of permanent stations along the Niger, it became apparent that this mission network would require its own administration, and in 1864 the former slave boy, Samuel Ajayi Crowther, became bishop of a vast diocese comprising all of West Africa save the already established British settlements.

It seemed an ideal arrangement. Crowther worked with purpose and diligence building up his missions, gaining converts both to Christianity and to the ideas for economic development of his friend and sponsor, Henry Venn. Spiritual rehabilitation through Christ and temporal regeneration through improved agricultural methods and technical training was the path of progress which he saw and followed with a clear eye. When his stations prospered but fitfully, he redoubled his efforts. When his mission workers from Sierra Leone fell short of expectations, he sought out better recruits. When some suggested that Africa might better make her own way without Europe's paternal guidance, he condemned such a view as madness which denied the fruits of mankind's progress to needy Africa. For Crowther, as well as for most of his generation of Westernized Africans, the material and spiritual development of Africa could only come in alliance with the progressive West. "Africa has neither knowledge nor skill . . . to bring out her vast resources for her own improvement," he informed his fellow workers on the Niger in 1869. ". . . Therefore to claim Africa for the Africans alone, is to claim for her the right of a continued ignorance. . . . For it is certain, unless help [comes] from without, a nation can never rise above its present state."

Such views did not preclude the vision of ultimately independent, economically viable West African communities, but it remained for second-generation liberated Africans to give more specific definition to the idea of political independence. Most eloquent among these was James Africanus Beale Horton who was born in Sierra Leone in 1835 the son of an Ibo recaptive. Horton showed early promise which aroused missionary interest and led to his education at Fourah Bay and eventual study at Edinburgh in the field of medicine. When he returned to West Africa in 1859, Horton came as a medical officer in the British army, serving for over twenty years in various stations from the Bights to the Gambia and thereby gaining an unusual familiarity with the peoples of West Africa.

Horton believed no less than Bishop Crowther in the importance of Western culture to the development of a modern West Africa, but he also took seriously statements emanating from England to the effect that the European presence in West Africa was temporary, limited both by the white man's susceptibility to killing fevers and the conviction that the end of the slave trade would also mean the end of Europe's intrusion in African affairs. Surveying the many traditional societies with which he came in contact, Horton enunciated two axioms of West African life. First, he said, there was no physical or intellectual difference between the African and the European. If the West had in fact developed a more advanced culture, this was due to historical and environmental factors which could be offset by introducing West Africans to the best elements of Western civilization. Secondly, Horton continued, the process of social improvement must end in the establishment of free nations in West Africa. Through education, technical training, and economic development the people of West Africa would eventually achieve a political and commercial stability, giving rise to a series of independent self-governing states, in the Gambia as well as Sierra Leone, among the Fante, the Yoruba, the Ibo, and other peoples. Horton's ideas, expressed in his extensive writings, were more than hothouse theorizing, for they were produced in conjunction with the effort of the Fante community to create an independent government through the Fante Confederation constitution of 1871. They also appeared, however, at a time when the authorities in Britain were shifting from a policy favoring withdrawal from West Africa to one of permanent occupation. With this basic change, West African dreams of independence went aglimmering.

WEST AFRICAN KINGDOMS IN
THE NINETEENTH CENTURY

As the nineteenth century opened, the people of West Africa in their vast majority were quite unaware either of the changing European presence or the doings of the rising coastal communities such as St. Louis or Freetown. The traditional way of life was as yet substantially untouched by such external developments which only gradually intruded on the affairs of the inland societies, for example, the great forest kingdoms with their dynastic and other intramural preoccupations. Indeed, by the early nineteenth century the main external concern of West Africa's forest people was with the slave trade which in various ways they sought to direct to their own advantage.

Slaving had little immediate effect on the destinies of the Yoruba people whose unhappy history of chronic civil war during the nineteenth century reflected an internal chaos unanticipated after the eighteenth-century triumphs of the Oyo empire. The conquest of Dahomey, the securing of a trade route from the capital of Old Oyo to the coast, and the establishment of the culturally homogeneous and politically stable metropolitan provinces of Oyo seemed an unlikely prelude to disintegration; yet the death of the *alafin,* Abiodun, early in the nineteenth century was followed by deep political cleavages involving the royal succession and the authority of the king's advisers, the *Oyo Mesi.* The consequent weakening of the state permitted the Fulani in the flood of their *jihad* to overrun Oyo, occupy Ilorin, and compel the *alafin* to the payment of tribute.

These events had major repercussions throughout Yorubaland. A vast migration southward ensued which upset the ethnic and political balance of the Yoruba forest states and triggered a series of wars and local rivalries. The town of Owu, vassal and ally to Oyo, was destroyed and disappeared from history; others like Ibadan and Abeokuta were born from the pangs of conflict, while Oyo was forced to relocate herself a hundred miles to the south on the edge of the rain forest. Ilorin, an important center within the Oyo empire, defected under its governor, Afonja, who made common cause with the Fulani as they spread southward under the impulse of their *jihad*. Even ancient Ife temporarily lost the protection of her privileged spiritual position and suffered attack. The southern remove of Oyo, which took place during the late 1830's, could not save the dwindling authority of the *alafin* who came increasingly under the influence of Ibadan which had grown rapidly as a refugee and war camp. Farther south, the Egba somehow evaded annihilation, and soon from their new city of Abeokuta they were competing with the Ijebu Yoruba as middlemen in the arms and slave traffic which had risen sharply as a result of the civil wars. Political stability disappeared in a complex of shifting alliances, and every man's hand was turned against all others as the desire for profit from slaving added its measure to the confusion and the agony. Ibadan soon became strong enough to check the Fulani push southward but not strong enough to unite Yorubaland. Out of control, the wars dragged on.

The immediate beneficiary of Yoruba strife was Dahomey. The decline of Oyo meant the realization of a long-standing national purpose to be free from the foreign yoke, an achievement which King Gezo (1818–1858) secured when he ousted an Oyo garrison during the early years of the Yoruba civil wars. Gezo was interested in more than political independence, however. Dahomey's economy, geared to the declining slave trade, needed fresh impetus which Gezo sought in the rich palm oil lands to the east where Yoruba civil conflict seemingly offered attractive prospects for easy success. Such hope proved illusory. Some early victories over the Egbado neighbors of the Egba were more than offset when Dahomey came to face the rising power of Abeokuta and was forced to accept defeat after a series of bloody attacks ended in decimation of the Dahomean forces. The last of these came in 1864, a savage thrust at Abeokuta by Glele, son and successor to Gezo, which was so disastrous to Dahomey's strength that she never again attempted large-scale military action and was compelled to simulate martial power by calculated acts of brutality against small communities and through baroque exhibitions of human sacrifice staged primarily for European

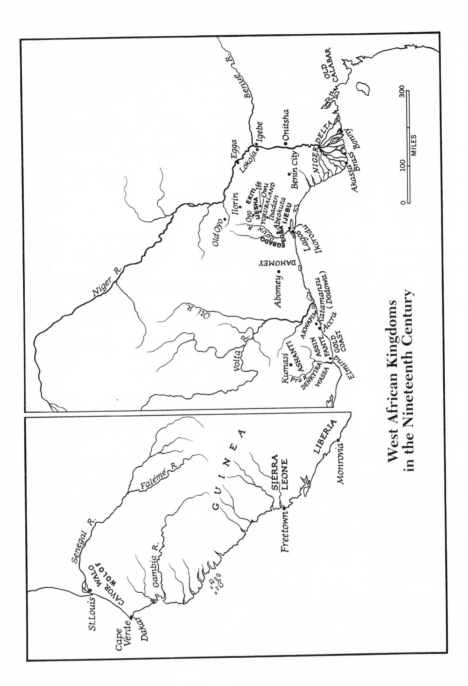

West African Kingdoms
in the Nineteenth Century

audiences. In fact, the failure to overcome the Egba denied the Dahomean economy its needed expansion, but Dahomey was still a formidable power when she finally bowed in 1892 to the superior strength of a French army which occupied her capital city of Abomey and put an end to her independence.

On the Gold Coast, the major states of Fante and Ashanti found themselves similarly caught up in the complications of a growing European presence. By 1800 Ashanti was emerging from the civil and constitutional difficulties which had beset her in the second half of the eighteenth century and was prepared both to strengthen her commercial outlets on the coast and to reassert her control over conquered southern provinces such as Wassa, Denkyira, Assin, and Akwapim. Beginning in 1806, a series of southern invasions ensued which would have gone badly for the disunited Fante had not the British authorities in the coastal forts taken sides against Ashanti, eventually forcing the abandonment of the southern provinces in 1831 after the northerners had been defeated with British help on the field of Katamansu (Dodowa).

Vexing as these developments were to Ashanti, there was little satisfaction evidenced among the coastal people, for the British, Dutch, and Danes pursued differing policies, and the British in particular seemed in African eyes to be guided by caprice as they alternated without apparent reason between indifference and interference regarding local affairs. In 1821, the British forts, which had been administered by an association of private merchants, were placed under the colonial authorities at Freetown. There followed a British disaster when the Ashanti overwhelmed the forces led by Sir Charles Macarthy in 1824, but just when this defeat was offset by the success at Katamansu, the forts once more were given over to private direction in an economy move which thoroughly perplexed and demoralized the coastal people. Next came an enlightened administration by George Maclean who served for a dozen years from 1830 as president of a council sponsored by the London merchants and whose tact and insight dissolved misunderstandings and went a long way toward establishing peace and increased trade between Ashanti and the coast.

Another seemingly inexplicable shift reintroduced in 1843 an official British presence in the forts and instituted a period of vacillating policy which undermined relations both with Ashanti and the coastal states. So disenchanted did the Fante become over the inconsistencies of British administration that they determined to form a political union capable of standing up to the Ashanti without reference to the government of the forts. In 1868, in the face of reviving Ashanti aggression, they formed the Fante Confederation as the basis for an independent state, but the Confederation soon collapsed when the British, in another unexpected change of direction, arrested its leaders as conspirators in 1871. This was but the prelude to a much firmer British colonial policy which was manifested three years later when the Gold Coast was annexed as a crown colony.

Part of the Fante trouble lay in their factious nature for they had great difficulty in working together even when a strong state would have provided desirable stability, defense equally against Ashanti invasion and British intervention. Such weakness was not unique. Other traditional societies also had their shortcomings which compounded the difficulties of dealing with the European enclaves along the coast. In this respect the Wolof kingdom of Cayor was particularly vulnerable; not only did it occupy the territory between St. Louis on the Senegal and the new port of Dakar founded by the French in 1857, but there were cleavages within the realm which invited intervention and conquest. Wolof society had long been ordered in a rigid hierarchy which placed the nobility at the top, followed by the mass of free peasants, and finally by the caste groups of which the *griots,* or praise singers, were particularly notable. Theoretically the bottom of the scale was occupied by the slaves, but slaves possessed carefully defined privileges which sometimes made their lot preferable to that of freemen; for example, the royal slaves from whom were drawn the *tyeddo,* or Cayor soldiery, had a military function which gave them the power to make and unmake kings.

By the middle of the nineteenth century a profound antipathy had developed between the farming population and the royal slave-soldiers who lived by plundering the yeomanry, an antipathy which gained strength from the fact that the peasants were Muslim and the *tyeddo* pagan. Between 1862 and 1886 the *damel,* or king of the Cayor, was Lat-Dior whose reign was interrupted periodically by French interference but who managed to maintain the independence of his realm for almost a quarter of a century, a tribute to his own tenacity and the toughness of his soldiers. The French pressed hard in their determination to join St. Louis and Dakar by telegraph and rail and to convert the Cayor into a peaceful protectorate devoted to groundnut culture. In the long run they were bound to prevail, but the break when it came was caused both by external interference and internal dissension. A split developed between the *damel* and his *tyeddo* arising from Lat-Dior's conversion to Islam and his consequent attempt to put an end to the traditional pillaging of the countryside by his troops. Thus it was that in the face of increasing French intrusion the beleaguered king found himself without the indispensable support of his throne slaves. In a last ditch encounter he was cut down by French troops and the Cayor annexed to Senegal.

THE VANISHING DREAM

The vision of a series of independent, prosperous African states, so vivid in the imagination of Fowell Buxton, Henry Venn, Samuel Crowther, and Africanus Horton, faded before the realities of individual ambition, human frailty, and economic motivation set in the rigors of the West African environment. European powers, economy-minded and dedicated to the anticolonial principles of laissez-faire, nevertheless found themselves drawn inexorably into a deepening entanglement in West African affairs. African peoples, eager for the opportunities of increased trade but jealous of their sovereignty, experienced increasing difficulty in segregating political from economic involvement, and slowly lost the sovereignty which was the source of their economic strength. The idea of independence finally gave way to the fact of colonialism, and the dream of free and modern West African societies was forced to await its realization until the mid-twentieth century.

The heart of the matter lay in the legitimate commerce sought by Europe's merchants and encouraged by her missionaries, the latter eager to develop a substitute for the slave trade. In the Senegal Valley the traffic in gum was a modest but exclusive occupation of the mulatto and European traders of St. Louis and as such formed a fragile prop for local prosperity and an inconsequential element in the French national economy. The trade, moveover, suffered the further complication in the eyes of the French government of requiring substantial military assistance to neutralize the mercantilism of powerful indigenous states controlling both banks of the river. Nevertheless, there were offsetting arguments favoring greater involvement—the long-lived illusion of untold wealth in the interior and the nationalism of the French Revolution added to the ancient

Bourbon dream of empire which began to revive during the 1850's with the rise of Louis Napoleon.

In 1854 a succession of ineffectual administrations came to an end with the appointment of Louis Faidherbe as governor of Senegal. Though sympathetic and informed regarding African civilization, Faidherbe nonetheless was a firm believer in the absolute superiority of French culture, nor did he shrink from the logic that commerce on the Senegal could not prosper without military support. Organizing the celebrated corps of African riflemen, the *Tirailleurs Sénégalais,* Faidherbe embarked on a series of campaigns which greatly expanded French influence beyond the coastal enclaves. The Trarza Moors were forceably persuaded to respect the river traders, forts were built southward along the coast, and the Cayor and other territories were subjected to military and diplomatic pressures. Even the formidable *al-Hajj* Umar, hesitating over the direction of his *jihad,* was diverted from the Senegal Valley by the defense of Medina in 1857, and turned his attention inland toward the Niger.

Faidherbe's lengthy administration (1854–1861, 1863–1865) converted Senegal's modest mercantile pretensions to dreams of glory. He founded the port of Dakar, improved the facilities at St. Louis, joined the two towns by telegraph in 1859, and laid plans for extensive agricultural developments in the Cayor and adjacent areas. His vision of a link between the Senegal and Niger basins led to negotiations with *al-Hajj* Umar which, though they produced no immediate results, showed the way to subsequent French penetration of the interior late in the nineteenth century. Thus, there emerged the image of a prosperous commercial and agricultural colony developing under the genial influence of French culture and the enlightened direction of French administrators. In the decades that followed Faidherbe, French influence spread inexorably. Chieftains like Lat-Dior were subdued, albeit often with difficulty, French commercial interests centered in Bordeaux gradually ousted the mulattoes from control of economic affairs, while the thoroughly gallicized mulattoes gained compensation by maintaining political ascendancy over the rising African population in the expanding towns.

Increasing British involvement in the affairs of West Africa was similarly connected with the rise of those trading activities which replaced slaving. In the Niger Delta, palm oil had proved a ready substitute, and by mid-century there existed a lively exchange between the Liverpool merchants and the Delta middlemen who had once been the principals of the slave trade. It was a rough and ready world, however; disputes were common, and in 1849 Britain agreed to the appointment of a consul, John Beecroft, to represent the English mercantile interests on the coast. A forceful individual, Beecroft was soon intervening in the affairs of local states like Bonny and Old Calabar, and his successors in the office of consul also found themselves drawn into intramural quarrels in their effort to protect the interests of the European supercargoes. Moreover, the temptation was always strong to increase outside pressure beyond the powers of mere persuasion, to introduce an element of force and to argue for the establishment of some form of protectorate in the Delta. The authorities in London would have none of this, however, and in 1865 the House of Commons produced the report of its Select Committee on West Africa which recommended, not further extension of British rule, but the preparation of Africans for self-government as a prelude to withdrawal from all territories except the repatriation center of Sierra Leone.

Such a view was out of step with events. In 1854 an expedition up the Niger under Dr. W. B. Baikie had demonstrated the efficacy of quinine as a malaria suppressant, and when regular steam navigation of the river was introduced three years later by Macgregor Laird, there developed the early prospect of direct commercial penetration of the interior and the eventual elimination of the African middlemen of Bonny, Brass, Old Calabar, and other city states in the Niger Delta. The opposition of these Oil Rivers communities was immediate, persistent, but unavailing, and even the widespread hostility of the inland people did not succeed for long in stemming the rising tide of Niger traffic. British official involvement followed the trade. A consul was placed up the Niger at Lokoja and warships were used for a time to escort the river steamers. The powers of the Delta consulate were increased and its influence rose accordingly. The logic of circumstances pointed to the establishment of a protectorate which was finally proclaimed in 1885.

In Yorubaland a different set of events was leading to the same growing British involvement. Widespread slaving caused by the Yoruba wars brought direct intervention in the affairs of Lagos in 1851 when Consul Beecroft deposed the reigning king, Kosoko, replacing him with a more tractable member of the royal house. Intervention raised more problems than it solved, however, for the consuls subsequently based in Lagos soon found themselves increasingly entangled by the diplomatic complexities of the Yoruba wars as they sought to develop legitimate commerce with the interior as a substitute for the outlawed slave trade. Lagos was annexed by treaty in 1861, but the wars, which flared up again at the same time, brought a breakdown of inland commerce, worrying the new government at Lagos which was expected by the authorities in London to foster trade while maintaining a policy of non-interference in Yoruba affairs.

During the 1860's the administration at Lagos was under the direction of the vigorous Lieutenant-Governor John H. Glover who viewed the Yoruba wars largely as a struggle on the part of the interior power of Ibadan to gain access to the coastal markets at Lagos despite the blockade of the trade routes by the Ijebu, and particularly by the Egba. Glover's tactics, therefore, called for pressure on Abeokuta to relax her restrictions while seeking alternate lines of communication between Lagos and Ibadan. This necessarily led to deteriorating relations with the Egba which degenerated into open hostilities in 1865 when Glover's troops drove an Egba army from its siege of Ikorodu, and in 1867 precipitated the expulsion of the C.M.S. mission from Abeokuta as a reaction to British interference. With the departure of Glover in 1872, tensions were eased somewhat, but intramural Yoruba disputes continued to be affected by the attitude of the Lagos government and merchant community, always intent upon increasing trade with the interior.

In part, these difficulties grew from the contradictions of a policy which encouraged an increase of trade but refused to admit the political consequences; in part, they reflected the gap between the statesmanship formulated in London and the way in which officials in the field interpreted their instructions and met the exigencies of daily problems. Such complications were particularly pronounced on the Gold Coast after 1843 when direct administration of the forts was resumed. In 1844 a series of bonds were signed with coastal states introducing English justice in their territories and abolishing such customs as human sacrifice, but stopping short of any direct intrusion in the government of these communities. The signatory chiefs, however, felt they were gaining British protection along with British law, and were nonplused when in 1868 the Dutch and English, without warning, exchanged a number of their forts in a move which increased administrative efficiency by creating contiguous stretches of coast under British and Dutch control, but which seriously upset the local power balance, particularly in relation to Ashanti.

States like Denkyira or Assin, traditional enemies of Ashanti, suddenly found themselves tied to the pro-Ashanti Dutch and thereby susceptible to attack from the north. Elmina, Ashanti's long-standing coastal outlet, moreover, now came under Fante pressure to break with Ashanti, a situation which greatly disturbed the northerners who dispatched a raiding party to the coastal area around Elmina in 1869. Britain refused to be provoked into action and, as her prestige slumped, the Fante Confederation was formally launched to oppose Ashanti. At this juncture the Dutch withdrew leaving the British in sole possession of all the coastal forts, including Elmina. While London continued to avoid direct confrontation with Ashanti, her government on the Gold Coast wrecked the Fante Confederation and thus destroyed any concerted local opposition to invasion.

In 1873 the Ashanti armies crossed the Pra and moved against the coast to retake Elmina and at last London decided upon strong military action in support of the coastal position. It was a major turning point in British West African policy. Once the English government and people faced the fact of Britain's long-standing and deepening involvement in Gold Coast affairs, the victory in the Ashanti war of 1873–1874 was quickly followed by annexation of the coastal settlements as the Gold Coast Colony, and a new chapter opened in the history of British relations in West Africa.

If Africanus Horton's image of independent West African states disappeared in the wreckage of the Fante Confederation, the failure of the humanitarians to create a new civilization in West Africa was best exemplified in the fate of Bishop Crowther and his Niger missions. Partly the difficulty lay in a shortfall between theory and practice—the impossible task of creating in a few short years communities of Christian, bourgeois, Westernized yeomen and merchants capable of demonstrating the values of a completely new and strange way of life and persuading their neighbors to partake of its fruits. Partly it reflected the force of circumstances which substituted imperialism for humanitarianism, converting the philanthropic ideals of the Buxtons and the Venns to the commercial designs of George Goldie Taubman, or the imperial dreams of Jules Ferry.

In building the Niger missions, Crowther faced an enormous task from the start. At once his appointment as bishop stimulated the jealousy of European missionaries and deprived him of effective control over the already established African churches in Yorubaland and Sierra Leone, a complication which blurred the conception of an indigenous church capable of propagating itself through missions founded by its own workers. In addition, there was the dependence of the Niger missions on traders, Europeans and Africans alike, for transportation and supplies, a dependence which strained relations between those interested in evangelization and those preoccupied with commercial gain. Nonetheless, the work went forward. Crowther had been instrumental in the establishment of stations at Onitsha and Igbebe (Lokoja) in 1857, and in time others followed—Akassa at the Niger mouth in 1861, Bonny and Brass in 1864 and 1868 respectively, and Egga beyond the confluence of the Niger and Benue in 1873.

Slowly, at first imperceptibly, a subtle change began to take form within the missionary movement. The rising interest in West African trade which led to the growing political involvement encouraged by men like Faidherbe, Glover, and Beecroft, led also to a redefinition of European-African relations. The older notion of the equality of all men before God had formed the basis for Henry Venn's program of African regeneration with its principle of partnership between European and African. Now, during the 1870's and 1880's, this view was giving way to a doctrine of Caucasian superiority which, though rooted in the pseudoscientific pronouncements of Richard Burton and his school of thought, had educated European missionaries to a skepticism over the capacity of the African to digest the benefits of Victorian civilization.

Venn died in 1873 and his successors retained little of his faith in African capability. The chronic complaint by traders that mission stations were inefficiently operated by lazy, drunken, dissolute agents was given a hearing in London, presumably because the Niger missionaries were all Africans and thus not considered fully tested. In 1877 the C.M.S. limited Bishop Crowther's authority by appointing a European lay worker to take charge of all temporal affairs connected with the Niger missions, and two years later financial control was vested in a committee of five Europeans and three Africans based in Lagos. Reports of mismanagement and irregularities on the Niger persisted, and in some cases were substantiated. In the changing context of the times these incidents prompted the conclusion at missionary headquarters in London that Crowther was an ineffective administrator overindulgent with his erring charges, while his missions were sadly in need of European supervision. Bit by bit, the old bishop's position was circumscribed, his agents charged with various offenses which were followed with suspension, transfer, or dismissal. By 1891,

Crowther, a now-ailing octogenarian, had been in effect superseded by a group of European missionaries, and in December of that year he died. With him also died the idea of a new independent Africa through the vehicle of an indigenous, self-propagating, Christian church. But by this time another age had dawned and the European scramble for Africa was in full flux.

Suggestions for Further Reading

There is a series of histories of West Africa, region by region, which are basic to this chapter, notably Michael Crowder, *The Story of Nigeria,* rev. ed. (London: Faber and Faber, 1966), *A Short History of Nigeria,* rev. ed. (New York: Praeger, 1966); W. E. F. Ward, *A History of Ghana,* 2nd. ed. (London: George Allen and Unwin, 1958); Christopher Fyfe, *A History of Sierra Leone* (London: Oxford University Press, 1962); and H. A. Gailey, *A History of the Gambia* (London: Routledge and Kegan Paul, 1964); this last to be combined with J. M. Gray, *History of the Gambia* (London: Frank Cass, and New York: Barnes & Noble, 1966). Senegal lacks a work in English; two histories in French are P. Cultru, *Histoire du Sénégal du XV Siècle à 1870* (Paris: Larose, 1910), and A. Villard, *Histoire du Sénégal* (Dakar: Maurice Viale, 1943). No satisfactory history of Liberia is available but information on its early affairs may be found in C. H. Huberich, *The Political and Legislative History of Liberia,* 2v. (New York: Central Book Co., 1947); P. J. Staudenraus, *The African Colonization Movement, 1816–1865* (New York: Columbia University Press, 1961); and J. F. A. Ajayi and I. Espie, eds., *A Thousand Years of West African History* (Ibadan: Ibadan University Press, 1965).

In addition to the above works, special treatment of early nineteenth-century European influences in West Africa is contained in R. W. July, *The Origins of Modern African Thought* (New York: Praeger, 1967 and London: Faber, 1968); while the abolitionist movement is dealt with in R. Coupland, *The British Anti-Slavery Movement,* 2nd. ed. (London: Frank Cass, 1964). To offset Coupland, see Eric Williams, *Capitalism and Slavery* (London: Andre Deutch, 1964). French assimilationist policy is traced in M. Crowder, *Senegal,* rev. ed. (London: Methuen, 1967). For a special study of Freetown society, see A. T. Porter, *Creoledom* (London: Oxford University Press, 1963).

French colonial activities in West Africa during the early nineteenth century are studied in G. Hardy, *La Mise en Valeur du Sénégal de 1817 à 1854* (Paris: Larose, 1921), and B. Schnapper, *La Politique et le Commerce Français dans le Golfe de Guinée de 1838 à 1871* (Paris:

Mouton, 1961); but see also J. D. Hargreaves, *Prelude to the Partition of West Africa* (London: Macmillan, 1963), and R. W. July, cited above.

The role of the missions is set forth in J. F. A. Ajayi, *Christian Missions in Nigeria, 1841–1891* (London: Longmans, 1965), and E. A. Ayandele, *The Missionary Impact on Modern Nigeria, 1842–1914* (London: Longmans, 1966; New York: Humanities Press). For the Sierra Leoneans returning to Yorubaland, see J. H. Kopytoff, *A Preface to Modern Nigeria* (Madison: University of Wisconsin Press, 1965). The ideas of Crowther and Horton are studied in R. W. July, cited above, and for Horton see also D. Kimble, *A Political History of Ghana, 1850–1928* (Oxford: Clarendon Press, 1963).

For West African kingdoms, see D. Forde and P. M. Kaberry, eds., *West African Kingdoms in the Nineteenth Century* (London: Oxford University Press, 1967) as well as the relevant citations listed above, particularly the chapters in Ajayi and Espie by A. A. Boahen and I. A. Akinjogbin on the Gold Coast and Dahomey respectively. See also S. O. Biobaku, *The Egba and their Neighbours, 1842–1872* (Oxford: Clarendon Press, 1957); S. Johnson, *The History of the Yorubas* (Lagos: C.M.S. Bookshops, 1921; New York: Humanities Press); J. F. A. Ajayi and R. Smith, *Yoruba Warfare in the Nineteenth Century* (Cambridge: Cambridge University Press, 1964); and I. A. Akinjogbin, *Dahomey and its Neighbours, 1708–1818* (Cambridge: Cambridge University Press, 1967).

The onset of the colonial period is the theme of Michael Crowder, *West Africa under Colonial Rule* (London: Hutchinson, 1968; Evanston, Illinois: Northwestern University Press, 1968), and J. D. Hargreaves, cited above, and there are many other works dealing with aspects of the subject, a few of which are W. W. Claridge, *A History of the Gold Coast and Ashanti*, 2v., 2nd. ed. (London: Frank Cass, 1964; New York: Barnes & Noble, 1964); K. O. Dike, *Trade and Politics in the Niger Delta* (Oxford: Clarendon Press, 1956); C. W. Newbury, *The Western Slave Coast and its Rulers* (Oxford: Clarendon Press, 1961); G. I. Jones, *The Trading States of the Oil Rivers* (London: Oxford University Press, 1963); G. E. Metcalfe, *Maclean of the Gold Coast* (London: Oxford University Press, 1962); J. E. Flint, *Sir George Goldie and the Making of Nigeria* (London: Oxford University Press, 1960); Martin A. Klein, *Islam and Imperialism in Senegal, Sine-Saloum, 1847–1914* (Stanford: Stanford University Press, 1968); and D. Kimble, already cited. For changing European attitudes toward Africa and Africans, see P. D. Curtin, *The Image of Africa* (Madison: University of Wisconsin Press, 1964).

13: Commerce and Statecraft in Eastern and Central Africa

THE RISE OF INTERNATIONAL TRADE

When the Ngoni forded the Zambezi in 1835 and penetrated the East African plateau, they brought revolutionary changes to a seemingly static pastoral scene. Their violent military tactics and novel political institutions meant annihilation for some, absorption into Ngoni life for others, and new social and political configurations for still others. Before their arrival, the peaceful countryside had been dotted with scattered villages sustained by a subsistence agriculture which provided a modest but adequate existence for a peasantry whose wants were simple and whose daily round had not greatly altered over the centuries. Although there were occasional fertile pockets, the rolling landscape was poor in soil and deficient in rainfall, and supported only a sparse population centered in tiny farming communities with little mutual economic and political contact, an isolation which greatly simplified the task of conquest for the invaders.

The impact of the Ngoni was shattering, but their long-range effect was no more profound and far less pervasive than that of its antecedent, which had begun to exert influence on the East African plateau well before the intrusion from the south. This was the vast Bantu migration spilling over subequatorial Africa and early reaching the eastern continental shores where it helped form the Swahili population of the coastal trading communities. On the western side of Africa the Bantu were in contact with Portuguese mariners by the fifteenth century in a relationship that gave rise to the slave traffic of Kongo and Angola. In the interior, however, the even tenor of bucolic life seems not to have stimulated the need either for revolutionary social reform or a more sophisticated economy involving systematic, long-range, intercontinental trade. Consequently, unlike the Sudanic regions, eastern Africa was characterized by only the slightest commercial and intellectual intercourse with the outside world. The early exchange by which Arab traders obtained the gold of Mutapa failed to expand beyond the Zambezi country, leaving the vast interior stretching from the upper reaches of the Nile to the Limpopo and beyond, isolated, remote, and introspective.

Isolation was never complete, however, nor were the people of the interior wholly content with their inward orientation. Slight but suggestive archeological evidence indicates an ancient trade in the Zambezi Valley exchanging local ivory for fabrics, beads, and other imported goods brought to the coastal ports of East Africa. There was, moreover, the substantial and long-lived gold trade of Mutapa and Changamire which finally foundered, not through African indifference, but from maladroit handling by the Portuguese after their occupation of the coastal entrepôts at the beginning of the sixteenth century. Furthermore, the Malawi people who took up residence at the southwest corner of Lake Nyasa (Malawi) probably by the beginning of the fourteenth century, had developed by the sixteenth century long-distance trading to coastal points such as Mozambique Island and Kilwa as the economic basis of their state. When the Malawi empire began to disintegrate, it was the Yao who replaced them by the end of the seventeenth century as the dominant traders to the coast. Finally, during the late eighteenth century, there were the Lunda kingdoms of *Mwata Yamvo* and of his vassal, who held the title of *Mwata Kazembe*. Both were focal points for a lively external trade east and west which saw slaves and ivory exchanged for a variety of manufactured goods, judging from the dishware, table silver, mirrors, and fabrics found at their courts.

The two kingdoms were located in the sparsely wooded country of the southern Congo watershed, that of *Mwata Yamvo* along the Kasai and Lulua tributaries and the *Kazembe's* in the valley of the Luapula within the copper-bearing Katanga. Their commerce was

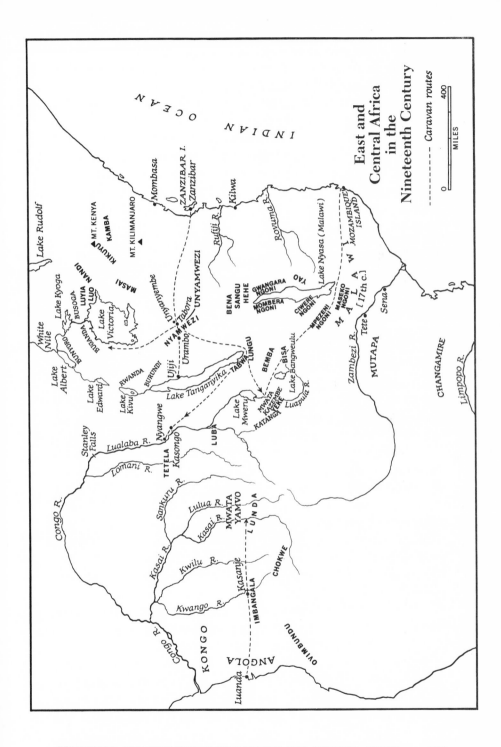

East and
Central Africa
in the
Nineteenth Century

----- Caravan routes

0   400
    MILES

INDIAN OCEAN

Lake Rudolf

Lake Kyoga

White Nile

Lake Albert

Lake Edward

Lake Victoria

Lake Kivu

BUNYORO

BUGANDA

BUSOGA

RWANDA

BURUNDI

NANDI

LUO

LUYIA

MASAI

KIKUYU

KAMBA

MT. KENYA

MT. KILIMANJARO

Mombasa

ZANZIBAR I.
Zanzibar

Kilwa

Rufiji R.

Rovuma R.

UNYAMWEZI

NYAMWEZI

Unyanyembe

Tabora

Urambo

Ujiji

Lake Tanganyika

TABWA

LUNGU

BEMBA

BISA

Lake Bangweulu

Luapula R.

Lake Mweru

MWATA KAZEMBE
KATANGA

MPEZENI
NGONI

MASEKO
NGONI

CIWERE
NGONI

MOMBERA
NGONI

GWANGARA
NGONI

BENA

SANGU

HEHE

YAO

Lake Nyasa (Malawi)

MALAWI
[17th c.]

MOZAMBIQUE ISLAND

Zambezi R.

Tete

Sena

MUTAPA

CHANGAMIRE

Limpopo R.

Stanley Falls

Lualaba R.

Lomani R.

Congo R.

Nyangwe

Kasongo

TETELA

LUBA

Sankuru R.

Lulua R.

Kasai R.

Kwilu R.

Kwango R.

Kasai R.

MWATA YAMVO

LUNDA

CHOKWE

Kasanje

IMBANGALA

KONGO

ANGOLA

Luanda

OVIMBUNDU

not handled directly or by the Portuguese and Arabs on the coast but rather by inland African middlemen, to the west the Imbangala, and in the east primarily the Bisa and Yao. The Bisa, who were related to the Lunda, sometimes sent their caravans straight through to the coast from their homeland east of Lake Bangweulu. Alternatively, they sold their goods to the Yao who took them from their own territory east of Lake Nyasa to Kilwa or Zanzibar. On the Atlantic side, the Imbangala monopolized the trade between *Mwata Yamvo's* kingdom and their capital of Kasanje from whence it was transshipped to the Angolan coast by *pombeiros*, trading agents of African or mulatto descent, who worked upcountry for the Portuguese at Luanda.

By the opening of the nineteenth century, these indications of interest in long-distance trade by peoples of the interior had been given additional affirmation by the activities of the Nyamwezi who occupied an extensive stretch of plateau country to the east of Lake Tanganyika. Organized into a series of decentralized chiefdoms and primarily concerned with farming and stock raising in their dry but fertile land, they nevertheless had developed a taste for commerce which gained them a widespread reputation as a trading people. These mercantile preoccupations arose from two factors. In the first place, the Nyamwezi country of Unyamwezi—poetically known as the Land of the Moon—was ideally situated to control a growing network of trade routes throughout the interior. From the principle center of Unyanyembe a major artery extended eastward to Zanzibar, five hundred miles distant. To the north was Lake Victoria and her bordering kingdoms, which by the late eighteenth century were receiving Indian calico and other goods via Unyamwezi. West and south beyond Lake Tanganyika lay the Katanga of *Mwata Kazembe* where Nyamwezi traders were active, exchanging manufactured goods for slaves, ivory, and copper, much of the copper going to the lake kingdoms in the form of ceremonial objects and articles of personal adornment.

Their strategic location aside, the Nyamwezi had developed a high competence as carriers, an occupation of prime importance in a land where in practical fact no other means of transportation existed. Pride in this skill reinforced a Nyamwezi monopoly of the carrying trade and manifested itself in the great caravans which wound their way, hundreds strong, to the coast each year. Though these expeditions contained donkeys, they were lightly loaded, the bulk of the merchandise being carried by the porters. Once on the coast, the men remained for some months busying themselves with odd jobs or raising crops on borrowed land. Thoroughly professional as porters, they were less impressive traders, lacking ability to bargain and generally unfamiliar with the institution of credit. In commercially sophisticated Zanzibar, this could have been a serious disability and an encouragement to the Swahili traders to venture inland, as indeed they subsequently did.

THE ECONOMIC IMPERIALISM OF SAYYID SAID

The outward commercial pressure of the Nyamwezi and other people of the deep continental interior soon led to a counterthrust from the outside inward, also primarily on behalf of trade. Among the first to show interest were the Portuguese—characteristically acquisitive but generally unsuccessful. Undismayed by the failure to gain control of the gold fields of Mutapa and Changamire, Portugal had subsequently looked northward where by the late eighteenth century her representatives were in commercial contact with the Lunda state of *Mwata Yamvo* via Angola, and *Mwata Kazembe's* kingdom by way of Tete on the Zambezi. In Lisbon the authorities had long contemplated the possibility of a transcontinental route which would connect Angola and Mozambique and bring forth great commercial and political dividends. With the occupation of South Africa by the British in 1795, this plan gained a new urgency and precipitated two expeditions in 1798 and 1806 with the purpose of surveying and securing a link across the continent.

The first reconnaissance, leaving Tete under the command of the explorer, Francisco de Lacerda, reached the capital of *Mwata Kazembe* but was permitted to go no further, for there was fear that the Europeans might arrogate authority and usurp the westward traffic to the land of *Mwata Yamvo*. In 1806 two *pombeiros* were sent from Angola to cross to the east coast, and after many delays, succeeded in reaching Tete and eventually in returning westward to their starting point. This journey brought no progress toward greater Portuguese influence in the interior; indeed, the earlier promise of trade between Tete and the Lunda states had failed to materialize, possibly because of competition from the Bisa and Nyamwezi. When in 1831 a third expedition was sent from Tete in quest of the

Kazembe's patronage, it failed utterly, the king pointing out that he already had satisfactory commercial contacts with the Zanzibar coast through the Bisa.

It was, therefore, the energetic merchandising of the Nyamwezi, Bisa, and Yao which was in large measure responsible for the buildup of an external trade, and more particularly for the guidance of that commerce away from the Portuguese entrepôts to the Arab and Swahili centers such as Kilwa and Zanzibar. At the same time a rising world demand for slaves and ivory stimulated along the coast a great curiosity concerning the continental interior as a source for those commodities. Like the Portuguese, the Arab and Swahili merchants sought to establish more immediate contacts with the inland people, but unlike the Portuguese they were largely successful in this effort. That this was so is closely related to the career of Sayyid Said, *Imam* of Muscat from 1806 to 1856 and suzerain of the Arab settlements on the East African coast, for it was Said who played a leading role in organizing and directing the commercial penetration of the interior during the years of his long reign.

To a considerable extent Said's presence in East Africa was circumstantial. As ruler of the Omani empire, he was primarily interested in strengthening the traditional control of Muscat over shipping in the Indian Ocean—from the Middle East to India and from India to East Africa. During the early years of the nineteenth century Muscat prospered as the great naval powers of France and England, locked in combat, permitted the Indian Ocean commerce to fall to the Arabs. With the defeat of Napoleon, however, Britain reasserted her naval supremacy, encouraging traders from India and extending her influence along the Arabian coast. Stymied at home, Said turned his attention to East Africa where he gradually brought his dependencies under more direct control, while he grew increasingly impressed with the commercial possibilities of the interior trade.

In 1837, the occupation of Mombasa broke the last resistance of the Mazrui family, thus securing Said's authority on the East African coast and setting the stage for his permanent move from Muscat to Zanzibar three years later. Long before this, however, Said, with consummate tact and a sure economic instinct, had begun to lay the foundations for a commercial empire which linked the coastal markets with the peoples of the interior via the extended network of caravan trails already established by the Nyamwezi and other inland traders.

The key to Said's success was coordination and expansion of available resources rather than the introduction of innovations. The trails, for example, were already in existence and Swahili or Arab traders had begun to travel them in small numbers during the early nineteenth century. Under Said, however, the frequency and size of coastal caravans were greatly increased, communities of Arab merchants were strategically placed along the routes, and agreements were solicited with groups like the Nyamwezi guaranteeing protection and exemption from tolls. In this way Arab centers developed at Ujiji on Lake Tanganyika and Tabora adjacent to Unyanyembe where they served as staging areas for further penetration and commercial advantage such as the contacts made with the Baganda in 1844 and after.

Furthermore, Sayyid Said well understood the relationship between commerce and capital; hence he was at pains to encourage immigration of Indian bankers, the so-called *Banyans*, who were granted religious toleration and given control of the financial administration at Zanzibar, including the all-important customs. The Indian and Arab communities in East Africa were naturally antagonistic and were able to cooperate neither before nor after the time of Said, but during his reign he was able to combine their assets—the financial acumen of the *Banyan*, the toughness of the Arab soldier and trader —to the advantage of all. Finally, Said greatly solidified the economy of Zanzibar by encouraging the culture of cloves already begun before his arrival, a move which expanded annual exports many fold while providing a local market for slaves from the interior needed to work the clove plantations. The resulting prosperity was demonstrated with dramatic clarity in export-import figures which increased enormously during the middle years of the century; by 1859, for example, Zanzibar stood as the world's foremost exporter of cloves, ivory, and gum-copal.

During Sayyid Said's day the Arab penetration of the interior was purely commercial and was meant to be no more. Caravans proceeding to the coast necessarily included armed guards, and the settlements such as Ujiji or Tabora could be defended if the occasion demanded, but basically these were peaceful, semipermanent settlements which rose and fell in numbers and activity with the volume of trade and which were characterized by comfortable houses, carefully cultivated gardens, flocks and herds, well-stocked warehouses, and quantities of slaves for domestic service or eventual sale in the coastal markets. In time this purely commercial character changed to something more political, partly because the death of Sayyid Said in 1856 deprived the merchants of his clarity of purpose, partly because mercantile objectives tended to suggest political means, and partly because new forces from Europe began to influence the decisions of the sultan at Zanzibar.

The exact nature of the Arab presence in the interior varied greatly from place to place, however. The traders numbered only two or three thousand widely scattered individuals whose influence necessarily was conditioned largely by the reaction of the local people. In Unyamwezi the settlers at Tabora were able for a time to interfere successfully in parochial affairs, in 1859 unseating Manua Sera as chief of Unyanyembe when he sought to tax Arab caravans. Later they found themselves greatly restricted by the rising power of a neighboring chief, Mirambo, who between 1876 and 1880 took control of the roads northwest to Buganda and founded a market which offered a lively competition to the Arab emporium at Tabora. In Buganda the burgeoning Zanzibari trade was consummated in 1869 by formal diplomatic representation which exercised important influence in local politics, but in the highlands to the east the Arabs made little headway until late in the century because of the hostility of people like the Kamba, Kikuyu, Masai, and Nandi. Far to the south they fared no better. East of Lake Nyasa, (Malawi) they came only as clients to trade with the Yao slavers, and a similar situation obtained north of the lake because of the strength of the Bena, Sangu, and Hehe people. To the west of Lake Tanganyika the Nyamwezi caravans kept the coastmen out of the Katanga, and it was not until the early 1880's, during the days of Tippu Tib, that the sultan at Zanzibar was able to assert authority south and west, an authority which on the eve of the European scramble for Africa, turned out to be extremely short-lived.

In any event, it was already an empty authority, for the sultan, Sayyid Barghash, had long since lost effective control of his realm. During the reign of Sayyid Said, the British had exerted pressure at Zanzibar through a permanent resident, but Said's considerable diplomatic skill had minimized this influence, even succeeding in maintaining the slave trade without hindrance despite a treaty of 1845 designed to put an end to the traffic between Zanzibar and Muscat. Said's son, Majid (1856–1870) proved to be a weak ruler, however, whose indecision and procrastination led him to rely intermittently on the British for support with a consequent loss of his independence.

Majid's successor, Barghash (1870–1888), though much more assertive, soon found himself under similar obligation, so that the British consul, John Kirk, quickly became a major voice in the Zanzibar government. In 1873 a treaty was forced upon Barghash putting an end to the slave trade throughout his territories, and from this point Kirk urged Barghash to greater military and diplomatic penetration inland, partly to extend the force of the slave trade treaty and partly to counter growing interest in the interior by other European powers. This was the basis for the 1882 arrangement with Tippu Tib in which Tib was to administer his own extensive holdings in the eastern Congo under nominal Zanzibari authority while diverting all the ivory of the region eastward to Barghash's coastal markets. Despite Tippu's energy this move was soon rendered obsolete by the Berlin Conference of 1884, leaving Barghash bereft of both empire and illusions. "I must beg your forgiveness," he informed Tib when the latter returned to Zanzibar in 1886. "I no longer have any hope of keeping the interior. The Europeans . . . are after my possessions. . . . Happy are those who died before now, and know nothing of this."

FIREARMS AND THE SHIFTING ECOLOGY OF THE INTERIOR

The Arabs came to the interior, prodded by the external market for ivory and slaves. At first they offered in exchange those age-old commodities, cloth and beads, but by the middle of the nineteenth century the inland people were demanding and receiving firearms. Guns for ivory and guns for slaves was a certain formula for increased warfare and a declining political stability. Arms encouraged the natural aggressiveness of some, helped others in the killing efficiency of their ivory hunt, and tempted still others to indulge their predatory inclinations through slaving. As time passed, the system fed upon itself—more guns and an ever-rising demand for diminishing supplies of ivory led to increased raiding and slaving with consequent breakdown of village life and the rise of bands of rootless adventurers all too ready to add their measure of violence to the turbulent times.

An oversupply of slaves developed as a result of the 1873 antislavery treaty, flooding the inland markets, cheapening life and compounding human suffering. Perhaps the more fortunate were those who became the agricultural workers and concubines for traders like the Yao or Nyamwezi. Many others were pressed into service as porters for the ivory bound toward the coast and, judging from the accounts of travelers and missionaries, these were callously butchered or left by the wayside to expire of starvation or exhaustion when they were unable to carry their loads farther. Finally there were those who fell before the initial onslaught, cut down while fleeing blindly from the attack on their homes, their rotting corpses and bleached bones soon the only testimony to the futility of their fate.

Warfare, slaving, and political disintegration were by no means uniformly distributed in the interior, the highest incidence occurring around Lake Nyasa (Malawi) and in the Congo basin, territories characterized by isolated villages incapable of uniting in self-defense. In a massive demonstration of the laws of natural selection, only those survived who could adapt to the changing times. The Yao, for example, were a decentralized people living under petty, independent chiefs early in the nineteenth century. Finding themselves imperiled by gun-bearing neighbors, they quickly gained firearms themselves, then responding a second time to environmental provocation, became the chief procurers of slaves for the Kilwa market, extending their territorial influence and centralizing their political authority. Kindred Malawi people were unable, for their part, to make similar adjustments and paid the price as they marched in the columns of the slave caravans their Yao neighbors sent to the coast.

Others also fared variously, although it was not always guns which played the decisive part. The Bisa, who had stimulated the early trade with *Kazembe*, succumbed to their warlike Bemba neighbors once the latter obtained guns, and it was these guns along with a newly united chieftainship which enabled the Bemba to turn aside the Ngoni when they attacked in 1856. In the case of the Sangu, however, cohesion came from opposing the Ngoni and mastering their superior military tactics, and the same would appear to be true of the Hehe, who with the Sangu occupied the area north of Lake Nyasa. Indeed, by learning well the military and political lessons of the Ngoni, the Hehe were able to keep Arab traders out of their country, thus denying themselves in their strength the very firearms which were so thoroughly transforming other groups. The effect of the Ngoni, like that of the Arab traders, was dual and contradictory —the weak were annihilated but the strong grew stronger in a setting of rising social disintegration and political anarchy.

Far to the north, beyond the limits of Ngoni penetration, the Arab traders encountered strong people, and their influence was limited accordingly. In the highlands between Mt. Kilimanjaro and Mt. Kenya were the Masai, Kikuyu, and Kamba, in their several ways all resistant to outsiders. The Kamba had trading pretensions of their own and thus monopolized the coastal routes, the Kikuyu were essentially xenophobic, and the Masai displayed their well-developed disposition toward warfare which led them to attack strangers with gusto. The traders were therefore obliged to approach the lake states in the Victoria region by way of Tabora in the south. Here they encountered a number of strong centralized kingdoms like Rwanda which forbade entry to foreigners or severely limited their movements, or the powerful nations of Buganda and Bunyoro. These last, though they were well disposed toward the Arabs, were also quite capable of controlling and defining the external trade to suit their own pleasure.

When traditional societies broke down, their demise was often precipitated and their authority replaced by new polyglot kingdoms led by Swahili, Arab or African opportunists taking advantage of the troubled times. Bringing together armies made up of fugitive slaves, deserting soldiers, refugees, detribalized brigands, and others torn loose from an orderly life by warfare and slaving, they moved about on massive elephant hunts, living off the land and terrorizing the local villages, or established more stable states on conquered lands. There were many examples. West of Lake Tanganyika along the upper Congo River, Arab and Swahili freebooters were particularly active as elephant hunters, raiding and pillaging on the strength of their superior firepower and eventually forming the basis for the more settled polity of Tippu Tib. To their south in the territory of *Mwata Kazembe,* the Nyamwezi state-maker, Msiri, carved out and maintained his own realm which lasted for a generation, until his death in 1891. Further west, the Chokwe, an obscure group of Lunda origin, rose for a time to dominate the ivory trade in the Zambezi-Congo watershed south of the Lunda kingdom of *Mwata Yamvo* which they eventually destroyed.

The rise of Msiri was based on the classic combination of guns, ivory, and slaves to which was added the Katangan specialty of copper, but it must also be understood in terms of internal decay within the *Kazembe* kingdom. Msiri first visited the land of *Kazembe* as a member of a Nyamwezi caravan, then returned about 1856 to settle permanently with a colony of Nyamwezi known locally as Yeke. It was at this time that a long, wasting civil war erupted over the royal succession, and Msiri, by taking sides, was able to build up strength which led to his emergence as an independent power about 1865. His military strength was based on his Yeke warriors, well armed with guns obtained through extensive trade connections and paid for with copper and ivory. Slowly the crumbling *Kazembe* kingdom was absorbed, and by 1885 most of the Luba kings to the north were paying Msiri tribute as well.

From the high point of his Luba campaigns Msiri's fortunes turned, essentially for the same reasons that had brought the *Kazembe's* downfall—excessive taxation and slaving practiced by a regime based solely on force. Msiri's rule was notoriously harsh. His palisades were festooned with skulls, not only of enemies, but also his subjects, for death was decreed often for trifling offenses. In 1886 a revolt broke out among the Sanga people but in the midst of this intramural difficulty, Msiri ran afoul of the forces of European imperialism bearing in upon Africa at this time. In 1891 he was shot by a member of an expedition sent by Leopold's Congo Independent State to occupy the valuable Katanga. From that point forward, pacification became Leopold's problem.

Msiri not only subjugated the Katanga but introduced many innovations into local society, not the least of which was smallpox vaccination. Nevertheless, in the long run it was the local culture which predominated, thoroughly absorbing its Yeke conquerers who finally lost even the knowledge of their native Nyamwezi tongue. To the west in the domain of *Mwata Yamvo,* a somewhat different situation unfolded during these same years. Oppressive royal taxation and a policy which arbitrarily designated villages to be sold into slavery had turned the Lunda population against its rulers at the very moment when the Chokwe to the southwest began to expand northward into the Kasai country. Originally a small group of seminomadic hunters, they had collaborated with Ovimbundu traders from Angola in collecting and marketing ivory, and with the aid of firearms had slowly expanded by a process of peaceful infiltration into new lands, followed by a struggle with the local inhabitants who were then absorbed into the widening Chokwe hegemony.

Internal dissension among the Lunda had reached the point during the early 1870's, that periodically the Chokwe were invited by contending royal aspirants to take sides, a development which greatly encouraged their northward migration into Lunda country. By 1885 they had occupied most of the state of *Mwata Yamvo*, sacked his capital, and sold its population into slavery. During the ensuing decade they consolidated their position and began to move against the Luba states. In 1898, the Lunda rallied and defeated the Chokwe in what might have been the beginning of an important counterattack, but at this point the military occupation by the Congo Independent State became effective, and the Chokwe remained fixed over a vast area astride the Kwilu and Kasai river basins and abutting on the western Katanga.

MIRAMBO, TIPPU TIB, AND THE DEMISE OF MERCHANT IMPERIALISM

At first blush, Mirambo, the Nyamwezi chief, and Tippu Tib, the Afro-Arab ivory trader, might seem to be antithetical figures—the latter a coastal Arab who made a career of extracting the wealth of Africa while forcing its people to be his unwilling accessories, the former an indigenous ruler intent on rallying his people against the encroaching invaders. Certainly Tippu was an entrepreneur and an opportunist who practiced exploitation on the grand scale, while Mirambo might be regarded as an early nationalist who brought cohesion to his people in the face of foreign intrusion.

Viewed from another perspective, however, both men may be seen as similar manifestations of the same process—the acquisition and consolidation of commercial advantage through political power. Flourishing during the later years of the nineteenth century, as the trade in ivory and slaves reached its climax, both Mirambo and Tippu Tib instinctively built states which enabled them to control that trade and protect it from competitors. The backbone of commercial traffic in eastern and central Africa was the line running inland from Zanzibar through Tabora and Ujiji, and across Lake Tanganyika into the eastern Congo. Interestingly, it was on that line that the two leaders fashioned their commercial empires, even joining in a brief, belated alliance to preserve their control of this major route.

Mirambo was born of chiefly parentage between 1830 and 1840

at the time when Arab excursions into the interior were changing from occasional speculations to the more systematic penetration encouraged by Sayyid Said. Competition between the new arrivals and the established Nyamwezi gradually sharpened, and it was only a matter of time before a purely commercial rivalry descended to the use of force. While the Arabs at Tabora were resolving the question of toll charges by eliminating Manua Sera, the troublesome chief at Unyanyembe, the Nyamwezi were developing their own strength to the west where Mirambo had succeeded to his father's chieftaincy and was beginning to assert himself both as a mercantile and a military power.

The Arab challenge with its modern armament and streamlined merchandising called for and received an imaginative response from Mirambo who jolted traditional Nyamwezi political standards with the concept of a centralized state supported by vigorous military tactics, a concept which gradually enabled him to extend his sway far beyond his original modest patrimony. A series of petty strikes subdued and absorbed neighboring villages, their loyalty assured by the moderate rule of their new prince. Speed and surprise in attack, personal courage, and the promise of spoils brought more than victory, however, for it also attracted large numbers of *ruga-ruga* (Ngoni mercenaries and detribalized adventurers uprooted by warfare) and these formidable warriors, armed with the guns which Mirambo was always at pains to obtain, soon developed into an army of unusual striking power.

Mirambo's objectives transcended booty for its own sake. He sought the establishment of a powerful Nyamwezi state which could stand off the intruding Arabs and control the growing interior trade to its own advantage. By 1871 he felt strong enough to give direct challenge to the Arab colony at Tabora, and there followed five years of warfare during which Mirambo was frequently reduced to extremity, managing to survive through tenacity of purpose while the superiority in arms of his foes was offset by their internal divisions. With the arrangement of peace in 1876, Mirambo was recognized as master of the region surrounding his capital at Urambo from which he quickly extended his control westward along the Ujiji route, and temporarily north toward Buganda. Though he never was able to challenge the Arabs successfully in the north, the Nyamwezi maintained their monopoly of the Katanga traffic and built Urambo into a market rivaling Tabora in importance.

During the years that Mirambo was consolidating and expanding his hegemony, his contemporary, Tippu Tib, was engaged in a similar exercise far to the west in the Congo area of the Lualaba and Lomani rivers. Born in Zanzibar about 1830, Tippu began trading as a young man for his father, a Tabora merchant, then struck out for himself during the 1860's in a series of wide-ranging ventures into Bemba and Lungu country at the southern end of Lake Tanganyika. Tippu Tib had early grasped the importance of armed retainers, and with these he was able to defeat Nsama, chief of the Tabwa people, adjacent to the Lungu, a coup which yielded Nsama's store of ivory and established Tib at once as a powerful and wealthy member of the immigrant trading class. Moving northward, the enterprising merchant prince combined trading and raiding, finally securing through a questionable claim of blood relationship a chieftaincy among the Tetela people in the Lomani area. By 1875 he had proceeded via Nyangwe on the Lualaba to Kasongo which became his headquarters. Here he reigned as a paramount chief among the Bantu people and as a governor chosen by the Arab traders, for none could challenge his force of arms.

Arabs had preceded Tippu Tib into the eastern Congo and by the time of his arrival, Nyangwe was recognized as a major entrepôt, filled with the harvest of raiding parties which roamed among the decentralized village communities hunting ivory and gathering slaves. Indiscriminate looting, however, by uncoordinated caravans was wasteful and untidy, and Tippu, who, like Mirambo, had a genius for political organization, soon had pacified a vast area in the Lomani and Lualaba basins, imposing taxes, building roads, staking out plantations, and regulating the hunting of elephants. He extended his authority downstream into the rain forest and in 1883 was already established at Stanley Falls. By 1890, although there were other important Arab traders in the area, Tippu Tib was preeminent; yet when he left the Congo in that same year on a trip to Zanzibar he was never to return, and a few short years later it was the Congo Independent State which controlled the lands over which he had once held sway.

Having established their commercial empires, neither Mirambo nor Tippu Tib was long able to hold and exploit the advantage they had gained, largely because of forces beyond their control. Mirambo had hoped for European support to secure the Nyamwezi state he was building, but this hope was seriously compromised in 1880 when he inadvertently killed two Europeans in the course of one of his campaigns and thus lost the confidence of John Kirk, the British consul at Zanzibar, who had been urging the sultan Barghash toward alliances in the interior. Even Mirambo's subsequent agreement in 1882 enabling Tippu Tib's caravan to pass safely through Nyamwezi territory failed to change opinions in Zanzibar. When Mirambo died in 1884, he still lacked European or Zanzibari backing for a strong and stable Nyamwezi kingdom, and with his death the people under his control soon reverted to their old parochial quarrels which continued until the area was occupied by the Germans in 1890.

In the case of Tippu Tib European conquest was also the ultimate consequence, ironically so because of Tippu's apparent awareness, even at the height of his power, that he could not long hold his domain. The Arab station at Stanley Falls was paralleled as early as 1883 with a European post founded there by H. M. Stanley on behalf of the International Association of the Congo, and the following year the Europeans attempted, albeit unsuccessfully, to prevent Tippu Tib from sending his caravans downstream beyond the Falls. Tippu had already agreed in 1882 to cooperate politically and commercially with Barghash, but within a few years he had evidently resigned himself to the fact that the Europeans could not be ousted; hence, in 1887 he contracted to serve the Congo Independent State as its governor at Stanley Falls with the understanding that Arab trade, except for slaving, would be unimpeded in the territory below the Falls. In this anomalous position he remained until 1890, distrusted both by the Arab traders and the Europeans. After his departure, even the fighting which broke out in 1892 between the Arabs and the Congo Independent State did not draw the aging political realist back to what he knew would be a futile defense of his domain. When Tippu Tib died in Zanzibar in 1905, his territories had already been incorporated into the Congo Independent State for over a decade.

BUGANDA AND THE INTERNATIONAL TRADE

When the first Arab trader arrived at the royal court of Buganda in 1844, he found a powerful, unified state, its exceptional strength arising from a number of related factors. To start with, an abundant and well-distributed rainfall combined with a soil fertility unusual by tropical standards to provide a plentiful food supply with a minimum of labor. Indeed, cultivation of plantains, the main crop, was largely left in the hands of the women, thus freeing the Baganda men for political and military pursuits which placed the state at a distinct advantage over its neighbors. As national institutions evolved, they tended to place authority centrally in the hands of the *kabaka* who was able to employ his power toward the further unification and extension of his kingdom. The royal succession, for example, was afflicted with less than the usual uncertainties, and once the king was firmly in control he became the unquestioned head of a military and administrative bureaucracy, each member of which held his position and wealth entirely at the *kabaka's* pleasure. Such a concentration of power in a relatively affluent, leisured society, offered unexampled opportunities for warmaking and economic imperialism. The result was that, by the early nineteenth century, Buganda had become, not only an absolute monarchy, but one which exercised extensive influence over the nominally independent adjacent peoples.

A despotism such as Buganda concentrated in the monarch's court, not only power, but the social and political nervous system of the country. Like the Versailles of Louis XIV, the *kabaka's* capital was filled with a domesticated aristocracy whose formula for survival was a shrewd mixture of obsequious flattery and palace intrigue. Here was dangerous ground as was amply illustrated by the oft-noted anecdote of the English explorer, J. H. Speke, who told of a Baganda shot arbitrarily on order of the *kabaka,* Mutesa, to demonstrate the properties of a newly acquired carbine. At the same time the court was the locus of opportunity in a land where the standard of success was achievement rather than status, and where the rewards of the *kabaka* were as great as his punishments were severe. Here, then, came the ambitious and quick-witted to try their fortune, and here was developed in its highest form the inventive, receptive turn of mind made possible by leisure among a people already noted for their adventurous, acquisitive nature.

In this effervescent milieu, traders from the outside world were welcome as the means to greater glory and prosperity for king and subject, and none feared the strangers for they represented no danger to these virile people. On the contrary, they strengthened expansionist tendencies already underway, for they brought new products—particularly cotton cloth and, later, guns—which were in immediate demand and which could be obtained for slaves and ivory wrested from neighboring peoples by Buganda's long-established military superiority. Repeated predatory expeditions sent out by the *kabakas* Suna, who reigned until 1856, and Mutesa, who succeeded him for another twenty-eight years, yielded rich rewards in the form of produce and cattle as well as slaves and ivory. These goods were converted into an expanding national prosperity which was based solely on a redistribution of wealth by military force, Buganda's economy at this time experiencing no growth of its own.

In time the acquisition of firearms was to combine with Baganda intellectual curiosity to effect a profound social and political revolution in Buganda society, but in the days of Mutesa the guns he collected merely reinforced his military dominance over weak neighbors as he established crack rifle companies recruited among young courtiers to supplement his peasant spearmen. Such added strength gave further assurance to Mutesa's diplomacy which was called upon during the 1870's to deal both with a renascence of power in Bunyoro and an imperialist thrust southward on the part of Egypt. In dealing with the Khedive Ismail's representatives, first Samuel Baker and then Charles Gordon, Mutesa consistently stressed an alliance against Bunyoro while the Egyptians spoke of an advance up the Nile which was initially thwarted by Mutesa's skillful combination of force and persuasion and eventually expired with the rise of the Mahdist state.

During the course of these events, the Buganda court was visited by the American journalist, H. M. Stanley, deep in the midpassage of his continental explorations, and when Stanley spoke of Christian missionaries coming to Buganda, Mutesa strongly encouraged what he evidently took to be potential European support which could be used to help stand off the Egyptians. As the Egyptian threat faded, therefore, C.M.S. missionaries arrived on the scene, but while they were to disappoint Mutesa as a means of military assistance, their long-run impact on Baganda society would prove considerable.

Suggestions for Further Reading

A general account covering the period dealt with in this chapter is found in K. Ingham, *A History of East Africa*, 2nd. ed. (London: Longmans, 1963; New York: Praeger, 1965). The coastal area and British policy are dealt with in two volumes by Reginald Coupland—*East Africa and Its Invaders* (Oxford: Clarendon Press, 1938), and *The Exploitation of East Africa* (London: Faber and Faber, 1939), as well as in J. M. Gray, *History of Zanzibar* (London: Oxford University Press, 1962). Best, however, are the chapters by Alison Smith and D. A. Low in R. Oliver and G. Mathew, eds., *History of East Africa,* I (Oxford: Clarendon Press, 1963). Material on the Congo is also contained in R. Slade, *King Leopold's Congo* (London: Oxford University Press, 1962). Useful, too, is E. A. Alpers, *The East African Slave Trade* (Nairobi: East African Publishing House, 1967).

Historical studies of indigenous African peoples are rare, but recent contributions in this area are B. A. Ogot, *History of the Southern Luo* (Nairobi: East African Publishing House, 1967); G. S. Were, *A History of the Abaluyia of Western Kenya* (Nairobi: East African Publishing House, 1967); and J. Vansina, *Kingdoms of the Savanna* (Madison: University of Wisconsin Press, 1966). Much material can also be gained from the accounts of nineteenth-century travelers such as Richard F. Burton, J. L. Krapf, J. Thomson, and J. H. Speke; for example, see Burton's *Lake Regions of Central Africa,* 2v. (London: Sidgwick and Jackson, 1961).

For Tippu Tib see H. Brode, *Tippo Tib* (London: Arnold, 1907), while Mirambo is examined in N. R. Bennett, *Studies in East African History* (Boston: Boston University Press, 1963).

14: The Partition of Africa

THE BERLIN CONFERENCE

On November 15, 1884, an international conference was convened in Berlin. Present was every nation of Europe, save Switzerland,
and the United States of America, fourteen nations in all. The European locale and membership were notable in view of the expressed
concern of the Conference, which was the continent of Africa. It was
proposed, first of all, to clarify the status of international trade on
the Congo and of navigation on the Niger. Second, an attempt was to
be made to define conditions under which future territorial annexa-
tions in Africa might be recognized.

Also in attendance was the ill-understood International Association of the Congo. This self-styled philanthropic organization had
been founded a few years earlier by King Leopold II of Belgium,
ostensibly to end slaving and substitute legitimate commerce in the
Congo basin, but in fact was the vehicle for Leopold's imperial dreams
in Africa. Lacking true sovereign status, it was already recognized by
the United States as a de facto government—ironically the nearest
thing to an African voice at the Conference. No African state was
represented.

That a conference concerned with Africa should be held in
Europe, by Europeans, and exclusively on behalf of European interests, was a natural consequence of events which by the late nine-

teenth century had projected the Western powers far beyond the strength of the world's other peoples, propelled by the twin forces of nationalism and industrialization. Indeed, the concerns of the Conference were essentially European concerns; the subject of Africa on the agenda was largely adventitious. Such a meeting might have dealt just as easily with free trade on the China coast and the rules of the game for acquiring islands in the Pacific. What was really at stake was the delicate balance of power among European nations, the projection of their rising mercantile interests throughout the world, and the nourishment of national pride which had recently begun to express itself through the acquisition of colonial territories in little-known, far-off places.

The history of the Berlin Conference amply bears out its European preoccupations. During the first half of the nineteenth century there had been no great interest among European nations in the Congo or Niger regions, but as ivory, rubber, and particularly palm oil, took on increasing importance in Western commercial and industrial development, mercantile activity grew apace and combined with the work of explorers to stimulate at least an unofficial enthusiasm on the part of European governments. Portugal, whose early importance in the Congo area had declined with her dwindling national strength, now sought control of the mouth of the Congo and to this end secured a treaty with Great Britain in 1884 which conceded Portuguese primacy along the coast while guaranteeing freedom of navigation on the river itself. Thus were served both British economic interests and Portuguese political goals. In addition, Britain was able to check French expansion in the Congo region.

Events had already overtaken the Portuguese, however, and the treaty at once aroused opposition everywhere. For some years French interest in Africa had been growing, fed by a desire both for economic gain and national prestige. By 1884 she had her own substantial claim to Congo territories as the result of a treaty which the explorer de Brazza had secured, giving France the north side of Stanley Pool at the head of the navigable Congo. At the same time, Leopold II was establishing the basis for his personal interests in the Congo area. Even as de Brazza was pursuing his explorations, Henry M. Stanley was engaged in similar activities for Leopold's International Association of the Congo; thus whatever the rival claims of Leopold and the French, both were of the same mind in opposing Portuguese pretensions in the area.

Into this situation of growing complexity was introduced the further complication of Prince Bismarck, chief minister of Imperial Germany which in the few short years since the Franco-Prussian War of 1870–1871 had established herself as the major power of Europe. Bismarck was essentially concerned with securing German preeminence in Europe, and consequently was at first indifferent to colonies as emblems of national prestige. He was, however, under increasing pressure from German commercial interests who wished to see the flag and the gunboat follow their widening trade, and in any case the artful chancellor was well aware that gains in Europe sometimes were best obtained through exertions in other latitudes. In this connection, he had gradually become uneasy as signs mounted that other European powers were edging toward territorial acquisitions in Asia and Africa. What if German trade should be denied access to these areas? How would German prestige weather a situation which found France and others controlling colonial empires while imperial Germany had none?

Beyond these considerations, Bismarck's foreign policy was based on soothing French national pride, rubbed raw by the disaster of Sedan, the German occupation of Paris, and the loss of Alsace-Lorraine. He thereby encouraged the French in colonial adventures which might compensate for humiliation in Europe, and sought to draw closer to France by controlled quarreling with her chief colonial rival, Great Britain. This could be done by laying claim in Africa and the Pacific to territories, the main value of which lay in the annoyance their occupation would cause Britain, while acquisition had the additional asset of placating the expansionist and commercially-minded groups within Germany. In 1884 Bismarck suddenly announced protectorates in South-West Africa, Cameroun, and Togo, as well as a portion of New Guinea in the South Pacific. At the same time the foundations for German East Africa were being laid even as the Berlin Conference met, a conclave called jointly by France and Germany at Portugal's suggestion in an effort to solve the Congo impasse which had resulted from the breakdown of the Anglo-Portuguese treaty.

If Bismarck's objectives in calling the Conference were centered primarily in Europe, they involved as well the formulation of a set of rules defining the orderly extension of European influence in Africa. During their three months of deliberations, the participating nations appeared to achieve much in this respect. First, they accepted not only freedom of trade and navigation in the Congo basin, but freedom of navigation along the Niger as well. Second, their final agreement, the Berlin Act, provided that any power henceforward annexing territory or instituting a protectorate would at once notify all signatories while guaranteeing effective occupation of the regions in question through the establishment of political stability.

These paper accomplishments, however, meant little in practice. Freedom of navigation was left to national, rather than international, control, while the concept of effective occupation proved unenforceable in any particular instance. Of greater moment were the agreements reached outside the regular sessions whereby the Congo region was partitioned. The German claim to Cameroun was recognized, the limits of Portuguese hegemony clarified, French rights along the north bank of the Congo River conceded, and most astonishing of all, the sovereignty of Leopold II over the Congo Independent State legalized by treaty.

In sum, the Berlin Conference neither precipitated nor regularized the so-called scramble for Africa; it merely punctuated the fact of Africa's partition. European encroachment had already been under way for a considerable time before the congress convened and the rapid occupation which followed was scarcely a direct result of its deliberations. Rather, it was the logical consequence of a larger historical evolution.

PARTITION—THE CAUSES

The partition of Africa is best understood as the culmination of those expansionist forces which shattered Europe's relative isolation at the dawn of the Renaissance, prompting her intrusion into other parts of the globe in a series of ever-widening waves. In Africa this was marked, first of all, by the search for trade which brought on the West African slave traffic; then, by the early nineteenth-century antislavery, humanitarian movement which attempted to atone for earlier sins through a program of rehabilitation, casting African societies in Europe's image.

Implicit in the humanitarian crusade was the conviction that Europe's presence in Africa was temporary and disinterested, that the development of prosperous African societies meant closer commercial attachment, but political divorce, between Africa and Europe.

If Portugal held stubbornly to her possessions on the Guinea coast, in Angola and Mozambique, France was largely indifferent to her West African holdings, while the official and public attitude in Britain, exemplified by the conclusions of the 1865 Select Committee of the House of Commons, was distinctly anti-imperial. Nevertheless, concurrent with the spirit of isolation were factors leading toward a steadily deepening entanglement.

The mere presence of European powers encouraged involvement. Sierra Leone, for example, had become a colony in order that slaves freed by the British naval squadron might be effectively rehabilitated, and the success of this venture was reflected in the thriving community of Freetown. But Freetown did not exist in a vacuum. She had growing mercantile relations with the inland people as well as territorial interests along the coast which necessarily drew her government into an active prosecution, here of boundary claims on the Liberian border, there of suspected slave trading in Portuguese Guinea, now of indigenous chiefs for alleged treaty violations, or again in reprisal for destruction of property or the death of British subjects caught in the chronic tribal skirmishing. Similarly, the French posts in Senegal and down the coast, however tentatively held, invited defense against apparent threats from Muslim revivalists of the interior, while the French continually entertained dark suspicions regarding British designs in their area. Far to the southeast, Britain had occupied Lagos in 1861 as a means of combatting the slave trade, a move which soon forced her to participate, unhappily but increasingly, in the complexities of Yoruba politics.

One source of growing involvement was the relative autonomy of colonial administrators whose freedom of action was directly proportionate to their degree of remove from home governments. Parliamentary questions or ministerial instructions could be ignored or subverted by energetic or strong-willed executives, while changing circumstances might necessitate actions not encompassed by initial instructions. "Insupportable pro-consuls," grumbled Lord Salisbury, the British foreign secretary during the height of the partition, but who could deny the influence on colonial policy of the energetic Governor Faidherbe and his disciple, Brière de l'Isle, advocate of *"le go-ahead des Americains,"* of that intrepid trail-blazer, de Brazza, whose popular appeals over the head of the government brought France into the Congo, or of the German adventurer-explorer, Carl

Peters, whose unsolicited exertions gave Germany an empire in East Africa?

The example of the Gold Coast is illustrative. There, British policy had clearly vacillated over the years, but there was no mistaking the differences in style and effectiveness of a series of colonial officials. In 1824 the ill-prepared expansionism of Sir Charles Macarthy led to death and defeat at the hands of the Ashanti and eventual abandonment of the coastal forts by the British government. Contrariwise, during the 1830's George Maclean's tactful diplomacy greatly revived British prestige and influence in the area, stimulating the local authorities to look to Britain for assistance and guidance which his successors were not always able to provide. Later, the liberal-minded Governor Sir Arthur Kennedy lent encouragement to the spirit of self-reliance among chiefs which culminated in the Fante Confederation movement, but unhappily the movement expired at the hands of others. First, the acting administrator, C. S. Salmon, arrested its leaders, convinced as he was that the Confederation was a conspiracy against British authority; then, as the Confederation showed signs of revival, it was smothered by the ineffectual sympathy of Kennedy's successor, J. Pope Hennessy, who approved its objectives but could not bring himself to recommend its acceptance in London.

The personal factor aside, expanding economic interests drew Europe inexorably into a deepening concern with African affairs. As the slave trade died, new demands for new products were generated by the growing industrial establishment of Europe. Palm oil came into prominence as a lubricant for machinery; there was a fast-rising consumption of cotton in the mill towns of England; ivory was found to have a wide range of ornamental and practical uses; gum was needed in the manufacture of paper and confectionery and as a dye fixative and fabric sizing; while a host of other products— groundnuts, tobacco, indigo, sugar, coffee, tea, tropical fruits— along with the generally vain hope of mineral wealth, stimulated European commercial enterprise. For their part, African societies developed an abiding desire for the manufactures of Europe—fabrics and utensils, but also alcoholic spirits and firearms, as well as the ever popular beads.

Mercantile activity more than implied political and military pressures which were exerted both inward and outward, for Africa was as quick, if not as adept, as Europe in prosecuting its commercial interests. A major factor in the difficulties encountered by the British on the Gold Coast during much of the nineteenth century was the unceasing urgency of the Ashanti thrust toward the coast in search of the European trade. It was the British decision to meet this pressure with force in the interests of political stability which led to the Ashanti War of 1873–1874 and the establishment of the British Gold Coast Colony. On the Senegal River, the Brakna and Trarza Moors had controlled the gum trade over the years through the force of their arms, a situation which was regularly deplored by the traders of St. Louis, but never resolved until Faidherbe subdued the Trarzas in 1858. Faidherbe's relations with *al-Hajj* Umar were also influenced by economic considerations as indeed were most of his programs for colonial development in Senegal.

Circumstances were much the same in other areas. Like Senegal, Sierra Leone existed on trade, and trade meant an aggressive policy toward the people of the interior, advocated by the Freetown merchants and prosecuted by vigorous governors like S. J. Hill who in 1861, despite misgivings in the Colonial Office, annexed territories in the hinterland in order that commerce might prosper. On the Niger, trade was even more completely a major factor touching all activity —the Christian missions, the social and political organization of the Delta states, the establishment of British consuls, and finally the breaching of the Delta and the mercantile-cum-political activities of George Goldie Taubman. When Bismarck made his sudden territorial moves in Africa in 1884 and 1885, the wonder is that he was able to base them on intramural considerations within Europe, ignoring in the main the growing clamor of the merchants of Hamburg and Bremen.

Yet Bismarck's motivation was characteristically sound. The African commerce, for all its rising importance, was but a minor matter compared with the great political and strategic factors generated by Europe herself. In 1882 Germany's West African trade represented only three-tenths of one per cent of her total imports, but by that date Germany had already become the most powerful nation in continental Europe, and Bismarck's main concern was to maintain and strengthen this position. The other colonial powers were no less preoccupied with European affairs. France looked for the day of revenge when the Germans would be humbled and Alsace-Lorraine regained. Britain, aloof from Continental involvements, was nonetheless intent upon preserving her world mercantile and industrial supremacy, a major requirement of which was the maintenance of open sea lanes for her shipping.

None of these matters had any direct connection with Africa although they were to play a decisive role in her final partition. Bismarck's decision to annex Alsace-Lorraine after the Franco-Prussian War was based primarily on considerations of military strategy, but this advantage was gained at the expense of a deep-seated bitterness in France. In time the French reaction took two antithetical forms. The first was a straightforward desire to regain the lost provinces and with them France's shattered national pride. This "doctrine of effacement" concentrated on Europe, equated colonialist arguments with national treason, and dreamed of the day of revenge. The other position was equally patriotic but saw a world changing before the force of industrialism, and argued that France's future greatness depended upon her ability to change with the times. Here was a doctrine of compensation which freed France from her myopic preoccupation with the "blue line of the Vosges" beyond the new Franco-German frontier, which spoke of markets and raw materials for France's growing industrial machine, and which offered imperial vistas to refresh the flagging spirits of all true French patriots.

The principal architect and theoretician of this new colonialism was Jules Ferry who as premier in 1880–1881 and again in 1883–1885, brought large areas under French control in Indo-China, Madagascar, and Africa. In Africa he engineered protectorates in Somalia and Tunisia, and supported explorations in the Niger and Congo basins. One such expedition, although not directly attributable to Ferry's encouragement, was that led by the young naval officer, Pierre Savorgnan de Brazza, who in 1880 secured a French protectorate over vast but ill-defined territories on the north bank of the Congo, and thus greatly stimulated in response the acquisitive instincts of both the Portuguese and Leopold II. At the same time, French activity on the West African coast alarmed Britain into a defensive posture regarding her commercial interests which led directly to her securing a protectorate in the Niger Delta area.

Such colonial adventures ideally suited Bismarck's objective of neutralizing the power of France in Europe and setting the French and British at odds as colonial competitors. The joint French and German invitation to the Berlin Conference was but another element in this complex diplomacy. Not only did it suggest closer Franco-

German cooperation, but it brought Bismarck squarely into the African scene where he might exercise a measure of control over the shape of Europe's impending occupation of Africa, not so much to guarantee an appropriate share for Germany as to insure that no difficulties might emerge in Africa to complicate Germany's European position.

The chief beneficiary of the Conference, however, was not the German chancellor but Leopold II of Belgium who has been aptly described as a "royal speculator . . . masquerading as a philanthropic society." This ambitious monarch, frustrated by the limitations imposed by his small kingdom, sought and eventually found expression for his imperial aspirations in the creation of the Congo Independent State with himself as its sovereign. He achieved this improbable objective in a series of artful maneuvers, first through the establishment in 1876 of the International Association for the Exploration and Civilization of Central Africa (International African Association), a private organization formed under Leopold's presidency with ostensibly scientific and humanitarian objectives, and then via the International Association of the Congo, controlled by Leopold and presumably interested in the commercial development of the Congo basin.

By the eve of the Berlin Conference, Leopold's Congo Association had laid claim to a large area through the treaty-making exertions of its agent H. M. Stanley, and the Belgian monarch was already hinting at the idea of a strong indigenous state in the Congo directed by Leopold himself. Such a concept was attractive to Britain and Germany as a check to French ambitions in the area, and all sides were cordial toward a scheme which blocked Portugal. France was finally brought into concurrence when she was assured the right to assume Leopold's obligations in the event he were unable to maintain the costs of administration. As the Conference proceeded, a series of bilateral agreements were concluded recognizing the sovereignty of Leopold's International Association of the Congo which thereby became a signatory in good standing when the Berlin Act was confirmed by the powers in February, 1885. Five months later the Association became the Congo Independent State.

In addition to Bismarck, Leopold, and France was a further factor, acting powerfully as a catalyst to partition. In 1798, when Napoleon invaded Egypt, Britain's reaction had been quick and unequivocal in the protection of her lifeline to India and the Far East.

Now, three-quarters of a century later, the stakes were that much higher in an era of rising industrial competition, and Egypt was even more the key to the East now that a canal at Suez had at last become a reality. The reign of the khedive, Ismail, which began in 1863 with high promise of fulfilling Muhammad Ali's program of modernization, soon foundered in mismanagement and extravagance. The Canal was completed in 1869, a fact which greatly intensified Europe's interest in Egyptian financial and political stability. Hence by 1879, when Ismail had brought the country to bankruptcy despite recourse to foreign loans, he was forced from power by his European creditors who took financial control of the country as advisers to Ismail's successor, Tawfiq. The economy measures they introduced struck hard at the Egyptian army, already a center of nationalist opposition to foreign interference. Disaffection among Egyptian officers led to the military revolt in 1881 led by Colonel Urabi Pasha, an uprising which was put down only when Britain invaded and occupied Egypt in 1882.

The occupation was to have been a joint French-British venture but France was prevented from participating because of a cabinet crisis, and Britain consequently found herself de facto ruler of Egypt, a role she accepted reluctantly as necessary to the protection of her communications to India and beyond. Such a situation, however, stimulated European rivalries already in motion as a result of economic competition, the rise of Imperial Germany, and the emergence of a spirited sense of nationalism. French confrontation with Britain, thwarted in Egypt, was thus intensified in West Africa while she vied with Portugal and Leopold's International Association of the Congo. Bismarck, in effect, exchanged his support of British intervention in Egypt for acquiescence in his African protectorates, while Britain and Leopold both responded to French pressures by developing their claims in West Africa and the Congo respectively. By 1885 the partition of Africa had indeed accelerated into a scramble.

PARTITION—THE PROCESS

The partition of Africa, then, was the result of a number of factors, primarily European in origin, which gradually accumulated momentum until by the time of the Berlin congress their combined force reached explosive proportions. To the early mercantilism which had brought the French occupation of the Senegal coast and the British posts on the Gambia River and the Gold Coast, were added the antislavery haven of Sierra Leone and the port of Lagos, annexed in 1861 also as a blow against the slave trade. In 1874 Britain gave up its efforts to withdraw from the Gold Coast, reversed its policy, and assumed the responsibility of governing the newly created Gold Coast Colony. For her part, France extended her authority far along the course of the Senegal during the administration of Faidherbe while the expansionism of Napoleon III pressed the conquest and occupation of Algeria, begun under the reigns of Charles X and Louis Philippe. Portugal maintained her holdings on the Guinea coast, along with Angola and Mozambique, and dreamed of empires her weakness would not allow.

For a time there was a pause in the formal extension of British and French authority in West Africa while privately inspired and semiofficial forces built up pressure for eventual occupation. French commercial enterprise, echoing Faidherbe, proposed railroad schemes for opening up the Niger watershed, connecting it alternatively with Algeria or the Senegal River system. Such proposals, which anticipated a deep penetration of the West African savanna, were followed by exploratory, quasi-military probes from Senegal which, however, were largely checked by the Tokolor state of Ahmadu to the east and the Mandinka power of Samori on Ahmadu's southern flank. Undaunted, French traders began to appear along the lower Niger where they at once came into conflict with the United African Company (later named the Royal Niger Company), formed in 1879 by the merchant prince, George Goldie Taubman, from several independent British mercantile establishments long active up the Niger beyond the preserve of the African trading states in the Delta. The consolidation by Goldie, the surname he preferred, had been frankly monopolistic and was followed by a commercial war which by the end of 1884 had succeeded in forcing out or absorbing the French.

Goldie's ultimate solution was political, however. He sought a charter, finally granted in 1886, giving him not only a commercial monopoly but political authority over the Niger territory in question. His treaties with local potentates in effect set up a sphere of influence which his Company administered by what later came to be known as indirect rule and which eventually was absorbed into the Niger districts protectorate. Proclaimed by Britain in 1885, this protectorate included the coast between the Lagos colony and German

Cameroun, extending inland as far as Lokoja and eastward two hundred miles along the Benue to Ibi. Thus was formed the basis for the modern state of Nigeria. Already this action had been preceded by the German protectorates in Togo and Cameroun in 1884, while the French, undeterred by their problems on the lower Niger, moved in 1883 to secure their Slave Coast trade by occupying Porto Novo and Cotonou, and therewith divorced Lagos from the Gold Coast by the intrusion of what eventually became the colony of Dahomey.

The Berlin Conference was also preceded by the reluctant British intrusion into Egypt in 1882, a temporary occupation which nevertheless dragged on in varying form until after the Second World War. In other parts of Africa, however, the Conference marked a new and accelerated stage in the partition. Brazza consolidated French claims to the territory between Gabon and the north bank of the Congo by the classic practice of treaty making, in this case with local chiefs in the Sangha and Ubangi river basins, thus providing a point of departure for subsequent explorations northward toward Lake Chad.

On the other side of the river, Leopold proceeded energetically to implement his successful claim at Berlin for control over the huge Congo basin. First, there was the business of exploration, already underway before the sovereignty of the Congo Independent State was achieved in 1885, but thereafter greatly intensified with the help of steam-powered river craft which were able to reach all parts of the huge Congo watershed. Interior river communications, however, were of little consequence as long as access to the sea was blocked by the rapids below Stanley Pool, and Leopold therefore very early began surveying a railroad link to the coast. Construction started in 1890 and the line was completed eight years later at a great cost in life, not only among the local people who were employed largely as porters between Leopoldville and the coast, but also among the West Africans, chiefly Krumen, brought in to help with the construction.

Leopold's problems were not entirely limited to extending effective communications over vast distances, for his hegemony was sharply contested in two major areas—the east and the Katanga. In the east were the Arab traders, well-established along the Lualaba River since the 1860's and headed by the redoubtable Tippu Tib. Their slaving activities extended far to the west and north of the Lualaba beyond Stanley Falls, and Leopold, weak in resources and

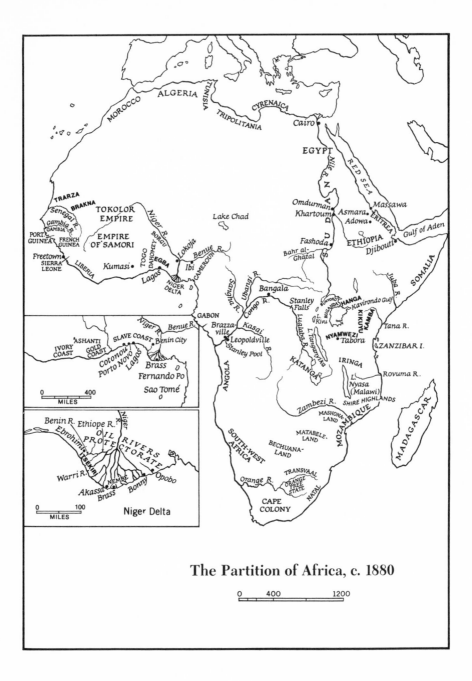

The Partition of Africa, c. 1880

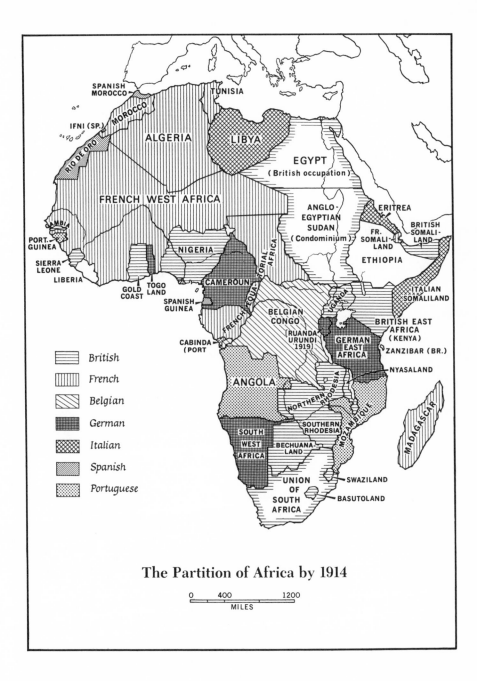

SPANISH
MOROCCO
TUNISIA
IFNI (SP.)
MOROCCO
RIO DE ORO
ALGERIA
LIBYA
EGYPT
(British occupation)
FRENCH WEST AFRICA
ANGLO-
EGYPTIAN
SUDAN
(Condominium)
ERITREA
FR.
SOMALI-
LAND
BRITISH
SOMALI-
LAND
GAMBIA
PORT.
GUINEA
SIERRA
LEONE
LIBERIA
NIGERIA
ETHIOPIA
GOLD
COAST
TOGO
LAND
SPANISH
GUINEA
CAMEROUN
FRENCH EQUATORIAL AFRICA
BELGIAN
CONGO
[RUANDA
URUNDI
1919]
UGANDA
ITALIAN
SOMALILAND
CABINDA
(PORT
GERMAN
EAST
AFRICA
BRITISH EAST
AFRICA
(KENYA)
ZANZIBAR (BR.)
NYASALAND
ANGOLA
NORTHERN RHODESIA
RHODESIA
MADAGASCAR
SOUTH
WEST
AFRICA
SOUTHERN
RHODESIA
BECHUANA-
LAND
MOZAMBIQUE
UNION
OF
SOUTH
AFRICA
SWAZILAND
BASUTOLAND

British
French
Belgian
German
Italian
Spanish
Portuguese

The Partition of Africa by 1914

0   400   1200
MILES

manpower, was unable to establish de facto authority farther than Bangala near the top of the Congo bend. In 1887 his agent, Stanley, managed to persuade Tippu Tib to become governor of the eastern region, an alliance of convenience based on Leopold's weakness and Tippu Tib's realization of the long-range power of the Europeans compared with Sultan Barghash's failing authority at Zanzibar. Tippu Tib could not control all the Arabs, however, and after he departed for Zanzibar in 1890, relations quickly deteriorated.

Not only were the Arabs suspicious of the European connection, but Leopold soon found himself embarrassed by his alliance with a notorious slave dealer when in 1888 Cardinal Lavigerie, founder of the White Fathers missionary movement, began a crusade to end the Arab slave trade. Converting a weakness into a strength, Leopold now came forward as the champion of African freedom and called an antislavery congress in Brussels in 1889 from which he extracted the right to charge import duties as a means of support for a campaign to end the Arab slaving once and for all. His mercantile and political objectives thus attractively concealed in humanitarian dress, Leopold abandoned further efforts to cooperate with the Arabs. In 1892 hostilities broke out and were largely ended three years later with the Europeans victorious under the leadership of Francis Dhanis, later made a baron by the grateful Leopold.

While the eastern provinces were being subdued, Leopold was similarly engaged in extending his rule to the Katanga. There Msiri had long held sway, but by 1890 he was under pressure from Cecil Rhodes and the British South Africa Company seeking control of the Katangan copper, an external complication added to the revolt of the Sanga people which had plagued Msiri since 1886. Msiri would have none of Rhodes' protection, nor was he any more receptive to Leopold's emissaries when they arrived in 1891 with similar overtures. Pressure by the Belgian king became so intense, however, that violence broke out and the uncooperative Msiri was killed. His death at once gave Leopold effective occupation of the Katanga although in the process he inherited the Sanga revolt which was not put down for another decade.

The Berlin Conference also marked, but did not greatly affect, a movement toward occupation in East Africa which was more particularly the result both of European international diplomacy and the activities of official and unofficial agents on the ground. The unsponsored harvest of treaties gathered by Carl Peters on the mainland back of Zanzibar in 1884 suited Bismarck's momentary purpose of embarrassing Britain, and a German protectorate was proclaimed just as the Conference concluded its deliberations in March, 1885. This development led to a British-German agreement in 1886 dividing the vast area between the Tana and Rovuma rivers along the line of the present Kenya-Tanzania frontier, Zanzibar, although not represented, being granted possession of the coastal islands and a shoreline strip ten miles deep. Zanzibari independence disappeared in 1890 when Britain gained the right to "protect" the island, at the same time being conceded primacy in the Great Lakes area which was to become the territory of Uganda. In return for this she ceded Germany the strategic North Sea island of Heligoland, and consented to outright German control over the Zanzibar coastal strip in Tanganyika, a foothold which was quickly extended inland to the region of Lake Kivu and Lake Tanganyika. Once again European diplomatic considerations had proved paramount in the partition of Africa.

As the decade of the eighties drew to a close, the quickening pace of partition came to southern Africa. Cape Colony and Natal had long been British possessions, but when Bismarck appropriated South-West Africa in 1884, Britain blocked possible German linkage with the Transvaal the following year by establishing a protectorate over Bechuanaland. Such a move also was to serve the imperial design of the Salisbury ministry, just come to power and dedicated to control of the Nile highway that would eventually expand into the idea of a Cape to Cairo axis. During the early eighties gold was discovered in the Transvaal, attracting, among others, Cecil Rhodes, already possessing a fortune in Kimberley diamonds, but Rhodes' enormous appetite for commercial and political conquest was scarcely satisfied thereby, and he pressed northward through his British South Africa Company toward the Zambezi and beyond. In 1890 his settlers founded Fort Salisbury in Mashonaland while company agents pushed on to contest the Katanga with Leopold. In 1891 protectorates were proclaimed in the trans-Zambezi area, as well as in the Shire highlands around Lake Nyasa where British missionaries had been gathering since the 1870's, inspired by the work and the example of David Livingstone.

British economic and political imperialism was now in full flower; Portuguese designs on Central Africa were rudely turned aside, while expansionists like Rhodes and Harry Johnston extended British primacy by treaty with the indigenous people. In Matabeleland and Mashonaland occupation resulted from military conquest in 1893 and suppression of a subsequent African revolt, leading in 1898 to the creation of a colony with an elected white settler minority in its legislative council. In South Africa, the determination of Britain to dominate the Transvaal and its growing economic strength led to the Boer War of 1899–1902, the defeat of the Boers, and the ultimate unification of South Africa under British rule.

French expansionism found its most fruitful expression in the great savanna belt of the western and central Sudan. Checked by the United States when in 1879 she proposed a protectorate over Liberia, France nevertheless emerged as master of vast stretches of West Africa and architect of an east-west axis which for a time challenged Britain's grand design from the Cape to Cairo. Her strategy was to link the valleys of the Senegal and Niger rivers, to connect these in turn with her North African centers in Algeria and Tunisia, then to push eastward to the Lake Chad region where French interests were aiming northward from de Brazza's Congo, and finally to press on to Djibouti on the Red Sea in a maneuver which would sever Britain's north-south line and loosen her hold on Egypt.

Britain, with no comparable territorial aspirations in West Africa, did not generally interfere with the French military operations which subdued Ahmadu's Tokolor empire between 1890 and 1893, established French rule in Guinea and the Ivory Coast by 1893, occupied Dahomey in a hard campaign in 1892, and finally put an end to Samori's prolonged resistance in 1898. The French advance to the east was forced to swing northward around the Fulani emirates when Captain Frederick Lugard, acting on behalf of Goldie's Royal Niger Company, occupied Borgu in 1894, a scant two weeks before the arrival of French forces. Another serious reversal occurred four years later far to the east when France's grand imperial strategy collapsed at Fashoda. A thrust into the Bahr al-Ghazal was approved by the French government in 1896, and two years later a small column under Captain J. B. Marchand arrived at Fashoda on the upper Nile after a fourteen-month march from Brazzaville. By this time, however, the British were well embarked on the process of taking the Mahdist Sudan, and in September, 1898, the *Khalifa* was defeated by General Kitchener at Omdurman, thus ending effective resistance from the Mahdist state. Kitchener immediately marched south to Fashoda where he threatened Marchand's much smaller contingent. After several uneasy weeks during which the two forces represented potential large-scale war, the French backed down, and with Marchand's departure so faded the threat to Britain's hold on Egypt and her control of the Nile.

In northern Africa, one other European power asserted herself. The process of Italian unification, achieved for practical purposes in 1861, now suggested the further embellishment of a colonial empire, and soon Italy was joining in the partition of Africa. Massawa on the Red Sea was taken in 1885, and then in 1889 the whole Eritrean coast and Asmaran highlands were occupied at the expense of Ethiopia. At the same time Somalia from Cape Guardafui to the Juba River became an Italian protectorate while the French established themselves at Djibouti and the British took that section of the Somali coast facing the Gulf of Aden. Italian pretensions were much greater than these modest acquisitions, but they also exceeded her strength, and she failed to occupy Ethiopia, checked by Menelik's stunning victory at Adowa in 1896. Later, however, in 1911–1912, she gained further African territories in Tripolitania and Cyrenaica. The last piece of independent Africa to fall was Morocco, divided between France and Spain in 1912.

On the eve of the First World War, the partition of Africa was complete. Only two territories—Liberia and Ethiopia—had escaped European colonization, and Liberia, at least from the viewpoint of the indigenous people of the area, might well have been regarded as a special version of the Western occupation of Africa.

PARTITION—THE AFRICAN RESPONSE

Throughout the process of partition, particularly during its climactic stages, the African people were little able to check the tidal wave of foreign control that swept over them. Unable to resist partition, they were by no means passive bystanders—impotent perhaps, but not passive and not unresponsive. There were, of course, many chiefs of small isolated communities who ill understood the significance of their mark on treaties which compromised their authority and potentially limited their freedom of action. Others, however, were quite well aware of their sovereignty and approached the Europeans, even as they were being approached in turn, as agents in the solution of economic problems or possible allies whose friendship might assist in the realization of a diplomatic victory at the expense of some belligerent neighbor. Africa therefore was not a dull, uncomprehending, inert mass, apathetic in the face of the force that bore in upon her; neither were African leaders necessarily high-minded romantic heroes fighting to the last drop of patriotic blood for national honor violated. They were human beings caught up in dynamics they could not control. Their eventual loss of land and liberty was due essentially to a want of technical sophistication, not to a lack of will or vigor to respond.

Examples abound. In Buganda, the *kabaka*, Mutesa, ruled with a firm hand, sure of his authority over a virile, imperialistically minded power. When, during the early 1870's, Egypt began to probe southward in search of trade and empire, both Bunyoro and Buganda saw the intruder, not as an object of fear, but as a means for gaining advantage in their intramural struggle. When the possibility of European support against both Bunyoro and Egypt later presented itself, Mutesa, like any resourceful statesman, reached out for help where he could find it, confident that in his strength he could use the Europeans to his own advantage.

Similarly, Mirambo in his struggle to establish a trading empire among the Nyamwezi, consistently regarded Europeans as his vehicle to success. Europeans had guns and understood mechanics, they possessed wide knowledge and influence; hence they could help him to gain power within his sphere, to control the passage of caravans, and with them, their wealth. His preference for Britain was a direct reflection of her influence in Zanzibar, even as his hopes for an enduring and powerful inland nation rested on the possibility of an alliance with the British state. Much the same considerations prompted the Hanga (Wanga) chief, Mumia, to encourage coastal traders and seek a British alliance during the 1880's as a means of offsetting a loss in local authority. So successful was Mumia's policy that his village north of Kavirondo Gulf grew in wealth and importance and later became the administrative center for Kavirondo while Mumia's influence increased proportionately.

These essays in international diplomacy by Mirambo and Mumia were made in the interests of political power linked to economic advantage. A profitable commerce was the aspiration of many an African people, and when that commerce involved Europe, as it frequently did, the European trade was assiduously wooed. When European merchants first appeared in West African waters in search of gold and then to barter for slaves, the goods they offered in exchange were exotic by local standards, but soon became necessities, not of life, but in the satisfaction of prestige and the desire for luxury. Spirits and tobacco developed into steady favorites; a taste spread for European and Indian textiles, for mirrors and ornamental jewelry, while firearms were quickly found to be indispensable to successful statecraft. When the slave trade was abolished, other products were substituted, and desolate indeed was the countryside which could provide no goods of interest to the Europeans. Far from opposing the arrival of traders, the local people frequently fought one another to gain access to the European commerce; as long as trade was the object, the European was more than welcome.

Commerce, therefore, was one of the forces leading to partition which found the African as quick as the European to press for advantage, and nowhere was he more resourceful than in the mangrove swamps of the Niger Delta coast. There, as elsewhere, the European trader was encouraged, but only to exchange his goods with the Delta middlemen who in turn monopolized the trade with the interior. When the Europeans attempted to penetrate upcountry and make direct contact with the inland markets, trouble resulted.

In the tidewater creeks, those familiar with the area were able to move swiftly and silently in their small craft, and when the occasion called for force, they could bring to bear large numbers of fully manned war canoes complete with cannon and riflemen. The prize was trade monopoly; in this respect the objectives and the tactics of George Goldie and the Royal Niger Company were identical with those of such Delta merchant princes as Jaja, king of Opobo, and Nana, the Itsekiri governor of the Benin River.

Both were hard-bitten realists, and Jaja in particular had risen from unpromising slave beginnings to become, first, head of one of the main trading houses of Bonny, and then, when the prospect of dominating Bonny faded, the founder of the new state of Opobo which soon emerged as the most important power in the Delta. Such pretensions with their corollary of mercantile dominance came under increasing pressure from British traders, particularly when the Berlin Conference proclaimed freedom of commerce on the Niger and a British protectorate was established throughout the Delta. Jaja had already secured a treaty sustaining his monopoly which he proceeded to implement by direct trade with England, threatening to destroy any upcountry producers who might try to deal with British merchants, and carrying on a vigorous diplomatic offensive to force Whitehall to honor the terms of his treaty. Since the British merchants in the area had formed a trading cartel, the issue was not free trade versus monopoly, but whether the monopoly would be African or British, and there was the further question of which government— British or African—in fact ruled the creeks. Reduced to these essentials, the dispute was clearly foreclosed against Jaja who, faced with the prospect of overwhelmingly superior force, surrendered in 1887 to the British consul, Harry Johnston, and was eventually deported.

The fall of Nana was also a history of mercantile competition played out in terms of political authority. In the far northwestern edge of the Niger Delta below Benin City, the Itsekiri traders had long been active, first in the slave traffic and later in the export of palm oil. In the 1850's on the urging of the British consul they had established the office of chief or governor of the Benin River as a check to unrest in the area. After a series of occupants, the post went in 1879 to Olomu, the most prominent Itsekiri trader of his day. His son, Nana, succeeded in 1883 on his father's death, using both his inherited wealth and his official position during the ensuing years to build up an impressive trade monopoly covering not only the creek region but the palm oil hinterland along the Benin, Ethiope, and Warri rivers.

Such a monopoly irritated many people. First, it was vexatious to the growing number of British traders coming into the area. Next, it was cited by the African oil producers as the chief cause for their falling prices during the 1880's. Further, there were disaffected elements among the Itsekiri who resented Nana's power. Finally, his strength was regarded by the British protectorate administration as a challenge by a local chief who was also strongly suspected of engaging in an illegal slave trade. In 1891 the Itsekiri country was placed under the new Oil Rivers Protectorate, now constituting the southern portion of the Niger districts, and shortly thereafter the mercantile and political opposition to Nana accelerated rapidly. In 1894 the acting consul-general reported to his government a virtual stoppage of trade due to unrest created by Nana's men. Nana was ordered to withdraw his war canoes and when the answer was unsatisfactory, a blockade was placed on his headquarters at Ebrohimi in the mangrove lowlands near the Benin River. The town was shelled and several attacks were mounted but these were driven off by well-armed and entrenched defenders. Finally, after adequate reinforcements had been called up, the town was taken in September, 1894, but by that time most of the population had melted into the forest. Nana escaped, later to give himself up in Lagos, and like Jaja, he was subsequently tried and banished.

In some instances the commercial-political opposition to European pressure ended more happily for the defenders; for example, with the Egba, who survived Governor Glover's energetic interference, maintaining their independence until 1914. Usually, however, the results were disastrous, as in the case of the Brassmen, who attacked the Royal Niger Company post at Akassa in 1895 in a desperate protest against the loss of their inland markets to the Company's monopoly, then were overwhelmed, despite determined resistance in their home Delta country of Nembe, and their town of Brass destroyed.

Occasionally what began as a matter of commerce took on a different color with the passage of time. Ashanti, defeated in 1874, soon endeavored to regain her old authority while European states during the 1880's stepped up their mutual competition in the extension of protectorate areas. The Gold Coast government, prodded by local African merchants on the coast, sought to impose its rule on Ashanti while Prempeh, the *asantehene,* moved to evade entanglement, his position progressively weakened by the defection of former allies asking for protection by Britain. In 1896 the British occupied Kumasi and deposed Prempeh, establishing a protectorate the following year. This action was deeply resented locally and, when in 1900 the Gold Coast governor committed an unpardonable blasphemy by demanding to sit on the golden stool, that ancient symbol of the Ashanti state and spirit, the people united in a rising which was put down only after months of hard campaigning. In 1901 Ashanti was annexed directly to the British crown.

The struggle of the Ashanti people to preserve the spirit and fact of national integrity was paralleled in other African societies. If Moshesh sought protectorate status as the means of national survival and Tippu Tib opted to join the forces he realized he could not beat, others fought stubbornly to stave off annihilation, their motivation often as diverse as their objective was identical. In the Katanga, Msiri paid with his life for refusing to give up the commercial advantage which Tippu Tib knew could not be held. In West Africa, the driving force behind the Senegalese Muslim leader, Mamadu Lamine, was partly religious zeal and partly pride in his Sarakole origins, while Ahmadu, son and successor to the great *jihad* leader, *al-Hajj* Umar, seems to have been preoccupied with the too-rigid defense of a Tokolor state that had seen its best days. With Samori it was the preservation of his Mandinka empire with a series of imaginative political and military maneuvers, as brilliantly conceived as they were ultimately futile.

East Africa also witnessed uncompromising resistance along with accommodation. If Mirambo had sought an alliance with Britain, his compatriot Siki was of another mind, and thwarted German occupation from his center at Tabora for several years until his defeat and death in 1893. Similarly, the Hehe chief, Mkwawa, held out against the Germans in the Iringa region of Tanganyika for the better part of a decade until he was overwhelmed in 1898. To the north, opposition was likewise variable—witness the Nandi in western Kenya who were not to be finally subdued until 1905, the Kikuyu who were sometimes cooperative, sometimes antagonistic, or the Kamba who generally were receptive to European penetration. Far in the south, resistance, though unavailing, was bitter and shaped an equally bitter course for the history of an unhappy land—the determined defense of the xenophobic Boer and the futile struggle of the ill-starred Lobengula against the irrepressible force of British penetration.

MODERNIZATION AND INDEPENDENCE IN ETHIOPIA

Political disintegration had settled over the Ethiopian highlands during the long royal residence begun at Gondar by Fasiladas in the mid-seventeenth century, and as such seemed to be preparing the ground for the accelerated process of partition which was to consume Africa during the nineteenth century. Intrigue and regicide were commonplace while monarchs degenerated into ineffectual puppets, corrupt and impotent within the remote splendor of their palaces. Only the Ethiopian Church managed a show of national cohesion, if not authority, while political power was captured by the nobility, the great princes of Tigre, Shoa, Amhara, and Gojjam ruling, for practical purposes, as independent sovereigns. Of these, Shoa, though peripherally located to the south and long beset by Galla pressure, had a particular destiny, for its royal house was to bring forth the men who would lead the country back to national unity and in the process protect it from annihilation by foreign powers.

Theodore, the first of the reformer-kings was not a Shoan, however, nor was he even of the main royal houses. The son of a minor chief in western Ethiopia, he was born about 1818, and given the name Kassa, coming to manhood in a period of growing chaos during which civil war degenerated into anarchy and brigandage was a plausible road to power. Living a life of chronic uncertainty in the unrelieved turmoil of the day, Kassa did indeed operate for a time as the chief of a band of highwaymen, a successful vocation that led eventually to political recognition and marriage with the daughter of the *ras* of Gondar in 1847. Within a few years he had gained control of both Gondar and Gojjam, and when this was followed by victory over the *ras* of Tigre in 1855, Kassa was able to have himself crowned *negusa nagast*, king of kings, with the throne name of Tewodros or Theodore. The king of Shoa having died shortly thereafter and his young son, Menelik, fallen into the emperor's hands, Theodore was established as the undisputed head of an Ethiopian nation once more united.

Theodore had unified the country by force, but, like Muhammad Ali, he now sought to build a modern state, making unity permanent through administrative reform and the nation powerful by means of an up-to-date army. He attempted to place civil control over the lands and the wealth of the Ethiopian Church, the state undertaking to pay the salaries of the clergy. He moved to break the power of the provincial nobility by instituting districts under his own appointed governors. He transferred his capital from the inaccessible center of Gondar, and instituted the first system of roads for better communication and military transport.

It was to military reforms that he gave chief attention, however, for he was aware of the shortcomings of the traditional means of warfare in Ethiopia in a context of growing imperial interest by European nations in the affairs of Africa. "I know the tactics of European governments," he announced. "First they send out missionaries, then consuls to support the missionaries, then battalions to support the consuls." As it happened, the missionaries became Theodore's own military vanguard when they were obliged by the emperor to bend their energies to casting cannon and shot rather than converting souls, finally producing a great mortar capable of firing a thousand pound shell, as well as several other artillery pieces of lesser caliber.

Such novelties as bronze cannon were much needed by the emperor who was beset, not only by foreign enemies actual or potential, but by rising opposition at home on the part of both nobility and clergy, unwilling to give up their long-standing authority to a central government, or to part with their vast accumulation of landed wealth. Deprived thus of an adequate financial base for his reforms, Theodore ultimately failed in his attempted modernization of Ethiopia, although the immediate cause of his downfall came from another quarter—a dispute with Britain over a request for technical assistance which involved misunderstanding and pride, tactlessness and arbitrary behavior.

In 1862 Theodore asked that artisans be sent to help him in his plans for military development. When this appeal was ignored, he took it to be an unfriendly act and responded by detaining the British consul and mishandling several other Europeans. Theodore's conduct was characterized by a lack of restraint which increasingly marred his later years, but his behavior may also have been caused by a single-minded determination to gain the help of craftsmen capable of manufacturing arms. In any event, relations gradually deteriorated between the two countries, and a military expedition was finally dispatched in 1867 under Sir Robert Napier to rescue the consul and his companions. By this time much of Ethiopia was in open revolt and the invaders had little difficulty reaching the fortress of Magdala where Theodore stood at bay. His small force was easily defeated in April, 1868, by the larger, better-equipped British expedition, and even his great mortar exploded on firing, thus punctuating the futility of Theodore's position. On defeat he committed suicide, and there ended this first attempt at Ethiopian modernization and unification.

For a time it appeared as though Ethiopia would revert to its earlier pattern of internal chaos, but in 1871 the *ras* of Tigre succeeded in outdoing his rivals, and early in 1872 he was crowned Yohannes IV, king of kings. Throughout his reign, the new emperor was to have little time for internal reform and, unlike Theodore, sought national unity by granting considerable local authority to regional princes in exchange for their loyalty to crown and nation. This loyalty left him free to deal with the mounting foreign threat to Ethiopia. Initially, there were the Egyptians who were subdued during 1875–1876 in their attempt to expand inland from the old Turkish coastal foothold at Massawa. More serious, however, were growing European interests in territories bordering Ethiopia. Particularly active in this respect was Italy, which first converted her Red Sea foothold of Assab into a colony in 1882, and then occupied Massawa in 1885 with British acquiescence, combining this expansionist policy with a diplomatic offensive designed to split Menelik, now king of Shoa, from his nominal overlord, Yohannes. Such machinations received a temporary setback when the Italians were defeated at Dogali in 1887, but Yohannes was now obliged to face yet another foreign enemy in the Mahdist armies of the *Khalifa* which attacked and burned Gondar in 1887. Two years later at Metemma (al-Qallabat), an Ethiopian victory was turned to defeat when Yohannes was mortally wounded, and his troops, suddenly demoralized, abandoned the field to the badly-mauled Sudanese. Once again the threat of disintegration faced Ethiopia.

Although the death of Yohannes was a blow to national security and unity in these parlous times, Ethiopia continued to enjoy good fortune in its succession of kings. Menelik II, who now proclaimed himself *negusa nagast* without serious dissent, had already served a royal apprenticeship since 1865 in Shoa, and for some years had been absorbing valuable experience in two activities vital to the survival of the Ethiopian state, the achievement and extension of national cohesion and the frustration of European aspirations in his country.

Menelik II's long career was characterized by good fortune leavened by an enlightened opportunism. Grandson of the celebrated Shoan king, Sahle Selassie (1813–1847), he became Theodore's prisoner in 1855 but profited from his confinement, observing at first hand the business of statecraft; then taking advantage of Theodore's failing hold on the government, he escaped from the fortress of Magdala in 1865. Back in Shoa, he assumed the crown of what was virtually an independent principality, and with the death of Theodore, claimed the title of king of kings. This placed him in direct confrontation with Yohannes, but potential civil war was avoided through negotiation in 1878 whereby Yohannes assumed the crown, and Menelik the succession, while the latter maintained all but the name of independence in the southern kingdom of Shoa.

Yohannes was thus free to turn his attention to foreign threats while Menelik busied himself in reasserting hegemony over what he regarded as Ethiopia's traditional tributaries to the south and west. "I shall endeavour," he was to inform the European powers some years later, "to re-establish the ancient frontiers of Ethiopia," and these he indicated to be Khartoum in the north and Lake Victoria to the west with all the Galla territories included. The process began with his accession to the Shoan throne. The Galla were cultivated by diplomacy or conquered by military action and an attack made on the Muslim state of Harar which still prevailed in the southeast. Menelik first subdued the Wello Galla located north of Shoa who had long isolated the Shoans from the rest of Ethiopia; then by both force and persuasion he formed the Shoan Galla Confederation around the area of what was later to become the capital city of Addis Ababa, finally pressing outward into Gurage and Kaffa to the southwest, Arussi, Sidamo, Bali, and Borana in the south, Wallaga in the west, and Ogaden to the east.

These areas were taken between 1875 and the end of the century—both before and after Menelik's accession to the Ethiopian throne—and were joined by the emirate of Harar which was subdued in 1887. Unlike previous conquerers, however, Menelik was interested in occupation, not ransom, and consequently introduced a permanent administration, either in the form of local rulers loyal to him or his own military garrisons where necessary. Hence his provincial government took on some of the quality of the European colonial regimes, at least in the eyes of those whose lands had been invaded, and in fact several of his campaigns were made expressly to forestall European colonial ambitions. "If powers at a distance come forward to partition Africa between them," he stated his philosophy to Europe, "I do not intend to be an indifferent spectator."

Whatever may have been Menelik's own imperial aims, he certainly was fully aware of the serious nature of the European threat, and his whole career as Shoan king and Ethiopian emperor was devoted to thwarting the expansion of western colonialism to his homeland. This objective he pursued with Theodore's classic tactic of securing modern arms, a process at which he was far more successful than his ill-starred predecessor. By purchase and through diplomacy he steadily accumulated firearms, particularly from Italy, whose fruitless attempts to seduce Menelik into a betrayal of Yohannes cost her dearly when the guns sent to the Shoan later were used in devastating force to repel the Italian invasion at Adowa.

By the time that Menelik succeeded Yohannes in 1889, the Italians were actively fanning out from their Massawa beachhead onto the Eritrean plateau and the French were entrenched in Djibouti. Vig-

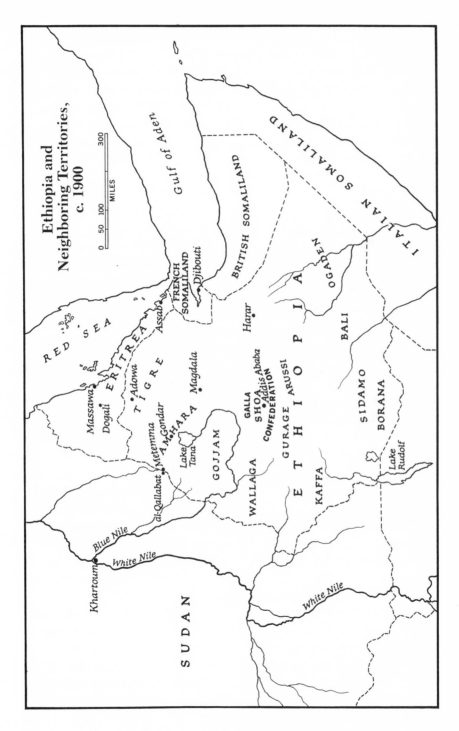

Ethiopia and
Neighboring Territories,
c. 1900

MILES
0 50 100   300

Gulf of Aden

FRENCH SOMALILAND

Djibouti

BRITISH SOMALILAND

ITALIAN SOMALILAND

RED SEA

ERITREA

Assab

Massawa

Dogali

Metemma

al-Qallabat

Adowa

TIGRE

Gondar

AMHARA

Magdala

Lake Tana

GOJJAM

WALLAGA

Harar

GALLA

SHOA

Addis Ababa

CONFEDERATION

GURAGE

ARUSSI

E T H I O P I A

OGADEN

BALI

SIDAMO

BORANA

KAFFA

Lake Rudolf

Blue Nile

White Nile

Khartoum

White Nile

S U D A N

orous countermeasures were therefore needed to check this latest manifestation of European expansionism. One of Menelik's first diplomatic acts was to sign the Treaty of Wichali (Ucciali) which conceded the Italian holdings in Eritrea but recognized Menelik's own imperial status in Ethiopia and guaranteed his access to the sea through Italian territory. The treaty, nevertheless, soon became a source of dispute rather than amity, for the Italians claimed that it bound Menelik to consult Italy in the conduct of his foreign relations, thereby converting Ethiopia into an Italian protectorate, whereas the Amharic version of the text made such consultation optional, not obligatory.

Menelik denounced the treaty in 1893 and, convinced of Italian designs on Ethiopia, prepared for the expected invasion with steady imports of weaponry for his growing army. When the Italian attack began in 1895, the situation was far removed from what had faced Napier almost thirty years earlier. In the first place, the Ethiopians were now better united behind their emperor and in opposition to the invaders whose appropriation of land for Italian colonists had particularly angered the local population in Tigre. Moreover, Menelik fielded an army of 100,000 well-armed troops, more than five times the Italian force, which was further embarrassed by unfamiliarity with the terrain, resulting in fatal tactical miscalculations against the Ethiopian battle plan which proved sound. The Battle of Adowa, fought in March, 1896, therefore, visited a crushing defeat upon the invaders, unique in the annals of the partition of Africa, which put the quietus for a long generation on European designs in the Abyssinian highlands.

Menelik's subsequent diplomacy, perhaps mistakenly, did not involve dislodging the Italians from Eritrea, but it did achieve the immediate, unqualified recognition in Europe of Ethiopian strength and independence, although it did little to diminish European interest in Ethiopia's economic possibilities. This was an important development for it enabled Menelik to enlist European assistance toward one of the major objectives of his reign, the modernization of Ethiopia. Always cautious of entanglements which might compromise his independence, the emperor began to entertain arrangements which would develop and open up his country.

Modernization was carried out along familiar lines. Bridges and roads were built and a railway projected in 1894 connecting Djibouti with Menelik's new capital of Addis Ababa, founded about 1886.

To this was added a postal service, as well as telegraph and telephone systems, all operating by the early years of the twentieth century. State administration was made more efficient, education modernized, and up-to-date banking facilities introduced along with the beginning of hospital and public health installations. These innovations, which were just a beginning and scarcely affected the daily existence of most Ethiopians, were invariably achieved with the help of Western technicians, a reflection of continuing European political interest in the area. Menelik, therefore, was at pains to arrange firm boundaries for his empire, and between 1897 and 1908 international frontiers were settled by treaty with all his neighbors.

To these formal developments, Menelik added a number of arrangements with private and public concessionaires designed to promote commercial, agricultural, or industrial development. Many of these grants were to prove illusory for the canny emperor was capable of awarding conflicting rights or claims to non-existent resources, pocketing the concession fees for the state, particularly in support of the excellent Ethiopian army.

Menelik's careful program, jointly standing off European efforts at economic and political domination while building up his internal resources, was sound policy. When in 1906 his health and vigor began to fail, Britain, France, and Italy, quickly reacting to a sign of weakness, concluded a treaty proclaiming their right to intervene in Ethiopian affairs "to protect their nationals" in the event of internal unrest. As the emperor grew progressively weaker, the possibility of a struggle for succession arose, and with it mounted the prospect of foreign interference. When Menelik died in 1913 on the eve of the First World War, however, the European powers were fortunately preoccupied at home, and Ethiopia survived intervention for another twenty years.

Suggestions for Further Reading

The complex subject of the partition of Africa has been treated in a large body of works, principally as an aspect of European diplomatic history. General studies include William Langer, *European Alliances and Alignments, 1871–1890*, 2nd. ed. (New York: Alfred A. Knopf, 1950), and *The Diplomacy of Imperialism, 1890–1902*, 2nd. ed. (New York: Alfred A. Knopf, 1951) by the same author, as well as A. J. P. Taylor, *The Struggle for Mastery in Europe, 1848–1918* (Oxford: Clarendon Press,

1954). The standard work on the Berlin Conference is Sybil E. Crowe, *The Berlin West African Conference, 1884–1885* (London: Longmans Green, 1942).

Reasons for the latter stages of partition seen in terms of British imperial policy are set forth in Ronald Robinson and John Gallagher, *Africa and the Victorians: The Climax of Imperialism in the Dark Continent* (London: Macmillan; New York: St. Martin's Press, 1961). French colonial policy is entertainingly if acidulously examined in Stephen H. Roberts, *A History of French Colonial Policy, 1870–1925* (London: Frank Cass, 1963), while Henri Brunschwig, *Mythes et Réalités de l'Imperialisme Colonial Français* (Paris: Armand Colin, 1960)—available in English as *French Colonialism, 1871–1914, Myths and Realities* (London: Pall Mall, 1966; New York: Praeger, 1966)—assesses the economic basis for partition. German colonial activity is studied along with aspects of British-German colonial rivalry in P. Gifford and W. R. Louis, eds., *Britain and Germany in Africa* (New Haven: Yale University Press, 1967).

Additional analyses of the factors leading to partition, taking particular account of happenings in Africa, include Henri Brunschwig, *L'Avènement de l'Afrique Noire* (Paris: Armand Colin, 1963); and J. Stengers, "L'Impérialisme Colonial de la Fin du XIXe Siècle: Mythe ou Réalité," *Journal of African History*, vol. III, no. 3, 1962, both stressing French involvement in the Congo. On the other hand, J. D. Hargreaves, *Prelude to the Partition of West Africa* (London: Macmillan, 1963; New York: St. Martins, 1963); and C. W. Newbury, "Victorians, Republicans, and the Partition of West Africa," *Journal of African History*, vol. III, no. 3, 1962, see rivalries in West Africa as a major factor.

Several works surveying Africa regionally, as well as biographies of individuals involved in the partition, are also useful. For example, see Ruth Slade, *King Leopold's Congo* (London: Oxford University Press, 1962), R. Oliver and G. Mathew, eds., *History of East Africa*, I (Oxford: Clarendon Press, 1963), as well as Hargreaves, which has been cited. Among biographies are several valuable works: John Flint, *Sir George Goldie and the Making of Nigeria* (London: Oxford University Press, 1960); R. Oliver, *Sir Harry Johnston and the Scramble for Africa* (London: Chatto and Windus, 1959); and Margery Perham, *Lugard*, 2v. (London: Collins, 1956, 1960; New York: Oxford University Press, vol. I, 1956).

The story of the African response to partition is scattered through many works, including several listed above. For Jaja, see K. O. Dike, *Trade and Politics in the Niger Delta, 1830–1885* (Oxford: Clarendon Press, 1956); and G. I. Jones, *The Trading States of the Oil Rivers* (London: Oxford University Press, 1963); as well as Roland Oliver, *Harry Johnston*, cited above. Nana is dealt with in P. C. Lloyd, "The

Itsekiri in the Nineteenth Century," *Journal of African History*, vol. IV, no. 2, 1963; the Brassmen in Flint, cited above, and E. J. Alagoa, *The Small Brave City-State* (Ibadan: Ibadan University Press, 1964); and the last independent years of the Ashanti in W. Tordoff, *Ashanti Under the Prempehs, 1888–1935* (London: Oxford University Press, 1965). There is much material on African response to the partition of East Africa in *History of East Africa*, already cited, but see also R. J. Harvey, "Mirambo," *Tanganyika Notes and Records*, Jan., 1950, no. 28; N. R. Bennett, *Studies in East African History* (Boston University Press, 1963); and G. W. Were, *A History of the Abaluyia* (Nairobi: East African Publishing House, 1967).

Further discussion of Ethiopia may be pursued in several standard works: Richard Greenfield, *Ethiopia* (London: Pall Mall Press, 1965; New York, Praeger, 1965); A. H. M. Jones and E. Monroe, *A History of Ethiopia* (Oxford: Clarendon Press, 1960); and E. Ullendorf, *The Ethiopians*, 2nd. ed. (London: Oxford University Press, 1965). See also articles by R. Pankhurst on Theodore and Menelik in *Tarikh*, vol. 1, nos. 1 and 4, as well as Sven Rubenson's *King of Kings, Tewodros of Ethiopia* (Addis Ababa: Haile Sellassie I University, 1966), and Mordechai Abir, *Ethiopia: the Era of the Princes* (London: Longmans, 1968; New York: Praeger, 1968).

15: The Rise of Nationalism in West Africa

ADAPTATION AND SURVIVAL

As the nineteenth century unfolded and European influence steadily reached out, probing ever deeper into the world of West Africa, the African reaction to Europe grew correspondingly, both in its extent and its force. It came from two distinct sources of the African population. On the one hand, there were the traditional societies, attempting to contain an alien presence within the definition of their time-tested way of life. On the other, there were those West Africans educated in Europe, who had already accepted in whole or in part the standards of Western civilization and who therefore sought to utilize their newly acquired skills both to strengthen their Africa and to protect it from annihilation at the hands of a foreign culture.

Traditional Africa was by no means inert or unproductive, but her rate and direction of change were scarcely relevant to the forces that bore in upon her, and her response, however determined, was thus foredoomed. Direct confrontation, diplomatic or military, was futile in the face of European technological superiority, and in West Africa the end was invariably defeat and submission, whether it was decided by the sword in the mangrove creeks of the Niger Delta and on the rolling plains of the West African savanna, or by negotiation in a chiefly compound. Jaja, defending his commercial monopoly at Opobo, Prempeh fighting to save his throne in Kumasi, or Samori in his desperate guerrilla action against the French all met the same fate, for in the final analysis they lacked the physical force to control their destiny. Survival, therefore, demanded accommodation—cooperation rather than conflict.

Accommodation with Europe promised much, but it also bristled with difficulties. Not only did it require a thoroughgoing knowledge of the two worlds of Africa and the West, it also called for a nice judgment of how far European civilization could be used to benefit African society without destroying it. Not only did it point the way to African independence from Europe through the very ideas and institutions of the West which were dominating Africa, but by the same token it posed the problem of keeping that domination from becoming permanent. Not only did it hold the promise of modernization and political freedom, it also contained the threat of cultural extinction. The men who practiced accommodation, therefore, were obliged to live at an advanced level of sophistication, to be able to move with easy assurance in the two worlds of Africa and Europe but never to forget their identity, to poise themselves between acceptance and rejection of the West without losing their sense of balance and proportion, to seek a secure marriage between those European institutions best suited to African growth and the most substantial elements of traditional African life.

It is not surprising that such demands brought varying responses. At one extreme were those Africans fully persuaded as to the superiority of European civilization, who saw African progress in terms of the degree to which Western culture could be absorbed and Western influence made dominant in Africa. At the other extreme were those who saw Europe as decadent and her attractions the siren song leading straight to perdition. The first group was exemplified by such assimilated Africans as Abbé Boilat and Paul Holle of Senegal, or, in a later generation, the Nigerian, Kitoyi Ajasa. Examples from the second group included the generation of cultural nationalists who professed the faith of *négritude* in the years following the Second World War. Between these two lay a wide range of opinion which was to a considerable extent a reflection of the differing approaches of Britain and France to the administration of their colonies.

Since the Revolution of 1789, France had based her colonial policy on the idea of assimilation which argued the superiority of French language and culture and the necessity that each colonial be converted with all dispatch into an unconditional Frenchman. Where French influence was directly felt—among the urban mulattoes of Senegal, for example—this policy was successful to a surprising extent. French-educated Africans tended to equate progress in Africa with mastery of European standards, to place status within the world-wide community of Frenchmen before the integrity of the Negro race, or to regard African nationalism as irrelevant to the reality of French cultural superiority.

British colonial practice, on the contrary, stressed, if anything, the differences between Africa and Europe, but at the same time unconsciously inculcated a wide range of Anglo-Saxon predilections extending from constitutional law to black silk umbrellas, and from Anglican theology to afternoon tea. The result was a greater independence of European standards and more diversity of response to colonial rule, combined with a degree of devotion to European culture as total as anything to be found within the French territories. Nevertheless, two main streams of thought were discernible among educated Africans in the British areas. The first held close to the French doctrine of assimilation, arguing that where European institutions were superior to those of traditional Africa, they should be introduced as quickly and thoroughly as possible, the better to get on with the business of social and cultural betterment. The other was much more self-consciously nationalistic, insisting that African civilization must develop along its own lines or perish, but often employing ideas and skills acquired in Europe to formulate its views and to attack the colonial policy and government it came to oppose.

POLITICS AND COMMERCE IN SENEGAL

The administration of Governor Faidherbe was pivotal in the development of French colonialism in West Africa. Before his time, the French presence, for all its longevity, had been tentative, and French commitment to her posts in Senegal remained equivocal. By the end of his tenure of office, the colony had been transformed, not so much physically as in its sense of mission. Instead of a precarious coastal foothold, Senegal had become a permanent base from which would one day be launched the conquest of an empire. Moreover, in the years following Faidherbe, there was growing assurance from the slow but steady development of the economy, while the second half of the nineteenth century saw the colony at last secure a definite participation in French political life, so long promised and so long withheld.

Faidherbe had laid the foundations for economic expansion both through his policy of pacification for the interior country and his program of public works designed to facilitate agriculture and commerce. To be sure, the gum trade of the early nineteenth century was little affected and exports rose with disappointing modesty from 2500 tons in 1854 to 4000 during the 1880's. This lackluster record was more than offset, however, by the emergence of groundnuts as a major product. In 1853 only 3000 tons were exported, but this figure rose dramatically in the years that followed—8700 tons in 1870, 34,000 in 1881, 45,000 in 1885, and 65,000 in 1894. Such statistics were accompanied by corresponding increases in the value of exports, a development which was nevertheless somewhat dampened by the fact that Senegal continued to be saddled with a single crop economy, groundnuts now having replaced gum as her major product. Although diversification was attempted fitfully with such crops as indigo, rubber, and cotton, little resulted; the groundnut yield of 1883, representing more than 70 per cent of the value of exports, typified the problem.

With expanding commerce came the rise of the city, slowly at first and then with increasing velocity in the decades preceding the First World War. St Louis was already an established center; by the end of Faidherbe's administration it had a population of approximately fifteen thousand, mostly Africans, with Europeans and mulattoes numbering but a few hundred each, the African community containing substantial numbers from the inland territories. Since St. Louis was situated on a small island in the Senegal River, the African neighborhoods had gradually spilled over to the suburbs of N'Dar Tout and Guet N'Dar on the Barbary peninsula which separated St. Louis from the Atlantic Ocean and which served as well as a terminus for the caravans from the interior. Here on the edge of the city were the compounds crowded with their traditional round straw huts, and the colorful noisy markets where the products of Africa and Europe changed hands to the accompaniment of shouted abuse and finally of mutual congratulations. In the middle of town, where the Europeans and mulattoes were dominant, the mood was vastly different—quiet streets lined with whitewashed buildings shimmered in the tropical heat, a scene which, according to the novelist Pierre Loti, invariably evoked a feeling of melancholy and lassitude.

St. Louis was not only the chief port by reason of its location at the head of the Senegal River; it served also as the seat of government for the colony. Nevertheless its preeminent position was challenged increasingly by other municipalities as the century drew to a close. While the island of Gorée gradually declined into picturesque decay, the nearby centers of Dakar and Rufisque were emerging in response to the new commercialism. Dakar, founded by the French administration in 1857, grew slowly at first. As late as 1881 it languished with fewer than 2000 inhabitants, but once the railroad to St. Louis had opened in 1885, growth was rapid. By 1895 the population had risen to 8000, in 1904 to 18,500 and on the eve of the First World War Dakar had become the first city of French West Africa, the capital and chief port for France's vast West African territories.

For its part, Rufisque experienced a growth only comparatively less spectacular. Arising spontaneously and without official assistance a dozen miles down the coast from Dakar, Rufisque was the result of the groundnut trade. With less than 1200 population in 1878, it rose to 4000 in 1883 and 8000 by 1891, almost doubling its size again by 1914. As early as 1885 this lively port controlled 40 per cent of Senegal's groundnut exports, and in the ensuing years she continued to develop, in 1914 still challenging Dakar's more diversified commerce with her mounting control of the groundnut trade. In the face of this economic expansion, St. Louis gradually faded, joining Gorée as a relic of days gone by.

The rise of Senegal's cities reflected political as well as economic growth, for it was in these communes that the French system of representative government was transplanted and developed during the second half of the nineteenth century. In both France and Senegal a brief experiment with democracy followed Europe's liberal revolutions of 1848; then after the autocratic reaction experienced during the regime of Napoleon III, parliamentary government was once again established as the French Third Republic launched itself in 1870. In Senegal this was reflected in a series of related moves. To begin with, the colony was granted the right of choosing through universal male suffrage a representative to the Chamber of Deputies in Paris. This privilege was made permanent in 1879, the same year that Senegal formed her first territorial General Council, also elected through universal suffrage and exercising substantially the same legislative responsibility for local administrative and financial matters as did the general councils of France's own metropolitan departments. In 1872, moreover, both Gorée and St. Louis were incorporated as full-fledged municipalities with their own democratically chosen municipal councils, Dakar at first sharing this authority with Gorée. In 1880 Rufisque was also elevated to this status of *commune de plein exercice*, and seven years later Dakar and Gorée were separated, thus forming the so-called Four Communes of Senegal. Since universal suffrage was defined through usage to include all individuals who could show a five-year residence in the communes, the vast majority of Africans was thus able to join the mulattoes and Europeans as electors, for deputy, for the general council, and for the municipal councils.

It did not follow, however, that the African vote meant African political power, since there were many complex facets to Senegalese politics during the decades leading up to the beginning of the First World War. First, there was France herself, whose rising interest was reflected both in the growing political and economic activities of the merchant houses of Bordeaux and in the colonial government concerned with the administration of an expanding empire. Bordeaux saw to it that her commercial stake in Senegal was protected by Bordelais agents on the ground, some European and some mulatto. For its part, the government introduced as much authoritarianism as the local traffic would bear, for it could not permit local parliamentary exercises in the general and municipal councils to interfere with its surveillance of the gradually expanding interior areas coming under its control.

These forces from France were offset by the mulattoes who, though they normally gave Bordeaux weak economic competition, were generally able to control local elections and offices, including the position of deputy to Paris. That they were successful in the face of an overwhelming African electoral majority was a measure of their control of the African vote, by reason of their wealth, position, and education through which they dominated former slaves and present servants. Election frauds were common during these years and African support was regularly bought to keep mulattoes in parliamentary control. Indeed, if they had been able to maintain a united front among themselves, the mulattoes would have been a great embarrassment to Bordeaux and the colonial administration;

instead intramural cleavages based on family feuds and economic competition kept them divided, thus simplifying the task of the French in maintaining their own political and economic influence.

One reason why political power was slow to develop among the Africans dwelling within the communes, was their laggard rate of assimilation into a French way of life. While the mulattoes had long since become completely converted to French culture, the Africans remained largely unabsorbed—speaking only Arabic or African languages, and on the whole illiterate in any tongue; Muslim in religious persuasion, and quite unfamiliar with the constitutional bases of government as imported from France. In 1857 Governor Faidherbe had guaranteed their special status as Muslims with an order which permitted the use of Islamic law in the settlement of civil disputes connected with such matters as inheritance and marriage. This decree, while protecting the personal status of the Africans, also tended to set them apart from the Europeanized population, an isolation which not only contributed to political exploitation but to other types of discrimination as well. Toward the close of the century, as French settlers arrived in Senegal in increasing numbers, it was alleged that these immigrants were being given preference in employment both by the government and in the commercial establishments of St. Louis, Dakar, and Rufisque.

Whatever the merits of these charges, there was no blinking at the move which gathered momentum, both in France and her colonies during the early years of the twentieth century, to abandon the concept of assimilation in favor of association, a doctrine which admitted the integrity of indigenous culture but only at a level inferior to French civilization. The consequence for people living under the policy of association was arbitrary rule, administrative justice, and forced labor imposed by a quasi-military colonial authority, and this was in fact the type of government which emerged in those areas of West Africa gained through France's late nineteenth-century conquests. In the Four Communes, however, the so-called African *originaires,* having long enjoyed political and civil rights guaranteed by the French constitution, considered themselves to be French citizens in good standing, and they therefore greatly resented official steps to limit their privileges by reducing them to the status of French subjects.

In Paris, nonetheless, it was argued that the special status as Muslims enjoyed by the *originaires* necessarily made them ineligible for French citizenship and its attendant obligations and privileges. In a complex series of administrative orders and court decisions taken between 1907 and 1914, the Africans of the Four Communes were systematically deprived of their French citizenship along with most of their civil and political rights, a development which was checked only by the outbreak of war in Europe and the rise of that master politician and defender of African rights, Blaise Diagne. Even before the advent of Diagne, however, the Africans had rallied in defense against their oppressors, organizing a mildly nationalist political party, the Young Senegalese, which was able to elect a few candidates to the local general and municipal councils but which had no pronounced effect in checking the new colonial policy. Interestingly, in view of Senegal's long-standing loyalty to France, the Young Senegalese demanded, not home rule or African independence, but a guarantee of their rights as Frenchmen, for the *originaires* had now come to regard themselves as full-fledged sons of the great revolution of 1789, as French as any citizen dwelling in France herself. Thus by 1914 the African population of the Four Communes, at any rate, viewed assimilation into French civilization as a major political, if not cultural, objective.

SIERRA LEONE AND AFRICAN NATIONALIST SELF-CONSCIOUSNESS

If African self-awareness in the French areas was emerging as an offshoot of French nationalism, a different set of circumstances in English-speaking West Africa was bringing forth a correspondingly different African response. The center for repatriated slaves in Sierra Leone continued to radiate influence wherever its people went, and most of these found their way eastward to parts of what later became Nigeria, in Yorubaland and the regions bordering the Niger River. What they brought in their intellectual baggage was partly a reflection of personal conviction and partly a measure of the Sierra Leone community they had left behind.

Already by mid-century the creoles of Freetown were shifting from the relatively uncritical acceptance of European civilization which had characterized the generation of Bishop Crowther to something more demanding, both of Europe and of their own African antecedents. If Crowther's son-in-law, the Reverend George Nicol, considered a Cambridge education as the ideal preparation for his son as a clergyman-to-be in Africa, Nicol's contemporary, the merchant, William Grant, would be satisfied with nothing less than the establishment of West Africa's own university designed to focus attention on African history and culture and thus avoid the emotional and intellectual confusion which so often accompanied education by a foreign set of standards. Again, James Quaker, trained for the ministry in London and for many years head of the C.M.S. grammar school in Freetown, could scarcely envision the development of an independent Christian church in West Africa except through continued and intimate association with British philanthropy. By contrast, the British-trained West Indian barrister and long-time Freetown resident, William Rainy, devoted himself during the same years to a career of exposing the extravagances and inequities of British rule in Sierra Leone, and found steady applause among the creoles for his exertions.

Such eclecticism was readily exportable. Bishop Crowther's great missionary work on the Niger on behalf of the "Bible and the plough" was carried out while another Sierra Leone émigré employed his own grasp of European institutions precisely to ward off prospective European influence. In Abeokuta, the Egba resistance to the belligerence of the Lagos administrator, J. H. Glover, found its most vigorous expression in the hands of George W. Johnson, sometime tailor and amateur musician, late of Sierra Leone. Colorfully known as Reversible Johnson, a name which did justice to his political prowess, he succeeded for a time in gaining a measure of support from the people of Abeokuta for his modernized Egba foreign office, the Egba United Board of Management, through which he mounted a successful diplomatic defense against the expansionism of the Lagos government.

Such action was scarcely appreciated by Crowther, the churchman, for it resulted among other things in the expulsion of the Church Missionary Society's European missionaries from Abeokuta in 1867. "Half-educated, unprincipled young men," Crowther described Johnson and his helpers, blaming them for the troubles of his co-workers, but the difficulty may have been in part caused by the Egba themselves, individualists to the core and non-partisan in their resistance to all alien efforts to save their souls. During the 1870's they forced the departure of another missionary, James Johnson, a Yoruba from Sierra Leone, dispatched to Abeokuta to re-establish the C.M.S. mission. Johnson was known as Holy Johnson among his contemporaries because of the puritanical nature of his Christianity, and it was his excessive zeal in progagating the faith in Egbaland which aroused the ire of the local people and led to his withdrawal.

This incident, which occurred early in Reverend Johnson's long career, was scarcely an accurate gauge of the man. Devoted Christian he was and his ecclesiastic abilities led ultimately to his appointment as assistant bishop in charge of a West African diocese. Moreover, during the last decades of the nineteenth century when African frustrations over the intrusions of colonial rule were sublimated in the form of independent church movements, Johnson remained staunchly loyal to his Anglican ties. Nevertheless he was one of the outstanding nationalists of his age, stressing the values of Africa's own culture, better suited to African needs than alien imports from Europe. Christianity was universal, insisted Johnson; it was no more European than it was African, but Western education, language, thought, and such external trappings as dress were parochial qualities to be imitated only at Africa's peril. Let the African cleave, therefore, to his ancient social practices, his time-tested ethical and moral codes. Johnson, the Christian cleric, had long been indulgent toward such indigenous customs as tribal markings, traditional marriage ceremonies, and local dress, while the use of African baptismal names was celebrated as part of his churchly ritual. Even domestic slavery he thought might be left to the "quiet ameliorative influence of the missionary's teaching," and late in his career he advocated the countenance of polygamy under certain circumstances as not incompatible with the teachings of Christ.

Preoccupation with Africa's welfare came in many guises. During this period, for example, the most distinguished name in the creole society of Freetown was without doubt that of Samuel Lewis. Widely known up and down the coast as learned barrister, member of the Sierra Leone legislative council, and Freetown mayor, Lewis exercised great influence in establishing standards of behavior and belief within his own community and beyond. His personal code was unquestionably Western—Christian faith, hard work, and public service with a modicum of personal profit to provide life's necessities, the very Victorian virtues which had been urged by Fowell Buxton and Henry Venn as the basis for social and economic reform in West Africa. As legal practitioner, he worked diligently for his clients who, he felt, also worked hard and deserved painstaking service in return. As appointed member of the legislative council which Lewis joined in 1882, nineteen years after its establishment, he saw himself as the servant of his community and constructive critic of official colonial policy. When he was knighted in 1893 he regarded this less as a personal honor than as a measure of West African progress, and took the occasion to urge greater public service on his contemporaries.

There was no gainsaying the extent of Lewis' own public service. During twenty-one years of faithful attendance in the legislative council until his death in 1903, Lewis was the guardian of popular rights—here forcing the withdrawal of an ill-advised law censoring the press, there criticizing executive usurpation of legislative functions, regularly calling for wide public representation on the council, and always filling the role of responsible spokesman for his people. As mayor of Freetown, he assumed the task of teacher, carefully instructing his fellow citizens in the obligations and privileges of self-government. As a public-spirited citizen, he conducted many experiments in the cultivation of new crops and urged agricultural improvement as a means to economic development. As a Sierra Leonean he regularly criticized a weak-willed colonial policy for failing to extend its influence into the interior, thus mortgaging, in his view, the economic and political future of his country. Withal, he called for sobriety, diligence, and responsibility from his people, for he saw no hope for ultimate self-government until they had in fact learned to govern themselves.

To many, Sir Samuel Lewis seemed too rigidly guided by an unreflective acceptance of European standards early instilled, perhaps, by a thoroughly British education. Nevertheless, a closer examination reveals something more—a careful mind at work, searching for the advancement of the African people and, backed by the courage to choose the unpopular over the expedient. Lewis was roughly handled at times, both by his own creole community and by the colonial administration, each of which tended to regard him as an occasional apostate, neither group really understanding his unfailing devotion to inner principle. Thus his desire to give legal service to his people was ever tempered by an unwillingness to sacrifice justice to cheap favoritism. Similarly, his principle of loyalty to constitutional authority did not preclude opposition to arbitrary rule. What appears in the works and working principles of Samuel Lewis, therefore, is a capsule version of West Africa's urgent problem of the nineteenth and twentieth centuries—how to build a modern society based on the best of both the African and European worlds.

EDWARD BLYDEN CREATES A PHILOSOPHY
OF AFRICAN NATIONALISM

Although, like Samuel Lewis, many West Africans wrestled with the difficult question of modernization and Westernization, few grasped the problem in its entirety or were aware of its massive complications, and only one seemed to see the necessity for creating a complete philosophy of African nationalism which permitted the full use of European ideas and institutions without damage to racial dignity or loss of a sense of African integrity. That one exception was Edward W. Blyden whose brilliance dominated the West African scene during the half century leading up to the First World War, and whose ideas not only aimed at the psychic security of Africa in the face of European intrusion, but anticipated the need far in the future for cultural and economic independence when African nations came to achieve political freedom in the mid-twentieth century.

Blyden was a West Indian by origin, born in the Danish island of St. Thomas in 1832. Though his antecedents were solidly West African—probably Ibo—he might never have come to the West Coast had it not been for the accident of an educational opportunity lost in the United States through racial prejudice, and a consequent trip to Liberia, where he settled in 1851, to gain the training denied. In Liberia, Blyden, whose scholastic aptitude had early been noted, quickly mastered Greek and Latin at school along with Hebrew as an extracurricular pursuit, his abilities earning him the editorship of the *Liberia Herald,* which he held for a year in the mid-fifties. Soon, however, he was teaching full time at his own school, becoming its principal in 1858, the same year he was ordained a minister of the Presbytery of West Africa. In 1862 Blyden took a chair as professor of Greek and Latin at the newly formed Liberia College, having journeyed to the Americas during the previous year in search of settlers for Liberia, the beginning of a long-lived career of public service and activity.

The recruitment trip was no accident, for Blyden was already formulating ideas regarding the role of Africa and Africans in the upward thrust of civilization; only in Africa, he argued, could the black race realize its own native genius, and this idea was to become one of the chief, albeit most controversial, aspects of his philosophy of African-ness. "I believe nationality to be an ordinance of nature," he declared at the time, "and no people can rise to an influential position among the nations without a distinct and efficient nationality. Cosmopolitanism has never effected anything."

Such a concept flowed from a more generalized philosophic stance. It was true that the races of the world differed physically and emotionally, shaped by long exposure to the forces of environment, agreed Blyden, accepting current European anthropological doctrine. They could not be ordered into a hierarchy of ability and achievement, however, as the white man invariably arranged them, placing himself at the head of the list; they were merely different. Indeed, continued Blyden, each race had its own peculiar assets, excelling in certain pursuits and less successful in others. Races were therefore not competitive or comparative so much as complementary, and in their totality they made up God's divinity. "Each race sees from its own standpoint a different side of the Almighty," said Blyden, "The whole of mankind is a vast representation of the Deity."

If the races were coequal but different, it followed that each had its own special contribution to make to the sum of human civilization. The white man had his virtues and faults—he was didactic and strong-willed, accomplished in the sciences and preoccupied with material betterment. This could lead to salutary ends; for example, in Africa it meant an end to the slave trade and intertribal wars, economic improvement, and the introduction of modern medicine. But, Blyden went on, these advantages came at a price. The European was also domineering and materialistic, selfish and essentially irreligious. Man, not God, became the sole object of human endeavor, the white race enslaved and bent others to its will, while religion was made to subserve material and temporal purposes.

Here was no person for the Negro to imitate, warned Blyden, particularly since the black man possessed uncommon characteristics of his own. First, there was the concept of community in African life. "What is mine goes; what is ours abides," Blyden quoted a Vai proverb to emphasize the harmony-in-unity of African society. Property was communal, and the fruits of the earth belonged equally to all. No competition separated people into antagonistic groups, no individuals gathered wealth at the expense of others, all were cared for—the aged, sick, and helpless along with the healthy—in the genial protective atmosphere of the family.

Secondly, there was the African's consonance with nature, his ability, said Blyden quoting the Book of Job, "to speak to the earth and let it teach him." Thus did the black race observe nature's rhythm of creation and recuperation as the model for a healthy polygamy, thus did the African follow the example of the industrious termite in constructing his own co-operative society, thus did he dwell outdoors, unburdened by clothing, using the whole book of nature for his school.

Finally, said Blyden, to communion with nature was added communion with God. Unlike Europe, African society made little distinction between the temporal and spiritual worlds—all existence was a continuum comprising the ancestors, the living, and the yet unborn. Religious thought and practice was no sabbath ritual but the essence of everyday life, reflecting a religious sense among the African people of highest refinement. That this had always been so, he insisted, was witnessed by the shelter which Africa had given the Jews and then the infant Jesus, as well as the cordial reception subsequently accorded the great religions of Christianity and Islam.

These special African qualities, Blyden continued, not only established the Negro as coequal and complementary to God's other people, it also gave a clue as to Africa's position in the upward thrust of civilization, a matter of the greatest importance to Blyden who insisted that racial achievement must be measured ultimately by its contribution to the sum total of human accomplishment. Clearly, said Blyden, past performance by the Negro suggested, not mastery but service. "Africa's lot resembles Him also who made Himself of no reputation, but took upon Himself the form of a servant . . . he who would be chief must become the servant of all, then we see the position which Africa and the Africans must ultimately occupy."

Service to humanity, harmony with nature, and communion with God, then, suggested to Blyden the unique and essential offering which Africa would make in a materialist, soulless world—"the mighty principle of Love." "Africa may yet prove to be the spiritual conservatory of the world," he rejoiced,

When the civilized nations, in consequence of their wonderful material development, shall have had their spiritual perceptions darkened and their spiritual susceptibilities blunted through the agency of a captivating and absorbing materialism, it may be, that they may have to resort to Africa to recover some of the simple elements of faith.

Thus, from his basic proposition describing the races as equivalent facets of a unitary godhead, each with its original and necessary contribution toward man's humanity, Blyden had secured African self-esteem in the face of Europe, but there were still some corollaries to be drawn from this scheme. First, there was the proposition that racial individuality called for social and biological segregation, and Blyden cited the American Negro and the Sierra Leone creole as flagrant examples of effete and confused people resulting from mis-cegenation. Nothing less than physical isolation and biological purity would therefore suffice, a point of view which evoked much contro-versy among Blyden's contemporaries even as it was to do in the days of Marcus Garvey and later.

Such radical notions, though they followed the logic of Blyden's argument, also had the practical advantage in his eyes of forcing the African to stand by his own cultural, intellectual, political, and eco-nomic institutions. Blyden insisted, for example, that education must necessarily be tailored to African needs—no foreign educational phi-losophy, no study of European heroes, no examination of alien bi-ology or geography could meet Africa's requirements—and it was he who greatly influenced William Grant through his own detailed plans for a West African university. In the same way, Blyden urged the importance of African history to signal past accomplishment and thereby reestablish the dignity of the Negro race. Finally, Blyden, the Christian minister, was one of the strongest critics of European mis-sionary practice in Africa. Citing the universality of Christ's message, he urged his people to organize their own churches—just as Christian but far less European—another declaration of racial independence.

Many of Blyden's pronouncements were highly theoretical, and he was frequently guilty of idealized history, anthropology, or biol-ogy. Nonetheless his ideas were developed in no vacuum, for he lived in daily acquaintance with the great issues of his day, as Europe subjected Africa to military conquest and political control; hence his philosophy had an immediacy for his contemporaries, helping to shape their actions and build their sense of racial identity in response to the European intrusion. His personal following was always small, for the educated Africans of his day were few in number, but his and their importance was disproportionate to their number and was ever growing. Consequently, he was able to exert a widening influence which ultimately transcended his own times, for Blyden's basic de-mand was the restoration of human dignity, a plea which has had continuing relevance in Africa, and indeed throughout the world.

LIBERIA AND THE TRIBULATIONS OF INDEPENDENCE

Throughout his writings Edward Blyden stressed the importance of Liberia as a haven for the rehabilitation of former slaves from America. Stimulated in part by his doctrines of racial segregation, but also by his image of an independent nation of black men, Blyden employed the most glowing terms in a recurring rhapsody over Liberia and her prospects. "It is the only spot in Africa where the civilised Negro—the American Negro without alien supervision or guidance is holding aloft the torch of civilisation," he stated. This theme sometimes was supplemented by more poetic flights: "I am kindled into ecstasy as I contemplate the future of that infant nation . . . The hills . . . covered with flocks, and the valleys with corn; the increase of the earth . . . fat and plenteous . . . Language fails . . . Imagination itself is baffled . . . and pauses with reverent awe before the coming possibilities."

This romantic expression of hope was scarcely supported by the fact of Liberia's faltering start as a self-governing nation. Independence had come initially in 1847 largely because a colony for repatriated American slaves was an embarrassment to the United States government, caught in the toils of its domestic slavery issue. When the colonists began to agitate for greater freedom from control by the American Colonization Society and Britain called into question the sovereignty both of Liberia and its parent organization, the slavery issue prevented any action by the American government, and Liberian independence followed.

Unhappily, the new state was ill-equipped to deal with problems which beset it from the start, many of them carry-overs from the colonial period. In the first place, immigration, chiefly from America, had always been low, producing a mere fifteen thousand colonists during the forty-year period from the founding of the colony to the time of the American Civil War, and gaining only a few thousand more thereafter as emancipated Negroes chose almost exclusively to remain in the United States.

Moreover, these arrivals from America had divided into factions based partly on mercantile-agrarian rivalries, but even more on social grounds with ancestry as the measure of acceptance. This unfortunate but understandable cleavage gave rise to a two-party system based largely on skin color, and at first it was the Republicans led by the octoroon, Joseph J. Roberts, who gained control of the government.

Roberts, a prominent merchant, served as governor during the last days of the Colonization Society and then became Liberia's first president during several successive terms. In 1870 the opposition True Whig Party was successful when Edward J. Roye, a full-blooded Negro became president. Victory nonetheless was brief. Roye first of all negotiated a disastrous foreign loan and then attempted to remain in office unconstitutionally, thus leading to a successful attempt by the Republicans to oust him and his supporters. Within a few years, however, the Whigs had returned to power and by 1884 were in such complete control that Liberia ceased to be a two-party state from that point forward. Gradually, the color issue died away, and by the end of the nineteenth century the mulatto faction among the settlers had quite lost its identity. Unfortunately, other related controversies had long since emerged to plague the struggling Liberian state.

From the earliest days there had been a basic cleavage between the settlers and the indigenous people of Liberia. The former with their Westernized background looked on the local inhabitants as uncivilized tribesmen much in need of spiritual and physical rehabilitation. This attitude, not unlike that of the European authorities assuming control in other parts of West Africa, looked to the development of a Liberian state under the leadership of a settler oligarchy with gradual participation by the indigenous population as its membership became absorbed into the Western culture of the immigrants. In fact, very little assimilation was encouraged or effected over the years, and relations between the Americo-Liberians and the local people remained at the level of unrelieved hostility punctuated by frequent outbreaks of violence. The settlers tended to adopt an attitude of superiority, based on culture rather than color, and they steadily extended their control inland, by treaty, land purchase, and protectorate, maintaining that control in many instances by force.

The administration of the hinterland was neither clearly defined nor efficiently managed, and the process by which political and civil rights were extended to the local people was complex and difficult to follow. A Department of the Interior was created in 1868, and five years later limited parliamentary representation was accorded the various tribal groupings. Not until the early years of the twentieth century did the people in the interior gain status as Liberian citizens, and it was to be almost another half century, during the administration of President William Tubman, before any concerted effort was made to bring the local African population into national life through genuine social and political reform.

Chronic financial difficulties were another burden which complicated Liberian national life, all the more so since they invited intervention by Liberia's British and French neighbors. Outright absorption through the establishment of a protectorate was probably prevented by the United States which expressed a "peculiar interest" in Liberia's independence, while making no attempt to impose its own colonial controls. When Liberian state finances reached an advanced level of chaos, as they did periodically, there was generally sufficient interest within the American government to arrange new financial terms without the necessity of European intervention. Nevertheless, although total absorption was avoided, Liberia lost several boundary disputes east and west to the French in the Ivory Coast and the British in Sierra Leone respectively. In 1882, for example, territory in the Gallinas district west of the Mano River was annexed to Sierra Leone after a protracted dispute. Ten years later, France absorbed into the Ivory Coast a large area claimed by Liberia, and further cessions along the Guinea and Ivory Coast borders were extracted in 1910.

THE DEMISE OF THE FOREST KINGDOMS

European expansionist activity at Liberia's expense was sometimes attempted through encouragement of tribal resistance, but the more usual European relationship with the traditional societies during the last decades of the nineteenth century was one of conquest, pacification, and absorption into expanding colonial territories. None was immune as European nations intensified their acquisitiveness in mutual competition. If smaller principalities like Nembe and the Itsekiri were overwhelmed, so too were such almighty but fading empires as Dahomey and Benin. The former, its illusion of military invincibility shattered on the walls of Abeokuta, gained some compensation during the 1880's in sacking the Yoruba kingdom of Ketu. Such victories were vain, however, in the face of a Dahomean economy no longer sustained by the slave traffic and unable to achieve economic security through legitimate commerce. French control of the coast introduced new complications concerning trading outlets and customs receipts which seemingly could only be resolved by military action.

Behanzin, succeeding to the throne at Abomey in 1889, provoked the French by calculated slave raiding and an attack on a French gunboat; then despite stubborn resistance was defeated and finally exiled in 1894, his kingdom converted into French colonial territory.

Benin, like Dahomey, with a reputation for human sacrifice, was brought under British protection in 1892 by a treaty which specifically abolished both slavery and sacrifice, while providing for trade relations. When the *oba,* Ovenramwen, appeared slow to comply, the acting consul-general proceeded inland in 1897 to investigate and was massacred with most of his party. The intruders had arrived with unfortunate timing at the moment of a great Bini festival marked by wholesale human sacrifice, and closed to all strangers on pain of the displeasure of the gods. A punitive expedition followed in 1897, Benin was captured and the *oba* exiled, and this once-great kingdom became just another part of Britain's Niger Coast Protectorate.

Such basic misunderstandings were not uncommon in the clash of unequal forces which punctuated the final colonial occupation of West Africa. In 1896 the British proclaimed a protectorate over the Sierra Leone hinterland beyond Freetown, an area defined by international treaty with France and Liberia but occupied without consulting the local chiefs. Administration of the protectorate was to be in the hands of the chiefs under the surveillance of a British district commissioner with governmental cost defrayed through a per capita levy, the so-called Hut Tax, of five shillings on each house. The tax was unfamiliar and unpopular, the protectorate government unwanted, and in 1898 mounting tension and mistrust erupted in war, the resistance led by Bai Bureh, a chief from Kasse on the Small Scarcies River. As Bai Bureh's forces were slowly reduced by a West Indian regiment, the revolt spread to other parts of the hinterland and a great many creoles and Europeans were killed in the spasm of resentment which welled up among the local people. The uprising, however, collapsed as quickly as it had arisen, and with Bai Bureh's capture and exile, all formal opposition ended. The Hut Tax remained and the protectorate continued to be administered indirectly through the numerous chiefs who had taken no part in the war.

The outburst which briefly shook Sierra Leone in 1898 was a minor reflex compared with the great and complex fratricidal struggle which had divided and devastated Yorubaland since the disintegration of the Oyo empire began toward the end of the eighteenth century. The first phase of the nineteenth-century Yoruba civil wars covered the period from 1820 to 1837 and was characterized by several factors—the destruction of Owu, the defection of Afonja, the *alafin*'s governor in Ilorin, and the consequent Fulani capture of that northern stronghold, the destruction of the ancient capital of Old Oyo and the remove of its people to the forest edge at the new Oyo, and the rise of independent Ibadan and Abeokuta. The second period, from 1837 to 1878, saw a complex struggle among the successors to Oyo which gradually polarized around Ibadan and Abeokuta. Despite her many opponents, Ibadan grew progressively stronger while Abeokuta was hard pressed to hold her own, faced as she was during this period by determined political and military attacks from Dahomey, as well as by the pressure of the British in Lagos who sought to reach the interior through Egba territory.

In their last stage, from 1878 to 1893, the Yoruba wars achieved new climaxes of complexity and animosity. By the 1870's, Ibadan had emerged as the most powerful of the Yoruba states, a fact which lent urgency to the formation of a coalition among her opponents. To the south, the Egba and Ijebu sought to limit Ibadan's power by blockade, forcing the Ibadans to gain their military supplies chiefly through Benin. To the east the Ijesha and Ekiti Yoruba were ready to join the alliance which also gained the support of Ilorin. Despite this formidable array, Ibadan more than held her own in a series of engagements, but neither side could gain the upper hand and the conflict dragged on.

With the Fulani no longer a decisive factor and Dahomey in decline, the combatants turned in upon themselves, preoccupied with their parochial quarrels; yet this was to be the period when a major external force would finally bring peace to the tortured land. Constant warfare, particularly in the interests of shutting off supplies to Ibadan, necessarily meant a serious dislocation of trade, a condition which greatly disturbed the merchants and government at Lagos. As early as 1882 the British intruded themselves as peacemakers, the urgency of their mission underscored by the rising threat which the wars posed to the survival of Lagos as a major entrepôt. By 1890 the cosmopolitan port with its polyglot population and its normally colorful, lively markets lay mournful and deserted, its shops empty and its trading canoes idle. There was a growing intensity, therefore, among the commercially minded Africans of the city that the authorities accelerate their quest for peace, by whatever means were required.

A negotiated peace concluded in 1886 almost succeeded in stopping the war, but the moment had not yet arrived and fighting broke out anew. Both the Egba and Ijebu tightened their blockade, the Ijebu adding a calculated insult to the government at Lagos, an incident which finally resolved the British to resort to force. An expedition under Governor Carter quickly subdued the Ijebu in 1892 and the following year the governor was able to establish a de facto protectorate over the various states of Yorubaland. At last peace had come to the prostrate country. Samuel Johnson, the Yoruba historian who had played an important role in the diplomatic offensive for peace, caught the sense of relief of an exhausted people. "To the vast majority of the common people," he reported, "it was like the opening of a prison door: and no one who witnessed the patient, long-suffering, and toiling mass of humanity . . . could refrain from heaving a sigh of gratification on the magnitude of the beneficial results."

ABORTIVE ALLIANCE—THE WESTERNIZED AFRICANS AND THE TRADITIONAL AUTHORITIES

In the face of the alien European intrusion, both traditional authorities and educated Africans sought effective means of response, whether in accommodation or opposition, and it was quickly evident that in the process some form of united effort by both old and new Africa would be attempted. In this respect it was the educated Africans who took the lead, representing themselves to the chiefs as Africa's most eloquent spokesmen before European governments, and to the colonial administrations as an ideal liaison between the alien worlds of Africa and Europe. This attitude was generally resisted by the traditional powers who were disinclined to share their dwindling authority with parvenu commoners, and by the colonial administrations, suspicious of educated elite as potential sources of disaffection, while seeking some sort of partnership in government with the long-established African leadership.

The French areas of West Africa scarcely knew the problem before the period of the First World War. In a few coastal points like the Four Communes of Senegal, the principle of assimilation, though under rising attack, still prevailed. In the hinterland a difficult conquest in the face of stubborn opposition led to a quasi-military regime imposed with rigid authority by French administrators.

The British approach was more flexible and pragmatic, but tended to begin with an effort to find legitimate African rulers through which the colonial administration could operate. The classic prototype was the Protectorate of Northern Nigeria, proclaimed in 1900 and placed under the governorship of Sir Frederick Lugard. Northern Nigeria coincided roughly with the Fulani empire, no longer in its virile expansive stage by the end of the nineteenth century, but still a well-knit and effectively administered state, its provinces clearly responsive to the authority of its ruler, the sultan of Sokoto. Lugard's first task, therefore, was effective occupation which was achieved through a series of military actions ending in 1903 in the dethronement and subsequent defeat and death of Sultan Attahiru I of Sokoto.

Faced with the problem of governing a huge territory with a massive fifteen million population, Lugard instituted the idea of indirect rule, already foreshadowed by Goldie and others, but now elevated to the level of a system of colonial government. With the pacification of the Fulani emirates, the established African administration was retained intact, British resident commissioners added at the apex, and a number of basic legal changes instituted such as the abolition of slavery and the introduction of British law to supplement the Muslim codes. Thus Lugard was able to impose his policies over a vast region without the necessity of an expensive network of administrators, while the emirs, in return for cooperation, were permitted to retain much of their traditional authority.

The concept of working with and through traditional authorities was tried in other British-held areas, its success varying to the extent that there were local administrations through which colonial policy could be applied. In eastern Nigeria where no chiefly system existed, indirect rule was necessarily an almost total failure. In western Nigeria where the chief was no autocrat, his sanction carefully defined by a complex system of customary law, district officers often weakened the fiat of a traditional ruler by inadvertance or carelessness. Ignorant of local usage, they might overlook the importance of royal ceremony or chastise a chief publicly before his people, thereby complicating the imposition of their own colonial authority.

On the Gold Coast a well-defined hierarchy of traditional leaders had long been a fact. Here south of Ashanti the British early attempted to impose their rule through the chiefly agency, and here the educated community made its most concerted effort to join with the chiefs in opposition to the colonial regime. There was already some precedent for this. The Fante Confederation had been an initial effort to marry the special attributes of the educated African to the chiefly power, while in his time Africanus Horton had devoted much attention as a member of the elite to the question of national independence in West Africa through the combined efforts of the educated and traditional leadership.

With the establishment of a colony and protectorate in 1874, the British sought to clarify the role of the chief in their government. Recognizing the organizational and fiscal economy of an administration which made use of the indigenous rulers, they introduced regulations which attempted to link the chief to the colonial power and redefine his jurisdiction. Greater definition necessarily meant limitation and supervision by a higher authority, however, while, at the same time, the more the chiefs were supported by the colonial government, the less their people came to look upon them as consequential units in that government. A series of ordinances made local rulers responsible for new but undignified and untraditional duties, removed the dispensing of justice from their hands, and gave the British governor the power to dismiss the native authorities who in the past had been responsible only to their own people. Other enactments by the officially controlled legislative council provided for municipal reforms which violated age-old township organization, and completely upset customary law regarding land ownership, that fundamental foundation of traditional African society.

Under these circumstances, a small but influential group of educated Africans from the coastal areas stepped forward to protect the authority of the traditional rulers, to push their own claims to increased participation in local affairs, and indeed to challenge the very right of the British to govern in the Gold Coast. Some were successful merchants like James H. Brew, John Sarbah, and J. W. Sey, but particularly active were a number of young English-trained lawyers, particularly T. Hutton Mills, John Mensah Sarbah, and J. E. Casely Hayford, whose understanding of the British constitution was matched by long study of Fante customary law, a combination ideally suited to a judicial challenge of the British presence in the Gold Coast.

Of particular prominence was John Mensah Sarbah, a Fante from Cape Coast of scholarly disposition and conservative habits, who utilized his training in English law to call into question both the legitimacy and the practicality of alien rule. The first Gold Coast African to be called to the English bar, Mensah Sarbah in a series of learned constitutional treatises pointed out that the British had resorted to force, not to law, in establishing themselves on the Gold Coast. They had pressed without justification the advantage which the bonds of 1844 had given to English jurisprudence in the administration of local justice. They had assumed quite unreasonably that in signing protection treaties African rulers willingly parted with their sovereignty. This, insisted Mensah Sarbah, was an arbitrary and unlawful imposition of colonial rule.

Moreover, the argument continued, having secured their position, the intruders instituted laws and procedures totally alien to local custom, thus enormously complicating, not only their own administration, but the lives of the people they had come to govern. "Gold Coast territory was not an uninhabited district . . . or [one] obtained by conquest or cession," Mensah Sarbah explained. "Whether the inhabitants were taken to be half or wholly savages, they had their aboriginal tribal government . . . invested with the rights of sovereignty and exercising its powers."

Nevertheless, Mensah Sarbah was forced to recognize the reality, if not the legality, of alien rule; better, then, to seek means for more effective African participation in government than to waste time in idle lamentation. To this end he urged expanding responsibilities for the educated African both as a leader bringing his people into a new changing world and as an individual "racy of the soil," in Mensah Sarbah's words, who would know how to preserve the best qualities of Africa's ancient communal virtues. Suiting the action to the word, he devoted his brief years—he died in 1910 when only in his mid-forties—to both the defense of traditional institutions and the demand for a larger degree of self-government.

As a private citizen and public petitioner, and later as a member of the legislative council, Mensah Sarbah consistently urged greater attention to the African and his institutions in the formulation of official policy. He argued for a wider utilization of community leaders as members of the legislative council, the better to represent the needs and desires of the people. He criticized British-imposed municipal government, based as it was on English, rather than African, experience. He pointed out the difficulty of enforcing taxation foreign to local usage. He spent long and frustrating years urging broader chiefly responsibility and independence in the administration of justice, one of the major strengths of traditional society. Undergirding all these practical everyday suggestions lay his painstaking studies in customary law produced in several massive volumes, of which *Fanti National Constitution,* appearing in 1906, represented his most mature philosophy of government.

Like so many West Africans of his day, Mensah Sarbah was particularly exercised over government policy concerning land ownership. In 1897 he helped to organize the Aborigines' Rights Protection Society as a focal point of popular protest, and led a determined fight before the legislative council in opposition to proposed legislation offensive to local customs of land usage. The administration had been concerned with the protection of African land from alienation by European concessionaires seeking timber, sub-surface, and other rights, and therefore introduced bills in 1894 and 1897 applying, in effect, British standards for determining ownership and inheritance of land in its Gold Coast colony.

There was at once sharp opposition within the African community, showing itself in public demonstrations, in a deputation sent to London in 1898 by the Aborigines' Rights Protection Society, and in learned briefs prepared by both J. E. Casely Hayford and John Mensah Sarbah. Mensah Sarbah used his material to support representations before the legislative council, the burden of his argument resting in the familiar claim that all land in Africa was always under ownership, that no lands were unoccupied no matter how long they appeared abandoned or remained out of cultivation. Hence, concluded Mensah Sarbah, there could be no legal expropriation of any territories to be classified as crown land. In this instance African customary law carried the day, and the legislation finally enacted was carefully defined to protect African land titles while still maintaining close preventive surveillance against alienation.

The defense of customary African rulers and traditional institutions mounted by John Mensah Sarbah and his educated contemporaries was based only partly on conviction, for there was also the growing desire to reach out for power in a changing society. Hence, in time the chiefly authority came to be as much a point of competition as of cooperation, the new and old elite locking in conflict over the leadership of their people in a fast-changing world. This struggle, which continued in parallel with the opposition to colonial government, did not reach its fullest dimension in the Gold Coast until the years after the First World War. By that time colonial rule had hardened everywhere in its most restrictive form, and West Africans of every definition needed all the mutual aid they could muster to keep in view the fading dream of national self-determination, a dream which had been one of the noble ideals of the war that hoped to make the world safe for democracy.

Suggestions for Further Reading

This chapter relies substantially on R. W. July, *The Origins of Modern African Thought* (New York: Praeger, 1967, London: Faber, 1968); other studies are helpful. See, for example, Michael Crowder, *West Africa under Colonial Rule* (London: Hutchinson, 1968; Evanston, Illinois: Northwestern University Press, 1968) and relevant sections in L. H. Gann and Peter Duignan, *Burden of Empire* (New York: Praeger, 1967; London: Pall Mall, 1967). For Senegal, see Michael Crowder, *Senegal, A Study in French Assimilation Policy*, rev. ed. (London: Methuen, 1967; New York: Barnes & Noble, 1967). Sierra Leone is covered in detail in C. Fyfe, *A History of Sierra Leone* (London: Oxford University Press, 1962); and in J. D. Hargreaves, *A Life of Sir Samuel Lewis* (London: Oxford University Press, 1958). H. R. Lynch, *Edward Wilmot Blyden* (London: Oxford University Press, 1967) deals with the great West African nationalist, and J. H. Kopytoff, *A Preface to Modern Nigeria* (Madison: University of Wisconsin Press, 1965) studies the role of the emigres returning home to Yorubaland from Sierra Leone. The best material on Liberia is found in R. L. Buell, *The Native Problem in Africa*, 2 vols. (London: Frank Cass, 1965; Hamden, Conn.: Shoe String Press, 1965), and in *Liberia: A Century of Survival, 1847–1947* (Philadelphia: University of Pennsylvania Press, 1947) by the same author. For the Gold Coast, see David Kimble, *A Political History of the Gold Coast, 1850–1928* (Oxford: Clarendon Press, 1963). The interaction between missionary policies and the response of African leadership is set forth in detail in J. F. A. Ajayi, *Christian Missions in Nigeria, 1841–1891* (London: Longmans, 1965; Evanston, Illinois: Northwestern University Press, 1965), and E. A. Ayandele, *The Missionary Impact on Modern Nigeria, 1842–1914* (London: Longmans, 1966 and New York: Humanities Press, 1967).

The best volume on the Yoruba wars is Samuel Johnson, *The History of the Yorubas* (Lagos: C. M. S. Bookshops, 1921), but this should be supplemented by J. F. A. Ajayi and R. Smith, *Yoruba Warfare in the Nineteenth Century* (Cambridge: Cambridge University Press, 1964), and S. O. Biobaku, *The Egba and their Neighbours, 1842–1872* (Oxford: Clarendon Press, 1957).

16: The Foundations of Progress and
Poverty in Southern Africa

THE BIRTH OF A NEW SOCIETY

The hard outline of South African society in the middle years of the twentieth century took its first firm shape during the half century preceding the unification of 1910. It began with the concluding stages of the great migrations of Boer and Bantu which thoroughly interspersed African and European communities across the vast southern veld. It continued as the European farmer appropriated new lands to his own use, denying them to the Bantu cattleman who was thus obliged to become a tenant farmer and rural laborer as the price of survival. It was given a dramatic thrust toward eventual prosperity as a modern industrial nation with the discovery of mineral resources in diamonds and gold. Despite parochial jealousies and a shifting British colonial policy, it moved uncertainly in the direction of the political unification which economic advance dictated.

Finally, unified and with national prosperity in sight, South Africa committed itself to a policy of social and economic discrimination based upon color. Asian, Coloured, and most especially, Bantu, were relegated to an inferior position, the latter fixed in the status of rural and urban pauper, denied the exercise of political and civil rights, and proclaimed unworthy of the fruits of his own labor. Thus did the long-lived Boer philosophy of the inequality of man achieve its logical conclusion in a way of life which was eventually to bring forth the apartheid state of the Republic of South Africa.

BRITAIN AND COMPLEXITIES OF COLONIAL STEWARDSHIP

The tragedy of Britain's colonial policy in South Africa emerged from the fact that she alone possessed the authority to deal with the complexities of government on the ground, yet her actions were dictated basically by domestic pressures irrelevant to the situation in South Africa. By projecting the Boer farmers far into the interior, the Great Trek gave an entirely new amplitude to the old problem of relations between white settlers and their Hottentot or slave laborers. Henceforward, there was to be a Boer-Bantu confrontation which dwarfed previous racial problems; moreover, by removing themselves from the jurisdiction of the Cape Colony, the trekkers had given geographic and political dimension to a social and cultural cleavage within the white population, long in development. The forces of racial antipathy and division had now been given new impetus. Only a strong, wise, and consistent policy might have succeeded in checking faction and replacing it with harmony and unity. Unfortunately, the British government was bound to pay greater attention to its constituents at home than to the necessities of the South African situation; worse still, British imperial and humanitarian impulses were a complex of contradictions which inexorably intruded their own ambivalence into the policies applied to South Africa.

Above all, one overriding consideration guided Britain's statesmanship in South Africa—the strategic position of that land athwart the route to the orient where British interests of long standing resided in India, the Antipodes, and the Far East. Beyond this was the concern of humanitarians for the indigenous African in need of conversion and regeneration, as well as the merchant's preoccupation with expanding commerce. Such matters were forced to contend, however, with the abiding absorption in London with economy in government and non-involvement in colonial entanglements. Hence supremacy had to be maintained and tribal rights protected without the financial commitment necessary to do the job. The Colonial Office was obliged to keep the peace without troops and to rule without power, while administrators on the ground found their assessments set aside by the exigencies of broader global strategies, and their policies reversed by local election results at home.

After the Great Trek, the balance of tensions set up by these conflicting forces emerged initially in an effort to exercise indirect control over the trekkers, by trying to extend the jurisdiction of Cape courts to the interior beyond the Colony's frontier, and by isolating the Boer farmers from coastal outlets and possible understandings with other European powers. Thus the annexation of Natal in 1845 served the double purpose of checking potential intervention from abroad while putting a stop to Boer commando raids into Zulu and Pondo country.

In 1848, a similar logic prompted the Cape Colony governor, Harry Smith, to annex and proclaim the territory between the Orange and Vaal rivers as the Orange River Sovereignty in a move to avoid Boer outbreaks in the Griqua states. This action meant deepening British involvement in the border dispute between the Boers and Moshesh along the Caledon River. Nevertheless, rising free trade, anticolonial sentiment at home led to a reversal of policy in 1852 and 1854 as the independence of the trekkers beyond the Orange River and in the Transvaal was recognized through the Sand River and Bloemfontein conventions. This withdrawal effectively freed the Boers to deal with Moshesh and led eventually to the wars between the Orange Free State and the Basuto which cost Moshesh most of his best land and reduced his people to desperation. To avoid the total breakup of the Basuto state and large-scale migrations of land-less wanderers into Natal, Cape Colony, and elsewhere, policy was once more reversed and Basutoland was annexed by Governor Wode-house in 1868.

Colonial administrators like Sir Harry Smith saw readily enough the need for coordinated policy which would unify weak European communities, poor in resources and manpower, and in their separate-ness incapable of solving the complexities of African relations. In 1858, the High Commissioner and Cape Colony Governor, Sir George Grey, stated the case with classic persuasiveness in his call for federation. The very weakness and isolation of the European com-munities, he said, encouraged an unrest among the African people which could not be contained by isolated, feeble governments. What-ever their differences, the European settler states could hope to survive only through fusion which would yield more than uniformity and wisdom to native policy; it would also bring political stability and economic strength to all. Fifteen years later, Lord Carnarvon, the Secretary of State for the Colonies, was arguing much the same thing. "The most immediately urgent reason for general union," he said, "is the formidable character of the native question, and the importance of a uniform, wise, and strong policy in dealing with it." Preoccupation in Westminster with economy in government had blocked Grey's proposal in its time, and now, in the mid-1870's, Carnarvon's urgings would go unheeded in the face of other factors which had arisen to complicate questions of union in South Africa.

THE REVOLUTION OF DIAMONDS AND GOLD

In 1867 diamonds were found in the alluvial soil of the Orange River near the Vaal confluence, and two years later the discovery of the 83 carat "Star of South Africa" lent drama to the inauguration of the world's greatest diamond industry and the beginning of South Africa's economic revolution. It also added a new dimension to the problem of political unity.

The diamond finds necessarily precipitated a stampede of claims over previously despised and ignored wasteland. The Griqua chief, Waterboer, and the Orange Free State both pressed their sovereignty, but the diamond rush which brought tens of thousands of fortune hunters from over the world led to the creation of a short-lived Diggers' Republic in 1870. Such an arrangement could not survive the pressures that closed in upon it. The Boer South African Republic in the Transvaal put forward its own claim while the Cape Colony somewhat reluctantly urged British annexation. The British government as usual viewed involvement with alarm, but finally in 1871 sanctioned annexation to the Cape of the territory which was called Griqualand West, realizing that if the diamond fields went to the Orange Free State, there could be little likelihood of subsequent confederation under the leadership of the Cape Colony.

The Cape Colony occupied a prominent position in imperial policy at the moment. Nineteenth-century political liberalism argued for colonial self-government, a condition which had already been achieved in Canada, New Zealand, and parts of Australia, and the Cape was expected to follow shortly. In 1853 Cape Colony had received a constitution granting representative, though not responsible, government; then in 1872 responsible government was instituted with

British control exercised only in external affairs. Britain now began to look once again toward union, stimulated by examples throughout the world—the American Civil War, Imperial Germany, Italian unification, and her own creation, the Dominion of Canada—as well as an awakening uneasiness over the rise of Germany as a world power.

There were also internal factors clamoring for unity, factors closely linked to the rise of the diamond industry. The dusty, untidy boom town of Kimberley became a magnet equally to men and to capital, both of which had long shunned South Africa. Imports in Cape Colony and Natal more than doubled between 1871 and 1875, interest rates on foreign investments declined sharply in response to a heavy capital influx, port facilities were improved by governments suddenly affluent through rising customs receipts, while railroad and telegraph lines reached out from the coast to tap the swelling resources of the interior. Within a few years the value of diamond exports had far exceeded the meager products of local agriculture. Financial unification seemed well on the way with the development of a regional banking system throughout Cape Colony; surely, circumstance had joined logic to demand political unification as well.

Lord Carnarvon, urged by Disraeli, moved to achieve confederation, and there was some prospect that the liberal-minded President Brand of the Orange Free State, President Burgers of the South African Republic in the Transvaal, and J. C. Molteno, first Prime Minister of Cape Colony, might prove cooperative. A differing native policy among the constituents appeared to be the most difficult, though not insuperable, obstacle, but in fact trouble, when it appeared, came in another guise. Both the Transvaal and Orange Free State were sulking for having been deprived of what they considered to be their valid claims to the diamond fields of Griqualand West. More crucial still, Cape Colony, newly raised to virtual independence and jealous of her status, her economy booming as never before, was in no mood to share her gains with others less fortunate. Molteno emerged as a tenacious though not very far-sighted politician whose vision of the future did not extend far beyond the immediacies of parochial Cape politics. Fearful of his position as first minister, and sensitive to possible interference from a former master, he declined to attend Carnarvon's federation conference in 1876, and the scheme collapsed.

In a fateful sequel, unification failed even more ominously in the north. There on the barren plains across the Vaal, the trekkers had squeezed an uncertain existence from the reluctant soil, hampered not only by the infertility of their country but also by rural isolation and a conservative resistance to modernity. A ruinously open-handed land policy yielded an inadequate revenue to the government and discouraged efficient cultivation, at the same time building expansionist pressures designed to bring conflict with neighboring Bantu peoples. In 1876 the xenophobic Transvaal settlers attempted to sever their connections to the south, with its rising industrialism and its custom duties, by seeking a rail outlet through Portuguese territory to Delagoa Bay, but this venture came to nothing. The same year war broke out with the Pedi over land claims, and resulted, not in victory or defeat, but in the financial and administrative collapse of the Transvaal. In April, 1877, Britain annexed the demoralized country, to the relief even of some in the South African Republic itself.

Carnarvon took over the Transvaal to avoid general war and to save the confederation he still hoped to create. In fact, events marched steadily toward disunity. Molteno had lost none of his earlier suspicions, and the Orange Free State was unenthusiastic despite a £90,000 award in compensation for her claims to Griqualand West. When in 1878 Carnarvon was replaced in a cabinet reshuffle, Sir Bartle Frere, the South African High Commissioner, became the chief protagonist for Britain's federation policy, but his exertions only succeeded in nudging that elusive objective even farther out of reach. Intent on gaining Transvaal friendship through the acquisition of territory in Zululand, Frere helped precipitate a war with the Zulu which led to the annihilation of a British column at Isandhlwana in 1879. The defeat, though later reversed at Ulundi, soured British public opinion over Disraeli's South African policy and added disrespect to Boer dislike of things British. Already Transvaal leaders, headed by Paul Kruger, had charged Britain with arbitrary rule and the frustration of Boer rights of self-determination; now, their demands for independence grew more insistent.

Basically, the difficulty lay in the same incompatibility which had plagued Boer-British relations throughout the century. The theory and practice of British imperial policy demanded support of each colony's administration through local taxation collected with the regularized efficiency of a modern government. Effective public finance and administrative orderliness, pursuing the trekkers beyond the Orange River, had now caught them and chastised them once again for their economic backwardness and organizational inefficiency.

Resentment over these matters was readily converted into patriotic outrage at sovereignty violated. When the Gladstone government, replacing Disraeli in 1880, withheld independence, frustration burst forth in a successful revolt which was followed by a grant of independence in all but foreign relations through the Pretoria and London conventions of 1881 and 1884. Another battle had been lost by the forces of unity, but with the discovery of gold in the Transvaal in 1884, the war was bound to be renewed.

At Kimberley, after the first wild rush had subsided, the task of sorting out thousands of claims began, to the end that the mines might be efficiently worked with modern equipment. Early in the process there arose two men whose energy and acuity enabled them to excel in the process of consolidation. Barney Barnato, an impecunious fortune seeker from East London, and Cecil Rhodes, the son of an English vicar, arrived in Kimberley when the initial waves of prospectors were already ebbing, drifting off in the face of barren claims and rising costs. Each pursued his goal of amalgamation, buying up digger rights and gradually forming larger companies until four major concerns emerged, one for each of the four Kimberley mines. Here Barnato stopped, content to control his share and enjoy his fortune. Rhodes was driven by the larger vision of empire in Africa, and in 1888 he succeeded in absorbing Barnato into his De-Beers Consolidated Mines at a price of £5,338,650. Two years later he had extended his control to all of South Africa's diamond mining.

"You want the means to go north," Barnato had observed in the face of Rhodes' persuasiveness, "so I suppose we must give it to you." Rhodes had been voicing his argument for empire beyond the Limpopo and across the Zambezi to the vast Congo watershed and perhaps onward toward Egypt. First, however, his attention was to be diverted by the Transvaal and the great gold-bearing veins of the Witwatersrand, where modern industrialism was clashing with Boer pastoralism.

The existence of gold deposits in the Transvaal had been known for some years, but only by the mid-eighties were they demonstrated to be economically viable, and then only under circumstances which were bound to create profound economic and cultural changes among the Boer farmers still searching for sanctuary from the implacable pursuit of British-imposed modernization. Suddenly they were descended upon by hordes of *uitlanders,* or foreigners, an Afrikaans term with pejorative overtones. Ten times the numbers that had invaded Kimberley fifteen years earlier, they arrived from far-off places —from Australia and New Zealand, America and the ports of Europe, as well as from the Cape and other points nearer at home. They sprawled across the veld, and at the site of the main reef a city sprang up with speed and without plan—noisy, dirty, busy, preoccupied with the business of gold, and indifferent if not impatient with the simple bucolic beliefs and customs of the Boer farmers.

From their capital at Pretoria, forty miles removed from Johannesburg, the Boers watched with mixed feelings, for wealth began to pour into the land along with the confusion and foreign ways. From the first, Johannesburg was destined to be no boom town, to rise up suddenly and die away as quickly, for the gold, though present in enormous quantities, could be obtained only by use of the most expensive, up-to-date equipment. Individual prospectors could not flourish here, only large-scale industrial complexes backed by vast capital resources, employing great gangs of labor, and penetrating deep into the earth by means of modern machinery and sophisticated scientific techniques. Tiny gold particles fixed in an ancient metamorphic rock were expensive to extract, and profits, though ultimately great, were small in margin and available only through a vast economic enterprise keyed to the subtleties of an international money market.

However distasteful this foreign intrusion may have been to the austere Boer farmer, it offered him at last an unparalleled opportunity for escape once and for all from the British to the south. At the same time it sharply increased the danger of imperial British interference. On the one hand, a bankrupt government was suddenly converted to affluence, and in the dozen years between 1883 and 1895 its revenues increased twenty-five fold. Nonetheless, the financial windfall came from tax levies on a wealthy, growing population, intense and dynamic, intolerant of Bible-reading farmers whose land it threatened to dominate. Again, the mines brought dramatic increases to the value of land and the price of foodstuffs, while the new industry introduced improvements in transportation and communication which had so long shunned the remote veld across the Vaal. These gains, however, threatened closer links with the south and with the British from whom the Boers had fled a half century earlier, and whose controls they had only recently shuffled off.

Shrewd, if isolated, the Transvaalers saw well enough that their new-found wealth was a means to political viability and independence, and, under the leadership of their president, Paul Kruger, they moved to exploit their greatly improved position. Kruger revived plans for a railroad to Delagoa Bay which would free him from dependence on southern outlets. He solicited advice and assistance from European powers, particularly Germany, who were always ready to embarrass the British when circumstances permitted. He sought room for expansion across the Limpopo, and in 1887 concluded the Grobler Treaty with the Ndebele king, Lobengula, which secured special privileges for Boers traveling and trading in Matabeleland. Thus, in strength, the Transvaal turned its back on union, but the very conditions which produced her strength were also to defeat her policy. In the end, it was the discovery of gold on the Witwatersrand which made certain the unification of South Africa.

THE ROAD TO UNION

British statesmen aside, there had been few serious moves toward consolidation in South Africa during the nineteenth century. Following the Great Trek, an effort by Andries Pretorius to bring Natal, Winburg, and the Transvaal Boers together had come to naught, and in 1860 his son, Marthinus, had attempted to join the South African Republic and the Orange Free State, resorting to the remarkable but nonetheless unsuccessful maneuver of securing election as president in both states. Such efforts were, to say the least, premature, since the South African Republic could scarcely maintain its own unity, while the Free State, contiguous with Cape Colony and containing many English settlers, had never shared the extreme sensitivity to British institutions of the trekkers to the north.

In the years that followed, the miscarriage of both the Grey and Carnarvon schemes complicated any subsequent attempts at unification. The aftermath of Lord Carnarvon's failure was the annexation and release of the Transvaal, the net result of which was a nascent Boer nationalism based on race, manifesting itself in a pronounced leaning toward Germany, with all the paraphernalia of foreign loans and advisers, of visiting war vessels and tariffs, all aimed at impeding internal South African unity. Unhappily, there were few offsetting factors at work among the Transvaal's neighbors. It is true, in Cape Colony, Jan Hofmeyr, through his Afrikander Bond, led the Cape Boers steadily away from racism to a doctrine of Boer-British cooperation, urging his people to greater participation in the public life of the Cape. Moreover, in the Orange Free State, President Brand, whose loyalties extended equally north and south, would not join Kruger in a proposed military and mercantile union which would have effectively isolated the two Afrikaner republics from their British-oriented neighbors.

Otherwise, Cape Colony and Natal seemed no more enlightened than the northerners. In 1885, Kruger, having failed momentarily to arrange for a rail line from Johannesburg to Delagoa Bay, asked for a customs union with the Cape which would have involved extending the Cape Town-Kimberley line to the Transvaal gold fields. Brand, sensing possibilities, urged a more general customs arrangement, but Cape Town was evasive, and Natal no less so. When the Cape belatedly suggested a conference in 1888, the moment had passed. Kruger had glimpsed the prospects which his gold deposits laid before him, and was already turning to the device of economic nationalism and a second, and this time successful, attempt to gain a rail outlet to Delagoa Bay. The others finally had their conference, without the Transvaal, which completed its line in 1894, but even then the Cape and Natal failed to reach agreement over uniform import duties. All that was salvaged was a customs union between the Cape and the Free State which gave the Cape railroads access to Free State territory.

Nevertheless the forces of unification were also in motion. The German protectorate over South-West Africa, proclaimed in 1884, stimulated the British to block a link-up with the Transvaal by annexing a portion of Bechuanaland to the Cape in 1885 and proclaiming a protectorate over the rest. This action not only eliminated German influence in the central plateau but checked Transvaal expansionism along its western frontier while maintaining control over the so-called Missionaries' Road which proceeded from the Cape Colony northward through Mafeking, skirting the western edge of the Transvaal on its way to Matabeleland and Mashonaland beyond the Limpopo. Such a move had been strongly urged by Cecil Rhodes, now a millionaire many times over with a fortune in diamonds and gold, and fully engaged in his ruthless and unswerving drive to promote British influence across Africa on behalf of wealth and empire.

To pursue his ends, in 1888 Rhodes intensified his participation in Cape politics, becoming the Colony's prime minister two years later, and in 1889 he succeeded in obtaining a royal charter for his

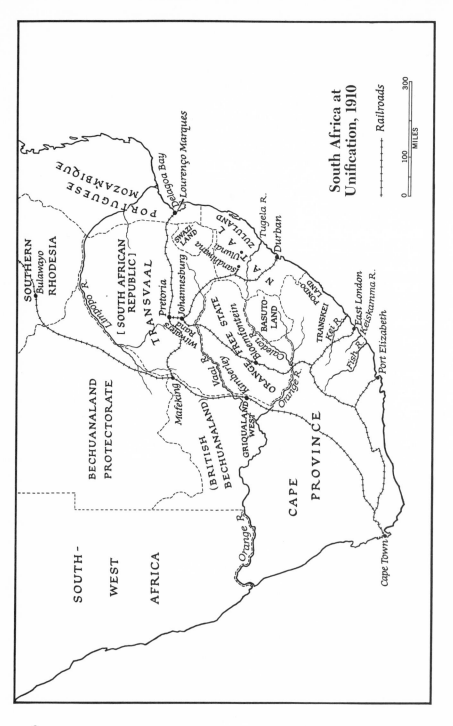

South Africa at
Unification, 1910

------- Railroads

MILES
0   100   300

SOUTHERN
RHODESIA
• Bulawayo

PORTUGUESE
MOZAMBIQUE

Lundopo R.

Delagoa Bay
• Lourenço Marques

[SOUTH AFRICAN
REPUBLIC]
TRANSVAAL

SWAZI-
LAND

Pretoria •
Johannesburg •
Witwatersrand
Isandhlwana
Tugela R.
ZULULAND
Ulundi •
Durban •

ORANGE FREE STATE
Bloemfontein •
Caledon R.

BASUTO-
LAND

PONDO-
LAND
TRANSKEI
Kei R.
Fish R.
Keiskamma R.
East London
Port Elizabeth

BECHUANALAND
PROTECTORATE

Mafeking •
Vaal R.
Kimberley
(BRITISH
BECHUANALAND)
GRIQUALAND
WEST
Orange R.

SOUTH-
WEST
AFRICA

Orange R.

CAPE   PROVINCE

Cape Town

British South Africa Company, the agency of his thrust to the north. In 1890 a column under Company direction arrived at the site of Salisbury to lay claim to Mashonaland and to open yet another chapter of British imperial history. The immediate objective, however, was further to contain the land-locked Transvaal in a tightening vise of British-controlled territories, thereby fastening her irrevocably to the British imperial interest. Rhodes had done his work well, and Kruger's persistent efforts to free his country from Britain's domination resulted only in deepening his involvement. In 1895 he succeeded in negotiating a protectorate over Swaziland which brought with it the long-sought territorial access to the sea, but simultaneously Kruger made such cordial overtures to the Germans as to frighten Britain with the specter of German primacy in the Transvaal. The Swaziland protectorate was forthwith revoked, Kruger lost his coastal outlet, and the Transvaal in effect was reduced to the position of a suzerain state, ringed on all sides by foreign territory, and dominated by Britain.

Rhodes now stepped up his pace, spurred by the growing competition among European nations in the partition of Africa and the knowledge that his own failing health left him little time. His objectives involved annexation of unclaimed territory in the interior through his chartered company, and the establishment of a customs union in South Africa which, he felt, the Transvaal would eventually be obliged to join. From this would follow South African political federation, the extension of British hegemony to the north, and finally a British steel spine down the eastern side of Africa, the Cape to Cairo railroad.

By 1895, therefore, unification seemed to be on the way despite the Transvaal, but Rhodes, ever in a hurry, was now prepared to force a showdown. The uitlanders, outnumbering the Boers by more than two to one, had been denied political rights and treated as aliens by their hosts who feared that a grant of political equality to the newcomers would cost them control over their own land. Responding to uitlander discontent over this state of affairs, Rhodes now helped organize a conspiracy to overthrow the Transvaal government by means of an internal uprising to be supplemented by a raiding party of five hundred Rhodesian police and volunteers under Dr. Jameson who would come in on appeal by the uitlanders. The Secretary of State for Colonies, Joseph Chamberlain, was privy to the plot, which, however, totally misfired when the ill-prepared and divided uitlanders lost heart and Jameson foolishly attacked despite instructions that he abandon the invasion.

The raid began on the last day of 1895, but without effective support within the Transvaal, Jameson and his men were speedily subdued. What did not end so quickly were the repercussions of this ill-starred adventure which, on the contrary, proceeded in ever increasing intensity until they burst forth in the Boer War four years later. The raid necessarily cast the Boers in the role of patriots defending their land, while Rhodes lost much prestige along with the support of Hofmeyr and the moderate Cape Boers, and was forced to retire from politics. The British government, suspected by many of complicity, appeared as an instrument of economic imperialism engaged in the establishment of a foreign financial and mining trust over the rightful Boer government. In sympathy, the Orange Free State finally concluded a military alliance with the Transvaal, whose leaders, for their part, were driven further toward a German entente while maintaining and adding to the vexatious restrictions on the uitlanders.

Steadily the chasm of misunderstanding widened as the area of accommodation narrowed. In 1897 Sir Alfred Milner was appointed Governor and High Commissioner of Cape Colony, and the following year Kruger was re-elected President of the Transvaal. From this point forward there ceased to be a basis for reconciliation. The Transvaal would not voluntarily give up its relations with European powers while Britain could not permit these alliances to threaten her predominance in South Africa. In the end, union was achieved, but only at the expense of war, which broke out in October, 1899.

The Transvaal and Orange Free State lost the Boer War quickly, although there was a long period of guerrilla action before a peace treaty was finally signed in May, 1902. The treaty terms were moderate, calling for large-scale rehabilitation of the country, and eventual responsible government in the two former republics, to be administered as crown colonies by Lord Milner, now colonial governor as well as high commissioner. Milner's policy was straightforward—economic rehabilitation based on the gold production of the Witwatersrand and political rehabilitation by means of a thoroughgoing anglicization of the predominantly Dutch population of the South African territories. Economic progress was at first halting, largely because of a shortage of labor on the Rand. The African miners, having been scattered during the war, were reluctant to work at the low wages offered, but they soon returned, possibly stimulated by the competition of contract Chinese labor utilized between 1904 and 1910.

Milner's political moves were revolutionary, given the South African situation with its population majority of Dutch antecedents, its long history of Boer discontent with British rule, and a bitter war just concluded in which two Boer republics had been defeated and occupied. Under these conditions Milner instituted a program of cultural assimilation involving the use of English as the official language and principal medium of instruction, the encouragement of English settlers, and an end to the acutely provincial Afrikaner school curriculum, all looking forward to an eventual federation of self-governing territories under the British crown. In fact, this policy was not ruthlessly pursued after Milner's departure in 1905 and the result was a sharp reaction against British cultural domination and the renascence of a particularly powerful brand of Afrikaner nationalism.

The most immediate nationalist manifestation was the formation of political parties—*Het Volk,* the People, in the Transvaal led by the Boer military figures, Louis Botha and Jan Smuts; the *Oranje Unie,* or Orange Union, of J. B. M. Hertzog, Abraham Fischer, and C. R. de Wet in the former Free State; and Jan Hofmeyr's revived Cape Colony Afrikander Bond under the name of the South African Party. The tides of nationalism and anti-imperialism were soon running so strongly that both the Transvaal and the Free State received new constitutions providing for self-government in 1906 and 1907 respectively, and by 1908 all these new Afrikaner parties were in complete control of their respective governments.

At last with the arrival to power of Boer governments, the time for union was drawing near. Britain looked on unification as strengthening her international position, especially in relation to Germany; by contrast, some Afrikaners saw it as the road to national independence, while moderate Afrikaners like Smuts and Botha thought in terms of a healthy merging of English and Dutch stocks to build a strong nation within the British Empire. In 1908 a convention met, finally producing a constitution which went into effect in May, 1910, eight years after the signing of the peace treaty. It provided for a unitary government under the British crown, the former colonies transferring their sovereignty to the central authority. It also provided for a legislature wherein only Europeans could sit, and for which, the Cape Province excepted, only Europeans could vote. Hence union came only for the European; it was not meant to include the 80 per cent of the South African population which was African.

THE OTHER UNION

The Union of South Africa had at last been achieved, emerging from the tensions of international politics and the necessities of economic development. The Boer War added forceful persuasion to the logic of modernization, and Afrikaner nationalism awoke in time to crown the process with its own unity. What seemed to be missing was that fundamental preoccupation of all South Africa, that other union which bound two races together in a common destiny—the relation between the African and the European.

Quite the contrary, it too was present. Spoken or unspoken, it had long since become part of each individual nervous system; consciously or unconsciously, it affected decisions, influenced attitudes, and determined the policies of state. When union was finally mooted, it might yet have failed had there been no agreement on so-called native policy. The Cape delegates were determined to sustain their long-standing tradition of a common voting roll without racial qualifications, while those of the Transvaal and Free State were equally unbending that no African might have the franchise. Union was salvaged only through compromise permitting local control of suffrage; in the end, the racial issue was the ultimate, irreducible obstacle which had to be circumvented to achieve political unity. With unification, moreover, came the principle that South African society was to be based upon racial privilege and exploitation, a principle that has shaped South Africa's affairs to the present, just as it had in turn been shaped by pressures over the long years stretching back to the first confrontation of Boer and Bantu on the Fish River.

The Great Trek had signaled the great change, that is, the beginning of the end for Bantu independence, the first steps in the disintegration of traditional Bantu society. The competition of rising populations, black and white, for decreasing supplies of arable land manifested itself in two forms. First and more dramatic, was the series of wars begun in the eighteenth century and concluded only in the early years of the twentieth, whereby the African resisted the engrossing of his land and the imposition of foreign control over his activities. Sometimes successful for a time but more often disastrous to the Bantu cause, African resistance usually ended with the European occupation of African territory and the compression of the indigenous people into more congested areas on ever poorer land.

Such a progression was particularly well marked on the eastern frontier of the Cape Colony. The old Xhosa area beyond the Fish River had been annexed by Governor Harry Smith in 1847, the former neutral zone contained between the Fish and Keiskamma being added directly to Cape Colony, and the territory between the Keiskamma and Kei rivers organized as the colony of British Kaffraria. Beyond lay the Transkei, a large area extending north to Natal, which would eventually become the main reserve for Africans under the latter-day policy of apartheid. Here, developed a vast refugee camp for uprooted people—Fingoes, Pondos, and Griquas, as well as broken remnants of Tembu and Xhosa retreating from the devastation of their self-inflicted genocide of 1857 in British Kaffraria. Such a multiplicity of insecure groups led to sporadic outbursts which in 1877 involved forces of the Cape government in an unwanted and expensive war. The sequel was not European colonization, but the extension by Cape Town of colonial controls which gradually introduced both Europeanization and a double standard both in the Transkei and in Cape Colony proper. By the 1890's there were stiff vagrancy laws on the books, no African could purchase alcohol, and the indigenous people were being encouraged to secure their land on the basis of survey and individual title. At the same time, the franchise was open to all, although literacy and property qualifications meant that most Africans, along with some Cape Coloureds and Europeans, were unable to vote.

Basutoland already having been taken over in 1868, the final annexation of Pondoland to the Cape in 1894 closed the gap between the Cape and Natal, and left only Zulu country and Swaziland unaccounted for south of Portuguese Mozambique. Swaziland lingered on until annexation by Britain in the mid-nineties, but in the Zulu territory where the Shakan *Mfecane* had instilled proud martial traditions, there were the makings of trouble with a renascent Zulu nation. The Zulu warriors chafed over their encirclement by colonial territories which limited their raiding and traditional "washing of spears." Moreover, Cetewayo, the Zulu king, was in dispute with the Transvaal over frontier land claims. When an arbitration commission found for him in 1878, the high commissioner, Sir Bartle Frere, insisted that the Zulu land cession be accompanied by the breakup of the Zulu military machine and the installation of a British resident in Zululand. Such terms led straight to the disaster at Isandhlwana early in 1879, a setback which was not recouped until six months later at Ulundi, when Cetewayo was defeated and exiled. For a time Zululand survived under the rule of thirteen chiefs established by the British, its final years marked by petty civil war and Boer incursions. In 1897 it was finally annexed to Natal.

During much these same years there was unrest and dissatisfaction among the Africans living in Natal. Not long after her annexation by Britain, the colony had established a series of reserves where Africans dwelt under traditional law administered by their own chiefs, but under the surveillance of European magistrates directed by Theophilus Shepstone, the Diplomatic Agent to the Natives. This policy of indirect rule, so different from that of the Cape, introduced a number of vexatious regulations and levies which were poorly administered and inadequately financed. In 1873 the situation led to a minor breach of the peace which resulted in the eventual banishment of a Hlubi chief, Langalibalele, the severe punishment reflecting a sense of European insecurity in the face of the thousands upon thousands of Africans residing in European-administered territories under circumstances which satisfied neither white nor black.

As always the essential problem was land. The Natal reserves seemed commodious, but their terrain was poor and was continually being chipped away to create white farms. The Europeans complained that the African locations drained off labor needed to cultivate their own fields, but the Bantu were in fact moving away from the reserves where they encountered only crowding, poor soil, and odious regulations. Despite the extensive acreage set aside for their use, more than half the Africans were squatters on private or crown lands.

Herein dwelt the second, less spectacular but more profound, competition for land. The Boer farmer thought in terms of a minimum tract of six thousand acres for each family, and with a rising population and absentee ownership, enormous acreages were quickly preempted. The original trekkers, moreover, had arrived in Natal, Transorangia, and the Transvaal at a time when the shock waves of the *Mfecane* had temporarily scattered the Bantu peoples so that there was an illusion of empty land which soon faded with the return of more peaceful times. Beyond this, European and African concepts of land ownership and utilization differed profoundly; what was alienation in the eyes of the one might to the other involve no more than a temporary right to pasturage. Such conditions led quickly to an intermingling of Africans and Europeans on the land, but in a pattern which usually relegated the African to the role of squatter or tenant on land he might have formerly occupied, now permitted to remain on by his new European landlord in return for labor or rent.

Rent and labor were as foreign to the Bantu as the concept of land ownership, but in the strange, evolving world into which he was plunged by the coming of the white man, he found increasingly that his labor was all he had with which to pay the rent and the taxes demanded of him, and to purchase the European manufactured goods —clothing, condiments, utensils, or luxuries—for which he had developed a taste which soon made them necessities. Losing possession of the land, he was obliged to work other men's gardens, to provide the muscle power by which other men might prosper. Yet despite the vast army of agricultural laborers which developed from this system, the wealth produced was meager, limited by the poverty of the land and the gross inefficiency of its management.

With the coming of diamond and gold mining, the pattern of an agricultural, rural proletariat was extended to these new urban industries where once again the Africans were compelled to work for the benefit of others under conditions of growing social, political, and economic limitations. They came, prodded by various motives. To the excitement of city life was added the desire for personal freedom and for money in pocket, denied on the farm with its monotony and its poverty. What they encountered as well, however, was a depressed wage scale which exploited their lack of skill and want of unity, and in fact based the industrial prosperity of South Africa as much on their unrewarded labor as on the presence of precious ores in the earth.

From the first, therefore, the double standard on the farm between European owner and African tenant was repeated in the industrial town. White labor came to mean skilled labor at high wages, whereas black labor was always unskilled and low paid. In the mines the white worker often was in fact skilled, his talents much needed in engineering the extraction of low grade ore. Nevertheless, the principle held that, regardless of skill, white labor must command a high price based on skin color, that the color bar when applied to industry decreed a continuing gap between African and European, with no prospect that the African could close that gap and gain access through excellence to the privileged class.

Such an arrangement made for great inefficiency, and was questionable economics as well. A large unskilled labor force was an ineffectual tool despite its cheapness, its depressed condition and easy availability a deterrent to increased competence, its low earning power an impediment to national prosperity. Yet, worse still was the utilization of a high-wage white labor supply, at first predominantly skilled but in the years after the First World War including more and more unskilled workers who, because of their color, had to be paid at a rate considered appropriate for so-called civilized labor. In 1936, for example, the earnings of 47,000 Europeans in the mining industries amounted to £16,700,000, £4,000,000 more than the combined income of 395,000 unskilled Africans. In economic terms this had several consequences. First, in times past, it had led to labor shortages caused by lack of African incentive, and the importation of contract workers like the Indian sugar indentures in Natal after 1860 and the Chinese brought into the Transvaal at the conclusion of the Boer War. Next, it encouraged industrial inefficiency through the use of cheap labor. Finally, the depressed African wage scale choked off a large potential purchasing power.

More than this, however, the double standard in labor meant an economic system wherein a large unskilled work force existed at submarginal levels in order that a small privileged segment of the population might achieve a standard of living comparable with that of the world's most advanced countries, despite the relative poverty of the South African economy. Hence, it was no wonder that the pattern of discrimination and segregation, which had emerged in the preindustrial years, should be perpetuated and strengthened when the center of economic life shifted from the farm to the city and South Africa's industry promised something more than the subsistence agriculture practiced so long by the *trekboer* farmer.

Such a drift of events might have been checked on several occasions by British intervention, the final opportunity coming at the conclusion of the Boer War. But Lord Milner's conviction that inferior blacks must needs be ruled by more advanced whites conceded the logic of the Afrikaner position regarding a franchise restricted to whites and foreclosed the possibility of genuine reform. Thus was the war won and the peace lost for the African population. Moreover, when the concept of federation gave way to a centralized government under unification, Cape liberalism was bound to be swamped sooner or later in facing contention from other quarters that the foundation and future of South African society rested in racial privilege.

Beyond the immediate circumstances, Britain's inadequacy was defined by the limitations of her own domestic and imperial necessities. As for the Africans themselves, their powers of resistance and range of action were even more acutely limited. Direct confrontation by tribal military force was futility conclusively demonstrated by the crushing of a Zulu uprising under Bambata in 1906. Africans therefore turned increasingly toward other means to compensate their growing sense of frustration.

First of all, there was the rise of an independent church movement which drew the sting from racial discrimination and permitted self-government in the world of religion where none was permitted in secular affairs. The earliest manifestations of these Ethiopian churches occurred during the 1870's and 1880's with such nationalist religious groups as Nehemiah Tile's Tembu Church. More significant, perhaps, was the later development of intertribal churches among mine laborers in the Transvaal organized by M. M. Mokone, James M. Dwane, and others. All these movements had the same motivation, however —to compensate for the restrictions of white rule by providing African organizations directed and controlled by Africans.

A second path led in the direction of more overt political action, but its first manifestations were mild and largely ineffective; witness the activities of John Tengo Jabavu, an enfranchised Cape Xhosa who sought unsuccessfully to extend political rights through an alliance with white liberals. Jabavu and others, like Walter Rubusana, were deeply disappointed by the discrimination against Africans contained in the Union constitution, taking their case in futile protest before the British people at the time of Parliamentary ratification in 1909. The shortcomings of Jabavu's program, with its misplaced reliance on black-white partnership, led to somewhat more vigorous measures in 1912 in the formation of the South African Native Congress which was later renamed the African National Congress. This organization, the work of Dr. Pixley Seme, Sol T. Plaatje, and others, sought full African citizenship through the franchise and the end of restrictions on landholding and personal movement—moderate objectives which were nonetheless anathema to a philosophy of white supremacy which would relentlessly steer the country in the direction of apartheid. During the years that followed, this educated African leadership, so moderate in its objectives and methods, might well have echoed the cry of anguish which had emanated some time earlier from the unhappy Africans of Natal, "If we Natives could only have feathers we would put on our wings and fly to another country."

BEYOND THE LIMPOPO—

The Union of South Africa united only the white South Africans. The black population remained outside, either physically in the territories of Bechuanaland, Basutoland, and Swaziland which came under British protection, or in the form of the Union's segregated African community—wanted only for its exploited labor, and denied all rights and privileges that a long residence in the land seemed to warrant. Beyond the Limpopo, however, another white community hesitated, and then declined to join, uncertain of its position and unready to lose its identity within the vast state taking shape to the south.

There was a certain historical logic to a unification which would have extended South Africa's hegemony to the Zambezi and perhaps eventually beyond. Both African and European had forded the Limpopo not many years earlier, occupying the vast territory that had once been the land of *Mwena Mutapa*, placing upon it the stamp of conquest that had become familiar during the days of the *Mfecane* and the Great Trek. In June, 1890, a column of pioneers, dispatched by Cecil Rhodes and accompanied by Rhodes' agent, Dr. L. S. Jameson, crossed the Macloutsi tributary of the Limpopo and marched to the site of Salisbury, thereby taking possession of Mashonaland. A half century earlier, the Kololo people of Sebetwane had finally reached safety in the waterlogged Aluyi country up the Zambezi above Victoria Falls. During much the same years, Mzilikazi and his Ndebele had abandoned their troubled land in the Transvaal in a final successful flight to security beyond the Limpopo, far from the reach both of the vengeful Zulu hordes and the guns and horses of the Boer trekkers. Now, it seemed, circumstances had again overtaken them; flight had gained, not sanctuary, but only respite, from the menace of the white man who once again confronted the Ndebele and challenged their rule.

The pioneer column which planted the British flag at Fort Salisbury in September, 1890 was the instrument of Cecil Rhodes' particularly virile form of European imperialism. The first step had been the establishment of the Bechuanaland protectorate blocking the Germans in South-West Africa and securing the Missionaries' Road north to Matabeleland, the domain of the Ndebele, or Matabele, people, led by their paramount chief, Lobengula. Having seen Imperial Germany checked, Rhodes next hastened to contain the move of the Transvaal across the Limpopo, set in motion through the Grobler Treaty of 1887. At his suggestion, the British South African high commissioner, Sir Hercules Robinson, negotiated the Moffat Treaty in February, 1888, which bound Lobengula to consult the high commissioner before undertaking any dealings with other powers involving territorial cession. The Moffat Treaty, thus, cancelled out the implications of a Transvaal protectorate contained in the Grobler agreement which, in any case, Lobengula had apparently regarded as no more than an expression of mutual friendship.

While the Transvaal government bitterly, but vainly, protested this serious check to its expansionist enterprise, Rhodes now moved to monopolize the economic exploitation of Matabeleland. Nine months after the Moffat Treaty, in October, 1888, Lobengula was induced to sign the Rudd Concession under which he assigned to Rhodes exclusive mineral rights throughout his domain in exchange for one thousand breech-loading rifles and a monthly stipend of £100. Both Lobengula and Rhodes regarded Ndebele suzerainty as effective within Mashonaland to the northeast as well as in Matabeleland proper.

The Rudd Concession not only provided Rhodes with important economic privileges in Ndebele country; it also enabled him to apply for a royal charter forming a company which could exploit the advantages gained through the Moffat and Rudd agreements. In 1889, the charter was granted, creating the British South Africa Company with powers to engage in various economic pursuits, to maintain its own police force, and to arrange political relations by treaty with African powers. Territorial definition did not exclude the possibility of expansion northward across the Zambezi. Thus Rhodes had gained the authority to occupy Central Africa, a step which he initiated during the dry season of 1890 when the pioneers crossed the Limpopo and, guarded by a Company police force of five hundred, headed into Mashonaland.

Lobengula was under no illusions as to the threat which these developments posed for his kingdom which was one of the major African powers south of the Zambezi. By the 1880's, the Ndebele nation had grown by accretion of conquered people to a population of 100,000, capable of fielding an army upwards of 20,000 disciplined spearmen. Here was a strong centralized state which had suffered none of the divisions that had plagued the Ngoni, which had reduced the Shona people to a condition of vassalage, and which showed a marked antipathy toward Europeans and a resistance to their way of life.

Nevertheless, the Ndebele position reflected basic weaknesses of which their king was only too well aware. The classic military tactics and traditional armament of the Shakan period were passing out of date as firearms became increasingly available. Ndebele society, however, had grown rigid, impeding any genuine military reform, while guns were expensive and difficult to keep in good operational condition. The Ndebele economy rested on cattle for food, for reward, and for prestige, but raiding was becoming more and more hazardous against well-armed neighbors, and prospective victims grew scarce as European control closed in from the south. Finally, many Ndebele, particularly among the young warriors, seem to have underestimated the magnitude of the European threat. Their hostility toward the white man led them on occasion to counsel annihilation of all whites in Matabeleland, a suicidal policy, as Lobengula fully realized, chiding his impetuous warriors with the remark, "You want to drive me into the lion's mouth." Such belligerence greatly complicated the king's diplomacy which was essentially designed to discourage the white advance without involvement in the direct military confrontation he knew would be fatal to his cause and people.

From Lobengula's point of view, then, he had conceded little in signing the Moffat Treaty unless he planned to give away his country, which was certainly not the case. Moreover, to Lobengula the Rudd Concession had the advantage of limiting foreign penetration to what the king mistakenly took to be one small group of ten miners under his royal authority, a grant for which he received in return a substantial supply of modern arms and a handsome monthly royalty. When Lobengula discovered his error, he moved to repudiate the Concession as contrary to his understanding, but events were already moving inexorably beyond his control. Caught between the militants in his own camp and the relentless pressure exerted by Rhodes, Lobengula in the autumn of 1889 granted Jameson limited prospecting rights which were promptly used as the excuse for the pioneer

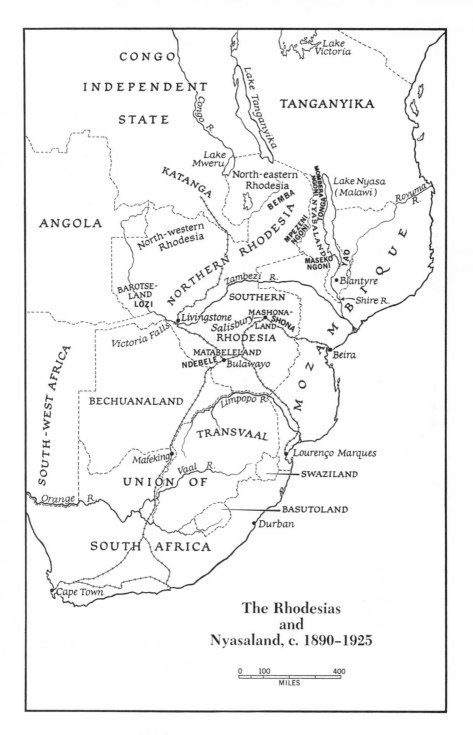

CONGO

INDEPENDENT

STATE

*Lake
Victoria*

TANGANYIKA

Congo R.

Lake Tanganyika

KATANGA

*Lake
Mweru*

North-eastern
Rhodesia

MOMBERA NGONI
NGONI NYASALAND

*Lake Nyasa
(Malawi)*

*Rovuma
R.*

ANGOLA

BEMBA

North-western
Rhodesia

NORTHERN RHODESIA

MPEZENI
NGONI

MASEKO
NGONI

•*Blantyre*

YAO

BAROTSE-
LAND
LOZI

Zambezi R.

SOUTHERN

M O Z A M B I Q U E

Shire R.

Livingstone
Salisbury
RHODESIA

MASHONA-
LAND

SHONA

SOUTH-WEST AFRICA

Victoria Falls

MATABELELAND
NDEBELE •*Bulawayo*

•*Beira*

BECHUANALAND

Limpopo R.

TRANSVAAL

Mafeking

Vaal R.

UNION OF

•*Lourenço Marques*

—— SWAZILAND

Orange R.

SOUTH AFRICA

—— BASUTOLAND

•*Durban*

•*Cape Town*

The Rhodesias
and
Nyasaland, c. 1890–1925

0   100   400
MILES

column which skirted Matabeleland to occupy Mashonaland. It was an action which clearly exceeded Lobengula's authorization, but it forced on him a fait accompli which the hard-pressed king could not undo short of a war which he realized could only end in disaster.

Indeed the situation, which threw the contempt and resentment of the Ndebele against the bumptious aggressiveness of the Europeans, seemed to lead straight to a single possible conclusion, one which Lobengula's tactics could not forestall indefinitely. The pioneers, a picked body of two hundred men including South Africans as well as British, Canadians, and Americans, were given three thousand acres each along with subsurface rights upon their arrival at Fort Salisbury. Thus a minor prospecting reconnaissance was converted into a major permanent colony. Jameson, the Company's administrator, attempted to introduce a modus vivendi by establishing a line between his group in Mashonaland, steadily growing with new settlers, and the Ndebele to the southwest; for his part, Lobengula accepted the fact of this arrangement, but steadily refused to admit the legality of the British occupation of his Mashona fiefdom, which, the Ndebele insisted, contained many of their cattle.

In July, 1893, Ndebele raiders appeared in force in Mashona country, firing villages and taking cattle, including some European stock. Demands and counter-demands followed, and Lobengula, yielding to the insistence of his more extreme advisers, mobilized, and some clashes ensued. In October, Jameson finally was given leave to invade Matabeleland, and in two sharp engagements the Ndebele were routed. Lobengula retreated northward toward the Zambezi, succumbing to smallpox in January, 1894. Thus the war ended and Matabeleland and Mashonaland fell to the South Africa Company of Cecil Rhodes by right of conquest.

Defeat brought no end to the tribulations of the Ndebele. Their lands were forfeit to the invaders and they were awarded two large but totally inadequate reserves, their difficulty compounded by African witnesses who unwisely told the investigating Land Commission what they felt the Commission wanted to hear—that these tracts were indeed satisfactory. Further, the Ndebele lost many of their cattle both to settlers and to Shona, and in early 1896 many more fell before an epidemic of rinderpest. There followed a bad drought and locust plague, all in all, an accumulation of afflictions which sorely tried the Ndebele. Beyond this, an African police force formed by the Europeans was guilty of high-handed methods in recruiting reluctant

Ndebele for mining work, Ndebele whose uncertainty and sense of humiliation were nurtured by a long-lived martial pride still virile despite the recent defeat. In March, 1896, resentment erupted into revolt, an outburst sanctioned by the priests of Mlimo, the supreme deity.

In June, the revolt spread to the Shona, incited by news of the Ndebele insurrection on top of their own resentment over the inequities and indignities of white rule. Both uprisings were bloody, involving far greater losses than those of the earlier war, and giving the prospect of long guerrilla action conducted by desperate men entrenched on strong ground. Indeed the Shona had to be blasted out of their hillside caves in a campaign which lasted until September, 1897, but the Ndebele capitulated a year earlier in October, 1896, as a result of patient negotiation conducted directly and personally by Rhodes himself. In this wise, armed African resistance ended, and a new era of African-European relations began.

The new relationship bore some resemblance to the racial pattern in South Africa, and some difference as well. The similarity was to large extent rooted in economic necessity—a small European population requiring a large African labor force in order to wrest even a modest return from the reluctant land. A few thousand settlers, straining to develop their mining claims and their fields, sought to induce the defeated Ndebele and Shona to become wage earners by making them both taxpayers and consumers of European manufactured goods. A 1902 ordinance governing employment conditions, for example, was designed to keep workers more permanently at their posts, while in 1904 the head tax was raised, not for revenue, but to compel Africans to take jobs.

In land policy there was also analogy to South Africa. Some effort had been made to provide for African needs, initially through the Matabeleland reserves of 1895, then through further land apportionment in 1902, and again in 1920. Through these various settlements 23 per cent of the land came to be set aside in African reserves, 32 per cent in European ownership, and 45 per cent as crown land open to purchase by anyone, but in practical economic terms limited to Europeans. Without taking account of the population ratio of one European for every twenty Africans (approximately 50,000 against 1,000,000 by 1930), there were the additional circumstances that European land was well served by railroads, was of generally good quality, and to a considerable extent unused. Still, the African allotments were considered adequate, particularly at a time when inaccessibility to a market meant little to people practicing subsistence agriculture.

Indeed, the reserves were in part a humanitarian gesture, a sanctuary for the African until he could be absorbed into a new society, for unlike South Africa, in Southern Rhodesia assimilation was the official policy. As soon as the African had learned through education and experience to deal with a Western, modern way of life, he would take his place as an equal in the new society, and there were electoral laws to prove the point, for from the first the only restrictions on the franchise were based on property and literacy.

Yet even here, as in other phases of Southern Rhodesian life, elements of discrimination could be detected. Property qualifications effectively excluded Africans from political activity, and were periodically raised to maintain that distinction; juries were necessarily white because they were drawn from the voting rolls, and a double standard came to obtain in the judgment of criminal cases; the constant and growing need for labor made for an insistent, though officially resisted, European demand that Africans be forced to work; while land apportionment, if not discriminatory by design, tended to favor white occupation. When the occasional African began to make economic and social progress, his advance was feared and blocked, first by custom and finally by official policy. In 1930 the Land Apportionment Act was passed whereby all Africans not under contract as laborers were relegated to the reserves. Thus did early humanitarianism expire as racial segregation in Southern Rhodesia finally gained the sanction of law.

Such legislation had been enacted by the European-dominated, self-governing colony of Southern Rhodesia which came into existence in 1923 after an administration by the British South Africa Company dating back to the days of the pioneer column. During this earlier period, economic development was a preoccupation to be punctuated by occasional constitutional advances which, though nominally for all, accrued essentially to the advantage of the European settlers. Development took place in various forms—railways which connected Southern Rhodesia to the south and brought an outlet as well through Portuguese Mozambique; gold mining which, modest in output, was yet the basis for the economy with an annual production worth £3,580,000 by 1914; agriculture which slowly provided exportable quantities of beef cattle, tobacco, citrus fruits, and some grains; and a gradually expanding population, the settlers rising from 13,000 in 1898 to 24,000 in 1911, and to 36,000 by 1923, the fast-growing African population being estimated in 1911 at 750,000 and over a million twenty years later.

Political advance, limited for practical purposes to whites, began in 1898 with the establishment of a legislative council providing for a popularly elected minority which became a majority in 1907 and was increased in 1913. By the time of the First World War, the settlers were demanding self-government, and in 1915 the Colonial Office agreed in principle. Over the years, the direction of the Company had grown irritating, and when a satisfactory formula was developed for its withdrawal, a draft constitution was prepared calling for responsible government, and in 1922 this was accepted by the electors who at the same time rejected the proposal that they be absorbed into the Union of South Africa. The next year Southern Rhodesia was annexed to the British Crown as a self-governing colony.

—AND ACROSS THE ZAMBEZI

The expansionist drive of Cecil Rhodes which produced the Moffat Treaty and Rudd Concession for Matabeleland had, by 1889, already crossed the Zambezi into Barotseland. There the Lozi king, Lewanika, actively sought a helping hand from Europe, for he was haunted by the possibility that he might be dethroned by his own people, as had occurred once before, or destroyed by the Ndebele, who were threatening a military invasion. Lewanika wrote to the administrator of Bechuanaland requesting British protection, but this overture was referred to Rhodes who had just obtained the charter of his British South Africa Company. Rhodes immediately dispatched a representative, F. E. Lochner, to Barotseland, and in 1890 this emissary concluded an agreement with Lewanika and his chiefs. Under the Lochner Concession, the Company obtained mineral and commercial rights throughout Barotseland and adjacent suzerainties, in return for which Lewanika was to receive a subsidy of £2000 a year.

This arrangement was conceived in misunderstanding. Lochner had implied that he represented the British government directly, whereas the protection for which Lewanika had contracted was provided only by the South Africa Company. Rhodes was interested in political control and commercial profit, but it soon became evident that there was no gold to be had in Barotse country, and interest in the area flagged. The Company defaulted on its annual payments to Lewanika and did not send him an official resident until 1897, by which time he had long since repudiated the Concession.

The arrival of the British resident, Major R. T. Coryndon, introduced a more active period of colonial administration, one which brought an end to Barotse sovereignty and a steady diminution of Lewanika's freedom of action. First of all, in 1898 and 1900, Coryndon renegotiated the old concession, adding the important provision that disputes involving whites would be judged by the Company which also might make farming grants to Europeans in the suzerain territories outside Barotseland proper. A few years later a hut tax was imposed, to be collected by Lewanika but only as an agent of the administration, and to be shared by him in a formula imposed by Coryndon. In 1904, Lewanika was obliged to surrender jurisdiction over civil and criminal justice for Africans outside the Barotse reserve, at the same time also losing control over certain types of cases within his own domain. Finally, two further agreements, reached in 1906 and 1909, forced the king to concede all authority over the disposition of lands outside Barotse country proper. Thus, by the time of his death in 1916, Lewanika had been reduced to the level of a local chieftain, wielding limited powers in his own territory, and even there, his sovereignty resting, at least in British eyes, with the English queen, not with the Barotse king.

Nevertheless, when Company rule was supplanted by a directly administered British protectorate for Northern Rhodesia in 1924, Barotseland identity had not been lost, and there were good reasons for this. In the first place, the Lozi vigorously challenged the legality of their various concessions, thereby at least forestalling further erosion of their authority. Secondly, the Company was careful to preserve some semblance of a Barotse state for it did not wish to jeopardize the legality of the mineral rights obtained from Lewanika in the original Lochner Concession. Moreover, it was during the 1920's that Sir Frederick Lugard's doctrine of indirect rule was at the height of its influence in shaping British colonial policy. Finally, in Rhodesia, there was the conviction that encouragement of traditional authorities might neutralize any movement toward larger, potentially dangerous, intertribal, racial cohesion.

Far to the east of Barotseland, events took a somewhat different turn, although imperial expansion was still at the heart of the matter.

In the Lake Nyasa area, for example, a series of European interests converged. There were the Scottish missionaries who arrived in the 1870's and who were soon calling for a British consul as protection against quickening Portuguese designs in the region. There were the Portuguese, long interested in extending their influence inland from their coastal possessions and connecting with a land bridge their holdings in Angola and Mozambique. Finally, there were Leopold of Belgium, the Germans in East Africa, and the omnivorous Rhodes, all expressing a lively preoccupation with central Africa. In the Nyasa country, however, it was the British who finally established themselves, proclaiming a Nyasaland protectorate in 1891.

As usual Rhodes had a hand in these developments although the principal agent was Harry Johnston, appointed British consul to Mozambique in 1889. To forestall the Portuguese, Johnston and his deputy, Alfred Sharpe, secured a number of protection treaties over a broad area west of Lake Nyasa and south of the Lake Tanganyika-Lake Mweru region. These pacts, along with additional treaties obtained concurrently by a representative of Rhodes' South Africa Company, assured British supremacy north of the Zambezi between Lewanika's domains and Lake Nyasa, but Portugal did not accept defeat until forced to acquiesce in the face of a British ultimatum in 1890. The following year, a treaty delineated the present Mozambique frontier, excluding Portugal from the Shire highlands south of Lake Nyasa where many of the Scottish missions were located. Prior to this, in 1890, an Anglo-German agreement had fixed the boundary with German East Africa, while, in 1894, the line of the Congo Independent State was established as it is today.

The Portuguese threat removed, there followed the problem of colonial administration. The South Africa Company agreed at first to finance the peacekeeping functions in Nyasaland of the African Lakes Company which had been organized originally as a commercial aid to the Scottish missions. Later this responsibility was given to Johnston, appointed commissioner in Nyasaland, and in 1891 a boundary was drawn west of Lake Nyasa, roughly parallel with the axis of the lake. Thus, in deference to the missionary distrust of Rhodes, Nyasaland was placed under separate administration as a British protectorate, although Rhodes' Company continued to finance its police-keeping functions. In 1895, however, Nyasaland was taken over completely by the British government, the Company maintaining responsibility for the interior territory, now called Rhodesia. In 1899, a further division was made between Lewanika's domains, officially named North-Western Rhodesia, and the vast plateau of North-Eastern Rhodesia lying west of Nyasaland and south of Lake Tanganyika. A final adjustment followed a few years later, placing what was to become the copperbelt within the North-Western zone.

The conflicting claims of colonial powers were not the only sources of contention within Nyasaland and North-Eastern Rhodesia. Harry Johnston, whose duties as commissioner included policing in both territories, used his South Africa Company subsidy to support a small army, primarily of Sikh soldiers, a force soon brought into play against local peoples unwilling to accept European domination. In the Yao country south and southeast of Lake Nyasa, for example, a number of chieftains confounded Johnston's troops between 1891 and 1893, and were not finally subdued until 1895 with the defeat of Makanjira, the most successful of the Yao warrior chiefs. In the Shire country, there was a brief uprising among the southern (Maseko) Ngoni in 1896, but resistance was light and easily put down. More difficult was the situation in North-Eastern Rhodesia, near the Nyasaland boundary. There the Ngoni of Mpezeni had been tricked into a fraudulent concession which opened up their country to white prospectors, brought deteriorating relations with the authorities, and ended in a revolt in 1898 which was crushed by military action, the Ngoni herds being confiscated in penalty.

Depending on circumstances and temperament, others were more amenable to foreign control. The Tonga welcomed missionary assistance that brought an end to their long-standing victimization by the northern (Mombera) Ngoni, and other Ngoni sections also made a successful transition from war making to peaceful existence. The outburst in 1896 among the southern Ngoni, for instance, was not typical of their attitude, for in fact they were attracted away from their traditional village life by the labor opportunities presented by the European plantations in the Shire highlands. Acknowledgment of a pax Britannica was also true of the powerful Bemba nation in North-Eastern Rhodesia. The Bemba, with a reputation for war making and an active alliance with Arab slavers from the coast, might have been expected to offer Johnston formidable opposition. Instead, they submitted to British control, perhaps because of the decline of the Arab caravan trade, perhaps, like the southern Ngoni, in response to the security and material advantages of peace.

The Arab slavers, intruders in their own right, were difficult to eliminate for they were well armed and tenacious adversaries. This was especially true of Mlozi, a Zanzibari trader, who established an armed village at the northern end of Lake Nyasa during the 1880's, from which he dispatched slave caravans to the coast. Over the years, he withstood a number of efforts to dislodge him, but in 1895 Johnston besieged him with an overwhelming force, and he was defeated and executed.

Resistance to European domination also emerged from another, entirely different, quarter. As in South Africa and elsewhere, African dissatisfaction with the limitations of white rule found release in religious expression through the independent church movement. In Nyasaland, a series of African revivalist churches appeared at the beginning of the twentieth century, stimulated by fundamentalist missionary activity and critical of many of the features of colonialism. Taxation and the calloused treatment of African labor on European plantations were sources of discontent which combined with pressure for land, and all became factors in the bloody but futile rising which the African preacher, John Chilembwe, set in motion in the neighborhood of Blantyre in January, 1915.

Encouraged and influenced by Joseph Booth, a British evangelist in Nyasaland, and exposed to American Negro protest during a residence in the United States, Chilembwe came to harbor a deep resentment against British colonial practice. In his small mission station near Blantyre, Chilembwe and his followers apparently lost patience bit by bit with white rule; then, when asked to fight in the British army during the First World War, they determined upon protest through violence. Their outbreak cost several European lives and many more African, but it was quickly crushed and Chilembwe was killed. More than the reaction of traditional societies his uprising pointed the way toward the independence movements of a later generation.

Despite such incidents, British colonial administration was firmly secured in Northern Rhodesia and Nyasaland by the turn of the century. With peace and stability, however, came the realization that Company rule might have outlived its usefulness in Northern Rhodesia. The settlers were demanding representation on a legislative council, and a complex series of problems concerning land ownership and mineral rights seemed to suggest the need for a direct colonial administration. The settlement which ended Company stewardship in Southern Rhodesia, therefore, was also applied to the north, and a protectorate over Northern Rhodesia, administered as a single unit since 1911, was established in 1924.

There was no comparable move toward settler self-government in the north, however. The number of Europeans remained low, only 3500 against a million Africans in 1921, and the concept within the British government of colonial trusteeship put a brake on moves toward settler domination. When, in the years prior to the Second World War, the development of the copper industry lent urgency to questions of political control, the white minority had not achieved a position of predominance as was the case in the south. Similarly, in Nyasaland over the years, the small white population gained no important political privileges which might have complicated the African independence movement which eventually emerged.

Suggestions for Further Reading

The basic works on South Africa are Leo Marquard, *The Story of South Africa*, 3rd. ed. (London: Faber and Faber, 1968; *A Short History of South Africa*, New York: Praeger, 1968), E. A. Walker, *A History of Southern Africa*, 3rd. ed. (London: Longmans, 1957; New York: Barnes & Noble, 1964), and C. W. De Kiewiet, *A History of South Africa, Social and Economic* (London and New York: Oxford University Press, 1941). For the Union of South Africa, L. M. Thompson, *The Unification of South Africa, 1902–1910* (Oxford: Clarendon Press, 1960) is definitive. Some information on early African nationalism in South Africa is available in Thomas Hodgkin, *Nationalism in Colonial Africa* (New York: New York University Press, 1957; London: F. Muller, 1956), and B. G. M. Sundkler, *Bantu Prophets in South Africa*, 2nd. ed. (London: Oxford University Press, 1961). The story of the Zulu nation is set forth in D. R. Morris, *The Washing of the Spears* (New York: Simon and Schuster, 1965), while the fortunes of other African societies may be followed in J. D. Omer-Cooper, *The Zulu Aftermath* (London: Longmans, 1966; Evanston, Illinois: Northwestern University Press, 1966). For Cecil Rhodes, see J. C. Lockhart and C. M. Woodhouse, *Cecil Rhodes* (London: Hodder and Stoughton, 1963; New York: Macmillan, 1963) and the older *Cecil Rhodes*, new ed. (London: Constable, 1938) by Basil Williams. Imperial policy is dealt with in R. Robinson and J. Gallagher, *Africa and the Victorians* (London: Macmillan, 1961; New York: St. Martin's Press, 1961) and C. W. De Kiewiet, *The Imperial Factor in South Africa* (Cambridge: Cambridge University Press, 1937; New York: Russell and Russell, 1937).

R. L: Buell, *The Native Problem in Africa*, 2v. (London: Frank Cass, 1965; Hamden, Conn.: Shoe String Press, 1927) contains much information on official policy regarding racial matters in South Africa.

A number of good general histories are available dealing with the Rhodesias and Nyasaland—A. J. Hanna, *The Story of the Rhodesias and Nyasaland*, 2nd. ed. (London: Faber and Faber, 1965; New York: Humanities Press, 1965),·A. J. Wills, *An Introduction to the History of Central Africa* (London: Oxford University Press, 1964), L. H. Gann, *A History of Northern Rhodesia* (London: Chatto and Windus, 1964; New York: Humanities Press, 1965) and *A History of Southern Rhodesia* (London: Chatto and Windus, 1965; New York: Humanities Press, 1965) by the same author, and Richard Hall, *Zambia* (London: Pall Mall Press, 1965; New York: Praeger, 1965). On racial matters in Southern Rhodesia, see Philip Mason, *The Birth of a Dilemma* (London: Oxford University Press, 1958), while both T. O. Ranger, ed., *Aspects of Central African History* (Evanston, Illinois: Northwestern University Press, 1968), and *The Zambesian Past* edited by E. Stokes and R. Brown (Manchester: Manchester University Press, 1966; New York: Humanities Press, 1966) present many of the events of the colonial and pre-colonial periods in the Rhodesias and Nyasaland from the African point of view. See also, T. O. Ranger, *Revolt in Southern Rhodesia, 1896–1897* (Evanston, Illinois: Northwestern University Press, 1968). A study of early nationalist resistance in Nyasaland is G. Shepperson and T. Price, *Independent African* (Edinburgh: The University Press, 1958; Chicago: Aldine, 1958), for which subject R. I. Rotberg, *The Rise of Nationalism in Central Africa* (Cambridge, Massachusetts: Harvard University Press, 1966) may also be consulted. The Portuguese side of the story of partition in Central Africa is found in James Duffy, *Portuguese Africa* (Cambridge, Massachusetts: Harvard University Press, 1959). See also P. R. Warhurst, *Anglo-Portuguese Relations in South-Central Africa 1890–1900* (London: Longmans, 1962).

17: Colonialism and Nation-Making

in East Africa

THE LOGIC OF EUROPEAN IMPERIALISM

The partition of Africa was set in motion by forces largely outside Africa's experience. National rivalries within Europe, a rising international commercial competition, the exigencies of geopolitical strategy, the aspirations and conceits of Western statesmen, even the exertions of European proconsuls, adventurers, and churchmen in Africa, all placed their imprint on the African land—here staking German claims, there intruding French interests, urging the rights of Britain, the sovereignty of Portugal, or the pretensions of Leopold of Belgium. For a time, the fate of the Nile highway passed from African into European hands, the Islamic way in the western Sudan was forced to accommodate Gallic and Anglo-Saxon Christian controls, while the vast Congo watershed faced the alien demands of a Belgian royal administrator.

If European occupation of Africa was largely unrelated to African circumstances, occupation nonetheless implied control, and control in turn demanded some form of government—an administration which would deal with alien peoples in ways which not only satisfied imperial strategies, but also sought to reconcile African and European views of the respective roles of ruler and ruled. Here there was little uniformity of governmental pattern. Colonial theory and practice varied enormously from power to power, but no more so than the African societies on which colonialism was imposed. The range extended from primitive hunter-gatherers to sophisticates thoroughly at home with European culture, from those who regarded the West as the key to progress in Africa to others who looked upon the colonial presence as meaningless and irrelevant to their way of life.

Nevertheless, some uniformities were discernible. First of all, there was the attitude of the European government seeking maximum control with minimum expense, tending to support the status quo, smiling on entrenched African oligarchies, and indifferent to costly and politically dangerous social reform. Secondly, as external power was extended across the African map, the diversity of indigenous societies was forced into unique conformities, artificial and arbitrary in their initial conceptions, to be sure, but the beginnings of the African nation-states which were to achieve national independence in the mid-twentieth century. Thus was modern Africa conceived, shaped in the uneasy union of two alien civilizations.

BRITISH PATERNALISM IN UGANDA

During the final decades of the nineteenth century, a number of factors combined to bring about extensive changes in Buganda, the nation which was to provide the foundation for the British protectorate of Uganda. First, there was the sense of skepticism, opportunism, and innovation which had long marked the national character of Buganda, particularly among the nobility of the *kabaka's* court. Next was a rising international commerce introduced by coastal Arabs who brought in their baggage not only Western firearms but also the Islamic faith. Beyond this was a more direct and immediate European influence represented by Protestant and Catholic clergy—missionaries who arrived respectively in 1877 and 1879, their object Christian conversion, but their effect Baganda parochialism and religious civil war. Finally, there were the imperial rivalries of Europe which led to the partition of Africa and the establishment in the Great Lakes region of a British protectorate over Uganda, agreed to by Germany and Britain in 1890 and formally instituted by Whitehall four years later.

The intellectual curiosity afoot in Baganda society and the concurrent weakness of Buganda's traditional religion made for easy conversion to new faiths, particularly among the lively, ambitious youth at court. Parties of adherents, Muslim, Catholic, and Protestant, quickly emerged among the young courtiers, already in a powerful position as special riflemen in Mutesa's armed forces. When the *kabaka* died and was succeeded in 1884 by his vicious and vacillating son, Mwanga, a potentially unstable situation disintegrated into open civil war, brought on by Mwanga's treacherous and maladroit statesmanship and encouraged by the ill-advised sectarianism of the missionaries.

In 1890 further complications developed when Captain Frederick Lugard, later to serve as colonial governor in Nigeria, arrived in Buganda representing the Imperial British East Africa Company which in turn embodied British interests in the area. There followed an involved series of military engagements and diplomatic thrusts which established British suzerainty while greatly reducing Mwanga's authority in relation to the Christian chiefs, especially those led by Apolo Kagwa, the *katikiro,* or first royal minister. When the British East Africa Company was dissolved and a British protectorate proclaimed over Buganda in 1894, Kagwa and his party acquiesced after some hesitation, riding with the British against the forces of Mwanga who was finally captured and exiled in 1899.

Throughout these developments, the *kabaka* had steadily lost authority to the religious factions among his followers, so that by the time of Mwanga's overthrow, Buganda was in fact a limited monarchy governed by an aristocratic oligarchy. At the same time the chiefs were admittedly dependent upon the British; hence, when Mwanga's departure removed the last opponent of the status quo, a long period of political stability ensued. Suddenly, the dynamism of Baganda society was replaced by a static rigidity which reflected both the contentment of the Baganda nobility and the disinclination of a new colonial administration toward change.

The mutual objectives of both the Baganda chief and the British administrator were embodied in the celebrated Buganda Agreement of 1900. In the first place, the Baganda undertook to collect and pay taxes to the colonial administration, thus acknowledging the sovereignty of the British Crown. In return for this, the traditional ruling hierarchy was retained complete with *kabaka, lukiko,* or legislature, *katikiro,* and other chiefly offices, all with full government func-

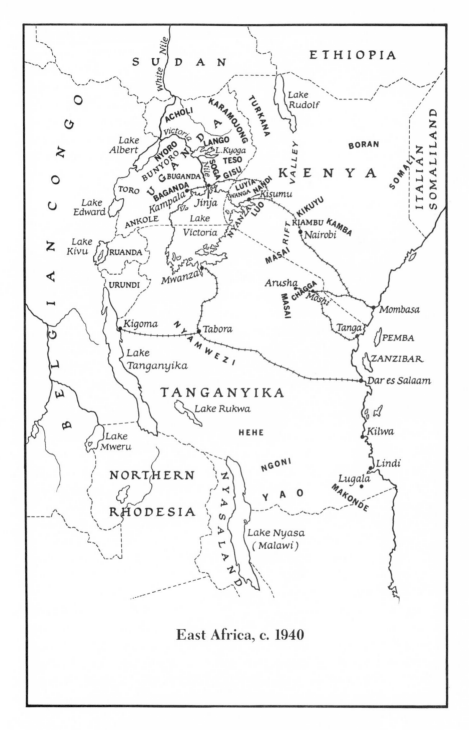

East Africa, c. 1940

tions subject only to the ultimate authority of Britain. Finally, Special Commissioner Harry Johnston, who negotiated the Agreement with the Baganda chiefs, instituted a revolutionary system of land tenure whereby all land was divided, half for the Crown and half for some four thousand chiefs, the chiefly portion henceforward to be maintained on the basis of individual private ownership. If the peasants did not resist this development, it merely indicated that their position as tribute-paying tenants remained unchanged. The aristocracy naturally regarded the change with the deepest satisfaction.

During the half century up to the conclusion of the Second World War, therefore, Buganda was administered by a cluster of British officials headed by the governor and superimposed upon an African chiefly hierarchy. The indigenous authorities were present in the person of the *kabaka* and his regional administrative chiefs called *bakungu*, in the *lukiko*, and the *katikiro*. To this the British added a series of minor district chiefs while broadening the functions of the *lukiko* chiefly council to include judicial and parliamentary responsibilities. The colonial administration laid down general policy but the details of government were left in the hands of the Baganda chiefs, and indeed the Baganda regarded the Agreement of 1900 as something like a treaty between sovereign states and managed over the years to maintain a show of autonomy although conceding ultimate authority to their British protectors. What emerged therefore was a system akin to what later was called indirect rule during Lugard's days in Nigeria, a system which worked with remarkably little friction, the chiefs secure in their dual role as rulers and as hereditary landed gentry. Thus when Buganda took her first steps toward modernization, they were made through the agency of traditional institutions, not through a new way of life, through acknowledged leaders like Apolo Kagwa, not through an educated elite divorced from the chiefs.

The Buganda government by hereditary ruler and appointed chief was extended without substantial alteration to the other territories which were gradually occupied to form the Uganda Protectorate. In such traditional kingdoms as Bunyoro, Toro, and Ankole, the new system fitted easily, especially since it brought with it the prestigious example of the formidable Baganda. Among the petty principalities of Busoga and the even less politically cohesive Gisu, Teso, Lango, Acholi, and others, adaptation to a strange political configuration came less easily, but in all cases the Buganda model was finally established, often with the assistance of Baganda agents who acted as advisers to the locally appointed chiefs. By the time of the First World War, a complete Baganda-style colonial administration had been substantially achieved in Uganda—a series of mutually exclusive African governments responsible only to the British protectorate authority at the apex. Few larger attachments thus emerged to compete with local loyalties, the Baganda proving particularly jealous of their sense of identity and prerogatives. Such parochialism was to prove a serious impediment to national cohesion during the trials of nation-making that were to come with independence.

Furthest advanced politically, Buganda also took the lead in the modest economic development that occurred during the years of British rule. Colonial policy, formulated as usual in terms of economy and local self-sufficiency, encouraged the emergence of a tax-paying peasantry, while prohibitive transportation costs, an unpromising world market, and a discouraging official attitude eliminated the possibility of European settlers and a plantation economy. Prodded by an administration in search of viable exports, the African farmer, though long accustomed to providing only for his own immediate needs, began to experiment with cash crop production. Led by Baganda peasants whose land purchases over the years gradually expanded the original four thousand freeholds of the 1900 Agreement to over fifty thousand, Uganda agriculture began to grow cotton, which quickly proved to be an outstanding success. From a mere £1000 in 1905–1906, cotton exports jumped in value to £369,000 in 1914–1915, stimulating total exports to a virtual sixfold increase over the same period.

Nevertheless, this early promise was not sustained. Other crops offered less prospect than cotton, and the few cash crops that were developed involved a relatively small number of producers. Transportation costs continued to impose severe limitations despite the rising activities of traders. Chiefs and landlords levied prohibitive requisitions on their tenants, while essentially the economy remained that of a subsistence peasant society. Not until the years after the Second World War would rising revenue and a colonial policy devoted to development and welfare bring about basic changes in the traditional pattern of leisurely rural poverty.

KENYA: RACIALISM IN A COLONIAL SOCIETY

As a colonial possession, Kenya offered few initial attractions, even to British imperialists of the Victorian Age. The main prize lay far inland where the Great Lakes held the strategic headwaters of the Nile, and the sophisticated Baganda offered the prospect of a fruitful partnership in colonial management.

The British East Africa Protectorate which was proclaimed in 1895 was regarded largely as a vast wilderness, inhabited by wild beasts and primitive peoples, which had to be traversed to reach the more consequential interior. The coastal strip above and below Mombasa was nominally under Zanzibar's suzerainty and coveted by her sultan, but it was also claimed by the Mazrui who, during 1895–1896, raised a brief but vexing rebellion that had to be put down by force. Inland for hundreds of miles were stretches of plains and hills, woodland and scrub, which Masai, Kamba, Kikuyu, and others contested with the great game herds and with each other. The Masai, in particular, seemed to have a penchant for civil strife, and all nations appeared to the British to lack even the rudiments of political organization. At the close of the nineteenth century, African energies were further eroded by famine and dulled by disease—precious cattle melting away before the dreaded rinderpest, crops devoured by locusts, and populations decimated by smallpox. This was country to be traversed, not occupied.

Yet to traverse was to occupy. Buganda and her neighbors had to be reached, first by road and then by railway, and to keep these lines open and protected required pacification, either by diplomatic agreement, as with the Masai, or by force, as imposed upon the Nandi who were subdued in a series of difficult campaigns between 1895 and 1905. A number of fortified posts were gradually established which were linked together in 1901 when the railroad from Mombasa reached Lake Victoria, thus providing a framework for the extension of British authority throughout the vast expanse of the East Africa Protectorate. Portentously, the railway also led directly to the increase in population of European and Asian settlers destined to play major roles in the future Kenya colony.

The Asians came up the rail line as traders, an extension of the ancient Indian mercantile connection with East Africa. The Europeans, for their part, were actively solicited by the government with the objective of developing the country through which the railroad ran, thus offsetting the costs of administration and public works. They came in various sorts—impecunious adventurers seeking a new stake in life, land-poor gentry from Britain, retired soldiers on pension, and Boers dissatisfied with conditions in South Africa—and they settled themselves on lands which careful and skillful British diplomacy had persuaded the Masai to vacate, the so-called white highlands stretching north and west from Nairobi along the line of the Rift Valley. Most lacked sufficient capital, and in any case, the initial tracts granted were too small for profitable farming. There were not many who could afford to wait the long years until coffee or sisal plantations began to yield profit, and few could engage in the extensive wheat and livestock production which characterized the handful of large holders like Lord Delamere.

There were additional complications. Even where European truck farming could be managed, it was undersold by African producers; beyond this, Europeans were not expected to engage in competition with native Africans nor to perform manual labor. Custom dictated, therefore, that farmers employ black workers, even if few could afford to pay wages attractive enough to entice the peasant from his familiar way of life. Similarly, custom forbade escape into small-scale commerce or a craft labor which were the province of the Asians and therefore considered socially demeaning.

The white settlers began arriving in numbers as the twentieth century opened, and in the years that followed, slowly and with difficulty, they began to make profit from their farming. Trial and error eliminated cotton, flax, and rubber culture, pointed up the viability of coffee and sisal, and discovered the value of maize. Because periodic depressions and the vagaries of world commodity markets presented their problems, gradually the small entrepreneurs were eliminated and land consolidated into larger, more economical units. In 1923 the authorities inaugurated a protective tariff which effectively subsidized cattle, dairy, and wheat producers, providing them with a local market, the expense of subsidy being passed on to the rest of the community in the form of higher prices.

Over the years, the settlers pressed the administration relentlessly for privileges they felt were theirs by right of position and talent, their demands developing a particular urgency regarding the question of labor. While London vacillated, various devices were introduced through the Protectorate government, the net effect of which was to lead or drive the African into the labor market.

In 1901 and on subsequent occasions head taxes were imposed, mainly to create a class of taxable, wage-earning African workers. It was not long, however, before this indirect compulsion had been supplemented by an informal system of manpower conscription, both for public and private use. In time the Kikuyu, on the edge of the white highlands, began volunteering their labor in return for grazing and cropping rights on European lands, but government action continued to tighten the bonds of coercion. In 1915 the Natives Registration Ordinance undertook to control labor movement in the interests of recruitment, and subsequent official interpretation of the law became tantamount to direct compulsion. Three years later the Resident Natives Ordinance decreed that only essentially full-time agricultural laborers might remain on European-held land, thus ruling out any possibility of a rising tenant or peasant proprietor class.

Finally, economic pressures were also exerted. Beginning in the 1920's, for example, African coffee culture was virtually forbidden, the chief reason being settler fear that rising agricultural prosperity among the Africans would force up the price of labor to prohibitive levels. The implications of these measures reached far beyond their immediate economic objectives. They helped set a pattern of two societies, segregated economically and socially, the one resting on the privilege of race and status supported by official fiat, the other locked in a position of inferiority and made to subserve the interests of the first.

The widespread view within the British government, which had originally encouraged white settlement and had envisioned a sturdy Anglo-Saxon yeomanry breathing life into a rich but unexploited land, was thus obliged to give way to the realities of racial discrimination. As in South Africa, a society arose dominated by a white minority which maintained its privileged position through manipulation of the machinery of government. By and large settler exploitation of the African was resisted by the home government sensitive to humanitarian pressures in Britain, but administrators in Kenya were more susceptible to settler demands, yielding to persistence or their own prejudices. Over the years favorable economic decrees were complemented by other official acts on behalf of the settlers; for example, in 1906 the introduction of a constitution and legislative council with unofficial settler representation, in 1907 the establishment of the protectorate capital at the former railway staging area and settler stronghold of Nairobi, and in 1908 the institution of an informal policy prohibiting the white highlands area to Asian settlement.

This last reflected a European settler attitude toward the Indian community as inflexible as that facing the African. Although there were chronic divisions among the settlers, they always presented a united front on racial issues and were implacable in their hostility toward the Asians, especially during the years following the First World War. They themselves received elected representation in the legislative council in 1920 as the East Africa Protectorate became the Kenya Colony, but in the face of similar demands on behalf of the Indians, the European view was simply that Asians might be represented by the official membership on the council, or, alternatively, by a specially appointed European. During the early twenties, the Indians pressed their demands while the settlers sought to dominate official policy. In 1923 a compromise British Government White Paper was issued which satisfied neither side. The Indians gained five council seats but were denied inclusion on a common voting roll; furthermore they could not obtain relaxation of the policy restricting non-European landholding in the white highlands. For their part, the settlers lost the monopoly of the franchise they had previously held, at the same time being rebuffed in their bid to have Kenya declared a self-governing colony on the Southern Rhodesian model.

These disappointing developments defined the highest point of settler influence which was further checked when the White Paper went out of its way to declare Britain's primary responsibility for Kenya's 2,500,000 Africans, not to be forgotten in the face of the articulate and self-serving exertions of 10,000 Europeans and 23,000 Asians. In 1924, the appointment of a European missionary gave the Africans a special representative on both the legislative and executive councils, and five years later African precedence was once again officially pronounced in a report which urged the principle of racial partnership, not racial domination.

That same year, 1929, the Labourites returned to power in Britain and soon made known their position on colonial matters in East Africa—rigorous protection of African land rights, an increase of African representation on the legislative council, and eventual responsible government only when all sections of the population were assured adequate representation. In 1931 a special committee of the two houses of Parliament in effect killed any lingering hope for local self-government under settler control, and a few years later European special privilege was further undermined by an income tax designed to redress what was officially regarded as an inequitable tax burden borne by the African population. If the outbreak of the Second World War in 1939 put a temporary end to politics, the War's end in 1945 also brought the ultimate realization that Kenya with its tiny European population would never fulfill that long-nourished settler aspiration, "white man's country."

KENYA: ALIEN RULE AND AFRICAN RESPONSE

If an early objective of British colonial administrators was the introduction of a white settler community, their philosophy of government was necessarily committed, consciously or unconsciously, to the idea of settler dominance with both African and Asian playing subordinate roles. Such a view could scarcely have raised humanitarian scruples in the minds of the first Protectorate officials as they compared their European skills and institutions with the apparently backward societies surrounding their early outposts. Unlike the people of the Great Lakes area, the Kenyan Africans appeared to possess little political sophistication and, indeed, most national groups (Mumia's small state of Wanga [Hanga] excepted) were organized primarily on kinship relations. This was as true of the Nilotic Luo and Bantu Luyia dwelling east and north of Lake Victoria as it was of the pastoral Nilotes–Masai and Nandi cattlemen of the Rift Valley region. It applied equally to seminomadic Boran and Somali herders roaming the arid stretches toward the Ethiopian and Somali frontiers, to Nilotic Turkana fishing the waters of Lake Rudolf, or to the Kikuyu and Kamba farmers of the central Kenya plateau.

Statelessness did not greatly confound the authorities, however. Within the first decade, military expeditions had brought large areas under control, and the threat of force extended the British fiat much farther still. Once peace had been secured, a profound ecological revolution ensued as embattled communities spread out of their fortress villages, hill dwellers were converted into plainsmen, and the voice of arbitration replaced strength of arms as a means of settling disputes. Moreover, the early rustication of the Masai in special reserves soon opened to cultivation by other African peoples, land previously regarded as too dangerous for occupation.

Occupation and pacification, nevertheless, proved simpler than on-going administration. Imposition of law and order, collection of taxes, introduction of public improvements, and recruitment of labor all required a hierarchy of officials in societies where none had existed traditionally and where appointed headmen were politically meaningless and personally irritating. Only the sanction of British authority backed by the presence of district officers gradually gave a degree of legitimacy to the administration-selected chiefs who continued to be an alien, albeit increasingly efficient, institution.

In one respect in particular, the matter of land policy, the Africans of Kenya never became reconciled to British rule. Their suspicions ever roused in defense of deep-seated attachment to the life-giving soil, they reacted as much to the potentiality as to the actuality of land alienation; fear of loss was at the bottom of much of their persistent sense of insecurity and injustice. Many groups were only lightly affected (those in the Kavirondo or Nyanza area, for example) but others had much more substantial grievances. The Masai became thoroughly disillusioned with their relegation to inadequate reserves, an experience which explains much of their apparent indifference to modernization and their retreat into xenophobic tribalism. In particular, the Kikuyu, closely attached to the land and with serious population pressures, suffered from both real and imagined alienation. Since their reserves were contiguous with the white highlands, many misunderstandings over ownership and occupancy arose over the years, and when, in the interest of more efficient scientific husbandry, the custom of Kikuyu residence and cultivation on settler lands was curtailed during the 1930's, long-lived resentment was given fresh impetus.

Land policy was linked to the system of territorial reserves, another sore point with the Africans. The Masai at an early date had been placed on reserves while Nandi and Kikuyu reserves were established before 1909, but most nations obtained no such guarantee. Moreover, the Crown Lands Ordinance of 1915 defined all land occupied and utilized by Africans as Crown land, and empowered the governor to sell portions of reserves if he felt they were no longer needed. Such legislation contributed no little to the widespread insecurity which, however, was somewhat alleviated in 1926 when reserves were proclaimed for all people throughout the country, and in 1934 when the Carter Land Commission recommended important extensions to lands already held in reserve.

Unfortunately, the strengthening of the reserves also stiffened lines of racial segregation, while ignoring the rising problems of urbanization manifest in centers like Mombasa and Nairobi. During the 1930's these towns began to attract numbers of rootless, unskilled Africans, poised uneasily between their traditional mode of life and a novel but insecure existence. Here then was a paradox of policy. Just as the separateness of white and black was being further defined by official decree, the two worlds of Africa and Europe were in fact being thrown together in a new and complex relationship.

KENYA: THE POLITICS OF CHANGE

During the half century concluding with the Second World War, colonial occupation brought extensive change to Kenya—a changing economy and a changing society—not all of which was welcome and little of which occurred without some measure of response from the African people. Slowly a wage-earning, money economy took hold, forced by the taxation and labor policies of the government and urged by a growing taste for European consumer goods. Accompanying this was a new individualism, fostered in part by missionary training, competing with traditional authority, and developing new sources of personal wealth and extra-tribal power along with a growing attraction toward middle class, Westernized social standards. To long-standing resentment over land were therefore added further misgivings concerning latter-day official policy seemingly designed to obstruct African advance toward economic sufficiency, toward educational opportunity, and toward a share in the standard of living introduced by the European.

As ever, social resentment found political expression. The earliest manifestations of political unrest took place within the traditional societies where young men, emancipated through education and escaping to the town or the European farm, began to take exception as early as 1912 to outmoded customary authorities or to chiefs owing their power to the European administration. The issues were various but one recurrent theme, at least among the Kikuyu, was the perennial question of land alienation. Between 1903 and 1906, during the initial wave of settlement in the white highlands, large tracts had been appropriated, particularly in the Kiambu district to the north of Nairobi, for which compensation was trifling or completely lacking, and where Africans were forced to become squatters on land they continued to regard as their own.

During the 1920's a number of protest organizations emerged, most of them founded by politically self-conscious Kikuyu. Although these groups enunciated specific grievances concerning such matters as land alienation, taxes, or labor policy, there was implicit in their protest a deeper sense of outrage over the basic implication of all official measures, namely that the African was a second-class human suitable only for exploitation. The first of these organizations to appear was the most moderate, however—the Kikuyu Association founded about 1920 by Kiambu farmers and headmen intent upon blocking any further alienation of their lands, but willing to work toward reform within the existing colonial structure.

Such sweet reasonableness was not for everyone. In Nairobi young clerks and domestics of various tribal origins came together in 1921 to form the East African Association under the Kikuyu leadership of such individuals as Jesse Kariuki and Harry Thuku. Thuku, literate and member of an influential Kikuyu family, held a clerkship in the Treasury, using his prestigious position to move into the front rank of those intent on challenging European authority. In 1921 he also founded the Young Kikuyu Association, apparently a temporary outgrowth of the East African Association, and the following year another Kikuyu, James Beauttah, was instrumental in the appearance of the Young Kavirondo Association in Nyanza, its membership made up of youthful educated Luo and Luyia. These organizations were uniform in rejecting the premise of white rule, basing themselves on the principle of political change. They attacked labor policy, the head tax, and land alienation, and were particularly opposed to the despised *kipande,* an identification card required of all Africans.

Thuku's militant program began to gain a following outside Nairobi, thereby insuring official concern and an early end for his movement. In 1922 he was arrested, this step leading directly to a protest rally that ended tragically when police fire killed over twenty members of the greatly excited crowd. On that note of violence the East African Association quickly collapsed, but in Nyanza, the Kavirondo Association experienced a somewhat different fate. Its initial political character was altered by missionaries who by 1923 had diverted its energies into welfare work, while political activities in the Kavirondo area tended increasingly over the years to degenerate into an unproductive intertribal rivalry irrelevant to any effective opposition against the inequities of colonial rule.

These were but temporary setbacks, at least in Kikuyuland. With Thuku in prison, leadership fell on others including Beauttah and Joseph Kangethe who helped found the Kikuyu Central Association in 1924 which listed among its several demands the release of Thuku, still the spiritual head of the protest movement. Gradually the K.C.A. gathered adherents, particularly among the younger generation, and within a few years of its appearance it was admittedly speaking authoritatively for the Kikuyu people as a whole.

Among its early recruits was Jomo Kenyatta who became General Secretary of the Association in 1928, as well as editor of its monthly journal, but Kenyatta was soon dispatched to London to present the grievances of his group directly to the British government. As Kenyatta later testified, these grievances centered on questions of education, of legislative council representation, and particularly of land ownership. "If you woke up one morning," said Kenyatta, "and found that somebody had come to your house, and had declared that house belonged to him, you would naturally be surprised, and you would like to know by what arrangement. Many Africans at that time," he continued, "found that, on land which had been in the possession of their ancestors from time immemorial, they were now working as squatters or as labourers."

Kenyatta remained almost continually in Europe until 1946, acting as K.C.A. representative in Britain and for a time pursuing postgraduate study at the London School of Economics. Thus, he avoided the crisis of leadership which threatened to destroy the K.C.A. movement in the 1930's. The schism developed with Harry Thuku's release in 1931, his by-then-moderate views appearing to disqualify him for K.C.A. membership, at least in the eyes of Jesse Kariuki, the Association's vice-president, and other activists. Thuku left to found the pro-government Kikuyu Provincial Association in 1935 but the K.C.A. survived the split and by 1940 was the most powerful and widely influential organization in Kikuyuland as well as the most radical. With the commencement of the Second World War it was proscribed and its leaders arrested, their release not coming until the closing years of the War.

In 1929, shortly before the outbreak of dissension within the K.C.A., Kikuyu society, slowly evolving before the pressure of Western ideas and institutions, was caught up in a crisis over the national custom of female circumcision. Attacked by the missionaries, the practice was held as an essential of Kikuyu culture, and the missionary censure was therefore widely interpreted as an effort to undermine that culture and gain further alienation of Kikuyu land. The great majority of people rallied in support of tradition and were led in this respect by the Kikuyu Central Association. The net result of the controversy was a temporary breaking away from the churches, but a permanent estrangement also arose between the missions and the schools, many of which thereafter came under the sponsorship of independent Kikuyu associations. Thus Kikuyu grievances against colonial rule found focus and release in the circumcision issue and the rise of African-controlled schools. The movement also served the postwar rise of Jomo Kenyatta who used the Kenya Teacher Training College, founded in 1939 in support of the independent schools, as a channel for the spread of his political influence.

By the outbreak of the Second World War, therefore, at least among the Kikuyu of Kenya, were to be found indications of the shape of things to come. Already evident were the lines of defense on behalf of tradition and the patterns of resistance against alien rule. What was also present, if less noticed, were the inter-tribal tensions which would eventually complicate the process of nation-making.

THE TANGANYIKAN COLONY AND MANDATE

Having gained a colonial empire in Africa as the by-product of Bismarck's powerful diplomacy, Germany undertook to administer her African holdings primarily as suppliers of raw materials for the German economy. In Togo and Cameroun the objects were ivory and palm products, and then cultivated crops such as coffee, cocoa, cotton, and rubber. Similarly, German East Africa was soon engaged in agricultural development—coffee, copra, and groundnuts, to which cotton and sisal were subsequently added.

To extract these products and govern their newly won territories, the Germans were at first guided by a policy of expediency which relied heavily on arbitrary, coercive methods of labor recruitment, but the completeness of colonial control was nonetheless compromised by a paucity of administrators and limited funds. Lack of personnel led to a system of indirect rule through local chiefs with whom treaties were signed wherever possible. In areas of former Arab influence, their officials, or *akidas,* were retained, each exercizing a degree of authority over several villages, often in concert with local headmen, or *jumbes.* If African governments appeared inconvenient, however, they were quickly reordered to different specifications, and always the ultimate authority was the German district officer. These officials were sometimes guilty of ruthless enforcement of the hut tax imposed first in 1897, a line of conduct which added fresh unrest to the chronic outbreaks of violence which had greeted German rule from its inception.

In 1888 the initial colonial government, the German East African Company, was challenged by a revolt of coastal Arabs fearing the end of their traffic in slaves, and when direct administration by the Imperial German government was instituted in 1890, there were other uprisings to command attention. The Hehe maintained a determined resistance for a half-dozen years after their initial annihilation in 1891 of a punitive expedition; in the Kilwa area Hasan bin Omari led a revolt during 1894–1895; while military action was required in 1893 to subdue the troublesome Chagga and the Nyamwezi chief, Siki. The Makonde of Lugala, followers of the Yao leader, Machemba, held off the Germans until 1899, and the Ngoni living back of Lindi had to be visited by a pacifying force in 1897.

In 1901 more flexible government policy was introduced. For example, an attempt was made to collect taxes by non-violent means; nonetheless, while this shift seemed at first to bring results, there was a fresh outbreak in the south in 1905 which quickly developed into a major rebellion. The initial manifestations of unrest in the Kilwa district seemed related to forced labor and the harsh methods employed by *akidas* in carrying out their duties. More particularly, there was objection to a government experimental program in cotton culture which the African farmer regarded as inequitable, uneconomic, and damaging to subsistence food production. When the movement received religious sanction in the form of a special water, or *maji,* given to the rebels, supposedly rendering them immune to gunfire, there developed a unity among diverse people, a fanaticism in battle, and a sense of commitment which quickly spread the Maji Maji Rebellion far beyond its original nucleus. Such circumstances joined with German unpreparedness to sustain the conflict during a two-year period before it was finally crushed in 1907, and then only through scorched earth tactics which supplemented military action in sub-

A Treasury of Knowledge and Cyclopedia History, Science and Art

32. Regent Village, a Freetown suburb, *c.* 1850

33. Monrovia
about 1875

Frank Leslie's Popular Monthly, JANUARY, 1876

34. Cape Coast
Castle, 1873

Illustrated London News, MAY 31, 1873

35. Edward W. Blyden

36. Samuel Lewis

37. James Johnson

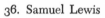

38. John Mensah Sarbah

39. Mutesa and members of his court

40. The Uganda Railway between Lake Victoria and Mombasa

41. A street in Gorée

42. Waterfront steps, Freetown

43. Lagos market

44. Herbert Macaulay

45. Nana Ofori Atta

46. J. E. Casely Hayford

K. A. B. JONES-QUARTEY

NATIONAL ARCHIVES OF SENEGAL, DAKAR

47. Lamine Guèye

48. Blaise Diagne

NATIONAL ARCHIVES OF SENEGAL, DAKAR

49. The Congo

duing the rebels with heavy casualties. It was estimated that at least seventy thousand Africans perished, many of disease and malnutrition.

By the end of the Maji Maji uprising, therefore, German administration in East Africa had been forced to conduct fully twenty years of warfare to secure pacification and African submission to colonial rule. There was a more positive side to the occupation, however. Despite limited resources, a number of public improvements were soon introduced—harbor development, bridge and road construction, and the establishment of institutions for scientific research. Some attempts were made to assist African agricultural production, while missionaries brought the beginnings of elementary educational instruction.

In 1907, a more liberal regime softened the harsher aspect of the earlier administration and concentrated on reform and economic expansion. Missionary schools were encouraged, public health services and further agricultural research inaugurated, while the arbitrary corporal punishment of Africans practiced in former times gave way to formalized judicial procedures. The development of settler plantations devoted to rubber, sisal, coffee, and cotton was assisted through special government institutes, pricing schemes, and improved communications. By 1914, a railroad line had been completed from the coast to Kigoma on Lake Tanganyika and another to the coffee districts around Moshi and Arusha. African farmers also benefited from these improvements, for they came in time to dominate the production of coffee, copra, and groundnuts. Hence, by the eve of the First World War, German administration had overcome many of its former limitations and converted an unsettled land, plagued by slaving and chronic warfare, to a peaceful colony with an expanding economy.

If latter-day German administration was enlightened as well as paternalistic, paternalism also characterized the period of international trusteeship that emerged from the Peace of Versailles under the mandate of the League of Nations. Most of the former German East African colony was placed under British responsibility and renamed Tanganyika while the tiny but heavily populated Hima-Tutsi kingdoms of Rwanda and Burundi became the Belgian mandate of Ruanda-Urundi. In Tanganyika, the new administration was at once characterized by a sense of commitment to protect colonial charges against exploitation while preparing them for eventual self-government. Laudable as was this attitude, it nevertheless tended to engender cautious, conservative trusteeship, and indeed during the immediate postwar period little was done in the Tanganyika mandate to fashion a new world in place of the dislocated society and ravaged land resulting from four years of hard military campaigning by German and Allied forces.

With the arrival of Sir Donald Cameron as governor in 1925, a more coherent and active administration emerged. The governor's personal temperament, his experience as Chief Secretary to the government in Nigeria, and his conviction that effective administration could only exist when based on indigenous institutions all contributed to his establishment of a system of indirect rule. The Native Authority Ordinance of 1926 undertook to govern through local authorities, investing them initially with responsibility for maintenance of order and collection of taxes, later adding judicial functions, while encouraging local financing and direction of community development projects.

Cameron's philosophy argued that the League mandate was a trust leading to ultimate self-rule; therefore, training of Africans in self-government was absolutely essential. Traditional authorities were the logical agents, he insisted, as was customary law the chosen vehicle, although precedent and accepted practice were always subject to adaptation on behalf of modern requirements. In his day, Cameron's policy was criticized by settlers in Tanganyika as suppressive of quick modernization under European leadership, and later it was argued that his selection of native authorities had been precipitous and maladroit, leading in fact to a confusion within traditional modes of government and their disintegration in the face of British procedures directed by British administrators. Although there may have been an element of justice in these charges, there were also a number of accomplishments to mark Cameron's stewardship.

In addition to invaluable experience in local government, the people of Tanganyika gained an expanded system of education adapted to their needs, aid toward agricultural development, particularly in teaching and research, and improved public health services especially designed to deal with endemic trypanosomiasis. Finally, there was progress in alleviating the distresses of forced labor which so sorely troubled African societies across the continent during the interwar period. A labor department was established in 1926 which encouraged better working conditions and provided medical care for workers, while at the same time wage payments in cash were guaranteed by law. Compulsory labor continued for public works but remuneration was usual, while the number of workers gradually declined in the face of rising voluntary employment. Nevertheless, although the government exerted no overt pressure on individuals to work either on public projects or private plantations, professed official neutrality was criticized in 1929 by the Permanent Mandates Commission of the League of Nations as tantamount to actual compulsion.

The departure of Cameron in 1931 marked no significant change in government policy. Even the world-wide depression of the 1930's and the crises of the Second World War lightly touched the sprawling mandate as yet so little affected by the stresses of Western civilization. There were of course changes. Education and public health moved forward very modestly, the economy slowly shifted from subsistence to cash crop production, porterage declined in the face of improved roads and motor transport, and a gradual rise in living standard was reflected in better domestic housing and the beginnings of public sanitation. Nevertheless, consequential economic changes were obliged to await the dynamics of the postwar years.

In much the same way, the pattern of traditional village life slowly evolved, giving ground before such pressures as British administration, population movements, and the rise of mixed urban centers. Regional loyalties and intertribal political configurations were still developments for the future, however. As yet few individuals conceived of themselves as members of a Tanganyikan nation.

MULTIPLE COLONIALISM IN ZANZIBAR

Colonization and colonial rule by alien groups had long been a fact of life in Zanzibar. For centuries, Arab merchants had maintained small communities up and down the East African coast, spreading Islamic culture along with their trade goods, and the Shirazi Persians in particular had through permanent immigration introduced a Middle Eastern and Muslim quality which came to be characteristic of the African population of Zanzibar and other island and coastal settlements. The resultant Swahili civilization maintained sufficient mercantile relations with inland Africans to interest traders, chiefly Arab and Indian, and eventually in the sixteenth century to attract the attention of Portuguese conquerers in process of asserting their commercial domination of the Indian Ocean. The ousting of the Portuguese by resurgent Omani Arabs at the end of the seventeenth century re-established Arab primacy along the coast, but this authority remained nominal until Sayyid Said succeeded to the Omani throne at Muscat in 1806 and then transferred his seat of government to Zanzibar in 1840.

Thus Zanzibar became the center of an Arab state on the East African coast, preoccupied at first with trade, particularly in slaves, and then during the second half of the nineteenth century, shifting to the cultivation of cloves as the British antislavery crusade spread into the Indian Ocean. This development had profound implications for the Africans of Zanzibar and to a lesser extent for the people of neighboring Pemba. First, it introduced an immigrant Arab aristocracy increasingly involved in plantation management. Next, it meant a thoroughgoing political and economic domination by the Arabs over the African population—their best lands alienated, their labor exacted by corvée, and their communities isolated from the ruling Arab class.

Beyond these groups there were plantation slaves and a small number of Asian clerks and shopkeepers. The latter were financially important but politically inactive, while the slaves gradually became converted into tenant farmers as servitude faded before the insistence of British abolitionism at the end of the nineteenth century. British officialdom, the smallest group of all, was at the same time of greatest consequence. Beginning with resident-advisers in the days of Sayyid Said, their representatives gradually increased their influence to the point of dominance during the consulship of James Kirk in the 1870's and 1880's; then in 1890, Britain imposed a protectorate which in practice became unadulterated colonial control.

As elsewhere, British colonial practice supported the status quo which in this case meant government through the agency of the Arab oligarchy. When at first the sultan's administrative machinery was completely overhauled in the interest of efficiency, Arabs were used to staff the new bureaucracy; then, in the 1920's a legislative council was introduced on which Arabs, despite their small numbers, had representation equal to that of the Africans and Asians combined. This was a particularly striking reflection of the unresponsiveness of official policy to changing times for it occurred during the interwar period which saw the rise of an African peasantry, steadily acquiring land from the failing Arab plantation aristocrats.

In the years following the Second World War, the general liberalization of colonial control in the British areas led in 1956 to popular election of half the unofficial legislative council members, a development which surprisingly was at first urged by the Arab minority rather than by the Africans who outnumbered all others by three to one. Arab leadership apparently hoped thus to maintain governmental control at the time of independence which was drawing near, and indeed in 1961 when responsible, ministerial government was instituted, the Arabs managed to form a coalition with sympathetic Africans. In time, however, political authority for the Arabs was to follow in the path of their economic decline.

BRITISH RULE AND NATIONALIST STIRRINGS IN THE NILE VALLEY

From ancient times, Egypt and the Sudan had been bound up in each other's affairs; now at the turn of the century as the *Khalifa's* armies fell before Kitchener's firepower, the Nile Valley was once again unified, this time within the embrace of British imperial power. Having occupied Egypt in 1882 at the time of the Urabist revolt, a move designed initially to protect European investments in Egypt, Britain remained as de facto ruler, her position reflecting both the quickening of the imperial pulse and concern for the safety of the Suez link with the East. When the Sudan fell to British arms in 1898, and France had been faced down at Fashoda in her effort to break the British hold on the Nile, the vast Mahdist state also came under Britain's control, to be administered through the device of the Anglo-Egyptian agreement known as the Condominium.

The Condominium was the creation of Lord Cromer, British consul-general in Cairo from 1883 to 1907, who governed Egypt indirectly through the local regime headed by the khedive. Nominally the khedive was both vassal of the Ottoman sultan and ruler of his own Sudanese dependency. To preserve these legal niceties, the Condominium proclaimed a dual sovereignty in the Sudan, Britain joining Egypt as co-ruler by right of conquest. Thus Cromer was able to impose effective control in both territories without the necessity of undisguised annexation. For the moment, at least, British control was unclouded by those qualifications which later came to embarrass her hegemony in the Nile Valley.

In Egypt and the Sudan, as in other areas, British imperial rule followed the familiar pattern of securing the status quo, content to insure protection of the Suez Canal and unwilling to embark on major social reforms which, it was felt in Whitehall, might bring unrest along with rising expectations. In Egypt extensive economic development was therefore undertaken only within the framework of the existing social order. Agriculture, particularly cotton production, was greatly stimulated by improved hydraulic engineering in the Nile floodplain, harbors were modernized and railroads built, and the economy thereby firmly directed away from subsistence farming to cash crop cultivation. Ownership of land, however, was permitted to accumulate in the hands of a local aristocracy which also monopolized the benefits of the modest, Western-oriented educational system, and exercised such limited parliamentary powers as were permitted by the British authorities.

In the Sudan, a combined British and Egyptian civil service conducted all official business, Sudanese at first having no share in the administration. As with Egypt, long-staple cotton production was encouraged, chiefly through an irrigation scheme begun in the Gezira before the First World War, while steam-driven river transport, railroads, and improved port facilities added their measure of modernization. These advances were financed, partly by Britain, but chiefly through interest-free Egyptian loans contributed at British insistence. Unlike cotton development in Egypt, the Gezira project was designed to encourage peasant farming, and indeed by the time it was nationalized in 1950, the scheme had grown into a large and successful agricultural cooperative involving the government, private concession companies, and tenant cultivators.

Despite its caution Britain's colonial policy of paternalism and limited reform provided the classic formula for nationalist discontent, a reaction which broke with particular violence in Egypt in the years following the First World War. Before the War some nationalist agitation had been apparent in the frustrations of European-educated civil servants who, in spite of their Westernized background, saw the wisdom of appealing to Egypt's Muslim peasantry, ever resentful over the inequities of taxation and land distribution. Nevertheless, it was the 1914–1918 conflict in Europe which crystallized local dissatisfaction—vexation over wartime sacrifices unrewarded, and bitterness in the knowledge that the great principle of national self-determination enunciated at Versailles was to be applied exclusively to European soil. The resultant rise of the Wafd party under Saad Zaghlul, and the rebellion that followed when Zaghlul and his aides were exiled to Malta, emphasized the seriousness of the Egyptian movement and led to a qualified grant of independence in 1922. Britain reserved for herself several important powers including security of imperial communications, responsibility for Egyptian national defense, protection of foreign nationals, and British preponderance in the Sudan.

In time the Wafd showed itself to be essentially conservative, representing affluent landed and financial interests; yet at this stage it was loath to accept any limitations imposed on Egyptian sovereignty, nor did it welcome recognition of Britain's paramountcy in the Sudan. In 1924, however, there expired any lingering Egyptian illusions concerning her share in the Condominium as her troops and officials were forced to withdraw from all Sudanese stations in retaliation for the assassination in Cairo of Sir Lee Stack, governor-general of the Sudan. The Condominium remained in name, but Egypt's interests in the south were thenceforward more appropriately to be reflected in the recurrent and vain Wafd assertion of Egypt's legal and historical position in the Sudan, rather than in any actual exercise of sovereignty.

British conservatism, responsible for the virtual end of Egyptian authority in the south, was also directed against a small but growing nationalist movement within the Sudan itself. As elsewhere in her African colonies, Britain was devoted during these interwar years to rule through traditional authorities who were treated with as much confidence and affection by administrators in the field as the educated Africans were mistrusted and shunned. Thus isolated in frustration, Westernized elite, already trained in such schools as Khartoum's Gordon Memorial College to extol European liberal and democratic values, came together in political opposition to the seeming hypocrisies of established authority. The first Sudanese to express a specific nationalism was Ali Abd al-Latif, a young Dinka whose political organization founded in 1921 brought him a jail term during which he developed the conviction that success could henceforth come only by making common cause with Egyptian nationalists. The result was a second party, the White Flag League, founded by Abd al-Latif in 1924 and dedicated, not to Sudanese freedom, but to unity with independent Egypt.

Ali Abd al-Latif's movement once again collapsed in the face of official displeasure, and the expulsion of the Egyptians in 1924 completed the isolation of his early nationalist followers. Moreover, the government pressed forward with its policy of indirect rule through the chiefly authorities, and educated Sudanese were actively discouraged from participation in government, even as minor members of the civil service. Nevertheless, circumstances were already developing which in time would not only produce a Sudanese nationalism, but one marked indelibly by the quality of Sudanese character and the necessities of Sudanese history.

This parochial manifestation was bound up with the particularities of Islam in the Sudan. In the days before the Mahdi, one of the most powerful sects was the Khatmiyya headed by the Mirghani family, its particular strength lying in the north and east. Long associated with Egyptian rule and resistant to the Mahdist impulse, the Khatmiyya and their Mirghani leaders were overshadowed during the years of the Mahdist state, re-emerging with the Condominium which gained their hearty cooperation as a return to the golden days of Egyptian influence in the south. For its part, Britain looked on the Mirghani as allies and influential leaders, in appreciation of which the head of the order, Sayyid Ali al-Mirghani, was knighted in 1916. During the interwar period, however, the Mahdists made a strong comeback as the British found another useful political friend in Abd al-Rahman, the posthumous son of the Mahdi. When political activity developed in the Sudan during the years of the Second World War, it quickly polarized around these two figures and their families.

In 1938, the Graduates' General Congress was founded by Sudanese government workers, now long established in the lower and medium ranks of the civil service. By 1942 the Congress was demanding self-determination for the Sudan at the end of hostilities, and when rebuffed, it split into two factions, the activist Ashiqqa founded by Ismail al-Azhari and a more moderate Umma party. The Ashiqqa, seeking Egyptian aid, also found themselves drawn to the Khatmiyya with its traditional orientation toward the north. The Umma responded by supporting Sudanese independence without Egypt, allying itself with the Sudan's leading nationalist symbol, Abd al-Rahman al-Mahdi. Thus each group gained mass strength among the politically inexperienced but devout Sudanese people. At the conclusion of the War, as Britain faced the multiple problems of relations with Egypt and the future of the Sudan, this basic political split within the Sudan conditioned her deliberations even as it was to shape Sudanese politics and relations with Egypt during the years leading to independence and beyond.

Suggestions for Further Reading

The standard works dealing with East Africa are Kenneth Ingham, *A History of East Africa*, 2nd. ed. (London: Longmans, 1963; New York: Praeger, 1965) and the second volume of the Oxford *History of East Africa* edited by V. Harlow and E. M. Chilver (Oxford: Clarendon Press, 1965). See also R. L. Buell, *The Native Problem in Africa*, 2v. (London: Frank Cass, 1965; Hamden, Conn.: Shoe String Press, 1965). The vast range of African affairs is examined in Lord Hailey's two massive surveys, *An African Survey* (London: Oxford University Press, 1938), and *An African Survey, Revised 1956* (London: Oxford University Press, 1957), but they are particularly useful for the period of colonial occupation. The most recent interpretation is contained in B. A. Ogot and J. A. Kieran, eds., *Zamani, A Survey of East African History* (Nairobi: East African Publishing House and Longmans, 1968).

For Uganda, there are a number of helpful studies including Kenneth Ingham, *The Making of Modern Uganda* (London: Allen and Unwin, 1958); D. A. Low and R. C. Pratt, *Buganda and British Overrule, 1900–1955* (London: Oxford University Press, 1960); and D. E. Apter, *The Political Kingdom in Uganda*, 2nd. ed. (Princeton, N. J.: Princeton University Press, 1967). Several more specialized works shed light on particular aspects of Uganda history; for example, R. Oliver, *Sir Harry Johnston and the Scramble for Africa* (London: Chatto and Windus, 1957); the same author's *The Missionary Factor in East Africa* (London: Longmans, 1952); M. Perham, *Lugard: The Years of Adventure* (London: Collins, 1956; New York: Oxford University Press, 1956); J. H. M. Beattie, *Bunyoro: An African Kingdom* (New York: Holt, Rinehart and Winston, 1960); and A. I. Richards, *East African Chiefs* (London: Faber; New York: Praeger, 1960).

Kenya is surveyed by many works, but see G. Bennett, *Kenya: A Political History* (London: Oxford University Press, 1963); and C. G. Rosberg and J. Nottingham, *The Myth of Mau Mau* (New York: Praeger; London: Pall Mall, 1966). Anthropological studies of local societies aside, histories based on oral tradition should be mentioned —B. A. Ogot, *History of the Southern Luo* (Nairobi: East African Publishing House, 1967); and G. S. Were, *A History of the Abaluyia of Western Kenya* (Nairobi: East African Publishing House, 1967). *Facing Mount Kenya* by Jomo Kenyatta (New York: Vintage, 1962) is a classic exposition of the Kikuyu point of view and may be supplemented by Kenyatta's *Suffering Without Bitterness* (Nairobi: East African Publishing House, 1968). The settler viewpoint is set forth in the works of Elspeth Huxley, among many others, but see particularly her *White Man's Country, Lord Delamere and the Making of Kenya*, 2v. (London: Macmillan, 1935; New York: Praeger, 1968).

For Tanganyika, see B. T. G. Chidzero, *Tanganyika and International Trusteeship* (London: Oxford University Press, 1961), Donald Cameron, *My Tanganyika Service and Some Nigeria* (London: Allen and Unwin, 1939), and the relevant chapters in P. Gifford and W. R. Louis, eds., *Britain and Germany in Africa* (New Haven, Conn.: Yale, 1967). For the Maji Maji revolt see J. Iliffe, "The Organization of the Maji Maji Rebellion," *The Journal of African History*, 1967, vol. VIII, no. 3. Zanzibari history leading to the political upheaval of 1964 is reviewed in M. F. Lofchie, *Zanzibar: Background to Revolution* (Princeton, N.J.: Princeton University Press, 1965). See also Iliffe's *Tanganyika Under German Rule, 1905–1912* (Cambridge: Cambridge University Press, 1969).

For Egypt and the Sudan, see John Marlowe, *Anglo-Egyptian Relations, 1800–1953* (London: The Cresset Press, 1954); Tom Little, *Egypt* (London: Ernest Benn, 1958), *Modern Egypt* (New York: Praeger, 1967); R. L. Tignor, *Modernization and British Colonial Rule in Egypt, 1882–1914* (Princeton, N.J.: Princeton University Press, 1967); P. M. Holt, *A Modern History of the Sudan*, 2nd. ed. (London: Weidenfeld and Nicolson, 1963; New York: Praeger, 1963); and K. D. D. Henderson, *Sudan Republic* (London: Ernest Benn, 1965; New York: Praeger, 1965).

18: Between Two World Wars:
Nationalist Frustrations in West Africa

WEST AFRICA AND THE FIRST WORLD WAR

Britain and France received both loyal support and material assistance from their West African colonies during the First World War. Supplies to help sustain the war economy were matched by substantial troop requisitions; indeed, more than 180,000 West Africans were recruited into the French forces during the four years of conflict. British-African soldiers fought ably in Togo and Cameroun as well as in East Africa, while French Africans were active not only in local campaigns to dislodge the Germans from their colonies, but also in Europe where many stood shoulder to shoulder with the French infantry on the western front. African troops were repeatedly cited for their bravery and effectiveness under combat conditions; beyond this, their presence in the ranks had a distinctly tonic effect on the morale of the hard-pressed Allies.

This psychological and material contribution was offered in a spirit of enthusiastic devotion to the mother country, and it was therefore not unnatural that West Africans, stimulated by the promise of Wilsonian self-determination at the war's end, began to look forward with rising expectations to the possibility of a new order which would substitute freedom for paternalism and introduce more of the benefits of modernization. It was this mood which characterized the pan-African congresses organized by the American Negro leader, W. E. B. Du Bois, which lent urgency to the program of J. E. Casely Hayford's National Congress of British West Africa, and which prompted nationalist leaders in their demands for extension of political rights, improvement of educational and public health facilities, or equality of economic opportunity between the white man and the black. Unfortunately, factors operating within the colonial powers of Europe were to render such aspirations vain. At the conclusion of hostilities, England, and particularly France, moved to strengthen and to systematize, not to weaken, their machinery of colonial government in West Africa.

THE THEORY AND PRACTICE
OF COLONIAL ADMINISTRATION

Both England and France had developed systems of colonial administration during the nineteenth century which differed markedly each from the other in their theoretical definition but which were not always so easily distinguishable in practice. French administrators had long followed techniques of colonial government based on the doctrine of assimilation, that view which held that French civilization should be shared by all people living under French rule, that those who dwelt in territories overseas were just as entitled to the exercise of full political and civil rights as were citizens of France itself. In practice this doctrine was applied only to limited portions of France's overseas holdings during the nineteenth century. In Senegal, the coastal communities were treated substantially like provincial districts of France, but in the hinterland French authority gradually extended itself primarily through force of arms, and led to a form of local government largely military in direction and nature.

Toward the end of the century, as French arms subdued larger and larger areas in Africa, colonial theorists in France became increasingly dissatisfied with the principle of assimilation. They argued that it was impossible to expect millions of people of totally different background and level of civilization to absorb the subtle qualities of French culture and to operate the democratic machinery by which Frenchmen governed themselves. They therefore proposed the alternative doctrine of association which encouraged colonial people to retain their traditional culture but which placed them in a clearly subservient position to their European masters. By the end of the war in 1918, association had become the dominant note in French colonial policy, and in West Africa a highly centralized, authoritarian regime emerged. At the apex stood the colonial ministry in Paris wherein originated all policy for the colonies. In the overseas territories were the colonial administrations, a hierarchy of officials from metropolitan France headed by a governor and charged with carrying into effect the designs of the ministry. At the bottom of the scale were the provincial, district, and village chiefs whose job it was to enforce the edicts of the administration—taxation, labor requisitions, and the maintenance of law and order. These chiefs were appointed by the colonial government which sometimes ratified the position of a traditional ruler or alternatively chose a chief arbitrarily where no appropriate indigenous authority existed. The standard of chieftaincy in the French African colonies was efficiency, not legitimacy; hence, French direct rule tended not only to be autocratic but erosive of native custom as well.

Administration in the British colonies was less responsive to any exact theory of colonization, but as with the French territories, lines of authority were tightening in the British possessions at the conclusion of the First World War. During the nineteenth century, England had administered her West African holdings in a variety of ways which reflected a characteristic pragmatism. By and large, however, colonial possessions were ruled arbitrarily by appointed governors assisted by their administrative staffs, and in the process no consistent or systematic attention was paid to the preservation or utilization of traditional customs and institutions. This lack of uniformity was checked, however, by Sir Frederick Lugard, who took charge of the Protectorate of Northern Nigeria in 1900, instituting the system of indirect rule which came to be the standard of Britain's administration in her West African colonies during the period following the First World War.

In theory, indirect rule was the antithesis of the French administration. It emphasized the maximum use of traditional law and governmental machinery, encouraging the people to continue in their traditional patterns of government, substituting only the ultimate appeal to the British crown for whatever had been the sovereign authority in the land. From the point of view of national self-determination for West Africa, however, indirect rule offered little more guarantee than did the direct administration of the French. For one thing, although indirect rule sounded superficially like virtual local autonomy, it was in fact a system whose ultimate authority clearly lay beyond the grasp of the Africans themselves. Such innovations as direct taxation, justice by administrative officers, and compulsory labor were often introduced arbitrarily to unwilling or uncomprehending African populations. Chiefs were normally chosen by their people, but their authority was known by all to reside in the British power which paid them salaries and advised them in their governmental duties through colonial administrators assigned for that purpose. Indirect rule, moreover, worked best in those areas like northern Nigeria where traditional governments most resembled European prototypes—large-scale states with a clearly defined centralized authority administering a system of direct taxation. In other regions like eastern Nigeria, with its decentralized societies and absence of chiefs, indirect rule was virtually impossible to initiate and an amended form of direct administration had to be substituted.

A second major shortcoming of indirect rule arose from the anomalous position in which it placed the growing body of educated Africans. By its nature, indirect rule emphasized the legitimacy of traditional authorities, but it was precisely the traditional chiefs who were least able to adapt themselves to the changing social and political conditions which followed the introduction of colonial rule. The small body of Africans trained in the West was best qualified to interpret the two worlds of Europe and Africa, each to the other; yet colonial administrators on the whole resisted the opportunity to make use of this source of African manpower. Partly, this was a defense of the traditional authority, but more often it emerged from a distaste for Africans capable of detecting and criticizing shortcomings in colonial administration. Educated Africans were said to lack the respect of their own people, but in fact it was the support of the colonial governments which was more often missing.

In one final respect both French and British colonial administration was antagonistic to West African nationalist aspirations after the First World War. France, emerging from the war economically prostrated, quickly rallied to the proposal put forward by the colonial minister, Albert Sarraut, for a massive exploitation of French colonies designed to rehabilitate the national economy. This latter-day mercantilism demanded a total political control, especially when it involved large-scale utilization of forced labor in the construction of major public works projects. While an analogous exploitation of the English colonies did not develop, a policy of laissez-faire in British West African trade was followed which meant in practice that economic power tended to fall into the hands of European firms. That the colonial government favored these large overseas corporations in its regulations may only have reflected administrative convenience, but the result nonetheless was a depressing effect on local West African economic enterprise.

NATIONAL POLITICS IN WEST AFRICA
BETWEEN THE TWO WORLD WARS

Colonial rule in West Africa in the years following the First World War permitted little effective political activity on the part of those Africans seeking broader economic and constitutional advantages. It was therefore a difficult era for African nationalists, an age in which the politics of accommodation with colonial governments often seemed to promise the greater reward. On the Gold Coast, for example, a decade of nationalist efforts to gain political, economic, and social reforms had led to little, whereas in Senegal local political leadership was content to develop a privileged position for a small section of the population by coming to terms with the French colonial administration. Only in Nigeria were the nationalists able to make some headway, and even there they had to be satisfied with modest achievement, while some of their countrymen more sympathetic to British rule were favored with honors and positions of responsibility in government.

It was in Senegal that the greatest shortfall developed between hopes for reform toward democratic self-determination and the crushing reaction of postwar French colonial policy. In the spring of 1914, just before the outbreak of hostilities in Europe, a remarkable event had appeared to signal the beginning of a major trend in political liberalism for French West Africa. For some years, the French had been moving to restrict the political and civil rights of the *originaires* (those Africans living in the four communes of Dakar, St. Louis, Gorée, and Rufisque), and by 1914 the French citizenship of these Senegalese had been revoked and inroads made on their voting privileges and their right to protection in French courts. The people of the Four Communes, accustomed to being treated as French citizens, had fought back for their rights and organized a small political party, the Young Senegalese, which made some modest gains in local elections. Political power in the communes, however, had always rested with the mulatto and French mercantile groups, and the Africans were not expected to be able to develop a political force of any consequence.

Fortunately for the African cause, there arrived in Senegal early in 1914 an obscure African customs official named Blaise Diagne, who had been born in Gorée many years earlier but who had lived away from his native country almost continuously throughout his adult life. Diagne returned at this time to contest the seat as representative from Senegal in the French Chamber of Deputies, a post which heretofore had always been filled either by a French or mulatto candidate. In an exciting election in which Diagne's own energetic and resourceful campaigning played an important part, he was elected Deputy, thus becoming the first African ever to fill that post.

Diagne's campaign had gone to the heart of the matter, accusing the Europeans and mulattoes of both economic and political discrimination against Africans, and pledging himself if elected to regaining the lost citizenship of his people. "The majority of the voters are black," he assured his rapt African audiences. "It is their interests which must be represented." True, his father had only been a cook, but he, Blaise Diagne, was proud to come from such humble surroundings. "Your candidate is the candidate of the people," he went on. "I am not ashamed to be a black man."

The election won, Diagne continued the assault. Hammering steadily in the public press on the subject of economic exploitation, social prejudice, and political discrimination against the Africans of the Four Communes, Diagne set a memorable example as an aggressive African capable of standing up to the European. At times he seemed obsessed by his campaign to gain respect for the black man; for example, when he almost precipitated a riot in Dakar, after taking violent offense when he discovered that a European resident had given his dog the name of Blaise. Later, during the last year of the war, he insisted on the strictest regard for protocol while traveling in West Africa on a recruitment campaign, in order that the dignity of the first African deputy might not be compromised. Most important of all, taking advantage of France's need for manpower from her colonies to fill the trenches in France, Diagne in 1916 secured a complete and unequivocal grant of French citizenship for the people of the Four Communes. "The natives of the incorporated communities of Senegal and their descendants," the law stated simply, "are and remain French citizens."

These were exciting days, not only for the citizens of the Four Communes, but for all the people of French West Africa. For the first time in the lives of many of Diagne's contemporaries, the age-old feeling of inferiority had been replaced with a sense of dignity and self-respect. What was more, Diagne did not appear ready to call a halt to his reform movement after he had regained the constitutional rights of the people of the Four Communes. Already idolized by a large following throughout the French territories of West Africa, he seemed on the verge of a fight to extend political and civil rights beyond the limited bounds of the Four Communes. In 1918 Diagne recruited over sixty thousand West Africans for the French army, and he was on public record as favoring the enlargement of the franchise to include those West Africans who had fought for the mother country in her needy hour. Moreover, he appeared capable of carrying out such a reform. A clever political tactician, he had quickly consolidated his position at the expense of the old conservative oligarchy in the Four Communes, and in 1919 was re-elected deputy. As the war ended, he was conspicuous in his support of a move by the colonial ministry to grant the privilege of municipal incorporation to a number of communities beyond the Four Communes, and at the same time he called for the extension to West Africa of labor legislation already in force in metropolitan France guaranteeing improved working conditions, greater leisure time, and the use of arbitration in industrial disputes.

In the years that followed, Diagne's proposals somehow never progressed beyond the talking stage. The plan for the extension of incorporated municipalities was dropped during the reaction of French postwar colonial policy, and in 1920 the old colonial General Council was replaced with Diagne's blessing by a Colonial Council, ostensibly more democratic but actually designed to give the administration a tighter control over colonial affairs. Throughout French West Africa, forced labor for public and private use was thrust on an indigenous population unable to defend its position in the face of the *indigénat,* the system of administrative justice which dealt arbitrarily with minor offenses and screened the African from the protection of French courts.

This was the situation which developed during the 1920's for the approximately fourteen million inhabitants of French West Africa. Classed as French subjects under the policy of association, these people had virtually no political or civil rights, and were represented only in the colonial council by chiefs whose own offices rested squarely on the sanction of the colonial administration. In the Four Communes, some fifty thousand citizens protected by Diagne's law, represented an island of privilege, and it soon became apparent that Diagne and his party had become disinterested in the needs of any outside this small group. In 1923 Diagne reportedly reached an agreement with the merchants of Bordeaux who had long held a major interest in the West African trade. Under this arrangement, the deputy received the support of Bordeaux for his political activities, in return for which he agreed not to interfere with Bordeaux's economic prerogatives in Senegal. Thereafter, though Diagne gave occasional lip service to a more liberal colonial policy—greater representation for West African territories in the French parliament, for example—most of his eloquence was utilized in eulogizing the French colonial system. In 1930 when France needed a defender of her colonial labor program at the conference on forced labor held by the International Labor Organization in Geneva, it is significant that she turned unhesitatingly to Blaise Diagne.

The changing attitude of the Diagne party in the postwar years brought a natural disillusion to many of its early followers who felt that their cause had been deserted by a political opportunist ready to exchange independence for the honors and perquisites of public office. In 1928, and again in 1932, Diagne's long-time lieutenant, Galandou Diouf, ran against his former chief, but the Diagne machine was too strong, the deputy was returned in both instances, and Diouf did not finally gain the parliamentary seat until 1934 after Diagne's death. On the face of it, the charge against Diagne of opportunistic capitulation to pressures from France appeared only too well substantiated, but in a deeper sense the problem was more complex. Diagne was a product of French assimilation and like most Africans educated by France, he had become thoroughly committed to a belief in the superiority of French civilization and the ultimate necessity for African absorption into the French way of life. For him, association was an interim state which would be followed in time by true assimilation. Ultimately, he was certain, there could never be any distinction between metropolitan and overseas France. "I belong to those," he once told a cheering Chamber of Deputies, "who believe that France's traditional posture . . . can only find its resolution in unity . . . of the spirit between France and the peoples or races scattered across her overseas territories." To Diagne there was much to be said for the policy of teaching young Africans about "our ancestors the Gauls."

One reason that Diagne's political opponents enjoyed so little success during his lifetime was that they were in essential agreement with his politics and philosophy, and consequently represented no basic change from his program. When Galandou Diouf had opposed Diagne, Diouf was accused of communist affiliation, Diagne of being an imperialist agent. Once Diouf succeeded to the position of deputy he became the established symbol of colonial rule and another opposition arose with the taint of radicalism.

Diouf's most successful opposition came from Lamine Guèye who during the twenties had been variously the ally and the foe of Diagne and of Diouf in the shifting pattern of local politics. When Diouf became deputy, Guèye moved into steady opposition, seemingly justifying the charge of radicalism leveled at him by aligning his local following with the French Popular Front from 1936 onward. This was no true reflection of leftist sentiments, however, for Guèye's party, like those of Diagne and Diouf, consisted of privileged African citizens, not of workers or peasants. To be sure, Guèye's Popular Front connections did prompt him to demand an extension of French citizenship beyond the Four Communes, a view which Diagne himself had once held. More significant, however, Guèye was at one with Diagne, Diouf, and other political leaders in the view that the future for Africa lay in assimilation into French culture. To a great extent the reactionary development of French colonial policy between the two World Wars was the result of policies determined in Paris. In some measure, however, its success was also caused by the deference to the basic principles of French colonialism accorded by the West African political leaders of the day.

In the British West African territories, the system of indirect rule was applied in differing degrees to suit local circumstances and the convictions of individual colonial governors. The result was a variety of administrations less rigorous and exploitative than those of the French, but essentially paternalistic in philosophy and resistant to local African movements for a greater share in the economic and political activities of the colonies.

In tiny Gambia, for example, the legislative council, first constituted in 1843 to advise the governor, contained only two Africans, both nominated by the administration from the port of Bathurst. It was not until 1932 that the people of the Protectorate hinterland were given any representation when provision was made to add a British Protectorate commissioner to the council.

In Sierra Leone, a legislative council had existed since the mid-nineteenth century, and Freetown had been a largely self-governing municipality since 1893 when the distinguished African barrister, Sir Samuel Lewis, had persuaded the government to create an elected municipal council with taxing authority, Lewis serving as the first mayor of Freetown. The experiment was no great success, however. As mayor, Lewis had labored diligently to instill in his creole neighbors both a sense of administrative responsibility and a willingness to submit to tax assessment for rating purposes, but to no avail. Few valued the franchise as something worth being taxed for, and in 1926, after a generation of inept and occasionally corrupt administration, the experiment in municipal self-government was discontinued by the authorities.

Representative government in the Colony and Protectorate fared better, and in 1924 the legislative council was enlarged to give greater African representation. Provision was made for eleven official and ten unofficial members, three of the latter elected by voters within the Colony possessing appropriate property and literacy qualifications. Of the remaining seven—all nominated by the governor—two were always Africans from the Colony, two representatives of the commercial interests, and three were paramount chiefs drawn from the three provinces of the Protectorate.

It was in Nigeria, where Lugard's system of indirect rule had originated, that the greatest opposition to British colonial practice developed, an opposition which was a combination of resistance by traditional authorities and an effort of educated Africans to introduce principles of democratic, representative government which they claimed were in the best traditions both of indigenous society and of their colonial masters. The opposition of traditional authorities was to a considerable extent a carry-over from the days of nineteenth-century independence when local rulers like Nana, the Itsekiri leader, or the emir of Kontagora, had unsuccessfully held out against the imposition of British protectorates. In 1918 the Egba people of Abeokuta had rioted and in 1929 there was an outbreak of violence among the market women in the Aba district of eastern Nigeria, both disturbances essentially protests against unfamiliar administrative practices imposed from above as part of the ostensibly indirect system of British rule.

The most persistent and effective reaction to the colonial administration came, however, from the educated classes located largely in Lagos. Their disaffection was complex and to a degree contradictory. In the first place, they were offended by the attitude of British officials, missionaries, and traders who introduced Western social and cultural standards, and then ridiculed African attempts to emulate the European. Further, they wished to introduce political reforms based on British democratic traditions and resented any efforts to impose arbitrary colonial rule. Finally, although they disliked indirect rule by indigenous authorities, they were troubled by the deteriorating effect which colonial government was having on traditional institutions.

During the years of the First World War, these Lagos nationalists had carried on an unrelieved campaign of opposition to the administration of Sir Frederick Lugard. Lugard's system of judiciary by administrative officers was for them no more than an inefficient tyranny, his policy of indirect rule a deception behind which British district commissioners might operate without hindrance, and the amalgamation of northern and southern Nigeria effected in 1914 but a device for the extension of military rule to the south where constitutional government had once reigned. When Lugard left Nigeria in 1918, the sense of relief among the nationalists was unrestrained, their attitude summed up by Thomas H. Jackson, editor of the *Lagos Weekly Record* and one of their leading spokesmen. "For six long years," Jackson complained, "we have lived under the cramped condition of military dictatorship when the law from being a means of protection had become an instrument of crime and oppression. . . . The last administration has made the very name of the white man stink in the nostrils of the native."

Such strong feelings reflected years of frustration, a frustration illustrated by the chronic dispute between the people of Lagos and the government over the king, or *eleko*, of Lagos. Lagos had been annexed in 1861 under a treaty with Docemo, the then-reigning *eleko,* wherein Docemo was given an annual stipend, but no provision was made for his heirs despite the fact that the sovereignty of the House of Docemo had been relinquished in perpetuity while the royal line continued to function as the traditional authority of the people of the city. The grievances of the Lagos nationalists came to be focused in this *eleko* issue and were pressed upon the administration by Herbert Macaulay, a civil engineer whose talents as a public speaker and polemic writer had made him the leading figure among the nationalists by the end of the First World War.

Macaulay and his followers had vainly urged Lugard to provide an adequate stipend to sustain the *eleko,* but instead the government had finally deposed the king and installed another candidate, accusing the *eleko* of having joined the Macaulay party to embarrass the authorities. This was in 1920, and from that point forward the *eleko* issue became an obsession to Macaulay and a major source of embarrassment for the administration. The Macaulay party circulated a petition for the reinstatement of the original incumbent, and, backed by public opinion in Lagos, continued to regard the "destoolment" (dethronement) as unconstitutional. Both Macaulay and Jackson carried on an incessant editorial campaign over the years against the colonial government, Macaulay's denunciations in 1928 gaining him conviction for criminal libel and a short prison term. Finally in 1933, under a more benevolent administration of Governor Sir Donald Cameron, recently arrived from Tanganyika, the *eleko* controversy was settled when the government agreed to the restoration of the popular claimant. It was a small victory in the sense that the position of *eleko* had long since become largely ceremonial. Viewed from another perspective, however, it showed the strength of a determined and resourceful African leadership, as well as the virility of traditional customs in the face of the forces of external change.

In part the *eleko* controversy reflected deep differences, not only between Nigerians and British, but between different groups within Lagos itself. Macaulay represented one extreme, a West African version of twisting the British lion's tail. Many educated Africans were out of sympathy with such undignified conduct, however. For them, British rule represented a major step forward and upward, and they regarded progress in West Africa in terms of how quickly Nigerians could absorb and utilize the best aspects of Western civilization. Theirs was a view not dissimilar from the assimilation theories put forward by French colonialists and embraced by Senegalese leaders like Blaise Diagne and Lamine Guèye. In Lagos this assimilationist position was typified by such respected members of the community as the eminent barrister, C. A. Sapara Williams, Dr. John Randle, the physician and political figure, Sir Kitoyi Ajasa, who founded the *Nigerian Pioneer* in 1914 to defend the policies of his friend Lugard, and the educator and public servant, Henry Carr.

Henry Carr had also been in the thick of the *eleko* fight, but on the opposite side from Macaulay, for Lugard had made Carr Resident of the Colony in 1918 and in this office he was obliged to defend the government's position. Not that Carr was reluctant to do so, for he was thoroughly unsympathetic with the views of the Macaulay party. To conservatives like Carr, the position of *eleko* was an anachronism which, having lost its original function, could only serve the antisocial purposes of attracting dissident groups within the community, providing them the opportunity to plot mischief within the *eleko's* compound. Encouraging such a weakened institution could only invite trouble, Carr insisted. It was better that the sons of the House of Docemo be given a sound Western education so that they might qualify to serve their people anew, not as faltering relics of a dead past but as well-integrated African members of a new Afro-European civilization. Such assimilationist ideas may have appealed to the authorities, but they were unequivocally rejected by most of the people of Lagos who preferred the more exciting approach of Macaulay and his followers.

One event which stimulated the Macaulayites and lent them a measure of success for a time was the constitutional change in 1922 which provided for the popular election of one member from Calabar and three from Lagos to a new and larger legislative council. This reform precipitated a flurry of political activity led by Macaulay and Jackson who founded the Nigerian National Democratic Party and placed three candidates before the Lagos electorate in 1923. Macaulay was ineligible for office, having been imprisoned over a misuse of trust funds ten years earlier, but his popularity proved transferable and his hand-picked candidates won the quinquennial elections for Lagos without difficulty between 1923 and 1938.

As it happened, winning three seats on a council of forty-six of which twenty-seven were government officials offered more electioneering excitement than actual political power as Macaulay and his Democratic Party soon discovered. In the first flush of enthusiasm, the Lagos members pledged themselves to cooperation and constructive criticism of official policy, but gradually their optimism was replaced with disillusionment. It became clear that the official majority on the legislative council was not to be influenced by unofficial opinion, and the elected representatives soon found themselves venting their frustration through exhaustive but fruitless questions in the council regarding governmental policy. Public interest in the elections gradually declined, and the work of the unofficial members became a sterile exercise in voicing their dissatisfaction with legislation which was forced upon them by the council's overwhelming official majority. This official majority, reported Dr. C. C. Adeniyi Jones, Macaulay's party colleague and long-time council member, "has practically reduced the unofficial members, especially the elected members, to the role of mere recording instruments of official sweet will."

In 1938 the Macaulay monopoly over the legislative council elections was broken by the Nigerian Youth Movement which signaled the beginning of a newer, more militant brand of nationalist politics. At the same time there returned to Nigeria Nnamdi Azikiwe, who soon added his journalistic dynamism to the new nationalism. Thus, on the eve of the Second World War, Nigerians were looking forward to nationalist politics well beyond the parochialism of the Herbert Macaulay era. But this was a development which was not to have consequence until the postwar period.

On the Gold Coast a similar set of circumstances was creating a somewhat analogous group of frustrations. Historically, the Gold Coast had been the first home of a West African independence movement, reflected by the Fante Confederation and the writings of Africanus Horton. Through the closing years of the nineteenth century and up to the beginning of the First World War, the Gold Coast educated elite had been especially active in pointing out their traditional constitutional and historical rights to a colonial administration then tightening its grip on the reins of government.

Influenced partly by Lugard's theory of indirect rule and partly by past experience, the Gold Coast governors of the war years and immediately thereafter followed the general British pattern in West Africa and sought to strengthen the chiefly authorities. In 1916 the legislative council was substantially enlarged, the most notable additions being three educated representatives of the coastal cities and three paramount chiefs to speak for the provinces, all to be nominated by the governor. In 1925 another constitution brought further changes. The urban representatives remained fixed at three and would henceforth be elected by manhood suffrage based on a property qualification. However, the number of chiefs was doubled, the six representatives to be elected by newly formed Provincial Councils made up of the leading traditional authorities.

Two years later, a Native Administration Ordinance gave the provincial councils specified administrative and judicial functions in a further effort to secure the power of the chiefs. British official policy at the time was based on the conviction that West African societies were evolving toward modern civilization only very slowly, and that until a greater degree of Westernization had been achieved, it was necessary to maintain the authority and integrity of the native authorities in order to prevent social disintegration.

Such a view was totally unpalatable to the educated classes in the Gold Coast, who had long fought to preserve traditional practice and authority but who felt increasingly that they were entitled to share in such local government as there was, first, because they represented a segment of the population of growing importance and, second, because they saw themselves as the most effective link between the old world of traditional Africa and the new world of Europe. By the close of the First World War most of the old leaders had disappeared from view, men like John Mensah Sarbah, James H. Brew, or T. Hutton Mills, but one of their most important spokesmen was more active and influential than ever. In J. E. Casely Hayford, the Cape Coast barrister and journalist, the Gold Coast African had a champion of long experience both in defending the virility of traditional institutions, and in arguing the qualifications for leadership of the educated classes.

If Casely Hayford's prewar exertions had concentrated on explaining the importance of traditional government to British administrators often too prone to discount the importance of native institutions, his postwar activities within the Gold Coast were devoted to checking the excessive growth of the chiefly authority encouraged by the British doctrine of indirect rule. At the root of the controversy lay a struggle for power between the leaders of the old Africa and those of the new. The chiefs felt their authority slipping away from them in the face of a Western intrusion which challenged them both in the form of a European administration and a Westernized African elite. The educated Africans, willing to protect the traditional authorities against the erosion of British government, were no longer content to submit to the dictates of unlettered chiefs. When the colonial administration attempted to strengthen the chiefs, therefore, a split developed within the Gold Coast between the chiefs and the elite.

The chiefly position was ably argued by Nana Ofori Atta, paramount chief of Akim Abuakwa and one of the representatives of the native authority appointed to the legislative council under the changes of 1916. Ofori Atta questioned the right of educated Africans to speak for the people. The chiefs, he insisted, were the rightful leaders in the land, and as long as they remained on their stools they were the appropriate medium through which local government should be conducted. Casely Hayford took a contrary view. According to tradition, he pointed out, chiefs were not the voice of their people; indeed, they were specifically denied this function which could either be expressed informally by any member of the community or officially by a specially chosen spokesman or linguist.

Beyond this, continued Casely Hayford, it was the educated African who was becoming a natural leader in a modern, changing world, for it was he who understood the Westerner and it was he whose literacy made him best qualified to deal with the alien presence in the land. "The educated class represents substantially the intelligentsia and advanced thought of British West Africa," he stated before the legislative council. "It also represents the bulk of the inhabitants of the various indigenous communities and with them claims, as sons of the soil, the inherent right to make representations as to extinguishing disabilities, and to submit recommendations for . . . necessary reforms."

Such logic failed to impress the administration which continued to support the role of the traditional authorities, much to the distress of the educated groups. The constitutional and administrative changes of 1925 and 1927 were received with extreme distaste by the elite who at first boycotted the new constitution and refused to cooperate in the choice of a legislative council. The progressive coastal cities were being discriminated against, they argued, and the chiefs encouraged beyond their capacity and their right to govern. It was nothing but an attempt to divide and rule. "That is no franchise at all," Casely Hayford cried out in protest. "It is a mockery. It is a sham, a humbug." Yet it was also a reality which the educated community eventually was forced to recognize.

Casely Hayford finally made his peace and stood successfully for election to the legislative council in 1927, pointing out the possibilities which lay before the educated African if he chose to exert his influence as an adviser to the chiefs. Others like J. B. Danquah, a younger brother of Ofori Atta and future head of the United Gold Coast Convention, agreed, observing that the real power in the Gold Coast was, after all, the British government which had to be endured in the form it chose to assume. A basic instability had been established, however, for the administration was attempting to rule indirectly through a traditional authority that no longer could sustain itself in the face of changing conditions and new forms of African leadership. The results of these uncertainties were to become manifest in the changing politics of the period following the Second World War.

THE NATIONAL CONGRESS OF BRITISH WEST AFRICA

During the period between the two World Wars, Casely Hayford was to a large extent preoccupied with a movement which went beyond the limited question of national politics within the Gold Coast. For many years he had come to regard international cooperation among Africans as the most effective means to the achievement of greater self-determination by the peoples of West Africa; hence, when democratic ideas at the end of the First World War stimulated nationalist aspirations in Africa, Casely Hayford saw his opportunity to translate his long-standing plans into actuality. Unity in thought, in aspiration, and in objective could best be served through unity in action, through a united West Africa. True patriotic love of country was love of mankind, he said. "I venture to commend . . . the coming together of entire West Africa as one man to think together, and to act together in matters of common need."

Following this conviction, Casely Hayford led a group of educated Africans in organizing a conference of West African leaders drawn from the Gambia, Sierra Leone, Nigeria, and the Gold Coast to be held in Accra in 1920. The conference was based on three major premises—that the educated African had become the natural leader of his people, that Wilsonian self-determination was a proper basis for political, economic, and social reform in British West Africa, and that community of interest would henceforth lead West Africans to work in close concert in achieving their mutual objectives.

These objectives proved to be many and various as they took shape through the resolutions of the conference. Constitutional reform was demanded in terms of municipal self-government, the end of courts presided over by British administrative officers, popular election of half the membership of the legislative councils, and the creation of special houses of assembly, containing popularly elected majorities, which would be responsible for colonial taxation and budget policy. Equality of opportunity between European and African was stressed in civil service, medical service, and judicial appointments. Similarly, there was urged the end of economic discrimination against Africans in favor of European business interests, especially in connection with indigenous land ownership and the right to sell or lease land without interference by the government. Further, it was argued that more efficient self-government might be fostered through a strengthened African press and particularly through more extensive, improved education capped by a West African university. Finally, the idea of national self-determination was given a special African relevance in the demand that no disposition of the former German colonies be made without reference to the wishes of the people of the territories involved.

As the conference concluded its work, it formed a permanent National Congress of British West Africa and subsequent meetings were held at Freetown in 1923, in Bathurst in 1925–1926, and at Lagos in 1929–1930. Much the same demands were put forward at these later conferences, an indication of the lack of practical success of the Congress' demands. Casely Hayford claimed that the Congress had been responsible for the legislative council reforms of the 1920's and for the founding of Achimota College in the Gold Coast, but beyond these questionable claims there was little concrete progress to show.

The fact was, the National Congress had been founded well ahead of its time. Not only did it get a cool reception from colonial administrations suspicious of a movement which challenged their authority and questioned their competence, but it never was able to capture the united backing of all indigenous groups within West Africa itself. In the Gold Coast, many chiefs were unsympathetic to a movement made up of educated Africans, whereas political divisions within the educated community of Nigeria robbed the Congress of effective support in that country. Moreover, the Congress never made clear its determination to speak for all the people. Its rallying cry that "taxation goes with effective representation," had a deceptively authentic ring, but what it seemed to mean in practice was that the rate-paying educated Africans wanted effective political control of the machinery of government they felt they were supporting through their taxes, and there was little indication of their genuine interest in true popular government. Be that as it may, political reform in British West Africa was not to be found in an interterritorial congress movement during the period between the two World Wars. When Casely Hayford died in 1930, the National Congress lost its chief supporter, and it too soon expired.

THE PAN-AFRICAN MOVEMENT

The National Congress of British West Africa had sought to secure greater economic, political, and social privileges for the people of the British West African territories. Nevertheless, it was also part of a larger movement for unity among members of the black race the world over, and it attempted as an organization made up of native Africans to give world leadership to this pan-African movement. Actually the Congress did little in a practical way to assume such leadership, although Casely Hayford, particularly through his journal the *Gold Coast Leader*, gave enthusiastic applause to evidence of Negro solidarity in various parts of the world, and laid claims for Africa as natural leader of worldwide pan-Africanism. His argument was simply one of antecedents. The black man originated in Africa, and it was to Africa that he might appropriately turn for refreshment and inspiration. Under African leadership, Casely Hayford argued, the Negro race could harness the discoveries of science, throw off the yoke of oppression, and eventually employ the Negro's elevated sense of right and wrong to assume moral leadership in a sick and materialist world.

As it happened, the guiding hand for a nascent pan-African movement came in another form from another source. First, there was the abiding interest in Africa maintained by New World Negroes throughout the nineteenth and into the twentieth century. For those burdened with slavery and the subsequent inequities of segregation and discrimination, Africa was a continuing source of inspiration for racial accomplishment and solidarity as well as a destination for emigration schemes put forward occasionally within the American Negro community. Next, the idea of racial solidarity transcending continental limitations was given specific manifestation in the first pan-African conference convened in London in 1900 by the West Indian barrister, Henry Sylvester Williams. This meeting, called to protest colonial rule in Africa, was attended by Negroes largely from the West Indies and the United States, but it gave concrete definition to the idea of black unity, for the first time expressed through the technique of a pan-African congress.

Finally, pan-Africanism reached full dimension in 1919 when W. E. B. Du Bois organized a pan-African congress in Paris coincident with the Versailles peace conference. Du Bois' objective was simple and clear—to seize the opportunity presented by the assembled delegates from the powers of Europe in order to demonstrate the solidarity of the black race, and to lay claim to the importance of Africa in the postwar world. Resolutions were passed calling on the great powers to establish codes of law, to be enforced by the League of Nations, which would protect the racial, economic, and political interests of Africans.

These were utopian hopes quite out of touch with the realities of postwar colonial policy in Africa. Indeed, Du Bois was fortunate to be able to gain permission from the French government to hold his conference at all, since martial law was still in force in France. He succeeded only because of Blaise Diagne's intercession with the French premier, Georges Clemenceau; yet, despite this modest beginning, Du Bois was pleased with the results. The conference had asked specifically that the German colonies be turned over to an international body rather than to various colonial powers, and in this suggestion Du Bois saw the germ of what came to be the mandates commission of the League of Nations.

Two years later in 1921, Du Bois brought together another, more ambitiously conceived pan-African conference which met in London, Brussels, and Paris with larger representation, particularly from Africa itself. This time, however, Europe was much less receptive. When a resolution criticizing the Belgian colonial regime was passed, there was sharp reaction in Brussels and an innocuous substitute was proposed and declared passed despite what Du Bois described as a clear majority in favor of the original version. This parliamentary maneuver was the work of Blaise Diagne who was acting as presiding officer at the time and who had now become a critic of Du Bois' pan-African movement. The second congress had taken as its theme the idea of racial equality as a basis for eventual self-government in Africa. Diagne declared himself opposed to any implied criticism of France's colonial policy, and succeeded in adding to the final resolutions of the conference a statement citing what Diagne regarded as the liberalism of France in dealing with her colonies.

Diagne claimed that Du Bois had become a dangerous and misguided man whose internationalist, bolshevist tendencies were obscuring the benefits which European powers had brought to their colonial peoples. Diagne had supported the first conference because he thought he saw an opportunity for Africans in the French colonies to educate their American brothers by comparing France's liberalism with the repressive measures used in the United States against American Negroes. The continued radicalism of the Du Bois contingent had made this difficult, said Diagne, although he felt that he had succeeded in some measure in forcing Du Bois to abandon his extremely critical stand on colonialism. For the assimilated Diagne, the only true cooperation in Africa was that between white and black. "To isolate the black race," he wrote, "and to let it work out its own evolution is ridiculous. . . . The evolution of our race . . . requires the cooperation of everybody."

This rebuff to American Negro pan-African aspirations was later underscored by the exchange which Diagne carried on with Marcus Garvey who had attempted to enlist Diagne's support for Garvey's pan-Negro movement with its strong criticism of European colonialism and its expressed purpose of creating a Negro empire in Africa. Once again Diagne cited the persecution of the American Negro in contrast to the African under French rule. Improvement in the conditions of Negroes living in America, said Diagne, could never come by preaching revolution, but only through emulation of the example in the French colonial territories of peaceful, progressive government. "We Frenchmen of Africa wish to remain French," he concluded, "for France has given us every liberty and accepted us without reservation along with her European children. None of us aspires to see French Africa delivered exclusively to the Africans as is demanded, though without any authority, by the American Negroes," at the head of whom Garvey had arbitrarily placed himself.

As with other efforts to effect social, economic, and political reform for Negroes during the interwar period, pan-Africanism eventually fell on hard times. Garvey's back-to-Africa movement collapsed in 1925 when he was convicted of fraud and finally deported by the United States to his native Jamaica. Meanwhile, the pan-African conferences of W. E. B. Du Bois continued to meet intermittently, without great achievement. A third convened in London and Lisbon in 1923 and another in New York in 1927, but neither of these had much success in terms of Negro solidarity or social progress for the black race. The London-Lisbon meeting was marred by the split in the Negro world occasioned by the Garvey movement and by the continued opposition of the colonial powers. The New York congress, which was sponsored by American Negro women's organizations, dealt largely with questions of social welfare in Africa but had little direct African representation. In 1929 a fifth congress had to be cancelled because of the economic crisis in the United States. It was not until the end of the Second World War that this fifth congress was finally held, by which time the course of world events had put an entirely new complexion on the pan-African movement and the nationalist aspirations of Africa's people.

LIBERIA AND AFRICAN NATIONALISM

The pan-African movement during the years after the First World War became involved with the affairs of the Republic of Liberia, pursuing her uncertain existence as the only independent Negro nation in West Africa. At his first pan-African congress, W. E. B. Du Bois had suggested an internationalized Africa formed of the former German colonies, to which could subsequently be added sections of Portuguese Africa and the Belgian Congo. Marcus Garvey had also talked of an independent African empire, and then had negotiated specifically with the Liberian government for a grant of land to accommodate his African colonization movement. Liberia was initially cordial to the idea which called for the repatriation of between twenty and thirty thousand Negro families from the Americas, each representing a worth of $1500, the whole operation to be financed by Garvey's Universal Negro Improvement Association to the extent of $2,000,000. The suspicion soon arose within the Liberian government, however, that Garvey might be conspiring to unseat the True Whigs who had long been the reigning party within the country; what was more, the Liberians seemingly were warned by neighboring colonial powers that there could be no toleration of an organization within Liberia which admittedly was working to overthrow European authority in Africa. In 1924, therefore, the Liberian pledge was rescinded in a move which was shortly followed by the general collapse of the Garvey movement.

Marcus Garvey was among the least of Liberia's troubles, however. After three-quarters of a century of independence, the country was still beset by the same problems that had long complicated healthy national growth—an inefficient, arbitrary, and often corrupt government, chronic insolvency resulting from an impoverished economy linked with administrative laxness, an uncertain national sovereignty threatened by European colonial expansionism, and a repressive native policy which maintained insecure but tyrannical control over the tribal areas. Politically, the country had continued under the domination of the descendants of the original Negro settlers from America who, by the conclusion of the First World War, numbered about twelve thousand against an indigenous population of perhaps as much as one million. Among the settlers, the True Whig Party formed an oligarchy, which not only denied the indigenous peoples any meaningful political representation or self-expression, but presented the Americo-Liberians with a bureaucratic regime perpetuated through such devices as election irregularities, political patronage, censorship, and arbitrary presidential rule.

Much of Liberia's trouble was financial. Inadequate and badly administered revenue policies had led to foreign loans in 1871, 1906, and 1912, negotiated on unfavorable terms which increased the country's debt burden and invited the possibility of intervention by creditor nations. In 1920 an American loan was tentatively arranged, but no final agreement was forthcoming, failure resulting in large measure from a lack of enthusiasm both in Liberia and in the United States. Nevertheless, the initial interest of the American government at least forestalled intervention by European powers, while the final breakdown in negotiations in 1922 forced Liberia into certain financial reforms at home. New tariffs and domestic taxes were imposed and methods of collection given a thorough overhaul. By 1925, revenue was almost three times that of 1918, and there was even a small budgetary surplus.

The basic problem of economic development remained, however, along with the need to liquidate expensive foreign loans. During the 1920's these pressures combined with a search by American industry for sources of natural rubber, and all these factors led ultimately to the conclusion of the well-known Firestone agreements of 1926-1927. With encouragement from the United States government, the American industrialist, Harvey S. Firestone, negotiated a series of concessions which enabled the Firestone interests to obtain ninety-nine year leasing rights to tracts totalling one million acres for development as rubber plantations. In return, Firestone paid rental fees and certain customs duties and agreed to construct harbor facilities at Monrovia. The total investment was protected by a controversial $5 million loan which funded previous Liberian foreign indebtedness, but at advanced interest rates, and in effect introduced American control over the collection of revenue in Liberia. Thus Liberia traded a loss of authority concerning national affairs for increased income from taxes and rentals, a measure of protection against potential intervention by neighboring colonial powers, and a general economic upturn based upon the introduction of American capital and organizational efficiency.

In fact, the Firestone connection did much to pioneer economic development, although initial miscalculations by Firestone over the availability of an adequate supply of workers raised the delicate question of compulsory labor such as was commonly practiced under the concession systems in the French and Belgian Congo and elsewhere. As it happened, in 1929 Liberia was accused by the United States of condoning a regimen of forced labor tantamount to slavery, and the following year an International Commission of Inquiry appointed by the League of Nations was invited to investigate. Although Firestone was shown to employ only voluntary labor, a number of prominent Liberian officials were charged in the Commission's report with conducting a system of compulsory labor "hardly distinguishable" from true slavery. The findings forced the resignation of highly placed government officers, including President Charles King, brought legislation designed to correct the abuses in question, and almost led to the imposition of a foreign protectorate under League of Nations auspices.

Aside from the reforms, which outlawed slavery, pawning, and the export of contract labor, international intervention was forestalled largely by Liberian determination to direct its own affairs. At the same time, administration of the hinterland continued substantially unchanged in its long-standing authoritarianism designed to maintain the ascendancy of the American-Liberians. Settler domination was assisted by the ignorance and isolation of the indigenous population hampered by a poor transportation and communications network and a rate of illiteracy exceeding 90 per cent. Nonetheless, other, more direct, means remained in effect.

Beginning in the first years of the twentieth century, a system of government through local rulers had been instituted which not only reduced the costs of administration but kept the interior divided and isolated along tribal lines. In addition there were hut taxes, labor requisitions for public works, and control of residence and population movements all imposed through recourse to military force. When necessary, moreover, there was no hesitation to reshape traditional institutions to suit official convenience, and to all these repressive measures was added an informal exploitation in the form of such tactics as unauthorized taxes, crop seizures, and illegal forced labor. All in all, the generally harsh and arbitrary policy induced a response of "sullen restless fury" punctuated by bloody outbreaks of violence.

With the inauguration of William V. S. Tubman as president in 1944, a fundamentally new approach was introduced in the form of Tubman's Unification Policy. The underlying philosophy of this approach was directed toward giving the traditional societies a sense of genuine participation in national life in place of their former exploitation. Extended suffrage and parliamentary representation, introduction of programs for health, education, and public works into the hinterland, guarantees against alienation of tribal lands, improvement of the professional quality of the interior administration, and a campaign to promote appreciation of traditional culture all combined to reduce the old animosities to the vanishing point. Thus, as the tide of African nationalism flooded in the years following the Second World War, Americo-Liberians were able to take the lead as patriots within their own country, avoiding the forces which, for example, relegated the creoles in Sierra Leone to a subsidiary role in national politics. For, despite the many changes which introduced vast social, economic, and political improvements for the indigenous people of Liberia, it was the settler minority which remained firmly in control of the sources of power and wealth as the era of African independence dawned.

Suggestions for Further Reading

Both British and French colonial policy is discussed in detail in
R. L. Buell, *The Native Problem in Africa*, 2v. (London: Frank Cass,
1965; Hamden, Conn.: Shoe String Press, 1965). British administration is
analyzed in Margery Perham, *Native Administration in Nigeria* (London:
Oxford University Press, 1937), and David Kimble, *A Political History of
Ghana* (Oxford: Clarendon Press, 1963; New York: Oxford University
Press, 1963). For the ideas on colonial administration of Lord Lugard see
Margery Perham, *Lugard: The Years of Authority* (London: Collins, 1960),
and Lugard's own *Dual Mandate in British Tropical Africa*, 5th ed. (London: Frank Cass; Hamden, Conn.: Shoe String Press, 1965). French policy
is set forth in S. H. Roberts, *History of French Colonial Policy*, 1870-1925
(London: Frank Cass, 1963), R. Delavignette, *Freedom and Authority in
French West Africa* (London: Oxford University Press, 1950 and Frank
Cass, 1968), and Michael Crowder, *Senegal, A Study in French Assimilation Policy*, rev. ed. (London: Methuen, 1967; New York: Barnes &
Noble, 1967).

National politics, covering both British and French West African
territories, are discussed particularly in terms of the ideas of nationalist
leadership in R. W. July, *The Origins of Modern African Thought* (London: Faber, 1968; New York: Praeger, 1967). There is also much material in Raymond L. Buell, *The Native Problem in Africa*, cited above.
Pre-World War II French West African politics are studied briefly in
R. S. Morgenthau, *Political Parties in French-Speaking West Africa* (Oxford: Clarendon Press, 1964). The standard history of the Gambia is still
J. M. Gray, *A History of the Gambia* (London: Frank Cass and New
York: Barnes & Noble, 1966) which may be supplemented by Harry A.
Gailey, *A History of the Gambia* (London: Routledge and Kegan Paul,
1964; New York: Praeger, 1965). For the Gold Coast see David Kimble,
A Political History of Ghana, cited above. Nigeria is covered by M. Crowder, *The Story of Nigeria*, rev. ed. (London: Faber, 1966), the American
edition, *A Short History of Nigeria* (New York: Praeger, 1966); J. Coleman, *Nigeria, Background to Nationalism* (Berkeley, California: University
of California Press, 1958); and T. N. Tamuno, *Nigeria and Elective Representation, 1923–1947* (London: Heinemann, 1966; New York: Humanities Press, 1966). Some of the flavor of West African nationalist thought
may be obtained from the writings of nationalist leaders; for example,
J. E. Casely Hayford, *Ethiopia Unbound* (London: C. M. Phillips, 1911);
Herbert Macaulay, *Justitia Fiat* (London, 1921); and Henry Carr, *Special
Report on the Schools of Southern Nigeria* (Old Calabar: Government
Press, 1900).

July, Coleman, Buell, and particularly Kimble discuss the National

Congress of British West Africa. See also Magnus J. Sampson, ed., *West African Leadership* (Ilfracombe, England: A. H. Stockwell, 1949).

The role of Blaise Diagne at the pan-African congresses after the First World War is discussed in July, but see also George Padmore, *Pan Africanism or Communism* (London: Dobson, 1956); W. E. B. Du Bois, *The World and Africa* (New York: Viking Press, 1947); and C. Legum, *Pan-Africanism,* rev. ed. (London: Pall Mall, 1965; New York: Praeger, 1965). For Diagne and the election of 1914, see G. W. Johnson, "The Ascendancy of Blaise Diagne and the Beginning of African Politics in Senegal," *Africa,* vol. XXXVI, No. 3, July, 1966.

On Liberia, Buell's *Native Problem* is full for the period he discusses, but his *Liberia: A Century of Survival, 1847–1947* (Philadelphia: University of Pennsylvania Press, 1947) is more up to date, as is the chapter on Liberia by J. G. Liebenow in G. Carter, ed., *African One-Party States* (Ithaca, New York: Cornell University Press, 1962). See also Liebenow's *Liberia: The Evolution of Privilege* (Ithaca, New York: Cornell University Press, 1969).

19: In the Heart of Darkness

THE BELGIAN CONGO

The Congo Independent State was Leopold's personal colony. Conceived in the fertile imagination of the Belgian monarch and brought into the world of nations in 1885 through his skillful machinations at the Berlin Conference, it was a unique phenomenon, the total creation of a remarkable man, the fulfillment of his imperial ambitions, and the outlet for his royal energies. "There are no small nations . . . only small minds," he pronounced, and not being one himself, proceeded to give shape and substance to the vast realm he had brought into being.

This was no mean task, even for an empire builder. Vague treaty rights had to be confirmed through effective occupation which meant, among other things, subduing the tenacious Arab slavers in the Lualaba country to the east and checking the energetic expansionism into the Katanga of that other African imperialist, Cecil Rhodes. Not content with mere consolidation, Leopold II sought, through the Anglo-Congolese agreement of 1894 to occupy the Bahr al-Ghazal, but this move was thwarted by the French, intent upon keeping the way open for their east-west axis. Such undertakings were enormously expensive, and their cost had to be added to already mounting outlays for routine exploration, occupation, and administration. During the five years following 1885,

Leopold was obliged to pay out twenty million francs of personal assets in support of his African adventure, a ruinous reversal even for a royal speculator.

This state of affairs could not long be endured by a man who regarded the Congo as his private property and who expected substantial returns on such valuable real estate. Beginning in 1887, Leopold granted extensive landholdings to a Belgian firm organized by Colonel Albert Thys who undertook to construct a rail line past the Congo River rapids, from Stanley Pool to the sea at Matadi, a link with the outside world essential to the exploitation of the Independent State's resources. The railroad was completed in 1898, by which time Leopold had hit upon other sources of financial assistance. At the Brussels Conference for the Abolition of the Slave Trade in 1889–1890, he succeeded in obtaining international agreement to a 10 per cent import duty, ostensibly levied as a means of combatting the Arab slave trade. At the same time, in 1889, Leopold II willed his African empire to Belgium, a calculated action which immediately yielded a ten-year, interest-free loan of twenty-five million francs.

This was a good beginning, but the Congo had much more to offer, and Leopold moved systematically toward a fuller exploitation of his domains. The initial policy adopted in 1885 had conceded commercial freedom to European traders as stipulated in the Berlin agreement, while providing that the State would claim title only to vacant lands, that is, lands not actually occupied by Africans. Such laissez-faire principles had brought little benefit to the Independent State, and soon were set aside in favor of a more remunerative regime. First, Leopold tightened up land policy by defining African land ownership in 1891 to comprise only areas under active cultivation, a most serious restriction considering indigenous agricultural practice which usually involved a periodic movement from exhausted lands to unoccupied, fresher tracts. Next, he earmarked all land now defined as vacant to be the *domaine privé*, the domain of the State, the natural products thereof, chiefly wild rubber and ivory, being the exclusive property of his government. In practice, this restricted zone came in time to comprise approximately half the total area of the Independent State, virtually all the territory north of the Congo River as far as Stanleyville, parts of the Kasai, and the vast Katanga which was divided between the State and the Katanga Company chartered in 1891. Other private concessionaires were licensed to assist with the harvesting of produce from these State lands, to which Leopold added a large tract of royal terrain, an enormous personal preserve staked out in the Lake Leopold region in 1896.

The commercial monopoly of Congo assets now safely in hand, for the Independent State was a stockholder in most of the private companies involved, Leopold now moved to the business of extracting the wealth of the land. First, there were the mineral resources of the Katanga, to be developed and controlled through a series of public and private bodies of which the *Union Minière de Haut-Katanga,* chartered in 1905, was to become most widely known. Next were the important resources of ivory, and particularly of rubber, their harvest resting heavily on the availability of indigenous labor. In 1892 a tax was imposed, payable in kind, expressly to encourage the gathering of rubber, and in 1903 Africans were required to work forty hours a month for the State or the private concessionaires, again with the harvesting of wild rubber particularly in view. Beyond these exactions were a variety of obligations involving construction labor, food requisitions, and military service.

One feature of this system of forced labor was the looseness of its administration which permitted wide discretion concerning methods of enforcement by local agents; another was the policy of production premiums paid to company employees and State officials, an open invitation to the abuses soon to become the hallmark of the Congo regime and the object of widespread international censure. Indeed, a constant, compulsive demand for rubber combined with few scruples about methods led straight to a system of unrivaled barbarism. The labor regimen meant virtual servitude for workers isolated far from home in strange and difficult surroundings; worse still, when villages failed to produce their assigned quota of rubber, chiefs and women were held captive against collection which was also urged by a liberal use of the *chicotte,* a hippo-hide lash of severely punishing qualities.

The variety of the atrocities and the vindictiveness of their perpetrators strain the limits of credibility. Armed African soldiers or company guards raided villages, looting supplies while taking hostages against deliveries of rubber. Others assigned the task of guarding villages, established themselves as local despots, making free with women and food supplies, killing and maiming those who resisted their tyrannies. Mutilation became a common practice, employed as punishment or even as a form of census, and stories were numerous of soldiers returning from expeditions to be congratulated on their collections of amputated right hands or garlands of ears festooned on a string. These obscenities added macabre punctuation to the rape, pillage, and murder which ravaged wide areas, and greatly reduced the population, in the process also effectively limiting the harvesting of rubber.

Such atrocities, reported in a rising chorus of protest by missionaries and other observers, led first to investigation and then to conversion of the Congo State into a Belgian colony. Much of the criticism originated in Britain where humanitarian scruples were combined with objections over Leopold's commercial monopolies violating the free trade guarantees of the Berlin Act of 1885. Both the Aborigines' Protection Society in London and the Congo Reform Association of E. D. Morel played their parts, but particularly damaging was the report filed in 1904 by Roger Casement, British Consul to the Congo. Casement's eyewitness account of brutal malfeasance was soon substantiated in the conclusions of Leopold's own investigating committee, and with international criticism mounting, the Belgian king finally capitulated. In November, 1908, his home government annexed the Congo Independent State which thenceforward became the Belgian Congo.

There had been humanitarian misgivings in Belgium itself over Leopold's Congo administration, but annexation was greeted with no great enthusiasm in the tiny country where a pragmatic view of the world could envision only trouble and expense in connection with this vast new acquisition. In fact, however, the main financial liability continued to fall on the Congo African, not on the citizen of Belgium. Under royal management, the king's private domain in the Lake Leopold area had yielded an estimated 71,000,000 francs between 1896 and 1905, much of this fortune expended for personal and public purposes in Europe. In transferring Congolese sovereignty to Belgium, Leopold also passed on assets valued at 110,000,000 francs along with assorted debts and liabilities amounting to 246,500,-000 francs.

Whatever income the Belgian state received from its newly acquired holdings of concession company securities and real property, it regarded the carrying charges on fully 200,000,000 francs of its Congo obligations as chargeable against the Congo itself. Thus the Congo, having contributed so generously to Leopold's personal wealth, was now obliged to service a heavy debt, much of which had been incurred by Leopold to finance lavish public works in Belgium. Moreover, for the time being, the shift from personal to colonial rule left unaffected the special position of the concessionaires which continued to control land in the Congo many times the size of Belgium unencumbered by any rental obligation to the Congo government.

Eventually Belgium renegotiated most of the Congo concessions on terms more favorable to the state, but the basic concept of economic advance primarily through private capital was not to be altered by a nation which believed so firmly in the balanced budget and the inflexible equation of private profit with public good. Under Belgian administration, therefore, economy in government and development through sound business practice became one basis for colonial policy. Another was reform of the abuses which had characterized the days of the Independent State combined with a thoroughgoing paternalism toward the Congo people which, it was felt, would eventually bring civilization where darkness reigned—the concept of "white man's burden" in its pure form. Finally, there was that well-developed Belgian pragmatism which emphasized practical solutions to specific problems, which frowned on articulated, long-range planning, and which denied colonial officers any recourse to guiding principles in moments of crisis.

What seemed in the abstract to be a well-ordered colonial administration devoted to human welfare emerged in practice, therefore, as an ill-designed authoritarianism based on misconception and fatally bound to the notion of human inequality. Examples abound. On the fundamental issue of land ownership and utilization, the colonial government made no essential changes from the policy of the Independent State. Occupation and ownership continued to be defined by European standards as large tracts were turned over to concessionaires and larger sections still reverted to state ownership. Moreover, Belgian concepts of economic advance in the Congo, formulated in terms of development by private European initiative, fully justified utilization of surface and mineral resources as a direct contribution to the improvement of African life, ignoring deepseated anxiety among the people over alienation of their land.

Political administration and local government were constructed on similar miscalculations. Traditional custom and the chiefly authority were to be the basis for local rule, but in 1910 a decree was passed providing for the division of the country into chiefdoms which bore little relationship to the actualities of indigenous life and frequently placed authority in the hands of minor headmen or nonentities while the leading chiefs went unrecognized. In 1920 and periodically thereafter new administrative units were created lumping together peoples of diverse origins to be governed by nominated chiefs lacking traditional sanctions and responsible for executive and judicial duties without precedent in traditional society. Quite probably these changes were designed to make the chief more the member of a colonial civil service than the representative of a traditional society for which Belgian administrative officers had small respect in any case. He thus came to occupy an anomalous position —an assigned leader of his people, yet without status at home or substantive authority in the colonial regime; an agent of the white man charged only with the administration of unpleasant tasks, such as road maintenance or law enforcement, meaningless in traditional society.

Labor policy was another fertile area for misunderstanding and mismanagement. The flagrant excesses of the Leopold era had been firmly suppressed, but recruitment continued unabated as concession companies competed in a rising demand for scarce workers. Inadequate administrative control resulted in malpractice such as manhunts and the custom of earlier times whereby women were made hostage until the men of a village agreed to sign on. A head tax instituted in 1914, and payable in cash, also encouraged men to leave their villages periodically, and in the Congo with its low population density (11.6 persons per square mile in 1923) there was always the danger of serious ecological dislocations if care were not exercised in restricting recruitment to allowable levels.

Programs regulating land, labor, and local government, however enlightened they might have appeared in the abstract, thus had little appeal for the African peasant. "What happiness have they brought us?" was the lament of one Congo chief. "They have given us a road we do not need, a road that brings more and more foreigners . . . causing trouble, making our women unclean, forcing us to a way of life that is not ours, planting crops we do not want, doing slave's work. . . . The white man . . . sends us missions to destroy our belief and to teach our children to recite fine-sounding words; but they are words we believe in anyway . . . And we live according to our beliefs, which is more than the white man does."

Chiefly hostility toward the missions was natural in view of the missionary role in undermining the basic tenets of traditional Africa. The missionaries, both Catholic and Protestant, were quite genuinely horrified by what they regarded as the depraved quality of daily existence—polygamy, slavery, drunkenness, slothfulness, cruelty—and they attached small merit to African values which ignored individual initiative and cared not what tomorrow might bring. Before Christianity could be introduced, they argued, such barbaric customs and practices would have to be destroyed; yet in their zeal, the missionaries were sometimes guilty of a heavy hand and a myopic view that confused European social standards with absolute truth and saw little virtue in African ways. Nevertheless, those Africans who left their villages to live in the mission-sponsored communities found modern medicine in place of witchcraft, and well-constructed houses and sanitary living conditions to counter the ramshackle squalor of the traditional village. The end of polygamy meant a rising status for women, a settled existence offered the possibility of a more refined agriculture, while education opened a new world of literacy and technical skills. The whole aspect of these Christian assemblages was one of comfort and prosperity.

To the missionary there were spiritual as well as material advantages. Christianity and literacy, he felt, meant liberation from ancient fears and taboos, the tyranny of the sorcerer was to be replaced with a new sense of hope in achievement and rational thought. In this realm of intangibles, however, the advantages may not have appeared so clear-cut to the African neophyte. Traditional beliefs broken down were not so easily replaced with something new. If the old standards lost validity, new ones, half-learned and ill-understood, were not necessarily more relevant to the simple, static, bucolic world into which they were introduced. For many, the confrontation of two ways of life caused complications enough in everyday affairs but this was nothing to the trauma of conflicting beliefs involving ancestors, the spirit world, and the hereafter wherein a false choice threatened eternal darkness in isolation from all that was familiar and loved.

For the African who did succeed in transferring to the European world, there was the disquieting suspicion that the faith preached by the missionaries was not so much a means of liberation as an engine of subjugation. There were many Africans in the Catholic priestly hierarchy (six hundred on the eve of independence in 1959) and Protestant missions had a similar record of ordination; yet had not these priests been relegated to inferior positions, were not congregations segregated by color and churches dominated by white missionaries, and did not the Catholic missions use their state educational subsidies to indoctrinate the African into a permanent subservience? In short, was not Christianity designed to perpetuate racial inequality and colonial domination?

Such misgivings may well have been related to the rise of separatist churches and prophet movements which enabled the African to throw off European missionary control in preference to a self-directed religious expression. This development first manifested itself in the spring of 1921 in the Thysville district of the Lower Congo with the appearance of Simon Kimbangu, a carpenter and evangelical preacher, who quickly gained a large following drawn by his alleged powers as a healer. Although he urged neither heresy nor civil disobedience, Kimbangu soon ran afoul of the authorities who came to regard him as an insurrectionary and imprisoned him later in the year along with some of his disciples.

While Kimbangu remained continuously in detention until his death in 1951, his movement retained its vitality, breaking out periodically during the twenties and thirties with the recurrent rumor that, although he was presumed dead, the victim of the authorities, the prophet would rise again and lead his people. Such neo-Kimbanguist revivals were especially related in the popular mind with the arrival in the Congo of the Salvation Army in 1935, its members being regarded as the reincarnation of Kimbangu and his disciples, their white faces the color of the departed spirits and the letter S on their uniforms the symbol for Simon Kimbangu himself.

This particular variant of Kimbanguism was partly propelled by a minor Salvation Army adherent, Simon Mpadi, whose movement, which concentrated during the late thirties in the French Congo, involved in outspoken form xenophobic and nationalist impulses which had always been implicit in the Kimbangu cult. Without doubt many purely religious factors explain the long-lived strength of Kimbanguism and other prophetic sects like the *kitawala*, or Watchtower, movement active in the Katanga during the interwar period. There was, for example, the insufficiency of emotional outlet in evangelical Christianity, or again, the inability of Christianity to deal satisfactorily with the problem of witchcraft or the role of ancestors.

Nevertheless, important extrareligious factors were present as

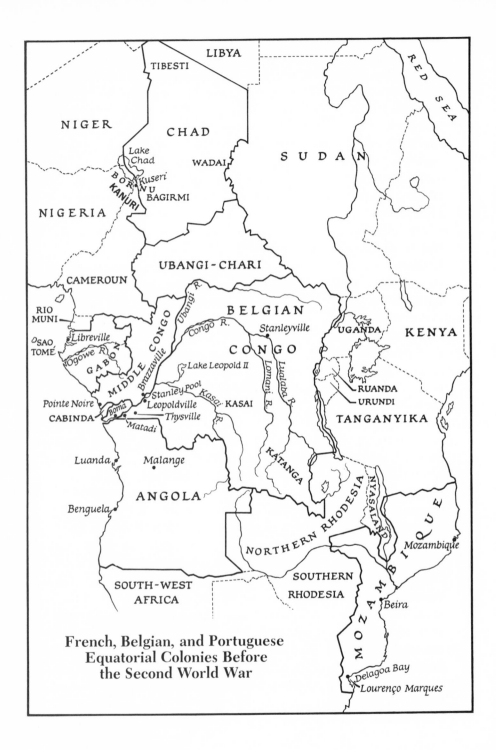

LIBYA

TIBESTI

NIGER

CHAD

Lake Chad

WADAI

SUDAN

RED SEA

NIGERIA

BORNU
KANURI
Kuseri
NU
BAGIRMI

CAMEROUN

UBANGI - CHARI

RIO MUNI

BELGIAN

Libreville
SAO TOMÉ

Ogowe R.
GABON

MIDDLE CONGO
Brazzaville

Ubangi R.

Congo R.

CONGO

Stanleyville

UGANDA

KENYA

Lake Leopold II

Lomani R.

Lualaba R.

RUANDA
URUNDI

Stanley Pool

Pointe Noire
CABINDA
Boma
Matadi

Leopoldville
Thysville

Kasai R.
KASAI

TANGANYIKA

Luanda
Malange

KATANGA

ANGOLA

Benguela

NORTHERN RHODESIA

NYASALAND

Mozambique

SOUTH-WEST
AFRICA

SOUTHERN
RHODESIA

MOZAMBIQUE

Beira

**French, Belgian, and Portuguese
Equatorial Colonies Before
the Second World War**

Delagoa Bay
Lourenço Marques

well. Some of Kimbangu's early followers had predicted the end of the world in a cataclysm which would destroy the white man, and this initial anti-European element had remained. Kimbangu's anticipated resurrection and return was partly a protest against Western political and religious domination, while his stature as prophet raised him to a level with such figures as Christ, Muhammad, and Moses. European rule with its forced labor and its destruction of traditional society had weighed heavily, but overt resistance was useless and dangerous. Converted to religious expression, however, political protest was possible and proved to be a not altogether unsatisfactory means of dissent.

Belgian paternalism, so manifest in political and religious matters, was reflected in economic and social affairs as well. The great industrial concerns, *Union Minière, Forminière,* and others, solved their labor problems during the twenties and thirties with expensive but well-conceived welfare programs. Workers lived in attractive communities complete with public health services, schools, and recreation facilities. Workers received good pay, hours and working conditions were carefully regulated, while transportation from home, rations, and medical attention were extended to all members of a family. The rising number of experienced workers living healthy contented lives emphasized the apparent success of this system.

Yet paternalism had very serious limitations. The schools were excellent but scarcely extended beyond the elementary level. Public health facilities and housing were modern and efficient, but they were also strictly segregated. Economic opportunity was unrivaled up to a point, but management and the professions were closed to the African. An informed populace was thwarted by press censorship, and education found no fulfillment in the creation of an African leadership. When independence came in 1960, the Congo possessed scarcely two dozen university graduates.

The problem was based in the paradox of Belgian policy—the mixture of administrative efficiency with blindness toward human aspirations, the attempt to improve the economic lot of the African while suppressing his political impulses, the practice of racial discrimination by representatives of a Western civilization which in its finer moments at least preached human equality and man's perfectibility. The paradox did not go unnoticed in the Congo. "We are helots," remarked one African observer. "There is no real intercourse between Belgians and Africans. The crudest, stupidest, most recently arrived Belgian *colon* regards himself as my superior . . . Officially there is no *racisme* in the Congo; but in practice we live in ghettos; in many shops we are served at separate counters; railway stations have separate entrances for *Européens* and *Indigènes*. Most of us in Leopoldville are too busy making money . . . to bother much about these things. But there is a *malaise*. Radical ideas reach us from across the Congo. . . . One day there will be an eruption. . . . We believe you mean to give us rights, but when?"

When the eruption finally came, the Belgian administration was no more ready than the Congo people. Belgian paternalism had stifled self-reliance and Belgian pragmatism could only precipitate the Congo into a sudden independence its people were ill qualified to sustain.

FRENCH EQUATORIAL AFRICA

The enormous sprawling territory which France designated as Equatorial Africa in 1910 was a complete anomaly. Stretching eighteen hundred miles from the coastal palm forests of Gabon to the mid-Saharan highlands of Tibesti, it formed an area as great as Belgium's' Congo but with little of the compactness, interior communication, and uniformity of its neighbor. In the north it contained desiccated wasteland, then stretches of such great savanna states as Wadai, Bagirmi, and Bornu—Muslim empires subsisting on slaving and the trans-desert trade, and including Arabs, Fulani, and Tuareg along with the local Kanuri, Wadai, and other peoples. Far to the south in the dense rain forests of the Ogowe, Congo, and Ubangi watersheds were numbers of small Bantu groups isolated in village communities and simple in their economies and sociology. With the exception of some hardwood stands in Gabon and wild rubber in the rain forest, the area was poor in resources, as indeed it was in population. In 1926, there were estimated to be but 3,100,000 inhabitants in all French Equatorial Africa, a density of only 3.5 to the square mile.

French occupation of this immense territory arose from the exigencies of late nineteenth-century European power politics rather than from any intrinsic local attractions. Initial contacts went back to the decade beginning in 1839 during which years France established trading posts and antislavery naval stations on the Gabon coast, of particular note being Libreville, founded in 1849 as a repatriation center for a cargo of freed slaves. This Gallic counterpart to Britain's Freetown constituted France's major achievement in the area before the arrival of the explorer Savorgnan de Brazza in 1875. Brazza conducted a series of explorations in the interior, first along the Ogowe River and then in other areas, capping his investigations by the treaty of 1880 with the Bateke king, Makoko, thus forming the basis for France's claims to the Gabon hinterland as far as the site of Brazzaville on the north side of Stanley Pool.

Brazza's activities, which included an infectious publicity campaign in Paris, stimulated a wave of expansionist enthusiasm in France and led to further explorations which, by the opening of the Berlin Conference in 1884, had firmly established French hegemony north of the Congo along the Ubangi River. France's imperial ambitions were now in full flood and further expeditions followed, culminating in the grand design to join central and north Africa at Lake Chad through which point an east-west axis would attempt to link Senegal with Ethiopia and Somalia. Such pretensions were only partially realized. During the 1890's both Britain and Germany forced their own colonial claims as far as Lake Chad, the former from northern Nigeria and the latter from its Cameroun protectorate. Moreover, in 1898, Captain Marchand was obliged to withdraw before Kitchener at Fashoda. Two years later, however, Major Lamy marched south from Algeria, linked up with Lieutenant Joalland's force coming east from Niger, and the two columns then joined Émile Gentil, already in Bagirmi country, where together they defeated the Sudanese conquerer, Rabih, at the battle of Kuseri in April, 1900.

This imposing pattern of conquest, followed more modestly by occupation and interior pacification, was forced to proceed slowly at first because of the difficult terrain, the scattered population, and the repressive tactics of the French forces which were at the same time so few in numbers. In 1905 four territories were organized, Gabon, Middle Congo, Ubangi-Chari, and Chad, all responsible to a governor-general at Brazzaville, and in 1910 a federation of French Equatorial Africa was formed. Poor communications, lack of personnel, and meager financing meant that administration was nominal, while public works, education, and health programs remained virtually non-existent.

Colonial theorists in metropolitan France nevertheless had no doubts about the necessity for introduction of European civilization into what they regarded as a primitive land, nor was there great hesitation within official circles over the virtues of economic exploitation; hence by 1912 when pacification had become general, vast tracts were already long since in the hands of private concessionaires. Most of these lands had been granted in 1899 in the rain forest areas of Gabon, Middle Congo, and Ubangi-Chari with their extensive growth of wild rubber, the more arid stretches of savanna in Chad proving less attractive. Forty companies with a combined capitalization of 59,000,000 francs received a total of 665,000 square kilometers, more than the area of France, for which they paid a trifling rental and over whose products they exercised complete ownership.

As in the Belgian Congo, a head tax and forced labor were imposed locally to insure collection of rubber and ivory, while no realistic attempt was made to protect African land ownership and utilization, even in restricted areas. An insufficiency of government officials and indifference to the niceties of justice soon combined with a need for porters and rubber workers to produce a systematic regimen of abuse. While yields remained low and most concession companies lost money, force became common practice in the gathering of rubber. Workers were rounded up by armed guards, women and children were taken hostage, and there were rising reports of villagers shot as recalcitrants, others perishing from disease and ill-treatment. At the same time, bloody reprisals broke out, directed against Europeans by the incensed local population.

An investigation headed by Brazza in 1905 substantiated many of the alleged atrocities and led to some reform of the concession system, if not to any marked improvement in the administration of France's four equatorial colonies. A good part of the difficulty lay in the essential poverty of the French Congo, a fact which soon dashed hopes of commercial profit if not dreams of empire, and probably stimulated brutality in civil servants and company agents, straining to squeeze wealth from a reluctant land. Unlike other areas, Equatorial Africa consistently ran deficits which had to be made up by the home government, while its sluggish economy showed little improvement over the years. In 1924 revenue amounted to 18,650,000 francs compared to 21,000,000 francs for tiny Togo and 195,000,000 for the Belgian Congo, a situation which reflected basic deficiencies in population and natural resources.

Beginning in 1910 the system of concessions was to some extent renegotiated by the French government but without any conspicuous benefit either to France or her central African colonies. Vast areas remained under private monopoly, while during the 1920's evidence accumulated pointing to fresh abuses in local administration. It had been established in 1910 that Africans would be guaranteed a portion of all produce gathered on company lands, and would have exclusive use of the areas designated as native reserves. No provision was made, however, for surveying the reserves, and no controls imposed to assure proper company payments for rubber gathered.

Beyond this, there appeared to be a recurrence of malpractices in connection with the requisition of African labor. During 1925–1926, for example, André Gide had visited Equatorial Africa in fulfillment of a childhood desire to see the Congo River, but this sentimental journey soon converted to a chronicle of rising indignation over repeated atrocities witnessed, and his classic *Voyage au Congo* emerged as an eloquent indictment of French colonial policy. Gide spoke of enforced rubber requisitions which ended in fines and imprisonment when not properly fulfilled, of beatings and killings, and of the infamous incident of defaulting rubber gatherers made to carry heavy beams the day long in the broiling sun, one of them finally collapsing and perishing in his tracks—a tale of cumulative terror which had left the country empty and its villages deserted.

Conditions in the forests of Ubangi-Chari, as described by Gide, were found to obtain generally through French Equatorial Africa, the result of the same poorly supervised practices of private concessionaires unchecked by inadequate numbers of civil servants working under a parsimonious colonial administration. Such circumstances were responsible for the loss of thousands of lives during the construction of the railroad from Brazzaville to Pointe Noire in the 1920's, and other tales of malfeasance and brutality continued periodically to emerge from the Congo. Nevertheless, although occasional adverse criticism helped put an end to particular abuses, up to the time of the Second World War no fundamental change had been brought about in this unhappy state of affairs.

Needless to say, African economic enterprise was not encouraged under French rule, and only a few lumbermen and cocoa farmers from Gabon were able to accumulate any appreciable capital before the era of independence. At the same time a tradition of exploitation by concession companies and an arbitrary if impecunious administration gave little encouragement either to the doctrine of assimilation or the rise of a class of educated Africans. A few small groups of elite had grown up in Libreville, Brazzaville, and Pointe Noire over the years, educated in mission schools and attracted to a modest political activity. In Libreville a branch of the French League for the Defense of the Rights of Man was active between 1918 and 1930, protesting governmental policy on such matters as land alienation and administrative justice. An allied group, Young Gabon, was founded in 1920, opposing the rule of tribal elders and demanding French citizenship. Generally these groupings tended to divide along ethnic lines and their effectiveness was reduced accordingly.

Of more consequence were the mass movements of semireligious origin which proved to be resistant equally to the direction of the colonial government and of the traditional authorities. The Kimbangu cult spread across the Congo River to gain a following among the Bakongo people living in Brazzaville, and it was in that same city that violence erupted in 1930 in connection with another popular leader, André Matswa. Matswa, a member of the Balali people, had formed an Association of Natives of French Equatorial Africa in 1926 while living in Paris. Starting life primarily as a social organization, his group soon developed political objectives, spreading at the same time to Brazzaville where it began to attack racial discrimination and the *indigénat,* or administrative justice, as well as demanding French citizenship for Africans.

Returning to Brazzaville to take leadership of his movement, Matswa attempted to organize a trade union, but was soon arrested and sentenced to three years in prison. He subsequently escaped, but was eventually recaptured and exiled to Chad where he died in prison in 1942 while serving a life sentence. Matswa's trial in 1930 was the scene of rioting, reflecting not only popular displeasure at the persecution of a local leader but a deeper discontent concerning political and social backwardness for which the colonial administration was held chiefly responsible. For years the Balali leadership, both educated and traditional, cooperated in a passive resistance to the authorities which was eventually crushed only by military action, and after the Second World War an antigovernment messianic cult arose in Brazzaville in the name of André Matswa.

For its part, the French regime showed little interest in basic reform until forced to do so by the pressure of events outside Equatorial Africa. The trauma of France's military collapse before

Hitler's armies in 1940 was followed by the slow rise of Free French resistance to the Vichy government in which Equatorial Africa played such a conspicuous role. Under her Negro governor-general from French Guiana, Félix Eboué, Brazzaville became the spiritual center of Free French activity; more than that, Eboué was able to inaugurate a fundamental change in colonial policy which looked to a completely new world-wide French union in the postwar period. Instituting improved medical and educational facilities, Eboué put an end to forced labor and moved toward the development of a peasant agriculture. Basing his system on a renascence of traditional sanctions, he encouraged authentic chiefs and strengthened indigenous institutions, offering the chiefs modern education to match their ancient status. Such changes were to be the foundation for a genuine partnership between European and African, and indeed, the Brazzaville Conference of 1944, over which Eboué exercised considerable influence, defined the future status of French African colonial peoples much along the liberalized lines he had suggested.

Nevertheless a long history of neglect and oppression left the people of French Equatorial Africa ill-prepared to deal with the new world which awaited them in 1945.

PORTUGUESE ANGOLA AND MOZAMBIQUE

Portuguese occupation of Africa—predatory and corrupt—did not change in character over the years. There remained the same concentration on slaving which had typified the early relations with the kingdom of Kongo and the region of Angola; after 1700, moreover, growing poverty and stagnation in Portugal insured parallel decadence for her African colonies. During the seventeenth and eighteenth centuries, Angola in particular was ruled by administrators who were expected to profit from their position, and frequently did so. Legitimate commerce and capital investment were insignificant, education and health facilities non-existent, and missionary work in full decline. Only atrophy and tyranny marked an unhappy land.

In Angola, the interior was under ineffectual occupation by military governors whose single-minded policy was exploitation without revolt, a controlled warfare which brought in slaves while avoiding a general uprising. In the towns, such as Luanda and Benguela, there was a small population of Europeans, trader-officials, adventurers, and so-called *degradados* drawn from the ranks of criminals and political exiles. By 1845 Angola contained only 1800 Europeans, most in Luanda. Benguela, for example, though important in trade, numbered only 39 whites including one woman. These settlers were politically important because of their control of the town councils, much of their exertions being directed toward pushing the administration into armed slave raiding in the interior. Indeed, slaving dominated all activity and was the sole support of the economy. Toward the end of the eighteenth century, it was estimated to account for 88 per cent of the colony's revenue, the rest coming from tithes and exports of ivory.

Mozambique presented a similar picture. By 1800 the coastal forts and trading posts had long since degenerated into centers of disease and decay, poverty-stricken slums matching the untidy dilapidation of Angola's ports. The towns contained Hindus and Goans along with Portuguese, most of them devoted to trade. Inland, during the seventeenth century, there had grown up a system of great feudal estates or *prazos,* held by Goan or Portuguese landlords who governed their holdings without reference to the Portuguese authorities, granting such allegiance as they did to the inland rulers of the Mutapa kingdom. Thus, as in Angola, Portuguese control over the interior was nominal; yet it was the *prazeros* who probably held Mozambique for Portugal when they successfully resisted the war bands coming up from the south, set in motion by the *Mfecane* during the early nineteenth century.

By mid-eighteenth century, the economic life of Mozambique had swung squarely to the marketing of exploitable African labor. Earlier coastal trade had languished and gradually given way to slaving, particularly in response to Brazilian needs, while many a *prazo* operated gangs of workers who were in fact slaves, although they were not always called such. Despite the British antislavery patrols, various international accords, and Portuguese government decrees, slaving flourished along the Mozambique coast as late as the 1870's. Some cargoes headed for Cuba, others went to Zanzibar and Madagascar, while still others were sent to the French sugar plantations of Reunion in the Indian Ocean.

During these same years there had been an increasing flow of workers on their way from the Delagoa Bay area to seek employment on the farms of South Africa. In 1875 Mozambique and the British in Natal and Cape Colony reached agreement regulating this movement, the Portuguese gaining considerable income therefrom by substantially raising their passport charges. During the 1880's, however, the opening of the gold mines on the Witwatersrand in the Transvaal greatly increased the demand for labor in South Africa and recruiters began systematically to take workers from Mozambique. Soon half the mine workers were Mozambique Africans, and by 1910 some 60,000 were laboring on the Rand.

Once again the Portuguese authorities insisted on regulating the supply, ostensibly on humanitarian grounds, but actually for the profit that could be gained. In 1901 an accord was reached which permitted controlled recruitment, and in 1909 a formal convention was signed to the same end. Service fees yielded substantial income which was supplemented by the provision of the 1909 convention that one-half of the total rail traffic from the Transvaal industrial area be channeled through Lourenço Marques on Delagoa Bay. Indirect gains were also impressive. Between 65,000 and 100,000 workers were contracted annually and each brought back accumulated savings which greatly stimulated the Mozambique economy. In 1903 the Portuguese estimated that 200,000 workers a year could mean an infusion of £3,000,000, and at that time it was reported that Africans were purchasing £600,000 worth of consumer goods a year, mostly in the southern districts where recruitment was heaviest.

Labor migration on this scale was much resented locally by public officials or private contractors relying on forced labor, for the workers clearly preferred the better conditions and assured wages of the Transvaal, and had to be coerced to work in Mozambique. In the Portuguese colonies, forced labor had long been considered an African birthright. When the government in Lisbon abolished the slave trade within Portuguese territory in 1836, there was such a violent reaction in Angola that for another decade no really effective action could be taken to implement this decision. Finally, in 1845 a prize court in Luanda put an end to the export of slaves, but only at the price of serious dislocations in an economy which was based largely on slaving.

During the 1850's, a series of decrees announced the gradual end of slavery in the Portuguese territories, but the provision of a transitional period of labor for each *liberto*, or freedman, was an invitation to abuse, and *liberto* soon became a euphemism for slave. In 1869 slavery was abolished immediately and without qualification, but again the law was evaded as masters made effective use of the uncertain status of the *liberto*. When the condition of *liberto* was finally terminated in 1876, workers were still obliged to contract their services, preferably with former masters, and vagrancy codes made continued forced labor an easy matter. Meanwhile, slave recruitment in the interior went on as before, now under the name of contract labor. The worst abuses and hypocrisy, however, were reserved for the labor market on the island of Sao Tomé, where, during the last decades of the nineteenth century, workers were shipped from Angola by the thousand each year to man the coffee and cocoa plantations. Many were listed as household servants, others as *libertos*, and some even came as freemen complete with passports, but all entered a world of virtual slavery.

Pressed from different quarters by British humanitarians and Angolan planters, the Portuguese had put an end to the worst abuses of Sao Tomé recruitment by 1915, and indeed the transitional years from the nineteenth to the twentieth century saw a concerted effort to institute a more comprehensive and coordinated colonial policy. First there was systematic pacification of the interior, not completed until 1919; then the imposition of an authoritarian regime under absolutist provincial administrators. During this process policies varied from a philosophy which frankly sanctioned white rulers exploiting black laborers, to that of a paternal humanitarianism designed to improve the African's lot materially and morally, and even to permit some few to achieve the status of *assimilados*, or thoroughly Westernized Portuguese citizens.

The changing fashion in colonial administration was largely responsive, not to circumstances in Africa, but to politics in Lisbon. In 1926 a military dictatorship was instituted and six years later the government of Antonio Salazar came to power. Over the years there had always been expectations in poverty-stricken Portugal that somehow her impecunious colonies would bring great wealth, but as always the colonies failed to throw off the weight of exploitation to which they were subjected. With Salazar, however, a more realistic economic policy began to yield modest results—colonial production tailored to the home and world markets, Portuguese immigration and capital investment, and improved agriculture. The African worker continued to be the basis for colonial production, but some attempt was made to avoid the worst abuses of the contract labor system. There was, however, something more. Salazar talked of Portugal's need for colonies in order to maintain a position of world importance, and there were many official references to the noble and uplifting mission of civilization and to the solidarity and glory of an imperial Portugal.

For the African, this policy meant slow assimilation into a Portuguese way of life, a long-lived process marked by extended periods of tutelage wherein he would require the protection of an enlightened but rigorous paternalism. Hence the principle of racial equality was subverted by the practice of cultural inequality, and reality unfolded in a repressive labor policy, continued economic backwardness, inadequate educational and medical facilities, and lack of technical development. A passbook system, the *caderneta*, enabled the authorities to keep all Africans under close surveillance while censorship, border patrols, controlled education, and ruthless police work prevented the development of cadres of local leadership. Hence, despite rural poverty and rising urban slums, there was little unrest in the years before the Second World War. A policy of calculated repression which discouraged literacy, withheld education, and isolated the African from the fast-changing world around him seemed ideally designed to maintain Portugal's colonial position indefinitely.

Nonetheless, a total quarantine could not be achieved. A number of Africans succeeded in gaining secondary school training, while Angolan towns like Luanda and Malange contained industrial and clerical workers aware of the advantages of modernization. There had been modest political activity even before the Second World War, but more forceful mass organizations emerged during the 1950's. In 1956 the *Movimento Popular de Libertação de Angola* (M.P.L.A.) was formed in Luanda to represent the urban dweller and to voice his rising discontent. Two years earlier, another political grouping, the *União das Populações de Angola* (U.P.A.) had taken shape in Leopoldville where numbers of Bakongo migrants from Angola had gone in search of employment.

Whatever the initial objectives of these parties, they soon were caught up in the continental thrust of African independence. First there was the example of Ghana in 1957, then in the following year, self-government for the people of the French Community territories, including the Bakongo north of the Congo River. In 1960 the Republic of the Congo came into being, as Nigeria also gained its freedom, and it was clear that other nations were soon to follow. In Angola, by contrast, the administration mustered troop reinforcements, arrested many of the M.P.L.A leaders, and sought to wipe out opposition by force. The Angolan African—his job and his land threatened by Portuguese immigration, his leaders imprisoned, his government at war with him—fought back, and the revolt of February, 1961 began its long, inconclusive course.

Suggestions for Further Reading

Beyond Lord Hailey's surveys of 1938 and 1956, there is no general treatment which deals with French Equatorial Africa, the Belgian Congo, and Portuguese East and West Africa. R. L. Buell's *The Native Problem in Africa*, 2 v. (London: Frank Cass, 1965; Hamden, Conn.: Shoe String Press, 1965) covers the French and Belgian territories up to the 1920's, but does not examine the Portuguese colonies. The most comprehensive survey for these is contained in James Duffy, *Portuguese Africa* (Cambridge, Mass.: Harvard University Press, 1959; London: Oxford University Press, 1959), but see also the same author's *A Question of Slavery* (Oxford: Clarendon Press, 1967); J. Vansina, *Kingdoms of the Savanna* (Madison, Wisconsin: University of Wisconsin Press, 1966); *Angola: A Symposium* (London: Oxford University Press, 1962); and R. J. Hammond, *Portugal and Africa, 1815–1910* (Stanford, California: Stanford University Press, 1967).

For the Belgian Congo, two works cover the period in question: Ruth Slade, *King Leopold's Congo* (London: Oxford University Press, 1962); and Roger Anstey, *King Leopold's Legacy* (London: Oxford University Press, 1966). A very brief assessment is found in Ruth Slade (with Marjory Taylor), *The Belgian Congo*, 2nd. ed. (London: Oxford University Press, 1961), while a more specialized study is available in R. Anstey's *Britain and the Congo in the Nineteenth Century* (Oxford: Clarendon Press, 1962). Some discussion of Congolese messianic movements is found in Thomas Hodgkin, *Nationalism in Colonial Africa* (New York: New York University Press, 1957; London: F. Muller, 1956). For anthropological analysis, see D. Biebuyck and M. Douglas, *Congo Tribes and Parties* (London: Royal Anthropological Institute, 1961), and A. Merriam, *Congo: Background of Conflict* (Evanston, Illinois: Northwestern University Press, 1961).

French Equatorial Africa is treated in Georges Bruel, *La France Equatoriale Africaine* (Paris: Larose, 1935); S. H. Roberts, *A History of French Colonial Policy, 1870–1925* (London: Frank Cass, 1963); and J. Suret-Canale, *Afrique Noire, Occidentale et Centrale: L'Ère Coloniale, 1900–1945* (Paris: Éditions Sociales, 1964). Early political and messianic movements are discussed in Georges Balandier, *Sociologie Actuelle de l'Afrique Noire*, 2nd. ed. (Paris: Presses Universitaires de France, 1963). There are many accounts of Congo atrocities but, for the French areas, see André Gide, *Travels in the Congo* (Berkeley, California: University of California Press, 1962), and the celebrated novel by Réné Maran, *Batouala* (Paris: Éditions Albin Michel, 1938).

20: The Two Societies of Southern Africa

APARTHEID—COLONIALISM IN SOUTH AFRICA

In South Africa the nineteenth century saw the establishment of a double economic standard whereby unskilled African labor was utilized by the European to accelerate his own rising prosperity. In the twentieth century the political capstone was placed upon the system of economic privilege, making certain through absolute control of the machinery of government that black labor would continue to perform its traditional function of sustaining the white man in his elevated status. This relationship between the races emerged eventually in the policy of apartheid which now characterizes South African society. Indeed, as the era of European colonialism drew to a close in the years following the Second World War, Afrikaner colonialism intensified, tightening its hold on its subject people, and attempting to place them physically in colonies where their long-standing service to the white South African community could be supervised and controlled.

In theory apartheid claims to be something other than political domination and economic exploitation. It argues that the races of the world develop best when physically separated from one another, and it seeks to have each go its own way, independent, and as nearly as possible, self-sufficient. Its apologists have been many, both white and black. Blyden was one; so too was Marcus Garvey.

Among its leading advocates in mid-twentieth century are the black nationalists in the United States, but its chief practitioners are incontestably the European leaders of the Republic of South Africa, its prime philosopher, Dr. Hendrik Verwoerd, head of the South African government from 1958 until his assassination in 1966.

During the 1950's when Verwoerd served as Minister of Native Affairs, he introduced a series of bills which gave legal sanction to much of the racial segregation then practiced, but which extended the concept much further to the establishment of Bantustans, or Bantu states, where Africans would live as separate, self-governing communities within the South African nation. The principle of physical separation extended as well to the Cape Coloured population—those descendants of seventeenth-century European, Hottentot, Malay, and West African Negro alliances—and to the Asian community of Natal, but theory was not to be carried at once to the point of economic dislocation. Where no actual homeland territory existed, as in the case of the Coloureds and the Asians, or where African labor was needed, for example, in the massive Witwatersrand industrial complex, other types of segregation could apply in the form of separate living areas, recreation facilities, transportation, schools, and places of worship. In the same way, white communities were segregated, and penalties awaited all transgressors of the segregation laws, Europeans and non-Europeans alike.

The apartheid legislation was various and comprehensive. In 1949 and 1950 miscegenation in or out of wedlock was outlawed, and in the latter year the Population Registration Act undertook to classify all persons in South Africa on a racial basis, thereby fixing the fate of each individual in relation to all subsequent and past racial legislation. Thus the Group Areas Act of 1950 provided for residential segregation by race; a series of Urban Areas Acts culminating in 1956 seriously limited the right of Africans to remain in municipal localities; the job reservation laws and decrees determined which sort of employment was open to white and which to black; the Native Labour (Settlement of Disputes) Act of 1953 forbade strikes by Africans and discouraged their unionization; and the Reservation of Separate Amenities Act of the same year concerned itself with standards of public facilities, from hospital beds to park benches, provided for the different races.

Such enactments, vexing and humiliating, largely ratified a discrimination already fixed by law and custom, but with the Promotion of Bantu Self-Government Act of 1959 the logic of apartheid was carried much further in the direction of absolute segregation. It was also brought to the point of paradox. The Verwoerd government proposed the establishment of eight Bantustans to be consolidated from the older African reserves, and to serve as the bases for eventual self-governing states to which Africans would gradually return from their present "temporary" residence in the white areas. The paradox rested in the realities of population and economic growth which were in fact constantly bringing larger numbers of Africans into the industrial cities where their labor was an essential element of national economic development.

Whether the official position regarding Bantustans was caused by cynicism or fanaticism, there was no mistaking the objective of that other major area of apartheid legislation, the establishment of schooling on a racial basis through the Bantu Education Act of 1953 and the Extension of University Education Act, passed in 1959. These laws in effect segregated instruction at all levels, placing the control of education for Africans under the central government's Department of Native Affairs, shifting their curriculum away from the European syllabus toward traditional African materials with particular attention to Bantu languages, and establishing special universities for Africans, Coloureds, and Asians who no longer were permitted to attend the European institutions. Critics pointed to the emphasis on vernacular languages which effectively limited communication and cohesion among Africans of different tribal origin, and argued that the rigid personal and academic regulations imposed within Bantu universities would surely stifle African development according to any internationally acceptable principles of university education. Under the guise of autonomy, for under apartheid an ostensible self-government was a pervasive feature of Bantustan administration, the Africans were being fixed in an economic, political, and educational status which would insure their continued subservience to the ruling white society.

Thus the framework for apartheid was conceived. According to the Bantu Self-Government Act each Bantustan was to operate on a system of representative government at local, regional, and territorial level with a parliament at the top governing in conjunction with a prime minister and cabinet. In the Transkei, the first Bantustan to be organized, the parliament is a combination of elected members and nominated chiefs, and its official language is Xhosa. Parliament has its own budget and treasury and is largely responsible for local affairs. A European commissioner-general is the link with the South African government, which allows no other form of African representation at the center and controls external matters along with surveillance of immigration, currency, and the Transkei constitution. What has emerged, therefore, is classic indirect rule with ultimate and absolute authority resting with the colonial Afrikaner government.

The policy of total apartheid in Bantustans contains a large element of unreality, for South Africa, like all developing industrial economies, shows a strong population drift toward the cities. The enormous and expanding industrial complex surrounding Johannesburg, the major port of Durban, and the manufacturing centers of Port Elizabeth and Cape Town continually attract people of all races and the figures show it. Between 1921 and 1960 the proportion of European city dwellers rose from 56 to 84 per cent; of Coloureds from 46 to 68 per cent; of Asians from 31 to 83 per cent; and of Africans from 12 to 32 per cent. Thus one-third of almost 12,000,000 Africans are now part of the so-called urban white areas compared with approximately a half million forty years ago drawn from a then African population of but 4,700,000. The number of urban Africans has therefore increased seven times in little more than a generation, and indications are strong that the 3,600,000 urban Africans of 1965 will have increased by another million within ten years.

Industrialization has of course meant a rising national prosperity, but its distribution is heavily weighted in favor of the European population which relies not only on superior education and training, but on color bar and job reservation legislation to maintain its privileged position. One study shows that the European standard of living rose almost 50 per cent between 1938 and 1953; the Asian and Coloured a more modest 11 per cent, while the African suffered a 6 per cent decline during the same years. In 1960 the European 19.3 per cent of the population gained 67 per cent of the national income while the African 68.4 per cent of the population earned but 26.5 per cent. The remaining 12.4 per cent accounted for by Asians and Coloureds received 6.5 per cent of South Africa's income. At the same time annual income for whites averaged $2800, for Coloureds $825, and for Africans about $520.

Certainly white South African living standards are among the best in the world today, characterized by comfortable homes, servants, free education, and frequently more than one automobile to a family. By contrast, the urban African lives a submarginal existence, depressed by his unskilled job and segregated status, hampered by a lack of opportunity for advancement into the better salaried, skilled positions, and plagued by the constant uncertainty that he may be sent back to the rural reserves at any moment. In response to rising industrial demand, some Africans have been able to move into higher and better paid levels of employment and there is steadily growing pressure by Africans on the limits of job reservation. Against this development stands the barrier of apartheid official policy (in the decade of the 1960's more commonly referred to as "separate development" and "separate homelands") but the doctrine of apartheid could in time give ground before the necessities of economic pragmatism.

With one-third of the Africans in the cities, another 30 per cent inhabit farms and villages in the white-owned countryside. In some areas the Africans are tenants who trade their labor for the right to utilize a plot of ground for cropping and grazing. Most receive an additional payment in kind or in cash, but income is so depressed that it must be supplemented where possible with work in town. Other Africans hire out as agricultural laborers paid in cash to which is added housing and sometimes a share in profits. This arrangement allows a good income in the skilled brackets, but frequently agricultural labor means the utilization of migrants and the appearance of abuses which normally attend rural unemployment. Everywhere rising population crowds out of the reserves, flooding the farming areas with an excess which is further intensified by foreign agricultural workers from Malawi, Mozambique, and Rhodesia.

Roughly 37 per cent of the African population live in the so-called homelands or reserves which are the Bantustan territories. These reserves comprise slightly less than 14 per cent of the South African land mass, and in addition to being scattered, broken, and interspersed with white farms, they are hopelessly overcrowded and scarred with erosion. The exhausted land gives little, and the endemic poverty would be much more severe were it not for the members of families constantly moving out to the town and white farm for supplementary income. In 1955 an official report estimated that half the income of rural families came from town wages. To make matters worse fully three-fifths of the African unemployed reside in the reserves and countryside, adding their weight to an already overburdened African economy.

Beyond poverty, segregation, and inequality of opportunity, there are the pass laws which require that every African carry a reference book containing identifying details along with a record of all permissions and endorsements involving freedom of movement, eligibility for employment, tax payments, or convictions for transgressions of the law. These books must be carried constantly and shown on demand, and are the major means by which labor movement is controlled and the government attempt to develop the Bantustans facilitated. Since the pass-law system strikes directly at the economic opportunity of subsistence earners, it has come to be the symbol and chief target of the African's resentment over the many inequities of his life.

THE GENESIS OF APARTHEID

If apartheid was the logical extension of long-nourished Afrikaner views on society and race, its particular form and appearance was a direct result of South African white politics in the years following unification in 1910. The fierce patriotism of Paul Kruger—his view of the Boers as the chosen people fleeing the world's corruption to follow God's will in a new land—was easily transferable to others of like background, particularly after the trauma of defeat in the Boer War and Lord Milner's subsequent campaign to convert South Africa into an English-oriented component of the British Empire. British cultural assimilation not only failed in its objectives but greatly encouraged the rise of an emphatic Afrikaner nationalism which was to culminate a half century later in the establishment of the South African republic, independent of any ties with Britain.

The move toward republicanism took time, for there were many, Boer and Briton alike, who were not immediately persuaded. The major figures in the years after Union were moderates—Jan Smuts, Louis Botha, and J.B.M. Hertzog, Boer generals who were nevertheless advocates of a joint British-Afrikaner effort in building a South African state. Smuts and Botha argued the synthesis of two cultures as the basis for a strong and productive society. Hertzog agreed, but saw an initial need for raising the Afrikaner position culturally and economically (greatly extending the use of the Afrikaans language, for example) before the two streams could come together in total harmony. The difference was largely a matter of emphasis, but in the view of hard-core Afrikaner nationalists, Hertzog offered much more attraction, and it was to him that they initially attached their allegiance.

Nevertheless, Botha and Smuts formed the first governments, organized through their South African Party with Botha becoming prime minister in 1910 and Smuts succeeding when the former died in 1919. Their pro-English orientation, involving support for Britain during the First World War, greatly stimulated Afrikaner nationalism, however, which rallied behind the Nationalist Party formed by Hertzog in 1912. By 1924, the Nationalists were strong enough to unseat Smuts, his downfall coming significantly after he had broken a 1922 strike by white miners, called to protest the intended use of Africans in skilled positions on the Rand. This introduction into politics of the so-called "native question" greatly strengthened the Afrikaner position, and Smuts fell from power, accused not only of an antilabor bias, but of indifference to white superiority as well.

From this point forward, Afrikaner and Nationalist Party control over South African politics slowly tightened. Somewhat unwittingly and unwillingly, Hertzog was maneuvered into contesting the 1929 general election on the issue of race relations. Advocating segregation of the African population economically, socially, and politically, he particularly urged the removal of Africans from the common voter rolls in Cape Province, a privilege they had enjoyed from the time of unification in 1910. Although the time was not yet ripe for such a step, the emotion-charged racial issue enabled the Nationalists to win the contest and Hertzog to remain as premier.

During the depression years of the 1930's, Hertzog and Smuts effected a rapprochement, forming the United Party and directing a coalition government from 1933 onward, each man still holding to the two-stream conception of South African society. Such a view necessarily put them at odds with the *Broederbond*, a quasi-secret society of deeply nationalistic persuasion, founded after the First World War as an agency for the establishment of an Afrikaner-controlled nation. Politically the *Broederbond* movement was reflected in an intense dislike for the Smuts-Hertzog coalition and in the crystalization in 1933 of a right-wing movement among the Nationalists, the *gesuiwerdes*, or purified, who eventually went into opposition as the new Nationalist Party under the leadership of a former Dutch Reform Church minister, Dr. D. F. Malan.

When Hertzog's bid for South African neutrality during the

Second World War failed, his coalition with Smuts ended, and Hertzog soon retired from politics, for he could find little common cause with the extreme, anti-British views of the Nationalists. For their part, Malan and his colleagues refused to compromise the principles of Afrikaner nationalism, and saw their determination rewarded by victory in the election of 1948. Smuts and the United Party were defeated by a Nationalist campaign of racism which introduced for the first time the term and the concept of apartheid. A rising industrialism had brought increasing numbers of Africans into the cities during the war while the world-wide liberalism of the immediate postwar years had encouraged African leaders to make political demands distasteful to white supremacy. The Malan victory was narrow, and indeed rested on coalition with a minor party, but once effected, it began a period of Nationalist Party domination backed by a steadily increasing support from all segments of the European population. Malan retired in 1954 and was succeeded by J. G. Strijdom who was replaced upon his death in 1958 by Dr. Verwoerd. Verwoerd's assassination in 1966 brought the Minister of Justice, John Vorster, to power as head of an all-powerful Afrikaner government.

Hertzog's views regarding racial segregation had finally forced a separate electoral roll for Cape Africans in 1936, but the period immediately following the 1948 general election found Malan unprepared to give specific definition to his campaign slogan of apartheid, and it remained for the Minister of Native Affairs, H. F. Verwoerd, to define the theory and implement the practice. At the same time the Nationalists were determined to press forward to their major objective of an independent republic. Once again it was Dr. Verwoerd who achieved success, engineering a winning referendum in 1960 which was followed in 1961 both by the formal proclamation of the Republic of South Africa and by her withdrawal from the British Commonwealth.

Neither the Bantustan policy nor republicanism would have been easy to achieve without the tacit support of South Africa's English population. The vote for the republic in 1960 was indeed close, but the drift away from the United Party to the Nationalists since 1948 has been unwavering and has finally resulted in an overwhelming Nationalist majority. The causes appear to rest ultimately in the broad-based support among Europeans for white domination and segregation, if not for apartheid. Since the proclamation of the Republic, moreover, a number of factors have brought the white community into closer cohesion. First, Nationalist ascendancy has muted the previously strident elements of Afrikaner nationalism, while increasing criticism abroad has driven South Africans together in mutual defense. Next, the European community has generally regarded the tribulations of the new nations of Africa as a clear indication of African incapacity for self-government. Finally, a growing spirit of militant nationalism among South Africa's own black population has stiffened the attitudes of those who may previously have entertained some degree of sympathy toward the grievances of the African masses.

AFRICAN NATIONALISM IN SOUTH AFRICA

The many factors which so greatly stimulated nationalist development throughout the continent at the conclusion of the Second World War were perceived as clearly in South Africa as in other latitudes. There too were Africans who had fought the good fight defending the Four Freedoms and who looked forward at war's end to the rewards of loyalty. There, sensitivity to the coming possibilities was, if anything, greater than elsewhere. Were not the black people of South Africa more advanced than those in other parts of Africa? Were they not earlier introduced and more thoroughly assimilated into the urban world and the industrialized complex of modern society? Did they not far surpass the people of Africa's many territories in numbers of university graduates, degree of literacy, political and social sophistication, and economic development? Were not their grievances deeper, of longer standing, than those of any other people?

Such thoughts were much in the minds of the Africans in South Africa at the very moment that Afrikaner leadership was achieving its political victory of 1948 and thereby opening the way for its greatly accelerated regimen of racial discrimination. Here in fact was the disheartening climax to years of unrelieved defeat, and it marked the beginning of a new trend by Africans toward positive action rather than petition to gain the better life and the freedom they sought.

Black nationalism in South Africa had been conceived in adversity, in the disappointment of John Tengo Jabavu, Dr. Pixley

Seme, and others, over the unification constitution of 1910 which denied the African the right to sit in the Union parliament and limited his franchise to those resident in the Cape Province. From the first their response was insufficient, ineffective. The modest objective of Dr. Seme's African National Congress (A.N.C.) which asked only for citizenship through constitutional means was no match for white opposition which reacted, not with concessions but with an increasing pressure of discrimination and segregation. As early as 1911, a Mines and Work Act reserved skilled jobs in the extractive industries for Europeans. Two years later, legislation was passed limiting the area of land available for African use to scarcely more than one-tenth of the whole South African land mass. At the same time, this Natives' Land Act directed the eviction of almost one million African squatters from white farms. The day after the bill was passed, as Sol Plaatje put it, "the African woke to find himself a pariah in the land of his birth."

Although the Afrikaner exponents of apartheid did not gain power until 1948, their work had largely been done for them by preceding governments. Directly after the First World War, for example, the Smuts ministry wielded an even hand in crushing labor unrest in Port Elizabeth, dispersing members of a millenarian religious sect in the eastern Cape Province, and chastising Hottentots in South-West Africa for tax default, all at a cost of hundreds dead and injured. In 1923, moreover, Smuts put through the Native Urban Areas Act permitting municipal authorities to control the number and location of Africans living in the city.

For its part, the administration of General Hertzog, between 1924 and the outbreak of the Second World War, proceeded with a systematic delimitation of African civil and political rights. In 1926, the Mines and Work Amendment Act extended and stiffened the definition of job segregation, while the Masters and Servants Act made it a criminal offense for Africans to break contracts. A year later the Native Administration Act gave the government the authority to appoint and depose chiefs, and threatened Africans with fines and imprisonment for causing "any feeling of hostility between Natives and Europeans." Other legislation circumscribed social and personal activity, virtually prohibiting the sale of alcohol to Africans, forbidding black-white extra-marital intercourse, and further limiting urban residence for Africans.

The culmination of these restrictions came in 1936 with the

Native Representation Act. This law relegated Africans in the Cape Province to a separate voting roll where they might elect three white men to represent them in parliament. Thus was the African vote segregated in the Cape, and brought a step closer to the total disenfranchisement which obtained elsewhere in the Union. The African community witnessed these reverses with growing anguish. "We have been denied all rights pertaining to human beings," cried an official of the African National Congress in 1929. "We are treated as aliens in the land of our fathers. . . . We are spoon-fed like children . . . denied all representation. . . . As a nation we are practically dead . . . We are a race of servants . . . for the white man."

While the Congress continued to base its strategy in delegations and petitions, others sought more militant solutions. In 1918, the Industrial and Commercial Workers' Union (I.C.U.) was founded by Clements Kadalie, an African migrant from Nyasaland of great energy and eloquence. At once Kadalie and the I.C.U. organized a series of impressive strikes which captured the admiration of the African population and raised membership to a claimed figure of 100,000. In the long run, however, administrative inexperience and implacable official opposition brought the Union's undoing. Kadalie was embarrassed by the infiltration of white communists whom he purged with difficulty, but whose departure deprived him of capable and experienced lieutenants. There followed an organizational deterioration which was hastened by defections, particularly that of the Zulu leader, Allison Champion, who established a separate I.C.U. in Natal. By 1930, the movement was finished; Champion was exiled from Natal, Kadalie was in obscurity, and only a handful of small unions, isolated and short-lived, signaled the passing of the once powerful I.C.U.

The appearance of the communists marked an important moment for it was the first of a series of efforts to organize and control black nationalism in South Africa, raising at once the question of whether leadership and objectives were to be exclusively African or whether they would be diverted to the service of international communism. For Kadalie the choice was clearly in favor of parochial objectives, the end of racial discrimination and the improvement of working conditions at home. Since that time, communism has maintained an uncertain influence, its revolutionary appeal clouded in the minds of African nationalist leaders by its association with white domination. At the same time, both before and after the outlawing of the South African Communist Party in 1950, communism has offered obvious attractions in competition with Western constitutional forms which suffer the liability of example in the government of South Africa.

General Hertzog's introduction in 1936 of separate voting rolls in Cape Province gave rise to another African nationalist organization, the All-African Convention formed by Dr. D. D. T. Jabavu, the son of John Tengo Jabavu. The Convention at once entered a vigorous if vain protest and refused to cooperate in the operation of the Natives' Representation Council, established concurrently with the change in voting procedures and given empty advisory functions connected with a broad range of African affairs throughout the Union. For a time, the African National Congress allowed its members to serve on the Council, but over the years so little heed was paid to the Council's deliberations that in 1946 its total membership resigned in protest, thereby signaling a virtual declaration of non-cooperation against the South African government. With war's end, African demands had become much more insistent, even within the moderate African National Congress, but in 1948 the white position had also stiffened, and the result was, not reform as in other parts of Africa, but rather the victory of Dr. Malan's Nationalist Party and the institution of apartheid.

Turning away from the traditional constitutional weapons of petition and representation, despairing of any ultimate prospect for political and economic emancipation, African leadership now began to shift toward direct action while avoiding recourse to outright violence. In 1946, a strike was called by the African Mine Workers Union which brought out 70,000 workers and paralyzed the Witwatersrand mines for several days. Two years later, the A.N.C. initiated two one-day work stoppages, and in 1953 the Congress collaborated with the South African Indian Congress in a campaign of civil disobedience. Over a six-month period, 8500 African and Asian demonstrators were jailed, chiefly for deliberately breaking the color bar in public facilities. In 1957, there was a bus boycott in Johannesburg, while 1957 and 1958 were marked with further demonstrations, these by African women against their inclusion under the pass laws.

Such activities drew their inspiration from Gandhian principles of passive resistance, but frequently they led to violence in the course of police response. There was bloodshed in 1946 as the police drove to break the great mine strike. One of the 1950 sit-down strikes ended with rioting in Johannesburg during which eighteen Africans were killed and over thirty injured. The defiance campaign of 1953 was called off after a series of clashes with the police resulted in numbers of Africans shot dead or wounded. To rigorous police methods the government added other measures—proscription of the Communist Party in 1950, the inclusion of women and adolescents under the pass law regulations in 1956, a massive treason trial of ninety-one Africans, Asians, and European sympathizers begun late in 1956, and finally the outlawing of the African National Congress in 1960. These actions were usually effective in hampering African opposition. Even the treason trial, which ended in 1961 without a single conviction, succeeded in neutralizing the activities of most defendants.

As the lines of official repression hardened, African reaction grew correspondingly extreme. The traditional Congress philosophy of racial equality achieved through nonviolence seemed bankrupt, its leadership, including Chief Albert Luthuli, vacillating and unrealistic, and its association with white liberals and communists no longer acceptable. Luthuli had been elected Congress president in 1952, but by 1958 he and other moderates were challenged by a group of young activists led by Robert Sobukwe, a lecturer at Witswatersrand University. Unsuccessful in capturing the Congress, they formed the Pan-Africanist Congress in 1959 with a program of Africa-for-the-Africans, and a strategy of strikes and demonstrations designed to bring the downfall of the Nationalist government. The result was the anti-pass law marches of March, 1960 which culminated in the massacre at Sharpeville where sixty-nine people were shot down and many more wounded by a panicky police force.

By 1961, both congresses, acting underground, appeared ready to turn to sabotage as a weapon. With Sobukwe in prison, the Pan-Africanists organized a movement called Poqo for purposes of sabotage, but its activities soon extended to political terrorism. In the A.N.C. Chief Luthuli had reluctantly but gradually acquiesced in the weapon of sabotage, the function of the Spear of the Nation subsidiary of Congress which came into being in 1962. In 1964, a number of younger Congress leaders, including Walter Sisulu and Nelson Mandela, were brought to trial for sabotage. Mandela freely admitted his participation, arguing that violence was the only recourse to the African, all other means of opposing white supremacy having been blocked by legislation. By the time of his sentence to life imprisonment, this seemed to be a majority view among the African population.

There were, however, exceptions. Despite widespread poverty a small African middle class had developed, while living standards in South Africa continued to be generally superior to those in other parts of the continent; hence there are many Africans who would lose much through all-out resistance and revolution. Moreover, even the radicals have generally eschewed communism in favor of Western democracy and have taken to violence with reluctance—witness Sobukwe's insistence on mass demonstrations rather than terrorism. Finally, there is evidence to suggest that a certain number of Africans are prepared to proceed with apartheid in a Bantustan government wherein they exercise local autonomy. The Transkei prime minister, Chief Kaiser Matanzima, has maintained his position largely through the votes of government-nominated chiefs, but his policy of accepting the Bantustan principle while constantly demanding more rights within the framework of separate development has its African supporters. Matanzima seems genuinely to subscribe to apartheid as the best prospect for African advance; in any case, a broad-based African nationalism appears of late to be giving ground to a more limited version based in Xhosa, Zulu, or Sotho cohesion, and Chief Matanzima, for one, has gained significantly in active and passive African support since he took office in 1963.

SOUTH-WEST AFRICA AND THE HIGH COMMISSION TERRITORIES

At the time of South African unification, it was generally assumed that less developed neighboring territories such as Basutoland, Bechuanaland, Swaziland, and even the Rhodesias, would ultimately be absorbed, and the South Africa Act of 1909 which set forth the details of union, provided machinery for eventual incorporation. Britain was reluctant to see an immediate and unqualified transfer, however, and insisted on provisions which would protect the interests of the territorial inhabitants after transfer. The matter was not pressed at the moment, and did not arise again until 1935 by which time action without the consent of the African people themselves appeared increasingly remote. With the accession to power of the Nationalists in 1948, the question was again mooted, but by this late stage South

African racial policies had thoroughly alienated world opinion, and the move toward incorporation was replaced by a growing demand within the territories for eventual independence.

The South African government's desire to absorb the High Commission territories was to a large extent bound up in the matter of apartheid and the administration of African reserves. Underdeveloped and impecunious, Basutoland, Bechuanaland, and Swaziland had long been heavily dependent upon South Africa, not only in economic terms but for many public services as well. Currency and banking, postal and telegraph facilities, and tariffs were all externally administered, while South Africa served as the chief market and principal source of goods coming into the territories. Significantly, a large proportion of the labor force from each territory found work in South Africa; for Basutoland over 50 per cent of her adult males at any one time were migrant workers in the Union.

Such close dependence involving much personal coming and going by individuals who suffered no economic or political color bar at home, was a source of embarrassment to the Afrikaner regime. Moreover, the Nationalists hoped through eventual absorption to reorganize the patchwork pattern of the Bantustans while adding vastly to their area of African reserves. In short, the South African government regarded the Trust Territories as native reserves in all but name, and sought to add them to the areas already held, thereby raising the proportion of the reserves from approximately 13 per cent to near 45 per cent of an enlarged South Africa.

In Basutoland, however, with its tradition of independence and its overwhelming African population, the British moved in 1959 to introduce a degree of internal autonomy which was designed as a first step toward total independence. Bechuanaland, largely African in population, gained limited home rule in 1961 and subsequently forced further reforms which set her on the road to complete autonomy. Swaziland, with its considerable European influence and land ownership, encountered greater difficulty in drafting a satisfactory constitution, and suffered thereby a period of uncertainty, but in 1964 the Swazi paramount chief organized his own party and took power in a way that forecast eventual independence in the form of a constitutional monarchy. Thus South Africa, with absolute economic ascendancy over its indigent neighbors, was yet obliged to stand aside while they moved steadily toward political independence.

In South-West Africa, events took a decidedly different turn. This German protectorate was mandated to the South African government at the conclusion of the First World War and administered as an integral part of South African territory. Over the years the League of Nations Mandates Commission repeatedly criticized South African stewardship, pointing to exploitation of African labor, discrimination in favor of the white population, and an absence of much needed educational and social development.

When in 1946 South Africa asked of the United Nations that South-West Africa be incorporated as part of the Union, her request was denied and the deficiencies of her previous administration cited as evidence of her unfitness. When the International Court of Justice handed down a non-binding advisory opinion in 1950 that the United Nations had inherited League of Nations responsibility for South-West Africa, the Malan government countered by declaring that no United Nations responsibility existed for South-West Africa since the mandate had lapsed with the disappearance of the Permanent Mandates Commission of the League of Nations. Subsequent efforts by the United Nations to assume her obligations have all been thwarted. In July, 1966, the International Court of Justice, in a surprising decision, refused to rule on the question of a United Nations mandate over South-West Africa. The following October, the General Assembly voted to end the South African mandate but this action was repudiated by Pretoria as an illegal intrusion into South African domestic affairs. In 1968 the United Nations renamed the territory Namibia and attempted to send a delegation to South-West Africa for the purpose of assuming control, but this move was blocked when South Africa refused to permit entry.

Clearly South Africa will not relinquish its hold on the territory in response to anything short of force. South-West Africa has been administered according to the principle of apartheid and its African population suffers the same disabilities while its Europeans enjoy the same advantages as their corresponding groups within the Republic of South Africa. In 1968 the South African government announced plans for the eventual establishment of separate homelands for the black people of South-West Africa, presumably a first step toward extending the Bantustan policy to that area.

THE THEORY AND PRACTICE OF PARTNERSHIP
IN CENTRAL AFRICA

For all its narrowness of vision, there is a certain perverse validity about the doctrine of apartheid. It offers the African little prospect but at least it tells him squarely where he stands. To the north in the Rhodesias there was from the first much high-minded talk about responsibilities and privileges, civilizing missions and the promise of the future, but along with the oratory there developed a pattern of discrimination onerous in its uncertainty and vexing in its deception. After the conquest and pacification in Southern Rhodesia, the official policy called for eventual assimilation of the African into European civilization, but circumstance imposed a de facto segregation based upon the differences between two cultures. When the African began to close the chasm, however, impediments were placed in his path as political rights were withheld that social and economic advantages might be maintained. Eventually discrimination was elevated to the status of a principle called "two pyramids" or parallel development.

In one essential this doctrine was philanthropic, enunciating the racial integrity of the African and the validity of his traditional institutions, and thereby providing a local argument both for the policy of indirect rule introduced by Sir Frederick Lugard elsewhere in Africa and the concept of trusteeship developed in the British Colonial Office. In another respect, parallel development stressed the antagonistic nature of the white and black races, confident in the superiority which the European felt regarding his civilization and the need he saw for paternalistic rule to bring the African from the abyss of ignorance and barbarism. This second facet appeared prominently in an address delivered in 1938 by the Southern Rhodesian prime minister, Godfrey Huggins, whose words gave eloquent expression to the convictions of his European constituents. Western civilization, said Huggins, had brought peace, prosperity, and progress, offering the African opportunities for advance which his own culture had long denied him. In this he should be given every encouragement, but his development should be separate and under no circumstances should it be permitted to interfere with progress in the white man's preserve. "To permit this would mean that the leaven of civilisation would be removed from the country, and the black man would inevitably revert to a barbarism worse than ever before. . . . The higher standard of civilisation cannot be allowed to succumb."

The "two pyramids" therefore became in fact a system of racial segregation imposed by the dominant European group. The establishment of Southern Rhodesia as a self-governing colony in 1923 provided the necessary constitutional authority, and legislation followed which insured that there would be no effective black challenge to white rule. First, there was the Land Apportionment Act, passed in 1930, which instituted a form of apartheid in land holding. To the African reserves of 21,600,000 acres, this law added special areas totalling 7,500,000 acres, open only to purchase by Africans. At the same time African squatters on 49,100,000 acres of European lands were obliged to vacate, or remain as contract labor. The purpose was partly philanthropic—to protect land from competitive European bidding and insure its acquisition by African farmers. Nevertheless, the underlying philosophy was segregationist, and the practical effect was to create a landless African labor supply. Those who remained on European farms constituted a rural proletariat, while those who could not purchase and maintain a farm competitively on the generally poorer African lands gradually drifted to the cities for jobs in industry and life in a growing ghetto slum.

The second piece of discriminatory legislation was the Industrial Conciliation Act of 1934 which was later amended in 1945. This bill provided for Conciliation Boards to be composed of European employers and trade unionists, their function to set wage scales and working conditions in local industries. Specifically excluded were African unionists, however, for they were regarded as unready for skilled work. Although African unions, therefore, had no legal status, African laborers could in theory command the going wages established by the Conciliation Boards, for they were fixed regardless of race. Nevertheless, in practice it was the rare African chosen in preference to a European, and so in the towns a high European wage scale was set against the unprotected, unskilled labor of the African. In the countryside this legislation did not apply. The resultant wage differential between skilled European and unskilled African labor was of the order to 15 to 1.

For a time it appeared as though a form of settler domination would install itself in Northern Rhodesia as well, particularly when the discovery of large deposits of copper attracted European capital and settlers, and transformed a vast and poor land into an economic prize worth fighting for. The Rhodesian copper fields had long remained unexploited in the face of the richer, more accessible ores in nearby Katanga. During the 1920's, however, more sophisticated prospecting techniques began to reveal substantial deposits, but just at the moment when large-scale investment appeared worthwhile, the world-wide depression of the early thirties broke the market and momentarily killed interest. A slow recovery ensued, however, culminating in all-out production during the Second World War and establishing the Northern Rhodesian copperbelt during the postwar years as the world's third largest producer. By 1952 government revenue had increased eighty fold over the figure for 1924 while the value of exports climbed from $2 million to more than $230 million during the same period.

These spectacular financial progressions inevitably attracted settlers; thus the 3600 white inhabitants of 1924 had risen ten times by 1951 and reached a total of 65,000 in 1956, this against an indigenous African population of something over 2,000,000. While such a proportion almost doubled the 20 to 1 black-white ratio in Southern Rhodesia, the prospect of economic gain joined hands with European consensus in racial superiority to bring pressure for preferential controls similar to those already exercised in Salisbury. When British South Africa Company rule was supplanted by a Protectorate government in 1924, a legislative council was formed with an unofficial minority of elected Europeans, but gradually the minority grew until in the years after the Second World War it had gained equality of numbers with the official members.

Nevertheless, there were complications in the Northern Rhodesian situation which had never been present in the self-governing colony to the south. A protectorate involved protection, in this case by the British Colonial Office on behalf of the African population, a fact enunciated most forcefully in 1930 by the secretary of state for the colonies, Lord Passfield (the celebrated Fabian, Sidney J. Webb). Thus a strong sense of colonial trusteeship combined with the fact of a smaller settler population to bring forth a doctrine, not of parallel development in racial isolation, but of cooperative partnership between white and black with the British government acting as a balance between the two. The net result of this complex of forces was a steady move toward settler domination and a degree of economic color bar which, however, never quite achieved the complete political control which was the basis for racial discrimination in Southern Rhodesia.

In 1948 the settlers achieved parity on the legislative council and were represented on the executive council in a manner which was tantamount to responsible ministerial government. Nevertheless, in the same year Africans had been given appointed representation on both councils and in 1953 as the settlers gained a qualified legislative council majority, the African membership was again raised, representing a modest but clear-cut gain on white membership. Similarly, European trade unions on the copperbelt monopolized the skilled jobs and commanded thereby during the postwar years elevated salaries fully twenty times the average of $25 a month which was paid the African miner. Such glaring discrimination, however, was never protected by law and was broken in 1955 by the major companies in a move which quickly brought Africans into a range of job categories hitherto controlled by white miners. At the same time the African Mineworkers' Union obtained substantial wage increases for the mass of unskilled labor. Color bar there was in Northern Rhodesia, but never was it absolute nor was it imposed through the legislation of a white-controlled government.

As a British protectorate, Nyasaland also enjoyed the sanctuary of trusteeship, but an even more powerful protection against white domination was her lackluster economic promise. A deficiency of mineral resources meant almost total reliance on agriculture, but even here production of coffee, cotton, tobacco, and groundnuts offered minimal attractions to European planters who numbered only a few hundred by the end of the Second World War. In 1946 approximately 5 per cent of the total land area of the Protectorate was still in the hands of white settlers, mostly in the Shire highlands, but much of these holdings was subsequently purchased by the government, thereby replacing a status of tenancy with one of freehold for thousands of African families.

Such apparent advantages were not unmixed. Poor resources induced but few public improvements and if a small European population (only nine thousand out of almost three million in 1961) removed the problem of settler domination, it also meant that the country's modest economic potentialities were hardly worth contesting. With the constitutional reforms instituted in African territories after the Second World War, it was clear that European influence would decline in Nyasaland in the face of increasing African activity. It was equally clear that no degree of political autonomy would gain the economic independence which a poor land could not sustain.

THE RISE AND FALL OF FEDERATION
IN CENTRAL AFRICA

Neither parallel development nor partnership appeared to offer much prospect for genuine multiracial cooperation in Central Africa. The "two pyramid" system of Godfrey Huggins was admittedly and irrevocably autocratic, while partnership as practiced in Northern Rhodesia evoked an image, not of equal responsibility, but of the paternal relationship between senior partner and junior apprentice. Moreover, where the economic stake seemed worth the effort, the European community had imposed an effective color bar which checked African progress in favor of its own advantage. Any amalgamation of Central African territories based upon a concept of racial partnership, thus seemed in the light of past experience to be in danger of a white domination and exploitation not unlike that already in effect in South Africa.

This was the opinion, at any rate, of the African community, particularly in the two northern protectorates, whenever the question of territorial merger arose. In Nyasaland and Northern Rhodesia, the Africans remained unmoved by arguments describing the economic advance and improved social services which would follow amalgamation. No more were they impressed with the guarantee that an interterritorial government would exercise no authority in the sensitive area of African affairs. For them the key was the potential withdrawal of Crown protection and the likelihood of eventual independence for a white-dominated Central Africa which would place them at the mercy of a settler government such as had been the case with the Africans of Southern Rhodesia ever since 1923. This was no idle concern with phantoms. Godfrey Huggins, the leading Southern Rhodesian advocate of fusion, had a notoriously low opinion of African capabilities which argued a long tutelage before racial partnership could mean racial equality. His chief supporter from Northern Rhodesia, the union leader, Roy Welensky, admitted publicly that white domination would necessarily characterize federation, for, in his judgment, the African was clearly unqualified for full partnership.

Implacable African hostility delayed and altered the shape of federation, but it could not prevent it, for there were powerful forces within the settler community, and to a lesser extent within Britain, which urged some form of union. Many of the arguments were economic and administrative. Amalgamation would coordinate the resources of the three territories, it was said, bringing together Southern Rhodesia's industry and capital, Northern Rhodesia's copper, and Nyasaland's labor. Economic union would also mean administrative convenience in the sharing of public services and diminished expenses through common planning and joint utilization of personnel.

There were political and psychological factors as well. The Europeans of Southern Rhodesia had at one time considered throwing in their lot with South Africa, but for many the Afrikaner racial policies were too doctrinaire and unification northward now seemed preferable. For their part, the settlers in Northern Rhodesia felt themselves frustrated in their quest for self-government, and looked to a southern alliance as a possible means whereby British protection might be neutralized. Within Britain there were many who favored amalgamation on economic grounds, but the vision of a strong multiracial state in Central Africa also had appeal as a barrier against the possible expansion of South African racialism. Perhaps most of all was the long-lived and long-frustrated desire among the Rhodesian settlers for true independence and dominion status. Could not unification of the three territories be the first step in a process which would end when Central Africa achieved her place within the world community of nations?

British uneasiness over the intensity of African opposition ruled out any centralized union such as that of South Africa, but introduced the alternative possibility of federation, and so it was that a series of conferences led to the final shaping of a new state which made its appearance in October, 1953, as the Federation of Rhodesia and Nyasaland (Central African Federation). Elections were held in each territory for a federal legislature of 35, the two protectorates holding 18 seats between them against 17 for Southern Rhodesia. Each territory elected 2 Africans as well as 1 European who was specifically charged with looking after African interests; thus, overall, the whites had 26 and the Africans 9 representatives. The election was marked by an emergent European opposition matching the African distaste for federation; in Southern Rhodesia a party formed to contest the election on the grounds that the new arrangement would undermine white supremacy. Nevertheless, the United Federal Party swept into power in all three territories and its leader, Godfrey Huggins, became the first federal prime minister while his lieutenant and eventual successor, Roy Welensky, was installed as minister of transport and development.

This initial success in no way meant the end of opposition which, on the contrary, continued to build up pressures in the ensuing years. The right wing among the settlers emerged as the Dominion Party, led by Winston Field, which set an antagonistic face against the concept of partnership. Too liberal on racial matters to suit the segregationists, the Federation leaders nevertheless impressed the African as implacably hostile to genuine racial partnership. Moreover, the African no longer was satisfied with partnership; increasingly he thought in terms of popular sovereignty—one man, one vote. Under fire from both the European right and the African left, the Federation ultimately fell victim to what appeared at first as the less formidable of these factors, the force of African nationalism.

In Nyasaland and Northern Rhodesia, African resistance to European controls had been early marked by the Ethiopian church movement which brought forth the futile rising of John Chilembwe at Blantyre in 1915. Later it shifted toward an effort to gain representation and redress through constitutional means; then with industrialization came labor discontent, specifically directed at the discriminatory wage structure in the copperbelt. By the time of federation, clearly defined nationalist movements in the northern territories had taken shape, the Nyasaland African Congress having been founded in 1944 while a Northern Rhodesia African Congress followed four years later. Within settler-dominated Southern Rhodesia, African nationalism crystallized later still, a militant Congress movement emerging only in 1957. The driving forces of nationalism were the usual ones—great social and economic changes leading both to self-awareness on a supra-tribal scale, and in the case of the people of Central Africa, to a resistance against the social and economic discrimination practiced by their white rulers. In nationalist eyes, the Federation was the capstone to the system of inequality which would place them in a position of permanent inferiority. At all costs it had to be destroyed.

In Southern Rhodesia there was some ambivalence in the African attitude toward federation. Nationalist leaders, like African National Congress president Joshua Nkomo, were firmly opposed, but others argued that a federal connection which brought them closer to the great African populations in the northern territories would eventually facilitate liberal reform in the south. The reaction in Nyasaland, however, was immediate and intense, its hostility explained in part by the experience of many Nyasa laborers with racial patterns in Southern Rhodesia and in part by the absence of a strong settler community. In 1955 a constitutional change permitted the election of five Africans to the legislative council, and Congress, led by the militant Henry Chipembere and M. W. K. Chiume, easily captured all five seats. Nonetheless, five votes out of twenty-three was a long way from political power, and the situation became more urgent in 1957 when Welensky, now federal prime minister, secured agreement in Britain for a review of the Federation constitution to take place in 1960, the probable outcome to be Central African independence within the British Commonwealth.

Extra-parliamentary tactics were clearly needed. Chipembere and Congress urged Dr. H. Kamuzu Banda to return to his native land and assume the leadership of the nationalist movement. Banda's qualifications were maturity and an ease in dealing with Europeans gained from long years as a medical practitioner in England. What he also provided was an incendiary leadership which touched off the emotion-charged atmosphere in Nyasaland, leading to outbreaks of violence in 1959, and then to the declaration of a state of emergency, the banning of the Nyasaland African Congress, and the detention of Banda and a number of his Congress lieutenants.

Explosions in Nyasaland were no isolated events during these fateful days; rather they were part of the upsurge toward independence in Africa which was quickly changing the map of the continent. In Kenya the Macmillan government provided for a new constitution early in 1960 which assured an African legislative majority, and shortly thereafter Dr. Banda was released from prison and invited to participate in a conference which introduced similar changes in Nyasaland. At the head of the newly formed Malawi Congress Party, Banda now gained full control of the territorial government as the result of general elections held in August, 1961. With this victory, the stage was set for secession and the eventual dissolution of the Federation.

In Northern Rhodesia, African discontent was no less pronounced, but here the nationalist drive against federation faced much more formidable obstacles. First there was a white settler community led by powerful European trade unions. Beyond this, there were important economic assets at stake. Welensky and the federalists could ill afford to let the copperbelt follow Nyasaland; moreover, federation and ultimate independence rested on the continued union between north and south, and Southern Rhodesia—right-wing extremists aside—was as determined as the north not to allow a fatal split to occur.

In 1951 the Northern Rhodesia African Congress came under the leadership of a militant former school teacher, Harry Nkumbula, who renamed it the African National Congress and conducted a vigorous, albeit futile, fight against the inauguration of federation in 1953. Congress feared both the prospect of increased discrimination and the growing influence of Southern Rhodesia, and its apprehensions were heightened by such developments as the choice of Salisbury for federal capital and the shift of the Northern Rhodesian Kafue dam project to the interterritorial Kariba site on the Zambezi. When Welensky became premier in 1956 and stepped up his fight to loosen the controls of the Colonial Office, the situation appeared desperate to Northern Rhodesian Africans, long smarting under the indignities of social and economic color bar and aware of the far greater disabilities of the Africans in Southern Rhodesia.

Congress' main weapon against discrimination during this period was the boycott which was employed extensively but without great success and which usually resulted in violence and government reprisals. Both Nkumbula and the Congress secretary-general, Kenneth Kaunda, were jailed briefly in 1955, a martyrdom which helped their cause but was more than offset by growing strains within Congress affecting its unity of purpose and action. Indeed, the two men were beginning to dispute leadership and tactics with each other, the popular Kaunda urging more vigorous political opposition, the less extreme Nkumbula losing rank-and-file support because of his apparent dictatorial manner.

Late in 1958 a formal split occurred when Kaunda and his militant colleague, Simon Kapwepwe, founded the Zambia African

National Congress, Kapwepwe inventing the name "Zambia" for the occasion. Z.A.N.C. immediately made serious inroads into Congress membership, but not enough to prevent Nkumbula's Congress from conducting an effective electoral campaign early in 1959 under a new constitution which, however, most Africans, Nkumbula included, considered thoroughly unsatisfactory in its African representation. Z.A.N.C. attempted to impose an election boycott by force, but this move was only partially successful as the new party was proscribed and its leaders placed in detention. Nevertheless, by 1960 they were all once more at liberty and a new party organized, the United National Independence Party (U.N.I.P.) with Kaunda as president.

Violence and unrest continued, largely stimulated by U.N.I.P. agitators, as gradually it became apparent that Northern Rhodesia, like Nyasaland, would sooner or later have its African-dominated government, an eventuality which could only mean secession and the end of the Federation. An African legislative majority in Northern Rhodesia was the recommendation of the Monckton Commission assembled by the British government in 1959 to advise on the future of federation, but such an unequivocal solution was as yet premature. Instead, the Colonial Secretary, Ian Macleod, put forward a complex constitution in the hope that neither Welensky's federalists nor the African nationalists would gain a clear majority, and federation would thereby be saved. Hence, as Banda and his Malawi Congress Party moved smoothly toward internal self-government, achieved early in 1963, and then proceeded with determination to total independence, elections were scheduled in Northern Rhodesia for October, 1962, in an atmosphere of uncertainty. The results of the voting under the Northern Rhodesian constitution of 1962 gave a clear majority neither to Kaunda's U.N.I.P. nor to Welensky's United Federal Party, and placed the balance of power with the African National Congress and Harry Nkumbula. Nevertheless, an African government was formed when Nkumbula joined Kaunda in coalition, the white United Federalists acting as opposition.

Welensky and his federalists had now been compelled to yield control of both protectorates to the forces of African nationalism. In December, 1962 they lost Southern Rhodesia as well, not to the Africans who were in firm check, but to the right-wing Rhodesian Front, a successor to the Dominion Party. In elections held that month, the Front defeated the United Federal Party when the latter proposed the end of color bar in public facilities. Hence all three territories had come under control of groups hostile to the concept and the fact of federation. There was no longer any basis for its survival, and at the end of 1963 the Federation of Rhodesia and Nyasaland ceased to exist.

Suggestions for Further Reading

For the recent history of South Africa involving the rise of Afrikaner nationalism and apartheid, a number of general works may be cited. See, for example, Gwendolen Carter, *The Politics of Inequality*, rev. ed. (New York: Praeger, 1959); L. M. Thompson, *Republic of South Africa* (Boston: Little, Brown, 1966); E. A. Walker, *A History of Southern Africa*, 3rd. ed. (London: Longmans, 1962; New York: Barnes & Noble, 1964); Pierre van den Berghe, *South Africa: A Study in Conflict* (Berkeley and Los Angeles: University of California Press, 1967); Leo Marquard, *The Peoples and Policies of South Africa*, 3rd. ed. (London: Oxford University Press, 1962); and John Cope, *South Africa*, 2nd. ed. (London: Ernest Benn, 1967; New York: Praeger, 1967).

The African perspective may be gained largely from literary sources, for example, Chief Albert Luthuli, *Let My People Go* (London: Collins, 1962; New York: McGraw-Hill, 1962); E. Mphahlele, *Down Second Avenue* (London: Faber, 1959); the fictional *Walk in the Night* by Alex La Guma (Ibadan, Nigeria: Mbari Publications, n.d.; Evanston, Ill.: Northwestern University Press, 1963); or even the jazz opera *King Kong* (London: Collins, 1961). For the African National Congress, see Mary Benson, *The African Patriots* (London: Faber, 1963) and particularly Edward Feit, *The Dynamics of the African National Congress* (London: Oxford University Press, 1962). The Communist role is described in E. Roux, *Time Longer than Rope* (London: Gollancz, 1948; Madison, Wis.: University of Wisconsin Press, 1964). See also Edward Feit, *African Opposition in South Africa* (Stanford: Hoover Institution, 1967).

Nationalism, both Boer and Bantu, is analyzed by E. S. Munger in *Afrikaner and African Nationalism* (London: Oxford University Press, 1967). See also W. H. Vatcher, *White Laager: The Rise of Afrikaner Nationalism* (New York: Praeger, 1965; London: Pall Mall, 1965). C. R. Hill discusses the logical outcome of apartheid in *Bantustans* (London: Oxford University Press, 1964), while Ruth First's *South West Africa* (Harmondsworth, Middlesex and Baltimore: Penguin, 1963), deals with the history of that territory. For the High Commission territories, Basutoland, Bechuanaland, and Swaziland, Jack Halpern, *South Africa's Hostages* (Baltimore: Penguin, 1965) is to be consulted.

Central Africa is well served with general histories. A. J. Hanna,

The Story of the Rhodesias and Nyasaland, 2nd. ed. (London: Faber, 1965; New York; Humanities Press, 1965); and A. J. Wills, *An Introduction to the History of Central Africa* (London: Oxford University Press, 1964) are supplemented by Richard Hall, *Zambia* (London: Pall Mall, 1965; New York: Praeger, 1965); L. H. Gann, *A History of Northern Rhodesia* (London: Chatto and Windus, 1964; New York: Humanities Press, 1965), and the same author's *History of Southern Rhodesia* (London: Chatto and Windus, 1965; New York: Humanities Press, 1965). Early nationalist stirrings in Nyasaland are described in detail in G. Shepperson and T. Price, *Independent African* (Edinburgh: The University Press, 1958; Chicago: Aldine, 1958) while the growth of nationalism in Northern Rhodesia and Nyasaland is traced in R. I. Rotberg, *The Rise of Nationalism in Central Africa* (Cambridge, Mass.: Harvard University Press, 1965).

Race relations in Central Africa is the subject of a trilogy produced under the auspices of the Institute of Race Relations in London: Philip Mason, *The Birth of a Dilemma* (London: Oxford University Press, 1958), and the same author's *Year of Decision* (London: Oxford University Press, 1960) which sandwich in time Richard Gray's *The Two Nations* (London: Oxford University Press, 1960).

For political analysis, see Colin Leys, *European Politics in Southern Rhodesia* (London: Oxford University Press, 1959); A. L. Epstein, *Politics in an Urban African Community* (Manchester: Manchester University Press, 1958; New York: Humanities Press, 1960); P. Keatley, *The Politics of Partnership* (Baltimore and Harmondsworth, Middlesex: Penguin, 1963); D. C. Mulford, *Zambia: the Politics of Independence, 1957–1964* (London: Oxford University Press, 1967); and James Barber, *Rhodesia: the Road to Rebellion* (London: Oxford University Press, 1967).

The African view of events in Central Africa may be measured through a number of works by African leaders. See, for example, Kenneth Kaunda, *Zambia Shall Be Free* (London: Heinemann, 1962; New York, Praeger, 1963); Kaunda's speeches edited by Colin Legum under the title, *Zambia, Independence and Beyond* (London: Nelson, 1966; New York: Internat'l. Publications Service, 1966); and a selection of his letters to Colin M. Morris, entitled *A Humanist in Africa* (London: Longmans, 1966). Also to be consulted are N. Sithole, *African Nationalism* (Cape Town: Oxford University Press, 1959; 2nd ed., London, 1968; New York, 1969); and Nathan Shamuyarira, *Crisis in Rhodesia* (Nairobi: East African Publishing House, 1967; London: André Deutsch, 1965; New York: Transatlantic Arts, 1965).

21: Toward Independence

THE FOUNDATIONS OF FREEDOM

Colonialism contained the germ of its own destruction; indeed, the whole colonial system was a vast engine for the creation of a modern self-governing Africa. By conquering, colonialism caused the desire to be free. By exploiting, it produced a rising resistance to tyranny. By introducing Africa to the modern world, it generated visions of a better life consummated in liberty. By demonstrating its own fallibility, it begot the hope that led to autonomy. By educating, it taught the skills of self-direction.

The educated African was the father of the independent African. Missionaries, commencing their work in West Africa early in the nineteenth century, introduced literacy as a necessary avenue to Christianity, but with education came ideas and ideals that were to change forever the African world. European humanitarianism exemplified in the abolitionist movement and Western liberalism enunciated by France's democratic principles of 1789 made quick converts of educated West Africans like Paul Holle, Bishop Crowther, and Samuel Lewis. Nevertheless, admiration for Western civilization joined with the desire to share in its material improvement and its principles of self-government, while later observers like James Johnson, John Chilembwe, or Harry Thuku were not slow to note the shortfall that had developed between Christian ideals and the realities of colonial rule.

In South Africa, the religion of humility and poverty evidently meant to reserve those qualities only for the black man. In the Congo, brotherhood was somehow converted to parental domination, while in West Africa, despite European democracy, the fruits of European technology appeared to be limited largely to the colonial ruler. European education, introduced by Europeans, came to liberate, but remained to command. The missionaries opened more and more schools but their products were permitted only to fill the lower ranks of governmental offices, of foreign trading establishments, of hospitals and schools, even of the Christian churches themselves.

Yet the effects of education could not be cut off at this subordinate, functional level. New ideas not only stimulated new hopes, they also provided the means for their realization. With education came the professional and technical skills necessary for creating the modern society the educated African desired. An educated group gained cohesion through literacy, and found a common objective in its appetite for the advantages of Western technology. The educated African, through the medium of his education, emerged as the new leader of African societies, a leader whose whole being strained toward revolutionary change.

As the network of education extended itself, it carried the doctrine of change farther, and deeper into the new African mentality. Traditional society appeared no longer acceptable in its poverty and sickness, its static tribalism and its antiquated values. Set against this unpromising picture was the European system with its powerful technology, its wealth, its modern medicine, its dynamism, and its optimism. Those who glimpsed the vision of modernization wanted more—more economic development, more public improvements, more political expression, and above all, more education as their prime prerequisite to political, social, and economic emancipation.

These demands came gradually, proportionate to the introduction of Western education, but there were other factors also militating for change which would lead to eventual national independence. Missionaries had come to liberate slaves and save souls but they remained to initiate social and economic reforms to which European mercantile interests and colonial governments likewise lent force in their time. One such change was the gradual but portentous shift from an economy based on subsistence agriculture to one which dealt with cash crops in an international market. In the long run this was to have ramifications well beyond the economic.

Not only did this changing economy introduce a common, compact currency, commercial agriculture, and prestigious, attractive manufactured imports, it had profound implications for ancient concepts regarding land tenure, the individual and the family, social status, and rules of inheritance. New principles of land utilization, new standards for labor incentive reached out into villages, and as increasing numbers developed a stake in the new system, they were increasingly determined to have a say in its operation as well. By the conclusion of the Second World War, the degree of growing involvement was considerable. On the Gold Coast, for example, cocoa exports rose between 1901 and 1951 from 1,000 to 230,000 tons, the value of timber exports over the same period from £70,000 to £4,977,000. In Nigeria by 1948 more than two of every five adult males were active participants in the cash economy. Uganda cotton produced but 500 bales for the outside market in 1906, but by 1953–1954 the figure had risen to 398,000 bales yielding an income of £12,750,000.

The same forces driving the economic revolution brought other fundamental changes. Colonial governments, not noted for their open-handed approach to public improvements, nonetheless built roads, constructed harbors, dredged rivers, installed telegraphic communication, and even introduced expensive networks of railroads. In East Africa the railway from Mombasa to Kampala created the economy of the Kenyan white highlands and established cotton production in Uganda. In Senegal, the line which was opened between Dakar and St. Louis in 1885 secured groundnut culture in the Cayor and converted Dakar from an insignificant administrative center into a great international port. Throughout West Africa railway and road systems were invariably directed toward the sea where they connected with a series of expanding entrepôts—Freetown, Dakar, Monrovia, Abidjan, Lagos, and others whose economic utility depended upon the breakwaters, channels, and other artificial devices introduced by European engineering.

These facilities did more than increase the economic activity which gave the African a growing stake in his new society. They also helped create nations out of the colonial territories which had been stamped across the African map in the council chambers of Europe. Typically, transportation and communication systems were internal and extended only as far as colonial frontiers, thus complicating international intercourse within Africa. Internally, however, they meant an easier movement of people and ideas—out of the isolation of village life, from countryside to city and back, from region to region, and among numbers of different ethnic and cultural backgrounds. If roads were a stimulant to commerce, they also helped spread the ideas which itinerant traders carried along with their goods, pollinating out-of-the-way communities with concepts that weakened their provincialism and broadened their experience. If rail lines were an aid to the administration of large areas by small cadres of European officers, they also moved Africans about in ever-increasing tempo, especially from the village to the town where the growing points of modernization were located.

The cities, crucial as a force driving toward independence, were essentially a new phenomenon, born out of the mercantile, cash crop economy. They wrenched the African from the comfortable familiarity of his rural community and thrust him into a strange world where he became dependent upon a salaried job and where he was lost in the impersonality and competitiveness of urban life. At the same time, however, the city offered excitement and freedom from traditional restraints. There, aggressiveness and ability were rewarded, and new ideas and relationships became a common fact of life. Where these urban centers were carefully regulated as in the Belgian Congo, their inhabitants under close surveillance as with South Africa or the Portuguese territories, it was difficult for overt nationalist activity to take shape, but in other areas—British West Africa, for example—the development of an assertive leadership and a devoted mass following was much more easily brought into being.

The importance of cities was out of all proportion to their share of national population. Even today African cities outside southern Africa contain no more than 15 per cent of the population of essentially agrarian states. The significance of the city rested in its strategic location at the center of power, of change, and of economic development. Even the tribal associations in the cities, arising out of a need to maintain connections with home, lineage, and the old way of life, played their part, for they were also important means for the dissemination of new ideas of urban origin back to the less sophisticated countryside.

Colonial rule was pointed toward self-destruction in yet another important way. Whether by direct administration through designated headmen or indirectly through established rulers, the regime steadily weakened the chiefly authority and the traditional sources of power.

Appointed chiefs had no standing with their people and legitimate princes gradually lost respect and authority as they were obliged to perform unchiefly and unpopular duties, like tax collection, road maintenance, and public health enforcement, at the instance of their colonial masters. This situation lent circumstantial authority to the argument of the educated elite that they, and not the chiefs, were best qualified to lead their people in these changing times. Consequently, while colonial governments were systematically weakening themselves at the grass roots, they were elevating, despite their intentions, a new class of leaders who were a potential source of disaffection.

This need not have been the case, for the African elite were confirmed in their attachment to European institutions and values, and would have been pleased by nothing more than a genuine partnership with Europeans in administering colonial territories. Rejected by European administrators, however, they began to take advantage of their Western education to formulate concepts of African freedom and to organize vehicles for political action. This process had been first set in motion by nineteenth-century leaders like Africanus Horton and Edward Blyden, and continued through *fin de siècle* critics like John Mensah Sarbah, James Johnson, or John Tengo Jabavu.

By the end of the First World War, educated Africans had become a thoroughly frustrated group, not only because they were forced to play what they considered to be an inadequate political role but because they chafed as well under a discrimination which checked their professional and economic ambitions and rubbed raw their social sensibilities. It is probably no accident that Herbert Macaulay, one of the few West Africans trained as an engineer and thus foredoomed to a subordinate post in the government, turned to political agitation as an outlet for his energy and sense of self-respect. During the period between the two World Wars, the African unofficial members of the legislative councils both in Nigeria and the Gold Coast maintained a continual barrage of complaints over discrimination against Africans in the appointment of magistrates, medical examiners, and other officials, over double-standard pay scales, and over economic policies which militated against the African businessman and in favor of his European competitor.

These complaints were accompanied both by an assertion of African cultural identity and a demand for political reform. Blyden had been an early advocate, though not practitioner, of the concept of an African personality, and he was followed in time by many others—the Nigerians, Majola Agbebi and James Johnson, the Gold Coast leaders, J. E. Casely Hayford and S. R. B. Attoh-Ahuma, and that later exponent of *négritude*, Léopold Senghor of Senegal—to name but a few. In the years after the Second World War and to a lesser extent before, African cultural identity found expression in literary and artistic output associated with such names as Ousmane Socé Diop, Mongo Beti, or Chinua Achebe, as well as with that lively advocate of Africanness, *Présence Africaine*.

Political expression came in the form of properly constituted and legal parties such as Macaulay's Nigerian National Democratic Party or Casely Hayford's National Congress of British West Africa, of less acceptable political organizations like the Kikuyu-inspired East African Association or the National Congress in South Africa, and of any number of journals with nationalist political sentiments. Where such developments were most thoroughly proscribed there were the nativist syncretistic movements, exemplified by Kimbanguism, to express nationalist discontent in sublimated form.

These organizations were part of a larger growth of so-called voluntary associations which arose throughout Africa in response to the developing needs of the new city dwellers. It was not merely a question of maintaining family or lineage links, although that was always important; these groups included as well trade unions, social clubs, sports associations, cultural fraternities, mutual aid societies, and religious movements, each with its special concerns. Whatever their origins, however, the voluntary associations came to have a political role as a training ground for leadership, as African-controlled information networks, as centripetal forces within a heterogeneous population, and finally as nuclei for political organization of the mass supporters of overt political action. Some like the Kikuyu Central Association were largely political in objective, to begin with. Others exerted influence by indirection—witness the connection between the Yoruba cultural society, Egbe Omo Oduduwa, and the Action Group of Chief Obafemi Awolowo or the subtle cohesion of ideas and objectives among the West African graduates of the Ecole William Ponty in Dakar.

Related to successful political organization was the public press with its ability to reach the growing numbers of literate individuals emerging from the expanding school systems. Newspapers had long been common in West African towns, but before the Second World War their appeal had been limited largely to the few educated elite. This pattern was destroyed forever in 1935 when Nnamdi Azikiwe, an Ibo representative of the new urban culture, became editor of the Accra *African Morning Post.* Two years later Azikiwe founded the *West African Pilot* in Lagos and a revolutionary brand of journalism had been launched.

Zik, as he was known to his contemporaries, was well endowed by temperament and training for the role he was destined to play in the rise of African nationalism. Born and reared outside the protective shell of traditional village life, he had gone to the United States during the mid-twenties for university study, receiving there not only his formal education but a liberal dose of survival techniques for a black man in a white-dominated world. When he returned to West Africa, he brought a practical knowledge of life and a first-hand experience with the race problem in America, its segregation, its lynchings, and its riots as well as the varying techniques of protest as practiced by such leaders as Marcus Garvey and W. E. B. Du Bois. Azikiwe had witnessed the spread of the back-to-Africa movement and the Negro flirtation with world communism, and he had watched the growth of a militant black press characterized by sensationalism and race consciousness.

Such experiences catalyzed personal energy and ambition to produce a different approach—demagogic and provocative—which replaced the urbane moderation of the established elite with the tactics of strident protest. Demands for measured constitutional reform were jettisoned, and in their stead were introduced appeals to racialism and positive action. Gone were the well-written but ponderous columns of Zik's predecessors, giving way to a fiery journalism which had great attraction for the growing numbers of urban dwellers with minimum education but expanding expectations. Azikiwe fixed upon specific grievances of farmers, clerks, unemployed, market women, and others, always associating their complaints in the popular mind with an anticolonial viewpoint. As imitators followed Azikiwe's lead, this lively penny press quickly extended its influence beyond local and ethnic limits, helped bring a new dynamism to nationalism in Africa, and in time served as a vehicle for the formation of actual political movements and parties.

The influence on Azikiwe of his foreign residence and experience was repeated in many other instances, which in their aggregate were an important factor in shaping the African independence movement. As always, it was a question of education, direct or indirect, which exposed observers from Africa to the many expressions of man's constant quest to be free. The Gold Coast barrister, John Mensah Sarbah, had learned Victorian liberalism along with his Blackstone during a long residence in England, while Blaise Diagne's early assertiveness stemmed as much from close familiarity with French attitudes and institutions as from personal predilections. In Britain there were long-established philanthropic organizations like the Anti-Slavery and Aborigines' Protection Society ready to encourage the resident aliens from Africa, while after the Second World War the Labour Party gave direct governmental sanction to the idea of African reform. France, too, had her philanthropic societies, but political connections were more influential as evidenced by Diagne's association with the Republican Socialist Party and by the formation in 1936 of a Senegalese branch of the French Socialists under the leadership of Lamine Guèye.

These were but individual examples in retail. During the First World War, thousands of Africans served as soldiers in Europe and gained first-hand knowledge of the West, an experience which was greatly intensified during the conflict from 1939 to 1945. Between the wars, moreover, increasing numbers of students passed an extended residence in Britain and America, if not in France, Portugal, or Belgium, where they were able to observe the theory and practice of democracy along with colonialism and racialism. Between 1925 and 1945 the West African Students' Union, organized by the Yoruba, Ladipo Solanke, provided Nigerians in Britain with a sense of racial awareness and thus influenced a whole generation of future West African public figures. Of equal importance was a small group of Africans living in the United States during the late thirties and forties. Some of them had been encouraged to study in America by Azikiwe and came in time to share many of his experiences in a land where political democracy joined hands with anti-imperialism, and lack of class consciousness with individualism, all these qualities fused with a pattern of segregation and discrimination which spread across the land. Thus were such future leaders as Kwame Nkrumah, Ozuomba Mbadiwe of Nigeria, and the Sierra Leonean John Karifa-Smart enabled to develop a spirit of aggressiveness to accompany their sense of pride in race.

During the years of the Second World War these Africans in America were particularly impressed by the high-principled idealism which characterized statements of President Roosevelt and others describing their vision of the postwar world. Indeed, the Second World War was in many ways a major stimulant to the African urge toward independence. Forgotten were the disillusionment and frustrations following the first war when colonies were specifically denied the right of national self-determination and the pan-African movement gradually degenerated into sterile futility. More particularly, thousands had ample opportunity to familiarize themselves with Asian resistance movements during campaigns in the Middle East, India, and Burma, while many others observed at first hand the behavior of European troops compared with their own capabilities. Especially memorable were the initial defeats and the humiliation of the Western powers in the Pacific by members of a supposedly inferior race, as well as the role of African *tirailleurs* in sustaining French freedom in Africa while the metropole lay prostrate under Nazi domination.

The War wrought other changes which had their impact in Africa. France defeated and Britain exhausted in victory marked a new era in the balance of international power. The United States and the Soviet Union emerged from the War as the two world leaders, each the head of a powerful bloc and each with its special reasons for disliking colonialism. As the era of the Cold War unfolded, the two appealed increasingly for the support of the peoples of Asia, Africa, and Latin America, and in the process made no secret of their disapproval of the colonial system. While Portugal remained fixed in her colonial possessiveness, and France withdrew but slowly from Indochina, the Dutch finally agreed to abandon Indonesia, and Britain arranged for independence in India, Pakistan, Ceylon, and Burma. The Atlantic Charter, pronounced by Roosevelt and Churchill during the years of conflict, had proclaimed the right of self-determination for all peoples, and when the British prime minister appeared later to repudiate his stand, this action merely stimulated further the rising aspirations to freedom in Africa.

At the conclusion of hostilities, the Labour government succeeded to power in Britain, and with Labour came a view of colonial stewardship that differed markedly from Churchill's concept of empire. Even as the French were reinterpreting colonial status in terms of partnership as enunciated at the Brazzaville Conference of 1944, the authorities in Whitehall were searching for new imperial definitions which would lead to eventual freedom for colonial people within a British commonwealth. By war's end, however, these vague assurances were no longer satisfactory to African nationalists. The Fifth Pan-African Congress meeting in Manchester, England, in 1945 demanded immediate independence for Africa, and thereby set the tone which would characterize the political aspirations of the African people in the postwar world.

INDEPENDENCE MOVEMENTS IN THE NORTHEAST

Ethiopia, the last African nation to lose her independence, was also the first to regain it. Menelik's failing health during his final years had introduced another period of political and dynastic uncertainty which was obliged to run its course through the brief, unsettled reign of the apostate to Islam, Emperor Lij Jasu (1913–1916), the accession to the throne of Menelik's daughter, Zauditu, under the regency of *Ras* Tafari, and finally the assumption of power in 1928 by *Ras* Tafari who was crowned Emperor Haile Selassie I in 1930 upon the death of Zauditu.

Haile Selassie's regency had been a period of slowly developing authority out of which he hoped to introduce reforms which would resume the modernization process begun by Menelik. Aside from progress in governmental administration and public works construction, a beginning was made toward the abolition of slavery and the replacement of feudal dues with controlled taxation. A ministry of education was formed in 1930, and the following year the emperor granted the country's first constitution, one, however, which provided only for an appointed parliament exercising limited advisory authority. Indeed, as emperor, Haile Selassie appeared to view his political role, not in terms of leadership toward democratic reform, but rather in the development of a loyal bureaucracy within the central government to offset the centrifugal force of the country's regional feudal barons.

These modest steps toward national strength were jolted to a standstill in 1935 by the rapid rise of a militant imperialism in Fascist Italy. Entrenched in Eritrea and Italian Somaliland, Mussolini precipitated a series of border incidents which were utilized as an excuse for invasion in October, 1935. By that time, Haile Selassie had already been forsaken, for all practical purposes, by the impotent League of Nations which Ethiopia had joined in 1923, and by those Western statesmen unwilling to challenge Italian aggression at the price of possible war in Europe. Unlike the days of Adowa, the Italian armies came fully prepared to wage a modern, mechanized war, whereas the Ethiopian levies were neither well equipped nor coordinated to mass their strength at crucial points. In the end, antiquated tactics offset personal bravery, and the spirited defence of difficult mountainous terrain yielded to Italian firepower and the devastation of repeated unopposed aerial bombardment. By the spring of 1936 the Italians were approaching Addis Ababa, and when it was clear that the shattered Ethiopian forces were incapable of defending the city, Haile Selassie left the country to place his cause directly before the League of Nations. Within a few days of his departure, the Italians were in Addis Ababa, and Mussolini could announce to the world the annexation of Ethiopia.

Despite continued guerrilla resistance, Ethiopia had finally become an Italian possession, but in fact, the triumph was short-lived. In 1941, in a campaign arising out of the Second World War, columns of British troops invaded Ethiopia from both Kenya and the Sudan, and, aided by guerrilla forces, were able within a few months to recapture the mountain kingdom. On May 5, 1941, five years to the day after Marshal Badoglio had entered Addis Ababa, Emperor Haile Selassie returned to his capital. Eritrea, taken at the same time, was administered by Britain under United Nations aegis until 1952, at which time it was federated as an autonomous unit with Ethiopia, the latter taking responsibility for external affairs. Such an arrangement appeared unlikely to endure in the face of economic interdependence, a mutual desire for union, and the ill-concealed pressures by the emperor's government to absorb the smaller territory. Despite growing misgivings within Eritrea over the absolutism of the Ethiopian regime, a series of steps brought the two units closer together until, in 1962, the Eritrean government announced that the country had become an integral part of the Ethiopian state.

The invasion of Ethiopia by Britain's military forces had been facilitated by her control of the neighboring Sudan, but in fact by the era of the Second World War colonialism was already reaching a dead end in that ancient land. The nationalist demands put forth by the leaders of the Graduates' General Congress, though peremptorily turned aside in 1942, arose at a time when the administration was already contemplating an extension of political responsibility. This was implemented in 1944 by the creation of a governmental advisory council of preponderantly Sudanese representatives, and by the end of the War, self-determination for the Sudan had been conceded in principle. What remained to be decided were details of timing and the matter of future relations with Egypt.

While the nationalists remained divided between the Umma party and the pro-Egyptian Ashiqqa of Ismail al-Azhari, the Egyptians continued to resist the idea of an independent Sudan until the military coup of 1952 brought the Nasser-Naguib group to power. The new military government, more flexible than its predecessor on the Sudan question, agreed in 1953 to immediate Sudanese self-government with self-determination to be settled within the following three years. This action, in effect ratifying what the British had already decided upon, set the stage for elections late in 1953 which resulted in a pronounced victory for Azhari and his Ashiqqa supporters, now reconstituted as the National Unionist Party.

The apparent preference of the Sudanese electorate for union with Egypt was in fact illusory, the strong support for Azhari reflecting rather a national dislike for the traditional Umma friendliness toward the British. The situation was misjudged by many outsiders including the Egyptians whose subsequent tactless diplomacy further alienated the Sudan, but Azhari correctly judged the popular tone and quickly converted himself from a unionist to the leader of the Sudanese independence movement. As prime minister, he moved without delay toward republican status which was formally declared on January 1, 1956. Autonomy brought little national unity, however. The old divisions remained between the Khatmiyya of Ali al-Mirghani and the *ansar*, or followers, of Abd al-Rahman al-Mahdi, while in the long run, Azhari's astute tactics in leading the country to independence deprived him of the rallying cry of union with Egypt which had hitherto kept his partisans united. The resultant deterioration of national politics into factionalism led to a fatal instability which was further aggravated by the growing problem of the southern Sudan.

This was another legacy of colonial policy. After the breakup of the Mahdist state, the British pacification and subsequent occupation of the southern provinces had been conducted quite separately from the administration of the Muslim, Arabic-speaking north. Islamic influences were not countenanced in the south; instead, indigenous institutions were encouraged, and Christian missionaries permitted to establish stations. As Sudanese independence approached, however, British officers were rapidly replaced with northerners whose policy of forced assimilation into the Islamic-Arabic cultural orbit of the north led to reaction and rebellion in 1955, peace being restored only with difficulty. Having rejected union with Egypt, the Sudan now faced centrifugal forces within its own land which were intolerable to a growing spirit of nationalism. It was imperative that cohesion be effected between two regions vastly different in culture and background, the north often prejudiced and eager to force closer ties through Islamic education and religious proselytization, the south suspicious and resistant to the point of open hostility.

The south and other problems of early independence seemed to elude the solutions of increasingly opportunistic politicians. Western parliamentary government appeared ill-suited to a land where traditions were rooted in long-lived personal loyalties and deep religious commitments. When, in 1958, a bloodless coup was engineered which installed the army under General Ibrahim Abbud as the new agency of government, there was little protest from a people long accustomed to authoritarian rule.

THE WEST AFRICAN CATALYST

While Ethiopia and the Sudan may have been the first to regain their liberty, it was West Africa, and particularly the Gold Coast, which provided the essential impetus for the wave of independence which swept over the African continent in the years following the Second World War. At the outset this was unlooked for, since the Gold Coast impressed its rulers as a model colony, steadily growing in political maturity and economic strength; one which in good time would doubtless achieve self-government, but surely only through an orderly, measured advance. In anticipation of this eventuality, a new constitution in 1946 had provided for a legislative council with an elected majority, a concession which was hailed alike by Englishmen and Gold Coasters as a fair indication of both past achievement and future promise.

In fact, appearances were deceptive, for the very state of progress on the Gold Coast was building explosive pressures which would not have been possible in a less developed land. First of all, there was a problem of rising commodity prices and scarcity of consumer goods caused by world-wide shortages at the end of the Second World War. Increasing numbers of urbanites with money to spend but few goods to buy suspected the government of using its position to assist European importers in manipulating the price structure for private profit, to public disadvantage. It was true that cocoa prices had risen with the rest, but at this point the outbreak of swollen shoot virus compelled the government to order the destruction of large tracts of diseased trees, consequently imposing great hardship on individual farmers. In many quarters the conclusion seemed inescapable—the government sought to ruin the farmer and take his land while encouraging the European merchants to make a killing out of the price spiral and market shortages.

In addition there were the numbers of soldiers returning home, their expectations unlikely to be met easily in a provincial West African society suffering economic dislocation. Beyond these immediate difficulties, however, was a basic shift in the community which upset long-standing social relations and encouraged a growing temper of opposition to authority within a large section of the population. The change was geared to an accelerating modernization which had more than doubled the numbers living in the major cities of the Gold Coast between 1931 and 1948, forced the commercialization of agriculture, and brought about the dramatic rise of a class of individuals, half educated by a few years of indifferent primary school training. Semiliterate, unskilled and often unemployable, dissatisfied with village life and unable to rise in the complex and unsettling world of the city, this new proletariat was resistant to the older chiefly authority and suspicious of a European-directed government. In January, 1948, a successful boycott of European goods indicated the prevailing mood of unrest. A month later, a serviceman's protest march in Accra got out of hand and developed into rioting which quickly spread to other centers, resulting in considerable loss of life and property.

In this situation, the older elite leadership group sought to exercise its leadership. A year earlier the United Gold Coast Convention had been formed by the merchant, A. G. Grant, the barrister and newspaper editor, J. B. Danquah, and other educated Africans as a national movement dedicated to eventual self-government; now under Danquah's direction, the U.G.C.C. declared the colonial administration bankrupt and suggested that the Convention be made the instrument of a new government. Such an action had little effect on the authorities who put Danquah and some of his colleagues in custody, but more significantly it left the African population unmoved, awaiting the leadership which it instinctively felt could not be provided by the exclusive, educated elite.

The administration reacted in another way. The findings of the Watson Commission which investigated the riots and the Coussey Committee which explored the possibility of political reform, in effect suggested nothing less than representative, responsible government as soon as practicable, but time was already running beyond this statesmanlike move, even as events overtook the ineffectual leadership of the U.G.C.C. In 1947, Danquah had appointed Kwame Nkrumah as secretary of the Convention in a move designed to spare its patrician leaders the details of party organization while freeing them for larger political strategies. The move had misfired as Nkrumah quickly built a national organization based on the captivating slogan of "self-government now", then took his new following with him in 1949 when he founded his own Convention People's Party, an exciting, revolutionary, nationalist movement with direct appeal to the growing dissidents in the Gold Coast population.

Had Danquah and his associates been more searching, they would never have offered Nkrumah the position of U.G.C.C. secretary, for his career up to that point strongly suggested a revolutionary leader of uncommon ability, determined and capable of far exceeding their limited goals. Born in 1909 near Axim along the western Gold Coast, he had, like Azikiwe, graduated from local schooling to pursue his higher education in the United States where he learned the techniques of self-support to supplement formal study in economics, sociology, and education. His political education began as well during these years when he served as president of the African Students' Association of the United States and Canada, at the same time learning something of revolutionary tactics, particularly from the West Indian Marxist, C. L. R. James.

Already Nkrumah was thinking of the means by which colonialism might be destroyed, and when he left America for England in 1945, he was referred by James to George Padmore, another West Indian and former Comintern member who had defected from the communist movement during the 1930's because he felt it to be insincere regarding national liberation in Asia and Africa. In London, Nkrumah and Padmore collaborated in organizing the Fifth Pan-African Congress at Manchester, with its ringing declaration for African independence which Nkrumah proposed to achieve through immediate organization of the African masses and the seizure of political power by means of strikes and boycotts. At the conclusion of the Manchester conference, Nkrumah busied himself with plans to implement the Congress resolutions, and it was at this point that he answered the call to return to the Gold Coast and accept the post of U.G.C.C. secretary. Beyond his education, his growing political experience, and his determination to succeed through immediate action, Nkrumah possessed personal charm, eloquence, and a sure instinct for leadership. Here was the spark which would bring to life the potential within the Gold Coast for a mass nationalist movement.

Nkrumah's instinct told him to rebuff at first the constitutional reforms recommended by the Coussey report; instead, in 1950, he called a general strike and boycott, peaceful in intention but marked by violence, the result of which was imprisonment for him and his top aides and great excitement within the country for his cause. From his martyred position in jail he was now able to campaign successfully in the 1951 elections under the new constitution, and his C.P.P. won a decisive victory at the expense of the U.G.C.C. As the country's leading political figure, Nkrumah was released from prison and quickly shifted to a policy of cooperation with the authorities. Clearly the chief delegate in the new assembly, he was given the formal title of Prime Minister in 1952, and in 1954 he obtained a new constitution which did away with all special and nominated categories in the assembly and with any officially sponsored ministers in the cabinet, the governor, however, reserving authority for external affairs and defense. Nevertheless, internal self-government was still but a way-station, and two years later Nkrumah was able to convince the British government that the country was ready for complete autonomy. On March 6, 1957, the Gold Coast became the independent state of Ghana.

In achieving his objectives, Nkrumah had been obliged to do

battle with more than the colonial administration. The 1951 constitution had provided for a substantial number of assemblymen chosen by regional chiefly councils, an arrangement anathema to one seeking exclusive national leadership. This impediment was removed by the 1954 constitution which provided for direct election of all assembly members, but at this stage another obstacle appeared in the shape of a rising opposition made up of various regional, ethnic, and religious interests—Muslims, Ewe, Ashanti, to name the major components—which argued for a federal-type government in order to achieve a proper balance between national and local interests. The chief organs of the opposition, the Northern People's Party and the Ashanti-based National Liberation Movement, banded together to contest the 1956 election, but the C.P.P. led by Nkrumah and his lieutenants, K. A. Gbedemah, Kojo Botsio, Krobo Edusei, and Kofi Baako, once again demonstrated its primacy with a solid victory, and this achievement convinced the British government that Nkrumah had the national support it regarded as a necessary prerequisite to independence.

Apparently Nkrumah himself felt no such confidence, for once in power as head of a sovereign Ghana, he proceeded to demolish the opposition and establish a single-party dictatorship, the Republic of Ghana proclaimed in 1960, with himself as president and eventually as life president. Whether he was motivated by a sense of personal infallibility or by a fear that the newly independent nation, intent on accelerating its thrust toward modernization, could not afford the luxury of a locally oriented political opposition, the party nevertheless came to be equated with the nation while Nkrumah began to look beyond his position as national leader to the role of spokesman for all of Africa.

If Nkrumah's one-party state was a counter to the threat of regionalism, it was this same parochial tendency that complicated the search for an independence formula in Nigeria. Here, as in the Gold Coast, economic and social changes arising out of the exigencies of the Second World War had pushed Nigeria along the road to modernization. Strategic and economic considerations had greatly stimulated local production which received additional impetus from the passage of the Colonial Development and Welfare Acts in 1940 and 1945, born of a changing conviction in Britain regarding the responsibilities of colonial stewardship. Demand for raw materials, moreover, continued to expand during the postwar years, and as exports of cotton, groundnuts, palm oil, cocoa, and timber increased in a rising world price structure, the possibilities for internal development of the economy grew accordingly.

The result was a changing socio-economic pattern characteristic of postwar Africa—the growth of industry, the expansion of cities, and the rise of organized labor; the steady extension of transportation facilities to meet insistent commercial needs; the frantic increase of the educational establishment in response both to popular demand and to shortage of skilled performers at all economic and technical levels; the involvement of ever widening segments of the population into a cash economy; the development of a significant internal market to parallel rising emphasis on exports and imports; the slow breakdown of a traditional way of life under attack by a new social dynamism.

Such changes were necessarily accompanied by emphatic nationalist impulses which were, however, complicated and diffused by Nigeria's historic heterogeneity. Despite the formation of the Nigerian federation in 1914, British administration between the two world wars had tended to emphasize regional diversity, especially the differences between north and south. The Muslim emirates, already isolated and xenophobic, were permitted to govern themselves according to obsolete feudal formulas, while the people of the east and west, although chafing under an ill-suited indirect rule, were nevertheless propelled forward into the contemporary world by their unwavering desire for the benefits of Western education. On the eve of the Second World War, the parochial politics of Herbert Macaulay were giving way to a broader nationalism exemplified both by the Nigerian Youth Movement of Ernest Ikoli, H. O. Davies, and others, and by the flamboyant exertions of Nnamdi Azikiwe.

For a time Azikiwe and the Youth Movement made common cause which, unfortunately, could survive neither the clash of personalities nor a sense of tribal identity, portentous in its implications—Zik with his solid Ibo support confronted by the large Yoruba block in the Youth Movement. In 1944 another attempt was made when Azikiwe formed the National Council of Nigeria and the Cameroons with himself as secretary and Herbert Macaulay as president. As the war ended, the N.C.N.C. set about building a national party dedicated to the achievement of internal self-government. As with the Gold Coast and the Sudan, Britain's postwar position regarding her colonies was not averse to a move toward self-determination, and the decade following 1945 was devoted, not so much to a struggle for independence, as to the search for constitutional stability in a land of centrifugal ethnic forces.

The first attempt was made by Governor Sir Arthur Richards whose constitution went into effect at the beginning of 1947. It was at once roundly criticized by nationalists, partly because it had been introduced without prior consultation within Nigeria and partly as a response to the undemocratic character of the new legislative council, its membership almost wholly chosen by indirection. The distinctive feature of the constitution, however, was its inclusion of the north in the central legislature and the establishment of three regional councils for north, west, and east. These bodies, though largely bereft of authority, were dominated by the chiefs and the British administration, and promised to become potential centers for a rising spirit of regionalism.

This initial effort to balance unity and diversity was soon followed by discussions which led eventually to a second constitution under which general· elections were held in 1951. This so-called Macpherson Constitution reflected the difficulties of formulating an effective government in a country of growing regional self-consciousness even as national developmental requirements called for increasing authority at the center. The constitution took effect at a time when cultural organizations like the Pan-Ibo Federal Union, the Ibibio State Union, and the Jam'iyyar Mutanen Arewa, or Northern Peoples' Congress, were proclaiming the ethnic integrity of their memberships and finding themselves in the process more and more involved with political activities. The Pan-Ibo Federal Union had been one of the founding members of the N.C.N.C., the Yoruba Egbe Omo Oduduwa sired its political wing, the Action Group, in 1951, while the Northern Peoples' Congress transformed itself into a political organ during the election campaign that same year.

The result of the new constitution, therefore, was a federation of three regional governments controlled by ethnic political parties all-powerful in their own areas and largely impotent elsewhere—the Action Group in the west, the N.C.N.C. in the east, and the Northern Peoples' Congress (N.P.C.) in the north. The federal legislature and its Council of Ministers, chosen from the regional assemblies, could not operate as an effectively coherent entity with conflicting regional priorities complicating its deliberations. This was especially marked on the question of national self-government, the eastern and western regions pressing for early independence while the northern leaders wished to go more slowly, fearful that in an autonomous state, their numerous but essentially illiterate people would be dominated by the more sophisticated, educated southerners.

In 1953 there were bloody riots in Kano reflecting local enmity toward the large numbers of literate southerners employed in the north as clerks in commercial establishments and government offices. When this outburst was followed by a motion in the northern parliament calling for the end of federation, the British government convened a new constitutional conference which met in an atmosphere of marked regional particularism, yet managed in its protracted deliberations to produce a new constitution which formed the basis for independence when it came in 1960.

This 1954 constitution seemingly placed the balance of power squarely in the three regions. The federal legislature was chosen according to electoral processes formulated by the regions; the central Council of Ministers was chosen on a regional basis; powers not delegated to the federation were reserved to the regions; each region was given a premier although none was designated for the federal government; and finally, although taxing powers were federal, distribution of revenue was made substantially proportionate to regional contribution. Lagos was designated a federal territory and the police remained federal, but other civil services, including the judiciary, were regionalized.

The strengthening of centripetal forces therefore remained a paramount necessity. For the moment, as the 1954 constitution came into effect, the major political figures were located in the regions— Dr. Azikiwe, the N.C.N.C. founder, as premier in Enugu, Chief Awolowo, head of the Action Group holding the same office in Ibadan, and Sir Ahmadu Bello, the Sardauna of Sokoto and leader of the N.P.C., the chief minister in Kaduna. Moreover, both the east and west looked to early self-government while the north still held back, thereby complicating the prospect of eventual national independence. At the same time, however, there were genuine efforts at unity. The N.C.N.C. and N.P.C. succeeded in combining to form a coalition federal government with Awolowo leading the Action Group as a loyal parliamentary opposition, and in 1957 the constitution was revised in an atmosphere of determined and growing cooperation. A major change was the creation of a federal prime minister empowered to choose his own cabinet, and this position was soon occupied by the moderate deputy leader of the N.P.C., Abubakar Tafawa Balewa. At the same time, the west and east accepted local self-government while the north agreed to follow suit in 1959.

Thus the ground was prepared for the independence of Nigeria which was proclaimed on October 1, 1960. Nonetheless, the essential divisiveness of the country remained. The regional political parties, despite repeated efforts, continued unable to build national followings, while within the regions themselves, signs of further fragmentation appeared as smaller ethnic bodies demanded local autonomy in their turn, free from the controls of the already dominant larger national groups.

INDEPENDENCE—THE FRENCH-AFRICAN VARIANT

The conference of some two score French colonial administrators who met at Brazzaville in January and February, 1944, marked an important turning point in French colonial policy. Recognizing Africa's contribution to the Free French cause, the provisional government of General Charles de Gaulle at once conceded a new kind of partnership, although equality between Frenchman and African was uncertainly defined by the delegates, now stressing the need for greater cultural assimilation, now arguing, with Félix Eboué, for the preservation of traditional values and institutions. Forced labor and the *indigénat* were to be abolished, modernization and French-style education greatly stepped up, and a broad-based franchise introduced along with a form of French citizenship allowing special cultural and religious status such as the *originaires* of the Four Communes of Senegal had long enjoyed. To a considerable extent the discussion centered on the question of administrative efficiency, with the federalists headed by Eboué arguing for decentralization on grounds of expediency. The conference finally urged the establishment of assemblies for various colonial territories, a decision which was of great moment in shaping the future independence of African peoples. Decentralization and democracy did not mean independence, however, as the delegates declared forever inadmissible the idea of self-government for France's colonies.

These recommendations comprised a major step forward even if all were not immediately brought into being. A liberal constitution was rejected by the French electorate in May, 1946, and a second, which became the constitution of the Fourth Republic five months later, was much less open-handed regarding colonial rights and status. The French Union which thereby came into being allowed no true confederation of states but classified former colonies as constituent territories of an indivisible republic. Greatest concessions were made in civil status and rights as the granting of French citizenship and its protection to all people of the Union meant a final end to forced labor and administrative justice. Nevertheless the franchise was for practical purposes limited to the 1,500,000 overseas citizens who met specified property and literacy qualifications. Each territory received its own assembly, both West Africa and Equatorial Africa were given regional Grand Councils, and there was a special assembly of the French Union seated in Paris, but all these bodies enjoyed only advisory powers. Real authority remained with the French parliament, to which the African territories now elected a number of representatives, and indeed to a considerable measure the old prewar controls remained, for parliamentary ministers were empowered to govern the territories by decree in the absence of contradictory legislation. Thus France had made major concessions and old-fashioned colonialism was dead, but the overseas territories were still tightly controlled from Paris. French assimilation did not extend to the sharing of authority.

High centralization of authority was in the best Napoleonic tradition, but there were also practical considerations in the maintenance of close French colonial controls. The postwar years saw a vast rise in metropolitan overseas investment, French West Africa alone receiving $1 billion between 1947 and 1956 in French treasury grants and public low-interest loans for developmental purposes, as well as considerable direct support from the mother country for the local civil and military establishments. Along with investment went a substantial emigration of *petits blancs,* French petty bourgeois who became permanent residents—government workers, shopkeepers, clerks, and artisans whose livelihood had to be protected. Finally, French mercantile control of the overseas economies was tightened in an economic union that directed fully 70 per cent of all exports to a protected metropolitan market, while receiving French goods on a similarly preferential basis.

That these benefits were reciprocal was affirmed by rising African affluence. In the decade following 1947, for example, West Af-

rican export of coffee and cocoa nearly tripled while groundnut shipments rose from 380,000 to 710,000 tons. To be sure these advances
greatly benefited European planters as well, especially in the Ivory
Coast where they had long been encouraged to settle and where
their competition with African farmers led to the formation in 1946
of a political movement, the *Parti Démocratique de la Côte d'Ivoire*
(P.D.C.I.), founded by a Baulé planter and physician, Félix Houphouet-Boigny. By 1949 Houphouet and the colonial administration
were locked in a struggle that involved police suppression and manip-
ulated elections designed to break the impact of African-organized
strikes and boycotts. After two bloody years, Houphouet, in a move
reminiscent of the earlier accommodation of Blaise Diagne, made
peace with the authorities and the French mercantile community, and
within a few years capital investment and economic expansion had
converted the Ivory Coast into one of the most productive territories
in French West Africa.

This early postwar antipathy to colonialism was shared in other
territories, although not on such explicit economic grounds. In 1946
Houphouet's party became a leading component of the grand interterritorial *Rassemblement Démocratique Africain* (R.D.A.) which
emerged from an historic meeting at Bamako called by several of the
West and Equatorial African deputies to the French parliament as a
reaction against the undemocratic constitution of the French Union.
The result was a series of R.D.A. sections organized within most of
the French-African areas, including the U.N. trust territory of Cameroun, each section acting as a local political party but with a considerable interterritorial allegiance to the R.D.A. caused by mutual
commitment to the idea of African emancipation. Yet, despite the
circumstances of its birth as well as its early association with the
French Communist Party, the R.D.A. maintained an essentially
moderate position regarding the French Union. Less accommodating
were the Senegalese Socialists, led first by Lamine Guèye and then by
Léopold Senghor whose *Bloc Démocratique Sénégalais* (B.D.S.)
founded in 1948 as a farmer-intellectual alliance quite independent
of the R.D.A., took the stand that some form of federation between
Africa and France was preferable to the insufficient political assimilation provided by the French Union.

While in Equatorial Africa political inexperience and French
overseas policy produced but faint echoes of events unfolding to the
west, the more sophisticated West Africans now moved to test the

strength of their affiliations with France, even as Paris was experiencing a fundamental change of heart regarding the nature of her overseas empire. Defeat in Vietnam in 1954, a reluctant grant of independence to the Tunisian and Moroccan protectorates in 1956, and the outbreak in 1954 of an increasingly ferocious civil war in Algeria all combined to shake the faith in French Union, as observers in Paris noted the growing power of national liberation movements all over the colonial world. Events in the Sudan and Ghana had their effect, the prospect of independence in the latter case leading to a new constitution granting internal autonomy to Ghana's neighbor, the United Nations trust territory of Togo.

This concession toward tiny Togo necessarily meant a fresh approach in all the French-African territories, and in 1956 there appeared a legislative *loi-cadre* which set forth the main outlines of a new policy for the overseas territories. The principle of assimilation was abandoned in favor of a revived concept of association in which a number of now semiautonomous territories with power over local affairs were placed in a federal relationship with France, the French government retaining control in external matters.

Local autonomy was granted, not as a step toward independence, but as its substitute; nevertheless the essential issue of the moment centered less on political liberty than on the fate of the two regions of French West Africa and French Equatorial Africa. These had been organized originally as administrative conveniences whereby the more productive areas could help defray the costs of government in the less developed territories. In time this situation became particularly vexatious to the more wealthy Gabon in Equatorial Africa and the Ivory Coast in West Africa, their accelerating development bringing with it a fast-growing burden in support of impecunious sister states. In 1954 the Ivory Coast was contributing over one-third of the total cost of administration in French West Africa and received back only half of that amount in local services. For its part, Senegal's record was distinctly better—a 30 per cent return for a 39 per cent output.

Under these circumstances it is not surprising that Houphouet, at this time serving as a French government minister, acted as a major influence in France's decision to establish a grouping based primarily on her direct relationship with each individual territory, the regional West African and Equatorial federations being considerably reduced in power and revenue. Against Houphouet was aligned

Léopold Senghor whose espousal of *négritude* and African culture and whose genuine belief in equal partnership between France and Africa led him to criticize the *loi-cadre* as what he termed "balkanization" of French Africa. Senghor was not alone. Within the R.D.A. were powerful elements led by Sekou Touré of Guinea and Modibo Keita of Soudan, who favored a strong federation as the prelude to independence for a massive and powerful West African state.

France now advanced an alternative, the celebrated offer of General de Gaulle, freshly come to power in the spring of 1958. He proposed that the African territories either ratify the constitution of the new Fifth Republic of France and thereby become autonomous states within a Community whose external affairs would be controlled by France, or take immediate and absolute independence. With Ghana now free and others clearly on their way, the idea of independence was much in the African air, but only Guinea led by Sekou Touré voted against the constitution thereby gaining immediate and total separation from France in September, 1958. The others accepted the constitution and the Community, reluctant both to sever their long association with France and to put an abrupt end to the substantial developmental assistance that had poured into their territories ever since the conclusion of the Second World War.

The sudden, brusque divorce of Guinea did not settle the twin questions of federation and independence. In Equatorial Africa, Barthélémy Boganda of Ubangi-Chari, president of the regional Grand Council, carried on a campaign for continuation of the old federation; nevertheless both African groupings were terminated by the formation of the Community, a move which merely intensified the search for unity. Senegal particularly dreaded isolation, not only on ideological grounds but because she was obliged to maintain and utilize the many federal installations at Dakar; for example, the port, the railroad to Bamako, and the university. In 1959, therefore, West African leaders formed the Mali Federation which initially included Senegal, Soudan, Upper Volta, and Dahomey, but which quickly reduced itself to the tandem of Senegal and Soudan when the others withdrew in the face of pressure from both Houphouet and the French.

The Mali Federation now moved toward total independence as France amended her constitution to permit complete autonomy within the Community. In June, 1960, the Federation became free, then, only two months later, split into the two independent nations of

Mali and Senegal, unity proving impossible between such diverse groups as the solemn, dedicated, austere Marxists of the poverty-stricken interior and the wealthier sophisticates living in Dakar.

Meanwhile, in 1959, Houphouet had helped form the Entente, a loose grouping made up of Niger, Dahomey, Upper Volta, and the Ivory Coast, and designed as a counterweight to the Mali Federation. Houphouet-Boigny had consistently argued against independence, partly because he regarded it as expensive and dangerous to African development and partly because he valued the cultural advantages of the French connection. When France gave Mali its freedom within the Community, however, his thesis was no longer defensible and the rush for independence began. Before the end of 1960 all of France's West African and Equatorial states had demanded and received their freedom. This included the United Nations trust territories as well. Part of Togo had already opted to join Ghana in 1957 and the remainder became an independent state in 1960, as did Cameroun. The following year a plebiscite in the British Cameroons resulted in the northern section remaining as part of Nigeria while the south voted to join the Federal Republic of Cameroun.

THE CRISIS OF INDEPENDENCE IN THE CONGO

Over the years Belgian paternalism effectively smothered any sense of Congolese nationhood, but it could not prevent Congo nationals from making note of the independence movements developing around them. Belgian efficiency wasted no energies training an elite for self-government which would never come, but it succeeded only in limiting the experience of those few leaders who did emerge. Belgian pragmatism rested secure in the knowledge of its realism and toughness, but in the crisis of independence it proved to be flaccid, purposeless, and unequal to the responsibilities that were thrust upon it.

The drive for independence came late in the Congo; having started tardily, however, it moved swiftly, borne along by African impetuosity and inexperience, matched with Belgian indecision. The independence of Ghana in 1957, General de Gaulle's dramatic *oui-ou-non* offer of independence or local autonomy within the French Community, the All-African Peoples' Conference held in Accra in December, 1958, and the widened horizons of Congolese attending

the Brussels international fair of that same year, opened prospects un-
dreamed of a few short years earlier. Inside the Congo, a modest and
controlled political activity begun in 1956 suddenly broke loose,
propelled by dawning ambition among the few educated elite, by
economic and social grievances in the cities, and by an ominous
tribalism springing up in diverse quarters of the country.

In 1957 limited reforms liberalizing representation in local
government and introducing elections for the city councils of
Leopoldville, Elisabethville, and Jadotville precipitated political organization—first, ABAKO (*Alliance des Ba-Kongo*), an ethnically-
rooted party which had originated in Leopoldville in 1950 as a
Bakongo cultural society, then, CONAKAT (*Confédération des Associations Tribales du Katanga*), another tribally-oriented confederation
based in the Katanga, and in 1958, the *Mouvement National Congolais* (M.N.C.) founded by a group of young educated Africans including Cyrille Adoula and Patrice Lumumba. ABAKO, led by Joseph
Kasavubu, and CONAKAT, associated from the beginning with the
name of Moise Tshombe, were necessarily regional in influence, but
the M.N.C. had gone beyond the limitations of parochialism and
supported the concept of a national party dedicated to a united
independent Congo. Local or national, however, all parties adopted
a rapidly accelerating demand for democracy and early independence.
ABAKO had called for an immediate grant of autonomy as early as
1956. The M.N.C. grew steadily more radical throughout 1959, presumably a reflection of Lumumba's meeting with Nkrumah at the
Accra conference. Each party found it expedient to step up its demands, fearful lest it be outdistanced by the others in the appeal for
votes.

The response of the Belgian authorities was a rapid series of
major concessions, culminating late in 1959 in the astonishing announcement that a conference would be held the following January,
its predetermined outcome to be independence for the Congo in
1960. Such precipitous action reflected divisions within the government in Brussels, as well as fears that the Congo might fragment into
a series of ethnic states if it were not allowed to go its way quickly.
In January, 1959, riots in Leopoldville had erupted, caused by resentment over unemployment and segregation, and profoundly unsettling to Belgian self-confidence. During the months that followed,
the early party groupings, now joined by others including the P.S.A.
(*Parti Solidaire Africain*) led by Antoine Gizenga, showed increas-

ing signs of regionalism along with their growing political extremism. Kasavubu and ABAKO were calling for virtual secession, the Katanga seemed to favor only a loose federalism, while rioting which occurred in Luluabourg and Stanleyville was based in ethnic animosities. Even the nationalist M.N.C. felt the strains of divisiveness and broke into two with the departure of an independent Luba section favorable to federalism.

Belgian authorities had expected to retain control over external affairs even after independence, but the weakness of their stand drew forth even more extreme demands from the Congolese. At the Round Table Conference held in Belgium during January, 1960, immediate independence was demanded and quickly granted along with the virtual assurance that the grant would be ratified by the Belgian parliament. Independence was set for June 30, 1960, with national elections to be held in May. Congolese leaders, momentarily united to face the Belgians at the conference, had found no opposition and, unopposed, had plunged on to gain even more than they had initially hoped for. It was a moment of missed opportunity. Lacking colonial resistance they also lost the necessity for a permanent unity which could have been the basis of a stable national government.

A constitution was drafted providing for a federal state of six provinces, the central government assuming such national responsibilities as military security, economic planning, federal currency, and higher education, while the provinces were given control in regional matters including local police and education at the lower levels. In the May election the strength of localism was all too apparent; although the M.N.C. and its related smaller parties gained a solid plurality in the national lower house, Lumumba and his advocates of a unitary state were far outnumbered by the sum of other parties, all regional in appeal and federalist in orientation. When a government was finally formed with Lumumba as prime minister heading a broad-based coalition, this move was made possible only through the last-minute cooperation of Kasavubu who was named Head of State.

The Republic of the Congo thus became a sovereign state under the most inauspicious circumstances. Indeed, on the day of national independence there was independence but as yet no nation. Fourteen million people drawn from over two hundred tribal groups had no sense of national identity, political leadership at the center was essentially dependent upon support in the regions, geographic diversity and enormous distances added their complications, while the sudden departure of a paternalist colonial regime removed restraints long endured and set free all of the centrifugal forces in this vast land. By the standards of Africa, the Congo was well developed in economic terms. There was a billion dollar annual production and one of the highest per capita incomes in the continent, but in its lack of political cohesion and its paucity of educated leadership it was certainly among the most poorly endowed of the new African nations.

The sequel to independence was virtual anarchy, succeeded by the four-year military occupation of a United Nations peace-keeping force, and then a slow, painful groping toward nationhood. Within a week of the celebration of independence, tribal disorders broke out, followed by a mutiny in the army which resulted in a number of European deaths and destruction of property. The ensuing panic and mass exodus of the predominantly Belgian European population deprived the country at its outset of much-needed trained personnel; then, less than two weeks after independence, Moise Tshombe announced the secession of the wealthy Katanga province which provided half the national revenue.

Lumumba and Kasavubu now appealed for intervention by a United Nations force which soon found itself caught up in a complex political and diplomatic tangle. There was the continuing influence of Belgian interests in the Katanga; the intrusion of international politics with unilateral Soviet encouragement and military supplies for Lumumba's government poised against strong American financial and logistical support for the U.N. action; the dismissal from office of Lumumba by Kasavubu in September, 1960, and his assassination the following February while in the custody of Tshombe; the near breakup of the state which was checked only when Cyrille Adoula formed a government in August, 1961; and the eventual occupation and reintegration of the Katanga in 1963 through United Nations action—all complicated by the continued incapacity of the Congolese army as an effective force for peace and security. On June 30, 1964, the United Nations mission and troops finally departed, but this was followed by another period of uncertainty during the 1964–1965 government of Moise Tshombe with its controversial white mercenary additions to the Congolese armed forces. Late in 1965 the Congo Republic was shaken by still another crisis when a bloodless coup installed General Joseph Mobutu at the head of a military government.

There is evidence that Mobutu may succeed in overcoming the divisive forces in his country. He can point to the growing longevity of his administration, his rising stature as an African leader, the effective elimination of Tshombe,* and most recently his defeat of a white mercenary insurrection which broke out in the summer of 1967, the insurgents being driven to refuge in Rwanda from whence they were finally evacuated to Europe in the spring of 1968.

As for Rwanda and neighboring Burundi, independence had come in 1962 after a lengthy Belgian administration of the Ruanda-Urundi mandate and trust territory. Here, as with the Congo, ethnic violence broke forth with the relaxation of colonial controls. In Rwanda the Tutsi, long-time aristocrats and traditional rulers, were massacred and driven out of the country by their subject Bahutu who pointedly established a republican government. In Burundi there was no comparable outburst and a limited Tutsi monarchy was established.

EAST AFRICAN *UHURU*

As in other parts of the continent, the move toward independence in British East Africa was closely linked to the problem of ethnic exclusiveness. In Uganda where the Baganda insisted on their own national integrity and in Kenya where the European community sought to maintain its dominant position, independence came slowly and painfully. In Tanganyika, far less developed in its economy and educational resources, little serious divisiveness emerged and it was there that the freedom cry, *uhuru*, was first converted into reality.

The British administration, not the African people, took the first steps toward Tanganyikan independence after the Second World War. Committed to a postwar liberalization of colonial controls and stimulated by its position as a United Nations trustee working toward eventual African self-government, Britain initiated several

---

* In October, 1965 Tshombe was dismissed from office by Kasavubu, then president of the Congo, and went into exile. In June, 1967, amidst speculation that he planned a return to the Congo, he was mysteriously kidnapped while on a flight in the Mediterranean, his plane being landed in Algeria. There he remained in custody, no final action being taken to extradite him to the Congo where he was wanted for trial on treason charges. In June, 1969, he died, still detained in Algeria. Kasavubu, deposed by General Mobutu in November, 1965, retired to his home at Boma where he died in March, 1969.

moves leading to greater local autonomy. In 1945 the legislative council was expanded to accommodate four African appointees along with the seven Europeans and three Asians. As investment in economic development and public works went forward, including heavy support for an ambitious but ill-fated scheme in mechanized groundnut production, there were further political advances. In 1951 an African was named to the executive council, and four years later the legislative council was again enlarged to include thirty unofficial nominees, ten representing each of the Asian, African, and European communities according to a principle of racial parity. Parity was the basis on which the governor, Sir Edward Twining, now moved to have the unofficial councilors brought to office through direct elections scheduled for 1958.

Such a liberalization of the political process, well ahead of the times in the late 1940's, was already out of date by the mid-fifties. In part, these constitutional reforms had been instituted to make more palatable the creation of the East African High Commission coordinating certain economic and administrative functions among the territories of Kenya, Uganda, and Tanganyika, but the fear of Kenya white domination made the move unpopular in Tanganyika. This opposition gradually took the shape of political parties, culminating in 1954 with the appearance of the Tanganyika African National Union (T.A.N.U.) under the leadership of a young African schoolteacher, Julius K. Nyerere, recently returned from his studies in Britain. T.A.N.U. and Nyerere at once opposed racial parity on principle and then further irritated the government by criticizing the prevailing system of indirect rule in the provinces, advocating an end to the old reliance on native authorities. Gathering overwhelming support throughout the country in competition with the interracial United Tanganyika Party, T.A.N.U. circumvented the parity qualifications during the 1958 elections by nominating and sweeping into office its own candidates in all three racial groups, thereby controlling the unofficial membership of the legislative council from that point forward.

With such overwhelming African support in a country where no large tribal groups existed as potential centers of regional disaffection, Tanganyika was suddenly projected to the forefront of the independence movement in East Africa despite her deficiencies in economic resources and trained manpower. The principle of parity was dropped and the franchise broadened as Asian and European

50. Nnamdi Azikiwe

51. Kwame Nkrumah

52. Emperor Haile Selassie

53. East African heads of state: From left to right,
Julius Nyerere, Milton Obote, and Jomo Kenyatta

54. Kenneth Kaunda,
President of Zambia

55. President Léopold Sédar
Senghor of Senegal

56. Agricultural modernization

57. Oil refinery, Senegal

58. Street scene, Lusaka

59. Aluminum plant, Guinea

60. Higher education: East Africa

61. High Court justices, Sierra Leone

fears were assuaged by Nyerere's moderation, and in 1960 T.A.N.U. again dominated the elections, now based on a single electoral roll. The following year came internal self-government which led to final independence in December, 1961. By this time, T.A.N.U.'s political ascendancy had become so complete that as the Tanganyikan nation achieved its freedom, it did so in the form of a single-party state.

In nearby Zanzibar, one-party rule came via the route of revolution. On the eve of independence, it appeared that the Islamic solidarity of the population would enable the Arab oligarchy to maintain its established political control. A coalition of the Arab-dominated Zanzibar Nationalist Party (Z.N.P.) and the African controlled but pro-Arab Zanzibar and Pemba People's Party (Z.P.P.P.) defeated the Afro-Shirazi Party (A.S.P.) in the 1963 elections, winning a majority of seats despite the A.S.P. poll of over 50 per cent of the popular vote. Intent upon putting an end to the economic and political domination of the Arabs, and despairing of achieving this end by constitutional means, an opposition began to take shape within the African population, its sentiments strongly Marxist, and its object revolution.

On January 12, 1964, the government fell before a coup engineered by a small group of ad hoc insurrectionaries only one month after independence had been achieved. As a result of this upheaval, the opposition forces were able to seize power, led by the A.S.P. president, Abeid Karume. At once, thousands of Arabs were arrested, much of their property confiscated or destroyed, the sultan banished, and the coalition parties proscribed. Beyond this, the new regime quickly instituted land reforms and other egalitarian moves designed to wipe out class privilege. In order to strengthen their political and economic program, the revolutionaries now looked abroad for aid through political alliance, and soon concluded an agreement with President Nyerere of Tanganyika which established the united republic of Tanzania in April, 1964. Although the union provided for a marked degree of centralization under a Tanzanian national government, the Zanzibaris have thus far retained in practice a considerable independence of action in both their domestic and international affairs and have probably also been responsible in part for Nyerere's own recent development into one of Africa's more militant advocates of state socialism.

The achievement of independence in Uganda was dominated throughout the period following the Second World War by the same

Baganda isolationism which had conditioned British colonial rule during the protectorate period. Therefore, as Britain began to consider the possibility of colonial autonomy, she was obliged to deal with the fundamental difficulty of separatism in Uganda; the more her administrators argued the case for unitary government, the more they stimulated national exclusiveness in Buganda. The first serious disagreement came in the 1950's as the governor, Sir Andrew Cohen, attempting to point Uganda in the direction of centralization, succeeded in precipitating a Baganda secession movement led by the *kabaka*, Mutesa II. Mutesa's deportation and subsequent restoration marked a paper agreement in 1955 which found neither side essentially moved from its position, Buganda proclaiming its own solidarity and Britain determined to have a unitary state.

In 1960 the *kabaka* again threatened secession, and the following year, as Britain studied plans for a constitution on which Ugandan independence might be based, it was agreed that Buganda should have special status as a federated state within an otherwise unitary Uganda. This development naturally brought demands for equivalent federal status from the other kingdoms, and in 1962 this was conceded to Toro, Bunyoro, Ankole, and Busoga, the less cohesive Acholi, Lango, Gisu, Teso and other peoples being accorded a more direct form of administration. Buganda had gained her point and the constitution allowed the Baganda *lukiko*, or assembly, to choose representatives to the national legislature and guaranteed Buganda local autonomy within a Uganda federation. When independence came in October, 1962, the *kabaka* was elected chief of state.

Indeed, the impasse was resolved, not so much by British acquiescence, as by the refined political maneuvers of Milton Obote, a Lango leader with pronounced leanings toward a centralized welfare state and therefore a natural enemy to Baganda particularism. As the possibility of independence approached during the late fifties, political parties began to appear to contest up-coming elections, but no party was able to gain more than a regional following and none from outside Buganda could penetrate the exclusiveness of Baganda parochialism. This was true of the Democratic Party based on the Catholic Church as well as the Bantu-supported Uganda People's Union. The nearest thing to a national party was the Uganda National Congress based on a farmers' cooperative, but it too was unable to maintain a following in Buganda. In 1960 Obote merged the Congress and

Union in the Uganda People's Congress (U.P.C.), thereby gaining wide support except in Buganda; then in 1961 he concluded an alliance with the *Kabaka Yekka* (K.Y.), an exclusively Baganda grouping emphasizing tribal solidarity, in the process risking his unionist support across the country. As it happened, the U.P.C. had no difficulty in holding its adherents as the coalition won the 1962 elections, thus bringing the country to independence with Obote as prime minister.

It was a loveless marriage of convenience, however—a poor agent with which to solve Uganda's long-standing problem of separatism. Obote had gained nominal unity and national autonomy, and hoped through coalition and the sobering responsibilities of independence to educate the Baganda away from their traditional aloofness. K.Y. no doubt felt it could continue to serve its parochial interests, the government requiring its support to remain in power. Accommodation did not succeed. In 1966, in an atmosphere of growing crisis, Obote arrested several K.Y. members in his cabinet, forced a unitary constitution through parliament which abolished the special position of Buganda, and drove the *kabaka* into exile by attacking his palace with troops of the predominantly non-Baganda army. Unity had been achieved, but its agent had been force, not consent.

Intramural differences among Africans would in time complicate the quest for independence in Kenya, but initially the problem lay elsewhere, in the legacy of colonialism. Here there were two discrete but complementary factors at work. First, there was the straightforward desire of the white settlers to maintain their dominant position, now greatly strengthened by the wartime production boom. Set against this was a long-standing sense of stewardship within the colonial administration which was heightened in the years after the Second World War by the conviction that colonial rule should be a guided path to ultimate independence. Hence the limited constitutional reforms which were instituted during the immediate postwar years reflected both the desire for a steady growth of African self-sufficiency and the paternalist conviction that political responsibility went hand in hand with Westernization—economic development and the mastery of Western ideas and institutions through Western education. Initially this course suggested multi-racial cooperation in Kenya, with the European community assuming major responsibility while awaiting the long, slow evolution of the African population. Without a doubt such views fitted neatly with settler aspirations concerning their own future.

Official policy was reflected in a series of moderate constitutional changes. In 1944 provision was made for an African appointee to the legislative council and a second was added in 1947. A year later Kenya gained an unofficial majority in the council, a majority to be sure dominated by eleven European elected members against five elected Asians, one Arab elected and one appointed, and four Africans nominated. In 1952 the total was raised to twenty-eight but the proportions remained substantially unchanged, Africans however achieving an appointment to the twelve-man colonial executive council.

Such modest concessions proved to be far from adequate for they failed to meet, let alone to liquidate, basic grievances long forming within the African population, particularly among the Kikuyu. As ever the problem was economic, rooted in the dislocations of a rapidly developing society. The essential problem was simple; in the face of a spectacular rise in national prosperity, the African standard of living was in actual decline. Between 1938 and 1952 Kenyan exports increased in value seven times, based mainly on the production of white settler cash crops. Over these very years the African contribution to national production was minimal—6 per cent in 1952, for example, compared with Uganda's 1951 figure of 63 per cent; at the same time African real income from the market economy grew at the rate of only 1 per cent per annum while the African population was rising at an annual rate of 3 per cent.

In the fifteen years following 1938 the African labor force doubled and by 1951 accounted, through wages, for two-thirds of African earnings; yet per capita income was less than $10 a year, one-quarter of the figure for Uganda. Labor was low paid because it was inefficient, but a plentiful supply of cheap labor, ideally fitting the needs of European farmers, kept incomes low and thus frustrated African attempts at gaining new skills through training. For survival, laborers were compelled to supplement their wages by maintaining a stake in the subsistence agriculture of their village and reservation; hence, the tribal areas continued to provide quantities of cheap labor, but shared only the most minimal portion of the national prosperity. Well aware of this condition, the African sought through political action to check his deteriorating economic position.

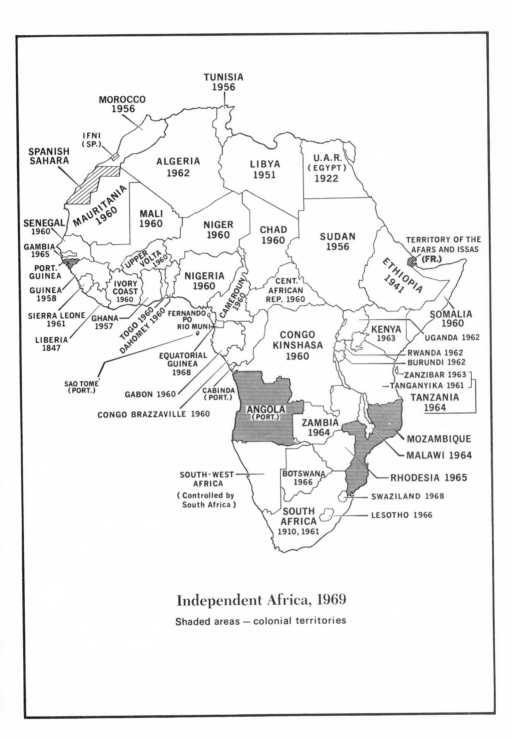

TUNISIA
1956

MOROCCO
1956

IFNI
(SP.)

SPANISH
SAHARA

ALGERIA
1962

LIBYA
1951

U.A.R.
(EGYPT)
1922

SENEGAL
1960

MAURITANIA
1960

MALI
1960

NIGER
1960

CHAD
1960

SUDAN
1956

TERRITORY OF THE
AFARS AND ISSAS
(FR.)

GAMBIA
1965

PORT.
GUINEA

GUINEA
1958

SIERRA LEONE
1961

LIBERIA
1847

UPPER
VOLTA
1960

IVORY
COAST
1960

GHANA
1957

NIGERIA
1960

TOGO 1960

DAHOMEY 1960

CAMEROUN
1960

CENT.
AFRICAN
REP. 1960

ETHIOPIA
1941

SOMALIA
1960

FERNANDO
PO
RIO MUNI

KENYA
1963

UGANDA 1962

SAO TOME
(PORT.)

EQUATORIAL
GUINEA
1968

GABON 1960

CABINDA
(PORT.)

CONGO
KINSHASA
1960

RWANDA 1962

BURUNDI 1962

ZANZIBAR 1963

TANGANYIKA 1961

TANZANIA
1964

CONGO BRAZZAVILLE 1960

ANGOLA
(PORT.)

ZAMBIA
1964

MOZAMBIQUE

MALAWI 1964

SOUTH-WEST
AFRICA
(Controlled by
South Africa)

BOTSWANA
1966

RHODESIA 1965

SWAZILAND 1968

SOUTH
AFRICA
1910, 1961

LESOTHO 1966

Independent Africa, 1969

Shaded areas — colonial territories

Led by the thin ranks of the educated, Africans in Nairobi and Mombasa began to form voluntary associations including an incipient labor movement, and out of this development emerged the Kenya African Union (K.A.U.) in 1944. With the old Kikuyu Central Association outlawed and Jomo Kenyatta, recently returned home from England, assuming the K.A.U. presidency in 1947, there seemed once again to be a vehicle for concerted African representations to government through a leadership of potentially supra-tribal appeal. As it happened the appeal was largely to the Kikuyu, located close to the government center at Nairobi and most directly affected by the land pressures from the white highlands.

Between 1945 and 1953, the Kenya African Union petitioned the government repeatedly for political and economic reform, particularly a change in land policy and a more direct representation in the councils of government. Land would have to be redistributed, said the Union, land which had been taken from the African to begin with and now desperately needed so that he might spread out from his overcrowded and overcropped reserves and put an end to the banishment of so many to starvation wages in the cities. At the same time, the argument continued, Africans were entitled to a higher proportion of the unofficial membership on the legislative council, a membership directly elected, not appointed by the colonial administration. Such appeals might have received a sympathetic hearing, especially from a Labour government in London, had not the settler oligarchy been quick and effective in guarding its own position. The result was that African representations were largely ignored, especially in the economic sphere. Specifically, there would be no land distribution, and no constitutional reform involving anything so radical as the single electoral roll demanded by the K.A.U. Failing to gain its objectives by peaceful petition, the African community slowly moved toward more violent means.

Disaffection grew gradually but inexorably as government policy continued to see progress only in terms of European leadership. Concurrently there arose among the Kikuyu the practice of oath-taking, the purpose, as with many people the world over, to generate social cohesion and total commitment to a cause. By the end of 1950 the K.A.U. leadership had recognized the emotional power of oathing and was using it as a conscious instrument of policy, hopeful of impressing their grievances on the government through mass unity. Now, however, the moderates in K.A.U. began to lose control in the face of urban militants like the labor leaders Fred Kubai and Makhan Singh, whose radicalism combined with the discipline of oathing to radiate the concept of violence outward from the city to the rural Kikuyu areas. In the Fort Hall, Nyeri, and other districts north of Nairobi there were growing outbreaks in late 1951 and on into 1952 —minor civil disobedience, arson, destruction of property, and finally, murder. In October, 1952, the progovernment Senior Chief Waruhiu was assassinated. Two weeks later a state of emergency was declared. Kikuyu complaints had at last gained official recognition through the resistance known as Mau Mau.

The Emergency, with its wholesale bloodletting and its savage campaigning, was the ultimate spasm of a society pushed to extremity. It was consequently not the moderate nationalists of the K.A.U. who were directly involved, as the administration believed, nor yet the ordinary peasant, but younger militants from Nairobi and the countryside whose flight to the forests of the Aberdares range and Mount Kenya was greatly accelerated by the declaration of emergency. The 1952–1953 trial and conviction of Kenyatta and his co-defendants as instigators of Mau Mau was therefore futile, and the resistance had to be stamped out by a military action which had largely completed its mission by the end of 1955, although the Emergency was not officially terminated until early 1960. Unsuccessful militarily, the resistance succeeded, however, where other methods had failed in forcing recognition of African grievances and producing a genuine effort to deal with them.

In the all-important area of land reform, scattered holdings were consolidated into unitary farms, soil conservation was stepped up, and a program of cash crop development instituted—all underway well before the end of the Emergency. All this might yet have been insufficient had it not been for political changes which were also instituted as early as 1954. Of these it was the introduction of the franchise for Africans in 1956 which overturned the administration program for controlled development of a multi-racial state, and set Kenya on the path to African self-government. First, political groupings began to take shape and a Luo leadership emerged to complement the Kikuyu. Next, by refusing to cooperate in a ministry based on racial electoral rolls, the African parliamentarians wrecked the idea of racial parity and hastened the changes of 1960. A convention was called which produced a complex constitution, but the essential feature was a common-roll franchise. The one-man-one-vote ideal, so effectively dramatized by Tom Mboya's eloquence at the 1958 Accra conference and elsewhere, had been achieved, and Kenya was on the way to becoming an autonomous African state.

An African-controlled government also marked the beginning of the end of land segregation in the white highlands. Nevertheless, as the obstacle of settler domination receded and the vision of independence grew brighter, a new complication materialized in the form of a disturbing disunity within the African community. Two parties emerged. There was the Kenya African National Union (K.A.N.U.) led by Kenyatta's old K.A.U. colleague, James Gichuru, the young labor organizer Tom Mboya, and Oginga Odinga, who had built up a large following in the Central Nyanza area. K.A.N.U. drew its strength mainly from Kikuyu, Luo, and Kamba, but another party, the Kenya African Democratic Union (K.A.D.U.), also appeared, headed by Ronald Ngala and Daniel arap Moi, and supported by a number of smaller ethnic groups fearful of Kikuyu and Luo domination. The election of 1961 was won by K.A.N.U. which, however, refused to form a government while its leader by acclamation, Jomo Kenyatta, was still in detention. K.A.D.U. then formed a government, but was embarrassed both by its minority position and by the release of Kenyatta in August, 1961. Finally, in 1963, a new federal state was created as K.A.N.U. and K.A.D.U. settled their differences, and after further elections Kenyatta became Kenya's first prime minister. In December, 1963, the country achieved independence, hopeful that, with the European question settled, a viable African nation was in the making.

BLACK AND WHITE INDEPENDENCE IN CENTRAL AFRICA

In Central Africa, the initial battle of African nationalists had been against federation, but the positive side of the antifederation struggle was national independence itself.

The combined strength of Nkumbula's African National Congress and Kaunda's U.N.I.P. easily insured an African legislative majority in the Northern Rhodesian general elections of October, 1962. Nevertheless the two parties worked together poorly during their short-lived 1963 coalition, and the resultant sense of national uncertainty was clearly evident in chronic outbursts of violence which African leaders, including Kaunda, were hard pressed to contain. In part the lawlessness reflected urban unrest and unemployment on the copper-belt, but it also arose from an atmosphere of political frustration wherein an African majority had somehow lost its advantage and dissipated its energies in intramural conflict.

Such uncertainties were removed, however, when a new un-complicated constitution was introduced in 1963 which broadened the franchise to include over one million Africans and thereby insured victory for Kaunda's popular United National Independence Party. As expected, the elections held in January, 1964, gave Kaunda and U.N.I.P. a solid legislative majority, although Nkumbula's Congress continued to show strength among the Ila-Tonga people in the southern districts and polled almost one-third of the 825,000 votes cast. With national leadership unambiguous at last, Kaunda moved steadily toward independence, using his new authority to regain the country's mineral rights from one of its major foreign concessionaires, the old British South Africa Company, while steps were taken at the same time to soothe the pride of the traditional royal house in Barotseland and thus forestall any separatist tendencies in the north-west. On October 24, 1964, independence was proclaimed in the new state of Zambia.

Once the antifederation spasms in Nyasaland had ended and Dr. H. K. Banda gained his overwhelming victory at the head of the Malawi Congress Party in August, 1961, the small highland territory moved smoothly toward independence. During 1962, Banda con-ducted the nation's affairs as unofficial head of government, he and his fellow ministers introducing numerous reforms with the coopera-tion of the governor, Sir Glyn Jones. In February, 1963 Banda be-came prime minister in name as well as in fact, and Nyasaland proceeded to the stage of internal self-government. A little over a year later, on July 6, 1964, complete independence came to the new country known as the Commonwealth of Malawi.

In Southern Rhodesia the achievement of independence had a far different history. Here the force of African nationalism developed late and here it was fully tested and contained by a strong group of white settlers long resident in the territory and long accustomed to directing national affairs without the assistance of those they con-sidered their inferiors. The controlling factors went back half a century and more, to the defeat of Lobengula and the subjugation of Ndebele and Shona, to the gradual emergence of a modern nation based on white management and black labor, and to the establishment of de facto segregation and discrimination by color which seemingly relegated over nine-tenths of the population to a permanently subordinate position.

Even under ideal circumstances it would have been well-nigh impossible to soften attitudes and relationships long since hardened into prejudice, to reverse the trend of decades and build a society based on genuine partnership. As it was, circumstances were much more conducive to the emergence of extremism, both European and African, an extremism which led to the crisis of U.D.I. (Unilateral Declaration of Independence) in November, 1965.

A number of factors were involved. First, there was the late but forced growth of African nationalism in Southern Rhodesia. The Southern Rhodesia African National Congress was not founded until 1957, when the one-time trade union leader Joshua Nkomo breathed new life into an older, moribund Congress movement. Spurred in its aspirations and demands by the example of nationalists in neighboring Nyasaland and Northern Rhodesia as well as by the rising tide of independence throughout Africa, the Congress soon became the target of an uneasy government which banned it in 1959 in order, it was said, to forestall the type of violence which was taking place at the time in Nyasaland. The nationalists immediately reappeared in new forms culminating in the Zimbabwe African People's Union (Z.A.P.U.), formed late in 1962 with Nkomo as president. In whatever form, however, the thrust of African nationalism was directed against the system of white supremacy. What it sought was majority rule, a political condition clearly unacceptable to the settler community.

Poised against the African was the European, but the white settlers were by no means united in their position. At one extreme was the Dominion Party led by Winston Field and dedicated to a European-dominated, independent Rhodesia. At the other were the liberals, exemplified by Garfield Todd, the Southern Rhodesian prime minister during the early Federation years, who favored the end of color bar and the institution of a multiracial society. Between these poles were the majority who supported Welensky's United Federal Party in its program of partnership, a policy which argued for the very gradual sharing of power with Africans over a long, evolving period of apprenticeship.

In 1958 Todd was replaced as Southern Rhodesian premier by

Sir Edgar Whitehead of the United Federal Party, and it was White-head who in 1959 proscribed the Congress movement and placed many of its members in detention. Somewhat paradoxically, he defended his action as a blow for multiracialism which, he said, could not survive fanaticism by either black or white, and concurrently Whitehead moved to do away with legal and customary color bar which he felt was an impediment to the healthy growth of a modern society. Under his guidance, the Land Apportionment Act was amended to allow for a degree of African residence in urban areas, and a campaign was instituted to do away with the social aspects of racial discrimination. In 1961, moreover, the Southern Rhodesian constitution was amended in such a way as to give modest legislative representation to Africans, but the prospect that they might eventually gain majority control was uncertain, estimates ranging from a dozen years to Ian Smith's not-in-my-lifetime declaration made in 1964.

Such tentative steps toward partnership were satisfactory neither to African nationalist nor to European conservative. Nkomo at first accepted with reluctance, then rejected, the constitution, yielding to the mounting criticism of Africans both inside and outside Southern Rhodesia. It was nothing but a device to perpetuate settler control, he insisted, and called for a boycott of the general election of December 1962, thus ruling out any possibility of racial partnership.

The white community, in its own eyes having made great concessions only to have them spurned by ungrateful Africans, was further upset by what it regarded as British duplicity and weakness in bowing to black pressure in Northern Rhodesia. There, Whitehall had granted a constitution in 1962 which, the whites felt, would establish an African state to the north and spell the end of the Federation of Rhodesia and Nyasaland. Having placed their faith in federation as a means to independence, the Southern Rhodesian settlers now turned in disgust from the ineffective moderation of the federalists and voted the newly formed Rhodesian Front into power. An outgrowth of the old Dominion Party, the Front in victory therefore could be expected to institute a right-wing segregationist regime, in every way anathema to African objectives.

Nevertheless the African nationalists regarded the Rhodesian Front victory as clearing the air of the ambiguities of federation, and prepared to do battle with their new opponents. While the Front lifted former restrictions and released numbers of detainees, Nkomo intensified his opposition, insisting that Southern Rhodesia was

African territory and that the Z.A.P.U. objective was nothing less than the end of minority rule. Even so, this was not enough for the more militant nationalists led by the Rev. Ndabaningi Sithole who formed the more belligerent Zimbabwe African National Union (Z.A.N.U.) in 1963, thereby splitting and seriously weakening the nationalist effort. The two groups vied with each other in pressing their demands and wasted much effort on an intramural struggle which played straight into the hands of the authorities.

The Rhodesian Front's initial amnesty may have deceived the nationalists into misjudging the essential inflexibility of the Front leaders on the issue of white supremacy, but they were soon disabused as the government put through legislation designed to contain any manifestations of African belligerence. Stiff laws were introduced against criminal acts of a political origin, nationalist leaders were kept under close scrutiny, and eventually both Nkomo and Sithole were placed in detention with numbers of the followers. While violence continued to break forth periodically, a good deal of it continued to stem from the rivalry between nationalist groups, and in any event the government was able to control concerted action by identifying and restricting new leadership as it emerged. By the end of 1964 the nationalist movement appeared well under control.

Having contained the Africans, the Rhodesian Front, led by Ian Smith after April, 1964, turned to the major issue of Rhodesian independence, an issue which was soon narrowed to the question of whether independence would be granted or seized. Successive British governments had uniformly insisted that the independence movement would have to show clear evidence of African backing as well as a guarantee of steady advance toward majority rule. Smith tried to prove African support through the testimony of chiefs, a tactic unacceptable in London. As for majority rule, he clearly had the settlers with him in setting his face against such heresy. In 1964 the Rhodesia Party was formed under the leadership of Roy Welensky, dedicated to moderation and constitutionalism and opposed to any extra-legal unilateral move toward independence. That October Welensky and his party were soundly beaten in two by-elections, and Smith's hand immeasurably strengthened thereby. Another year of intensive negotiation followed, but there appeared to be no basis for compromising the essential quarrel over whether power would ultimately rest with the majority, which would mean African rule, or with the settler minority and their position of racial supremacy. On November 11,

1965, the Unilateral Declaration of Independence was broadcast by Smith, and the last of the Central African territories found its independence.

THE HAVES AND THE HAVE-NOTS

For the African population of Rhodesia, U.D.I. meant anything but independence, and there were others placed about the continent who saw themselves in similar condition. In South Africa, whatever their views about the Bantustans, few Africans deluded themselves with the thought that they possessed independence or even true self-government. In the Portuguese territories of Mozambique, Angola, and Guinea, a classic colonial regime still prevailed, scarcely altered since the heyday of the slave trade, while, in 1965, Spain still held minor and little-publicized African territories in varying stages of colonial status. In a different category, far to the east on the Somali "Horn," the Djibouti enclave, now known as the Territory of the Afars and Issas, remained under French protection, having so voted in March, 1967, in preference to absorption into neighboring Somalia.

For the rest, independence came early and late. With United Nations assistance, Libya had secured her freedom in 1951, while to the west Algerians fought their way to liberty in 1962 after seven years of bitter warfare with France. If the Afar and Issa people of the former French Somaliland preferred their protected status, those in the Italian and British Somaliland protectorates opted for independence which arrived in 1960 as the two territories merged to become the Republic of Somalia.

In West Africa, the smaller British colonies followed the path trod by Ghana and Nigeria. Sierra Leone achieved independence in 1961 and the tiny enclave of the Gambia in 1965. In both territories, smallness of size posed the problem of economic viability, a question which arose again in connection with the High Commission Territories embedded in the South African land mass. Nevertheless, Moshesh's Basuto nation became the kingdom of Lesotho in 1966 with his direct descendant, Moshoeshoe, as constitutional monarch and Chief Lebua Jonathan as prime minister. In the same year the vast but impecunious Bechuana protectorate gained its freedom as the Republic of Botswana led by its president, Seretse Khama. Two years later, Swaziland followed her sister territories to independence.

Finally, there was Equatorial Guinea—the small enclave of Rio Muni nestled between Gabon and Cameroun, and the nearby island of Fernando Po—which gained its freedom from Spain in October, 1968.

Suggestions for Further Reading

The literature on nationalism and independence in Africa is indeed extensive, and only a portion of it is listed here.

General works include Thomas Hodgkin's classic, *Nationalism in Colonial Africa* (New York: New York University Press, 1957 and London: F. Muller, 1956); the interesting essay, *Africa, the Politics of Independence* by Immanuel Wallerstein (New York: Vintage, 1961); and the relevant sections of Guy Hunter, *The New Societies of Tropical Africa* (London: Oxford University Press, 1962). See also Thomas Hodgkin, *African Political Parties* (Harmondsworth, Middlesex: Penguin, 1961); and G. A. Almond and J. S. Coleman, eds., *The Politics of Developing Areas* (Princeton, New Jersey: Princeton University Press, 1960). A number of group studies dealing with a variety of African nations before and after independence include two edited by Gwendolen Carter, *African One-Party States* (Ithaca, New York: Cornell University Press, 1962) and *National Unity and Regionalism in Eight African States* (Ithaca, New York: Cornell University Press, 1966); as well as J. S. Coleman and C. G. Rosberg, eds., *Political Parties and National Integration in Tropical Africa* (Berkeley and Los Angeles, California: University of California Press, 1964); and W. J. M. MacKenzie and K. Robinson, eds., *Five Elections in Africa* (Oxford: Clarendon Press, 1960).

For northeastern Africa see Richard Greenfield, *Ethiopia* (London: Pall Mall Press, 1965; New York: Praeger, 1965), E. Ullendorff, *The Ethiopians*, 2nd ed. (London: Oxford University Press, 1965); K. D. D. Henderson, *Sudan Republic* (London; Ernest Benn, 1965; New York: Praeger, 1965); P. M. Holt, *A Modern History of the Sudan*, 2nd ed. (London: Weidenfeld and Nicolson, 1963; New York: Praeger, 1963); I.M. Lewis, *The Modern History of Somaliland* (London: Weidenfeld and Nicolson, 1965; New York: Praeger, 1965); Tom Little, *Egypt* (London: Ernest Benn, 1958), revised as *Modern Egypt*, (New York: Praeger, 1967); John Marlowe, *Anglo-Egyptian Relations, 1800–1953* (London: The Cresset Press, 1954). See also Mohamed O. Beshir, *The Southern Sudan, Background to Conflict* (London: C. Hurst, 1968; New York: Praeger, 1968).

Histories of British West African nations already mentioned in other chapters deal with independence individually, but special attention should be given to J. S. Coleman, *Nigeria: Background to Nationalism* (Berkeley and Los Angeles, University of California Press, 1958); D. Austin, *Politics in Ghana, 1946–1960* (London: Oxford University Press, 1964); David Apter, *Ghana in Transition,* rev. ed. (New York: Atheneum, 1963); R. L. Sklar, *Nigerian Political Parties* (Princeton, New Jersey: Princeton University Press, 1963); Kalu Ezera, *Constitutional Developments in Nigeria,* 2nd. ed. (Cambridge: Cambridge University Press, 1964); and for economic material, P. T. Bauer, *West African Trade* (London: Routledge and Kegan Paul, 1963; New York: Kelly, 1963). The writings of nationalist leaders include George Padmore's two works, *Pan-Africanism or Communism* (London: Dennis Dobson, 1956) and *The Gold Coast Revolution* (London: Dennis Dobson, 1953); Kwame Nkrumah's autobiography, *Ghana* (Edinburgh: Thomas Nelson, 1959); Sir Ahmadu Bello's *My Life* (Cambridge: Cambridge University Press, 1962); and *Awo, the Autobiography of Chief Obafemi Awolowo* (Cambridge: Cambridge University Press, 1960). See also J. R. Hooker, *Black Revolutionary* (London: Pall Mall, 1967; New York: Praeger, 1967).

The French-African territories are served by the two volumes of V. Thompson and R. Adloff, *French West Africa* (London: George Allen and Unwin, 1958; Stanford, Cal.: Stanford University Press, 1958) and *The Emerging States of French Equatorial Africa* (London: Oxford University Press, and Stanford, Cal.: Stanford University Press, 1960); R. S. Morgenthau, *Political Parties in French-Speaking Africa* (London: Oxford University Press, 1964); Michael Crowder, *Senegal: A study of French Assimilation Policy,* rev. ed. (London: Methuen, 1967; New York: Barnes & Noble, 1967); and A. R. Zolberg, *One-Party Government in the Ivory Coast,* rev. ed. (Princeton, New Jersey: Princeton University Press, 1969), as well as the relevant sections of the group studies mentioned above.

For the Congo, see Roger Anstey, *King Leopold's Legacy* (London: Oxford University Press, 1966); E. W. Lefever, *Crisis in the Congo* (Washington: Brookings, 1965); Crawford Young, *Politics in the Congo* (Princeton, New Jersey: Princeton University Press, 1965); and Catherine Hoskyns, *The Congo Since Independence* (London: Oxford University Press, 1965), which may be supplemented with A. P. Merriam, *Congo: Background to Conflict* (Evanston, Illinois: Northwestern, 1961); and Colin Legum, *Congo Disaster* (Baltimore and Harmondsworth, Middlesex: Penguin, 1961).

There is considerable literature on the independence background in East Africa. In addition to K. Ingham, *History of East Africa,* 2nd. ed. (London: Longmans, 1963; New York: Praeger, 1965), which for Uganda may be supplemented by the same author's *The Making of Modern Uganda* (London: George Allen and Unwin, 1958); Zanzibar is dealt with in M. F. Lofchie, *Zanzibar: Background to Revolution* (Princeton,

New Jersey: Princeton University Press, 1965); and Kenya is served by G. Bennett, *Kenya: A Political History* (London: Oxford University Press, 1963), and C. G. Rosberg and J. Nottingham, *The Myth of Mau Mau* (New York: Praeger, 1966; London: Pall Mall, 1966). A number of works present the views of African nationalists, for example, Jomo Kenyatta, *Suffering Without Bitterness* (Nairobi: East African Publishing House, 1968); Oginga Odinga, *Not Yet Uhuru* (London: Heinemann, 1967; New York: Hill & Wang, 1967), Tom Mboya, *Freedom and After* (London: Andre Deutsch, 1963; Boston: Little, Brown, 1963); and Julius Nyerere, *Freedom and Unity* (Dar es Salaam: Oxford University Press, 1967).

Nationalism and independence in Central Africa has been treated in a variety of recent works. See, for example, such standard histories as A. J. Hanna, *The Story of the Rhodesias and Nyasaland,* 2nd. ed. (London: Faber, 1965; New York: Humanities, 1966); and Richard Hall, *Zambia* (London: Pall Mall, 1965; New York: Praeger, 1965). These may be supplemented by R. I. Rotberg, *The Rise of Nationalism in Central Africa* (Cambridge, Massachusetts: Harvard, 1965); D. C. Mulford, *Zambia: The Politics of Independence, 1957–1964* (London: Oxford University Press, 1967); and James Barber, *Rhodesia: the Road to Rebellion* (London: Oxford University Press, 1967). An African view of events may be seen through Kenneth Kaunda, *Zambia Shall Be Free* (London: Heinemann, 1962; New York: Praeger, 1963); and Nathan Shamuyarira, *Crisis in Rhodesia* (Nairobi: East African Publishing House, 1967; New York: Transatlantic Arts, 1965; London: André Deutsch, 1965).

22: Modern Africa: The Quest for
Power and Prosperity

AFRICA IN MIDPASSAGE

The achievement of independence was both an end and a beginning. A most satisfying climax to the nationalist struggle, it was also the point of departure toward goals which had necessarily eluded the grasp of a colonial people.

Colonialism had introduced revolutionary concepts of economic development, but material sufficiency would escape the African until political freedom had insured that the fruits of African economies first served African ends. European domination had been responsible for new territorial configurations and unprecedented propositions concerning the size and function of government, but ultimate political stability was a condition which could emerge solely through the discipline of self-direction. Western imperialism had opened a wider world to African experience, but a constructive role in international affairs was perforce reserved for those who governed themselves at home. Increasingly over a century and a half, the West had dominated widening aspects of African life; consequently, political independence was but the first step toward a greater social, economic, and intellectual freedom leading to the creation and establishment of a genuinely African identity in world civilization. Finally, independence itself was not yet fully achieved. There remained the vexing problem of the European-dominated south—the arbitrary rule over African majorities by white oligarchies in Rhodesia and South Africa as well as continuing colonial control in the Portuguese territories. Even in the flush of enthusiasm and pride which marked the independence celebrations in Accra and Lagos, in Dakar and Brazzaville, in Dar es Salaam and Lusaka, there were many sobering thoughts of the future. Clearly, much work remained to be done.

MODERNIZATION—THE FIRST PRIORITY

Modernization—in good measure, the utilization of experimental science and technological proficiency for economic and social development—has been a growing preoccupation of Africa's people over the past 150 years, and unquestionably represents for independent Africa today her most compelling priority. Political liberty, for all its appeal, has stood second to the vision of the good life, a life of rising material prosperity. Freedom is hollow that does not bring with it the schooling and the medical services, the better roads and the new housing, the electricity, water, and sewage systems, and by no means the least, those necessary luxuries—motorbikes, cinema, radio, non-essential dress, or an evening's entertainment. Politicians who flourished by bringing their people to independence were not likely to remain long in power if they could not deliver prosperity in the wake of freedom; hence the governments of independent nations have been at once preoccupied with the problems of modernization.

Economic development for Africa, however, presents many difficulties, difficulties which bear close relationship to the nature of the African environment. Although this environment is often and correctly described in terms of the caprices of the weather acting on a generally barren land, it is probably the very geniality of Africa's climate which has constituted a major impediment to progress and growth. Tropical temperatures, lacking a period of winter frost, encourage proliferation of species and heavy population expansion, but the resultant multiplicity of animal and plant life has meant an intense competition for survival and a consequent limit on the numbers and geographic concentration of any particular species.

Each organism encourages in its existence a natural enemy which flourishes by feeding on its victim but which eventually declines in numbers as the population of its prey is destroyed. In Africa, therefore, survival of species ultimately has rested upon small numbers spread over wide areas, and this limitation has applied equally to all. Thus, when man in Africa graduated from hunting and gathering to the stage of cultivation, he was compelled to practice a shifting agriculture and to be content with subsistence production in the face of voracious pests which limited his harvests while he himself continued to endure the lethal and enervating attack of tropical diseases.

During the era of colonial control, the development of modern medicine and scientific agriculture introduced for the first time the possibility of overturning this dismal balance of nature and converting crop production into a major engine for a rising standard of living. Since, throughout the world, economic growth has usually sprung from a base in agriculture, and since today nine out of ten Africans are still farm dwellers, modernization in Africa must first of all achieve a revolution in crop production. Not only is this a shorter route than industry provides toward increasing total exports and building budget surpluses, it also levels the most direct attack on the problem of unemployment while stimulating other sectors of the economy—service industries, transport, and, ultimately, manufacturing.

Realization of the prior claims of agricultural development has not escaped the economic planners either in the colonial or independent African governments, but achievement is beset with complications. Beyond the ecological balance of a tropical environment with its downward-leveling pressures, Africa suffers widely from a thin and infertile soil cover which is alternately washed away by excessive rains and burned out by a remorseless sun. Further, though generally lacking the conservatism of the peasant with deep attachment to a particular parcel of land, the African farmer is nonetheless hampered by limitations of technique and outlook. The pressures of environment had forced him to adopt a migratory, subsistence cultivation, a system which exploits land instead of improving it, which produces for survival but nothing more, and which emphasizes security and discourages innovation. Since production even today is linked in the main to local consumption, the concepts of a market economy, of cash crops, the accumulation of surpluses, and production specialization have grown but slowly. Furthermore, traditional patterns of land tenure have militated against the idea of private ownership, thereby inhibiting any tendencies by individual farmers to introduce physical improvements or to invest capital and labor in anticipation of a greater productivity.

Environment and custom, therefore, have combined to frustrate the development of scientific cultivation and commercialized production in a money economy, but there have also been factors working for change. The growth of urban markets, the introduction of a system of cash exchange, the rise of part-time farming linked to migratory labor, and the development of export crops beginning during the colonial period, have all pointed African farming in the direction of market production, and African governments have increasingly added the thrust of their own economic planning.

Official activity has attacked the problem on many fronts. The identification and encouragement of cash crops was an early activity of colonial regimes—cocoa, groundnuts, and palm products in West Africa, coffee and tea in East Africa, cotton in the Anglo-Sudan, and rubber in the Congo as well as in independent Liberia. In Kenya the government's land resettlement program begun in 1954 was accelerated after African political ascendancy was assured in 1960, and large blocks in the white highlands came under African control in the form of permanent holdings; similarly, freehold tenure and settled farms have been widely established through legislation in various countries across the continent.

State-directed pest control, better transportation, irrigation and erosion projects, the production of fertilizers, government agricultural credit and crop storage facilities, as well as improved genetic strains resulting from publicly-supported research are all widely employed to increase productivity, while the demonstration farm and extension service are standard devices for educating the individual farmer and for identifying and attacking his problems. Some government efforts have come in the form of vast projects like the Gezira cotton growing scheme which evolved successfully in the Sudan over the early years of the twentieth century. Several of these large-scale ventures have been spectacular failures—witness the disastrous attempt to grow groundnuts in Tanganyika between 1948 and 1950; hence, more modest steps are generally favored as less costly and more viable.

Whatever the particular form of any specific project—a fertilizer plant in Senegal, a palm tree nursery in Nigeria, an irrigation demonstration farm for Ghana, a program for rural development in Tanzania, or a self-help housing scheme in Kenya—the ultimate objective is always the same. Agricultural production must be dramatically increased, greatly improved in quality, and concentrated on essential crops. Food must be produced to meet the needs of the home market, thus eliminating costly imports, while agricultural exports are steadily developed as an essential prerequisite to economic growth.

Fundamental though it is, economic growth through agricultural development is painfully slow and difficult. At present, production is barely matching population increase, there is a discouraging lag in the application of modern methods and technology, while droughts and other natural disasters continue to take their toll, forcing the import of food which in turn brings inflation. The new states of Africa have therefore turned where possible to other sources of wealth, in particular to the continent's vast mineral resources which now comprise almost 15 per cent of world output.

Providing there is sufficient capital available for development, the exploitation of sub-surface assets offers many roseate prospects. It was diamonds and then gold that financed modernization in South Africa, while copper mining in Zambia has placed that country's production—normally averaging over 700,000 tons a year—behind only the United States and the Soviet Union and about on a par with Chile. In Congo-Kinshasa, mining, principally of copper, cobalt, and industrial diamonds, provided over four-fifths of all exports in 1967 and projects a brilliant national future once political and financial stability have been achieved.

Other territories bristle with possibilities. Gabon, already relatively affluent because of its timber, now exports every year a million tons of crude oil and a million tons of high-grade manganese, along with about 1500 tons of uranium. To this must be added the Mekambo iron deposits, a massive field containing well over half a billion tons of 60 per cent or better iron content, which will begin to produce in 1974, thus adding significantly to a gross national product that already sustains the highest per capita income in black Africa. Similarly, if less spectacularly, the Mount Nimba deposits lying in Liberia and Guinea contain 250 million tons of 66 per cent ore and have already made Liberia the third largest exporter of iron in the world. Iron has also rescued Mauritania from a desert poverty, and huge uranium deposits in the Agades region may do as well for impecunious Niger. Bauxite, which is the industrial arm of Ghana's

Volta River power project, is present in Guinea in extensive, high-quality reserves, Sierra Leone has long been a diamond and iron ore producer, while rich stores of phospates have been identified and developed in Togo and Senegal.

The export of minerals not only earns foreign exchange and invites investment; it also requires sophisticated harbor, transportation, and power facilities which are of value to agricultural and industrial producers who might not otherwise be able to afford their construction. In the past the need for such expensive facilities has been an impediment to development, but more recently improved techniques of mineral extraction and dwindling world supplies have worked in favor of Africa in this respect. A more serious challenge to African aspirations comes from other quarters—competition between nations inside and outside Africa or from new products, the wastage caused by man-made political unrest, or the sad fact that some nations simply lack the natural resources for development or find their supplies running out. For example, a drastic fall in world prices threatens Nigerian tin and columbite, while in Ghana some gold mines have been earmarked for shutdown due to declining supplies. Such countries as Mali, Chad, Malawi, or Tanzania presently show little evidence of any important mineral resources, but faint hopes are sometimes realized as in the case of recent uranium reserves discovered in the parched wastes of Somalia.

Perhaps most frustrating of all are the situations where development has been blocked, not by lack of resources but by human frailty. In Nigeria a substantial oil production yielding 13 million tons and a government revenue of $50 million in 1966 was severely affected by the ravages of civil war. Investment capital from abroad at first quietly melted away, the national growth rate seriously declined, while an inestimable burden was introduced by war expenses mostly chargeable against hard-earned foreign exchange. Similarly, economic advance was badly compromised in the Congo by the civil unrest following independence, Zambia has suffered substantial economic dislocation from the political necessity of supporting sanctions against Rhodesia since the Unilateral Declaration of Independence in November, 1965, and the United Arab Republic (Egypt) has been obliged to pay a heavy price as a result of the Arab-Israeli war in June, 1967.

While the base line for modernization in Africa rests in agriculture and initial economic stimulus wherever possible seems best provided by mining, it is the development of industry which is the ultimate goal of her planners, for industrialization is the key to a breakthrough from poverty to affluence. It is also far and away the most difficult and elusive aspect of African development. There are several reasons for this. First of all, since African nations are primarily agricultural, their internal market is small and inelastic, made up of numbers of farmers with limited income and desire for manufactured goods. Moreover, an export market offers few alternative prospects, involving international competition with fully industrialized nations whose productive capacity, technical sophistication, and management experience cannot be matched by neophytes.

Worse still, there are limits at any given moment on the total world consumption of so-called primary products such as food and raw materials for manufacturing, which often suffer the additional disability of drastic international price fluctuations from year to year. Industrial products, however, are much less vulnerable to such pricing changes and can be consumed virtually without check other than the ability to pay. Under these circumstances, an exchange of African primary products for the manufactured goods of the developed nations leaves Africa in an increasingly unfavorable market position. It is forced into a disadvantageous international exchange of foodstuffs and raw materials which have a limited demand for expensive machinery and other processed materials; thus Africans are hampered in their attempt to accumulate foreign exchange and improve their standard of living through a conversion to industrialization.

This is a difficult situation which is being met in a variety of ways. One approach is to inherit the manufacture of cheap, easily produced commodities increasingly abandoned by the more advanced nations. Another is to establish processing industries associated with mining or agriculture, thus reducing the bulk of raw materials for easier, cheaper transport. Still another is to engage in the final assembly of products more economically shipped in semifinished form. This tactic has been particularly notable in the automotive industry as road transport in Africa has expanded since the Second World War. Assembly plants have been supplemented, moreover, by the manufacture of spare parts, and, as the consumption of gasoline has risen, with the construction of refineries and the multiplication of service stations. In all these cases, where the cost of labor forms a large proportion of the total cost of production, Africa enjoys a competitive edge over the developed nation because of her cheap labor supply.

Examples abound, as industry has inched up to account for 9 per cent of the continent's gross domestic product as of 1966. Zambia no longer exports unprocessed copper ore, substituting a finished product, electrolytic refined copper, and Liberia has begun to produce iron ore pellets of high purity and uniformity much in demand for iron and steel manufacture. Ghanaian gold is also refined as is sugar in Nigeria and Tanzania and petroleum in the Congo and several other countries. Many industries are small and geared primarily for local consumption as in the case of textiles in Togo and the Sudan, soap in the Ivory Coast, processed foods, tobacco, and footwear in Ethiopia, or bottling works and distilleries in a wide range of locations. In Nigeria a cement plant takes advantage of local limestone deposits, while Ghana has begun to develop an industrial complex situated at the port of Tema. Here are ten establishments including a flour mill, margarine plant, fish cannery, oil refinery, and a factory for the production of animal feed, each installation designed to utilize by-products from the others.

Poor planning or political motivation have been responsible for failures like the abandoned paper mill at Jebba in Nigeria or the shoe factory in Kumasi which has been unable to produce at competitive prices. Perhaps the best example, however, of what can be accomplished despite meager natural resources is offered by Kenya. Lacking significant mineral deposits or unusual soil fertility, it has nonetheless developed one of the best growth rates in Africa, largely by attracting foreign investment in a range of processing industries related to agriculture and by a careful promotion of tourism.

Economic development in Africa, of course, relies heavily on good transportation and communication facilities as well as on adequate water-driven electric power, but there is a growing conviction among national leaders that one of the essentials of modernization is international economic cooperation such as tariff unions, common markets, or production coordination. Pan-Africanism is an old idea, even in its post-independence form of actual associations among African states, but these early groupings had strong political coloration while the continental Organization of African Unity (O.A.U.) founded in May, 1963, has been only slightly concerned with economic matters. The Economic Commission for Africa (E.C.A.), established by the United Nations in 1959, has a solid record of useful services in coordinating economic and financial policy among nations, but its activities necessarily stop short of executive action by sovereign states. Until recently, moreover, international associations with strong economic interests were to be found mainly within the former French areas of Equatorial and West Africa, for example, the Afro-Malagasy Common Organization (O.C.A.M.) with its European Economic Community (E.E.C.) connections or the Entente states of Ivory Coast, Dahomey, Upper Volta, Niger, and Togo.

The year 1968 marked an important shift away from the more vaguely-defined and loosely organized pan-African coalitions to essentially economically motivated communities. Already, Kenya, Uganda, and Tanzania had established the East African Community (E.A.C.) in December, 1967, as a cautious, hopeful step back to the common market they once enjoyed in the days of the British East African High Commission, and shortly thereafter they began to consider membership requests from Ethiopia, Somalia, Rwanda, and Zambia, while initiating talks for a trade link with E.E.C. In March, 1968, Senegal, Guinea, Mali, and Mauritania formed the Organization of Senegal River States (O.E.R.S.) primarily for the development of the river basin, and scarcely a week later the short-lived United States of Central Africa (U.E.A.C.) came into being comprising Chad, Congo-Kinshasa, and the Central African Republic in an effort to step up mutual economic cooperation. Finally, at the end of April, the West African Regional Group was created by nine states (Gambia, Ghana, Guinea, Liberia, Mali, Mauritania, Nigeria, Senegal, and Upper Volta) as a first step toward desired but elusive economic unification.

Not only were the relatively affluent Ivory Coast and Gabon conspicuously absent from these last regional unions, but there continued to be enormous practical impediments to genuine unity despite the most serious of intentions. Some of these were the heritage of colonial days; for example, internally oriented networks of transportation and communications, differences in national language, in organization of government offices, in systems of bookkeeping, and in a pervasive cultural infusion which so readily identifies the Gallic tone of Cotonou or Brazzaville, the Belgian quality of Kinshasa, the Muslim character of Khartoum or Bamako, or the Anglo-Saxon spirit of Lagos or Kampala, each blended with a large helping of local ethos.

Beyond such intangibles lie the practical problems of sorting out a variety of national customs regulations based on different tariff systems which in turn are related to current international agreements such as the O.C.A.M. preferential rates for imports from the European Common Market. Finally, joint planning must necessarily entail difficult decisions regarding the location of industrial plants, particularly as much needed investment capital from abroad wishes to locate in the more advanced territories. Thus a good measure of statemanship will be required, and some of this has already been in evidence; witness the E.A.C. distribution of customs which allows disproportionately larger shares to Uganda and Tanzania at the expense of more developed Kenya.

Although all independent African states attempt to manipulate their economies through varying degrees of public controls and direct government participation, there are discernible two differing approaches to national economic planning, one essentially idealist, the other leaning toward the pragmatic. For their part, the idealists hold clearly in view at all times the vision of a perfect society which is to be realized through an economic revolution controlled and directed by a rigorous state authority. Before he was ousted in the military coup of February, 1966, Kwame Nkrumah was probably the leading exponent of the idealist school, having been succeeded since his downfall by the Tanzanian chief of state, Julius Nyerere. As prime minister and president of Ghana, Nkrumah continually emphasized the close relationship between political action and economic development, a major function of the state being to force the pace of modernization. While this meant total war on such traditional institutions as the power of chiefs, the extended family, nepotism, and "dash," and while it entailed massive infusions of capital aid from abroad to revolutionize subsistence agriculture and press forward with industrialization, it also produced a highly ambivalent attitude toward foreign economic assistance. Wanting and needing help, Nkrumah was nonetheless suspicious of the "neo-colonial" domination which he felt such help entailed, and his continued advocacy of pan-African unity was designed to create a third force in the world which would compel the developed nations to grant massive aid without conditions, either economic or political.

Nyerere's lofty image of a great egalitarian society in Africa has also brought forth a strong state authority engaged in rigorous economic planning, while his principle of self-help added to disappointments over the nature and extent of foreign assistance has evoked a growing disillusionment with Europe and America and a corresponding reorientation toward Communist China. Such doctrinaire interpretations of Africa's destiny are, however, not for the pragmatists, who encourage investment from abroad as the quickest route to African development while defining state socialism to allow more leeway for private capital.

By the opening of 1969, Tanzania found herself virtually alone as the exemplar of socialist idealism, for the ranks of the committed had been thinned by events—Nkrumah's fall duplicated late in 1968 when Modibo Keita was ousted by the army in Mali, Sekou Touré's continuing search for rapprochement with France, and a growing economic eclecticism in countries like Algeria and Zambia. Already the rest of the continent was made up of pragmatists in varying degree with perhaps Félix Houphouet-Boigny's Ivory Coast as their most conspicuous and successful example. Houphouet indulges in no philosophic flights, concentrating rather on development through a rising outflow of exports balanced by an influx of foreign capital and technical assistance. Unlike many African leaders, he refuses to compromise efficiency and replace expatriates with partly trained Africans, and unlike the idealists he welcomes close association with the West, particularly France; like Léopold Senghor, he sees African progress in terms of Eurafrican partnership. The results, he points out, are a buoyant economy, a growth rate close to 8 per cent during the 1960's, and one of the highest per capita incomes in tropical Africa.

Whatever the varying attitudes within Africa, economic development across the continent has relied heavily upon foreign assistance and intimate commercial contacts with the industrialized world. Even if such devices as forced labor and mandatory savings were politically feasible, the domestic financial and technical resources of Africa are scarcely capable of sustaining economic growth unaided. At the same time, foreign outlets are essential to supplement the small and weak home market, absorbing substantial portions of a production which must expand continually if development is to be achieved. There are difficulties, however, which emerge from a series of related circumstances.

In the first place, the wealthy nations, both East and West, gain relatively little from their association with the developing world of Africa, not even from foodstuffs and raw materials which are increasingly threatened by substitutes; for example, polypropylene for sisal, plastics for metals, or synthetic fabrics for cotton. Further, investment capital in the final analysis is deployed for selfish purposes within the creditor nation—corporate profit, national prestige, or cold war strategies—and need not necessarily benefit the borrower. Even genuinely humanitarian considerations tend to become lost when challenged by political necessities at home, and the intensity of interest in foreign aid can change abruptly in the face of economic compulsion or the constantly shifting pressure of events in different parts of the globe. In 1964 and 1968 two international meetings of the United Nations Conference on Trade and Development (U.N.C.T.A.D.) produced no measurable progress toward a proposed global redistribution of wealth that was to be effected first, by the promise of aid from the affluent to the impecunious to the extent of one per cent of their gross national product; second, by the raising and stabilization of the prices of primary products; and finally, by the preferential entry for manufactured goods originating in the emerging areas. Agreement in principle was not followed by any positive action among the wealthy nations.

Although economic aid to Africa rose to $1 billion annually during the early independence years, 1960–1965, this effort began to reverse itself thereafter as major aid nations were forced to respond to the pressure of domestic and other events. Britain, for example, was obliged to institute austerity at home in order to rally the pound and strengthen her international trade pattern. Similarly, American aid fell before the urgency of domestic problems and the mounting costs of military commitments in Vietnam. France, while maintaining a high level of aid in Africa, tended to concentrate her efforts largely in the most successful of her former colonies.

Furthermore, such aid as was forthcoming did not always provide the assistance it seemed to promise. The most absolute aid is that which comes as an outright unencumbered gift or in the form of a price for primary products artificially fixed above that of the world market. Loans can be classified as genuine aid only when they are arranged on a long-term basis at an interest rate below what is normal. Short-term loans at standard interest rates are no more than a business proposition usually highly unfavorable to the poorer nation which needs time as well as money for development. Outright gifts have been in fact rare, although pricing arrangements are not infrequent, but the bulk of direct aid to Africa has come in the form of interest-bearing loans. Already the developing states are repaying old loans at a rate in excess of new borrowing; in short the flow of capital as far as loans are concerned has reversed itself from the poor to the rich.

Even more distressing, many loans have been tied to special arrangements requiring that purchases be made in the creditor nation, usually at prices above the level set by international competition. Thus the real value of the loan is substantially reduced although interest charges are based on its face value. Barter agreements, popular among Communist-bloc countries, also present pitfalls to the unwary. An offer of capital goods in exchange for an agricultural product may involve inefficient or obsolete machinery of inflated value, and unless careful prior agreement is reached, the crop can be resold on the international market with disastrous effect on the world price. Direct trade with the West offers its problems too, for industrial prices tend to rise while those of primary products have declined in recent years. Increased production, the basic prerequisite to modernization, is thereby compromised by an unfavorable international price structure. From 1963 until mid-1966, exports from the developing world rose approximately 6 per cent a year, but over the same period their import prices increased by 2 per cent. Consequently the advantage of this accomplishment was reduced to 4 per cent while debt servicing further eroded purchasing power to a net increase of only 3 per cent.

This gloomy picture is intensified by growing food shortages due to a population increase which also threatens to wipe out hard-earned national growth rates. Meanwhile as the industrialized nations, East and West alike, have continued to rise in prosperity, their aid and concern for the poor nations has declined relatively, if not absolutely. By 1968 expenditures on defense were almost seventeen times greater than economic assistance to the developing world. Unless the trend can be reversed with a substantial growth in foreign aid, the fulfilment of rising expectations will be greatly complicated. Self-help, laudable and necessary though it may be, cannot do the job alone.

THE PROBLEM OF POLITICAL STABILITY

Economic development is of course closely linked to political stability. Clearly, the process of modernization cannot take place in an atmosphere of unrest, while economic planning requires a high degree of control in the hands of a centralized authority. Not surprisingly, therefore, African leaders since independence have consistently stressed political strength, not only because of their natural desire to remain in power but because a vigorous and durable government is the necessary prerequisite for an economic advance which they are expected to deliver. More than that, there are many divisive forces at work among peoples whose sense of national identity is as yet feeble and uncertain, and who are easily persuaded to support factious movements, even to the point of secession. It is not surprising under these circumstances that democratic processes have sometimes suffered while political freedom is regarded as an expendable luxury at this initial stage of independent growth.

It was in Ghana, which had led Africa to independence, that the issue of centralization was first joined. Nkrumah's Convention People's Party, for all its popularity, was obliged to endure widespread voter apathy during the national elections held in 1954 and 1956. Moreover, regional movements were urging a federated government which would guarantee protection of local economic interests in the more affluent areas, while the traditional authorities hoped they might continue to wield the powers they had exercised under the indirect rule of the British. To Nkrumah, intent upon creating a modern state, such centrifugal tendencies were intolerable, and he quickly moved to head them off. In this he was successful and Ghanaian unity was preserved, but only in the form of a one-party state and a one-man dictatorship which permitted no opposition, driving dissenters into exile or imprisoning them without judicial process under the notorious Preventive Detention Act.

Such arbitrary rule might have gone unchallenged had it not been accompanied by an inflexible and impatient determination to modernize which failed to take account of the realities of Ghana's economy, overstressing industrialization and neglecting agriculture, and thereby converting $500 million of reserves at independence into a national debt of more than $1 billion by 1965. In February, 1966, a coup by combined army and police forces ousted Nkrumah while he was absent on a state visit to Communist China, its leaders accusing him of bringing the country to the brink of disaster through economic mismanagement and political tyranny. The military formed a National Liberation Council headed by Lieutenant-General J.A. Ankrah which governed the country by decree, but in 1969 a new constitution prepared the way for a return to civil government. Elections held in August of that year gave a majority in the new national assembly to the Progress Party of Dr. Kofi Busia who formed a government with the major opposition centered in the National Alliance of Liberals headed by Nkrumah's former finance minister, K. A. Gbedemah. Under the constitution, presidential powers were to be exercised temporarily by an army and police triumvirate; hence, in effect, the military retained ultimate authority during the early stages of parliamentary rule. Among many pressing problems, the new government faced the possibility that ancient divisive forces might re-emerge, typified by the rivalry of Busia and Gbedemah as prominent representatives respectively of the Ashanti and Ewe communities. Meanwhile, Nkrumah waits in exile, hoping for the reappearance of just such internal particularist strains which might bring him back to power.

Far across the continent to the east other struggles between centralism and particularism have been in motion. In Uganda the new constitution ratified in September, 1967, has enabled the country's determined president, Milton Obote, to check the divisive pull of regional loyalties. The old kingdoms of Buganda, Bunyoro, Toro, and Ankole have been dissolved, and the government has set its sights on economic development of truly national dimension. Whether the centrifugal forces in Uganda have been destroyed or merely checked for the moment, her northern neighbor, the Sudan, is experiencing her latest spasm of factionalism in a country where strong religious and regional differences have long complicated true national unity. Although the military regime of General Abbud was replaced by civilian rule in 1964, political leaders have been unable to resolve long-standing differences which have impeded economic and social progress. In 1967 the old Mahdist Umma party lost its effectiveness by splitting into liberal and conservative wings, while the National Unionist Party of Ismail al-Azhari amalgamated with the pro-Egyptian People's Democratic Party which had departed the N.U.P. in 1956 after al-Azhari turned away from his original support for union with Egypt.

These shifts and schisms, based partly on the old Mahdiyya-Khatmiyya division, partly on a family quarrel among the Mahdist *ansar* followers, and partly on the recurrent issue of relations with Egypt, have retarded national development, but nonetheless remain secondary to the unresolved problem of relations between the north and the southern provinces of Bahr al-Ghazal, Upper Nile, and Equatoria. There, the Nilotic people have long argued neglect both during colonial times and since independence while claiming that the northerners in control of the government in Khartoum have tried to thrust their Islamic way of life on the Christian and pagan south. In 1961 long-lived discontent broke out in the form of a guerrilla revolt which has brought bitter fighting and driven over 100,000 refugees out of the country, mostly into Uganda. Some southerners have tried to secure concessions by working within the government and this has further complicated and intensified the revolt which has also been the source of border problems and strained relations with Uganda. By early 1969 final agreement on a constitution had yet to be reached because of uncertainties as to whether the Sudan should be a centralized state as favored by the north or a federation preferred by the southerners. Unfortunately, these parochial differences have turned energies away from major developmental problems such as balance of payment deficits, trade losses, and unemployment, as well as recurrent educational and religious issues. In May, 1969, discontent among army officers over continuing political and economic frustrations brought a second military coup, the new regime apparently leaning toward a stricter state socialism to help solve national problems.

The strength of local allegiance has plagued national development in a number of other newly independent countries. Civil war in Nigeria, which broke out in 1967, was spawned in tribal animosities, and Zambia has experienced the stress of both tribal and religious exclusiveness. For example, President Kaunda briefly threatened to resign his office in 1968 in a moment of exasperation over tribalist tendencies among political leaders, while at the time of independence the nation experienced a stubborn defiance of governmental authority arising from a dispute with the Lumpa Church of Alice Lenshina Mulenga. Concentrated in the Bemba country to the northeast, the 50,000 Lumpas reacted violently during 1964 against pressures to bring them into the reigning United National Independence Party, fighting neighboring tribes incited to attack them, resisting government troops with heavy loss of life, a large contingent finally retreating into the nearby Congo.

In Congo-Kinshasa, where zionist churches have long flourished, numbers of prophetic sects pose a threat to civil order, abandoning village life, refusing to pay taxes, and sometimes resorting to brigandage and kidnapping as in the case of the Kitawalistes in Equateur province to the northwest. Elsewhere tribal loyalties still threaten slowly growing political stability. The insurrection of white mercenaries in 1967 gained the immediate support of Katangese gendarmes bent on achieving the secession that had eluded Moise Tshombe after independence, and touched off local unrest when the mutineers marched through Kivu and Orientale provinces. Between independence in 1960 and the advent of General Mobutu's government five years later, the Congo had known far more anarchy than order, an order essential to national development and prosperity. Under Mobutu, however, the country has enjoyed a lengthening period of stability.

The search for political strength and unity has stimulated African leaders to resort increasingly to the device of a one-party government, either officially as with Nkrumah's C.P.P., the Tanganyikan African National Union (T.A.N.U.), and many others, or informally in the numerous cases where opposition parties are simply not encouraged. In Kenya, for example, President Kenyatta for a time harassed but tolerated the opposition Kenya People's Union led by Oginga Odinga. However, Luo unrest following the assassination of Tom Mboya in July, 1969, eventually led to the proscribing of K.P.U. and Odinga's house arrest.

The numerous states which make up the great bloc of former French colonies have leaned heavily on the single-party government as an instrument of national strength, but they have relied even more on French friendship and financial support to provide them with cohesion and stability. Ivory Coast development stems from the early fifties when Félix Houphouet-Boigny terminated his militant opposition to French economic interests in his country, and others have also prospered in direct proportion to their degree of harmony with France. Before his death in 1967, President Léon Mba of Gabon consistently promoted ties with France which he regarded as a second fatherland. In 1964 French paratroopers were on hand to restore him to power after he had been ousted in a military coup, and his gratitude was expressed in granting French access to Gabon's rich uranium deposits. The new president of Gabon, B.-A. Bongo, has proclaimed his own single-party government, but otherwise maintains the intimate French connection instituted by his predecessor.

Senegal is another nation which has profited from a warm relationship with her one-time ruler. Like many French-speaking Africans, President Leopold Senghor deeply admired General de Gaulle, who gained great prestige in 1960 when he granted independence to France's former African colonies. Nevertheless, admiration has been buttressed by much-needed economic assistance in support of a single-crop economy which unaided would be hard-pressed to maintain Senegal's national establishment with its large civil service, its university, and its great harbor installations. Groundnuts account for virtually 85 per cent of Senegal's exports; hence, when French groundnut subsidies ended in 1968, the question of national prosperity once again arose in terms of long-standing economic dependence and political friendship toward France.

Those who have chosen to proceed free of the French connection have been obliged to suffer the consequent blight of Gaullist disfavor. Guinea's declaration of independence in 1958 if anything strengthened her sense of national solidarity, but it also removed the prop of France's financial help, trade preferences, and technical assistance, and thereby greatly complicated Sekou Touré's attempts to accelerate the development of his economy. A decade of economic decline has been characterized by a halting productivity, a growing external debt, and an unstable currency which substantial foreign aid, chiefly from Communist sources, could not overcome. In 1968 Guinea appeared at last ready for rapprochement with France as well as with her neighbors, Senegal and the Ivory Coast, which have remained within the French orbit.

Similarly, Mali has paid with continuing poverty for a freedom of action. Although she remained within the French community, she left the franc zone in 1962, established her own currency, and accepted foreign aid from Russia and China among others as the basis for an independent social and industrial development. Five years later her balance of payment difficulties had become so acute that it was evident her slender resources could no longer sustain economic independence. Growing debts and need for a hard currency led to negotiations in 1967 for a series of stages returning Mali to the franc zone the following year.

Still another form of national divisiveness has long been apparent in Liberia. From its earliest days, the country has been dominated by its American colonists who gradually extended their control over the indigenous population, ruling arbitrarily and culminating their exploitation of land and people during the period between the two world wars when the ugly charge of slaving reached as far as the president's office. With the accession of William V.S. Tubman as chief of state in 1944 there has been a steady improvement in relations, and local leaders have been encouraged to join with the settler aristocracy in government. Since 1964 representation of one million indigenous Liberians in the legislature has equaled that of the thirty thousand Americo-Liberians, a degree of parity which, however, takes little account of President Tubman's absolute political control and the economic ascendancy of the settlers. That dissatisfaction with this state of affairs exists became apparent in 1968 when a government official of tribal origin was charged with treason for plotting to incite revolution designed to overthrow the settler oligarchy and return the country to its original inhabitants. This government action was accompanied by President Tubman's denunciation of tribalism and his firm declaration that all Negroes and all Liberians were Africans and that Liberia belonged equally to all of her citizens.

THE PAN-AFRICAN MOVEMENT

If strong national governments have been sought as the necessary basis for economic development, pan-African unity since independence has been Africa's means for overcoming the limitations of national weakness in a parlous world. Although most African statesmen have consistently urged pan-African unity, it was Kwame Nkrumah who was its most articulate early spokesman. In their individual frailty, said Nkrumah, the new states of Africa could do little to influence the great powers, neither to dissuade them from a senseless and dangerous arms race nor to cause them to divert defense expenditures toward solution of the economic problems of the developing countries. In unity, however, Africa could accomplish much. It could be a powerful voice in the United Nations, a third force to balance the giants of West and East, and an economic community which would raise Africa from a depressed supplier of raw materials to an industrialized, modernized region, healthy and prosperous in its own right. Nkrumah therefore decried political and economic association with former colonial masters, arguing, for example, that an African common market was the proper alternative to associate membership in the E.E.C. favored by France's former colonies.

During the pre-independence years immediately following the Second World War, the pan-African movement was directed primarily against the political restrictions and racial indignities of colonial rule. The Fifth Pan-African Congress in 1945 was concerned with anti-colonialism and the rights of black men in general, these themes converging in the demand for national independence in Africa. At the same time French-speaking colonials from Africa and the West Indies developed the idea of *négritude* and founded the journal, *Présence Africaine,* which extolled African cultural achievements in a manifestation culminating in the two conferences of black writers and artists held in 1956 and 1959. By 1957, however, with the independence of Ghana achieved and freedom for other territories clearly in sight, the emphasis of pan-Africanism shifted quickly toward a search for international unity in pursuit of the objectives so persuasively set forth by Kwame Nkrumah.

The year 1958 marked several important developments, most of which were directly connected with Nkrumah and Ghana. In April, the Conference of Independent African States met in Accra where it recognized the revolutionary National Liberation Front (F.L.N.) as the legitimate representative of Algeria and emphasized African unity in practice by forming a special African group among the African ambassadors at the United Nations. September saw another grouping come into being, the Pan-African Freedom Movement of East and Central Africa (P.A.F.M.E.C.A.), designed to encourage independence movements in its defined area; then, after Guinea had opted for freedom from France, there came the Ghana-Guinea Union in November, 1958, which gave dramatic indication of the capacity and desire of Africans to unite in mutual assistance.

The high point of the year was reached, however, in December with the All-African Peoples' Conference in Accra attended by delegates representing political groups and trade unions in twenty-eight countries, most still colonies. It was at this meeting that Patrice Lumumba gained the impetus which helped precipitate the rapid movement toward independence in the Congo, while the conspicuous role played by Tom Mboya as Conference chairman focused attention at a crucial moment on the nationalist struggle in Kenya.

After this first flush of enthusiasm, the pan-African movement began to change character once again. The growing number of independent nations created both local problems of first priority and an expanding group of African leaders whose personal ambition, temperament, or training made international cooperation increasingly difficult. The Congo crisis of 1960 drove the first ideological wedge into African unity by dividing the support of African states between Lumumba and Kasavubu; hence, subsequent pan-African groupings took on a less universal quality. Toward the end of 1960, the Brazzaville Group, or African and Malagasy Union (U.A.M.), came into being briefly, comprising most of France's former sub-Saharan colonies and Malagasy. In 1965 it re-emerged as the Afro-Malagasy Common Organization (O.C.A.M.), and in both guises it was characterized by a desire for concerted political action and for economic association, through France, with the European Common Market. The political position of the Brazzaville bloc which supported Kasavubu and adopted a restrained position on the Algerian war, was balanced by the January, 1961, meeting of the Casablanca nations (Ghana, Guinea, Mali, Morocco, and the United Arab Republic) who rallied to Lumumba and invited the provisional government of Algeria as a full-fledged participant. This polarization, in ideological terms a debate over the right of revolution against established governments, caused the ultimate demise of the All Africa Peoples' Conference which never met after 1961.

At this stage there were already over two dozen independent African states to question the appropriateness of revolution; hence, the grouping of legitimate governments which met at Monrovia in 1961 and 1962 was dedicated both to non-interference in internal affairs and to a renewed attempt at continental unity. There followed, moreover, the settlement of the Algerian war, the end of Katangan secession, and the defeat of federation in the Rhodesias, all of which eased the way toward reconciliation between the Casablanca and Monrovia points of view. Gradually it came to be recognized that freedom of the white-dominated south, not the unseating of conservative African governments, was the continent's first political priority, and required absolute pan-African unity. In May, 1963, thirty states met at Addis Ababa and signed the charter which brought into being the Organization of African Unity (O.A.U.).

There were some initial successes, largely at the expense of South Africa and Portugal who were forced from membership in several international bodies, South Africa, for example, resigning from the International Labor Organization and the Food and Agriculture Organization. There was also the establishment of the African Liberation Committee designed to assist liberation movements in the south. Further, the O.A.U. was able to quench the Algerian-Moroccan war which flared briefly in the autumn of 1963. Finally, patient O.A.U. diplomacy led to the eventual agreement late in 1967 by which Kenya and Somalia finally settled their long-standing border dispute. Nevertheless, the immense difficulty in finding common ground and courses of action for nations of differing and shifting interests has frequently strained African faith in O.A.U. effectiveness although it remains a potentially powerful force for diplomatic action leading to continental harmony and unity.

Particularly it has been the inability of the O.A.U. to deal satisfactorily with major African crises which has most clearly delineated its present limitations. First, it was impotent in the face of civil unrest which broke forth in the Congo at the end of 1963. Unable to devise a viable course of action, the nations of Africa were obliged to stand by helplessly while peace was restored by Moise Tshombe, that pariah of African leaders, acting as Congolese prime minister during 1964–1965 and employing white mercenaries. Next, on the occasion of U.D.I. in Rhodesia, the O.A.U. resolved that its membership break off diplomatic intercourse with Britain if she failed to bring down the Rhodesian government by force. Initially, only ten of thirty-eight states responded to the resolution, and by the close of 1968 all had resumed normal relations.

Finally, there is the civil war in Nigeria which broke out in 1967 when the Ibo-dominated eastern region seceded as the independent state of Biafra. While the O.A.U. delicately skirted the issue, several member states eventually recognized Biafran sovereignty, thereby violating the O.A.U. charter providing for non-interference with internal affairs of constituent nations. This action caused Nigeria to withdraw her considerable financial support of the African Liberation Committee based in Dar es Salaam, an evident reprisal against Tanzania which was the first to recognize Biafra. Nevertheless, the O.A.U. continued to deploy its prestige and influence in search of a peaceful solution for Nigeria despite the divisions among its founder nations over an appropriate policy.

THE NIGERIAN CIVIL WAR

If pan-African accord has been elusive, so too has the ability of legitimate governments to forestall internal disunity and protect themselves against revolution, particularly by their military establishments. Between 1952, the year that Colonel Nasser staged the revolt which overthrew the government of King Farouk, and 1968, which closed out with a bloodless coup in Mali, there were over seventy incidents, either staged or planned with military collusion, and twenty of these led to the institution of new army-led governments. Dahomey endured five successful coups through 1969, and General Mobutu twice took charge of the government in Congo-Kinshasa where lack of public order and indiscipline in the armed forces had been chronic. It was an army revolt in June, 1965, which unseated Ahmed Ben Bella and installed Colonel Houari Boumedienne in his stead as chief of state in Algeria, while military revolts swept away civilian rule in Burundi, Upper Volta, and the Central African Republic in 1966. President Sylvanus Olympio was assassinated in 1963 during a successful coup in Togo, and President Nkrumah was deposed by his army and police in February, 1966, scarcely a month after a major upheaval in Nigeria had overthrown the federal and regional administrations and instituted a period of growing instability in that unhappy land. Sierra Leone experienced two successful military coups, the first which did away with civilian rule in March, 1967, and the second which re-established it in April, 1968. Late in that same year, the long-lived government of Modibo Keita came to an abrupt, but peaceful, end when the president's army deposed him in favor of a military administration.

This unstable character in African political life reflects the complexities of a society in process of great charge. One major problem in many areas has been a tenacious tribalism which complicates all efforts to build a sense of national unity and pride. In part this is a legacy of colonial times when territories were formed without regard for ethnic cohesion, but it also reflects the great diversity of peoples in Africa where loyalties have traditionally been centered in the smaller units of family or clan. A second factor is found in the rising frustration of people who looked upon independence as the total solution to the problem of poverty, only to find an improved standard of living still beyond reach. When this sense of frustration reached the armed forces, it touched individuals able to translate their sentiments into action, and revolution followed. That there have been many instances in which control was returned to the civilian authorities attests to a genuine desire for reform rather than an arrogation of power, but unviable economic units like Dahomey and intractable problems of development everywhere have perpetuated and intensified political unrest. It was in Nigeria that these uncertainties burst forth in most violent form on the fateful night of January 15, 1966.

During the following morning, the most incredible events were rumored and then confirmed. A mutiny by young army officers had unseated the government, and while the country slept, the prime minister, Sir Abubakar Tafawa Balewa and his finance minister, Chief Festus Okotie-Eboh, had been kidnapped in Lagos, the Western Region premier, Chief Samuel Akintola, was dead in Ibadan, while in Kaduna, Nigeria's most powerful politician, Sir Ahmadu Bello, had been shot down and killed. Before the day was out a panicky federal cabinet had handed over its authority to the military, and the army chief, Major-General Aguiyi-Ironsi, found himself the new head of state.

As these developments were revealed, disbelief gave way to rejoicing, for Nigeria had long suffered growing frustrations over her economic and political difficulties. While statistics described a healthy growth rate, the period since independence had been marked by unemployment, rising rent and food prices, labor unrest, and ugly rumors of corruption in high places. Political uncertainty was concentrated in the Western Region where an intramural struggle within the Action Group pitted Chief Akintola against Chief Awolowo, and ended in victory for the former in 1962 when Awolowo was convicted and jailed for plotting to overthrow the government, a decision which was widely discredited throughout the country.

Akintola formed a new grouping, the Nigerian National Democratic Party (N.N.D.P.) and developed close relations with Bello's N.P.C. which dominated the Northern Region. Irregularities connected with federal elections in 1964 were compounded by open manipulation of the Western Nigerian elections in the autumn of 1965, as Akintola sought to maintain his control of the regional government. There was a growing wave of reaction throughout the country calling into question the competence and probity of political leadership because of the encroachments on personal and journalistic freedom and the cynical disregard for the results of the electoral process. In the Western Region the months preceding the coup were marked by a rising round of looting, arson, rioting, and killing. It was a moment marked for revolution, and when the army plot succeeded, it released in one emotional burst the pent-up feelings born of long years of frustration.

For a time the country was united in enthusiasm as regional suspicions and jealousies were forgotten, and Ironsi's condemnation of tribalism along with his abolition of the four regions were applauded as the initial steps toward a new era of Nigerian unity and progress.

It was not long, however, before past misgivings re-emerged. Those assassinated (Balewa and Okotie-Eboh were later found dead) included no Ibos; yet the plot had been concocted chiefly by Ibo officers, it was said. Many Nigerians in the north and west saw the coup as an attempt by the aggressive Ibo people to take control of the country. Anti-Ibo riots erupted in the north as the backdrop to a second revolt, staged on July 29, 1966, this time by a group of northern officers. General Ironsi was deposed and assassinated, and a new military head of state emerged in the person of Lieutenant-Colonel Yakubu Gowon, a northern Christian from one of the smaller tribal groups.

Unfortunately, some northern troops mutinied at this juncture and led a pogrom against Ibos living in the northern towns which eventually spread in the weeks that followed, a massive blood bath in which thousands of Ibos perished, their homes and property destroyed. Those that survived returned to the east where the military governor, Lieutenant-Colonel Ojukwu, had already announced his intention to act without submitting to the authority of Colonel Gowon's government. In this declaration, Ojukwu appeared to reflect an Ibo determination henceforward to have no more than a minimal contact with the people of Nigeria who had caused them such misery.

Throughout the remainder of the year and into 1967 the determination of the easterners hardened, and they insisted that Nigeria could only exist in the future as a loose federation of virtually sovereign states. Gowon, however, was pledged to national unity, to be preserved by force, if necessary. A series of constitutional talks were unproductive as was a summit consultation between Ojukwu and the Gowon government held at Aburi, Ghana, early in 1967. The drift apart continued, and Gowon's announcement that Nigeria would become a federation of twelve states in place of the old regions was interpreted in the east as a veiled attempt to re-impose northern dominance. A few days later, on May 31, 1967, the east seceded as the independent Republic of Biafra. The Nigerian civil war had begun.

Although Biafra enjoyed some initial successes, by the spring of 1968 after almost a year of conflict, it appeared that the federal forces were on their way to a military victory. The major cities of Enugu and Onitsha had fallen and Port Harcourt seemed certain to follow, while the area still under Biafran control had been reduced to less than half the original Eastern Region. Great punishment had been absorbed by the Ibo population, both from direct military action and through disease and famine, the Biafrans were sealed off by a tightening blockade, and ultimate victory appeared to have vanished. Up to April, 1968, not one government had given diplomatic recognition to the new state of Biafra, while military aid from Britain was instrumental in the achievement of federal successes in the field. At the same time, it was clear that the Ibos were determined to fight on indefinitely in the face of what they regarded as an attempt at total extermination, and were capable of maintaining their fight in the form of a guerrilla action, at least, for many months or even years.

The sense of purpose within the federal government was no less determined. There could be no thought of abandoning the oil-rich Niger delta without a serious struggle; moreover, were the Biafrans permitted to go their way, there was little likelihood the faction-ridden country could survive as a nation. It seemed probable that the Gowon twelve-state plan was a genuine effort to solve the federal problem, to break the power of the major ethnic groups, particularly the Fulani-Hausa in the north, by creating local governments of considerable authority in areas defined roughly along ethnic lines. The north was divided into six states, the west into two, and the mid-west left intact, while the east was to be split into three states. Such action was widely commended within Nigeria, particularly when civilians were brought into the Federal executive council, but it failed to impress the Ibos and the war dragged on.

The Biafran cause gradually impressed others in Africa, and in mid-April, 1968, Tanzania gave the new state official recognition. In explaining this action, President Nyerere pointed out that the wholesale massacres in the north had convinced the Ibo people that they were rejected by the rest of the country and that they could no longer feel safe outside their own region. Their decision to leave, he continued, was met with further recourse to violence in the form of civil war, while suggestions that peaceful negotiations replace military action were ignored. There being no evidence of existing Nigerian unity, Nyerere concluded, there was nothing to do but recognize the existence of a Biafran nation. The Tanzanian action was followed with similar diplomatic recognition by Zambia, the Ivory Coast, and Gabon. At the same time military assistance developed from diverse sources, Federal Nigeria gaining help from the Soviet Union and the United Arab Republic while France began to provide small arms to

Biafra, a supply which momentarily enhanced Biafran prospects. Nevertheless, expanding Federal forces, well equipped with arms obtained chiefly from Britain, exerted pressures which combined with famine and disease to wear down the Ibo people. On January 12, 1970, the Biafrans capitulated and the Nigerian civil war came to an end.

FRUSTRATIONS IN THE SOUTH

Modernization, national strength, and pan-African unity were followed by yet another priority—the liberation of the south. The march toward independence, impressive though it was, had stopped short of absolute success, and those Africans who had gained their freedom could not rest with it until they had helped those still under what they regarded as continuing colonial domination. One of the first actions of the O.A.U. in 1963 was the formation of the African Liberation Committee designed to coordinate and assist liberation movements throughout the continent, which meant, as a practical matter, those concerned with South Africa, South-West Africa, Rhodesia, and the Portuguese territories of Mozambique, Angola, and Guinea. Since the governments in these countries differed basically from Britain, France, or Belgium in their attitude toward African independence or majority rule, it was clear that militant action was required.

The difficulty was not only with the temper of white resistance. There were rival revolutionary groups claiming legitimacy for Rhodesia and Angola and a similar schism later developed for Mozambique. It was often difficult to determine who should be supported and who ignored, while the member nations of the O.A.U. were seldom at one over questions of tactics, both military and diplomatic. Further, the Liberation Committee was often resented by nationalists who felt it was interfering with their internal affairs. Finally, many states of the O.A.U. were vexed by an early policy decision to delegate a share of the Liberation Committee's responsibilities to independent nations bordering the countries under attack, thereby, it was said, giving these neighboring states too much control over the Liberation Committee policy and activities.

These organizational difficulties caused problems, but it was the basic strength of the regimes under attack which has presented the freedom movement with its essential complication. South Africa is a virile modern state with a government long experienced in dealing with African dissent, and an army quite capable of containing any military invasion short of assault by a major power. Similarly, the Rhodesians have expressed confidence in their ability to neutralize either internal unrest or guerrilla infiltration as well as to offset the effects of economic pressures applied through U.N. action. Moreover, the threats and criticisms aimed from the outside have had the effect of consolidating the white minorities of South Africa and Rhodesia behind the racial policies of their leaders. As for Portugal, despite the illness and retirement of General Salazar in 1968, she continues to regard her colonies as areas which can be developed under Portuguese leadership into highly prosperous multiracial societies.

Nevertheless, it is Portugal's African territories which appear most vulnerable to the liberation movement. Small and poverty ridden, Portugal has been obliged to put over 100,000 men on active service in Africa and to devote nearly one-half of her annual budget to military expenses as she strives to defeat the revolts in her colonies. In Angola, she was able to regain much of the northern areas occupied during the initial outbreak of 1961, but the guerrillas have shifted to other districts in the eastern and central provinces, launching their attacks from bases in the Congo and Zambia. Were it not for the continuing split between the M.P.L.A. movement and the Bakongo U.P.A. led by Holden Roberto, the Portuguese position might be much more critical after years of difficult fighting. As it is, Portugal remains determined to hold Angola, particularly in light of important recent discoveries of oil and iron ore.

An analogous situation has developed in Mozambique. Since 1964 an insurgent group, the *Frente de Libertação de Moçambique* (FRELIMO) led by Eduardo Mondlane until his assassination early in 1969, has been slowly extending its control over the northern provinces adjacent to Tanzania, and is attempting to gain ascendancy in the Tete region as well. The war is a difficult one for the Portuguese but they remain in control of the towns and highways, and as with Angola, their resolve is stiffened by rising prospects for development based on iron ore and water power. In Guinea, rebellion has been more effective and Portugal has succeeded in maintaining itself with certainty only in the urban areas. Unable to gain the initiative, the Portuguese might eventually abandon this small country, although its loss would have the effect of encouraging the independence movements in the more important territories of Angola and Mozambique.

If Portuguese Africa offers some prospect for successful revolution, Rhodesia is the point on which the independent African nations have concentrated their greatest diplomatic and military pressures. The Unilateral Declaration of Independence (U.D.I.) of 1965 was declared illegal by the British government which sought economic sanctions through the United Nations, obtaining a partial trade embargo voted in the Security Council in 1966. A ban was placed on the sale of oil to Rhodesia while import of a number of her products (tobacco, asbestos, sugar, chrome, meats, hides, and others) was prohibited to U.N. member states. Such partial action was unsatisfactory to African nations who demanded direct military intervention, a step which Britain was not prepared to take. At first the embargo appeared to have effect and Rhodesia's exports fell by over one-third, but her minerals and other goods continued to be in world demand and trade revived, albeit in clandestine form, while oil continued to flow into Rhodesia freely via South Africa.

This unsatisfactory situation was compounded by the fact that Zambia, which relied heavily on imports from Rhodesia, was more injured by the embargo policy than Rhodesia herself, undergoing economic hardships in applying the sanctions, yet placed in the humiliating position of having to continue imports for which she had no alternative source of supply. In May, 1968, the U.N. voted a total trade and travel embargo against Rhodesia in a move which was likely to have more psychological than practical effects as long as South Africa and the Portuguese territories continued to provide avenues for exports and imports. Moreover, the action was likely further to embarrass Zambia which, for example, was dependent upon Rhodesian coal for the refining of her iron ore.

Economic pressure has therefore been thoroughly unsatisfactory to African leaders who continue to urge armed intervention by Britain and to sponsor harassment by guerrilla squads filtering across the Zambezi River from Zambia. Africans from Rhodesia, trained in China, Cuba, and elsewhere, moved into the Zambezi Valley in considerable numbers during the spring of 1968, but were brought under control by security forces with the help of a South African police contingent after a campaign of several weeks. While these raids are expected to persist, they seem unequal to the task of overturning the present government, nor were the sanctions likely to persuade the Rhodesian whites to revoke their unconstitutional declaration of independence and renegotiate their position based on eventual majority rule. Quite the opposite, in June, 1969, Rhodesia's primarily white electorate voted to create a republic, thereby severing any lingering formal ties with Britain through her monarchy. At the same time, the voters approved the introduction of a new constitution first put forward by Ian Smith and the Rhodesian Front Party in July, 1968, a constitution which proposes separate provincial assemblies based on race, operating under firm white surveillance at the center. Such action will institute a form of apartheid in this northern neighbor of South Africa.

Difficult as is the Rhodesian situation, it offers some grounds for hope which the freedom movement can scarcely entertain about the Republic of South Africa. There the white citizens clearly support official policy on apartheid, or separate development, while the black population remains securely controlled by a widespread and efficient police force. The South African economy is booming—the gross domestic product rose 7.5 per cent in 1968—and inflation, because of rapid national development, is a major economic problem. Far from presenting an attractive target for subversion, South Africa appears on the contrary to be mounting a political, diplomatic and economic offensive of her own designed to neutralize African hostility at home while spreading her influence among the independent black nations of Africa.

While general prosperity in South Africa has begun to raise living standards for black as well as white, the Bantustan idea offers the appeal of real, if limited, political gains. The government of John Vorster insists that there need be no isolation of South Africa because of her policy of separate development. Reversing the older view regarding eventual absorption of the High Commission territories, Vorster sees them as independent black nations which anticipate the eventual status of the Bantustans—politically free but bound to South Africa by close and beneficial economic ties. Thus Botswana is already being used to channel South African manufactured goods to previously closed African markets, while economic dependence has caused the prime minister of Lesotho, Chief Leabua Jonathan, to declare publicly that sanctions against South Africa would be far more injurious to Lesotho than to the economy of their chief target.

Indeed, South Africa has extended her influence well beyond these neighboring enclaves. Her annual exports to the rest of Africa exceed $250 million, much of this, to be sure, going to Rhodesia since U.D.I., but much also flowing into such nations as Zambia and

Ghana. Malawi has been particularly responsive to South Africa, which, along with Rhodesia, absorbed 300,000 Malawi workers and thereby contributes decisively to the fragile economy of an impecunious country. A new capital for Malawi has been approved on the basis of advice from South African planners, a South African company will build a railroad linking Malawi with Mozambique, and the South African government has provided a $15.4 million loan toward this project. Both Malawi and Botswana have opened diplomatic relations with South Africa and Vorster is confident that, sooner or later, other African states will follow.

If relations do not develop along these lines, there is another alternative which has haunted the leaders of independent Africa. Both Angola and Mozambique have large numbers of Portuguese settlers who might declare their own U.D.I. and turn to South Africa for assistance. While it is not likely that South Africa would view this development with favor, political unrest in these territories would almost certainly draw a military response from the south to add to the collaboration which already exists between South Africa and Rhodesia. Far from liberating the south, independent Africa would thus find itself facing a large and powerful state dominating the southern third of the continent and capable of extending its influence further north at the expense of newborn and defenseless nations.

THE MENACE OF SPECIAL PRIVILEGE

In February, 1967, President Julius Nyerere of Tanzania announced the Arusha Declaration which described the process of national development through self-reliance and frugality, to be practiced in an atmosphere free of ostentation and exploitation. Viewed from one perspective, the Declaration was essentially an attempt to relate development to the resources and needs of the nation; hence, agricultural production was stressed and hard work by the Tanzanian people placed above the efficacy of foreign aid. At the same time, the Declaration clarified President Nyerere's view that the end product of an improving economy must be distributed evenly throughout the population; there could be no priviledged class, no concentration of wealth in the hands of the few, no reverence demanded and received by leadership. Thus, those individuals associated with T.A.N.U. or the government would be obliged henceforth to live solely on their modest salaries, divesting themselves of all outside income-producing connections or property.

Herein lay another problem for the new nations of Africa to be added to questions of economic development, political strength, and the end of colonial rule. Basic to the Arusha Declaration was a determination not to lose the advantage of independence through the substitution of one privileged group for another. There would be small gain for the people as a whole if former colonial rulers moved out simply to be replaced by a new aristocracy native to the land whose educational advantages or position in government were used to provide them with a standard of living out of all proportion to national wealth while little advance was to be found in the general per capita income. In fact, there were indications that during the early independence years, just such a special class of Africans was taking shape.

In East Africa, the Swahili term *wa Benzi* emerged to describe this new class, a word which focuses without pity on the fondness shown by so many of the new elite for Mercedes Benz automobiles. Despite national individual incomes which rarely average as much as $200 a year, small but evident numbers in all countries are apparently able to afford such indulgences, one way or another utilizing their position for private economic gain. Numerous accusations have been leveled at public officials, for example, charging irregularities which range from bribery and embezzlement to the selling of influence or misappropriation of allocations. The report of the Forster Commission into the activities of ministers in the Sierra Leone government prior to the military take-over of March, 1967, is replete with allegations of malfeasance which amounts to the use of public position for private advantage; convictions have been obtained in Nigeria for corrupt practice by state officers; in Congo-Kinshasa there have been charges of embezzlement in connection with public corporations; while the military government in Ghana has conducted investigations into the activities of ministers in the previous government in response to complaints of malpractice. The charge of corruption even reached the Ghanaian army officer corps which had pledged itself to stamp out such activity. In April, 1969, General Ankrah admitted using for political purposes funds collected from foreign firms, and was therefore compelled to resign as head of state.

The problem has not been limited to overt irregularities. In taking over from colonial administrations, African officials have assumed elevated salaries and perquisites originally designed to attract skilled specialists for work in Africa and usually far out of scale with the economic resources and salary standards of the new country. In Kenya, for example, while the salaries of members of parliament have been doubled since independence, civil servants are paid according to the old colonial schedule, a situation which has caused critics of this system to argue that it must necessarily give rise to a propertied, self-entrenched, politico-economic group. Even the university student is affected. Those familiar with the African university have often been struck by the essentially economic motivation of so many students who appear to regard their education primarily in terms of how well-paying a job it will provide. To be sure, the system is such that job placement and salary scale are too rigidly geared to formal academic achievement, but it is nevertheless disappointing to see such a self-centered attitude among the youth in countries which have more need for a measure of idealism to face the exigencies of the future. It was therefore no accident that President Nyerere was exercised in 1966 when university students protested their obligation to perform national service, for this attitude embodied the very sense of special privilege he was determined to destroy.

THE SEARCH FOR AN AFRICAN IDENTITY

If President Nyerere's declaration at Arusha was a call for self-help, it was also part of a search which he and other Africans have conducted to develop a new, modern African civilization with its own values and its own validity. Just as Edward Blyden a century earlier was seeking an African identity in a world that seeemd to be collapsing before European technological strength, so today the same process is to be seen—the utilization of those tools from the rest of the world which will help Africa become strong, but a selective utilization combined with revived values and institutions from traditional Africa.

The process is not easy because African civilization has been profoundly affected over the past century and a half by ideas and institutions, chiefly from the West, and this development, if anything, is accelerating. Moreover, it is difficult to be selective, to take, for example, the principle of capital accumulation without the incentive to personal profit, or the desire for material plenty while avoiding spiritual aimlessness. Finally, throughout its history Africa has contained a great variety of social and political groupings, until recently isolated and only now reaching out toward national unity, continental cooperation, and racial identity.

Nevertheless, the early years of political independence have been characterized by a determination to achieve cultural independence as well, to re-examine the moral tenets of the past, to sing again the old songs of love and hope, to regain the ancient life force of the ancestors, and to rediscover in the tested values of traditional Africa a spiritual thrust which will help propel the new societies of modern Africa. The search takes many forms. In Senegal, the philosopher-poet-statesman, Léopold Senghor, speaks of the intuitive judgment and sympathetic harmony with nature which the black man brings to human knowledge and argues that contemporary society cannot reach perfection until all the races have contributed toward what he terms the "Civilization of the Universal." In Nigeria the medical school of the University of Ibadan operates a psychiatric center in a village near Abeokuta which makes effective use of the age-old African sense of family and arts of healing. In Tanzania, Julius Nyerere sees African socialism as an expression of genuine human equality, drawing on the ideas of mutual ownership and community sharing which evolved in traditional society and applying them to instil *ujamaa,* or family-hood, in the mind of the modern African striving to better his lot.

The concept of human dignity occurs again and again, as Africans seek to establish an African world presence and to gain the respect of others through the development of respect among Africans for their own way of life. This comes in many forms—the study and performance of traditional music, dance, and sculpture, the writing of African history, the search for a fresh African idiom in con-temporary artistic expression, the reshaping of Western-style educa-tional standards and values, the turning to indigenous forms of Christianity, and the continuing debate over national language. In the African universities there is a sea drift away from the curricula bequeathed by colonial administrators toward one suited to African needs. Institutes of African studies examine the old arts and experi-ment with the new, scholars explore past civilizations and present politics, while departments of pedagogy debate the degree and nature of schooling needed to put sinew into developing societies.

One of the most virile expressions of the new African identity is found in the creative arts and letters. Schools of art and design attached to universities are numerous, in Kenya, Uganda, Nigeria, and Ghana, for example, but they are supplemented by informal clubs, theaters, and ateliers whose activities are frequently more productive and original. In Ghana there is an interesting experimental theater and an excellent traditional dance group. In Nigeria the playing companies of Ogunmola and Duro Ladipo as well as the Mbari societies of Ibadan and Oshogbo have stimulated much writing, painting, and theatricals. *Black Orpheus* has long been an important vehicle for new African writing, while the revue, *Transition,* has presented original works along with literate comment on a wide range of affairs relating to Africa. Senegal played host to an immense international congress on African culture in 1966, and Abidjan offered itself as the locale for the annual meeting of the International PEN club in 1967, while a pan-African cultural festival was held in Algiers in the summer of 1969.

Africa has achieved a substantial literary production in the years since the Second World War. The work of authors like Camera Laye, David Diop, and Cheikh Hamidou Kane differ as much from each other as they do from the writing of Chinua Achebe, James Ngugi, or Ezekiel Mphahlele, but all are attempting to explain the phenomenon of Africa to themselves as well as to the world around them. One of their problems is the recurring search for a language of expression. They are torn between the desire to describe their world in its own authentic tones and to communicate what they have to say to others. Thus far virtually all African writing has been done in foreign European idiom, but if this is a limitation, it is one which seemingly can be overcome by the talent of the artist.

This matter of mode of expression arises more generally in Africa over the question of national language. There is an overwhelming desire to have a national tongue native to the land, but the practicalities appear to be insuperable. While Tanzania has established Swahili as her official language, others have been obliged to settle for French or English, in order that their people may communicate with one another and all with the world beyond. In fact, this may be a most appropriate development since the search for an African identity is made precisely so that Africa can knit herself more tightly into the world community. When the Nigerian playwright, Wole Soyinka, says he wants to be a good writer, not a good African writer, he is expressing what is in the mind of every African. For Africa has indeed become part of the modern world.

Suggestions for Further Reading

There are necessarily but few book-length examinations of the post-independence period in Africa, and one must turn instead to news media for information. A number of reviews are informative, for example, *West Africa* (London), the *East Africa Journal* (Nairobi), the *Journal of Modern African Studies* (London), *Ibadan* (University of Ibadan), *Black Orpheus* (Ibadan), *Transition* and *Mawazo* (both Kampala), and *Présence Africaine* (Paris).

An important source is to be found in the writings of contemporary African leaders. These are scattered in newspapers and periodicals, but there are available a number of collections and autobiographical pieces. Most extensive among these are the writings of Kwame Nkrumah including the autobiography, *Ghana* (New York: Thomas Nelson, 1957; Edinburgh: Thomas Nelson, 1959); *I Speak of Freedom* (London: Heinemann, 1961; New York: Praeger, 1961); *Africa Must Unite* (London: Heinemann, 1963; New York: Praeger, 1963); and *Neo-Colonialism: The Last Stage of Imperialism* (London: Thomas Nelson, 1965; New York: International Publishing Service). See also K. A. Busia, *The Challenge of Africa* (New York: Praeger, 1962); Julius Nyerere, *Freedom and Unity* (Dar es Salaam: Oxford University Press, 1966); Oginga Odinga, *Not Yet Uhuru* (London: Heinemann, 1967; New York: Hill and Wang, 1967); Kenneth Kaunda, *Zambia: Independence and Beyond* (London: Thomas Nelson, 1966; New York: International Publishing Service); Kenneth Kaunda, *A Humanist in Africa* (London: Longmans, 1966); N. Sithole, *African Nationalism, 2nd ed.* (London: Oxford University Press, 1969); Jomo Kenyatta, *Suffering Without Bitterness* (Nairobi: East African Publishing House, 1968); Tom Mboya, *Freedom and After* (London: André Deutsch, 1963; Boston: Little, Brown, 1963); and Ali Mazrui, *Towards a Pax Africana* (London: Weidenfeld and Nicolson, 1967; Chicago: University of Chicago Press, 1967). For West Africa there are L. S. Senghor, *On African Socialism* (New York: Praeger, 1964); Mamadou Dia, *The African Nations and World Solidarity* (New York: Praeger, 1961); *Awo: The Autobiography of Chief Obafemi Awolowo* (Cambridge: Cambridge University Press, 1960); Sir Ahmadu Bello's *My Life* (Cambridge: Cambridge University Press, 1962); Abubakar Tafawa Balewa's *Nigeria Speaks* (Ikeja, Nigeria: Longmans, 1964); and *A Selection from the Speeches of Nnamdi Azikiwe* (Cambridge: Cambridge University Press, 1961).

A number of works may be cited for their discussion of political and economic developments. See, for example, Guy Hunter, *The New Societies of Tropical Africa* (London: Oxford University Press, 1962; New York: Praeger, 1964); Njoroge Mungai, *The Independent Nations of Africa* (Nairobi: Acme Press, 1967); W. Arthur Lewis, *Politics in West Africa* (London: Allen and Unwin, 1965); Colin Legum, *Pan-Africanism*, rev. ed. (London: Pall Mall, 1965; New York: Praeger, 1965); and edited by the same author, *Africa: A Handbook to the Continent*, rev. ed. (New York: Praeger, 1967). See also Helen Kitchen, ed., *A Handbook of African Affairs* (New York: Praeger, 1964; London: Pall Mall, 1964); Immanuel Wallerstein, *Africa, The Politics of Unity* (New York: Random House, 1967); K. W. Grundy, *Conflicting Images of the Military in Africa* (Nairobi: East African Publishing House, 1968); and Andrew M. Kamarck, *The Economics of African Development* (London: Pall Mall, 1967; New York: Praeger, 1967). The *Oxford Regional Economic Atlas, Africa* (Oxford: Clarendon Press, 1965) is also useful.

For African literature one should turn to the substantial output of African writers, but see also Lilyan Kesteloot, *Les Écrivains Noirs de Langue Française* (Brussels: Free University of Brussels, 1963); Claude Wauthier, *The Literature and Thought of Modern Africa* (London: Pall Mall, 1966; New York: Praeger, 1966); and R. W. July, *The Origins of Modern African Thought* (New York: Praeger, 1967; London: Faber, 1968), the last chapter of which attempts to assess the search for identity in contemporary Africa.

Bibliographical Note

Each chapter has been provided with a list of readings particularly relevant to the material in that chapter. These lists are not so much complete as suggestive, and readers who wish to explore further are urged to consult the bibliographies of the volumes indicated. In the main, articles from scholarly journals have not been included in the chapter listings, and the same holds true for works in foreign languages, their occasional appearance usually occurring when there was no full-length study in English available.

There follows below a compilation of works appearing in paperback which bear in whole or in part on the subject of Africa's history. This is necessarily a partial listing, the chief purpose of which is to facilitate the acquisition of historical and related studies at modest cost. Each title is available from the publisher indicated,* and the reader will see at once that most originated in the United States, others in Britain, while a few were published in African countries. Publication dates have not been included since the date of a paperback reissue is not usually of consequence, while, in all cases, titles have been chosen for their timeliness and bearing on the subject of African history.

* As of October, 1968 in Britain (*Paperbacks in Print,* Summer, 1969, London: J. Whitaker and Sons), and February, 1969 in the United States (*Paperbound Books in Print,* October, 1969, New York: R. R. Bowker Co.).

APTER, D. E., *Ghana in Transition,* rev. ed., (New York: Atheneum; London: Trans-Atlantic Book Service).

————, *The Political Kingdom in Uganda,* rev. ed., (Princeton, N.J.: Princeton University Press; London: Oxford University Press).

AWOLOWO, OBAFEMI, *Awo: The Autobiography of Chief Obafemi Awolowo,* (Cambridge: Cambridge University Press).

AZIKIWE, NNAMDI, *Zik: A Selection from the Speeches of Nnamdi Azikiwe,* (Cambridge: Cambridge University Press).

BALEWA, ABUBAKAR TAFAWA, *Nigeria Speaks,* (New York: Humanities Press; Ikeja, Nigeria: Longmans).

BASCOM, W. R. and HERSKOVITS, M. J., eds., *Continuity and Change in African Cultures,* (Chicago: University of Chicago Press).

BELLO, AHMADU, *My Life,* (Cambridge: Cambridge University Press).

BENNETT, G., *Kenya: A Political History,* (London: Oxford University Press).

BOHANNAN, P., *Africa and the Africans,* (New York: Natural History Press).

BREASTED, J. H., *A History of Egypt,* (New York: Bantam).

COLE, SONIA, *The Prehistory of East Africa,* (New York: New American Library).

COLLINS, R. O., and TIGNOR, R. L., *Egypt and the Sudan,* (Englewood Cliffs, N.J.: Prentice-Hall).

CRONON, E. D., *Black Moses,* (Madison, Wis.: University of Wisconsin Press).

CROWDER, M., *Senegal: A Study in French Assimilation Policy,* rev. ed., (New York: Barnes and Noble; London: Methuen).

————, *The Story of Nigeria,* rev. ed., (London: Faber and Faber).

CURTIN, P. D., ed., *Africa Remembered,* (Madison, Wis.: University of Wisconsin Press).

DAVIDSON, B., ed., *The African Past,* (New York: Grosset and Dunlap; Harmondsworth, Middlesex: Penguin).

————, *The African Slave Trade,* [orig. *Black Mother*] (Boston: Little Brown).

————, *The Lost Cities of Africa,* (Boston: Little Brown).

DE KIEWIET, C. W., *A History of South Africa, Social and Economic,* (London: Oxford University Press).

DUFFY, JAMES, *Portugal in Africa,* (Baltimore: Penguin).

EMERSON, R., and KILSON, M., eds., *The Political Awakening of Africa,* (Englewood Cliffs, N.J.: Prentice-Hall).

EMERY, W. B., *Archaic Egypt,* (Baltimore and Harmondsworth, Middlesex: Penguin).

EZERA, KALU, *Constitutional Developments in Nigeria,* (Cambridge: Cambridge University Press).

FLINT, J. E., *Nigeria and Ghana,* (Englewood Cliffs, N.J.: Prentice-Hall).

FORDE, D., ed., *African Worlds,* (London: Oxford University Press).

FORTES, M., and EVANS-PRITCHARD, E. E., eds., *African Political Systems,* (New York and London: Oxford University Press).

GARVEY, MARCUS, *The Philosophy and Opinions of Marcus Garvey,* (New York: Atheneum; London: Cass).

GHAI, D. P., ed., *Portrait of a Minority, Asians in East Africa,* (Nairobi: Oxford University Press).

GIDE, ANDRE, *Travels in the Congo,* (Berkeley and Los Angeles, Cal.: University of California Press).

HANCE, W., *African Economic Development,* rev. ed., (New York: Praeger).

HARGREAVES, J. D., *Prelude to the Partition of West Africa,* (London: Macmillan).

———, *West Africa: The Former French States,* (Englewood Cliffs, N.J.: Prentice-Hall).

HERSKOVITS, M. J., *The Human Factor in Changing Africa,* (New York: Random House).

HILL, C. R., *Bantustans* (London: Oxford University Press).

HODGKIN, T. L., *Nationalism in Colonial Africa,* (New York: New York University, Press).

HOLT, P. M., *A Modern History of the Sudan,* 2nd. ed., (London: Weidenfeld and Nicolson).

HUNTER, G., *The New Societies of Tropical Africa,* (New York: Praeger).

INGHAM, K., *A History of East Africa,* rev. ed., (New York: Praeger).

KAMARCK, A., *The Economics of African Development,* (New York: Praeger; London: Trans-Atlantic Book Service).

KAUNDA, K., *Zambia Shall Be Free,* (London: Heinemann).

KEATLEY, P., *The Politics of Partnership,* (Baltimore and Harmondsworth, Middlesex: Penguin).

KENYATTA, J., *Facing Mount Kenya,* (New York: Random House; London: Heinemann).

———, *Suffering Without Bitterness,* (Nairobi: East African Publishing House).

KIMBLE, G., *Tropical Africa,* vol. II, (New York: Doubleday; London: Trans-Atlantic Book Service).

KITCHEN, H., ed., *A Handbook of African Affairs,* (New York: Praeger).

KOHN, H. and SOKOLSKY, W., *African Nationalism in the Twentieth Century,* (Princeton, N.J.: Princeton University Press; London: Van Nostrand).

LANGER, W., *European Alliances and Alignments*, (New York: Random House).

LEWIS, B., *The Arabs in History*, (New York: Harper; London: Hutchinson).

MAIR, L., *Primitive Government*, (Baltimore and Harmondsworth, Middlesex: Penguin).

MARQUARD, L., *The Story of South Africa* rev. ed., (London: Faber).

———, *The People and Policies of South Africa*, 4th. ed., (London: Oxford University Press).

MBOYA, T., *Freedom and After*, (London: Deutsch).

MOOREHEAD, A., *The Blue Nile*, (New York: Dell; London: Four Square).

———, *The White Nile*, (New York: Dell; Harmondsworth, Middlesex: Penguin).

OGOT, B. A., *History of the Southern Luo*, (Nairobi: East African Publishing House; Evanston, Ill.: Northwestern University Press).

———, and KIERAN, J. A., eds., *Zamani, A Survey of East African History*, (Nairobi: East African Publishing House and Longmans; New York: Humanities Press).

OLIVER, R., ed., *The Dawn of African History*, 2nd. ed., (London: Oxford University Press).

———, ed., *The Middle Age of African History*, (London: Oxford University Press).

———, and FAGE, J., *A Short History of Africa*, (Baltimore and Harmondsworth, Middlesex: Penguin).

———, and MATHEW, G., eds., *History of East Africa*, vol. I, (London: Oxford University Press).

PARRINDER, E., *African Traditional Religion*, 2nd. rev. ed., (London: Seraph, Society for Propagation of Christian Knowledge).

PERHAM, M. and SIMMONS, J., *African Discovery*, (London: Faber).

POST, K., *The New States of West Africa*, rev. ed., (Baltimore and Harmondsworth, Middlesex: Penguin).

ROBINSON, R., and GALLAGHER, J., *Africa and the Victorians*, (New York: Doubleday; London: Macmillan).

ROSBERG, C. and NOTTINGHAM, J., *The Myth of Mau Mau*, (Nairobi: East African Publishing House).

ROUX, E., *Time Longer than Rope*, 2nd. ed. (Madison, Wis.: University of Wisconsin Press).

RUDWICK, E. M., *W. E. B. Dubois: Propagandist of the Negro Protest*, (New York: Atheneum).

SHAMUYARIRA, N., *Crisis in Rhodesia*, (Nairobi: East African Publishing House).

SLADE, R. *The Belgian Congo*, 2nd. ed., (London: Oxford University Press).

SUNDKLER, B., *Bantu Prophets in South Africa*, 2nd. ed., (London: Oxford University Press).

THOMPSON, L., *Politics in the Republic of South Africa*, (Boston: Little Brown).

VAN DEN BERGHE, P., *South Africa, A Study in Conflict*, (Berkeley and Los Angeles, Cal.: University of California Press).

VANSINA, J., *Kingdoms of the Savanna*, (Madison, Wis.: University of Wisconsin Press).

WALLERSTEIN, I., *Africa: The Politics of Independence*, (New York: Random House; London: Trans-Atlantic Book Service).

————, *The Politics of Unity*, (New York: Random House).

WARD, W., *A Short History of Ghana*, 7th ed., (New York, Humanities Press).

WERE, G., *A History of the Abaluyia*, (Nairobi: East African Publishing House; Evanston, Ill.: Northwestern University Press).

WILLIAMS, E., *Capitalism and Slavery*, (New York: Putnam; London: Deutsch; New York: Putnam).

WILLS, A. J., *Introduction to the History of Central Africa*, 2nd. ed., (London: Oxford University Press).

YOUNG, C., *Politics in the Congo: Decolonization and Independence*, (Princeton, N.J.: Princeton University Press; London: Oxford University Press).

ZOLBERG, A., *Creating Political Order: The Party States of West Africa*, (Chicago, Rand McNally; London: Eurospan).

Index

Ahmadu, son of *al-Hajj* Umar, 200, 205, 322, 334

Ahmed Ben Bella, Algerian leader, 590

Ahmose, Egyptian pharaoh, 33

Ain Farah, Darfur, 98; *map*, 92

Aja, states and people, West Africa, 113, 114; *map, 106*

Ajagbo, Oyo Yoruba king, 110

Ajasa, Kitoyi, Nigerian leader, 345, 451

Akan, language and people, West Africa, 105, 115, 116, 117, 118

Akassa, Niger Delta, 290, 333; *map, 282, 324*

Akidas, German East Africa officials, 420

Akintola, Samuel, Nigerian political figure, 592

Akwamu, Akan state, 117; *map, 106*

Akwapim, Akan state, 117, 283; *map, 282*

Akyem, Akan state, 117; *map, 106*

Albert, Lake, Congo/Uganda, 143; *map, 6, 136, 215, 295, 407*

Algeria, region and state, 322, 328, 539, 545n., 565, 588, 589, 590; *map, 324, 325, 557*

Algerian-Morocco War of 1963, 589

Ali, Kanem-Bornu king, 203

Ali Abd al-Latif, eastern Sudan nationalist, 435

Ali Ghaji, Kanem-Bornu king, 71

Ali Khurshid, Egyptian Sudan governor, 218

Alkalawa, Gobir, 192; *map, 193*

Allada, city state, West Africa, 110, 113, 114; *map, 106*

All Africa Peoples' Conference, Accra, 541, 560, 588, 589

All-African Convention, South Africa, 499

Almoravids, Berber group, 62–3

Aluyi (Lozi), people, Central Africa, 242, 390; *map, 240*

Alvarez, Father Francisco, Portuguese missionary, 89, 93

Alwa, eastern Sudan state, 97, 98; *map, 92*

Amanitare, Kushite queen, 37

Amanto states, Ashanti, 117, 119–20

Amda Seyon, Ethiopian king, 93

Amenemet II, Egyptian pharaoh, 30

Amenhotep III, Egyptian pharaoh, 33

American Colonization Society, 272, 359, 360

Americo-Liberians, 360, 463

Amhara, Ethiopian region, 47, 90, 93, 94, 95, 96; *map, 31, 92, 339*

Amharic, Ethiopian language, 90

Amina, Hausa queen, 74

Anglo-Congolese agreement of 1894, 466

Anglo-Portuguese Treaty of 1884, 313, 314

Angola, region, 137, 142, 155–6, 163, 294, 297, 304, 322, 399, 483, 565, 599; and Portuguese colonialism, 481–2, 484, 485–6, 596; African resistance, 486; *map, 136, 153, 295, 324, 325, 393, 474, 557*

Ankole, state, East Africa, 143, 408, 554, 583; *map, 407*

Ankrah, Lt. Gen., J. A., Ghana officer, 582, 600

Annuak, Nilote people, 221; *map, 215*

Ansar, Mahdist followers, 227, 527, 583

Antislavery and Aborigines' Protection Society, Britain, 469, 522

Antislavery patrol, British, 271, 278

Apartheid, South Africa, 158, 370–1, 385, 389, 488–93, 495, 499, 501, 503, 504, 598; legislation, 489–91, 497–8; in Rhodesia, 598

Apolo Kagwa, Baganda leader, *see* Kagwa, Apolo.

Aqaba, Gulf of, 5

Arabia, 13, 45, 47, 76, 91; *map, 92*

Arabs, 24, 53, 87, 197, 298, 476; in East Africa, 79–82, 87, 139, 177, 294, 298—303, 400, 405, 420, 431–3, 553; in Egypt and eastern Sudan, 98–9, 214, 217, 222; in Central Africa, 124, 131; in eastern Congo, 307–8, 323, 326, 466, 467

Aragon, Iberia, 150; *map, 153*

Arguin Island, West Africa, 150, 151, 157, 195; *map, 153*

Arma, Moroccans, 185

Aro Chukwu Oracle, Iboland, and slave trade, 167, 169

Arqamani (Ergamenes), Kushite king, 37

Arusha, Tanzania, 429; Arusha Declaration, 599, 600, 601; *map, 407*

Arussi, Ethiopian region, 338; *map, 339*

Ashanti, people and kingdom, West Africa, 103, 115, 116–17, 118, 119–20, 195, 283, 289, 333, 532, 583; and golden stool, 117, 333; and coastal trade, 117, 283, 318; government, 117, 119–20, 239, 283; British war of 1873–4, 289, 318; *map, 25, 106, 153, 193, 282, 325*

Ashiqqa party, eastern Sudan, 436, 527

Ashmun, Yehudi, Liberian official, 272

Ashraf, Mahdist group, eastern Sudan, 229

Asians, in South Africa, 388, 489, 490, 491; in East Africa, 410, 413, 414, 546, 556; in Mozambique, 482

Asmara, Eritrea, 329; *map, 324*

Aspelta, Kushite king, 36

Assab, Eritrea, 337; *map, 339*

Assegai, spear, South Africa, 235, 252, 254, 259

Asselar, Sahara, 12

Assimilados, Portuguese Africa, 484

Assimilation, 137; Portugal and Kongo, 154; in Zululand, 236; and Ngoni, 239, 241; Kololo and Lozi, 242, 251; Ndebele, 251; Basuto, 254–5; French colonial doctrine and policy, 267–8, 273–4, 345–6, 440, 446, 536, 537, 538, 539; in British West Africa, 271, 275–6, 289–91, 354, 450–1; in Senegal, 350, 351; in South Africa, 382–3, 493; and Southern Rhodesia, 395, 504; in French Equatorial Africa, 480; in Portuguese areas, 484, 485

Assin, Akan state, 115, 283, 289; *map, 106, 282*

Association, French colonial doctrine, 350, 441, 447, 539; Parallel development, Rhodesia, 504

Association of Natives of French Equatorial Africa, 480

Assyrians, 34–5

Asurbanipal, Assyrian king, 35

Aswan, Egypt, 28, 37, 211, 213, 216; *map, 31, 92, 215*

Atbara River, eastern Sudan, 36, 38; *map, 31, 92, 215*

Atlantic Charter, 524

Atlas Mts., Morocco, 4, 42; *map, 6, 39*

Attahiro I, Sultan of Sokoto, 365

Attoh-Ahuma, S. R. B., African nationalist, 521

Awdoghast, West Africa, 55, 57, 58, 62; *map, 39, 54*

Awolowo, Obafemi, Nigerian nationalist leader, 521, 535, 592

Axim, Gold Coast, 163, 530; *map, 153*

Axum, kingdom, Abyssinia, 37, 38, 43–8, 90, 91, 96, 97; overruns Kush, 38, 97; and Christianity, 46, 91; and Indian Ocean trade, 45, 46, 47, 76; *map, 31, 81*

Azande, people, eastern Sudan, 222; *map, 25, 215*

al-Azhari, Ismail, political leader, eastern Sudan, 436, 527, 583

Azikiwe, Nnamdi, Nigerian nationalist leader, 452, 522, 523, 530, 533, 535

Azores, 150

Baako, Kofi, Ghana nationalist, 532

Bab el Mandeb, straits, 45, 77; *map, 31, 81*

Badagry, West Africa, 278

Badi, Funj king, 211

Baganda, people, East Africa, 144, 309, 405, 408–9, 410, 554, 555, 596; *map, 25, 407*

Bagirmi, state, central Sudan, 187, 202, 207, 476, 477; *map, 25, 193, 474*

Bahr al-Ghazal, region and Nile tributary, 143, 207, 211, 220, 221, 223, 224, 228, 230, 328, 466, 583; *map, 215, 324*

Bahr al-Jebel (Upper White Nile), 222, 224; *map, 215*

Bahutu, people, East Africa, 545

Bai Bureh, Sierra Leone chieftain, 362

Baikie, W. B., British explorer, 287

Baker, Samuel, British explorer, 224, 310

Bakongo, Congo people, 480, 485

Brazzaville Conference, 1944, 481, 525, 536
Brazzaville Group (African and Malagasy Union), 589
Brew, James H., Gold Coast leader, 366, 453
Brière de l'Isle, G., Senegal governor, 316
Britain, in Yorubaland, 110; in Benin, 113, 362; on Gold Coast, 116, 119, 283-4, 365-6, 368, 528-32; in South Africa, 162, 237, 255-7, 260, 262-3, 327-8, 371-8, 379-84, 388, 482, 493, 501-2; in West Africa, 162-3, 205, 270-1, 275-80, 286-7, 319, 321, 322, 361, 363, 365-6, 440, 448-55; in central Sudan, 208, 477; in eastern Sudan, 228, 230, 328-9; in Zanzibar, 300-1, 327; and Congo, 313, 320; and Egypt, 320-1, 323; in East Africa, 326-7, 405-9, 410-16, 417-19, 432-3, 511, 545-6, 553, 554, 555-6, 558-9; in Somalia, 329; in Ethiopia, 336; in Sierra Leone, 270-1, 362; in Central Africa, 401-2, 504, 509, 513, 561, 563, 564, 597; after Second World War, 524-5; in Nigeria, 533-6, 594; and economic aid, 532, 580
British Cameroons, U.N. trust territory, 541
British East Africa (Kenya), 410, 413; map, 325
British Kaffraria, South Africa, 385
British Somaliland, 565; map, 339
British South Africa Co., 326, 327, 381, 391, 394, 396, 397, 399, 400, 401, 506, 561
Broederbond, South Africa, 494
Brussels Conference for Abolition of the Slave Trade, 467
Buddu, state, East Africa, 143, 144; map, 136
Buganda, state, East Africa, 135, 143, 303, 306, 308-10, 330, 405, 410, 554, 583; government, 144, 308-9, 406; trade, 144, 300, 309-10; economy, 310; society, 308-9, 406, 408; map, 136, 295, 324, 407
Buganda Agreement of 1900, 406

Bulala, Central African people, 71
Bulom, Sierra Leone region, 103
Bunyoro, state, East Africa, 135, 143, 144, 303, 310, 330, 408, 554, 583; government, 143, 408; map, 136, 295, 324, 407
Burgers, T., Orange Free State president, 374
Burton, Richard, British explorer, 290
Buruli, state, East Africa, 143; map, 136
Burundi, state and region, East Africa, 143, 429, 545; map, 295, 557
Bushmen, 11, 24, 43, 77, 123, 133, 134, 161, 162, 164, 233, 262; map 25, 153
Busia, Kofi, Ghana prime minister, 583
Busoga, state, East Africa, 143, 408, 554; map, 136, 295
Butha Buthe, Basutoland, 253; map, 261
Buxton, T. F., British philanthropist, 277, 285, 353

C-Group, people, eastern Sudan, 30
Caderneta, Portuguese Africa, 485
Caillié, René, French explorer, 276
Cairo, Egypt, 327, 328; map, 325
Calabar, Nigeria, 451
Caledon River, South Africa, 260, 262, 372; map, 261, 380
Calicut, India, 151
Cameron, Sir Donald, British colonial governor, 430-1, 450
Cameroons, Mt. and range, 5, 41; map, 39, 193
Cameroun, state, 101, 439, 566; German protectorate, 314, 315, 323, 419, 477; U.N. trust territory, 538; independence, 541; map, 324, 325, 474, 557
Cão, Diogo, Portuguese explorer, 151
Cape Coast, Ghana, 275, 366, 453
Cape Colony, South Africa, 158, 162, 232, 237, 255, 256, 260, 262, 263, 264, 327, 371, 372, 373-4, 378, 379, 384, 385, 388, 483; early society, 158, 160; map, 261, 324
Cape Coloured, people, South Africa, 161, 164, 385, 489, 490, 491
Cape Province, South Africa, 494, 497, 498, 499; map, 380

Cape Town, South Africa, 24, 88, 160, 162, 176–7, 256, 262, 379, 491; *map, 159, 240, 261, 380, 407*

Carnavon, Lord, British political figure, 373, 374, 375, 378

Carr, Henry, Nigerian leader, 451

Carter, Sir Gilbert, Lagos governor, 364

Carter Land Commission, Kenya, 415

Carthage, North Africa, 40–1; *map, 39*

Casablanca Group, 589

Casely Hayford, J. E., Gold Coast leader, 366, 368, 440, 453–5, 457; and National Congress of British West Africa, 455–7, 521

Casement, Roger, British consul, Congo, 469

Castes, 105, 107

Castile, Iberia, 150; *map, 153*

Cataracts, Nile, 8, 28, 29, 30, 33, 36; *map, 31, 215*

Cattle culture, 138, 142, 233, 251, 252

Caulkers, mulatto chiefs, West Africa, 165

Caucasoids, 11, 13, 21, 22, 24, 30

Cayor, Wolof kingdom, 284–5, 286; region, 518; *map, 282*

Central Africa, 391, 508, 560

Central African Federation (Rhodesias and Nyasaland), 509

Central Saharan language group, 23; *map, 25*

Cetewayo, Zulu king, 237, 385

Ceuta, Morocco, 150, 152; *map, 153*

Chad, state and region, French colony, 477, 480; economy, 574; *map, 474, 557*

Chad, Lake, 23, 70, 192, 207, 221, 323, 328, 477; *map, 6, 39, 193, 324, 474*

Chadic languages, 24; *map, 25*

Chagga, people, East Africa, 135, 138, 420; *map, 136, 407*

Chamberlain, Joseph, British political figure, 381

Champion, Allison, Zulu leader, 498

Changa, Mutapa governor, 131

Changamire, state, Central Africa, 123, 131, 132, 238, 252, 294, 297; *map, 136, 261, 295*

Chari-Nile languages; *map, 25*

Chari River, Cameroun/Chad, 221

Chiefly authority, 105, 113, 114, 119, 132, 140, 144, 236, 252, 365, 471, 519–20, 578

Chilembwe John, Nyasa churchman, 401, 510, 516

China, 79, 82, 131

Chinese, in East Africa, 80; in South Africa, 383, 388

Chipembere, Henry, Nyasaland nationalist, 511

Chiume, M. W. K., Nyasaland nationalist, 511

Chokwe, Congo people, 142, 303, 304, 305; *map, 136*

Christianity, Coptic, 91; Ethiopian, 46, 91, 93; and eastern Sudan, 97–8; Portugal and Kongo, 152, 154; in Senegal, 166; in British West Africa, 271, 275, 277–9, 289–91; and Buganda, 310, 405–6; and African churches, 353, 358, 389, 401, 584; in Belgian Congo, 472–3, 475

Church Missionary Society (C.M.S.), 271, 277, 278, 288, 290, 352

Chwezi, Hima clan, 142

Cibinda Ilunga, Lunda king, 141, 142

Cilool, Lunda official, 142

Cities, western and central Sudan, 57–60, 73; Benin City, 112; West African coast, 275–6, 347–8; East African coast, 77–82, 87–8; and African independence, 519

Citizenship, French, 274, 351, 443, 445, 447, 480, 536, 537

Civilizations, African, Egyptian, 13–20, 28–34; in western and central Sudan, 55–60, 60–1, 62, 64–5, 69–70, 71, 72, 73, 74; East African coast, 78–83, 164; Ethiopian, 43–4, 47–8, 90–1, 96–7; eastern Sudan, 97–9, 213–14, 226; West African forest, 103–8, 112; Mutapa and Changamire, 122–4, 131–3; Bantu, 137–40, 145, 234, 236, 239, 241, 242, 251, 252, 264, 293–4; Luba-Lunda, 141–2; and Islam, 56–7, 64–5, 67, 187–8; westernized, 271, 273–4, 275–6, 277–80; present day, 601–4

Clapperton, H., British explorer, 195, 276

Dan, West African people, 103

Danaqla, people, eastern Sudan, 214, 223, 224, 225, 227, 229; *map, 215*

Danes, 116, 163, 283

Danquah, J. B., Gold Coast nationalist, 455, 530

Darfur, region, eastern Sudan, 12, 29, 38, 40, 71, 72, 98, 212, 214, 216, 222, 224, 226, 227, 228, 229; *map, 31, 39, 92, 215*

"Dash," 169, 578

Daud, Songhai king, 68-9

Daura, Hausa state, 73, 201; *map, 54, 193*

Davies, H. O., Nigerian nationalist, 533

De Beers Consolidated Mines, South Africa, 376

Degel, Gobir, 190, 191; *map, 193*

Degradados, Angola, 482

Delagoa Bay, Mozambique, 236, 238, 375, 378, 379, 482; *map, 261, 380, 474*

Delamere, Lord, T. P., Kenya, 411

Delgado, Cape, Mozambique, 87, 134; *map, 81, 136*

Democratic Party, Uganda, 554

Dendi, West African region, 69; *map, 54*

Denham, Maj. D., British explorer, 276 ✓

Denkyira, Akan state, 115, 116, 117, 118, 283, 289; *map, 106, 282*

Denyanke, Fulani, Senegal, 188

Department of Native Affairs, South Africa, 490

Desert, 4; *map, 7*

Dhanis, Francis, Belgian soldier, 326

Diagne, Blaise, Senegalese parliamentary deputy, 351, 444-7, 451, 458-9, 523, 538

Diamonds, South Africa, 373, 374, 376, 387

Diara, ancient Ghana, 67

Dias, Bartolomeu, Portuguese explorer, 84, 151, 156

Diggers' Republic, South Africa, 373

Dingane, Zulu king, 237, 252, 258, 259

Dingiswayo, southern Bantu leader, 234, 235

Dinguiray, Guinea, 199; *map, 193*

Dinka, people, eastern Sudan, 220, 221, 222, 223; *map, 25, 215*

Diop, David, African poet, 603

Diop, Ousmane Socé, African writer, 521

Diouf, Galandou, Senegalese parliamentary deputy, 446, 447

Direct rule, 415, 441, 442, 470-1

Dirma, West Africa, 69; *map, 54*

Disraeli, Benjamin, 375, 376

Divine kingship, in Egypt, 19, 28; in Kanem-Bornu, 70, 71; among Wolof and Serer, 105; in Central Africa, 132, 140, 141, 142; and Bunyoro, 143

Djibouti, Somalia, 328, 329, 341, 565; *map, 324, 339*

Doaro, Muslim Ethiopian state, 91, 93; *map, 92*

Docemo, Lagos royal family, 449-50, 451

Dodowa (Katamansu), battle, Gold Coast, 283; *map, 282*

Dogali, battle, Ethiopia, 337; *map, 339*

Domesticated animals, 13, 14, 22

Dominion Party, Southern Rhodesia, 510, 513, 562, 563

Dongola, eastern Sudan, 97, 211; *map, 92, 215*

Dongola reach, eastern Sudan, 30, 33, 216; *map, 31*

Dowa, Malawi, 241

Drakensberg Mts., South Africa, 4, 232, 234, 241, 242, 253, 258; *map, 6, 261*

Du Bois, W. E. B., American Negro leader, 440, 522; and pan-African congresses, 458-60

D'Urban, Benjamin, Cape Colony governor, 257

Durban, Natal, 491; *map, 380, 393*

Dutch, 88, 116, 156, 157, 162, 163, 168, 283, 288, 289; in South Africa, 156-60, 162

Dwane, James, M., South African churchman, 389

Dyalo, Fulani clan, 196

Dyula, Mandinka traders, 104, 186, 187, 204; expansionism, 204

East Africa, 24, 135, 138, 518, 600;

high plains, 177–8, 293–4; European occupation, 326–7
East Africa Protectorate (later Kenya), 410, 413
East African Association, Nairobi, 417, 521
East African Coast, 44, 45, 46, 77–79, 83, 134, 162, 410; civilization, 78–83, 293–4; trade, 37, 76, 78, 82–3, 88–9, 177, 298; and Portugal, 82–5, 164; Omani Arabs, 85–9
East African Community (E.A.C.), 577, 578
East African High Commission, 546, 577
East India Co., Dutch, 156, 158, 160, 255
Eboué, Félix, French-African administrator, 481, 536
Ebrohimi, Itsekiri center, 332; map, 324
Ecole William Ponty, Dakar, 521
Economic Commission for Africa, (E.C.A.), 576
Economic development, 354; and West African missions, 278; in Uganda, 409; in Kenya, 416; in German East Africa and Tanganyika, 429; in Egypt, 434; and eastern Sudan, 434; Belgian Congo, 470; French Equatorial Africa, 478–9; in Portuguese Africa, 482–4; in South Africa, 388, 491–2; in Nyasaland, 508; and environment, 570–1; and agriculture, 571–3; and minerals, 573–4; and industry, 574-6; and pan-Africanism, 576–8; theories of, 578–9; and foreign aid, 580–1
Economy, national, Ghana, 529, 573–4, 576 582; Nigeria, 533, 574, 576; French West Africa, 537–8; Congo-Kinshasa, 544, 573, 576; Kenya, 556, 576; Uganda, 556; Chad, 574; Ethiopia, 576; Egypt, 574; Gabon, 573; Guinea, 573, 574; Ivory Coast, 576, 579; Liberia, 573, 576; Mali, 574; Malawi, 574; Mauritania, 573; Niger, 573; Senegal, 574; Sierra Leone, 574; Somalia, 574; Sudan, 576; South Africa, 377, 495, 573;

Togo, 574, 576; Tanzania, 574, 576; Zambia, 573, 574, 576; Uganda, 583
Edo (Bini), Nigerian people, 102, 111, 112
"Educated Africans," 176, 271, 275–80, 345–6, 351–4, 355–8, 365–9, 389–90, 435–6, 442, 448, 456, 484, 517; in Nigeria, 449–52; in Gold Coast, 452–5; in French Equatorial Africa, 480; in Congo, 544
Education, European, 353, 358, 456, 481, 485; in South Africa, 489–90; and independence, 516–17, 519–20, 533, 555
Edusei, Krobo, Ghana nationalist, 532
Efik, Nigerian people, 167, map, 153
Egba, Yoruba people, Nigeria, 110, 115, 281, 283, 288, 333, 352, 363, 364, 449; map, 282, 324
Egbado, Yoruba people, 281; map, 282
Egba United Board of Management, 352
Egbe Omo Oduduwa, Yoruba association, 521, 534
Egga, Nigeria, 290; map, 282
Egypt, 13–20, 21, 37, 38, 40, 224, 230, 310, 336; predynastic, 13–14; early civilization, 13–20, 28–34; early influence on eastern Sudan, 28–34, 37; connections with Axum, 44; government, 14, 19; and modernization, 179–83, 218–19, 321; occupation of Sudan, 210–13, 217–20, 221–3, 224–5, 433; and the Mahdi, 227–8; European occupation, 320–1, 323; and Condominium, 433–7; independence movement, 435; economy, 574; map, 31, 215, 324, 325, 557
Egyptian, language, 20, 24
Egyptians, pharaonic, 11
Ehangbuda, Benin king, 113
Eighteenth Dynasty, Egypt, 33
Ekiti, Yoruba people, Nigeria, 363; map, 282
Eleko controversy, Lagos, 449–50, 451
El Fasher, Darfur, 29; map, 31, 39
Elisabethville, Congo, 542

Fezzan, North African region, 42, 55, 71, 195; *map, 39, 54*

Field, Winston, Southern Rhodesia political figure, 510, 562

Fifth Cataract, Nile, 33; *map, 31, 215*

Fiftieth Ordinance, South Africa, 256, 257

Fingoes, South African people, 385

Fire, developed in Africa, 10

Firearms, 69, 112, 117, 164, 169, 178, 199, 205, 206, 227, 252, 254, 259, 309–10, 330, 340, 405; and East African interior, 301–2, 303–4, 309–10

Firestone, Harvey S., American businessman, 462

First Cataract, Nile, 28, 29, 30; *map, 31, 215*

Fischer, Abraham, Boer leader, 383

Fish River, South Africa, 162, 232, 257, 387; *map, 106, 240, 261, 380*

Food and Agriculture Organization (F.A.O.), United Nations, 589

Foreign aid, 580–1

Forminière Belgian Congo, 475

Forster Commission, Sierra Leone, 600

Fort Jameson, Zambia, 241

Fort Jesus, Mombasa, 85, 87

Fort Hall, Kenya, 559

Fourah Bay College, Freetown, 278, 279

Four Communes, Senegal, 349, 351, 364, 443–4, 445, 447, 536

Fourth Dynasty, Egypt, 29

France, 116; in West Africa, 162–3, 205, 206–7, 321, 322, 328, 361, 364, 440, 579; in Senegal, 166, 268, 273–4, 284–5, 286, 346–7, 348–51, 364, 443–7; in Egypt, 180, 320–1; in central Sudan, 208, 328; in eastern Sudan, 230, 328–9, 466; in Dahomey, 283, 323; and Congo, 313, 319, 320; and North Africa, 319, 328, 329; in Somalia, 329; in Equatorial Africa, 476–81; after Second World War, 525, 536–7, 539–41; and economic aid, 537, 585–6; and former colonies, 585–6, 589; and Biafra, 594

Franchise, South Africa, 383, 384, 494, 495, 497, 498, 499; French territories, 536; Kenya, 559–60; Northern Rhodesia, 561

Franco- Prussian War, 314, 319

Free French, 481, 536

Freetown, Sierra Leone, 102, 176, 270, 275–6, 277, 278, 351, 352, 353, 448, 456, 476, 518; *map, 153, 193, 324*

French Community, 540, 541

French Equatorial Africa, 476–81, 537, 538, 539, 540; concessionaires, 477–8, 479; atrocities, 478, 479; and Free French, 481; *map, 325, 474*

French League for the Defense of the Rights of Man, 480

French Revolution, 176, 267, 345, 351, 516

French Somaliland, 565; *map, 325, 339*

French Union, 481, 536–7, 538, 539

French West Africa, 537, 538, 539; *map, 325*

Frente de Libertação de Moçambique (FRELIMO), 596

Frere, Sir Bartle, British colonial administrator, 375, 385

Frumentius, Syrian monk, 46

Fulani, West African people, 43, 52, 55, 67, 69, 72–3, 74, 113, 186, 187, 188, 189, 194, 280, 281, 363, 476, 594; in Hausaland, 189–90, 191–2, 195, 365; and Islam, 186–8, 189–90, 192, 194; in Macina, 196–7; and Kanem-Bornu, 201–2; *map, 54, 193*

Fulanin Gida, house Fulani, 189

Funj, state and people, eastern Sudan, 98, 211, 213, 214; *map, 92*

Futa Jalon, region, West Africa, 5, 102, 188, 199; *map, 106, 193*

Futa Toro, region, Senegal, 186, 188, 198, 199; *map, 193*

Ga, people, Ghana, 116, 118; *map, 106*

Gabon, region and state, 205, 273, 323, 476, 477, 479, 539, 566, 585; economy, 573; recognizes

Good Hope, Cape of, 84, 151; *map, 6, 153, 159*

Gordon, Charles George, administrator in eastern Sudan, 224, 228, 310

Gordon Memorial College, Khartoum, 435

Gorée Island, Senegal, 157, 163, 166, 268, 274, 348, 349, 443; *map, 153*

Gowon, Col. Yakubu, Nigerian head of state, 593, 594

Gqokoli Hill, battle, South Africa, 235

Graaf-Reinet, South Africa, 162; *map, 159*

Graduates' General Congress, eastern Sudan party, 436, 527

Grain Coast, West Africa, 272

Granada, Iberia, 149; *map, 153*

Grand Bassam, Ivory Coast, 273; *map, 193*

Grant, A. G., Gold Coast nationalist, 530

Grant, William, Sierra Leone Creole, 276, 352, 358

Great lakes, East Africa, 134, 135, 138, 140, 143, 178, 327, 405, 410, 414

Great Trek, South Africa, 237, 257-9, 262, 263, 264, 372, 378, 384, 390; *map, 240*

Grey, Sir George, Cape Colony governor, 372, 378

Griots, praise singers, 284

Griqua, states and people, South Africa, 252, 254, 258, 260, 262, 372, 385

Griqualand West, South Africa, 373, 374, 375; *map, 380*

Grobler Treaty, Transvaal, 378, 391

Groundnuts, 101, 284, 317, 347, 348, 429, 507, 518, 533, 538, 546, 572, 586

Group Areas Act, 1950, South Africa, 489

Guadeloupe, West Indies, 273

Guardafui, Cape, Somalia, 77, 329; *map, 31, 81*

Guari, Hausaland, 194; *map, 193*

Guet N'Dar, Senegal, 347

Guèye, Lamine, Senegal nationalist, 447, 451, 523, 538

Guinea, state and region, West Africa, 102, 204; and French, 328, 361, 586; independence, 540, 586; economy, 573, 574, 586; *map, 153, 324, 557*

Guinea Coast, West Africa, 164-5

Guinea, Gulf of, 101; *map, 6*

Gum, 219, 273, 285, 317, 318, 347

Gurage, Ethiopian region, 338; *map, 339*

Guro, West African people, 103; *map, 106*

Gwandu Hausaland, 192; *map, 193*

Gwangara, Ngoni section, 241; *map, 240, 295*

Gyaman, region, West Africa, 117; *map, 106*

Habe, Hausa dynasties, 189, 194

Habitants, Senegal, 166

Hadya, Muslim Ethiopian state, 91; *map, 92*

Haile Selassie (*Ras* Tafari), Ethiopian emperor, 525-6

Hamdallahi, Macina, 197; *map, 193*

Hand axe, 9, 10

Hanga (Wanga), state, East Africa, 330, 414; *map, 324, 407*

Hannak, Nubia, 99; *map, 92*

Hanno, Carthage admiral, 41

Harar, Muslim Ethiopian state, 94, 338; *map, 92, 339*

Hasan bin Omari, of Kilwa, 420

Harkhuf, Egyptian trader, 29

Hatshepsut, Egyptian queen, 33, 44, 76

Hausa, West African people and states, 43, 52, 67, 72, 185, 186, 189-90, 191-2, 196, 201, 202, 594; *map, 25, 54, 193*

Hausaland, West Africa, 55, 58, 72, 73, 74, 112, 116, 178, 189-92, 194-5, 196, 200; *map, 54, 193*

Hehe, people, East Africa, 300, 302, 334, 420; *map, 295, 407*

Heligoland, 327

Hellenistic civilization, and Kush, 37; and Axum, 46, 90

Henry, Prince of Portugal, 84, 150

Herodotus, 41, 42, 53

Hertzog, J. B. M., Boer leader, 383, 493, 494, 495, 497, 499

Het Volk, Boer political party, 383

Hicks, William, British soldier, 228

in Rhodesia, 563–5; and African culture, 601–4

Independent Church Movement, 353; in West Africa, 358; in South Africa, 389; in Nyasaland, 401, 510; in Congo, 473–5, 584; in Zambia, 584

India, 151, influence on Kushitic culture, 37; and international trade, 46, 76, 79, 82, 84, 89, 131, 298

Indian Ocean, 76, 84, 88, 89, 139, 152, 156, 298, 432, 482; trade, 44, 46, 76, 78, 82–3, 88–9; *map, 136*

Indigénat (administrative justice), 446, 480, 536, 537

Indirect rule, 322, 365–6, 398, 441–2, 447, 449; in Natal, 386; in Buganda and Uganda, 408–9; in German East Africa, 419; and Tanganyikan mandate, 430, 546; in eastern Sudan, 436; in Gold Coast, 452–4, 582; under Félix Eboué, 481; and South African Bantustans, 490; and chiefly authority, 365, 471, 519–20; in Nigeria, 449, 533

Indonesia, 80, 131

Induna, military leader, southern Bantu, 236, 252

Industrial and Commercial Workers' Union (I.C.U.), South Africa, 498

Industrial Conciliation Act, 1934, Southern Rhodesia, 505

Industrialization, in Egypt, 181–2; in South Africa, 377, 495; in Ghana, 573–4, 582; and modernization, 575–6

International Association for the Exploration and Civilization of Central Africa (International African Association), 320

International Association of the Congo, 308, 312, 313, 320, 321

International Court of Justice, and South-West Africa, 503

International Labor Organization, 446, 589

Iringa, Tanganyika, 334; *map, 324*

Iron, and Assyrians, 35, 40; and Meroe, 36, 40; in West Africa, 40, 43, 52, 133; in North Africa, 40; and East African coast, 79; sub-

Equatorial Africa, 123, 134; and modernization, 573, 574, 576

Irrigation, in Egypt, 20, 181

Isandhlwana, battle, South Africa, 375, 386; *map 380*

Islam, 24, 149, 150, 183; in ancient Mali, 64–5; and Songhai, 67–8; in Kanem-Bornu, 70–2; in Hausaland, 73–4, 178, 189–95, 201–2; on East African coast, 79–82; and East African interior, 406; and Ethiopia, 90, 91, 93–4; and Samori, 205–6; in West Africa, 55–7, 64–5, 66, 111, 150, 186, 187–8, 189–90, 196–7, 198–200, 203–4, 205–6, 208, 274, 284–5; 350, 532; in eastern Sudan, 98, 178, 214, 217, 226, 436

Ismail, Egyptian general, conquers eastern Sudan, 211–12

Ismail, Egyptian khedive, 223–4, 310, 321

Ismail al-Azhari, eastern Sudan nationalist, 436

Italian Somaliland, 526, 565; *map, 325, 339, 407*

Italy, 230; and European expansionism, 329, 337, 340

Itsekiri, people, Niger Delta, 332–3, 361, 448; *map, 324*

Ivory Coast, region and state, West Africa, 107, 116, 273, 361, 538, 539, 541, 585; and French, 328; economy, 576, 579; recognizes Biafra, 594; *map, 324, 557*

Ivory trade, 30, 33, 34, 41, 42, 44, 45, 53, 59, 77, 78, 82, 89, 157, 167, 177, 294, 296, 313, 317, 419, 467, 468, 478; in eastern Sudan, 221, 222–3; in East Africa and Congo, 301, 303–4, 307–8, 309–10

Ja'alayyin, people, eastern Sudan, 214, 223, 227, 229; *map, 215*

Jabavu, D. D. T., South African Bantu nationalist, 499

Jabavu, John T., Xhosa, nationalist, 389, 496, 499, 520

Jackson, T. H., Nigerian nationalist, 449, 450

Jaga, people, Congo, 86, 137, 155, 156; *map, 136*

Modernization (*Cont.*)
theories, 578-9; and foreign aid, 580-1

Moffat Treaty, Ndebele, 391, 392, 397

Mogadishu, Somalia, 80, 83, 84; *map, 81*

Moi, Daniel arap, Kenyan political leader, 560

Mokone, M. M., South African churchman, 389

Moltena, J. C., Cape Colony prime minister, 374, 375

Mombasa, island and city, East Africa, 77, 80, 83, 85, 86, 87, 298, 410, 416, 518, 558; *map, 81, 295, 407*

Mombera, Ngoni leader, 241, 400; *map, 240, 285, 393*

Monckton Commission, Northern Rhodesia, 513

Mondlane, Eduardo, Mozambique nationalist, 596

Monomotapa, (see also *Mwena Mutapa* and Mutapa kingdom), 83, 124

Monrovia, Liberia, 275, 462, 518; *map, 193*

Monrovia group, 589

Montesquieu, C. L., on slavery, 269

Moors, 149, 188, 273; Brakna, 318; Trarza, 286, 318

Morel, E. D., British reformer, 469

Morice, Capt., French trader, 88

Morocco, region and state, 42, 62, 69, 150, 185, 329; independence, 539; *map, 54, 153, 325, 557*

Moshesh, Basuto leader, 258, 260, 262, 333, 372, 565; statesmanship, 253-5, 262-3

Moshi, Tanzania, 429

Moshoeshoe, Lesotho king, 565

Mossi, people and kingdoms, West Africa, 60, 65, 67, 185, 186, 197; *map, 54, 193*

Mount, Cape, West Africa, 119, 164; *map, 153*

Mouvement National Congolais, (M. N.C.), 542, 543

Movimento Popular de Liberação de Angola, (M.P.L.A.), 485, 486, 596

Mozambique, region, 84, 87, 88, 238, 297, 322, 396, 399, 492, 565, 599; Island, 294; and Portuguese colonialism, 482-3, 596; *map, 295, 324, 325, 380, 393, 474, 557*

Mpadi, Simon, African evangelist, 473

Mpande, Zulu king, 237, 259

Mpezeni, Ngoni leader, 241, 400; *map, 240, 295, 393*

Mphahele, Ezekiel, African writer, 603

Msiri, Katangan leader, 303-4, 326, 333

Mthethwa, people, South Africa, 234, 235, 242; *map, 261*

Muhammad Ahmad, 225, 226. *See also* Mahdi

Muhammad ibn Ahmad, Muslim scholar, 74

Muhammad Ali, 99, 198, 217, 219, 220, 223, 321, 335; establishes Egyptian rule, 180; occupation of Sudan, 210-13; Egyptian modernization, 179-83

Muhammad Bello, Sultan of Sokoto, 191, 192, 194, 199, 201

Muhammad D'ao Songhai king, 66

Muhammad Rimfa, Hausa king, 74

Muhammad Said, Egyptian ruler, 220

Mohammad Sharif, Muslim scholar, 225

Mohammad Toure, Songhai king, 56, 59, 67, 68, 74, 196, 203

Mulattoes, in Senegal, 166, 274, 349-50, 444

Mumia, Hanga king, 330, 414

Muscat, Arabia, 85, 87, 89, 298, 300, 432; *map, 81*

Mutapa, kingdom, 83, 131, 132, 164, 294, 297, 482; civilization, 124, 131, 132-3; trade, 131; and Portuguese, 131; *map, 136, 295*

Mutesa I, Buganda king, 309, 310, 330, 406

Mutesa II, Buganda king, 554

Mutota, Rozwi king, 124, 132

Mwanga, Buganda king, 406

Mwata Kazembe, Lunda king and state, 294, 296, 297, 298, 302, 303, 304; *map, 295*

Mwata Yamvo, Lunda king and state, 142, 294, 295, 297, 303, 304, 305; *map, 285*

Mwene Mutapa, (Monomotapa), royal title, 124, 133, 390

Mweru, Lake, Congo/Zambia, 399; *map, 6, 136, 240, 295, 393*
Mzilikazi, Ndebele king, 251–3, 258, 259, 390

Nafata, Gobir king, 191
Nairobi, Kenya, 413, 416, 417, 558; *map, 407*
Namibia (South-West Africa), 503
Nandi, people, East Africa, 300, 334, 410, 414, 415; *map, 295, 407*
Nana, Itsekiri leader, 331, 332–3, 448
Napata, Kush, 33, 34, 36, 37; *map, 31*
Napier, Sir Robert, British soldier, 336
Napoleon I, 179, 320
Nasser, Col. G. A., Egyptian president, 590
Natal, South Africa, 236, 237, 253, 258, 259, 260, 327, 372, 374, 378, 379, 385, 386, 483, 489; *map, 261, 324, 380*
Native Administration Act, South Africa, 497
Native Administration Ordinance, Gold Coast, 453
Native Authority Ordinance, Tanganyika, 430
Native Labour (Settlement of Disputes) Act, 1953, South Africa, 489
Native Representation Act, South Africa, 498
Native Urban Areas Act, South Africa, 497
Natives' Land Act, South Africa, 497
Natives Registration Ordinance, Kenya, 412
Natives' Representation Council, South Africa, 499
National Alliance of Liberals, Ghana political party, 583
National Congress of British West Africa, 440, 455–7, 521
National Council of Nigeria and the Cameroons, (N.C.N.C.), political party, 533, 534, 535
National Liberation Council, Ghana, 582
National Liberation Front (F.L.N.), Algeria, 588
National Liberation Movement, Ghana political party, 532

National Unionist Party, (N.U.P.), Sudan, 527, 583
Nationalism, 346, 455–6, 518–19, 525; Afrikaner, 161, 375, 378, 383, 493, 494, 495; Egyptian, 183, 434–5; and Samori, 206, 207; Zulu, 236; Ngoni, 239; and Mirambo, 305; and the churches of Africa, 353, 358, 389, 401; in Kenya, 417–19; in eastern Sudan, 435–7; in Senegal, 443–7; in Nigeria, 449–52, 533–6; and Gold Coast, 452–5, 530–2; in Congo, 473, 475, 541–3; South African Africans, 496–7, 498–501; in Central Africa, 510, 511–13, 561, 562, 563, 564; in French Africa, 536–41; in Tanganyika, 546, 553; in Kenya, 558–60; in Zambia, 560–1
Nationalist Party, South Africa, 494, 495, 499, 501
N'Dar Tout, Senegal, 347
Ndebele (Matabele), people, South and Central Africa, 137, 251, 254, 258, 378, 390, 391–2, 394–5, 397, 561; *map, 240, 393*
Ndongo, state, Angola, 155
Ndwandwe, people, South Africa, 234, 235, 236, 238, 239, 242; *map, 261*
Negritic languages (Niger Congo), 23, 40; *map, 25*
Négritude, 345, 521, 540, 588
Negroids, 11–12, 21–2, 24, 26, 43, 50, 124, 133, 214; at Khartoum, 11–12, 21–2, 33, 43; in West Africa, 42–3, 52
Nembe, Niger Delta state, 333, 361; *map, 324*
Neolithic period, 11, 12, 13, 21, 22, 23, 33, 50–1, 137–8
Netekamani, Kushite king, 37
New Kingdom, Egypt, 32–3, 44
Newspapers, and African nationalism, 522
Ngala, Ronald, Kenya political leader, 560
N'gazargamu, Bornu, 72, 201, 202; *map, 54, 193*
Ngoni, people, Central Africa, 123, 131, 137, 177, 178, 238–41, 293, 302, 303, 420; divisions, 239, 240, 400; *map, 240, 295, 407*

Ngugi, James, African writer, 603
Nguni speakers, South Africa, 86, 140, 177, 232, 233, 236, 237, 242, 251; *map, 240*
Ngwane, people, South Africa, 234; *map, 261*
Niani, Mali empire, 63; *map, 54*
Nicol, George, Sierra Leone clergyman, 351–2
Niger Coast Protectorate, 362
Niger-Congo language group (Negritic), 23, 40; *map, 25*
Niger Delta, 5, 101, 102, 286–7, 319, 331–3; society, 166–8; *map, 282, 324*
Niger Districts Protectorate, 322–3
Niger Expedition, 1841, 262, 277, 278
Niger Missions, C.M.S., 289–90
Niger River, 8, 42, 52, 53, 62, 66, 69, 199, 286, 290, 314, 328, 351; *map, 6, 7, 39, 54, 106, 153, 193, 282, 324*
Niger, state, 541; economy, 573; *map, 474, 557*
Nigeria, state, 485, 518, 541, 592–5, 600, 602, 603; as British colony, 365, 449; Northern protectorate, 365, 441, 477; Western region, 365; Eastern region, 365; and African nationalism, 449–52, 455, 533–6; Federation, 499, 533; independence, 532–6, 565; economy, 574, 576; civil war, 584, 590, 591–5; *map, 325, 474, 557*
Nigerian Civil War, 584, 590–5; background, 592
Nigerian National Democratic Party, (first), 451, 521; (second), 592
Nigerian Youth Movement, 452, 533
Nile Delta, 13
Nile River, 14, 28, 38, 43, 144; cataracts, 8, 28, 29, 33, 36; *map, 6, 7, 25, 31, 39, 81, 153, 215, 324*
Nile Valley, 13, 14, 20, 24, 33
Nilotes, people, 23, 24, 134, 135, 139, 143, 221–2, 414, 583; and government, 143, 221, 414
Nilotic language group, 23, 221; *map, 25*
Nimba, Mt., Liberia and Guinea, 573
N'jimi, Kanem-Bornu, 71
Nkomo, Joshua, Southern Rhodesian

Nationalist 511, 562, 563, 564
Nkrumah, Kwame, Ghanaian nationalist leader, 524, 532, 578–9, 582, 583, 591; and Gold Coast independence, 530–1; and modernization, 578, 582; and pan-Africanism, 531, 587, 588
Nkumbula, Harry, African nationalist, 512, 513, 560, 561
Nok, culture, Nigeria, 103
North Africa, 40–3, 149, 187, 195, 223; and European penetration, 322, 329
Northern Peoples' Congress (N.P.C.), Nigerian political party, 534, 535, 536, 592
Northern People's Party, Ghana, 532
Northern Rhodesia, 398, 401, 402, 505–7, 509, 510, 562, 563; and "partnership," 506, 508, 509; and federation, 509, 512, 513; and African nationalism 510, 512, 513; independence, 560–1; *map, 325, 393, 407, 474*
Northern Rhodesia African Congress, 510, 512
Nova Scotians, Sierra Leone settlers, 270–1, 275
Nsama, Tabwa leader, Congo, 307
Nsuta, Ashanti state, 117
Nuba Hills, eastern Sudan, 220, 221, 225; *map, 215*
Nubia, region and kingdom, eastern Sudan, 22, 28, 29, 30, 32, 33, 34, 97; *map, 31, 92, 215*
Nubian (Nuba), people, eastern Sudan, 97, 214
Nuer, people, eastern Sudan, 221, 222; *map, 215*
Nupe, people and kingdom, West Africa, 110, 192, 194; *map, 54, 106, 193*
Nyamwezi, people, East Africa, 241, 301, 304, 305–6, 308, 420; as traders, 296–7, 298, 299, 300; *map, 240, 295, 324, 407*
Nyangwe, eastern Congo, 307; *map, 295*
Nyanza, Kenyan region, 415, 417, 560; *map, 407*
Nyasa, Lake, (Malawi), 5, 86, 237, 239, 241, 294, 296, 300, 302, 327,

Port Natal, South Africa, 237, 260; *map*, *261*

Porto Novo, Dahomey, 323; *map*, *324*

Portugal, 150, 156, 157; and East African coast, 84–6, 87, 89, 93, 124, 131, 238, 294, 297, 431; and Ethiopia, 93; and West Africa, 111–12, 116, 151, 162, 164–5, 294; and Mutapa state, 131, 132, 164; imperial expansion, 150–2, 154, 156, 297, 313, 320, 321, 327, 399; and Kongo, 152–5; in Angola, 155–6, 163, 297, 481–2, 483–6, 596; in Mozambique, 482–3, 596; in Guinea, 596; *map*, *153*, *324*, *325*, *474*, *557*

Portuguese Guinea, 101, 107, 164–5, 322, 565; *map*, *324*, *325*, *557*

Potgieter, Andries, Boer leader, 258, 260

Pra River, Ghana, 115, 116, 118, 289; *map*, *106*, *282*

Pratt, W. H., Sierra Leone Creole, 275–6

Prazos, Mozambique, 482

Prempeh, king of Ashanti, 333, 345

Présence Africaine, revue, 521, 588

Prester John, 89, 93, 152, 154

Pretoria, Transvaal, 251, 376, 377; *map*, *380*

Pretorius, Andries, Boer leader, 259, 378

Pretorius, Marthinus, Boer leader, 378

Preventive Detention Act, Ghana, 582

Progressive Party, Ghana, 583

Promotion of Bantu Self-Government Act, 1959, South Africa, 489–90

Province of Freedom, Sierra Leone, 270

Ptolemy, Claudius, geographer, 78, 134

Punt, region, Somali "Horn," 33, 44, 76; *map*, *31*

Pygmies, 24, 29, 133, 134

Qadir, Kordofan, 225, 226; *map*, *215*

Qadiriyya, Muslim brotherhood, 187, 190, 196, 198, 200

al-Qallabat (Metemma), battle, 337; *map*, *215*, *339*

Qarri, eastern Sudan, 216; *map*, *215*

Quaker, James, Sierra Leone Creole, 352

Queen Adelaide Province, South Africa, 257; *map*, *261*

Quran, 187

Quz Rajab, eastern Sudan, 216; *map*, *215*

Raba, Nigeria, 194, 195; *map*, *193*

Rabih Fadlullah, Sudanese conquerer, 203, 204, 207–8, 477

Racial discrimination, in South Africa, 161–2, 384–7, 388, 488–93, 495, 497, 498, 509; in West Africa, 290, 350; in Central Africa, 396, 504, 506, 507, 508, 510, 512, 562; in East Africa, 412, 415–16, 417, 560; in Belgian Congo, 472–3; in French Equatorial Africa, 480; in Portuguese Africa, 484–5

Racial policies, in South Africa, 384, 385, 386, 387–9, 488–93, 495, 497–8; in Southern Rhodesia, 395–6, 504, 506, 562, 564; in Kenya, 412, 416, 560; in Belgian Congo, 475–6; in Portuguese Africa, 484–5

Railroads, 284, 323, 340, 379, 410, 429, 467, 479, 518

Rainfall, African, 3–5; in Congo basin, 4; in West Africa, 4, 5, 101; desert, 4; in Ethiopian highlands, 4; in South Africa, 4; *map*, *7*

Rain forest, 4, 10, 11, 21, 23, 24, 52, 101, 133, 476; and human habitation, 22; *map*, *7*

Rainy, William, Sierra Leone Creole, 352

Randle, John, Nigerian leader, 451

Rano, Hausa city state, 73; *map*, *54*

Rassemblement Démocratique Africain (R.D.A.), French Africa, 538, 540

"Recaptives," Liberated African slaves, 271, 275

Red Sea, 5, 14, 33, 43, 44, 47, 76, 89, 90, 210, 214, 228; *map*, *6*, *31*, *39*, *81*, *92*, *215*, *324*

Red Sea Hills, 28, 30, 90, 228; *map*, 215

Regimento, Portuguese, and Kongo, 154-5

Republic of South Africa, 371, 489, 493, 495, 503

Reservation of Separate Amenities Act, South Africa, 489

Resident Natives Ordinance, Kenya, 412

Retief, Piet, Boer leader, 258-9

Reunion Island, Indian Ocean, 88, 273, 482

Rhapta, East African coast, 77, 78, 79

Rhodes, Cecil, British empire builder, 326, 327, 376, 379-82, 390-2, 395, 397, 399, 466

Rhodesia, region, 122, 399, 492; North-Western, 400; North-Eastern, 400; *map*, 393

Rhodesia, state, 564-5, 599; republic, 598; apartheid policy, 598; *map*, 557

Rhodesia Party, 564

Rhodesian Front, Southern Rhodesia, 513, 563, 564, 598

Richards, Sir Arthur, Nigerian governor, 534

Riebeeck, Jan van, and South Africa, 158

Rift Valley, East Africa, 5, 135, 411, 414; *map*, 407

Rio Muni, Equatorial Guinea, 566; *map*, 557

Roberts, Joseph J. Liberian president, 359

Robinson, Sir Hercules, British South African administrator, 391

Rome, ancient, in Africa, 37, 41-2, 45

Round Table Conference, and Belgian Congo, 543

Rovuma River, East Africa, 327; *map*, 81, 295, 324, 393

Royal Africa Co., British, 163

Royal Niger Co., 322, 328, 331, 333

Royal seclusion, in Benin, 112-13, and Zimbabwe, 123, 132; in Kongo, 154; in Kanem-Bornu, 203

Roye, Edward J., Liberian president, 360

Rozwi, Mutapa rulers, 124

Ruanda-Urundi, Belgian mandate, 545; *map*, 325, 407, 474

Rubber, 313, 347, 411, 419, 462, 572; in Belgian Congo, 467, 468; in French Congo, 476, 478, 479

Rubusana, Walter, South African Bantu nationalist, 389

Rudd Concession, Ndebele, 391, 392, 397

Rufiji River, Tanzania, 78; *map*, 81

Rufisque, Senegal, 348, 349, 443

Ruga-ruga, irregulars, East Africa, 306

Rwanda, state, East Africa, 134, 303, 429, 545; *map*, 295, 557

Saad Zaghlul, Egyptian nationalist, 435

Sabakura, Mali king, 64

Sahara Desert, 4, 10, 11-12, 13, 21, 22, 23, 24, 40, 42, 50-2, 476; *map*, 39

as-Sahili, Muslim architect, 64

Sahle Selassie, king of Shoa, 337

Said, Sayyid, Sultan of Zanzibar, 88, 89, 298-300, 306, 432

Saif, Kanem-Bornu king, 70

Saifawa Dynasty, Kanem-Bornu, 70, 203

St. Louis, Senegal, 163, 166, 176, 199, 268, 274, 275, 284, 285, 286, 318, 347, 349, 443, 518; *map*, 153, 193

Salazar, Gen. Antonio, Portuguese prime minister, 484, 596

Salim Qapudan, Turkish explorer, 220, 222

Salisbury, Rhodesia, 122, 381, 390, 512; *map*, 393

Salisbury, Lord, British political figure, 316, 327

Salmon, C. S., Gold Coast official, 317

Salt trade, 53, 55, 64, 103-4, 116, 195, 204

Sammaniyya, Muslim brotherhood, 225

Samori Toure, Mandinka empire builder, 204-7, 334, 345; early career, 204; statemaking, 204-5, 206; relations with Europeans, 205, 322, 328; character and achievements, 206-7; *map*, 324

Sand River Convention, South Africa, 262, 372

Soudan, French West Africa, 540

South Africa, region and state, 177, 233, 264–5, 598–9; and Dutch, 157–60, 162, 164; and British, 237, 255–7, 259, 260, 262–3, 327–8, 371–3; and unification, 372–3, 374–5, 379–83; and racial policies, 384, 385, 386, 387–9, 488–93, 495, 497–8, 509; pass laws, 493, 500; treason trial, 500; and High Commission territories, 501–2; industrialization, 377, 495, 573; and independent Africa, 595–6, 598–9; and Rhodesia 597; *map, 159, 261, 380, 557*

South Africa Act, 1909, 501

South Africa Communist Party, 499, 500

South African Indian Congress, 499

South African Party, 494

South African Republic (Transvaal), 373, 375, 378, 598; *map, 380*

Southern Rhodesia, 510; and "native policy," 395–6, 504–5, 508, 562; and land policy, 395–6; self-governing colony, 397, 401, 413; and federation, 509, 512, 513–14; and African nationalism, 510, 561, 562, 563, 564; and independence, 564–5; *map, 325, 380, 474*

Southern Sudan (of eastern Sudan), 527; environment and people, 221–2; and slave trade, 223; and secession, 583–4

South-West Africa, 4; German protectorate, 314, 327, 379, 391; South African mandate, 503; *map, 324, 325, 380, 393, 474, 557*

Soviet Union, 524, 544, 594

Soyinka, Wole, Nigerian playwright, 603–4

Spain, 85, 156–7, 329, 565, 566

Spear of the Nation, South Africa, 500

Specialization, technological and economic, 10–11, 12, 14, 19, 104

Speke, J. H., British explorer, 309

Stack, Sir Lee, British colonial official, 435

Stanley, H. M., American explorer, 308, 310, 313, 320

Stanley Falls, Congo, 307, 308, 323; *map, 295, 324*

Stanley Pool, Congo River, 8, 313, 323, 467, 477; *map, 324, 474*

Stanleyville, Belgian Congo, 467; *map, 474*

Stel, Simon van der, 158, 160

Stel, Willem van der, 158, 160

Stellenbosch, South Africa, 158; *map, 159*

Stephen, James, British abolitionist, 269–70

Stone Age, 43, 44, 133, 161; Old Stone Age (Paleolithic), 10; New Stone Age (Neolithic), 11

Strijdom, J. G., Afrikaner leader, 495

Suakin, eastern Sudan, 214, 216, 228; *map, 215*

Sudan, region, 42, 178, 188; central, 40, 207; eastern, 11, 22, 24, 29, 207, 208, 210, 211–13, 224–8, 229–30, 433; and southern provinces, 221–3; western, 22, 52–60, 104, 194, 208; and African imperial administration, 60–1, 71; and European penetration, 328–9; *map, 39, 324*

Sudan, Anglo-Egyptian (eastern), 433–7; and independence, 526–8, 539; and Egypt, 433–7, 527, 528; and the South, 528; economy, 576; political stability, 583–4; *map, 324, 325, 407, 474, 557*

Sudd, Nile River, 36, 212, 213, 220, 221; *map, 31*

Suez Canal, 321, 433, 434

Sufism, saint worship, Islam, 187, 216, 225, 226

Sulaiman Bal, Torodbe leader, 188

Sulaiman Dama, Songhai king, 66

Sulb, Kush, 33; *map, 31*

Sultan-bin-Seif, Omani ruler, 87

Sumaguru Kante, Soso leader, 63

Suna, Buganda king, 310

Sunday River, South Africa, 162; *map, 159*

Sundiata, Mali king, 60, 63–4, 67

Sunni, Songhai Dynasty, 66

Sunni Ali, Songhai king, 56, 59, 65, 66–7, 68

Susenyos, Ethiopian king, 95

Susu, people, Futa Jalon, 188; *map, 193*

Swahili, language, people, and culture,

Vet River, South Africa, 260; *map*, 261

Victoria Falls, Zambezi River, 242, 390; *map, 240, 383*

Victoria, Lake, East Africa, 5, 23, 135, 142, 143, 296, 338, 410, 414; *map, 6, 7, 136, 240, 407*

Volta River, West Africa, 102, 115; *map, 54, 106, 193, 282;* Black Volta, 115; *map, 54, 106, 193;* industrial complex, 573

Voluntary associations, 521

Vorster, John, South African prime minister, 495, 598, 599

Wadai, kingdom, central Sudan, 71, 187, 203, 476; *map, 25, 54, 193, 474*

Wadi Halfa, eastern Sudan, 213, 229; *map, 31, 215*

Wafd, Egyptian nationalist party, 435

Wagadugu, Mossi state, 185; *map, 193*

Wahabiyya, Muslim reformers, 198, 210, 225

Walata, Western Sudan, 57, 58, 63, 65; *map, 39, 54*

Wali, Mali king, 64

Wallaga, Ethiopian region, 338; *map, 339*

Walo, region, Senegal, 105; *map, 106, 282*

Wanga (Hanga), state, East Africa, 330, 414; *map, 407*

Wangara, region, West Africa, 53, 62, 63, 64; *map, 54*

Warden, H. D., British South African official, 263

Warri River, Nigeria, 332; *map, 324*

Waruhiu, Chief, Kikuyu leader, 559

Wassa, Akan state, 115, 283; *map, 106, 282*

Wassulu, West African region, 205; *map, 193*

Waterboer, Griqua leader, 373

Watson Commission, Gold Coast, 530

Webb, Sidney J., 506

Welensky, Roy, Rhodesia Federation prime minister, 508–9, 510, 511, 512, 513, 562, 564

West Africa, 22, 23, 24, 40, 43, 52, 119, 133, 163, 267; savanna civilization, 55–60, 60–1, 62, 64–5, 69–70, 71, 72, 73, 74; trans-Saharan trade, 41, 51, 53, 55, 64, 66, 69, 72, 73; forest civilization, 103–8, 112, 280; forest trade, 103–4, 112, 116, 118; slave trade, 162–3, 165, 169–70, 269–70; European trade, 168–70, 271; and westernization, 177, 268, 271, 273–4, 275–80; and partition, 316, 317, 318, 321, 322–3, 328; French territories, 346–51, 443, 445; British territories, 351–4, 365–9, 447–55

West African forest, 11, 22, 52, 101–2, 111

West African Pilot, Lagos, 522

West African Regional Group, 577

West African Students' Union, Britain, 523

West Indies, 458; British, 270; French, 273

West Indies Co., French, 163

de Wet, C. R., Boer leader, 383

Wet phase, Sahara, 11, 13, 21, 50

White Fathers, missionaries, 326

White Flag League, eastern Sudan, 435

White highlands, Kenya, 412, 413, 415, 518, 558, 560, 572

White mercenaries, Congo-Kinshasa, 584–5, 590

White Nile, 21, 36, 43, 97, 143, 213, 216, 220, 221, 224, 225; *map, 6, 31, 215, 339, 407*

Whitehead, Sir Edgar, Southern Rhodesia prime minister, 563

Whydah, Dahomey, 113, 273; *map, 106, 193*

Wichali (Ucciali), treaty, Ethiopia, 340

Wilberforce, William, British abolitionist, 270, 271, 277

Winburg, South Africa, 260, 378; *map, 261*

Witwatersrand, Transvaal, 376, 378, 483, 489, 499; University, 500; *map, 380*

Wodehouse, Sir P., Cape Colony governor, 372

Wolof, Senegal people, 105, 166, 274, 284; *map, 25, 106, 282*